INTERNATIONAL &
TRANSNATIONAL CRIMINAL LAW

Other books in the *Essentials of Canadian Law* Series
Intellectual Property Law
Income Tax Law
Immigration Law
International Trade Law
Family Law
Copyright Law
The Law of Equitable Remedies
Administrative Law
Ethics and Canadian Criminal Law
Securities Law
Computer Law 2/e
Maritime Law
Insurance Law
International Human Rights Law
Legal Research and Writing 2/e
The Law of Trusts 2/e
Franchise Law
Personal Property Security Law
The Law of Contracts
Pension Law
Constitutional Law 3/e
Legal Ethics and Professional Responsibility 2/e
Refugee Law
Mergers, Acquisitions, and Other Changes of Corporate Control
Bank and Customer Law in Canada
Statutory Interpretation 2/e
The Law of Torts 3/e
National Security Law: Canadian Practice in International Perspective
Remedies: The Law of Damages 2/e
Public International Law 2/e
The Law of Evidence 5/e
Criminal Procedure
Individual Employment Law 2/e
Environmental Law 3/e
Bankruptcy and Insolvency Law
Criminal Law 4/e
The Law of Partnerships and Corporations 3/e
The Charter of Rights and Freedoms 4/e
Youth Criminal Justice Law 2/e
Civil Litigation

ESSENTIALS OF
CANADIAN LAW

INTERNATIONAL &
TRANSNATIONAL
CRIMINAL LAW

ROBERT J. CURRIE
Schulich School of Law, Dalhousie University

IRWIN
LAW

International and Transnational Criminal Law
© Irwin Law Inc., 2010

Published in 2010 by

Irwin Law Inc.
14 Duncan Street
Suite 206
Toronto, ON
M5H 3G8

www.irwinlaw.com

ISBN: 978-1-55221-162-5

Library and Archives Canada Cataloguing in Publication

Currie, Robert J. (Robert John), 1970–
    International and transnational criminal law / Robert J. Currie.

(Essentials of Canadian law)
Includes bibliographical references and index.
ISBN 978-1-55221-162-5

    1. International offenses. 2. Transnational crime. 3. International criminal
courts. I. Title. II. Series: Essentials of Canadian law

K5015.4.C87 2010   345   C2010-900447-7

The publisher acknowledges the financial support of the Government of Canada through the Book Publishing Industry Development Program (BPIDP) for its publishing activities.

We acknowledge the assistance of the OMDC Book Fund, an initiative of Ontario Media Development Corporation.

Printed and bound in Canada.

1 2 3 4 5   14 13 12 11 10

Mixed Sources
Product group from well-managed forests,
controlled sources and recycled wood or fiber
www.fsc.org Cert no. SW-COC-000952
© 1996 Forest Stewardship Council
FSC

SUMMARY
TABLE OF CONTENTS

FOREWORD   *xix*

PREFACE AND ACKNOWLEDGMENTS   *xxv*

ABBREVIATIONS   *xxxi*

CHAPTER   1:   Introduction: Convergence of Disciplines   *1*

CHAPTER   2:   Jurisdiction Over International and Transnational Crime   *48*

CHAPTER   3:   The Core Crimes   *104*

CHAPTER   4:   Direct Enforcement Against the Core Crimes: International and Internationalized Criminal Courts   *159*

CHAPTER   5:   Indirect Enforcement: National Prosecution of the Core Crimes   *214*

CHAPTER   6:   Other International Crimes   *269*

CHAPTER   7:   Transnational Crimes of International Concern   *303*

CHAPTER   8:   Transnational Crimes of Domestic Concern   *407*

CHAPTER   9:   International Criminal Cooperation   *445*

CHAPTER 10:   International Criminal Cooperation, Human Rights, and the Application of the *Charter*   *497*

CHAPTER 11:   Immunities from Criminal Prosecution   *539*

TABLE OF CASES   *601*

INDEX   *619*

ABOUT THE AUTHOR   *647*

DETAILED
TABLE OF CONTENTS

FOREWORD   *xix*

PREFACE AND ACKNOWLEDGMENTS   *xxv*

ABBREVIATIONS   *xxxi*

CHAPTER 1:
INTRODUCTION: CONVERGENCE OF DISCIPLINES   *1*

A. Introduction   *1*

B. History   *3*

C. Distinguishing International and Transnational Criminal Law   *12*

    1) Analytical Models of ICL and TCL   *12*
    2) International Crimes   *17*
    3) Transnational Crimes of International Concern   *19*
    4) Transnational Crimes of Domestic Concern   *20*

D. Enforcement   *21*

E. International Cooperation in the Suppression of Crime   *23*

F. The Impact of Human Rights   *25*

G. Sources of International and Transnational Criminal Law   *27*

    1) Domestic Sources   *27*
    2) International Law Sources and Their Reception in Canada   *29*
        a) Treaty Law   *30*
            i) Creation and Legal Effect   *30*
            ii) Reception   *32*

    b) Customary International Law *33*
      i) Creation and Ascertainment *33*
      ii) Reception *35*
    c) Other Sources *37*
    d) Section 11(g) of the *Charter* *41*

G. **Subjects of International and Transnational Criminal Law: State Responsibility versus Individual Liability** *42*

Further Reading *46*

CHAPTER 2:

JURISDICTION OVER INTERNATIONAL AND TRANSNATIONAL CRIME *48*

A. **Introduction** *48*

B. **Essential Definitions and Concepts** *50*

    1) Jurisdiction Defined *50*
    2) Domestic, Extraterritorial, and Concurrent Jurisdiction *50*
    3) Prescriptive and Enforcement Jurisdiction *53*

C. **Prescriptive Jurisdiction** *56*

    1) Introduction: "Allocating Competences" *56*
    2) The Territorial Principle *59*
      a) Conduct within Territory *59*
      b) Qualified Territoriality *62*
    3) Principles of Extraterritorial Jurisdiction *66*
      a) Nationality *66*
      b) Passive Personality *68*
      c) Protection of State Interests *69*
      d) Universal *71*
      e) A Global Test: Substantial and *Bona Fide* Connection *78*
    4) Jurisdiction at Sea *82*
      a) Internal Waters and the Territorial Sea *84*
      b) Contiguous Zone *86*
      c) Exclusive Economic Zone *87*
      d) Continental Shelf *88*
      e) High Seas *88*
      f) Hot Pursuit *89*
    5) Jurisdiction in Space *91*
    6) Jurisdiction over the Internet *92*

D. **Enforcement Jurisdiction** *92*

E. **Treaty-Based Prescriptive and Enforcement Jurisdiction: *Aut Dedere Aut Judicare* and "Conditional" Universal Jurisdiction** *96*

F. Jurisdiction of International Courts   99

Further Reading   102

CHAPTER 3:
THE CORE CRIMES   104

A. Introduction   104

B. Genocide   105

1) History   105
2) Definition and Jurisdiction   108
3) The Mental Element of Genocide: *Dolus Specialis*   109
4) Defining the Protected Group   111
5) Acts Constituting Genocide   112
    a) Killing   113
    b) Causing Serious Bodily or Mental Harm   113
    c) Deliberately Inflicting Conditions of Life Calculated to Destroy
        the Group   113
    d) Imposing Measures Intended to Prevent Births   114
    e) Forcibly Transferring Children   114
6) Inchoate and Incomplete Offences   115
7) Genocide in the *Rome Statute*   116

C. Crimes Against Humanity   117

1) History   117
2) Definition and Jurisdiction   119
3) Contextual Elements   121
    a) Civilian Population   121
    b) Widespread or Systematic Attack   122
4) Mental Element   123
5) Prohibited Acts   124
    a) Murder   124
    b) Extermination   125
    c) Enslavement   125
    d) Deportation   126
    e) Imprisonment   126
    f) Torture   126
    g) Rape   127
    h) Persecution   128
    i) Other Inhumane Acts   129
6) Crimes Against Humanity in the *Rome Statute*   129

D. War Crimes   130

1) History and Definition   130
2) Jurisdictional Requirements   133

a) Existence of and Nexus to Armed Conflict   *133*
b) International versus Internal Armed Conflict   *134*
3) Mental Element   *137*
4) The *Geneva Conventions* and *Additional Protocols I* and *II*   *138*
a) Introduction   *138*
b) The Grave Breaches Regime   *140*
c) Common Article 3 and *AP II*   *144*
5) Violations of the Laws or Customs of War   *146*
6) War Crimes in the *Rome Statute*   *149*

E. Aggression   *152*

Further Reading   *157*

CHAPTER 4:

DIRECT ENFORCEMENT AGAINST THE CORE CRIMES: INTERNATIONAL AND INTERNATIONALIZED CRIMINAL COURTS   *159*

A. Introduction   *159*

B. The Nuremberg and Tokyo Tribunals   *160*

C. The United Nations *Ad Hoc* Tribunals   *165*

1) The International Criminal Tribunal for the former
Yugoslavia (ICTY)   *165*
a) Creation and History   *165*
b) Structure   *169*
c) Jurisdiction   *170*
2) The International Criminal Tribunal for Rwanda (ICTR)   *171*
a) Creation and History   *171*
b) Structure   *175*
c) Jurisdiction   *175*

D. The International Criminal Court (ICC)   *176*

1) Creation and History   *176*
2) Structure   *185*
3) Jurisdiction   *187*
a) Subject Matter Jurisdiction   *187*
b) Territorial Jurisdiction   *188*
c) Personal Jurisdiction   *189*
d) Non-party States   *190*
e) Temporal Jurisdiction   *191*
4) "Triggering" Proceedings before the Court   *192*
a) State Party Referral   *192*
b) Referral by the Security Council   *193*
c) Prosecutor's *Proprio Motu* Powers   *195*

       d) Deferral by the Security Council *195*
   5) Admissibility *196*
       a) Complementarity *196*
       b) Gravity *199*
       c) "Interests of Justice" *200*
       d) *Ne Bis In Idem* *201*

E. Internationalized Courts *202*

   1) The Special Court for Sierra Leone *203*
       a) Creation and History *203*
       b) Structure *205*
       c) Jurisdiction *206*
   2) Cambodia Extraordinary Chambers *207*
   3) Special Tribunal for Lebanon *208*
   4) East Timor *209*
   5) Kosovo *210*
   6) Former Yugoslavia: Bosnia and Herzegovina War Crimes Chamber and Serbian War Crimes Chamber *211*
   7) Iraqi High Tribunal *211*

Further Reading *213*

CHAPTER 5:

INDIRECT ENFORCEMENT: NATIONAL PROSECUTION OF THE CORE CRIMES *214*

A. Introduction *214*

   1) Overview: The Post-war World *215*

B. Canada, 1945–1999 *223*

   1) Post–WW II Developments *223*
   2) The Deschênes Commission Report *227*
   3) Response to Deschênes: The 1987 *Criminal Code* Amendments *228*
   4) The *Finta* Case and Its Fallout *230*

C. The *Crimes Against Humanity and War Crimes Act, 2000* *233*

   1) Introduction *233*
   2) The Act *234*
       a) Jurisdiction *234*
       b) Crimes *237*
          i) Genocide and Advocating/Incitement to Genocide *243*
          ii) Crimes against Humanity *246*
          iii) War Crimes *250*
       c) Command/Superior Responsibility *252*
       d) Liability, Complicity, and Inchoate Offences *253*

e) Procedure and Defences 255
f) Other Provisions 258
3) The *Munyaneza* Case 259

D. **Immigration-based Mechanisms** 263

1) Exclusion from Immigration 264
2) Exclusion from Refugee Status 265
3) Loss of Citizenship 267

Further Reading 268

CHAPTER 6:

OTHER INTERNATIONAL CRIMES 269

A. **Introduction** 269

B. **Torture** 270

1) History and Definition 270
2) Jurisdiction over Torture 272
3) Mental Elements 274
4) Acts Constituting Torture 275
5) The Public Official Requirement 277
6) Other State Obligations 277
7) Torture in Canadian Law 278

C. **Piracy** 281

1) History and Definition 281
2) Jurisdiction over Piracy 285
3) Piracy in Canadian Law 286

D. **Slavery** 288

1) History and Definition 288
2) Jurisdiction over Slavery 291
3) Slavery in Canadian Law 292

E. **Apartheid** 293

F. **Terrorism as an International Crime?** 295

Further Reading 301

CHAPTER 7:

TRANSNATIONAL CRIMES OF INTERNATIONAL CONCERN 303

A. **Introduction** 303

B. **The Suppression Conventions** 305

1) History and Development   *305*
2) Central Features   *307*
3) Human Rights Concerns   *311*

C. **Transnational Organized Crime**   *314*

1) Introduction   *314*
2) The Organized Crime Offences   *317*
   a) International Law   *317*
   b) Canadian Implementing Legislation   *321*
3) Trafficking in Persons   *324*
   a) International Law   *324*
   b) Canadian Implementing Legislation   *327*
4) Smuggling of Migrants   *330*
   a) International Law   *330*
   b) Canadian Implementing Legislation   *332*
5) Illicit Manufacturing of and Trading in Firearms   *333*
   a) International Law   *333*
   b) Canadian Implementing Legislation   *335*
6) Corruption   *336*
   a) International Law   *336*
   b) Canadian Implementing Legislation   *340*

D. **Terrorism**   *343*

1) Civil Aviation   *344*
2) Maritime Terrorism   *346*
3) Hostage-Taking   *349*
4) Internationally Protected Persons   *352*
5) UN and Associated Personnel   *353*
6) Terrorist Bombings   *356*
7) Terrorist Financing   *359*
8) Nuclear Terrorism   *364*
9) The "New" Terrorism: Part II.1 of the *Criminal Code*   *367*

E. **Drug Trafficking**   *370*

1) International Law   *370*
2) Canadian Implementing Legislation   *377*

F. **Proceeds of Crime and Money Laundering**   *379*

1) International Law   *379*
2) Canadian Implementing Legislation   *384*

G. **"Child Sex Tourism"**   *388*

1) International Law   *388*
2) Canadian Implementing Legislation   *391*

H. **Cybercrime**   *392*

1) International Law 392
2) Canadian Implementation 403

Further Reading 405

CHAPTER 8:

TRANSNATIONAL CRIMES OF DOMESTIC CONCERN 407

A. Introduction: "Purely" Domestic Crimes with a Transnational Element 407

B. Qualified Territoriality in Canadian Law 409

1) The *Libman* Test 409
2) "Real and Substantial Connection" 412
3) International Comity 417
4) *Libman* and Extraterritoriality 420
5) Summary 423

C. Prescriptively Transnational Crimes: Extraterritorial Criminal Jurisdiction 425

1) Canada and Extraterritorial Jurisdiction 425
2) Implementing International Treaties 428
3) Avoiding Lawlessness and Territorial Gaps 429
4) Controlling the Behaviour of Representatives of Canada 430
5) Protection of Canadian Interests 432
6) "Non-extraterritorial" Offences 433
7) Ships, Aircraft, and Fixed Platforms 434

D. Conspiracy 437

Further Reading 443

CHAPTER 9:

INTERNATIONAL CRIMINAL COOPERATION 445

A. Introduction 445

B. Extradition 447

1) International Law 447
   a) History 447
   b) Principles of Extradition Law 449
      i) Double Criminality and Extraditable Offences 450
      ii) Reciprocity 452
      iii) Specialty and Re-extradition 453
      iv) Evidentiary Requirements 453
      v) Political Offence Exception 454

vi)   Discrimination   *457*
vii) The "Rule of Non-inquiry"   *457*
viii) Military/Fiscal Offences   *458*
ix)   Double Jeopardy/*Ne Bis in Idem*   *459*
2) Canadian Law   *460*
a) Part 2 of the *Extradition Act*: Canada As Requested State   *462*
i)   Authority to Proceed   *462*
ii)   The Judicial Phase   *463*
iii) The Ministerial Phase   *467*
b) Part 3 of the *Extradition Act*: Canada As Requesting State   *471*

C. "Alternatives" to Extradition: Abduction and Extraordinary Rendition   *472*

1) Abduction   *473*
2) Extraordinary Rendition   *479*

D. Mutual Legal Assistance   *482*

1) International Law   *482*
2) Canadian Law   *485*
a) The Legislation   *485*
b) Part I of the *Mutual Legal Assistance in Criminal Matters Act*: Canada As Requested State   *486*
i)   Issuing of Search Warrants   *486*
ii)   Challenging the Warrant: The Sending Hearing   *487*
iii) Issuing Evidence-Gathering Orders (EGOs)   *491*
iv)   Challenging the EGO   *492*
v)   Appeals   *494*
vi)   Costs   *494*
vii) Other Modalities in Part I of the Act   *495*
c) Parts II and III of the Act: Canada As Requesting State   *495*
i)   The Making of the Request   *495*
ii)   Admissibility of Evidence Received   *495*
iii) Foreign Witnesses   *496*

Further Reading   *496*

CHAPTER 10:

INTERNATIONAL CRIMINAL COOPERATION, HUMAN RIGHTS, AND THE APPLICATION OF THE *CHARTER*   *497*

A. Introduction   *497*

B. Extradition, Deportation, and Mutual Legal Assistance   *498*

C. Admissibility of Evidence Gathered in Foreign States   *509*

1) Evidence Gathered by Foreign Officials   *509*
2) Evidence Gathered by Canadian Officials   *515*

3) Other Investigative and Enforcement-Type Actions by State
Officials *523*
4) Concluding Observations on *R. v. Hape* *530*

Further Reading *537*

CHAPTER 11:

IMMUNITIES FROM CRIMINAL PROSECUTION *539*

A. **Introduction** *539*

B. **Immunity in International Law** *541*

1) General Comments *541*
2) Immunity *Ratione Personae* *543*
3) Immunity *Ratione Materiae* *544*

C. **Immunities before International Tribunals** *546*

1) International Military Tribunal: Removal of Personal or Functional
Immunity or Both? *546*
2) The *Ad Hoc* Criminal Tribunals *549*
   a) General *549*
   b) *Milosević* (ICTY) *551*
   c) *Karadžić* (ICTY) *552*
   d) *Kambanda* (ICTR) *554*
3) Internationalized Tribunals: The Special Court for Sierra Leone *555*
   a) General *555*
   b) Charles Taylor *555*
4) The International Criminal Court as a Special Case *558*
   a) General *558*
   b) Article 27 *559*
   c) Article 98 *560*
   d) *Bashir* *562*
5) Conclusions *566*

D. **Immunity before Domestic Courts** *567*

1) Introduction *567*
2) War Crimes *568*
   a) The *Geneva Conventions* *568*
   b) *Eichmann* *569*
   c) *Yerodia* *572*
3) Genocide *577*
   a) The *Genocide Convention* *577*
   b) Customary International Law *578*
4) Crimes against Humanity *579*
5) Torture: *Pinochet* *580*

E. **Canadian Implementation** *589*

1) General Comments   *589*
2) War Crimes   *590*
3) Crimes against Humanity   *592*
4) Genocide   *593*
5) Interpretation   *593*
6) Diplomatic Immunity as a Special Case   *596*

F. Conclusion   *598*

Further Reading   *599*

TABLE OF CASES   *601*

INDEX   *619*

ABOUT THE AUTHOR   *647*

FOREWORD

This book is an innovation as far as Canadian legal practitioners, scholars, and law students are concerned. Academics from France, for example, have for many years published lengthy manuals covering the field of *Droit international pénal*, but I cannot think of a country from the common law tradition with anything similar. The Americans have their case books, containing lengthy excerpts from judgments and hypotheticals for classroom discussion, but nothing along the lines of a comprehensive monograph.

Nothing could seem more appropriate today, given Canada's profound, and in some ways, pioneering role in the related disciplines that Robert Currie accurately distinguishes with the labels "international criminal law" and "transnational criminal law." In recent times, Canada has been very much at the forefront, but this was not always the case.

Although essentially idiosyncratic developments concerning international criminal prosecution date back to the Middle Ages, there was nothing resembling the field as it now exists until the Paris Peace Conference of 1919. Ambitious plans to prosecute war criminals for the ancestors of what we now call genocide, crimes against humanity, and aggression were set out in the post-war treaties, but these plans were never properly implemented. Nothing significant is known about the Canadian position in this area. Our country was present at Versailles, but fledgling Canadian diplomats were still to some extent operating in the shadow of the British Empire. International criminal law must have been a remote concern to them.

This hardly changed even after WW II, when the first genuinely international prosecutions took place at Nuremberg and Tokyo. The war crimes trials had been prepared by a body known as the United Nations War Crimes Commission, which began meeting in London in late 1943. All of the Allied nations were welcome to participate, and most of them did, but not Canada. Somebody in the Canadian High Commission had a watching brief, and the Canadian copy of the documents of the War Crimes Commission eventually found its way into the national archives. But while the Poles, the Czechs, and the Australians were actively involved, Canada was nowhere to be seen. We do not know why.

The *Charter of the International Military Tribunal*[1] was negotiated by the four "great" powers, and there was no place for Canada, had it wanted to participate. But once the *Charter* was adopted, other states were welcomed to ratify. Nineteen of them did so, including Australia and New Zealand. In its final judgment, the International Military Tribunal noted these ratifications, which provided evidence of the widespread acceptance of the law contained in the *Charter*. But again, for reasons that nobody has ever explained, Canada sat this one out. The only sign of Canadian interest in this activity is the presence of a judge among the eleven-member bench of the Tokyo tribunal, E. Stuart McDougall, who was on loan from the Quebec Superior Court.

This absence is probably not very surprising when it is placed within the broader context of Canada's disinterest in the nascent human rights movement in the late 1940s. Notoriously, when the vote was taken in the Third Committee of the United Nations on the final draft of the *Universal Declaration of Human Rights*[2] on 7 December 1948, Canada was one of the few abstainers (along with Saudi Arabia and the Soviet Union). Lester Pearson lamely told the General Assembly that the federal government was concerned about imposing obligations on the provinces. In fact, the archival records show that the federal Cabinet was simply hostile to the promotion of human rights. But whatever the explanation for this initial estrangement from both international human rights law and international criminal law in what were their formative years, Canadian policy changed dramatically decades later.

The transformative influence seems to have been the drafting and adoption of the *Canadian Charter of Rights and Freedoms*.[3] It stimulated debates about the role of international law within the Canadian judi-

---

1   82 U.N.T.S. 279.
2   A/RES/217, 10 December 1948.
3   Part I of the *Constitution Act, 1982*, being Schedule B to the *Canada Act 1982* (U.K.), 1982, c. 11.

cial system. The one direct reference to international law in the *Charter*, in section 11(g), bears directly on the subject matter of this book, as it concerns issues of retroactive war crimes prosecution. Canadian NGOs, including the Canadian Jewish Congress, lobbied successfully for the text, hopeful that trials under universal jurisdiction might take place at some point in the future. Something was in the air.

Hardly had the *Charter* been adopted than Quebec judge Jules Deschênes was mandated to hold a Royal Commission about alleged Nazi war criminals resident in Canada. We now know that many hundreds of them had found their way to Canada in the post-war years, at a time when growing right-wing hysteria prompted immigration officials to look the other way when "anti-communists" with suspicious war records sought immigration status. Justice Deschênes provided a trenchant legal analysis that paved the way for amendments to the *Criminal Code*.[4] He also compiled a list of suspects for potential prosecutions. By the late 1980s, Canada had suddenly become a hotbed of activity for international criminal law.

More or less in parallel with these developments, Canadian courts confronted some of the more challenging issues of transnational criminal law in the new legal context of the Canadian *Charter*. But initially at least, judges were rather conservative. In *Cotroni*,[5] the Supreme Court of Canada held that the right to remain in Canada, enshrined in section 6, did not protect a Canadian citizen from extradition to the US. Then, in 1991, the Court refused to block the return of two individuals to the US where they faced the death penalty. An important and unanimous precedent set by the European Court of Human Rights two years earlier, in *Soering v. United Kingdom*[6] (in which Canadian Judge Ronald St. John Macdonald participated), was essentially ignored by the Supreme Court.

The establishment of the International Criminal Tribunal for the former Yugoslavia by the United Nations Security Council in May 1993 signalled a golden age for Canadian activity. Jules Deschênes was elected to the first bench of the tribunal. With three of his colleagues, he signed the majority judgment of the Appeals Chamber in the *Tadić Jurisdictional Decision*[7] of October 1995. The word "landmark" does not begin to convey the importance of the ruling for modern international criminal law. In 1996, Louise Arbour joined the tribunal as its Pros-

---

4   R.S.C. 1985, c. C-46.
5   *United States of America v. Cotroni*, [1989] 1 S.C.R. 1469.
6   Series A, No. 161 (1989) (Eur. Ct. Hum. Rts.).
7   *Tadić* (IT-94-1-AR72), Decision on the Defence Motion for Interlocutory Appeal on Jurisdiction, Appeals Chamber, 2 October 1995.

ecutor. Many other Canadian lawyers were active in and around the tribunal and its partner, the International Criminal Tribunal for Rwanda, including Bill Fenrick, Payam Akhavan, Norman Farrell, Luc Côté, Robert Petit, and Eugene O'Sullivan. Two Canadians, Sharon Williams and Kim Prost, served as *ad litem* judges.

While the Yugoslavia and Rwanda tribunals were struggling to become operational, the United Nations ploughed ahead in its effort to establish the International Criminal Court. There was no substantial Canadian participation in the early phase of the work, which was mainly undertaken by the International Law Commission. But when the focus shifted to the General Assembly in 1995, Canada became one of the main players. Canadian diplomats and justice department lawyers, including Jon Allen, John Holmes, Darryl Robinson, Alan Kessel, and Don Piragoff, made vital contributions, earning the respect of experts around the world for their professionalism and commitment. A few months before the Rome Diplomatic Conference, a seasoned Canadian diplomat, Philippe Kirsch, was called upon to preside over the proceedings. And preside he did, navigating the draft statute through to the successful conclusion that many had thought was impossible. Kirsch went on to chair the Preparatory Committee and was elected the court's first president.

Much more could be said about Canadian involvement in international judicial mechanisms, and this is not the place for a thorough review. Suffice it to say that almost everywhere that there is some activity in this field, Canadian experts will be found, be it United Nations–sponsored "hybrid" courts, newer *ad hoc* tribunals like the Special Court for Sierra Leone and the Special Tribunal for Lebanon, and even national truth commissions.

Less spectacular, and less visible, is the field of transnational criminal law. It continues to function in the background, ensuring vital features of law enforcement that make the headlines less often than the war crimes trials. In the area of extradition, the Supreme Court of Canada eventually got it right, effectively reversing its earlier precedent on extradition for capital offenders in *Burns*.[8] In recent years, Canadian courts have provided an invaluable level of judicial review and supervision over a government that has at times been rather cavalier about its international obligations in the field of human rights. It is in transnational criminal law, especially its counterterrorism wing, where fundamental rights and freedoms have been most threatened, and where judicial fidelity to the principles of the *Charter* is most essential.

---

8   *United States of America v. Burns*, [2001] 1 S.C.R. 283.

Thus, over the ninety years or so that we can truly speak of a Canadian foreign policy, the country has moved from the periphery in the field of international and transnational criminal law to its very centre. Robert Currie's book is both a description of this process, and a part of it. It weaves together the different themes, which are not easy to connect, into a comprehensive overview of the field. This study provides us with both an invaluable reference and a source of much insight into the complexities of the field.

William A. Schabas OC MRIA
Oughterard, Ireland
17 October 2009

PREFACE AND ACKNOWLEDGEMENTS

As I began to tell friends and colleagues that I was writing a book on international and transnational criminal law, the response tended to be that this sounded very interesting, "war crimes stuff and all that." A few ventured that this must be something of a rarified field of law, even obscure. Twenty years ago, they would have been correct; international criminal law rested on the aging edifice of the *Charter of the International Military Tribunal (Nuremberg)* and the *Eichmann* trial, as well as a few war crimes treaties that rarely saw any traffic; the International Criminal Court was still just an idea; and transnational criminal law was a mixed bag of treaties on specified acts, along with old extradition treaties and some scratchings at inter-state evidence-gathering cooperation. The Canadian law and practice on point was mostly moribund.

What a difference two decades can make. As I write this preface, the world is celebrating the anniversary of the fall of the Berlin Wall, twenty years ago to the day. While the end of the Cold War was not the only prime mover in the revival of this field, it is a historical marker that prefaced a time of significant development in international as well as transnational criminal law. As this book was going to press, a sitting head of state was under indictment by a permanent and functioning International Criminal Court, a former head of state was being tried by the Special Court for Sierra Leone, and Radovan Karadzić was tangling with the International Criminal Tribunal for the former Yugoslavia over his conduct of his own defence on genocide charges. In Canada, a bill was going through Parliament that was designed, in part, to allow Canada to live up to its obligations under the *European Cybercrime Convention*;[1] some of our first post-9/11 terrorism prosecutions were lurching along in Ontario; and federal prosecutors had indicted a second Rwandan individual for crimes allegedly committed during the 1994 genocide, just weeks after the first person had been sentenced to life imprisonment. This subject matter is obscure no longer. It is in the public eye and before the conscience of Canadians, and the world, every day.

I was motivated to write this book in no small part by the sense that there was a hole in the literature around this field that could usefully be filled. There is, of course, no lack of academic writing on international criminal law, even general survey texts such as this one. Since 2003, a number of excellent books have been published by such reputable and learned commentators as M. Cherif Bassiouni;[2] Antonio Cassese;[3] Ilias Bantekas and Susan Nash;[4] and Robert Cryer, Hakan Friman, Darryl Robinson, and Elizabeth Wilmshurst.[5] However, all of these works, though of high quality, are dominated by their attention to the prosecution of truly *international* crimes — genocide, crimes against humanity, war crimes — by international courts and occasionally by states. This is a worthy, exciting, and fascinating field, and indeed a great deal of this book is dedicated to exactly this. However, this is, in relative terms, a rarified area. There are simply not that many international criminals, and even fewer trials of international criminals; when such trials do happen, they are momentous occasions.

The prosecution of these international crimes stands in sharp contrast to the vast majority of everyday criminal justice work that involves international law, which is done either around what this book calls *transnational crimes of international concern*, such as terrorism, money laundering, organized crime, and human and narcotics trafficking, or *transnational crimes of domestic concern*, which are simply ordinary domestic crimes that involve the jurisdiction of more than one state. Thus, *international* and *transnational* criminal law are related, but increasingly distinct, areas of law and practice, and the literature on the transnational side is much more scarce and diffuse. My hope is that this book, which gives roughly equal time to both sides of the equation, will make a modest contribution to redressing the imbalance.

---

1   E.T.S. No. 185 (2001).

2   *Introduction to International Criminal Law* (Ardsley, NY: Transnational Publishers, 2003).

3   *International Criminal Law*, 2d ed. (Oxford: Oxford University Press, 2008).

4   *International Criminal Law*, 3d ed. (New York: Routledge-Cavendish, 2007).

5   *An Introduction to International Criminal Law and Procedure* (Cambridge: Cambridge University Press, 2007).

A second aspect of my sense that there was a place for this book arose from a belief that something was needed on the Canadian side, both for international and for transnational criminal law. Canada is an increasingly important player in a world where crime is as globalized as the economy, yet there is only a small amount of scattered literature on various topics, with no attempt to bring it together and give the "big picture" from the Canadian point of view. Moreover, working with broad legal concepts from the purely inter-state level is one thing, but wrestling with the various treaty regimes, customary norms, and implementing legislation when one is actually trying criminal cases at the domestic level is entirely another. Given that both the international and the transnational are increasingly touching on domestic criminal law practice, there is a pressing need to make sure that international lawyers and criminal lawyers are speaking the same language. The goal, then, was fairly simple: to have a book in which practitioners and judges could have access to the relevant law (or at least a broad cross-section of it), explored, analyzed, and occasionally criticized in a useful manner. Also, as a teacher of international and transnational criminal law at a Canadian law school, my own approach has been to combine the international with the transnational and explore their application within the Canadian context. This book is designed to facilitate that kind of inquiry, and my modest hope is that other professors and their students will find it useful.

However, while I hope the book will be useful, I am by no means presenting it as being complete. When one begins saying *something* about a particular subject, it is difficult to resist the temptation to try to say *everything*, and figuring out the most relevant and salient points that will appeal to the broadest base of potential readers is a Herculean task. While the "Essentials" series has very properly become known for having produced high-quality books, I am not yet convinced that it is not a scheme to secretly torture struggling textbook writers. In any event, an effort to try to distil the "essentials" of both the relevant international law and the Canadian law on point has led to some necessary selectivity. In particular, trying to keep much of the focus on the transnational necessarily truncated treatment of the international. So, for example, there is no significant attention to several topics that tend to be discussed in international criminal law texts, such as principles of liability or modes of committing offences. Nor is there any focus on procedure and evidence before international criminal courts, nor on cooperation with those courts, which are better left to specialized texts on those subjects. Nor is there any treatment of the increasingly salient topic of civil liability for acts constituting international crimes and the necessary piercing of state immunity which this entails.

It will be clear that this book and its author owe a great intellectual debt to the pioneering work of Professors Sharon A. Williams and Jean-Gabriel Castel. Their book, *Canadian Criminal Law: International and Transnational Aspects*[6] was the first solid Canadian effort in the field, and though it is now regrettably out of date, it must be viewed as one of the more formidable and influential Canadian international law texts ever produced. I can only hope that the many litigators, jurists, and scholars who viewed that book as an invaluable resource will find the present book to be a worthy successor.

I have tried to state the law as of around 30 June 2009, although later developments have been incorporated where possible. There will undoubtedly be deficiencies, and I will welcome (at robert.currie@dal.ca) any comments that readers wish to provide.

ACKNOWLEDGMENTS

In the fall of 2006, I attended the Canadian Council on International Law's annual conference in Ottawa. One of the featured speakers that year was James Crawford, the Whewell Professor of International Law at the University of Cambridge and a world-renowned international law scholar. In the midst of his speech, Professor Crawford recalled getting and giving what he considered to be the most useful piece of advice about writing an international law textbook of any kind: "Don't do it." There was the expected appreciative chuckle from the audience. I noticed that Professor Crawford was not smiling.

Having now completed this project, I have some sense of what he meant. However, working on this book has, on balance, been one of the greatest pleasures of my legal career. This is in no small part because it allowed me to experience the generosity and kindness of a substantial number of people.

The peer review process for the manuscript was carried out by way of a unique effort on the part of lawyers at Justice Canada, all of whom practise in the various disparate areas dealt with herein. I was lucky that John McManus of the War Crimes Program had the energy and patience to coordinate this process, and I am extremely grateful to him and to the anonymous peer reviewers. A number of other Justice Canada personnel patiently answered questions, provided advice and documents, and generally supported my efforts for no other reason than interest and goodwill—despite the fact that in places I am quite critical regarding Crown

---

6   (Toronto: Butterworths, 1981).

positions on various points. I wish to thank them here: Terry Beitner, Tom Beveridge, Barbara Kothe, James Martin, Chris Ram, Amos Donahue, Lucie Angers, and Peter LaPrairie. I save for last my friend Joseph Rikhof, also of the War Crimes Program, who has been a tireless source of feedback and without whose encyclopedic knowledge of international criminal law this book would be much poorer.

A number of friends and colleagues read parts of the book (sometimes rather large swathes of it) and/or offered advice and criticism where it was most needed: Bill Fenrick, Hugh Kindred, Steve Coughlan, Jonathan Coady, Christine Hanson, Gib van Ert, Bill Gilmore, Judge John Joy, and Neil Boister. I am also grateful to Professor William Schabas for writing a foreword that so successfully enhances the Canadian flavour of the book. Many of my colleagues at Dalhousie, past and present (including those named above), have provided the rich intellectual atmosphere that challenged me to write this book, and the moral support that allowed me to continue the effort. I wish particularly to thank Phillip Saunders, Dawn Russell, Teresa Scassa, Diana Ginn, Bill Lahey, Rollie Thompson, David Blaikie, Chris Nicholls, Meinhard Doelle, Aldo Chircop, Elizabeth Hughes, and Michael Deturbide. My friends Gordie MacDonald and Scott MacPhail asked for and patiently listened to blow-by-blow updates on "how the book is going," and I will always be grateful to him for that.

I gratefully acknowledge that the research for this book was funded in part by a grant from the Foundation for Legal Research, as well as summer research funding provided by Dalhousie Law School (now the Schulich School of Law at Dalhousie University). That funding allowed me to retain the practically superhuman research assistance of Jessica Reekie (LL.B. Dalhousie, 2006) and Gillian MacNeil (LL.B. Dalhousie 2006, LL.L. University of Ottawa 2007, LL.M. University of Cambridge 2008), whose contributions are reflected on virtually every page of this book. In Gillian's case, I was grateful to take her on as the leading co-author of Chapter 11, which benefited greatly from her substantial knowledge on the difficult topic of immunities from prosecution. I am also grateful to Fiona Campbell, Emily Dwyer and Jim Janson, all of whom made research contributions in the later stages of writing. The library staff at the Sir James Dunn Law Library at Dalhousie were always helpful, particularly David Michels, whose ability to dive into the bowels of the UN document system is awe-inspiring. I must also express my appreciation and gratitude for the solid backing and indulgence I received from Irwin Law, and in particular from Jeff Miller, Alisa Posesorski, Heather Raven, and Anita Levin.

I wish to thank publicly the students of the International Criminal Law seminar course at Dalhousie Law School, 2005–2009, for being a source of inspiration and for cheerfully accepting having draft chapters of the book forced on them as required reading. There are a number of students who have passed through Dalhousie while this book was being written, both within and outside of the seminar, who have produced written work that I was fortunate to have been able to supervise and/or consult: Andrew Gough, Lee Seshagiri, James Miglin, and Daniel Watt. Some of their published work is cited in these pages. Those whom I have forgotten to thank will, I hope, forgive the omission. All of those mentioned above are naturally absolved of any responsibility for the book's weaknesses, the burden of which is mine alone.

This book is dedicated to the memory of my teacher, mentor, and friend, Ronald St. John Macdonald, without whose guidance and encouragement I might not have sought out this path; and to my wife, Donna Davis, and my daughters, Meg and Katherine, without whom nothing else would have any significance.

Robert J. Currie
Halifax, Nova Scotia
9 November 2009

ABBREVIATIONS

APC	All People's Congress
AP I	*First Protocol to the Geneva Conventions*
AP II	*Second Protocol to the Geneva Conventions*
AFRC	Armed Forces Revolutionary Council
ASP	Assembly of States Parties to the International Criminal Court
AU	African Union
CAH Act	*Crimes Against Humanity and War Crimes Act* [Canada]
CAT	United Nations *Convention against Torture*
CBSA	Canadian Border Services Agency
CDSA	*Controlled Drugs and Substances Act* [Canada]
CFATF	Caribbean Financial Action Task Force
CFPOA	*Corruption of Foreign Public Officials Act* [Canada]
CIA	Central Intelligence Agency [US]
CIC	Department of Citizenship and Immigration Canada
CICAD	Inter-American Drug Abuse Control Commission
CIDA	Canadian International Development Agency
CSCE	Conference for Security and Cooperation in Europe
CSIS	Canadian Security Intelligence Service
CTC	Counter-Terrorism Committee
CoE	Council of Europe
DFAIT	Department of Foreign Affairs and International Trade Canada

DRC	Democratic Republic of the Congo
ECCC	Extraordinary Chambers in the Courts of Cambodia
ECHR	*European Convention on Human Rights*
ECOSOC	United Nations Economic and Social Council
EEZ	exclusive economic zone
EGO	evidence-gathering order
EU	European Union
FATF	Financial Action Task Force
FIU	financial intelligence units
FRY	Federal Republic of Yugoslavia
GC I	*First Geneva Convention*
GC II	*Second Geneva Convention*
GC III	*Third Geneva Convention*
GC IV	*Fourth Geneva Convention*
IAEA	International Atomic Energy Agency
IAG	International Assistance Group, Justice Canada
ICAO	International Civil Aviation Organization
ICC	International Criminal Court
ICCPR	International Covenant on Civil and Political Rights
ICC Elements	*International Criminal Court, Elements of Crimes*
ICJ	International Court of Justice
ICJ Statute	*Statute of the International Court of Justice*
ICL	international criminal law
ICRC	International Committee of the Red Cross
ICTR	International Criminal Tribunal for Rwanda
ICTY	International Criminal Tribunal for the former Yugoslavia
IGO	inter-governmental organization
IHL	international humanitarian law
IHT	Iraqi High Tribunal
ILC	International Law Commission
ILO	International Labour Organization
IMO	International Maritime Organization
IMT	International Military Tribunal [Nuremberg]
IMTFE	International Military Tribunal for the Far East
INTERPOL	International Criminal Police Organization
IRPA	*Immigration and Refugee Protection Act* [Canada]
ISS	International Space Station
IWGTIP	Interdepartmental Working Group on Trafficking in Persons
ITLOS	International Tribunal on the Law of the Sea

JCE	joint criminal enterprise
JICJ	Journal of International Criminal Justice
KYC	"know your customer"
LRA	Lord's Resistance Army
MLA	mutual legal assistance in criminal matters
MLA Act	*Mutual Legal Assistance in Criminal Matters Act* [Canada]
MLAT	mutual legal assistance treaty
NAFO	Northwest Atlantic Fisheries Organization
NATO	North Atlantic Treaty Organization
NGO	non-governmental organization
OAS	Organization of American States
OAU	Organization of African Unity
Ocean YB	Ocean Yearbook
OECD	Organisation for Economic Co-operation and Development
OSCE	Organization for Security and Co-operation in Europe
PCIJ	Permanent Court of International Justice
POWs	prisoners of war
PREPCOM	Preparatory Committee for an International Criminal Court
RCMP	Royal Canadian Mounted Police
RIDMDG	Revue de droit militaire et de droit de la guerre/The Military Law and Law of War Review
RPE	*Rules of Procedure and Evidence*
RUF	Revolutionary United Front
SALW	small arms and light weapons
SCSL	Special Court for Sierra Leone
SOFA	Status of Forces Agreement [NATO]
STL	Special Tribunal for Lebanon
TCL	transnational criminal law
TOC Convention	*United Nations Convention against Transnational Organized Crime*
UKSIA	*State Immunity Act* [United Kingdom]
UN	United Nations
UNCAC	*United Nations Convention against Corruption*
UNCLOS	*United Nations Convention on the Law of the Sea*
UNCRC	United Nations *Convention on the Rights of the Child*
UNDCP	United Nations International Drug Control Program
UNGA	United Nations General Assembly
UNMIK	United Nations Interim Administration Mission in Kosovo

UNODC	United Nations Office on Drugs and Crime
UNSC	United Nations Security Council
UNTAET	United Nations Transitional Administration in East Timor
USSC	United States Supreme Court
VCLT	*Vienna Convention on the Law of Treaties*

CHAPTER 1

INTRODUCTION: CONVERGENCE OF DISCIPLINES

A. INTRODUCTION

To the person who says he knows nothing about international and transnational crime, the reply would have to be, "But of course you do; it is all around us; it is constantly in the media." Indeed, it is not hyperbole to state that over the last decade international and transnational crime have come to permeate a large part of the modern political, legal, and social agendas of both states and the world at large. As a case in point, what is arguably the most prominent and far-reaching socio-political event in modern history—the attacks on the World Trade Center and the Pentagon on 11 September 2001—was a manifestation of international terrorism, a phenomenon already well known to the world community. It was "transnational" in the truest sense of the word: it involved, as is well known, an attack in the US by a group of mostly Saudi nationals who were members of a shadowy organization that was being at least loosely run from Afghanistan. The victims of the attacks were nationals of several countries. Persons allegedly involved in planning the attack have been apprehended and subjected to trial in the US, the UK, and France. Others have been transported to secret detention sites in still other states (sometimes without the knowledge of these states), interrogated, and subjected to torture—which is itself an international crime.[1]

---

1   For example, Khalid Sheikh Mohammed, believed to be one of the chief lieutenants of Osama bin Laden and the planner of the 9/11 attacks, was apprehended

This horrendous crime was a forceful reminder that crime is not now (if it ever was) a matter only of concern to domestic victims, police, and prosecutors, and that crime suppression cannot stop at the borders of any one state. The reactions to and effects of 9/11 have been global in scope; they have included armed attacks on two sovereign states, increased and sometimes dubious enforcement of "security" goals by governments worldwide, the undermining of international human rights standards, and attempts to squelch legitimate public debate about the efficacy of these efforts.[2] Other horrendous crimes have led to significant international reaction. The international media has been full of reports about the atrocities which occurred during and after the breakup of the former Yugoslavia, the genocide that took place in Rwanda in 1994, and more recently the horrific carnage wrought by government and militia forces in the Darfur region of Sudan.

And yet it is not just international and transnational crime, but the bodies of law attaching to these phenomena, which are alive in the media and in the public imagination. In particular, the enforcement of what has traditionally been called "international criminal law" (ICL) has been very visible. One need only consider the prosecutions undertaken against former heads of state alone, which would have been unheard of twenty years ago: the arrest of former Chilean dictator Augusto Pinochet in the UK on the basis that he was wanted for crimes by a Spanish magistrate;[3] the trial of Serbian strongman Slobodan Milosević

---

in Pakistan in March, 2003. He was turned over to US authorities, who transported him to be questioned at an "undisclosed location," and he was later reported to have divulged information that led to the capture of other high-ranking Al-Qaeda figures (see Andrew Buncombe, "Attacks in Riyadh: Saudi Bombs Expose Myth of American Victory in Terror War" *The Independent* (14 May 2003) at 5). The US government recently disclosed that Mohammed had been subject to the "waterboarding" torture technique 183 times while in custody: Scott Shane, "Waterboarding Used 266 Times on 2 Suspects" *The New York Times* (20 April 2009), online: www.msnbc.msn.com/id/30302830/. At the time of writing, Mohammed was on trial at Guantanamo Bay.

2   "[T]he events of 11 September 2001 became a catalyst for the systematic disregard of established international rules on human rights, the treatment of combatant prisoners and the use of military force around the world . . . . " (Philippe Sands, *Lawless World: Making and Breaking Global Rules*, rev. ed. (London: Penguin, 2006) at 21). See also International Commission of Jurists, *Assessing Damage, Urging Action: Report of the Eminent Jurists Panel on Terrorism, Counterterrorism and Human Rights* (Geneva: International Commission of Jurists, 2009), online: www.icj.org/IMG/EJP-report.pdf.

3   *R. v. Bow Street Magistrate, ex parte Pinochet (No. 3)*, [2000] 1 A.C. 147 (H.L.). See also Michael Byers, "The Law and Politics of the Pinochet Case" (2000) 10 Duke J. Comp. & Int'l L. 415.

before the International Criminal Tribunal for the former Yugoslavia (ICTY), the first sitting head of government to be indicted and tried by an international criminal tribunal;[4] the trial, conviction, and execution of deposed Iraqi dictator Saddam Hussein before an Iraqi court for international crimes committed while he was in office;[5] the conviction of former Rwandan Prime Minister Jean Kambanda by the International Criminal Tribunal for Rwanda;[6] the trial of former Liberian President Charles Taylor before the Special Court for Sierra Leone;[7] the conviction of former Peruvian President Alberto Fujimori for torture, kidnappings, and enforced disappearances;[8] and the recent indictment of Sudanese President Omar Al-Bashir by the International Criminal Court (ICC).[9]

Even the making of international law, not always a matter of significant public interest, has had a high profile when international crime is involved, as evidenced by the prominent coverage of the 1998 United Nations conference in Rome that led to the conclusion of the *Rome Statute of the International Criminal Court*.[10] The *Rome Statute* is, in many senses, the pinnacle of the modern history of efforts to ensure accountability for international crime. That history, and the concurrent history of inter-state cooperation in suppressing transnational crime, will be briefly surveyed below.

B. HISTORY

While ICL in its modern form truly emerged in the twentieth century, some of the ideas and themes which underpin it can be traced back several thousand years and brought forward through the ancient empires

---

4　Which was brought to an untimely end by the defendant's death due to illness on 11 March 2006. See Michael Scharf & William Schabas, *Slobodan Milosevic on Trial: A Companion* (New York: Continuum, 2002).

5　Mariam Karouny, "Saddam Executed at Dawn" *The Globe and Mail* (30 December 2006) A1. See Michael Scharf, *Saddam on Trial: Understanding and Debating the Iraqi High Tribunal* (Durham, NC: Carolina Academic Press, 2006); Michael Newton & Michael Scharf, *Enemy of the State: The Trial and Execution of Saddam Hussein* (New York: St. Martin's Press, 2008).

6　*Kambanda* (ICTR-97-23-A), Appeals Chamber Judgment, 19 October 2000.

7　*Taylor* (SCSL-03-01-T). Taylor's trial is currently under way before a special panel of the Special Court for Sierra Leone, sitting in The Hague.

8　"Fujimori Gets Lengthy Jail Term" *BBC News* (7 April 2009), online: http://news.bbc.co.uk/2/hi/americas/7986951.stm.

9　"Warrant Issued for Sudan's Leader" *BBC News* (4 March 2009), online: http://news.bbc.co.uk/2/hi/africa/7923102.stm.

10　UN Doc. A/CONF.183/9; Can. T.S. 2002 No. 13 [*Rome Statute*].

of Egypt, Persia, Greece, and Rome, as well as the thought and cultures of India, China, Islamic countries, and medieval Europe.[11] It is first important to understand that modern international law itself is usually traced to the *Peace of Westphalia* of 1648,[12] and that the classic, "Westphalian" model of international law is based on a system of independent, sovereign states. The law which governs relations between these states is framed around consent, mutual recognition of sovereign equality, and mutually accepted obligations to both act in specific ways and to refrain from specific kinds of acts. Emerging from antiquity, however, was one of the earliest limits on state sovereignty: the "laws of war"[13] as a means of limiting the kinds of behaviour which could be engaged in during armed conflicts between states. Moreover, by the nineteenth century a broad consensus had emerged that individuals who violated the laws of war could be subject to prosecution, though these prosecutions were undertaken by state courts under national law at that time.

Significant formation of the primary rules of this body of law came with the adoption of the *First Geneva Convention* in 1864,[14] which dealt with ameliorating the condition of the wounded soldiers on battlefields, and with the various *Hague Conventions* that emerged from the International Peace Conferences held in 1899 and 1907, which imposed limitations on methods of warfare that could be employed by states. These treaties were among the earliest, and perhaps the first, to significantly place individuals under the protection of international law, which had until that point governed and protected only the rights and obligations of states. They eventually gave rise to modern international humanitarian law (IHL), particularly in the form of the *Geneva Conventions* of 1949,[15] which along with their two protocols[16] provide for criminalization of grave breaches of humanitarian standards during wartime.[17]

---

11   For a succinct and well-referenced account, see Robert Cryer, *Prosecuting International Crimes: Selectivity and the International Criminal Law Regime* (Cambridge: Cambridge University Press, 2006) c. 1 [Cryer]. See also William Schabas, *An Introduction to the International Criminal Court*, 3d ed. (Cambridge: Cambridge University Press, 2007) c. 1 [Schabas].

12   For a compelling critique of this, see Stéphane Beaulac, *The Power of Language in the Making of International Law: The Word "Sovereignty" in Bodin and Vattel and the Myth of Westphalia* (Boston: Martinus Nijhoff, 2004).

13   Now generally referred to as "international humanitarian law" (IHL) or the "law of armed conflict."

14   *1864 Convention for the Amelioration of the Condition of Wounded in Armies in the Field*, 1 Bevans 7; Can. T.S. 1942 No. 6.

15   (1950), 75 U.N.T.S. 31, 85, 135, and 287 [*Geneva Conventions*].

16   (1977), 1125 U.N.T.S. 3 and 609.

17   See Chapter 3 for more detailed treatment.

Some of the first actual movement towards liability of individuals for breaches of international law, however, emerged in the aftermath of WW I.[18] The "Commission on the Responsibility of the Authors of War and on the Enforcement of Penalties" was set up by the victorious Allies in 1919 as a means of investigating the potential for prosecuting those who violated the laws of war and, notably, for those who started and waged the war. Its report[19] took a robust approach, recommending prosecution of perpetrators under "the principles of the law of nations" (sourced, in part, in the *Hague Conventions*) and included among those to be tried the Kaiser of Germany and other high officials.[20] In rough accordance with the Commission's recommendations, the 1919 *Treaty of Versailles*[21] provided for the set-up of Allied Tribunals to try German perpetrators. However, the effort was mostly ineffective and in the end, only twelve trials were held at Leipzig, under questionable criminal processes, and the stiffest sentence imposed was four years. The Kaiser, the prosecution of whom article 227 of the *Treaty of Versailles* had specifically anticipated, escaped to the Netherlands, which refused to extradite him to face the charges. A similar attempt to prosecute Turkish war crimes perpetrators was aborted by the 1923 *Treaty of Lausanne*, which imposed a general amnesty.[22]

It is generally agreed that true international criminal justice came into being after WW II. In 1945 the United Kingdom, France, the US, and the Soviet Union signed *The Agreement for the Prosecution and Punishment of Major War Criminals of the European Axis*, establishing the *Charter of the International Military Tribunal* (IMT),[23] to which nineteen other states later adhered. The IMT was convened in the German city of Nuremberg in November 1945 to try twenty-two prominent Nazi leaders for the three crimes within its jurisdiction: crimes against peace, war crimes, and crimes against humanity. The tribunal was made up of four judges and four alternates, appointed by each of the four Allied Powers. Ultimately, nineteen of the defendants were convicted and

---

18   See, generally, James F. Willis, *Prologue to Nuremberg: The Politics and Diplomacy of Punishing War Criminals of the First World War* (Westport, CT: Greenwood Press, 1982).

19   Report of the Commission to the Preliminary Peace Conference, reprinted in (1920) 14 A.J.I.L. 95.

20   Though the Commission did conclude that the waging of aggressive war was not a crime under international law; *ibid.* at 118.

21   *Treaty of Peace between the Allied and Associated Powers and Germany*, [1919] T.S. 4.

22   *Treaty of Lausanne between Principal Allied and Associated Powers and Turkey* (1923), 28 L.N.T.S. 11.

23   82 U.N.T.S. 279; the *Charter of the IMT* was annexed to the Agreement.

twelve of these were sentenced to death.[24] Subsequently, a number of other trials of suspected German war criminals were held in various parts of the country occupied by the Allies, the most important held pursuant to Allied Control Council Order No. 10.[25]

The IMT was faced with a formidable legal task. It was by no means certain, and is still open to question, whether the "crimes" within its purview were indeed crimes under international law at the time the acts were committed—or indeed whether there was such a thing in international law as "the direct imposition of liability without any intercession of domestic legal orders."[26] Nonetheless, it is beyond doubt that both the principle of individual liability under international law and the crimes themselves were conclusively established by the IMT's judgment.[27] The tribunal rejected arguments that the crimes themselves had been created by the *Charter of the IMT* and thus were retroactive. It defined "crimes against peace," or the making of aggressive war, as "the supreme international crime" and found its basis for so doing in the *Kellogg-Briand Pact* of 1928,[28] which had renounced war as an instrument of national policy. War crimes were founded in the *Hague Conventions*, while crimes against humanity were closely linked to the laws of war but essentially founded on the fact that in large part these were acts committed upon people by their own governments, or by governments acting outside the scope of armed conflicts, and that "it would fly in the face of justice to leave Nazi crimes unpunished."[29] These aspects of the Nuremberg legacy were carried on through the post-war period by other courts, including those set up in Germany under Allied Control Council Order No. 10.[30] The IMT's "sister court," the International Military Tribunal for the Far East (IMTFE), tried the most senior Japanese war criminals under similar law as was applied at Nuremberg.[31]

---

24 See, generally, Telford Taylor, *The Anatomy of the Nuremberg Trials* (New York: Knopf, 1992).

25 *Control Council Law No. 10, Punishment of Persons Guilty of War Crimes, Crimes Against Peace and Against Humanity*, 3 Official Gazette Control Council for Germany, 50–55 (1946) [Allied Control Order No. 10].

26 Cryer, above note 11 at 39.

27 Reprinted in *France et al. v. Göering et al.*, reprinted (1947), 41 A.J.I.L. 172 [*Göering*]. See also (1947), 22 I.M.T. 203, 13 I.L.R. 203, 1 Trial of the Major War Criminals 171 (Int'l Military Trib.).

28 Can. T.S. 1929 No. 7.

29 Schabas, above note 11, Introduction at 6. See, generally, M. Cherif Bassiouni, *Crimes Against Humanity in International Criminal Law*, 2d rev. ed. (The Hague: Kluwer, 1999).

30 Above note 25; see, for example, *In Re Ohlendorf and Others* (1948), 15 I.L.R. 656.

31 Though there has been considerable scepticism and criticism with regard to the legality and the fairness of the IMTFE, which has not withstood as readily

There was a rush of enthusiasm and activity immediately following the major post-war prosecutions. The General Assembly of the newly formed United Nations passed a resolution affirming "the principles of international law recognized by" the *IMT Charter* and the tribunal's judgment,[32] and directing the International Law Commission (ILC) to formulate the *Nuremberg Principles*.[33] The *Genocide Convention*[34] was formulated in 1948, while 1949 saw the adoption of the four *Geneva Conventions*.[35] Article VI of the *Genocide Convention* specifically envisioned the founding of "an international penal tribunal" to try perpetrators, and the ILC and a special committee of the General Assembly worked on this question for several years, as well as on the drafting of a "Code of Crimes against the Peace and Security of Mankind."[36] By 1954, however, it had become clear that the tensions of the Cold War would prevent any further substantive work on the ICL agenda, and the General Assembly suspended its efforts.

Over the next few decades there were a few trials of war criminals, notably the prosecution of Adolf Eichmann by Israel[37] and that of Klaus Barbie by France.[38] Also, the work of the ILC on its draft code of crimes was revived by the General Assembly in 1981.[39] On the whole, however, the development of international criminal justice was moribund at best, with little progress made despite the continued occurrence of conflicts and atrocities.[40]

---

as the IMT the charge of "victor's justice." See Richard Minear, *Victor's Justice: The Tokyo War Crimes Trial* (Princeton: Princeton University Press, 1971); R. John Pritchard, "International Military Tribunal for the Far East and the Allied National War Crimes Trials in Asia" in M. Cherif Bassiouni, ed., *International Criminal Law*, 2d ed. (Ardsley, NY: Transnational, 1999) vol. III at 109 [Bassiouni 2d ed.]. See Chapter 4.

32   GA Res. 95(I), UN GAOR, 1st Sess., UN Doc A/64/Add.1, (1946) 188.

33   Which it did in 1950: (1950) Yearbook of the International Law Commission, vol. II, para. 97.

34   *Convention for the Prevention and Punishment of the Crime of Genocide* (1951), 78 U.N.T.S. 277, Can. T.S. 1949 No. 27 [*Genocide Convention*]. See Chapter 3.

35   Above note 15. See Chapter 3.

36   See D.H.N. Johnson, "Draft Code of Offences against the Peace and Security of Mankind" (1955) 4 I.C.L.Q. 445.

37   *Attorney-General of Israel v. Eichmann* (Jerusalem Dist. Ct. 1961), reprinted (1968), 36 I.L.R. 18. See Chapter 5.

38   *Fédération Nationale des Déportés et Internés Résistants et Patriotes et Autres c. Barbie* (1985), 78 I.L.R. 125 (Fr. Ct. Cass.).

39   GA Res. 36/106 (1981).

40   Geert-Jan Knoops, *An Introduction to the Law of International Criminal Tribunals: A Comparative Study* (Ardsley, NY: Transnational, 2003) at xxv.

The end of the Cold War, symbolized in some sense by the fall of the Berlin Wall in 1989, spurred on a great number of social forces. An unfortunate aspect was the unleashing of ethnic and religious tensions that had quietly been simmering during the years of superpower dominance, most brutally exemplified by the atrocities committed during the breakup of Yugoslavia that commenced in 1991. A Commission of Experts was established in 1992 by the Security Council to investigate and gather evidence on the crimes being committed and continuing in the area.[41] The Commission echoed earlier calls[42] for the establishment of an international criminal tribunal to prosecute responsible individuals, and as a result the Security Council created the International Criminal Tribunal for the former Yugoslavia (ICTY).[43] The mandate of the ICTY was to prosecute "persons responsible for serious violations of international humanitarian law committed in the territory of the former Yugoslavia since 1991,"[44] and its founding statute drew on the work being done by the ILC to define both the crimes and the makeup of a court which could administer them.

The ICTY was the first of what are often referred to as the "UN *ad hoc* tribunals," *ad hoc* in the sense that each was created for a limited time[45] to deal with a specific conflict rather than being a permanent institution. The second was created in 1994 in response to genocide and other atrocities committed primarily in Rwanda; the Security Council was galvanized by international condemnation for its failure to intervene early enough to prevent the killings. The International Criminal Tribunal for Rwanda (ICTR) was, like the ICTY, an exercise of the Security Council's powers under Chapter VII of the *UN Charter*, which are designed to allow the Council to intervene in matters that jeopardize international peace and security. Its statute is similar to that of the ICTY, and the two tribunals share an integrated Appeals Chamber.

The year 1989 also saw the re-invigoration of the idea of a permanent international criminal tribunal.[46] The General Assembly asked the

---

41   See William J. Fenrick, "In the Field with UNCOE: Investigating Atrocities in the Territory of Former Yugoslavia" (1994) 34 RIDMDG 33.

42   Schabas, above note 11, Introduction at 11.

43   UN Doc. S/RES/827.

44   SC Res. 808 (1993).

45   The ICTY's current completion strategy plans for the conclusion of trials by 2010, and of appeals by 2011.

46   See M. Cherif Bassiouni, "The Making of the International Criminal Court" in M. Cherif Bassiouni, ed., *International Criminal Law*, 3d ed. (Leiden: Martinus Nijhoff, 2008), vol. III at 117 [Bassiouni 3d ed.]; Gerhard Mueller & Douglas Besharov, "Evolution and Enforcement of International Criminal Law" in Bassiouni 2d ed., above note 31, vol. I at 257.

ILC to re-examine the potential for such a body,[47] at the request of Trinidad and Tobago and a group of similarly minded Latin American states which hoped to have an independent mode of prosecuting narcotics traffickers. By 1994 the ILC had produced a draft statute for a court, which was complemented in 1996 by a final version of the *Code of Crimes against the Peace and Security of Mankind.*[48] Despite intense controversy and disagreement, matters progressed quickly (by international law standards) and in 1995 the General Assembly set up the Preparatory Committee for an International Criminal Court (PREP-COM) to formulate proposals for a treaty that would be placed before an international conference of states. That conference, as noted above, was held in Rome in the summer of 1998. At the end of what was by all accounts a remarkable negotiating session[49] that was chaired by Canadian diplomat Philippe Kirsch, the *Rome Statute*[50] was adopted by a strong majority vote and came into force on 1 July 2002 after it had been ratified by sixty states; it currently has 109 parties. The court ended up having jurisdiction essentially over the core Nuremberg crimes—crimes against humanity, war crimes, genocide, and aggression—though, ironically, proposals to include narcotics trafficking were dropped, as were suggestions that the court prosecute other transnational crimes such as terrorism. The crime of aggression was, as it had been after WW II, a political hot potato and was left to be defined in future efforts of the state parties.[51]

As will be seen in more detail in Chapter 4, the ICC has jurisdiction over criminal conduct only where states that have jurisdiction over the crimes are unwilling or unable genuinely to do so, a mechanism referred to as "complementarity." However, states that are parties to the *Rome Statute* also have an obligation to make the crimes under the ICC's jurisdiction crimes under their domestic laws, so as to be able to at least decide whether to prosecute in the first place. This has led to a re-invigoration of state efforts to criminalize and, to some extent, prosecute these "enemies of humanity." In 2000 Canada passed its own legislation in this regard, the *Crimes Against Humanity and War Crimes Act*[52] (*CAH Act*), along with various amendments to related statutes,

---

47   GA Res. 44/39 (1989).

48   UN Doc. A/51/10 (1996).

49   See Philippe Kirsch & John T. Holmes, "The Rome Conference on an International Criminal Court: The Negotiating Process" (1999) 93 A.J.I.L. 2.

50   Above note 10.

51   The negotiating process to conclude a definition is currently under way; see Chapter 3.

52   S.C. 2000, c. 24 [*CAH Act*].

and an alleged participant in the Rwandan atrocities has been tried under this statute.[53] Also, the demonstrated successes of the *ad hoc* tribunals and the founding of the ICC have spurred on other efforts at internationalized criminal justice, and special courts or chambers have been set up in Sierra Leone, Cambodia, East Timor, Kosovo, Iraq, and Lebanon.[54] As will be seen, as was the case with Nuremberg, each of these efforts has attracted controversy, and the current situation is far from an idealized vision of what international criminal justice might be. Nonetheless, it is undeniable that the last six decades have seen significant, even momentous, developments in the establishment of mechanisms of accountability for the most heinous of crimes.

Parallel to the creation and growth of ICL, however, have been legal developments that deal with less dramatic but still pernicious brands of crime, the kinds of crime that states must deal with on a daily basis and which consume the bulk of law enforcement resources. This body of law will be referred to here as transnational criminal law (TCL), for reasons explained more fully in Section C, below in this chapter.

Writing just prior to the creation of the *Charter of the IMT*, Professor A.N. Trainin wrote of international crimes in the ICL sense, but also noted that "conventions are quite possible for combating individual crimes which are not of an international character . . . but which require coordinated measures of struggle."[55] To some extent this was stating a not only obvious but well-established fact; states had long since seen the light of "coordinated measures of struggle" against certain brands of criminals and crime that tended to use state sovereignty to their advantage, and both formal and informal cooperation in suppressing these activities had been in place for well over a century.[56] Pirates, for example, had long been declared enemies of humanity and by mutual agreement of states were susceptible to prosecution by any state which could apprehend them, regardless of their nationality or where their crimes had taken place. Slavery had been formally outlawed throughout most of the world by the end of the nineteenth century, and

---

53   RCMP, News Release, "RCMP Charges Foreign National with War Crimes" (19 October 2005). See Chapter 5. Desiré Munyaneza was convicted of genocide, war crimes, and crimes against humanity in May 2009 (*R. c. Munyaneza*, 2009 QCCS 2201, leave to appeal granted, 2009 QCCA 1279).

54   See Chapter 4.

55   A.N. Trainin, *Hitlerite Responsibility under Criminal Law*, trans. by A. Rothstein (London: Hutchinson, 1945) at 42.

56   For a general account, see Ethan Nadelmann, "Global Prohibition Regimes: The Evolution of Norms in International Society" (1990) 44 International Organization 479.

various international treaties prove a substantial level of international cooperation to suppress the trade in human beings.[57] There were several centuries' worth of treaties between states on extradition, allowing the transfer of fugitive criminals back to states where they had committed crimes in order that prosecution take place.[58] The International Criminal Police Organization (INTERPOL) was founded in Vienna in 1923,[59] an early example of an inter-governmental organization designed to fight transnational crime.

Nonetheless, as Professor Roger Clark points out, the distinctions made by Trainin "do seem to cover the field since 1945 fairly well."[60] In the years following WW II, and corresponding with developments in communications and transportation technology, there has been an exponential increase in the amount of crime that crosses borders and in the successful frustration of the efforts of law enforcement personnel. These are, for the most part, garden-variety domestic criminals who are breaking domestic laws, but increasing sophistication and the resource base that comes with operations of an international scope can confer advantages on them. Similarly, the response has been (again, by international law standards) an exponential increase in the number of international treaties designed to deal with these trends. For example, there are over a dozen treaties designed to facilitate inter-state cooperation in suppressing various terrorist acts, and there are similar and widely adhered-to instruments to suppress everything from organized crime, narcotics trafficking, and money laundering to currency counterfeiting, attacks on submarine cables, and unlawful use of the mail. These "suppression conventions" and their domestic manifestations in Canada are dealt with in Chapter 7.

On some occasions the level of cooperation and adherence by states in these treaties has led to particular suppression regimes achieving truly global status. For example, the United Nations *Convention against Torture (CAT)*[61] was concluded in 1984 in an effort to combat torture by persons acting in an official capacity. The convention was widely adhered to, and today it is well settled that the prohibition of torture

---

57   See M. Cherif Bassiouni, "Enslavement: Slavery, Slave-Related Practices, and Trafficking in Persons for Sexual Exploitation" in Bassiouni 3d ed., above note 46, vol. I at 535.

58   See Section D, below in this chapter and Chapter 9.

59   "INTERPOL History," online: www.interpol.int/Public/icpo/governance/sg/history.asp.

60   Roger Clark, "Offenses of International Concern: Multilateral State Treaty Practice in the Forty Years Since Nuremberg" (1988) 57 Nordic J. Int'l L. 49 at 84.

61   Can. T.S. 1987 No. 36.

is a *jus cogens*, or non-derogable, norm under customary international law and is binding on all states regardless of whether they are a party to the *CAT*. Similarly, the *Apartheid Convention*[62] was created in order to deal with the particular situation of South Africa, but is now settled as having created an international crime that binds all states and individuals. Additionally, both of these treaties have informed further efforts at codifying international criminal law, since each is defined in the *Rome Statute* as a form of crime against humanity.

Even beyond its role in formulating treaties, the United Nations has devoted significant resources to assisting and coordinating international cooperation in suppressing various forms of transnational crime. The UN Commission on Crime Prevention and Criminal Justice is an active body that has a membership of forty states at any given time, and is responsible for setting policy directions for combating crime and strengthening state criminal justice systems, as well as for arranging periodic international congresses on crime prevention and criminal justice. Its directives are carried out by the United Nations Office on Drugs and Crime (UNODC),[63] which provides significant resources to states towards information sharing, assistance with treaty implementation, and facilitating technical cooperation projects.

The remainder of this chapter reviews the analytical approach to be taken to international and transnational criminal law in this book, and then sketches out some of the fundamental concepts and core developments which underpin the subject matter.

C. DISTINGUISHING INTERNATIONAL AND TRANSNATIONAL CRIMINAL LAW

1) Analytical Models of ICL and TCL

The various legal doctrines and instruments that are under consideration in this book have historically been labelled "international criminal law," and articles, books, and law school courses have borne this name consistently for decades. However, whatever ICL was, it was in no way an internally consistent system or doctrine of law, international or otherwise; it had no unique methodology and none of the characteristics of a proper legal discipline, and its most illustrious proponents

---

62 *International Convention on the Suppression and Punishment of the Crime of Apartheid*, 30 November 1973, 1015 U.N.T.S. 243 [*Apartheid Convention*].

63 Online: www.unodc.org/unodc/index.html.

disagreed even on what the boundaries were.[64] It is true enough to say that, topically, ICL is concerned with the suppression of crime and that it has some international law content. However, by the time the first legal scratchings emerged on the idea of a "world criminal court" that would give firm foundation to the idea of individual criminal liability under international law,[65] various networks of states had already been dealing for some time with crime and criminals that crossed borders—phenomena that created a different order of international law problems and required different kinds of solutions. For the latter kind of behaviour, the criminology discipline has developed the term "transnational crime," and this terminology has gained a great deal of acceptance among politicians and policy-makers.[66] International lawyers, by contrast, simply "embrace the division of criminal law, based on the legal order of reference, into national and international."[67] Thus, using the label ICL immediately precipitates inquiry into what *type* of "international criminal law" the speaker intends to deal with. This is unsatisfactory, and yet the relationships between these two streams of ICL are significant enough that it is intuitive and efficient to deal with them as, loosely, one subject matter—and, more to the point, in one book. What is required is an analytical framework that allows us to separate and identify the various features.

The analytical model used here stems in no small part from the fact that this text, as part of a series of books about "Essentials of Canadian Law," is taking a view of international and transnational criminal law largely from the perspective of one state, Canada. The goal here is not simply to do the conventional survey of the various penal regimes in international law and refer only lightly to enforcement at the domestic level, though some overview of the broad corpus of international criminal law and practice is necessary. Rather, this book attempts a fairly detailed survey of the interaction between domestic criminal law and the international law norms that both inform it and to some extent are incorporated into it.

---

64   Some doubted that it even existed; see Georg Schwarzenberger, "The Problem of an International Criminal Law" (1950) 3 Curr. Legal Probs. 263.

65   See James Brierly, "Do We Need An International Criminal Court?" (1927) 8 Brit. Y.B. Int'l L. 81; 1937 *Convention for the Creation of an International Criminal Court* (1938) League of Nations Official Journal Special Supp. 156; Manley O. Hudson, "The Proposed International Criminal Court" (1938) 32 A.J.I.L. 549.

66   Gerhard O.W. Mueller, "Transnational Crime: Definitions and Concepts" in Phil Williams & Dimitri Vlassis, eds., *Combating Transnational Crime* (London: Frank Cass, 2001).

67   Neil Boister, "'Transnational Criminal Law'?" (2003) 14 E.J.I.L. 953 at 953.

This is necessary and desirable for two reasons. First, as the globalization of criminal law has proceeded, it has been observed that international lawyers and criminal lawyers often do not speak each other's language very well. This is understandable, given that international law is a stand-alone legal system that has traditionally been concerned with the rights and obligations of states rather than individuals, while criminal law systems are as varied as the cultures from which they emerge and are focused on both prosecuting crimes and protecting the human rights of individuals. Each discipline has its own language and its own distinct methodology. However, as international law becomes an increasingly important part of domestic legal frameworks, while at the same time criminal law concepts are being developed at the international level, the need for cross-disciplinary communication is intensifying. Today's domestic criminal practitioner needs to be alive to inter-state jurisdictional problems, treaty norms, and the impact of international human rights obligations. Conversely, those who would see international crimes prosecuted at the state level must have a solid understanding of how the domestic criminal law operates and how it implements and deals with international law norms.

Second, the traditional use of the label "international criminal law" has arguably passed its prime. To describe the legal regimes dealt with in this text as a "mixture of international and criminal laws" is far too glib and simplistic. A better starting point is to identify the utility of being able to understand "the convergence of two disciplines: the penal aspects of international law and the international aspects of national penal law."[68] Yet at each point of this "convergence" there are unique and even systemic developments that are complex, far-reaching, and worthy of individualized study. In fact, it may be said that there are various streams of what is traditionally referred to as "international criminal law" and that these streams are diverging and developing distinct characteristics, to the point that it is helpful and necessary to examine them separately.

The most thorough and successful doctrinal work to date on international and transnational criminal law has been done by Professor Cherif Bassiouni.[69] Under the rubric "international criminal law," Bas-

---

68   Jordan Paust *et al.*, *International Criminal Law: Cases and Materials*, 2d ed. (Durham, NC: Carolina Academic Press, 2000) at 3.

69   See generally M. Cherif Bassiouni, *Introduction to International Criminal Law* (Ardsley, NY: Transnational, 2003), and "The Discipline of International Criminal Law" in Bassiouni 3d ed., 46, vol. I at 3. See also Barbara Yarnold, "Doctrinal Basis for the International Criminalisation Process" (1994) 8 Temple Int'l & Comp. L.J. 85.

siouni includes all international law, both substantive and procedural, that has some penal characteristics. These he breaks down into certain categories: international crime *stricto sensu* (i.e., crimes for which there is individual liability under international law itself), crimes of international concern (i.e., crimes which are the subject of international treaties that coordinate state efforts to suppress them), and associated procedural and enforcement modalities which operate both under domestic laws and via international law obligations between states.

Why depart from such a well-developed attempt to resolve "international criminal law" as a distinct discipline? Even Bassiouni, noting the complexities inherent in such a broad scope of subject matter, reflects that "a doctrinal framework reflecting the polyvalent nature of ICL is difficult to formulate because the disciplines from which its components originate are inherently different."[70] For the purpose of examining this body of law from the domestic stable, at least, it is analytically convenient to take the "polyvalence" to its ultimate end and break its constituent parts into separate analytical categories.

In an important essay,[71] Professor Neil Boister has made a compelling case for the decoupling of international criminal law and transnational criminal law. Building on Philip Jessup's use of the phrase "transnational law" in reference to "all law which regulates actions or events that transcend national frontiers,"[72] Boister proposes using the phrase "transnational criminal law" (TCL) as a descriptive analytical phrase separate from "international criminal law." It would cover "the indirect suppression by international law through domestic penal law of criminal activities that have actual or potential trans-boundary effects,"[73] and focus specifically on the network of "suppression conventions" that have developed since the nineteenth century in order to coordinate inter-state efforts to combat certain types of crime.[74] This system, Boister argues, is highly distinguishable from the legal norms that attempt to suppress international crimes *stricto sensu*. True international criminal law usually emerges from customary international law, and individual criminal liability under international law can now be directly enforced by, *inter alia*, the International Criminal Court. Transnational crimes, by contrast, basically operate under an indirect suppression regime wherein states agree by treaty to criminalize cer-

70   Bassiouni, "The Discipline of International Criminal Law," *ibid.* at 9.
71   Boister, above note 67.
72   Philip Jessup, *Transnational Law* (New Haven: Yale Univ. Press, 1956) at 2, as quoted in Boister, *ibid.* at 954.
73   Boister, *ibid.* at 955.
74   See, generally, Chapter 7.

tain kinds of conduct and to assist each other in combating and enforcing—the goal being to facilitate domestic prosecution of domestic crimes, albeit in response to international concerns. Also, true international criminal law deals with conduct that is deemed to offend or threaten the most important interests of the international community or to "shock the conscience of humankind," while transnational criminal laws respond either to state concern regarding criminal conduct that crosses borders or to shared cosmopolitan values regarding the harmfulness of some brands of crime.[75] It seeks to achieve these shared aims "through the suppression conventions projecting substantive criminal norms beyond the national boundaries of the state in which they originated."[76] Finally, as will be seen, international crimes can be prosecuted by any state regardless of where they occur under the principle of universal jurisdiction, whereas jurisdiction over transnational crimes is more limited.

Boister distinguishes transnational crimes from purely domestic crimes by noting that domestic crimes "are criminalized solely at the election of the state and are not initiated through international treaty."[77] While this correctly separates out those domestic crimes which have no international law *source*, it is not unusual for an otherwise purely domestic crime to have international law *implications* and present unique problems with which governments, courts, and defence lawyers must wrestle. For example, a criminal operation in Canada fraudulently sells securities by telephone to US residents, who send their money to other members of the operation located in Panama and Costa Rica; does Canada have the jurisdiction to prosecute, or should it cede jurisdiction to another affected state?[78] Or another: Canadian police investigating a money-laundering operation engage in search and seizure activities in the Turks and Caicos Islands. At the trial of the individual alleged to have controlled the operation, does the *Canadian Charter of*

---

75   Boister, above note 67 at 966–68.

76   Boister, *ibid.* at 968. Boister does note, however, that these "substantive norms" of domestic law become diluted as they are projected onto the transnational level, as the suppression conventions tend towards vaguer descriptions of the kinds of offences to be dealt with and leave it to the state parties to continue to define the substantive content of the offences as they wish. This "doctrinal weakness" in TCL is in marked contrast with international crimes *stricto sensu*, the content of which is (or is meant to be) universally defined under international law; see *ibid.* at 958.

77   Boister, *ibid.* at 963.

78   See *Libman v. The Queen*, [1985] 2 S.C.R. 178.

Rights and Freedoms (Charter)[79] apply to potentially exclude the evidence seized offshore?[80] While these matters are domestically focused, the international law issues raised can be complex and are frequently misunderstood. Any study of the transnational dimensions of criminal law should give this area specific attention.

Accordingly, this book will approach the subject matter using the set of analytical categories detailed below.[81] There is no intent here to present this structure as a means to redefine international and transnational criminal law as a discipline or to displace the significant work by Bassiouni and others. Rather, the goal is to present the salient features of this emerging area of law in a way that highlights the distinguishing features but allows appreciation of the interplay between the various streams; and to provide teachers, students, and practitioners with a set of convenient "leaping off" points for engaging with what can be extremely complex subject matter. The categories are framed around classification of the "crimes" involved, but obviously the subject matter here is equally concerned with the entire bodies of law which are in place for prohibition, prosecution, and enforcement.

2) International Crimes

International crimes are crimes that are deemed by the international community to transcend the domestic criminal law of any state, and that call for suppression and enforcement either directly under international law or by permissive use of the widest bases of state jurisdiction. These are acts which strike at the most central concerns and interests of the entire world community, states and individuals alike, and justify bringing to bear the entire weight of the international legal system. They will, variously or in combination, "shock the conscience of humanity" because of their pernicious nature, or threaten international peace and security. They will often have an element of state involvement in the criminal act, making the suppression and prosecution of the crime more difficult and justifying a significantly higher level of condemnation than would otherwise be necessary. The perpetrators are, to use the conventional phrase, *hostis humani generis*, the

---

79   *Canadian Charter of Rights and Freedoms*, Part I of the *Constitution Act, 1982*, being Schedule B to the *Canada Act 1982* (U.K.), 1982, c. 11 [*Charter*].

80   See *R. v. Hape*, [2007] 2 S.C.R. 292 [*Hape*].

81   For a somewhat similar framework, see Edward Wise & Ellen Podgor, *International Criminal Law: Cases and Materials* (New York: Lexis, 2000).

enemies of humankind. The prohibition of an international crime will most usually be a *jus cogens*[82] norm under international law.

There are essentially two subcategories of international crime. The first is covered by the idea of international crimes in the strict sense, that is, crimes for which there is individual responsibility under customary international law, and which can be prosecuted directly by an international court as well as by domestic criminal courts. These criteria are met by the offences of genocide, crimes against humanity, war crimes, and aggression (or "crimes against peace"), which are often referred to as the "core crimes."[83] Note two points. First, individual liability for these crimes under international law may be codified in a treaty, such as the *Rome Statute*, or in an instrument such as the statutes of the ICTY and ICTR, which were created pursuant to resolutions of the UN Security Council. Also, as in the case of the crime of genocide, a treaty creating a crime may itself pass into customary international law.[84] However, liability for an international crime is not dependent on such an instrument because it proceeds directly from customary international law, and accordingly, no state may question it. Second, states may enter into treaties that oblige them to actively prosecute these core crimes, and in some cases there may even be obligations to prosecute under customary international law.[85] However, the *prohibition* of each of these crimes remains a matter of customary international law and is binding upon all states, and each may be prosecuted by any state under the customary international law principle of *universal jurisdiction*[86] as well as by truly international criminal tribunals.

The second subcategory of international crime covers those offences for which there is no direct liability of individuals under international law, but which are of a sufficiently odious nature that they may permissively be prosecuted by any state under its domestic criminal law system. Even a state which has no direct tie to the criminal act itself is deemed to be acting on behalf of the entire international community in enforcing against such offences, and may utilize the principle of *universal jurisdiction* in so doing. These crimes—torture, piracy, apartheid, and slavery—have not attracted the status of the core crimes, but are deemed to be sufficiently egregious to justify prosecution of the perpe-

---

82   See Section G(2)(b), below in this chapter.

83   As will be seen in Chapters 3 and 4, these are the four crimes over which the International Criminal Court has jurisdiction.

84   *Genocide Convention*, above note 34.

85   As appears to be the case for grave breaches of the *Geneva Conventions*; see Chapter 2, Section C(3)(d) and Chapter 3.

86   See Chapter 2, Section C(3)(d).

trators wherever they may go, so as to ensure they can find no safe haven. With some crimes, such as torture, the prohibition of the offence is a *jus cogens* norm, and states must at least have a law that prohibits torture in their domestic systems in order to comply with international law. With others, such as piracy, there may or may not be an obligation to prohibit the crime, but virtually universal interest in suppressing the crime means that international law nonetheless provides a broad jurisdictional basis for interested and affected states to prosecute.

3) Transnational Crimes of International Concern

This category of crime covers those referred to by Boister as operating under the framework of "transnational criminal law." It covers crimes that, firstly, are not properly considered "international crimes." There is no direct liability under international law for an individual convicted of these acts, nor may any state utilize the universal principle of jurisdiction in a permissive manner to prosecute any offender whom it can apprehend. However, these are types of crime that affect the interests of several, and sometimes a large number, of states, whether those interests are criminal, economic, social, or cultural. Most importantly, they generally have a transboundary element or effect of some sort, where any or all of the acts, perpetrators, proceeds of crime, harm, or other effects touch on the jurisdiction of more than one state. Accordingly, states enter into agreements (typically referred to as the "suppression conventions") to cooperate with each other in order to ensure that offenders have more difficulty finding safe haven from authorities wishing to prosecute them, and to pool prosecutorial and enforcement resources in a way that ensures a common base level of ability among partner states to actively suppress the criminal activities.

These objectives are accomplished by imposing three main types of obligations on partner states. Each must: change its domestic law in order to criminalize a particular kind of conduct; establish a broad regime for taking jurisdiction over offences and offenders on both territorial and extraterritorial bases; and either prosecute any offender whom it apprehends or extradite the offender to another partner state which is willing to do so (a device usually called *aut dedere aut judicare*). The *aut dedere* mechanism, in one way, makes the exercise of jurisdiction over these crimes broader than state jurisdiction over international crimes since, for the most part, exercising universal jurisdiction over international crimes is permissive but not mandatory. Under most of the suppression conventions, by contrast, any state which apprehends an offender must exercise jurisdiction over that person by either prosecuting or extraditing. However, an *aut dedere* provision operates only as between states which are party to the treaty, rather than as a customary international law obligation on all states, and thus is narrower in that sense.

Put simply, an offence is a "transnational crime of international concern" because there is a treaty or set of treaties in place between groups of interested states that deal with the crime. There are a large number of these treaties, and the range of crimes they cover is broad, including narcotics smuggling and trafficking, corruption of foreign officials, fraudulent use of the mails, terrorism, and human trafficking. These are not crimes under international law, though there is international law dealing with these crimes. The overall goal is to coordinate the efforts of states in prosecuting transnational crimes, but the prosecutions themselves are still done under each state's domestic criminal laws.

4) Transnational Crimes of Domestic Concern

Transnational crimes of domestic concern are crimes under domestic law which involve, in some way, more than one state. The criminal prohibition involved does not arise from an international law source but is simply part of the state's own criminal law system. However, in the commission of the crime, the interests (and thus the sovereignty) of more than one state are engaged, and therefore the state's domestic law requires a set of rules to deal with the international law issues that arise as a result.

Primarily, courts before which individuals may be prosecuted need to be able to determine whether or not they have jurisdiction over the subject matter, that is, the commission of the crime itself.[87] In a non-transnational case, jurisdiction is automatic; the crime was committed in Canada, for example, and the offender is now before a Canadian court. In transnational situations, the jurisdiction inquiry is more complex. Typically, there are two types of situations that will fall under this category. The first is where a court must examine the criminal law that it must apply and ascertain whether it can take *extraterritorial* jurisdiction over a crime that has been committed wholly in another state. The second is where a court is faced with a crime that was committed partly in Canada and partly in another state, or where some aspect of the acts

---

87   As we will see in Chapter 2, this kind of analysis involves the courts exercising their judicial jurisdiction in order to determine whether the legislature has awarded them with the competence to hear a particular case. Jurisdiction over the offender (enforcement jurisdiction) will usually not be an issue at this stage, since a court will generally not be deciding whether to hear a matter before the individual charged appears before it.

or conduct involved in the crime has some kind of impact on Canada. In this situation, the court must determine whether the crime can be said to have been committed in Canada, despite the transnational aspects, as a matter of *qualified territorial jurisdiction.* Under both of these inquiries there are international law issues at play, since conceivably more than one state may have an interest in prosecuting the offender. Accordingly, the court will often have to apply international law rules in making its determination, albeit in a "domesticized" form.

D. ENFORCEMENT

Effective suppression of international and transnational crime cannot stop with simply creating laws, be they domestic or international. The laws themselves must be enforced, and the offenders captured and prosecuted. With regard to ICL, a distinction is usually drawn between *direct* and *indirect* enforcement.[88] As we have seen earlier, international and transnational criminal law developed initially in a decentralized system of sovereign states, each of which was reluctant to cede any jurisdiction over its criminal law and process to any other state or body. Even after international norms came into being that provided for individual liability under international law, the primary forum for prosecuting offenders was the domestic courts of states which had implemented the international criminal prohibitions into their own domestic laws. This is referred to as "indirect enforcement"—the enforcement of substantive international law norms by the courts of domestic law systems.

"Direct" enforcement of international criminal law would be accomplished by a truly "international" criminal tribunal, one that is created and draws its powers from international law and operates at a supra-national level. The first true example of an international court prosecuting individuals for international crimes occurred with the establishment of the Nuremberg and Tokyo tribunals set up after WW II, and it was only in the late twentieth century that more direct enforcement of ICL was undertaken by the ICTY, the ICTR, the ICC, and to some extent the internationalized courts. Even these tribunals are features of systems that combine both direct and indirect enforcement. As will be seen in Chapter 4, the jurisdiction of the ICC is "complementary" to that of states, and direct enforcement by the court occurs

---

88   The terminology appears to be Bassiouni's; see Bassiouni 2d ed., above at note
       31, vol. I, Introduction at xiv.

only where there is no state willing or able to genuinely assume jurisdiction over a particular matter.[89]

Two additional points are worth making. First, a court can be international and provide direct enforcement without being in any way universal. All of the international criminal tribunals which have been established to date have been limited in their jurisdictions according to, *inter alia*, when and where the alleged offences took place and the nationality of the offenders. There appears to be no political will among the international community of states to create an international criminal court that would have a generalized, universal jurisdiction over any particular international crimes.

Second, direct enforcement against a particular offence by an international criminal court usually reflects the fact that the offence has attained "international crime" status. More prospectively, the agreement by states to include a particular crime within the jurisdiction of an international court may be the act that crystallizes this crime as international in nature. Neither situation is watertight, and crimes which are otherwise transnational crimes of international concern can become international crimes by way of their inclusion within the jurisdiction of an international court.

The ICC best illustrates the complicated nature of these dynamics. It has jurisdiction over genocide, crimes against humanity, war crimes, and aggression, all of which were established as international crimes prior to the founding of the court. However, serious consideration has been given by the state parties to the *Rome Statute* to the inclusion of both narcotics trafficking and terrorism as crimes within the court's jurisdiction. If this occurs, then both of these offences will become international crimes, at least functionally, in the form in which they are criminalized, by any revision to the *Rome Statute*, and subject to the ICC's "complementary" direct enforcement. The point at which they become international crimes substantively would be more difficult to pinpoint; while inclusion in the *Rome Statute* would certainly underscore the view of states that such crimes are important and worthy of international prosecution, it would not automatically enshrine them as international crimes under customary international law, subject to

---

89 The ICTY has recently begun to transfer some of the matters within its jurisdiction to special courts set up in the states that emerged from the Yugoslav conflict, thus substituting indirect enforcement for direct. See Michael Bohlander, "Last Exit Bosnia—Transferring War Crimes Prosecution from the International Tribunal to Domestic Courts" (2003) 14 Crim. L.F. 59. See also Chapter 4, Section E(6).

universal jurisdiction. At best, it would "set them on the road," await-ing further political will from states.

The systems of direct enforcement under international law are examined in Chapter 4, which surveys the important features of the various international and "internationalized" criminal tribunals. Chapter 5 deals with indirect enforcement, that is, the prosecution of international crimes at the state level, with specific reference to Canada and the "core crimes" covered under the *Crimes Against Humanity and War Crimes Act*.[90]

E. INTERNATIONAL COOPERATION IN THE SUPPRESSION OF CRIME

Enforcement as against international and transnational crime is ultim-ately accomplished by states, either because they prosecute the crimes themselves (indirect enforcement) or because they cede this particular sovereign capacity to a supra-national criminal tribunal (direct enforce-ment). Unlike a purely domestic prosecution, these brands of crime most often involve matters within the territorial jurisdiction of more than one state. This can be as simple as an offender murdering a victim in one state, then fleeing to another state to evade capture; or as com-plicated as an international drug-trafficking scheme where planning takes place in one state, narcotics are grown and processed in a second state and transported through a third, while the drugs are distributed in a fourth state, then the proceeds are laundered in a fifth state, and finance other criminal activities in a sixth. In each kind of case, two or more states each has pieces of the enforcement puzzle but may well be unable to successfully prosecute without assistance. The state which has custody of the offender may not have the jurisdiction to prosecute, or even if it does, all of the evidence may be in other states.

Accordingly, states have historically cooperated with each other to facilitate the procedural aspects of prosecution of transnational crime out of mutual interest in crime suppression. The oldest form of this cooperation is probably *extradition*, the formal rendition of fugitive of-fenders from a state that apprehends the offender to a state that wishes to prosecute, a practice which by some accounts dates back to ancient Egypt.[91] There is now a large network of bilateral extradition treaties

---

90   Above note 52.

91   I.A. Shearer, *Extradition in International Law* (Dobbs Ferry, NY: Oceana, 1971) at 5.

and several major multilateral ones, and multilateral arrangements are sometimes built into the suppression conventions. Police officers have been engaged in active cooperation for some time, certainly since the nineteenth century, both informally and by way of inter-government-al organizations such as INTERPOL. In the twentieth century, states began to strike treaties on *mutual legal assistance* in criminal matters, under which one state could request of its treaty partner state that the latter gather evidence that was in its territory and transmit it to the requesting state, for use in a criminal prosecution in that state. Again, there are both bilateral and multilateral arrangements in place among states. Subsequent arrangements have dealt with the freezing and seizure of proceeds of crime, the transfer of prisoners and of criminal proceedings, and the recognition of foreign penal judgments. It is be-coming increasingly common to see integrated arrangements that put these mechanisms into place on a regional basis, the European Union being the most prominent example.

While these cooperation methods developed primarily to facilitate prosecution of transnational crime (in both its forms), cooperation of states is also key to systems of direct prosecution. Again, the ICC pro-vides an instructive view. The court, while it has direct enforcement powers in terms of prosecuting offenders, has little in the way of direct procedural abilities analogous to domestic police powers over investi-gation, evidence-gathering, and arrest.[92] It must rely upon cooperation from the states that are party to the *Rome Statute*, and the treaty itself contains obligations for these states to, *inter alia*, surrender accused offenders to the court and gather and transmit evidence. The court is also empowered to enter into cooperative arrangements with non-party states.

It is useful to discuss these sorts of cooperative arrangements sep-arately from the categories of crime, since they are employed in various ways no matter what category of crime is being dealt with. The crime committed by a fugitive running from one state to another might as well have been a common domestic crime as a transnational crime of international concern, but the extradition process will essentially be the same though the treaty basis for it might vary. The most important aspects of these cooperative mechanisms are dealt with by way of sur-veying Canada's participation, in Chapter 9.

---

92   The *Rome Statute* does contain some provisions under which state parties are obliged to allow the ICC Prosecutor to conduct investigations in the state's ter-ritory. See Valerie Oosterveld, Mike Perry, & John McManus, "The Cooperation of States with the International Criminal Court" (2002) 25 Fordham Int'l L.J. 767.

F. THE IMPACT OF HUMAN RIGHTS

It has been correctly observed that "the international criminal process is inextricably linked with the development and application of human rights."[93] Both areas of law strive to achieve essentially the same goal, which is the protection of persons and the upholding of the fundamental standards and values of the international community regarding how human beings are treated, both by states and by each other. Both are often reactive in effect, but each strives to have a prophylactic function—to motivate states and individuals to treat persons humanely, and to deter inhumane treatment.

As can be drawn from the historical overview above, the goal of ICL from its outset (and the even earlier goal of IHL) was the protection of some core of fundamental rights which were held to be possessed by all individuals. Criminal law at the international level was the first and perhaps the blunter instrument to use in this regard, but the three crimes adjudicated at Nuremberg and Tokyo represented a significant and new effort to protect people from depredations at the hands of the state and its agencies, in particular. The *Genocide Convention*, which has been described as "a quintessential human rights treaty,"[94] went even further and required states to enact prohibitions on this "crime of crimes" in their domestic laws that would catch both public and private offenders. "The crimes that are deemed to attract this level of opprobrium are primarily those which *entail* human rights violations, both in the sense that they offend very basic aspects of human dignity (race, freedom, gender, etc.) and that they are most likely to be carried out by state actors or persons in a position of quasi-governmental power."[95] In light of modern developments, and particularly the founding of the ICC, it can safely be said that if ICL and the tribunals which apply it are not "human rights courts" in some sense, they are nonetheless fundamentally directed towards protecting human rights by using criminal prohibitions.

As the international criminal process has become operational, however, a slightly ironic twist has been that human rights concerns are increasingly raised in defence of those against whom ICL and TCL are most directed: offenders. This is an entirely logical and appropriate

---

93   Ilias Bantekas & Susan Nash, *International Criminal Law*, 3d ed. (New York: Routledge-Cavendish, 2007) at 19.

94   "Report of the International Law Commission on the work of its forty-ninth session, 12 May – 18 July 1997," UN Doc. A/52/10 at para. 76.

95   Robert J. Currie, "Abducted Fugitives before the International Criminal Court: Problems and Prospects" (2007) 18 Crim. L.F. 349 at 371.

development, of course, since for these legal systems to have any legit-imacy they must uphold human rights standards in the treatment of offenders. To compromise criminal process guarantees or other funda-mental rights while enforcing laws that, at least in the case of ICL, are geared towards enforcing human rights values, would be hypocritical and undermine the whole idea of international criminal justice.[96]

Yet both ICL and TCL display a certain tension in regards to the human rights of offenders. While the statutes of both of the *ad hoc* tribunals require adherence to the highest standard of international human rights law, there have sometimes been problems in execution.[97] Also, the Appeals Chamber of the ICTY has recently shown willingness to compromise human rights standards regarding legality of arrest and treatment of an accused, citing the importance of prosecuting persons accused of "Universally Condemned Offences."[98]

Treatment of accused persons is also a significant source of ten-sion within the law and practice of TCL. While the international law regime devoted to inter-state assistance in the suppression of trans-national crime has become quite advanced, it has been observed that the protection of the rights of offenders has rather lagged behind.[99] TCL brings into sharp relief the fact that human rights norms are not mono-lithic, as well as the fact that there are major differences among states as to how offenders should be handled from a criminal process point of view. The impact of these questions on inter-state cooperation can be profound. For example, in 2001 the Supreme Court of Canada broke with its previous caselaw and ruled that extraditing an individual to face the death sentence in another state would almost always violate the protections of section 7 of the *Charter*.[100] There has recently been con-troversy over the Canadian Security Intelligence Service (CSIS) using

---

96 See Lorenzo Gradoni, "You Will Receive a Fair Trial Elsewhere: The Ad Hoc International Criminal Tribunals Acting as Human Rights Jurisdictions" (2007) 54 Netherlands Int'l L. Rev. 1.

97 David Paciocco, "Defending Rwandans Accused before the ICTR: A Venture Full of Pitfalls and Lessons for the International Criminal Law" in Hélène Dumont & Anne-Marie Boisvert, eds., *The Highway to the International Criminal Court: All Roads Lead to Rome* (Montreal: Les Éditions Thémis, 2004) at 97. See also *Barayagwiza* (ICTR-97-19-AR72), Decision (Prosecutor's Request for Review or Reconsideration), 31 March 2000, with commentary thereon by William Schabas, "*Barayagwiza v. Prosecutor*" (2000) 94 A.J.I.L. 536.

98 *Nikolić* (IT-94-2-AR73), Decision on Interlocutory Appeal Concerning Legality of Arrest., 5 June 2003. See discussion of this case in Chapter 9.

99 Neil Boister, "Human Rights Protections in the Suppression Conventions" (2002) 2 Hum. Rts. L. Rev. 199.

100 *United States of America v. Burns*, [2001] 1 S.C.R. 283 [*Burns*].

information obtained from foreign authorities which was extracted by torture.[101] On the other hand, recent US-led efforts to combat terrorism have put prosecutorial interests in the ascendancy, and the state that was once the beacon of freedom in the world has rendered suspects to secret offshore prisons and torture chambers[102] and engages in criminal trials before secretive military tribunals.[103]

Accordingly, it can be seen that human rights have been and continue to be an animating force behind the development and application of ICL and TCL. Paradoxically perhaps, they are a source of both unity and division among states, and this tension explains many of the twists and turns of the international community's efforts to balance prosecution with rights protection.

G. SOURCES OF INTERNATIONAL AND TRANSNATIONAL CRIMINAL LAW

1) Domestic Sources

While one normally thinks of ICL and TCL as being based in international law (thereby creating obligations on states to do or refrain from doing certain things), domestic criminal laws can reach outside the territory of a state in many ways and be properly classified as "international" or "transnational" in effect, if not in origin. For example, it may be against the law in Canada to commit a certain act anywhere outside Canada, or to commit the act against a Canadian national who is outside Canada.[104] As another example, in order to extradite a fugitive

---

101 See Colin Freeze & Bill Curry, "Spy Chief Dismisses Witness' Remarks on Torture" *The Globe and Mail* (3 April 2009). A good account can be found online: http://legalift.wordpress.com/2009/04/04/csis-head-dismisses-subordinates-remarks-on-use-of-torture-evidence/.

102 See Margaret Satterthwaite, "Rendered Meaningless: Extraordinary Rendition and the Rule of Law" (2007) 75 Geo. Wash. L. Rev. 1333; Parliamentary Information and Research Service, Library of Parliament [Canada], "Extraordinary Rendition: International Law and the Prohibition of Torture," Doc. No. PRB 07-48E (2008), online: www.parl.gc.ca/information/library/PRBpubs/prb0748-e.htm.

103 This reference is to the courts set up at the US facility in Guantanamo Bay. The legislation underpinning the trials was struck down two times by the US Supreme Court: *Rasul v. Bush*, 542 U.S. 466 (2004); *Hamdan v. Rumsfeld*, 126 S. Ct. 2749 (2006).

104 This would be an assertion of extraterritorial jurisdiction by Canada; see Chapter 2.

to another state, Canada must have a domestic law in place that provides for extradition in appropriate circumstances.[105] Both of these examples would also engage Canada's international law obligations owed to other states. In the first, if Canada seeks to prosecute an offender for an offence committed outside of Canada, this could create conflict with another state or states which also wish to prosecute, and/or which question Canada's entitlement to prosecute under international law. In the second, if Canada declined to extradite a fugitive to a state with which it had a treaty and which had requested extradition, that state might have an international law claim against Canada for its failure to abide by the terms of the treaty.

The three main domestic sources of criminal law in Canada are (1) the Constitution of Canada, including the *Charter*;[106] (2) legislative statutes that create offences, most prominently the *Criminal Code*;[107] and (3) judge-made common law regarding criminal matters, which, while it does not create offences, can create certain defences and generally interprets both the legislation and the Constitution.

There is a dynamic interplay between these three sources of law. The Constitution is the overarching law of the land, and both legislation and common law regarding criminal matters must be consistent with it. Section 91 of the *Constitution Act, 1867*[108] provides that the federal Parliament has sole jurisdiction to make criminal law, which it does both through the *Code* and through other regulatory legislation that creates offences (sometimes called "quasi-criminal law"). The provinces may also enact regulatory statutes that create offences within their areas of constitutional competence. Further, all criminal and quasi-criminal statutes (substantive law), and enforcement thereof by police, prosecutors, and regulatory officials (procedure), must comply with the rights and freedoms guaranteed under the *Charter*. Particularly important for criminal law are section 7, which protects life, liberty, and security of person and the right not to be deprived thereof except in accordance with the principles of fundamental justice; section 8, which provides the right to be free from unreasonable search and seizure; section 9, which protects people from arbitrary detention; section 10, which provides for rights upon arrest; and section 11, which ensures fair trials.

The courts police both the maintenance of the division of powers and compliance with the *Charter*. Thus, if a court finds that a provincial regulatory statute is, in pith and substance, actually an attempt to cre-

---

105 *Extradition Act*, S.C. 1999, c. 18.

106 Above note 79.

107 R.S.C. 1985, c. C-46 [*Code*].

108 (U.K.), 30 & 31 Vict., c. 3, reprinted in R.S.C. 1985, App. II, No. 5.

ate a criminal offence, it can strike down the statute or the offending portions. If a court finds that a criminal statute is vague, overbroad, or impinges on *Charter* rights to a degree that cannot be reasonably and demonstrably justified (in accordance with section 1 of the *Charter*), that statute can be struck down or "read down"[109] as a remedy. Courts can also find that either of the investigative or trial processes have violated a person's *Charter* rights and provide a broad range of remedies, including dismissal of the case or exclusion of improperly taken evidence. On the other hand, the legislatures can make laws that override court holdings, so long as they are consistent with the *Charter* in so doing.

2) International Law Sources and Their Reception in Canada

The relationship and interrelationship between domestic law and international law has been a delicate and contentious matter for decades[110] and continues to inspire intense study and debate.[111] For the purposes of this text, it is sufficient to sketch out the major sources of international law[112] and provide a basic account of how they become the law of Canada (a process usually referred to as "reception").[113]

Article 38(1) of the *Statute of the International Court of Justice*[114] contains what is generally viewed as the most authoritative statement of the sources of international law:

---

109 This means "giving the law a sufficiently narrow interpretation to bring it into line with the demands of the constitution" (Robert Sharpe & Kent Roach, *The Charter of Rights and Freedoms*, 3d ed. (Toronto: Irwin Law, 2005) at 349).

110 The foundational essay is Ronald St. John Macdonald, "The Relationship between International Law and Domestic Law in Canada" in Ronald St. J. Macdonald, Gerald L. Morris, & Douglas M. Johnston, eds., *Canadian Perspectives on International Law and Organization* (Toronto: University of Toronto Press, 1974).

111 See, generally, the excellent collection of essays in Oonagh Fitzgerald, ed., *The Globalized Rule of Law: Relationships Between International and Domestic Law* (Toronto: Irwin Law, 2006); Gib van Ert, *Using International Law in Canadian Courts*, 2d ed. (Toronto: Irwin Law, 2008); Hugh Kindred & Phillip Saunders, eds., *International Law: Chiefly as Interpreted and Applied in Canada*, 7th ed. (Toronto: Emond Montgomery, 2006) c. 4; and Jutta Brunnée & Stephen Toope, "A Hesitant Embrace: The Application of International Law by Canadian Courts" (2002) 40 Can. Y.B. Int'l L. 3.

112 On the creation of international law, see Alan Boyle & Christine Chinkin, *The Making of International Law* (Oxford: Oxford University Press, 2007).

113 For more in-depth treatment, see John Currie, *Public International Law*, 2d ed. (Toronto: Irwin Law, 2008) cc. 3–6; Mark Freeman & Gibran van Ert, *International Human Rights Law* (Toronto: Irwin Law, 2004) cc. 3, 8, 9, and 11.

114 Can. T.S. 1945 No. 7 [*Statute of the ICJ*].

a.   international conventions, whether general or particular, establishing rules expressly recognized by the contesting states;

b.   international custom, as evidence of a general practice accepted as law;

c.   the general principles of law recognized by civilized nations;

d.   subject to the provisions of Article 59, judicial decisions and the teachings of the most highly qualified publicists of the various nations, as subsidiary means for the determination of rules of law.

Still matters of debate are whether this formulation of international law sources was meant to be exhaustive or is simply meant to be indicia of the *kinds* of obligations imposed on states, as well as whether there is a hierarchy between them (except insofar as paragraph (d) is expressly intended to be "subsidiary" to paragraphs (a) through (c)). On a broad reading at least, this formulation is capable of encompassing the sources of international law to be surveyed here.[115]

a)   Treaty Law

i)   *Creation and Legal Effect*

Treaties (also referred to as agreements, conventions, pacts, and protocols, *inter alia*) are written agreements between states[116] by which those states undertake a legal obligation to act in accordance with the treaty's terms.[117] The obligation is one under international law, and the substantive law rules that govern treaties are codified in the *Vienna Convention on the Law of Treaties* 1969 — which is itself binding on all states as a matter of customary international law (see Section G(2)(b), below in this chapter). States which enter into treaty obligations must perform and otherwise honour the terms of the treaties, a principle known as *pacta sunt servanda*.[118] This represents a surrender of sovereignty of the states which are parties to the treaty, by mutual agreement, and states are not permitted to invoke their own domestic law as a means of escaping their treaty obligations.[119]

---

115 Currie, *Public International Law*, above note 113 at 96.

116 And sometimes between states and international organizations. For example, the United Nations has international legal personality and has the capacity to enter into treaties with states. See, generally, Philippe Sands & Pierre Klein, *Bowett's Law of International Institutions*, 6th ed. (London: Sweet & Maxwell, 2009); Finn Seyersted, *Common Law of International Organizations* (Leiden: Martinus Nijhoff, 2008).

117 *Vienna Convention on the Law of Treaties*, 1969; Can. T.S. 1980 No. 37, art. 2 [*VCLT*].

118 *Ibid.*, art. 26.

119 *Ibid.*, art. 27.

With most treaties, an appropriate state official will sign the treaty and render the state a *signatory*, which indicates that the state is expressing its intention to become bound by the treaty. The state will then make whatever changes to its domestic legal framework that are required to give effect to the treaty, and subsequently give a formal notice of its acceptance to be bound by the treaty (usually referred to as "ratification"), at which point the state is properly a "party" to the treaty. Treaties contain terms that indicate the time at which they will "come into force"—that is, have binding effect on all ratifying states—and this usually happens upon a specified number of ratifications being entered. Thus, a treaty is binding on a state once the state itself has ratified the treaty and the treaty has come into force as between all state parties. A state which did not participate in the formulation of the treaty may nonetheless become a member, a process known as "accession."

States will sometimes enter "reservations" when they sign or ratify a treaty, indicating that they are accepting the treaty's obligations only in part or modifying the legal effect of some provisions.[120] Other state parties may object to reservations, which has the effect of nullifying the reservation as between the reserving state and the objecting state.[121] States may also make "statements of understanding," which indicate a state's interpretation of particular provisions of the treaty.

Since treaties are fundamentally based on consent, states may withdraw their consent to be bound by a treaty, either temporarily ("suspension") or permanently ("termination"), though particular treaties may have rules governing these processes. Otherwise treaties can be suspended or terminated by the occurrence of material breach of the terms of the treaty, supervening impossibility of performance, fundamental change of circumstances, or conflict with a newly developed *jus cogens* norm.[122]

Treaties may be either bilateral (between two states) or multilateral (between three or more states), and the treaty-making process may range from being highly formalized to a simple *ad hoc* agreement between states. ICL and TCL treaties cover this entire ground. For

---

120 *Ibid.*, art. 2. Canada often uses a "federal state clause" with regard to treaties, indicating that the federal government (which has Canada's treaty-making power) only accepts to be bound to the extent it exercises jurisdiction over the subject matter of the treaty. In practice, the federal government usually attempts to gain full agreement with the provinces on implementing the treaty prior to ratification.

121 *Ibid.*, art. 20(b).

122 Currie, *Public International Law*, above note 113 at 179–84. On *jus cogens*, see Section G(2)(b), below in this chapter.

example, Canada is a party to both the *Genocide Convention* and the *Rome Statute*, both of which were concluded under the auspices of the United Nations and involved highly structured negotiations between large numbers of states. The Organisation for Economic Co-operation and Development (OECD) organized the concluding of the *Convention on Combating Bribery of Foreign Officials in International Business Transactions*.[123] By contrast, Canada's treaties regarding extradition and mutual legal assistance are usually bilateral.

ii)   Reception

Treaty-making is an act of the executive branch of government, a "Crown prerogative," but under Canada's constitutional monarchy all law-making must be done by the legislative branch, that is, Parliament. Therefore, a treaty is not part of Canadian law until a law of some sort has been made to give effect to the treaty, which is called "implementation."[124] The implementing law can be either statutes of the federal or a provincial or territorial legislature, forms of subsidiary legislation such as regulations, or administrative or indirect methods. The legislation can be implemented only by the governmental entity that has the constitutional ability to do so, and thus any treaty which touches upon provincial powers must be implemented by each province separately.

Canada employs no single method for implementing its treaty obligations. Sometimes a statute will be passed for the explicit purpose of implementing a set of treaty obligations. This could be done for a specific treaty or a range of treaties. For example, the *Crimes Against Humanity and War Crimes Act*[125] was intended primarily to implement Canada's obligations under the *Rome Statute*. By contrast, the *Extradition Act*[126] and the *Mutual Legal Assistance in Criminal Matters Act*[127] are intended to implement Canada's obligations under all treaties in those subject areas. With some treaties, however, the federal government will take note of legislation that has the effect of implementing a certain treaty provision and rely upon it as having done so, even if the legislation was not expressly intended for that purpose.[128]

---

123 Can. T.S. 1999 No. 23.

124 *Baker v. Canada (Minister of Citizenship and Immigration)*, [1999] 2 S.C.R. 817 at para. 69.

125 Above note 52.

126 Above note 105.

127 R.S.C. 1985 (4th Supp.), c. 30.

128 See, generally, John Mark Keyes & Ruth Sullivan, "A Legislative Perspective on the Interaction of International and Domestic Law" in Fitzgerald, ed., above note 111 at 277.

Since treaties are part of the laws of Canada, the courts must apply, interpret, and give effect to them. The legal principles on this question are complex and unsettled in some areas, but two points can succinctly be made. First, the courts must take judicial notice of all of the laws of Canada which they have jurisdiction to administer, and this includes all legislation that is deemed to implement treaty law, whether it originates in a treaty or not. Second, Parliament is ultimately sovereign in its law-making capacity and has the ability to legislate in violation of international law.[129] However, as a matter of statutory interpretation, courts are bound to interpret domestic law as being in conformity with international law,[130] "unless the contrary clearly appears."[131] With specific regard to treaties, this means that virtually all forms of legislation (including delegated legislation and prerogative acts) should be interpreted in a way that is consistent with any applicable treaty obligations, whether or not the legislation explicitly implements the treaty. This will be so unless the legislation expressly contravenes the treaty obligation, or does so by necessary implication.[132] The presumption should, in theory, apply equally to treaties which have been ratified but not implemented, and treaties which have been signed but not yet ratified.[133]

As will be seen throughout this text, treaties are a significant source of ICL and TCL for Canada, both in terms of obligations Canada has undertaken to other states, and in terms of substantive and procedural criminal law that is part of the domestic legal landscape. This is particularly true as regards transnational crimes of international concern, as Canada is a party to numerous treaties aimed at suppressing these forms of crime. Section 7 of the *Criminal Code*, which implements most of the extraterritorial jurisdiction requirements of the suppression conventions, is easily one of the most voluminous parts of the entire statute.

---

129 See Chapter 8.

130 *Ordon Estate v. Grail*, [1998] 3 S.C.R. 437 at para. 137; *Hape*, above note 80 at paras. 53–56.

131 D.C. Vanek, "Is International Law Part of the Law of Canada?" (1960) 8 U.T.L.J. 251 at 259.

132 Ruth Sullivan, *Sullivan and Driedger on the Construction of Statutes*, 4th ed. (Markham, ON: Butterworths, 2002) at 422*ff*.

133 Particularly given that art. 18 of the *VCLT*, above note 117, requires signatory states to refrain from actions which would defeat the intent or purpose of the treaty; see Freeman & van Ert, above note 113 at 157. Whether it applies to the common law is unsettled; *ibid.* at 153.

b) Customary International Law

i) Creation and Ascertainment

Customary international law is an entirely different order of international-al obligation than treaties, which are based on explicit agreement and formal provision of consent between states. Customary obligations, by contrast, are based on the behaviour of states and their demonstrated belief in the normative force that behaviour contains. This is captured by the two formal requirements for finding a customary international law obligation: (1) that there is a state practice which is general (though not necessarily universal[134]) and uniform and (2) that the state practice is accompanied by a belief on the part of states that the practice is obligatory, referred to as *opinio juris*.[135]

If both of these elements are present, then the obligation is one that is universally binding on all states, even those which have not expressly accepted the obligation. In fact, acquiescence to state practice is acceptable evidence that the practice is legal. States which protest particular practices on a consistent basis from the time of the inception of the norm are able to escape the force of the obligation, and are known as "persistent objectors." In certain circumstances, a group of states in a particular region may develop "local" or "regional" customary norms which will apply as between themselves only, and even diverge from more generalized customary obligations.

Customary international law contains within it a subset of norms, known as *jus cogens* or "peremptory norms," that represent the highest order of international law obligation. *Jus cogens* norms are "non-derogable," that is, they cannot be displaced by either treaty or persistent objection, and can be modified only by a subsequent *jus cogens* norm.[136] So great is the universal acceptance of these norms that a treaty which attempts to escape their obligatory effect is automatically rendered void,[137] and if a new peremptory norm emerges, it voids any existing treaties which are inconsistent with it.[138] The prohibitions of a number of international crimes have risen to *jus cogens* status, including genocide, crimes against humanity, slavery, and, arguably, piracy.[139]

---

134 *Case Concerning Military and Paramilitary Activities in and against Nicaragua (Nicaragua v. United States of America)*, [1986] I.C.J. Rep. 14 at 98.

135 Which is itself short for *opinio juris sive necessitates*, a Latin phrase which translates to "opinion that an act is necessary by rule of law."

136 *VCLT*, above note 117, art. 53.

137 *Ibid.*

138 *Ibid.*, art. 64.

139 Ian Brownlie, *Principles of Public International Law*, 6th ed. (Oxford: Oxford University Press, 2003) at 488–89.

There is a great deal of interplay between customary international law and treaty law, as the relationship is a dynamic one. Treaties may *declare* or *codify* an existing body of customary international law; treaties may represent the *crystallization* into custom of the obligations contained in the treaty if the treaty is widely adhered to after its formation; and treaties may build on an existing body of custom and perform a *law-making* function.[140] The *United Nations Convention on the Law of the Sea*,[141] for example, served all three of these functions. Also, treaties and customary international law that have identical content can coexist. For example, a state might have three obligations in a treaty, one of which also reflects a customary international law rule. If the treaty was breached by the partner state, the first state could repudiate the two non-custom obligations but could not escape the one with customary force.

ii) Reception

Customary international law is part of the law of Canada by way of the doctrine of "incorporation" or "adoption." Consistent with English tradition, custom is deemed to be incorporated into the Canadian legal framework (specifically the common law) automatically and generally does not require implementation by statute. It is not treated as being foreign law; rather, it is "part of the law of the land."[142]

As with treaty law, Canadian courts are obliged to take judicial notice of customary international law and apply it in the same manner that domestic law would be applied.[143] Because customary international law is not as easily ascertained as domestic law, this can and should lead the courts on a sometimes wide-ranging inquiry as to what Canada's customary obligations are.[144] Equally, when interpreting and applying

---

140 Currie, *Public International Law*, above note 113 at 207–13.

141 10 December 1982, 1833 U.N.T.S. 3.

142 Sir William Blackstone, *Commentaries on the Laws of England*, vol. 4 (Chicago: University of Chicago Press, 1979) at 67. See *Re Foreign Legations*, [1943] S.C.R. 208; *Saint John (City) v. Fraser-Brace Overseas*, [1958] S.C.R. 263; *Re Canada Labour Code*, [1992] 2 S.C.R. 50. See also *Hape*, above note 80 at paras. 35–39.

143 See *Re Regina and Palacios* (1984), 45 O.R. (2d) 269 (C.A.).

144 This has led to the odd practice of having international law scholars testify as expert witnesses in court hearings, giving their opinion on the state of the international law which courts then rely on as "evidence" as to what the international law is. This is methodologically unsound. Since customary international law is part of the law of Canada, the courts are meant to ascertain for themselves what the law is and then take judicial notice of it. The parties may, of course, retain experts to assist them in making their submissions to the court on the content of the law, but it is not a proper topic on which expert opinion

legislation, the presumption of conformity with Canada's international law obligations applies, and courts must read the legislation as being in conformity with custom unless there is a conflict that is either express or necessarily implied.[145] For example, in *Mugesera v. Canada* (*Minister of Citizenship and Immigration*),[146] the Supreme Court of Canada had to determine how to define the elements of the offences of incitement to genocide and crimes against humanity. Both of these offences were contained in the *Criminal Code* at the relevant time, but the Court defined the offences in accordance with the customary international law definitions of each.

With respect to Canadian criminal law specifically, it should be noted that Parliament has expressly declared (in section 9 of the *Code*) that no person can be prosecuted for a common law offence.[147] Since customary international law is incorporated as part of the common law, this would seem to mean that for any act to be a criminal offence it must be legislated as such;[148] if it is not, then it is not a crime in Canada, even though it may be a crime under customary international law. As noted in Section F(2)(a)(ii), above in this chapter, Parliament is free to legislate in violation of international law so far as the *domestic* effect of this legislation goes, but this would not prevent Canada from being open to an international claim from another state if it failed to criminalize, for example, war crimes or crimes against humanity.[149]

In practice, this is generally not an issue, both because Canada tends to act in conformity with its international obligations, and because most offences under international law are now codified under treaties to which Canada adheres.[150] The two different kinds of inter-

---

evidence should be received. See, generally, Gib van Ert, "The Admissibility of International Legal Evidence" (2005) 84 Can. Bar Rev. 31.

145 *Hape*, above note 80 at para. 39.

146 [2005] 2 S.C.R. 100 [*Mugesera*].

147 *Code*, above note 107, s. 9(a).

148 Or, at least, there must be legislation or other legal instruments to prohibit it. For example, the prohibition on slavery is a *jus cogens* norm. There is no provision of the *Criminal Code* or other statutes which criminalizes slavery, but it is clear under the *Charter*, *inter alia*, that slavery is not permitted in Canada.

149 See Section H, below in this chapter.

150 Though it is not beyond the realm of possibility. The crime of genocide, as set out in the *Genocide Convention*, above note 34, passed into customary international law within a few decades after the conclusion of the *Convention*. Despite being a party to the *Convention* and having a coterminous customary international law obligation, until the coming into force of the *CAH Act*, above note 52, Canada had only criminalized the offence of incitement to genocide. Accordingly, Canada was arguably not in compliance with its international law obligations for that time.

national law obligations can also be used to supplement each other. For example, the *CAH Act* criminalizes genocide, crimes against humanity, and war crimes both as those crimes are defined in the *Rome Statute* and as they are defined in customary international law.[151] Thus, Canada can meet its obligations under the *Rome Statute* but will also be able to prosecute offenders by applying the most current versions of the offences under customary international law, which will be advantageous to the extent that these are broader than the *Rome Statute* crimes.

Because *jus cogens* norms are essentially ingrained rules of customary international law, they should be applied with full force and effect in Canadian law unless a clear intention to the contrary can be found. The current status of *jus cogens* in Canadian law is a matter of some uncertainty, due in no small part to the confusing manner in which the Supreme Court of Canada dealt with the issue in *Suresh v. Canada (Minister of Citizenship and Immigration)*.[152] In terms of criminal prohibitions which have *jus cogens* status, section 9 of the *Criminal Code* appears to indicate that they must be explicitly provided for by law in order to have domestic effect. Practically speaking, this is usually not an issue, since *jus cogens* crimes are typically part of Canadian law in any event.

Parliament can, of course, still legislate in violation of *jus cogens* norms as a matter of legislative supremacy, but the presumption of conformity should be applied more assiduously, if anything, as regards *jus cogens*. Logically, if Parliament is presumed to be legislating in conformity with *any* of Canada's international law obligations, then this presumption should operate with more force when it comes to peremptory norms.

c) Other Sources

There are several other sources of international law that contribute to Canada's legal framework vis-à-vis ICL and TCL. The first, per article 38(1)(c) of the *Statute of the ICJ*,[153] is "general principles of law recognized by civilized nations." The most generally accepted view of this source[154] is that it consists of general principles of law that are held in

---

151 *CAH Act, ibid.*, ss. 4(3) and 6(3); though the available international law defences seem to be only those provided for in the treaty, except insofar as the domestic law defences also reflect customary international law on point; *ibid.*, ss. 11 and 14.

152 [2002] 1 S.C.R. 3. See van Ert, above note 111 at 205–6 and 347–48.

153 Above note 114.

154 Though there are several competing views; see Currie, *Public International Law*, above note 113 at 101–6.

common under the domestic law system of a strong plurality of states. They are used essentially by courts to fill in the gaps left by treaty and/ or customary law on particular points where a solid international rule cannot be discerned.[155]

When looking at both ICL and TCL, in particular, there are a number of principles of criminal law which can be said generally to have international law status of this sort,[156] and as Schabas and Beaulac have pointed out, "Because, by definition, such rules are derived from domestic law, most if not all of them are already recognized by Canadian courts."[157] For example, the principle that ignorance of the law is no excuse can safely be said to be a general principle of international law,[158] and in Canada this is reflected in section 19 of the *Criminal Code*.[159] Also, the principle against the retroactive application of criminal law (*nullum crimen sine lege*) is a general principle of international law, both as a consistent principle of criminal law in the major domestic systems, and as a matter of international human rights law. In Canada, this principle finds its expression in section 11(g) of the *Charter*.

Article 38(1)(d) of the *Statute of the ICJ* refers to two secondary sources of international law, which, though not primary sources, may nonetheless aid in determining a legal norm. The first is "judicial decisions," which means the decisions of both international and national

---

155 So, for example, in *Kupreškić* (IT-95-16-T), Trial Judgment, 14 January 2000, a Trial Chamber of the ICTY stated: "[I]t is now clear that to fill possible gaps in international customary and treaty law, international and national criminal courts may draw upon *general principles of criminal law as they derive from the convergence of the principal penal systems of the world*. Where necessary, the Trial Chamber shall use such principles to fill any *lacunae* in the Statute of the International Tribunal and in customary law" (at para. 677, emphasis added). See also *Kunarac et al.* (IT-96-23-T and IT-96-23/1-T), Judgment, 22 February 2001 at para. 439.

156 Professor Cassese has proposed, with particular reference to the caselaw of the ICTY, that a class of rules referred to as "general principles of international criminal law" can be discerned, which forms part of the system of truly *international* prosecution of crime—as distinct from "general principles of criminal law recognized by the community of nations," which can nonetheless also be applied by the international criminal tribunals. See Antonio Cassese, *International Criminal Law*, 2d ed. (Oxford: Oxford University Press, 2008) at 32–52.

157 William Schabas & Stéphane Beaulac, *International Human Rights and Canadian Law: Legal Commitment, Implementation and the Charter*, 3d ed. (Toronto: Thomson Carswell, 2006) at 83.

158 *R. v. Finta*, [1994] 1 S.C.R. 701 at 763, La Forest J. Oddly, it is an excuse in South African law; see *S v. De Blom* (1977) 3 SA 513 (A).

159 For another example, the protection against "double jeopardy" embodied in the principle *ne bis in idem*, see *R. v. Van Rassel*, [1990] 1 S.C.R. 225 at 233.

courts as well as arbitral tribunals. In international law there is no system of *stare decisis*, so international caselaw is not binding in the manner that cases are in common law systems. However, judicial decisions are nonetheless highly persuasive evidence of the state of the law and can also reflect state practice if they emerge from domestic courts. Canadian courts have often used the decisions of both foreign and international courts to determine both domestic and international law points.[160] In *Mugesera*,[161] the Supreme Court of Canada relied extensively on the caselaw of the ICTY and ICTR in order to determine the content of the offence of crimes against humanity.[162]

The other secondary source in article 38(1)(d) is the "teachings of the most highly qualified publicists of the various nations," which basically refers to the writings of international law scholars. Again, this is not an independent source of law, but is rather a tool for courts to use when determining the content and scope of international law norms. In *R. v. Finta*, La Forest J. noted the distinction between scholarly writings which explain and summarize the content of international law obligations, and the views of the writers as to what the law should be — the latter to be viewed as a "subsidiary" source.[163]

A further source of international law is what is known as "soft law" or *lex ferenda*. Even calling it a "source" perhaps confers too much weight, as Professor John Currie notes, "the most widely accepted view is that *lex ferenda* or soft law is not truly law at all but rather a category of potentially significant legal developments or materials."[164] These developments and materials can come from a wide variety of sources, such as resolutions of the UN General Assembly, the work of the International Law Commission, draft treaties and codes of conduct, and multilateral "Declarations" under which states can agree broadly on principle if not on obligation. Much soft law will at least provide evidence of state practice and indicate *developing* international law norms which have not yet crystallized, and will even play a proactive role in facilitating the development of new norms, a good example of which is the ILC's Articles on State Responsibility, which are now widely regarded as codifying customary international law on this contentious

---

160 See, for example, *Burns*, above note 100.

161 Above note 146.

162 The Court was arguably too enthusiastic in this regard, as it seemed to accept the tribunal findings as *authoritative* declarations on the law, as opposed to simply being persuasive findings that would assist the Court to reach its own decision on the content of the law.

163 Above note 158 at 761–62.

164 Currie, *Public International Law*, above note 113 at 120.

subject. In the ICL area, an important soft law instrument was the *Draft Code of Crimes against the Peace and Security of Mankind*,[165] the result of decades of work by the ILC that still serves as an important reference point on certain aspects of ICL.

Soft law, of course, does not have any binding authority on states and is not applied as "law" *per se* by Canadian courts. Nonetheless, particularly in recent years, the courts have made liberal reference to various sources of soft law in order to make determinations on "hard" legal matters that touched on Canada's international law obligations. A good example is *United States of America v. Burns*,[166] where the Supreme Court of Canada was called upon to define the "fundamental principles of justice" under section 7 of the *Charter*, in the context of whether Canada should extradite individuals to face the death penalty in a foreign state. In deciding that this practice was generally unconstitutional, the Court made extensive use of soft law instruments, including declarations of the UN Human Rights Committee, a Report of the UN Secretary General, and the UN's *Model Treaty on Extradition*.[167]

An important source of international law which does not easily fit into any of the above categories is the concept of international *comity*. Comity is best described as an attitude of respect and deference as between states, and a firm determination not to act in a manner that interferes with this respect and deference unless strictly necessary, despite there being no obligation to defer in this way. In *R. v. Hape*, the Supreme Court of Canada set out its fullest explanation of comity to date, defining it as "informal acts performed and rules observed by states in their mutual relations out of politeness, convenience and goodwill, rather than strict legal obligation."[168]

Comity has an odd normative status; as Estey J. suggested in *R. v. Spencer*, comity is "neither a matter of absolute obligation, on the one hand, nor of mere courtesy and good will, upon the other."[169] In *Hape* the Court noted that "[w]hen cited by the courts, comity is more a principle of interpretation than a rule of law, because it does not arise from formal obligations."[170] Without a doubt, however, it informs the courts' interpretation and application of Canadian law, to the point that

---

165 Above note 48.

166 Above note 100.

167 *Ibid.* at paras. 82–89. See also Suresh, above note 152.

168 *Hape*, above note 80 at para. 47, citing Robert Jennings & Sir Arthur Watts, *Oppenheim's International Law*, 9th ed. (Harlow, UK: Longman, 1996), vol. I at 50–51.

169 [1985] 2 S.C.R. 278 at 283.

170 *Hape*, above note 80 at para. 47.

a presumption of conformity can be said to apply, at least to the extent that there is a presumption that legislation is intended to preserve comity.[171] It is noteworthy that in *Libman v. The Queen*,[172] La Forest J. incorporated comity into the test for territorial jurisdiction under Canadian criminal law in a manner that effectively transformed comity into a "hard" law obligation.[173] Otherwise, however, "comity ceases to be appropriate where it would undermine peaceable inter-state relations and the international order."[174]

d) Section 11(g) of the *Charter*

Section 11(g) of the *Charter* is worth a few brief remarks, as it seems to play a couple of noteworthy roles. The paragraph provides for the right of a person charged with an offence "not to be found guilty on account of any act or omission unless, at the time of the act or omission, it constituted an offence under Canadian or international law or was criminal according to the general principles of law recognized by the community of nations." This provision appears designed to implement the freedom from the retroactive application of criminal law contained in article 15(1) of the *International Covenant on Civil and Political Rights (ICCPR)*.[175] Concurrently, since this particular freedom is one of the "general principles" of international law (i.e., *nullum crimen sine lege*, or the principle of legality) as described above in this chapter, the provision doubles as Canada's own domestic expression of this principle.

The inclusion in the section of "international law" and "general principles of law recognized by the community of nations" (despite its facial redundancy)[176] reflects the wording of article 15(2) of the *ICCPR* and provides that prosecution would not be retroactive if the act were an offence under international law, even though it had not been criminalized by the state. Accordingly, Parliament may enact criminal offences with retroactive effect—but probably better called "retrospective"—where the point of the statute is to criminalize conduct which was already a crime under international law.[177] The provision has not been tested often, but in the decision of the Supreme Court of Canada

---

171 *Daniels v. White*, [1968] S.C.R. 517 at 541, Pigeon J. See also *R. v. Zingre*, [1981] 2 S.C.R. 392 at 401.

172 [1985] 2 S.C.R. 178.

173 See Chapter 8.

174 *Hape*, above note 80 at para. 50.

175 GA Res. 2200A (XXI), 21 UN GAOR, Supp. No. 16 at 52, UN Doc. A/6316 (1966), 999 U.N.T.S. 171, entered into force 23 March 1976 [*ICCPR*].

176 Freeman & van Ert, above note 113 at 182 and 273.

177 *Ibid.* at 273.

in *R. v. Finta*,[178] both the majority and the dissent found that Canada's domestic offences for war crimes and crimes against humanity, created in 1987, did not offend section 11(g) even though Finta was charged with acts that allegedly took place in WW II. In fact, the court read the provision broadly, the majority finding that it was sufficient that the acts in question were "illegal" under international law at the time, even though they were not formally "crimes," because justice demanded such a result.[179]

Since the reference is to "international law," this would seem to apply both to treaty crimes and to customary international law crimes. Thus, if in 2001 Canada signed a treaty which criminalized a certain act but did not implement the treaty until 2007, a person could be prosecuted for committing the offence anytime after the signing of the treaty in 2001. This is almost an academic point, since most criminal law treaties do not create crimes, though they do require states to create them.

However, Canada ratified the *Genocide Convention*, which created the crime of genocide, in 1952, but as noted earlier,[180] it did not implement genocide as a crime until 2000. Nonetheless, section 11(g) of the *Charter* allowed Parliament to create a retrospective offence of genocide, specifically genocide outside Canada,[181] which will allow prosecution for extraterritorial genocide that occurred after the earlier of 1952, the date the *Genocide Convention* came into force for Canada, or the date that genocide became a customary international law crime.[182]

G. SUBJECTS OF INTERNATIONAL AND TRANSNATIONAL CRIMINAL LAW: STATE RESPONSIBILITY VERSUS INDIVIDUAL LIABILITY

Because international law emerged as a largely consensual system of rules that governed the interactions of states, it was traditionally understood that states were the only entities which had rights and obligations that could be exercised and enforced, and indeed this is still

---

178 Above note 158.
179 *Ibid.* at 870–74.
180 See above note 150.
181 *CAH Act*, above note 52, s. 6.
182 Similar treatment is given to crimes against humanity.

largely the case today.[183] States are still the primary movers and actors in the international legal system, and even the development of international organizations with this "international legal personality," such as the UN, can be seen as stemming from collective agreement among states to surrender their respective sovereignty. This state of affairs is usually expressed by referring to the states as the primary "subjects" of international law, that is, the primary entities with legal personality.

In contrast to this, to the extent that individuals had any status under international law, they were generally viewed as the "objects" of the law. Individuals had no standing to make any claims or pursue remedies against states,[184] though states could bring claims on behalf of their nationals against other states—the theory being that the rights of the state of nationality itself had been violated. In the twentieth century this began to change, and individuals began to acquire a certain level of international legal personality along two fronts which are relevant here. First, international human rights law has bestowed rights upon individuals as against states, which makes the individual a "subject" of international human rights law as an entity who is at least formally entitled to invoke that law in his own protection. The primary issue has been the lack of fora in which the individual actually has standing to pursue a remedy, and thus "[t]he expression of these rights . . . is still not matched by equally effective measures to implement them."[185]

Second, as international criminal law initially developed, and certainly by the time of the Nuremberg and Tokyo tribunals, it was recognized that individuals had obligations under international law and thus were "subjects" of the law for that purpose as well. Indeed, this is the necessary corollary of the idea of a crime under international law—that international law contained duties which individuals must fulfill, and they could be liable for breach of those duties.

To properly comprehend ICL and TCL, and against the foregoing background, the important point can be made that international law imposes obligations on and awards rights to both states and individuals, but that redress for violations proceeds in different ways. The liability of states for breaches of international obligation is dealt with primarily under the doctrine of *state responsibility*, which has at its base the fundamental idea that a breach of an international obligation by

---

183 See, generally, Bengt Broms, "Subjects: Entitlement in the International System" in Ronald St. J. Macdonald & Douglas M. Johnston, eds., *The Structure and Process of International Law* (The Hague: Martinus Nijhoff, 1983) at 383.

184 Unless such was expressly granted by treaty; see *Jurisdiction of the Courts of Danzig* (1928), P.C.I.J. (Ser. B) No. 15.

185 Kindred & Saunders, above note 111 at 70.

a state "entails the international responsibility of that state."[186] These principles cover responsibility for breach of both treaty obligations and customary international law norms, though the former is governed by the customary international law of treaties as codified in the *VCLT*. In the course of resolving claims, states have recourse to international courts (such as the ICJ) which have jurisdiction over the states and the dispute, or to formal dispute-resolution methods set up under specific treaties (for example, the International Tribunal on the Law of the Sea (ITLOS)). They also may resort to arbitration or may simply agree to settle the dispute between themselves.

By contrast, if an individual engages in conduct that amounts to an international crime such as genocide, then the individual is directly liable under international law and is truly the subject of the law. As the Nuremberg Tribunal famously stated, "Crimes against international law are committed by men, not by abstract entities, and only by punishing individuals who commit such crimes can the provisions of international law be enforced."[187] As noted above, while the liability is direct in the sense of being personal to the individual, the enforcement can be by direct means (trial before and punishment rendered by an international court) or indirect means (trial for an international law crime before domestic courts). The court must be one which properly has jurisdiction over the individual and the crime, and this too is determined by the applicable rules of international law as well as any relevant state law relating to jurisdiction.

Since the international criminal law under which an individual is liable is based either in custom or treaty, it is necessarily created by states. Thus, the individual is subjected to penalty under law which imposes direct duties upon her, but which was created by a law-making process in which she had virtually no input. At best, any individual input into international law-making is indirect, insofar as individuals may have some opportunities to affect their own government's contribution to international law-making, but it is not at all a democratic process. Recognition of this emerged in the late twentieth century in the form of non-governmental organizations (NGOs)[188] which expended great efforts towards influencing the process of creating international

---

186 Articles on State Responsibility, Article 1. See, generally, James Crawford, *The International Law Commission's Articles on State Responsibility: Introduction, Text and Commentaries* (Cambridge: Cambridge University Press, 2002); René Provost, ed., *State Responsibility in International Law* (Aldershot, UK: Ashgate, 2002).

187 *Göering*, above note 27 at 223.

188 See Boyle & Chinkin, above note 112 at 52–97.

criminal law, in particular, so as to ensure appropriate protections of the individuals. These efforts were sometimes quite successful; for example, it has been acknowledged that NGO input played a significant role in the creation of the ICC.[189]

What is fascinating about these distinctions is what can be observed at the points at which they converge. For example, the individual's ability to invoke human rights protections will vary with the prosecuting court and the law which governs it. With international courts such as the ICC, ICTY, and ICTR, human rights protections are built into the statutes of courts, which means both that the courts must uphold human rights standards during the trial, and that the accused may apply to the court for relief for any other human rights violations he may have suffered. In national courts, on the other hand, the accused nominally enjoys the international human rights obligations which bind the prosecuting state, whether they emerge from treaty or custom. However, to invoke these international law protections, the accused must first have recourse to the domestic courts, which may or may not provide a level of protection that accords with the international obligations. If it does not, the individual is left to any recourse which may be pursued at the international level, such as a right of petition to a supra-national body. In the case of states which are party to the *European Convention on Human Rights*,[190] the decisions of the European Court of Human Rights must be directly implemented by the state. If it fails to do so, it is liable to the other state parties as a matter of state responsibility. Under the *ICCPR*, by contrast, the individual has a right of petition, but the Human Rights Committee can only express "views" which do not bind the state or require it to reverse an offending decision. Formally speaking, the state would be responsible to the other state parties for a breach of the treaty, though in practice, claims are not made by states on this basis.

The distinction between state responsibility and individual liability also comes into relief when examining transnational crimes of international concern, though they operate in more of a parallel fashion in that setting. Under the suppression conventions, state parties take

---

189 See Vincent Del Buono, "International Advocacy Networks and the International Criminal Court" in International Centre for Criminal Law Reform and Criminal Justice Policy, *The Changing Face of International Criminal Law: Selected Papers* (Vancouver: International Centre for Criminal Law Reform and Criminal Justice Policy, 2002) 201–16. Also noteworthy is the work of the International Committee of the Red Cross (ICRC), which has been in the vanguard of the creation and ascertainment of international humanitarian law for over a century.

190 213 U.N.T.S. 222.

on the obligation to ensure that particular offences exist within their criminal laws. Accordingly, the individual will be liable for an offence under the state's domestic law and not under international law, even though the crime itself may initially emerge from the treaty regime — it is a crime under international law only in an indirect sense, which is part of the reason these offences are best described as "transnational." If the state party fails to enact the particular offence in its domestic law, it will be responsible to its treaty partners for this breach of treaty obligation. Similarly, if it fails to extradite or prosecute and instead gives haven to an offender, then this is a breach of international law by the state itself. The individual will not be liable for this failure on the part of the state, though if he is apprehended in another state which is party to the treaty, he may be prosecuted for the crime which is the subject matter of the treaty.

These distinctions are best kept uppermost in mind when operating within ICL and TCL, as each stream of law in this area necessarily engages a complex mixture of both state responsibility and individual liability. It is important to sort out which brand of obligation is engaged when examining any discrete issue within the discipline, and an effort will be made hereafter to highlight the distinction as it arises.

FURTHER READING

BASSIOUNI, M. CHERIF, "An Appraisal of the Growth and Development of International Criminal Law" (1974) 45 Rev. I.D.P. 405

———, *Introduction to International Criminal Law* (Ardsley, NY: Transnational, 2003) cc. 1–3

BOISTER, NEIL, "'Transnational Criminal Law'?" (2003) 14 E.J.I.L. 953

CASSESE, ANTONIO, *International Criminal Law*, 2d ed. (Oxford: Oxford University Press, 2008), cc. 1–3

CRYER, ROBERT, *Prosecuting International Crimes: Selectivity and the International Criminal Law Regime* (Cambridge: Cambridge University Press, 2005) c. 1

CRYER, ROBERT et al., *An Introduction to International Criminal Law and Procedure* (New York: Cambridge University Press, 2007)

FITZGERALD, OONAGH, ed., *The Globalized Rule of Law: Relationships between International and Domestic Law* (Toronto: Irwin Law, 2006)

McCORMACK, TIMOTHY L.H., "From Sun Tzu to the Sixth Committee: The Evolution of an International Criminal Law Regime" in Timothy L.H. McCormack & Gerry J. Simpson, eds., *The Law of War Crimes: National and International Approaches* (The Hague: Kluwer, 1997)

NADELMANN, ETHAN, "Global Prohibition Regimes: The Evolution of Norms in International Society" (1990) 44 International Organization 479

VAN ERT, GIBRAN, *Using International Law in Canadian Courts*, 2d ed. (Toronto: Irwin Law, 2008)

TOMUSCHAT, CHRISTIAN, "The Legacy of Nuremberg" (2006) 4 Journal of International Criminal Justice 830 (plus other articles in the same volume)

WILLIAMS, SHARON A., "The *Criminal Law Amendment Act 1985*: Implications for International Criminal Law" (1985) 23 Can. Y.B. Int'l Law 226

WILLIAMS, SHARON A., & J.-G. CASTEL, *Canadian Criminal Law: International and Transnational Aspects* (Toronto: Butterworths, 1981) c. 1

CHAPTER 2

JURISDICTION OVER INTERNATIONAL AND TRANSNATIONAL CRIME

A. INTRODUCTION

It is impossible to engage fully with international and transnational criminal law without a solid understanding of jurisdiction. Specifically, it is important to comprehend both the international law principles that govern when and how states may exercise criminal jurisdiction, and the manner in which the domestic law implements, incorporates, and otherwise interacts with these principles.

Why is this so? Over a century ago, Lord Halsbury wrote that "all crimes are local . . . jurisdiction is only territorial."[1] The former statement was not true even at the time; the historical record bears out that by the late nineteenth century both crime and criminals were mobile — on foot, by mail, by train, and by ship. Malfeasants in old movies portraying the American "Old West" often headed to Mexico in order to escape the domestic law enforcers. It is even less true now, as advances in transportation and communication technologies have meant that the world is, at least potentially, the oyster of the modern criminal.

While Lord Halsbury's latter *dictum* certainly spoke to the approach the English criminal law traditionally took towards jurisdiction, the international perspective was and is far more complex. From early days both domestic and international law regimes were required to develop means to deal with crimes that occurred, as La Forest J. once

---

1   *Macleod v. Attorney-General for New South Wales*, [1891] A.C. 455 at 458.

put it, "both here and there."[2] States shared among them the desire to reach and prosecute crimes which had negative effects on whatever they deemed to be their national interests, though they often disagreed over the methods to be employed and the interests to be protected. Certainly some elasticity was required, both in terms of *making* laws that applied to crimes that had some international or transnational aspect, and of *enforcing* those laws against the perpetrators by obtaining physical custody of them. However, national chauvinism regarding criminal law regimes generally meant that the exercise of criminal jurisdiction was hard fought and jealously guarded among states, and the criminal element was usually able to exploit the gaps that resulted. In more modern times, conflict often arises regarding the application of human rights to criminal process, which varies significantly among certain groups of states.

Today, the international legal framework displays the great strides that have been made in enhancing inter-state cooperation as governments have sought to draw the net around international and transnational crime more tightly. Yet the bulk of the entire edifice still rests, as it probably must, on trying to coordinate the exercise of jurisdiction on the *national* level, and the criminals are still able to exploit the weaknesses. Many treaties have been concluded that provide some elasticity of jurisdiction, though these have been done on a crime-by-crime basis and, with certain exceptions, bind only those states which agree to be bound. The attempts at supra-national jurisdiction embodied in the *ad hoc* tribunals, the International Criminal Court (ICC), and the various hybrid courts[3] are admirable, but limited in scope. Jurisdiction still causes problems, and states need rules, embodied in international law, to solve these problems.

From a historical perspective, it might seem odd to start from the level of international law, since the domestic criminal law jurisdiction of states clearly operated, at least in some prototypical form, well before the first tentative gropings of the inter-state legal order. Specific to this text, it is necessary to grasp some of the foundations of Canadian criminal law, not to mention our constitutional structure, in order to ascertain how international and transnational criminal law manifest themselves in (and as) Canadian law; certainly, Canadian criminal law can be entirely understood with little, if any, reference to international law sources. However, it is the interaction of the two bodies of law which is key. As explored in the previous chapter, both customary and treaty-based

---

2   *Libman v. The Queen*, [1985] 2 S.C.R. 178 at para. 63.

3   See Chapter 4.

international law are the law of the land to the extent that they bind Canada on the international level and are implemented or incorporated. Thus, as soon as the inquiry is taken beyond our borders in some way, jurisdictional problems emerge that possibly would never occur at the purely domestic level, or at least cannot (or should not) be solved without some recourse to international law. The relationship is symbiotic.

This interrelationship, in turn, makes jurisdiction a very fluid concept, as its various features and manifestations are interrelated. Jurisdictional problems can be very complex and can be difficult to trace through in a linear manner. This chapter will lay out the basic concepts that will allow the reader to understand what jurisdiction is and how it is exercised. It will then review the international law regarding the exercise of criminal jurisdiction by states, which will provide greater insight into the jurisdictional issues that arise on the domestic level.

B. ESSENTIAL DEFINITIONS AND CONCEPTS

1) Jurisdiction Defined

The way in which the term "jurisdiction" should be defined depends a great deal on the context in which it is used. At domestic law, generally speaking, "jurisdiction" simply refers to the ability of the state to exercise some form of power, coercive or otherwise, over persons, places, things (including property), and events. This power may be exercised by various agencies of the state—the legislature, the executive, the courts, or regulatory bodies that receive delegated power from one of those sources—and is defined and delimited by whatever the powers of those agencies happen to be.

At international law, "jurisdiction" similarly refers to the legal powers of the state, but more importantly, determines what one state legally may do vis-à-vis other states. It is "the term that describes the limits of legal competence of a State or other regulatory authority . . . to make, apply and enforce rules of conduct upon persons."[4]

2) Domestic, Extraterritorial, and Concurrent Jurisdiction

The ability and entitlement of a state to exercise its powers is a function of state sovereignty. At international law, all states are sovereign

---

4   A.V. Lowe, "Jurisdiction" in Malcolm Evans, ed., *International Law* (Oxford: Oxford University Press, 2003) at 329.

equals, and each has a duty not to interfere with the domestic affairs, and thus the sovereignty, of other states.[5] What is deemed to be a state's "domestic" affair, however, is not a simple matter. In the international legal system, the state is essentially a territorial entity, and each state has plenary jurisdiction over its territory and every person and thing that is within its borders.[6] Therefore, Canada's territory is the place where other states may not act in a sovereign manner, at least without Canada's permission. Other states may not exercise their criminal jurisdiction on Canadian soil.

To be sure, Canada may give up some of its ability to exercise its criminal jurisdiction by way of international agreement. For example, when foreign soldiers are posted to Canada, Canada often enters into "status of forces" treaties whereby Canada agrees that the foreign state may be the first to exercise jurisdiction over its own nationals, even for crimes committed on Canadian soil.[7] Moreover, the way in which Canada exercises its jurisdiction may be regulated by international law; even though a particular exercise of jurisdiction may be a unilateral act by Canada that is legal at domestic law, it may violate some international legal norm and expose Canada to liability to other states on the basis of state responsibility.[8]

As explored in further detail in Section C, below in this chapter, what constitutes a state's domestic jurisdiction may extend beyond persons or events on its territory. Canada may wish to exert jurisdiction over the actions of one of its nationals abroad, for example, on the basis that the conduct of its national is a matter of domestic concern.[9] Be-

---

5   Hugh Kindred & Phillip Saunders, eds., *International Law: Chiefly as Interpreted and Applied in Canada*, 7th ed. (Toronto: Emond Montgomery, 2006) at 547; *R. v. Hape*, [2007] 2 S.C.R. 292 at para. 68 [*Hape*].

6   Compare discussion of the "territorial principle" of jurisdiction in Section C(2), below in this chapter.

7   See, for example, the 1951 *North Atlantic Treaty Status of Forces Agreement*, Can. T.S. 1953 No. 13, as implemented in Canada by the *Visiting Forces Act*, R.S.C. 1985, c. V-2. For a case where Canadian criminal jurisdiction was alleged to conflict with that of a state hosting Canadian forces, see *R. v. Saunders* (2005), 232 N.S.R. (2d) 249 (Prov. Ct.). For other examples, see the *Protocol Concerning Frontier Controls and Policing, Co-operation in Criminal Justice, Public Safety and Mutual Assistance Relating to the Channel Fixed Link*, signed between the UK and France on 25 November 1991; and the *Israel–Jordan Treaty of Peace*, 1994, Annex I(b) & (c).

8   *Anglo-Norwegian Fisheries Case*, [1951] I.C.J. Rep. 116. States cannot plead their domestic law as a defence to a violation of international law (*Vienna Convention on the Law of Treaties*, 1969; Can. T.S. 1980 No. 37, art. 27).

9   Although, as discussed in Section C(3)(a), below in this chapter, and in Chapter 8, typically Canada does not employ the "nationality principle."

cause the integrity of state territory is one of the foundational norms of international law, such a use of power is referred to as an exercise of *extraterritorial jurisdiction*.

No principle of international law prohibits *ab initio* the establishment of extraterritorial jurisdiction by a state, but attempts to exercise it will usually engage the sovereign interests of other states that are also connected to the relevant exercise by events, persons, or places. The system of state sovereignty, then, imposes limits on the exercise of extraterritorial jurisdiction by states. Specifically, since all states are equally sovereign, it follows that as soon as Canada exerts power in a way that has effect outside its borders, it may face legal limitations and/or practical opposition from other interested states. Any act that exerts power outside the state's territory necessarily implicates the interests of other states. This is manifestly so where the act in question affects another state's territory or citizens, as this quite directly engages the interests of the second state. It is equally true, however, even for areas such as the high seas or outer space. Because no state has plenary jurisdiction in these areas, all states have at least a conceptual interest in regulating the manner in which any state acts, so as to safeguard their own interests. In any event, one state's exercise of extraterritorial jurisdiction "cannot interfere with the rights of other states, whether by involvement in their domestic affairs or by some other means."[10] Most inter-state jurisdictional conflicts arise from states asserting extraterritorial jurisdiction, and the bulk of the discussion in this chapter deals with extraterritoriality.[11]

It is not uncommon for more than one state to have and to claim criminal jurisdiction over a particular transaction. For example, if a Spanish citizen shoots and kills an American citizen in Edmonton, then three states might claim jurisdiction: Spain because the killer is its citizen, the US because the victim was its citizen, and Canada because the murder occurred in its territory. This is referred to as a situation of *concurrent jurisdiction*, that is, two or more states concurrently have at least a potential interest in exercising jurisdiction. Obviously, situations of concurrent jurisdiction are a likely source of legal conflict.

---

10   Robert Currie & Steve Coughlan, "Extraterritorial Criminal Jurisdiction: Bigger Picture or Smaller Frame?" (2007) 11 Can. Crim. L. Rev. 141 at 145.

11   It is worth noting that when discussing the exercise of criminal jurisdiction, there is a distinction to be made between offences which take place entirely outside the territory of a state (thus necessitating an exercise of *extraterritorial* jurisdiction) and offences which take place only partly within a state's territory (necessitating an exercise of *qualified territorial* jurisdiction). The latter is discussed in further detail in Section C(2)(b), below in this chapter, and in Chapter 8.

Sections C and E, below in this chapter, will explore how assertions of jurisdiction by states are justified under international law, and how conflicts are managed.

3) Prescriptive and Enforcement Jurisdiction

In his much-cited essay, Professor Michael Akehurst distinguished three different ways in which jurisdiction was exercised by states:

> the power of one State to perform acts in the territory of another State (executive jurisdiction), the power of a State's courts to try cases involving a foreign element (judicial jurisdiction) and the power of a State to apply its laws to cases involving a foreign element (legislative jurisdiction).[12]

These three categories are analytical and are not watertight. Some writers prefer to maintain Akehurst's separation,[13] while others variously treat judicial jurisdiction as part of legislative or executive[14] jurisdiction, or dismiss it altogether.[15] A more efficient and usable framework for international and transnational criminal law, and the one that will be utilized in this book (as it is employed in international law generally), distinguishes *prescriptive* jurisdiction from *enforcement* jurisdiction.[16]

Prescriptive jurisdiction refers to the state's ability to prescribe or make criminal law, that is, to pass domestic laws that govern (or purport to govern) the conduct of individuals or otherwise affect their rights or property. Another way of stating it is to ask whether the legislative authority of the state encompasses the subject matter; does the state have "jurisdiction over the crime"?[17] These domestic laws may be wholly territorial, or partially or fully extraterritorial in terms of to whom and to what they apply, and all three of these categories are

---

12   Michael Akehurst, "Jurisdiction in International Law" (1972–73) 46 Brit. Y.B. Int'l L. 145 at 145.

13   Malcolm Shaw *International Law*, 5th ed. (Cambridge: Cambridge University Press, 2003) at 576; Ilias Bantekas & Susan Nash, *International Criminal Law*, 3d ed. (New York: Routledge-Cavendish, 2007) c. 4. See also *Restatement of the Law, Third: Foreign Relations Law of the United States* (St. Paul, MN: American Law Institute, 1987–) vol. 1 at 232, §§ 401, 402, and 404 [*Restatement*].

14   Sharon A. Williams & Jean-Gabriel Castel, *Canadian Criminal Law: International and Transnational Aspects* (Toronto: Butterworths, 1981) at 5.

15   Roger O'Keefe, "Universal Jurisdiction: Clarifying the Basic Concept" (2004) 2 JICJ 735 at 736.

16   Kindred & Saunders, above note 5 at 547. See also *R. v. Cook*, [1998] 2 S.C.R. 597 at para. 131; *Hape*, above note 5 at para. 58.

17   Williams & Castel, above note 14 at 5.

relevant to a proper understanding of international and transnational criminal law. Even a domestic law that covers only domestic territory may have a transnational aspect. For example, the *1988 Narcotics Convention*[18] requires Canada to criminalize certain drug offences, but Canada is required only to (and does only) exercise territorial jurisdiction over these crimes. By contrast, the provisions of the *Rome Statute for the International Criminal Court*[19] require Canada to criminalize war crimes, crimes against humanity, and genocide wherever in the world they occur—a fully extraterritorial prescriptive jurisdiction.[20]

Enforcement jurisdiction, as the name suggests, refers to the state's ability to give effect to its criminal law, "to enforce the fruits of their legislative or judicial labour."[21] In the criminal context it can be useful to separate this phrase into the following subcategories: "investigative jurisdiction," referring to the ability of the state to initiate and carry out criminal investigation, as well as to seize evidence; and "jurisdiction over the person," referring to the ability of the state to obtain custody over (usually by way of extradition), arrest, and prosecute an individual.[22]

The state activities encompassed by the term "judicial jurisdiction" are highly relevant to both prescriptive and enforcement jurisdiction. The legislature can empower the courts to apply laws, and the courts themselves are often called upon to make determinations as to whether or not they have jurisdiction. On the other hand, in applying laws, the courts could be said to be enforcing them, and the state also uses courts to enforce by acting as prosecutor. It is submitted that categorizing the specific activities of national courts is too dependent on national constitutional arrangement to have any general application, so the exercise of judicial jurisdiction simply will be referred to as needed here.[23]

It is worth noting that as between prescriptive and enforcement jurisdiction, it is possible for a state legally to have one, both, or neither,

---

18   *UN Convention against Illicit Traffic in Narcotic Drugs and Psychotropic Substances*, Can. T.S. 1990 No. 42 [*Narcotics Convention*].

19   UN Doc. A/CONF.183/9 (17 July 1998), (1998), 37 I.L.M. 99, Can. T.S. 2002 No. 13 [*Rome Statute*].

20   Implemented by the *Crimes Against Humanity and War Crimes Act*, S.C. 2000, c. 24, s. 9. See Chapter 5.

21   Bantekas & Nash, above note 13 at 71.

22   This description (in particular the subcategory of "investigative jurisdiction") was initially proposed in Stephen Coughlan *et al.*, "Global Reach, Local Grasp: Constructing Extraterritorial Jurisdiction in the Age of Globalization" (2007) 6 C.J.L.T. 29 at 32, and adopted by the Supreme Court of Canada in *Hape*, above note 5 at para. 58.

23   Accord, Lowe, above note 4 at 333.

depending on the context and facts of a particular case. "In order to validly prescribe and enforce its laws . . . a state must have jurisdiction over both the subject matter and the person involved."[24] Canada would have prescriptive jurisdiction over a murder that took place on Canadian soil and can enforce its jurisdiction by arresting and prosecuting the murderer. As soon as an extraterritorial element is introduced, complications ensue. For example, if the murderer flees to the US, then Canada cannot immediately enforce its jurisdiction. However, if Canada made an extradition request for the fugitive, the US would recognize Canada's prescriptive jurisdiction over murders taking place in Canada as being consistent with international law, and would likely extradite the fugitive back to Canada.[25] In this hypothetical situation, then, Canada has a legal claim to prescriptive jurisdiction and can use legally valid means to enforce it.

On the other hand, the Parliament of Canada is constitutionally competent, as the saying goes, to outlaw smoking on the streets of Paris.[26] However, while this might be a valid legislative act in domestic law, France would certainly condemn this law as being an illegal exercise of prescriptive jurisdiction under international law. It would most likely refuse to extradite anyone to face the Canadian criminal law as a result. As will be explored below, Canadian police could not enter onto French territory to arrest the individual, as this would violate French sovereignty. In this example, as a matter of international law, Canada has no legal claim to either prescribe or to enforce its criminal law.

Even a valid exercise of prescriptive jurisdiction might not end the matter, as another state (or states) may have a concurrent, and thus competing, jurisdictional claim over the same subject matter and/or person. In these kinds of situations, who determines whether either state's claim is legal and which state's claim should take priority? How will the individual be delivered to a jurisdiction where she can be prosecuted? International law has developed both customary international law rules and treaties to address these problems, which will be explored in the remainder of this chapter.

---

24 Kindred & Saunders, above note 5 at 548.

25 Assuming the terms of the extradition treaty were complied with; see Chapter 9.

26 Peter W. Hogg, *Constitutional Law of Canada*, student ed. (Scarborough, ON: Thomson/Carswell, 2003) at 301, citing Sir Ivo Jennings, *The Law and the Constitution*, 5th ed. (London: University of London Press, 1959) at 170–71 and *British Columbia Electric Railway Co. Ltd. v. The King*, [1946] A.C. 527 at 541–42. See Chapter 8.

C. PRESCRIPTIVE JURISDICTION

1) Introduction: "Allocating Competences"

Criminal law, and the exercise of criminal jurisdiction, are matters about which states have historically tended to be quite chauvinistic. In some sense the criminal law is deemed to be one of the important ways in which a state safeguards both the security of its citizens and its own national interests. The prevailing view that the exercise of criminal jurisdiction is a direct function of sovereignty has meant that states jealously guard it and are not favourable to extraterritorial assertions of jurisdiction by other states. This view likely took hold as a function of the classical Westphalian system and would work well in an ideal world where all crime took place entirely within the bailiwick of one domestic criminal law regime. Of course, as a means of effective management of criminal conduct, it was doomed and outdated from the start, since crime has never respected borders. The view prevails nonetheless, as can be seen from the fact that most, if not all, of the inter-state cooperation in criminal matters that exists is geared primarily towards resolving problems and conflicts that relate to jurisdiction.

When can a state legally exercise prescriptive jurisdiction, in particular on an extraterritorial basis? The starting point is easy enough to frame: a state may exercise jurisdiction only when so doing does not infringe upon the sovereignty of other states.[27] The foundational statement of this international law doctrine is usually located in the decision of the Permanent Court of International Justice (PCIJ) in the *Lotus* case.[28] The case arose from the collision of the French ship *Lotus* and the Turkish vessel *Boz-Kourt* on the high seas, which caused the *Boz-Kourt* to sink and eight passengers and crew members to be killed. The *Lotus* made it into a Turkish port, where the ship's officer of the watch was arrested by Turkish authorities (and eventually tried and convicted) for involuntary manslaughter. The French government brought a case before the PCIJ in which it argued that Turkey did not have jurisdiction over the offence.

The case was resolved in favour of Turkey on a particular jurisdictional ground.[29] However, the court famously spoke to the general

---

27   *Hape*, above note 5 at para. 62.

28   *The Case of the SS "Lotus" (France v. Turkey)* (1927), P.C.I.J. (Ser. A) No. 9 (Permanent Ct. of International Justice) [*Lotus*].

29   Specifically, that the ship was essentially floating in Turkish territory for jurisdictional purposes, and thus Turkey had a territorial jurisdiction claim. This particular legal fiction was later rejected as the law of the sea was codified.

principles of law underpinning the exercise of prescriptive jurisdiction as follows:

> International law governs relations between independent states. The rules of law binding upon States therefore emanate from their own free will as expressed in conventions or by usages generally accepted as expressing principles of law and established in order to regulate the relations between co-existing independent communities or with a view to the achievement of common aims. Restrictions upon the independence of States cannot therefore be presumed . . . .
>
> Far from laying down a general prohibition to the effect that States may not extend the application of their laws and the jurisdiction of their courts to persons, property and acts outside their territory, [international law] leaves them in this respect a wide measure of discretion which is only limited in certain cases by prohibitive rules; as regards other cases, every State remains free to adopt the principles which it regards as best and most suitable . . . .
>
> In these circumstances, all that can be required of a State is that it should not overstep the limits which international law places upon its jurisdiction; within these limits, its title to exercise jurisdiction rests in its sovereignty.[30]

The court's approach to the entitlement of states to exercise prescriptive jurisdiction was extremely broad and permissive. In fact, the court found that to rebut the wide discretion to which states were entitled, it would be necessary for a contending state to *prove* the existence of any "prohibitive rules" that somehow constrained the exercise of jurisdiction.[31] This latter view was opposed with some force in the decades after the judgment, the general view being that "the emphasis lies the other way around."[32] Nonetheless, this pronouncement in *Lotus* definitely "set the tone"[33] for the way in which states' competence to exercise prescriptive jurisdiction has been treated, and it is generally held that "few rigid limits on jurisdiction over the offence are set down by customary international law."[34] On the other hand, state practice reveals that states are clearly uncomfortable with the idea of unbridled permission to extend prescriptive jurisdiction extraterritorially, and

---

30 *Lotus*, above note 28 at 15–16.

31 *Ibid.*

32 Shaw, above note 13 at 582; see, in particular, sources cited at notes 44 and 45. Professor Lowe refers to this as "a tiresome and oddly persistent fallacy"; above note 4 at 334.

33 John Currie, *Public International Law*, 2d ed. (Toronto: Irwin Law, 2008) at 341.

34 Kindred & Saunders, above note 5 at 555.

the specific currency of *Lotus*-based permissiveness probably extends only to situations where the event in question has some nexus to the state asserting jurisdiction.[35]

There is a certain Scylla and Charybdis dynamic at work here. State A cannot interfere with State B's exercise of its domestic jurisdiction, because to do so would impinge on B's sovereignty. Yet B, however it determines what makes up its "domestic jurisdiction," cannot exercise that jurisdiction in a manner that infringes on A's sovereignty. Determining where either of these lines are crossed is a delicate matter, brought to a head in any case where both A and B (and possibly other states) make concurrent claims to criminal jurisdiction over the same subject matter; that is to say, where two or more states not only have laws that purport to regulate the conduct of a particular individual, but make claims to their entitlement to enforce those laws. Since so many criminal acts may have transnational elements, and since different theories of prescriptive jurisdiction exist in the domestic laws of states, conflict and lacunae are inevitable. It is unsurprising, then, that what rules there are to address jurisdictional conflicts emerge from the criminal law stable.

There are two primary responses to this situation in international law.[36] First, as explored in Section E, below in this chapter, states can negotiate treaties that set rules about which state will have primacy of jurisdiction in predefined situations. Second, what are often referred to as "principles" of jurisdiction have developed in international law,[37] the goal of which is to broker multiple concurrent state claims to jurisdiction and try to manage conflict between them. Each has the effect of legitimizing, to a greater or lesser extent, a state's claim to exercise jurisdiction over persons, places, and things beyond its territory.

The international law regarding the exercise of prescriptive jurisdiction—in fact, the entire notion of jurisdiction itself—can in this way be seen as essentially a problem-solving mechanism. It stems from the very nature of the international legal system, where each sover-

---

35   See Cedric Ryngaert, *Jurisdiction in International Law* (Oxford: Oxford University Press, 2008) at 26–30.

36   The third response, it might be suggested, is to simply go "outside" international law, i.e., a state may simply assert and enforce its jurisdiction despite conflicting claims, backed perhaps by force of arms, political or trade influence, etc.

37   See, generally, Harvard Research, "*Draft Convention on Jurisdiction with respect to Crime*" (1935) 29 (Supp.) A.J.I.L. 435. While these principles are usually regarded as being matters of customary international law, it has also been suggested that they reflect "general principles of national law" (Bantekas & Nash, above note 13 at 72).

eign state has complete internal control over its domestic affairs but inevitably bumps up against other, equal sovereigns when dealing with any extraterritorial matter. Hard and fast rules are difficult to come by. Since no hierarchical ordering can be made of their respective powers, the fallback position has been to generate principles that regulate their claims as against, and between, each other.[38] This system of "allocating competences"[39] is a direct outgrowth of the need to manage interstate relations, and while it is normative in character it is functionalist in practice. As Professor Ian Brownlie has written, "the sufficiency of grounds for jurisdiction is an issue normally considered relative to the rights of other states and not as a question of basic competence."[40]

The point should also be made that, while concurrent jurisdiction presents at least the potential for conflict between states, disputes do not always emerge; the mutual interest of states in cooperating to combat crime means that some conflicts are easily managed. As Williams and Castel have written, "In cases of concurrent jurisdiction all the states concerned may legitimately be able to lay claims. In practical terms the state which has the most interest and also that which has custody of the person of the alleged offender will do so."[41] As we examine these various problem-solving methods, what will become clear is that they are all means by which to assess the strength of the connection between the state and the matter over which it seeks to prescribe its criminal law.[42] As we will see, this has led some to postulate a more generalized test.

2) The Territorial Principle

a) Conduct within Territory

As noted above, states are essentially territorial entities, and complete and plenary jurisdiction over all matters occurring within a state's territory is a function of statehood.[43] As Lord Macmillan stated in *Compania Naviera Vascongado v. SS Cristina*,

---

38 "Jurisdiction . . . is concerned with what has been described as one of the fundamental functions of public international law, viz., the function of regulating and delivering the respective competencies of states . . . " (F.A. Mann, "The Doctrine of Jurisdiction in International Law" (1964-I) 111 Rec. des Cours 1 at 15).

39 Rosalyn Higgins, *Problems and Process: International Law and How We Use It* (Oxford: Clarendon Press, 1994) at 56.

40 Ian Brownlie, *Principles of Public International Law*, 6th ed. (Oxford: Oxford University Press, 2003) at 297–98.

41 Williams & Castel, above note 14 at 7.

42 John Currie, above note 33 at 341.

43 Bernard Oxman, "Jurisdiction of States" (1997) 3 Encyclopedia of Public International Law 55 at 55.

It is an essential attribute of the sovereignty of this realm, as of all sovereign independent states, that it should possess jurisdiction over all persons and things within its territorial limits and in all cases, civil and criminal, arising within those limits.[44]

Territorial jurisdiction is the bedrock rule, the default or starting point for criminal jurisdiction, and there are practical reasons beyond lofty assertions of state sovereignty that make this state of affairs desirable. States are most interested in protecting their nationals and residents, and maintaining public order within their boundaries. Their legislatures are also best able to establish and tailor offences to suit local conditions. They will "ordinarily have little interest in prohibiting activities that occur abroad,"[45] and they may in fact wish to avoid any political conflict that might result from trying to regulate conduct that occurs in other states.[46] Having a trial in the place the crime occurred enhances accountability of the domestic criminal law system, both in the sense that the community can more closely scrutinize local judges and prosecutors than foreign ones, and that a greater chance exists for catharsis and healing to occur among the victims and the larger community.[47] Also, in an ordinary criminal case the accused, victims, witnesses, and evidence will usually be in the state where the offence occurred, which will save police and judicial resources. All parties will most often speak the same language, saving on translation expenses. The accused will normally be a national or at least a resident, and will be familiar with the local law, including fair trial rights.

The state therefore has jurisdiction over all conduct by all individuals on its territory, whether or not those individuals are nationals of the state,[48] and accordingly, when an individual leaves his home state, he is subject to the criminal law and procedure of whatever foreign state he enters.[49] This jurisdiction extends over the state's land mass (including the subsoil) and its inland and internal waters, including lakes and

---

44   [1938] A.C. 485 at 496.

45   *Libman*, above note 2 at para. 11.

46   *Ibid.*; see also Bantekas & Nash, above note 13 at 72.

47   Antonio Cassese, *International Criminal Law*, 2d ed. (Oxford: Oxford University Press, 2008) at 336 n. 1 [Cassese, 2d ed.].

48   Though if the perpetrator is a foreign national, then the state of his nationality may have a concurrent claim; see Section C(3)(a), below in this chapter.

49   As the Supreme Court of Canada has held, "individuals who choose to leave Canada leave behind Canadian law and procedures and must generally accept the local law, procedures and punishments which the foreign state applies to its own resident" (*United States of America v. Burns*, [2001] 1 S.C.R. 283 at para. 72). See also *Schreiber v. Canada (Attorney General)*, [1998] 1 S.C.R. 841 at paras. 23–25, Lamer C.J.

rivers; jurisdiction at sea is considered under a separate heading in Section C(4), below in this chapter. Territory also encompasses any foreign territories that are controlled by the state, for example, land occupied after being seized in war.

With regard to the airspace above a state's territory, the starting point is that the state[50] has jurisdiction over it.[51] However, concurrent jurisdiction may be created by customary international law or by a treaty that allows the state of registration of an airplane to assert jurisdiction over it. Canada is a party to the *Chicago Convention on International Civil Aviation,*[52] which provides that an aircraft has the "nationality" of the state where it is registered, and is also a party to the *Tokyo Convention on Offences and Certain Other Acts Committed on Board Aircraft,*[53] articles 3 and 4 of which distribute jurisdiction over crimes onboard aircraft between the state of the aircraft's nationality and other states which may be affected. Canada asserts prescriptive jurisdiction over offences committed on its aircraft under section 7(1) of the *Criminal Code.*[54] Assertion of jurisdiction on this basis is widespread, particularly as geared towards terrorism offences, and it is likely that states are permitted to do so as a matter of customary international law.

As an arctic state, Canada also has to face the issue of whether "territory" includes ice. The discrete issue of criminal jurisdiction in the arctic region is not often discussed, but Canadian sovereignty and jurisdiction over its arctic islands and the waters around and outside them has been a source of controversy primarily due to disagreement between Canada and the US as to the status of the Northwest Passage and the waters of the Arctic archipelago.[55] The current position appears to be that the waters off Canada's arctic islands are to be treated as

---

50   Often referred to as the "subadjacent state" in such circumstances.

51   See *Smith v. Socialist People's Libyan Arab Jamahiriya* (1997), 113 I.L.R. 534 at 541 (US Ct. App. 2d Circ.). It was on this basis, for example, that the government of the UK asserted jurisdiction over the Pan Am flight that exploded over Lockerbie, Scotland, even though the alleged perpetrators were Libyan and the plane was American. Of course, the UK also had a claim due to the wreckage of the plane striking its territory and killing some of its nationals, under the principles of "qualified territoriality" and "passive personality"; see Sections C(2)(b) and C(3)b), below in this chapter.

52   Can. T.S. 1944 No. 36, art. 17.

53   Can. T.S. 1970 No. 5 [*Tokyo Convention*].

54   R.S.C. 1985, c. C-46 [*Code*].

55   Kindred & Saunders, above note 5 at 457–64; Gillian MacNeil, "The Northwest Passage: Sovereign Sea Way or International Strait? A Reassessment of the Legal Status" (2006) 15 Dal. J. Leg. Stud. 204.

conventional ocean waters despite the presence of ice, and thus the international law of the sea regime applies.[56]

b) Qualified Territoriality

Successful prosecution of criminal offences requires the state to prove that the accused person committed certain acts which attract liability under the state's criminal law. In Canadian criminal law, the Crown must prove that the accused possessed the necessary intent (*mens rea*) and completed the prescribed physical acts (the *actus reus*).[57] The application of the territoriality principle becomes more complex when the acts or results that make up the offence occur in more than one state.[58] The classic example is where A, who is in state X, fires a gun and kills B, who is standing across the border in state Y. Which state has territorial jurisdiction? Suppose A shoots B in state X, but B goes across the border to Y and dies. Does the consummation of the murder in Y give Y jurisdiction?

More modern and realistic examples can be mooted, often made more complex by the presence of an inchoate crime. Suppose A and B conspire in Canada to traffic cocaine in the US; B delivers cocaine to a buyer in the US but receives payment in Mexico; B then returns to Canada where he and A bank and spend the profits. Can Canada prosecute B for trafficking, even though neither the delivery of nor the payment for the drugs took place there? Can the US prosecute A for conspiracy to traffic, even though he never entered that country? To deal with these sorts of problems, international law allows for the "stretching" of the territorial principle in order to formulate solutions. Though there is no solid observable rule, to the extent there is a principle of law underlying such cases it is often referred to as "qualified territoriality."[59]

Historically, qualified territoriality has been broken into subsets. Under the *subjective territoriality* principle, a state may assert jurisdiction over an offence that begins on its territory but is completed outside the territory. The rationale is that states have an interest in preventing

---

56   See Section C(4), below in this chapter.

57   See, generally, Kent Roach, *Criminal Law*, 4th ed. (Toronto: Irwin Law, 2009).

58   Though this is not dealt with here, similar problems arise in Canada when crimes take place in more than one province; see Tim Quigley, *Procedure in Canadian Criminal Law*, 2d ed. (Toronto: Thomson Carswell, 2005), updated to 2008-Release 2 at §3-17.

59   For a leading study of the principle as used by the US, UK, and several states in continental Europe, see Cedric Ryngaert, "Territorial Jurisdiction Over Cross-frontier Offences: Revisiting a Classic Problem of International Criminal Law" (2009) 9 Int'l. Crim. L. Rev. 187.

criminal acts from taking place on their territory, both as a matter of local public order and in the interest of controlling activities that may harm the interests of another state.[60] It may also serve to deter criminal conduct that is "not penalized or inadequately policed in the country where its consequences are felt."[61] What is meant by the commission of an offence having "begun" in a state will naturally vary with the circumstances. In a US case,[62] an American national was prosecuted for a first degree murder that took place in Mexico, on the basis that the element of premeditation had taken place in Arizona. In *R. v. Reyat*, the accused was convicted of manslaughter and possession and use of explosives for planting a bomb in an airplane in Vancouver that exploded and caused the deaths in Tokyo, Japan.[63]

It should be noted that court decisions often do not explicitly invoke the language of subjective territoriality, but employ it substantively in determining that an offence was "committed" in the state for the purpose of prosecution. In *Re Chapman*,[64] for example, the Ontario Court of Appeal held that the accused could be tried for conspiracy in Canada because the fraud conspired had been committed in Canada — even though the fraud was engaged through the mailing of letters from Canada to the US.[65]

Under the *objective territoriality* principle, "a state has jurisdiction over a crime which is completed within its territory. This is also known as the injured forum theory or the effect within the territory principle."[66] Not a great deal rests on the notion of the offence being "completed" in the state, though this is the way the principle is usually phrased. The manner in which this principle is used varies widely among states; some require that an element of the offence be committed in the state, while others require only some harmful impact. Even the latter criterion usually indicates some actual conduct within the state, even if that conduct does not amount to an element of the offence. For

---

60   *Libman*, above note 2 at para. 77.
61   Bantekas & Nash, above note 13 at 74.
62   *State of Arizona v. Willoughby* (1995), 114 I.L.R. 586 (Ariz. S.C.).
63   (1993), 20 C.R. (4th) 149 (B.C.C.A.). The jurisdictional issue was first raised on appeal but not pressed by the accused's counsel, moving the Court of Appeal to comment, simply, "We are not persuaded that the Courts of this Province did not have jurisdiction to try the accused for these offences" (at para. 8).
64   [1970] 3 O.R. 344 (C.A.).
65   Today this case would be resolved on the basis of the "real and substantial connection" test put forward in *Libman*; see Chapter 8.
66   Williams & Castel, above note 14 at 29.

example, US courts have found jurisdiction over a perpetrator who did not operate within that country, but used agents to carry out an act.[67]

The most far-reaching extension of the objective territorial principle is in the "effects doctrine," an extremely controversial approach propounded by American federal courts in the mid- to late-twentieth century.[68] Geared towards enforcement of US anti-trust law,[69] the effects doctrine holds that courts may impose liability on individuals outside the US who have engaged in activities that have had economic or other consequences within the US.

In terms of the objective territorial principle, the effects doctrine is highly controversial, and no case can be made for its acceptance as a rule of customary international law. Nor has it had any significant impact on international and transnational criminal law. It is perhaps more accurate to say that an assertion of criminal jurisdiction on the basis of objective territoriality will likely be uncontroversial at international law where some harmful effects *stemming directly from the criminal act* are felt within the state. Whether other states would recognize the asserting state as having the best claim to jurisdiction on this basis, however, is a separate question that will be considered in Section C(3)(e), below in this chapter.

The point is often made that while several states may concurrently have legitimate international law claims to territorial jurisdiction over a matter, "[i]t is more efficient if the investigation and prosecution of an offence is concentrated largely in the hands of a single State,"[70] and that this state is most likely to be the one that has custody of the offender.[71] In addition, it should be noted that, in this era of increased criminal cooperation between states, the governments of states often cooperate in such a way as to avoid conflict over jurisdiction. In situations of concurrent territorial jurisdiction, it is not unusual for national prosecutorial authorities to consult each other with a view to determining which state has the better chance at successfully convicting the individual, and thus reach agreement on who should defer.[72] This, in turn, can de-

---

67   See Jordan Paust *et al.*, *International Criminal Law: Cases and Materials* (Durham, NC: Carolina Academic Press, 1996) at 124. In Canada, see *R. v. Dos Santos* (1992), 96 Nfld. & P.E.I.R. 13 (Nfld. S.C.T.D.).

68   See, generally, Kindred & Saunders, above note 5 at 568–70; John Currie, above note 33 at 343–45.

69   Called "competition law" in Canada.

70   Lowe, above note 4 at 337.

71   Williams & Castel, above note 14 at 30; John Currie, above note 33 at 342–43.

72   This describes the situation where a person may be prosecuted by any of the states with concurrent jurisdiction for the same criminal acts; prosecution in one will ideally end the matter, because the rule of double jeopardy (the princi-

termine whether the individual will stand trial in the custodial state or be extradited to another state that is asserting jurisdiction. Such cooperation can even precede arrest, and agreement on jurisdiction can be the first step in a joint plan that will include the making of an extradition request, arrest, surrender, and prosecution.[73]

As to how states may reach a negotiated decision about which state should prosecute, a recent UN report on fraud and economic crime offers a thoughtful and practical template of inter-state considerations.[74] It suggests that the following factors be taken into account:

a) the state which has suffered the greatest direct and indirect harm,
b) the state in which most of the elements of the offence were committed,
c) the state that has the greatest investment of investigative efforts in the case,
d) the location of witnesses and evidence,
e) the state that has the strongest case,
f) the state with the best capacity,
g) the nationality of the offender and whether she can be extradited,
h) other offences involved or which may be prosecuted,
i) other offenders that are involved or may be prosecuted, and
j) the respective sentencing regimes.

The Canadian approach to qualified territoriality stems from the Supreme Court of Canada's decision in *Libman v. The Queen*,[75] and is dealt with separately in Chapter 8.

---

ple of *ne bis in idem*) would prevent extradition to another state to face criminal charges arising from the same conduct. In fact, *ne bis in idem* provides a further incentive for consultations. In most cases, the efforts of one state to prosecute will foreclose further attempts by others, which creates an incentive to make sure that the state with the best chance of success has the lead, and also that others provide whatever cooperation is required. This is distinguishable from situations where the same individual is wanted by different states, but for two different crimes, though this too will give rise to inter-state consultation.

73 For a case where the Supreme Court of Canada felt such consultation was pushed so far that it operated unfairly to the accused, see *R. v. Larche*, [2006] 2 S.C.R. 762.

74 Results of the Second Meeting of the Intergovernmental Expert Group to Prepare a Study on Fraud and the Criminal Misuse and Falsification of Identity, Addendum, Economic Fraud, UN Doc. No. E/CN.15/2007/8/Add.2 (2 February 2007) at para. 50 [UN Fraud Experts' Report].

75 Above note 2.

3) Principles of Extraterritorial Jurisdiction

Because it stems from the sovereignty of the state under international law, territorial jurisdiction over criminal conduct is a super-added principle; it is the starting point, universally accepted and unarguable. The only reason that other principles of jurisdiction have developed is because states sometimes claim jurisdiction over a matter when they are *not* the territorial state. The following bases for jurisdiction are thus all extraterritorial in scope, and enjoy varying amounts of support at international law. Canadian practice regarding the extension of extraterritorial criminal jurisdiction is analyzed in Chapter 9.

a) Nationality

The nationality principle (also called "active nationality" and "active personality") allows the assertion of jurisdiction by the state of which *the accused person* is a national, without regard to where the offence took place. It has been suggested that this principle is underpinned by the natural allegiance that is owed by an individual to his state of nationality.[76] Historically, it was employed primarily by civil law countries as a means of accommodating their (typically constitutional) inability to extradite their nationals to face criminal process in foreign countries. "If, for example, a German national were to commit a crime in Canada and then flee back to Germany, he/she would never face criminal process if nationality-based jurisdiction was not asserted, since the fugitive could not be returned to the *locus* state,"[77] which would create impunity for the offender.[78]

Stemming from England's strict adherence to the territorial principle, common law states historically did not utilize the nationality principle to assert jurisdiction, though its use by other states was not controversial. As the need to combat international and transnational crime became more pressing during the twentieth century, these states became more flexible in approach and began to make greater use of the nationality principle — the essential interest being to close jurisdictional gaps and avoid the creation of "safe havens" for offenders. As is the case with subjective territoriality, it is also a useful means for a state to control the conduct of its nationals when the crime is not criminal-

---

76 Harvard Research, "Draft," above note 37 at 519. Determining who is a "national" is largely left to domestic law, but is regulated as between states by international law. See, generally, Kindred & Saunders, above note 5, c. 8.

77 Currie & Coughlan, above note 10 at 146–47.

78 See *Public Prosecutor v. Antoni* (1960), 32 I.L.R. 140 (Sweden Ct. App.).

ized or treated seriously in other states.[79] Conversely, some states will exercise nationality-based jurisdiction on a "double criminality" basis, that is, only where the conduct which is criminal under their domestic law is also criminalized in the foreign state.[80] This allows the avoidance of the vexing problem of prosecution for acts that are legal in one state but criminal in another, which would offend the *nullum crimen sine lege* principle.[81]

The nationality principle has generally been used by common law states for more serious crimes, and often in conjunction with other bases for jurisdiction, such as the protective principle (see Section C(3)(c), below in this chapter). It is also found in the numerous international conventions geared towards the suppression of particular crimes, and signing such a treaty either obligates or allows a state to employ nationality-based jurisdiction. Canada utilizes this principle sparingly, usually for serious crimes such as treason[82] and to implement various international agreements which require it.[83] So, for example, Canada has begun to prosecute Canadian nationals for sexual crimes against children that take place in other countries, as it has accepted an obligation to do under the *Optional Protocol to the Convention on the Rights of the Child on the Sale of Children, Child Prostitution and Child Pornography*.[84] Section 7(4.1) of the *Criminal Code*, which provides for this nationality-based jurisdiction, was recently upheld as being valid under international law and *Charter*-compliant.[85]

There is an international trend towards extending the nationality principle, or something like it, to persons who have nationality-type links to the state, such as resident aliens,[86] foreign citizens who are employed by the government or armed forces, and permanent residents.[87] Canada is part of this trend; provisions that implement treaty obliga-

---

79   Though obviously, a state could not push this kind of thinking too far, and would certainly be constrained by international human rights norms. For example, a conservative religious theocracy that outlaws the consumption of alcohol domestically would have trouble getting a nationality-based claim recognized if it wished to prosecute its citizen for consuming alcohol abroad.

80   For example, Egypt; see Cassese, 2d ed., above note 47 at 337, n. 2.

81   *Ibid.*, n. 3

82   *Code*, above note 54, s. 46(3).

83   See *ibid.*, s. 7. For further discussion, see Section E, below in this chapter, and Chapter 8.

84   UN Doc. A/RES/54/263 (2000).

85   See *R. v. Klassen*, 2008 BCSC 1762.

86   Akehurst, above note 12 at 156–57.

87   Robert Jennings & Arthur Watts, *Oppenheim's International Law*, 9th ed. (Harlow, UK: Longman, 1992), at 1156–57.

tions often assert jurisdiction over any person who "is not a citizen of any state and ordinarily resides in Canada."[88] Section 7(4) of the *Code* deems an indictable offence to have occurred in Canada if it is committed by anyone "while employed as an employee within the meaning of the *Public Service Employment Act* in a place outside Canada." The provision of the *National Defence Act*[89] dealing with service offences under the *Code of Service Discipline*[90] gives jurisdiction "whether the alleged offence was committed in Canada or outside Canada,"[91] and section 273 of the same Act gives criminal jurisdiction where a person covered by the *Code of Service Discipline* commits an offence "while outside Canada" that would be an offence in Canada.[92] To the same effect is section 39 of the *Royal Canadian Mounted Police Act* as regards that organization's "Code of Conduct."[93]

b) Passive Personality

Under the passive personality principle (also called "passive nationality"), a state may assert jurisdiction over an extraterritorial criminal offence where the *victim* was one of its nationals. The basis for claiming jurisdiction under this principle is the state's interest in protecting the interests (usually the physical safety) of its nationals when they are abroad, as well as the state's (at least potential) lack of faith in a foreign legal system.

The unilateral use of this principle by states is highly controversial and does not reflect an accepted customary international law principle.[94] The US has made some use of the principle, for example, for hijacking offences,[95] though it was one of the earliest protestors when other states did so.[96] It has been suggested that there are "fears that

---

88 See *Code*, above note 54, s. 7.

89 R.S.C. 1985, c. N-5.

90 *Ibid.*, Part III. It regulates the behaviour of "(a) an officer or non-commissioned member of the regular force; (b) an officer or non-commissioned member of the special force" (*ibid.*, s. 60(1)).

91 *Ibid.*, s. 67.

92 *Ibid.*, s. 273. In effect, members of the Canadian military (as well as their dependents and persons accompanying the forces) bring Canadian criminal law with them wherever they go, at least in terms of being liable for breaches of it.

93 R.S.C. 1985, c. R-10, s. 39.

94 This was certainly so at the time of the *Lotus* case, above note 28; see the dissent of Moore J.

95 *Hostage Taking Act*, 18 U.S.C. §1203 (1984); see *United States v. Yunis (No. 2)*, 681 F. Supp. 909 (D.D.C. 1988). See also the "Special maritime and territorial jurisdiction of the United States," under 18 U.S.C. § 7(7).

96 Shaw, above note 13 at 590.

passive personality jurisdiction favours powerful States at the expense of weaker States."[97] Williams and Castel aptly describe the traditional discomfort with use of passive personality:

> [A] national of state A may be subject to punishment in state B (if state B applies this principle) for an act done in state A to a national of state B, even though the act may be lawful under the law of state A. In other words, in today's cosmopolitan society, in major cities one could be subject to exotic foreign laws through dealing with aliens even though the law of the place where the act occurs would not make it a criminal offence.[98]

In practice, passive personality, like nationality, is often used on a "double criminality" basis.

Use of passive personality is less controversial with regard to transnational crimes of international concern, particularly terrorism, and the suppression treaties often allow states to utilize it in combination with other jurisdictional grounds, though it is generally available as an option rather than made mandatory.[99] This is viewed to be justified as a means of avoiding "safe havens" for offenders and ensuring that the grounds for prosecution are as wide as possible. Canada's use of this principle is confined almost exclusively to this setting, and is virtually always found in combination with other jurisdictional grounds. For example, section 7(3.7) of the *Criminal Code* provides for passive personality jurisdiction over torture, as well as nationality and "custodial universal jurisdiction" (see Section C(3)(d), below in this chapter). Passive personality has also been accepted as a basis on which to prosecute war criminals.[100]

c) Protection of State Interests

The protective principle, like the territorial principle, is also an incident of state sovereignty, but as the name suggests it is more defensive than proactive.[101] At international law it is accepted that states are justified in acting to protect or prevent harm to their vital national

---

97   Robert Cryer *et al.*, *An Introduction to International Criminal Law and Procedure* (Cambridge: Cambridge University Press, 2007) at 42.

98   Williams & Castel, above note 14 at 130.

99   For example, art. 5(1)(c) of the United Nations *Convention Against Torture and Other Cruel, Inhuman or Degrading Treatment or Punishment*, 1465 U.N.T.S. 85, Can. T.S. 1987 No. 36 [*Torture Convention*].

100 *Rohrig, Brunner and Heinze* (1950), 17 I.L.R. 393 (Neth. Ct. Cass.).

101 See, generally, Iain Cameron, *The Protective Principle of International Criminal Jurisdiction* (Brookfield, VT: Aldershot, 1994).

interests, and thus in limited circumstances they may assert jurisdiction over extraterritorial acts which threaten or subvert these interests. Traditionally, these interests were somewhat ephemeral, more in line with old-fashioned notions of the "dignity of the sovereign," but in the modern era are geared more towards a (sometimes expansive) view of "security, territorial integrity and political independence."[102] Examples justified under this principle are treason, espionage, counterfeiting of national currency and passports, and some immigration offences.[103] Beyond these central state interests, however, "state practice is uneven."[104] Like nationality and passive personality, protective-type provisions are found in suppression conventions.

The main problem with the protective principle is the potential for its abuse. In the famous *Eichmann* case,[105] the Israeli District court held that Israel was entitled to try Eichmann under this principle on the basis that it was entitled to act to protect the "vital interests" of the Jewish people—despite the fact that Israel had not existed as a state until after Eichmann's criminal conduct took place.[106] In the latter part of the twentieth century the US has made expansive use of this principle in "protecting" itself from the international trade in narcotics, and in the wake of the 9/11 attack, the language of protection certainly has underpinned much of that state's anti-terrorism activity. In an era dominated by talk of security, the international community will inevitably see interplay on what constitutes a vital interest; and as Professor Lowe comments, "the pressure to expand the use of this principle, and the danger of unshackling it from the protection of truly *vital* interests and of permitting its use for the convenient advancement of important interests, is clear."[107]

As with the passive personality principle, Canada has made infrequent use of the protective principle. The *Security Offences Act* provides for extraterritorial jurisdiction over "an offence under any law of Canada" where the conduct in question constitutes "a threat to the security

---

102　Kindred & Saunders, above note 5 at 559.

103　For some classic cases, see *In re Urios* (1919–22), 1 Annual Digest 107 (France Ct. Cass.); *Joyce v. D.P.P.*, [1946] A.C. 347 (H.L.); *R. v. Neumann*, 1949 (3) SA 1238 (Sup. Cr. Ct. Transvaal).

104　John Currie, above note 33 at 349.

105　*Attorney-General of Israel v. Eichmann* (Jerusalem Dist. Ct. 1961), reprinted (1968), 36 I.L.R. 18.

106　See D. Lasok, "The *Eichmann* Trial" (1962) 11 I.C.L.Q. 355 at 364. Much stronger was Israel's claim under the universal principle, considered in Section C(3)(d), below in this chapter, which was emphasized by the Supreme Court, see below note 124.

107　Lowe, above note 4 at 342.

of Canada."[108] It is at play with the forging of passports,[109] fraudulent use of a certificate of citizenship,[110] treason and high treason,[111] certain offences in the *Citizenship Act*[112] involving false representations concerning citizenship,[113] and can also be found in the various provisions that implement anti-terrorism treaty obligations.[114]

d) Universal

The functional idea behind universal jurisdiction is that *any* state can extend its prescriptive jurisdiction to cover certain criminal acts, even without any territorial, nationality, or protective-type links between the state and the accused or her conduct. That is, Canada could assert prescriptive jurisdiction over a criminal act committed in Indonesia, by a national of Turkey, against a national of Japan, which was in no way directed against Canadian state interests. This is an extremely broad basis on which to exercise jurisdiction and operates quite differently from the other accepted principles. In historical perspective, the expansion of the use and acceptance of the universal principle by states over the last several decades has been breathtaking, given that well under a century ago it saw only very limited use by the international community. Currently, however, determining when it is legal at international law for a state to exercise universal jurisdiction is complex, and ascertaining the scope and limits of this doctrine is at once one of the most fluid and controversial exercises in the field of international and transnational criminal law.[115]

The general principle underlying universal jurisdiction is that "any state may exercise criminal jurisdiction over individuals accused of

---

108 R.S.C. 1985, c. S-7, s. 2, which cross-references the definition of "threats to the security of Canada" to s. 2 of the *Canadian Security Intelligence Service Act*, R.S.C. 1985, c. C-23; the latter definition contains the extraterritorial provision. See also the *Security of Information Act*, R.S.C. 1985, c. O-5, s. 26.

109 *Code*, above note 54, s. 57.

110 *Ibid.*, s. 58.

111 *Ibid.*, s. 46.

112 R.S.C. 1985, c. C-29.

113 *Ibid.*, s. 30. It may also be engaged in the immigration context (see *Immigration and Refugee Protection Act*, S.C. 2001, c. 27, ss. 124–135), but see Chapter 7.

114 See Chapter 7, Section D(9).

115 As Higgins J., Kooijmans J., and Buergenthal J. wrote in their joint separate opinion in the *Yerodia* case, below note 130, "That there is no established practice in which States exercise universal jurisdiction, properly so called, is undeniable . . . . [N]ational legislation and case law, that is, State practice, is neutral as to the exercise of jurisdiction" (para. 45). See, generally, Stephen Macedo, ed., *Universal Jurisdiction: National Courts and the Prosecution of Serious Crimes under International Law* (Philadelphia: University of Pennsylvania Press, 2006).

those crimes that have attracted a significant level of international opprobrium to allow it."[116] Like much of international and transnational criminal law, universal jurisdiction has developed in a piecemeal fashion. The usual starting point is the crime of piracy.[117] As travel by ship became a cornerstone of both the economies and military apparatuses of Britain and other states, there was elevated concern about the harm wreaked by pirates. The jurisdictional problem was that pirate attacks most often took place on the high seas, where no state had authority to prescribe any law except that controlling its own ships, and that even those pirate ships which flew a state's flag generally did not enter port except under secretive circumstances. The solution was a generalized agreement among seagoing nations that any state could arrest, and enforce its criminal law against, pirates. The pirate was declared to be, at international law,[118] "no longer a national, but *hostis humani generis* [enemy of all humankind] and as such he is justiciable by any State anywhere."[119] This was a practical method for dealing with a practical problem, in the special case of a large geographical area over which no one state could exercise sovereignty. The availability of universal jurisdiction over pirates developed into a customary international law norm, and was restated in article 105 of the *United Nations Convention on the Law of the Sea (UNCLOS)*,[120] which itself has customary law status.

The second skein of universal jurisdiction was based on the nature of the crime. Certain crimes have been deemed by the international community to be so horrendous and abhorrent that they represent an attack on the international community itself. The Nuremberg Tribunal after WW II recognized that the crimes within its jurisdiction, namely crimes against peace, war crimes, and crimes against humanity,[121] were all susceptible to universal jurisdiction and many of the post-war trials arguably proceeded on this basis.

---

116 Kindred & Saunders above note 5 at 579.
117 See Chapter 6. See, generally, D.H. Johnson, "Piracy in Modern International Law" (1957) 43 Transactions of the Grotius Society 63.
118 Note that universal jurisdiction attaches only to the international crime of piracy, i.e., piracy *jure gentium*. States may have domestic laws regarding piracy that, to the extent they exceed the scope of the international crime, could not be successfully enforced under universal jurisdiction. See Chapter 6.
119 *Re Piracy Jure Gentium*, [1934] A.C. 586 at 589, Lord Macmillan. See also *Lotus*, above note 28 at 70, Moore J. (dissenting).
120 UN Doc. A/CONF.62/122, reprinted (1982), 21 I.L.M. 1261[*UNCLOS*].
121 *Charter of the International Military Tribunal*, 82 U.N.T.S. 279, art. 6.

In the post–WW II era, the substantive content of war crimes was defined by the 1949 *Geneva Conventions*,[122] which also required states to exercise jurisdiction over these crimes on a universal basis. As these Conventions (and their Protocols)[123] crystallized into crimes under customary international law, so too did the entitlement of states to exercise universal jurisdiction over them. By the time of the *Eichmann* trial, the Supreme Court of Israel was able to find that universal jurisdiction was available over crimes against humanity and war crimes, grounded on the entitlement of states to act "in the capacity of a guardian of international law and an agent for its enforcement."[124] There is currently little doubt that both war crimes and crimes against humanity are subject to universal jurisdiction. Despite the controversy around defining crimes against peace[125] these crimes (now commonly referred to as the crime of "aggression") remain at least formally subject to universal jurisdiction today, stemming from the Nuremberg precedent.

While the entitlement of states to assert universal jurisdiction over certain crimes is a matter of customary international law, either the criminal prohibitions themselves, the jurisdictional entitlement, or both may originate in treaty and develop into principles of customary international law. An example is the *Geneva Conventions* regime referred to above, where both the crimes and universal jurisdiction over them have become principles of customary international law. Another example is the crime of genocide, which originated in the 1948 *Genocide Convention*.[126] Article VI of the *Genocide Convention* provides for jurisdiction by the territorial state or by "such international penal tribunal as may have jurisdiction with respect to those Contracting Parties which shall have accepted its jurisdiction." The latter phrase anticipated the foundation of an international criminal tribunal with inherent jurisdiction over the crime of genocide, which did not arise until the founding of the International Criminal Court in 1998. Even then, the ICC did not have universally based jurisdiction over genocide. However, there is today a powerful argument that states may exert universal jurisdiction over genocide as a matter of customary international law.[127] In 2001, an ambitious study out of Princeton University

---

122 (1950), 75 U.N.T.S. 31, 85, 135, and 287; see Chapter 3.

123 (1977), 1125 U.N.T.S. 3 and 609.

124 *Attorney-General of Israel v. Eichmann* (1962), 36 I.L.R. 277 at 304 (Israel Sup. Ct.).

125 See Chapter 3, Section D.

126 *Convention on the Prevention and Punishment of the Crime of Genocide* (1951), 78 U.N.T.S. 277, Can. T.S. 1949 No. 27 [*Genocide Convention*].

127 *Restatement*, above note 13 at § 404, reporters' note 1; and see the survey by William Schabas, *Genocide in International Law: The Crime of Crimes*, 2d ed.

suggested that the following crimes are subject to universal jurisdiction: piracy, slavery, war crimes, crimes against peace, crimes against humanity, genocide, and torture.[128]

Generally speaking, universal jurisdiction is exercised in one of two ways. In the first, states will enforce universal jurisdiction over a perpetrator where that person is apprehended in their territory. This is often called "custodial universal jurisdiction." The second, and more controversial means, is "absolute universal jurisdiction,"[129] whereby a state will initiate proceedings without waiting until the offender is present on its territory, as under custodial universal jurisdiction, and may initiate some kind of enforcement action, such as making an extradition request or issuing an arrest warrant. The exercise of absolute universal jurisdiction is a highly contentious matter, which has sparked inter-state claims before the International Court of Justice (ICJ). In the *Yerodia* case,[130] the Democratic Republic of the Congo (DRC) brought a claim against Belgium for initiating criminal proceedings against its sitting Foreign Minister for war crimes and crimes against humanity, even though Yerodia was not in Belgium. The case was ultimately resolved on the question of immunities from jurisdiction of sitting state officials, though three of the judges issued a separate opinion wherein they explored the universal jurisdiction principle in detail.[131] The is-

---

(Cambridge: Cambridge University Press, 2009) at 409–35, wherein he concludes: "There is simply too much State practice and judicial authority to support a credible challenge to the principle of universal jurisdiction where genocide is concerned" (at 435). Canada used the principle of universal jurisdiction to prosecute and convict a Rwandan national of genocide in 2009; see the discussion of *R. c. Munyaneza*, 2009 QCCS 2201 in Chapter 5.

128 The "Princeton Principles" are set out and discussed in Macedo, above note 115 at 15–38.

129 Antonio Cassese, *International Criminal Law*, 1st ed. (Oxford: Oxford University Press, 2003) at 286–91 [Cassese, 1st ed.].

130 *Case Concerning the Arrest Warrant of 11 April 2000 (Yerodia Case) (Congo v. Belgium)*, [2002] I.C.J. Rep. 3 [*Yerodia*].

131 Specifically, the separate opinion of Higgins J., Kooijmans J., and Buergenthal J. considered the issue of whether, by laying charges and issuing an arrest warrant on the basis of universal jurisdiction (what the judges termed "the assertion of universal jurisdiction" (para. 53), but what I would consider acts of "investigative jurisdiction"), even though Yerodia was not in Belgium at the time, Belgium had acted in excess of its jurisdiction at international law. The judges concluded that state practice did not disclose any limitation on so doing, essentially because these acts by themselves had no impermissible extraterritorial effect. The reasons do contain the following odd statement: "In criminal law, in particular, it is said that evidence gathering requires territorial presence. But this point goes to *any* extraterritoriality, including those that are well established and not just to universal jurisdiction" (para. 55). It is difficult to tell what the

sue appears to be squarely before the ICJ in a currently pending case, that of *Certain Criminal Proceedings in France (Republic of the Congo v. France)*,[132] where DRC has alleged that a French exercise of absolute universal jurisdiction is unlawful.

Why the controversy? Prosecution under universal jurisdiction is an intrusive act by a state. Even where a state asserting jurisdiction under this principle can be said to be acting as the sword of the international community, the territorial and national states will also have strong interests in such crimes and may object to interference with their own exercises of jurisdiction. Moreover, the territorial or nationality states may have no wish to prosecute the individual in question, and may even view the exercise of universal jurisdiction by the foreign state as political interference.[133] In state practice, absolute universal jurisdiction tends only to be exercised in situations where at least the territorial state, and often the national state, has not initiated (or has refused to initiate) criminal proceedings.[134] Beyond this avenue of restraint, some states will exercise jurisdiction only where the offender is apprehended in their territory,[135] while others will conduct investigations[136] and sometimes trials[137] in the absence of the accused.

It is important to distinguish true universal jurisdiction under customary international law from the entitlement of states under certain

---

judges meant by "evidence gathering" in this context, since it is clear in state practice that investigation by police is frequently done in the absence of the accused. In fact, this is the process which gives rise to the majority of extradition requests—the state has to assemble evidence which discloses a case against the accused prior to ever laying charges or requesting extradition.

132 2003, General List No. 129 (I.C.J.). DRC's application initiating proceedings can be found online: www.icj-cij.org/docket/files/129/7067.pdf.

133 In 2009, the European Union (EU) and the African Union (AU) began talks surrounding the political friction that has been generated by EU states assuming universal jurisdiction over what the AU views as an excessive number of African accused persons; see Council of the European Union, "The AU–EU Expert Report on the Principle of Universal Jurisdiction," Doc. 8672/1/09 (16 April 2009).

134 See the *Guatemalan Generals Case*, Sentencia 327/2003 (Tribunal Supremo, Sala de lo Penal), reprinted (2003), 42 I.L.M. 686; Hervé Ascensio, "Are Spanish Courts Backing Down on Universality? The Supreme Tribunal's Decision in *Guatemalan Generals*" (2003) 1 JICJ 690; C. Kreß, "Universal Jurisdiction over International Crimes and the Institut de Droit International" (2006) 4 JICJ 561; Cassese, 1st ed., above note 129 at 285–87.

135 This tends to be the Canadian approach; see Chapter 5.

136 For example, Spain, under its 1985 *Law on Judicial Power*, Organic Law 6/1985, art. 23.

137 For example, Italy, *Criminal Code*, R.D. No. 1398 (19 October 1930), as am., art. 7.5; Cassese, 1st ed., above note 129 at 287.

international treaties, without any links to the offence, to prosecute offenders where the state apprehends the offender on its soil. The latter refers to the treaty-based entitlement to a form of custodial universal jurisdiction—called "conditional" universal jurisdiction—under the suppression conventions, which is dealt with further in Section E, below in this chapter.

What will be apparent is that most of the crimes which do attract universal jurisdiction share two characteristics: each is a crime under customary international law (that is, it imports personal liability under international law regardless of the criminal law of states), and the criminal prohibition is itself a norm with *jus cogens* status (that is, it is a peremptory, non-derogable norm under international law).[138] Two methodological questions arise. First, does an international crime attaining *jus cogens* status *automatically* confer universal jurisdiction on all states? And second, if so, can it be said that states are not only permitted to exercise universal jurisdiction, but are obliged to do so on an *erga omnes* basis?

Current practice would indicate that the answer to the first question is no,[139] and thus the answer to the second must be academic for the moment.[140] For example, in the *Pinochet* case,[141] Spain had requested the extradition of Chilean former dictator Augusto Pinochet to face charges of torture, *inter alia*. Lord Millet proposed that international crimes attracted universal jurisdiction if they met two criteria: (1) that they had *jus cogens* status, and (2) that they were "so serious and on such a scale that they can justly be regarded as an attack on the international legal order."[142] His Lordship concluded that the "systematic use of torture on a large scale and as an instrument of state policy," because its prohibition was *jus cogens*, had attracted universal jurisdiction in at least 1973.[143] The majority of the House of Lords disagreed, however, holding that jurisdiction had accrued only when the *Torture Convention*[144] was implemented by the UK. It seems, currently, that *jus cogens*

---

138 Piracy is exceptional here, in that it is the principle of universal jurisdiction over piracy which is customary international law. See Eugene Kontorovich, "The Piracy Analogy: Modern Universal Jurisdiction's Hollow Foundation" (2004) 45 Harv. Int'l L.J. 183.

139 Accord, Cassese, 1st ed., above note 129 at 301.

140 See M. Cherif Bassiouni, "International Crimes: *Jus Cogens* and *Obligatio Erga Omnes*" (1996) 59 Law & Contemp. Probs. 63.

141 *R. v. Bow Street Magistrate, ex parte Pinochet (No. 3)*, [2000] 1 A.C. 147.

142 *Ibid.* at 274, Lord Millett.

143 He found support for this in the ICTY Trial Chamber's decision in *Furundzija* (IT-95-17/1-T), Judgment, 10 December 1998.

144 Above note 99.

status is not enough to confer universal jurisdiction; state practice must also reflect *opinio juris* among states that they are obliged to acknowledge the legality of the universal jurisdiction claim.[145]

The exception here may be the obligation on states under the *Geneva Conventions* to actively seek and prosecute those who commit grave breaches of these instruments.[146] Given the customary international law status of these instruments,[147] the exercise of universal jurisdiction must not only be permitted, but operate as a binding obligation on all states. That is not to say that the obligation has been honoured, as war crimes prosecutions by states have been sadly small in number.[148]

A third, albeit rarely invoked, thread of universal jurisdiction exists whereby states will sometimes exercise universal jurisdiction over common crimes in order to deal with situations where impunity for the offender might otherwise result. For example, in two cases in the 1950s, the Austrian Supreme Court held it had jurisdiction to try foreign nationals for acts on foreign territory that were crimes under the foreign state's law, so long as Austrian law contained the same offences, where extradition was not available.[149] Such universal jurisdiction may be appropriate for exercise over stateless persons or stateless vessels in some *res communis* area such as the high seas.[150] It is suggested that universal jurisdiction on this basis is likely to be contentious and seems open to abuse. It is far preferable, and more in keeping with modern trends, to regulate such conduct on the basis of traditional principles that at least demonstrate a link between the asserting state and the perpetrator. Better still is managing jurisdiction by treaty; for example, the *Antarctic Treaty*[151] provides that states will assert jurisdiction over their own nationals for crimes committed in Antarctica, an area of *res communis*.

To the extent that such a difficult topic can be summed up, the following can be offered: states are entitled to exercise universal jurisdiction over conduct that amounts to a crime under customary international law, which has attained *jus cogens* status, and where state

---

145 Accord, Bantekas & Nash, above note 13 at 86.
146 See Richard van Elst, "Implementing Universal Jurisdiction over Grave Breaches of the *Geneva Conventions*" (2000) 13 L.J.I.L. 815.
147 *Legality of the Threat or Use of Nuclear Weapons*, [1996] I.C.J. Rep. 226 at para. 79.
148 See Chapter 5.
149 *Universal Jurisdiction Case* (1958), 28 I.L.R. 341 (Austrian Sup. Ct.); *Hungarian Deserter Case* (1959), 28 I.L.R. 343 (Austrian Sup. Ct.). See also *Universal Jurisdiction over Drug Offences* (1987), 74 I.L.R. 166 (Germ. Fed. Sup. Ct.).
150 See Harvard Research Draft, above note 37, art. 10; *United States v. Marino-Garcia*, 679 F.2d 1373 (11th Cir. 1982).
151 (1959), 402 U.N.T.S. 71.

practice supports the legality of the state taking jurisdiction. This category includes piracy, genocide, crimes against peace, war crimes, and crimes against humanity, and may include torture. More uncertain is whether a state is permitted under customary international law to exercise universal jurisdiction when the alleged perpetrator is not present in the state.

Canada's extension of universal jurisdiction has traditionally been fairly conservative, and like all Canadian applications of extraterritorial jurisdiction, it tends to conform to either customary international law entitlements or treaty obligations. There are actually very few provisions in Canadian criminal law that provide for absolute universal jurisdiction. One is found in the *Geneva Conventions Act*,[152] which implements Canada's obligations under those instruments by criminalizing grave breaches of the Conventions.[153] Section 3(2) expressly provides that proceedings may be commenced, "whether or not the person is in Canada." Also, section 74 of the *Criminal Code* criminalizes acts of piracy "while in or out of Canada." Unlike other extraterritorial provisions of the *Code*, it does not require that the accused be found in Canada before jurisdiction crystallizes, and so this provision amounts to full-fledged universal jurisdiction.

Canada's jurisdiction over other crimes which attract universal jurisdiction under international law, namely genocide, war crimes, and crimes against humanity, is provided for in section 8 of the *Crimes Against Humanity and War Crimes Act*.[154] However, jurisdiction may be exercised only in custodial fashion, where "after the time the offence is alleged to have been committed, the person is present in Canada."[155] Accordingly, this provision is properly understood as implementing conditional universal jurisdiction as regards those crimes as they are defined in the *Rome Statute*.[156] To the extent that the definitions of the crimes are broader than those contained in the *Rome Statute*, however, this provision reflects an assertion of prescriptive universal jurisdiction, but without the fullest capacity to enforce it as may be permissible under international law.

e)   A Global Test: Substantial and *Bona Fide* Connection

As we have seen, the entitlement of a state to legally exercise its criminal jurisdiction bears some resemblance to the old saw about the right

---

152 R.S.C. 1985, c. G-3 (as am.).
153 *Ibid.*, s. 3(1).
154 S.C. 2000, c. 24, s. 8. See Chapter 5.
155 *Ibid.*, s. 8(b).
156 Above note 19.

to swing one's fist ending where the nose of another begins. In the absence of a treaty that entitles or obliges contracting states to assume jurisdiction over a particular matter (regarding which, see Section E, below in this chapter), international law is essentially permissive. The *Lotus* case[157] stands, at least arguably, for the proposition that only an actual prohibitive rule of international law can constrain a state where it wishes to assert criminal jurisdiction on a prescriptive basis. Its ability to do so is a function of state sovereignty. Of course, the major prohibitive rule[158] is that the sovereignty of other states must be respected; the "nose begins" notionally as soon as a state's exercise of jurisdiction collides with the interest of another state, and conflict can ensue where one state objects to another's extraterritorial reach. Such conflict is more likely to crystallize when states attempt to enforce their jurisdiction, to be sure, since a prescribed but otherwise inactive jurisdiction is unlikely to cause trouble. Nonetheless, the analytical starting point is whether the state's prescriptive jurisdiction over person or subject matter was itself legal.

The passages above have described the various principles of jurisdiction that have been used by states to legally justify their assertions of qualified territorial and extraterritorial jurisdiction and to iron out jurisdictional tangles with other states. These problem-solving tools are spoken of as "principles," not rules, perhaps because they have only limited normative effect. Despite some efforts, there is no general treaty regime on criminal jurisdiction.[159] The customary international law on point is, as we have seen, coherent but disunified. In state practice, disputes are as often resolved by practicality (the state with custody prosecutes), *realpolitik* (powerful state threatens/induces weaker states into yielding jurisdiction), or outright illegality (one state illegally abducts fugitive from the territory of another)[160] as they are by purely legal arguments. The fact that the increasingly dated *Lotus* case is regularly cited as the basis for the law of prescriptive criminal jurisdiction highlights the fact that these are not the kinds of conflicts which states care to litigate.[161] The fallback is to the decisions of domestic courts, which will often have recourse to these principles in determining whether they have domestic jurisdiction over an offence or in evaluating the claim

---

157 Above note 28.
158 Another set of prohibitive rules are those regarding immunities; see Chapter 11.
159 Though for regional efforts, see, for example, the 1998 *Amsterdam Treaty Amending the Treaty on the European Union* (reprinted (1998), 37 I.L.M. 56), art. K3(d).
160 See Section D, below in this chapter, and Chapter 9.
161 Which, incidentally, speaks to the intense attention the *Yerodia* case received.

of an extradition partner.[162] However, due to varying levels of comfort with international law among the national judiciaries, the caselaw sometimes obscures as much as it illuminates.

It is important not to overemphasize the conflict aspect of jurisdictional questions. After all, inter-state cooperation in criminal matters occurs every day, and a great deal of the work is accomplished through generous application of inter-state comity underpinned by joint interest in ensuring crime is prosecuted. On the purely legal plane, however, the problem to be solved is how to determine which state has primacy in situations of concurrent jurisdiction, or at least to determine when one state's exercise of jurisdiction will not infringe the sovereignty of other states. As noted above, what is clear about each of the traditional principles of jurisdiction is that they are geared towards demonstrating a connection of some sort between the state and the criminal act and offender in question. This has led some distinguished jurists to develop a more global "test" for legality of jurisdiction based on the idea of connection.[163] Professor Brownlie's formulation[164] is probably the most reflective of law and practice as it stands. On his reading of international law and practice on point, states will have a legally cognizable (and probably primary) claim to jurisdiction where (1) the state exercising jurisdiction has a substantial and *bona fide* connection to the subject matter of the case, (2) the domestic or territorial jurisdictions of other states are not infringed,[165] and (3) the elements of accommodation, mutuality, and proportionality are applied. This framework recognizes that the exercise is essentially a two-part one: the principles of jurisdiction are used to determine whether a state has a *prima fa-*

---

162 Canadian courts are beginning to employ international law methodology in answering such questions For example, they determine the jurisdictional principles under international law (either customary or treaty): if customary, it is treated as being incorporated directly into Canadian common law (e.g., *Cook*, above note 16, and *Hape*, above note 5), and if treaty-based, the relevant statute implementing the jurisdictional law into the domestic law is cited and applied (e.g., *Klassen*, above note 85).

163 See F.A. Mann, "The Doctrine of Jurisdiction in International Law" (1964-I) 111 Rec. des Cours 1, at 82; Myres S. McDougal & W. Michael Reisman, *International Law in Contemporary Perspective* (Mineola, NY: Foundation Press, 1981) at 1274. And see Andreas Lowenfeld, "International Litigation and the Quest for Reasonableness" (1994-I) 245 Rec. des Cours 9 at 77; *Barcelona Traction, Light and Power Company, Ltd. (Belgium v. Spain)*, [1970] I.C.J. Rep. 3, Separate Opinion of Fitzmaurice J.

164 Brownlie, above note 40 at 309.

165 This is most likely to occur where one state attempts to *enforce* its jurisdiction on the territory of another by, for example, kidnapping a fugitive there; see Section D, below in this chapter.

cie claim to jurisdiction, and then a more global set of factors is balanced to determine the overall strength of the claim.[166] The test could be called one of "reasonableness," which is the label applied to a similar version most famously put forth in the *Restatement (Third) of US Foreign Relations Law*[167] and which has been followed by American courts.[168] As Professor Cedric Ryngaert has noted, this kind of test allows assessment of jurisdictional claims on a holistic basis, but allows for the incorporation into the analysis of such legal norms as the principle of non-intervention, genuine connection, equity, proportionality, abuse of rights, and the responsibility or duty to protect.[169]

On this view, the traditional principles of jurisdiction can be used as means for demonstrating the "substantial and *bona fide* connection" required. The territorial state will usually have the most significant connection, but the other principles can be used individually or combined to demonstrate other states' connectedness. Thus, to take one example:

> If a French national commits murder in Canada, then both states have a legal claim to prescriptive jurisdiction: France on the nationality principle and Canada as the territorial state. To ensure the individual escapes double jeopardy, clearly one state must prosecute and the other must forbear, but no serious argument could be made that either state is infringing upon the other's sovereignty. If the victim of the murder was Brazilian, then this third state might also have prescriptive jurisdiction on the passive personality principle. It is at this point that "accommodation, mutuality and proportionality" would come into play; if neither France nor Canada accepted passive personality as a legal basis for jurisdiction over murder, and given that territoriality and nationality are the more generally-accepted juris-

---

166 In terms of its operation, this is essentially the test used by La Forest J. in *Libman v. The Queen*, above note 2, to assess whether Canada can legally assert qualified territorial jurisdiction over cross-border offences, though with an initial emphasis on territorial links. However, it bears emphasizing that the *Libman* test determines whether Canada has territorial jurisdiction over a matter under its domestic law, while Brownlie's test referred to here is for whether a state's claim to jurisdiction (particularly where extraterritorial jurisdiction is being asserted) is lawful under international law. This point is often misunderstood in the literature. See Chapter 8.

167 *Restatement*, above note 13 at § 403.

168 For a thorough analysis of the international law status of the "reasonableness" test, both as provided in the *Restatement* and in other formulations, see Ryngaert, *Jurisdiction in International Law*, above note 35, c. 5. Professor Ryngaert posits an interesting alternative, an "efficiency and justice analysis"; *ibid.*, c. 6.

169 *Ibid.* at 142–53.

dictional principles, then any attempt by Brazil to enforce its jurisdiction would likely be (properly) rebuffed.[170]

It is suggested that this is a more than reasonable legal solution to conflicts over concurrent jurisdiction, though offering a legal solution to a political problem has its own difficulties. However, management of criminal jurisdiction by way of international agreement has been demonstrably superior to *ad hoc* decision-making, as the network of suppression conventions indicates. This approach has the advantage of setting out norms for problem-solving in advance of the problem actually arising, and minimizing instances of conflict by instituting a regime for exerting jurisdiction that is both permissive (in the sense of providing equally valid claims for jurisdiction to virtually all of the contracting states that might have an interest in the matter) and obligatory (in that states are obliged to either exercise jurisdiction or prosecute once they have custody over an offender). Many of the suppression conventions also contain specific mechanisms for the resolution of jurisdictional conflicts, which usually only amount to an obligation for the contesting states to negotiate, but do provide a further means of settling conflicts.[171]

More on the latter topic is found in Section E, below in this chapter, but suffice it to say for present purposes that while the power of the principle of state sovereignty has been undermined significantly in recent years, the news of its death has been greatly exaggerated—particularly in the realm of public policy concerning states' criminal law culture and powers. This being the case, the "substantial and *bona fide* connection" test is best viewed as a stop-gap or fallback, for use while the important work goes on towards securing further international agreement on "elastic jurisdictional principles which can be molded to fit the realities of modern-day crime."[172]

4) Jurisdiction at Sea

The ability to extend criminal jurisdiction out to sea, particularly beyond those maritime areas that are considered part of Canadian territory, is a function of state sovereignty much like any exercise of extraterritorial jurisdiction. What is unique about the international law of the sea is that states can enjoy certain sovereign rights over some

---

170 Currie & Coughlan, above note 10 at 151.
171 In terms of practical application, reference might be made to the UN Fraud Experts' Report, above note 74.
172 Williams & Castel, above note 14 at vii.

sea areas without actually having sovereignty there. Also of interest is jurisdiction over vessels, both domestic and foreign, as the legal regime relating to each is different. Vessels, too, can sometimes be said to enjoy rights in maritime areas, including some areas which are otherwise within the sovereignty of a state. However, while the vessels may "enjoy" such rights, entitlement to them belongs to the sovereign state whose flag they fly.

The international law of the sea is itself a unique and complex body of international law that predates the modern Westphalian system of state sovereignty. Presently it is centred primarily around the 1982 *United Nations Convention on the Law of the Sea (UNCLOS)*,[173] which is a multi-layered and comprehensive legal regime governing the uses of the sea and maritime areas by states. A great deal of *UNCLOS* is considered to be customary international law, but it is also supplemented by other customary law and state practice on various topics. The entire body of the law of the sea is essentially designed to regulate the rights and obligations of *coastal states*, that is, those states which have coastal areas; *flag states*, that is, states which have ships registered under their laws engaged in international shipping activity; and *port states*, particularly as regards foreign vessels in domestic ports. It also regulates the use of *res communis* areas such as the high seas, which fall under the exclusive jurisdiction of no state. Canada ratified *UNCLOS* in November 2003, and its immense amount of coastline makes this an extremely relevant area of law.

Exploring jurisdiction over maritime areas is one of the instances, mentioned in Chapter 1, where there is significant interplay between the applicable principles and obligations under *international* law, the extension of Canadian *criminal* jurisdiction, and the extension of domestic *regulatory* or *quasi-criminal* jurisdiction. The object here is to focus on the extent to which international law allows the extension to maritime areas of criminal jurisdiction, and to explore Canada's criminal jurisdiction at sea.[174] As will be seen, the most relevant statutes are the *Oceans Act*,[175] which implements most of Canada's obligations under *UNCLOS*, and section 477.1 of the *Criminal Code*, which extends criminal jurisdiction to all marine areas beyond the territorial sea over which Canada has jurisdiction. There will be reference to various quasi-criminal/regulatory jurisdictions where appropriate, but this section

---

173 Above note 120.

174 See, generally, Andrew Gough, "Canadian Criminal Jurisdiction over the Seas: Current State and Present and Future Sources for Expansion" (2008) 22 Ocean YB 479.

175 S.C. 1996, c. 31.

does not contain a complete survey as regards jurisdiction for offences under, for example, customs, fisheries, immigration, or environmental protection legislation, and recourse should be had to the appropriate sources in these areas.

a) Internal Waters and the Territorial Sea

The notion of "territory" must be defined differently as between states with coastlines and those without, since sea borders are necessarily different from land borders. As the international law of the sea developed, it was recognized that there had to be some way to delimit where the coastlines of states, which were inevitably uneven, ended and the maritime zones began. This was particularly important because a state's legal entitlement to exercise jurisdiction over the maritime areas off its coast declines or shrinks the farther out from the land it seeks to go. The answer has been the development of a system of "baselines," which define the "point of departure for the seaward measurement of a coastal state's maritime zones."[176]

The area to the landward side of a coast's baseline is referred to as "internal waters,"[177] and includes the seabed and subsoil under the waters, ports,[178] and river mouths.[179] Internal waters are assimilated to a state's territory in every way, and for the purposes of criminal jurisdiction they are treated as land. Therefore, for example, Canada has complete jurisdiction over foreign ships and their crews which are in a Canadian port, though in practice it might cede jurisdiction to the flag state if the incident is wholly contained on the ship itself.[180]

The state's "territorial sea" begins on the seaward side of the baselines and extends outward for 12 nautical miles.[181] Jurisdiction over this area is generally of a plenary nature, and in Canada the *Oceans Act* provides that the territorial sea (as with internal waters) "forms part of Canada."[182] However, jurisdiction is qualified by international law norms regarding the right of "innocent passage" for foreign[183] vessels through the territorial sea, whether they are transiting through

---

176 John Currie, above note 33 at 290. See, generally, Kindred & Saunders, above note 5 at 924–29.

177 *UNCLOS*, above note 120, art. 8(1); *Oceans Act*, above note 175, s. 6.

178 *UNCLOS*, ibid., art. 11.

179 *Ibid.*, art. 9.

180 Kindred & Saunders, above note 5 at 932.

181 *UNCLOS*, above note 120, art. 3; *Oceans Act*, above note 175, s. 4.

182 *Oceans Act*, ibid., s. 7. This includes the arctic region.

183 State criminal jurisdiction over state-registered vessels is dealt with in Section C(4)(e), below in this chapter.

the waters or heading for the coastal state's ports.[184] A state's criminal jurisdiction is expected to be enforced over foreign commercial vessels in the territorial sea only where a crime on board the ship during its passage disturbs or has some impact on the coastal state; the Master or flag state of the ship requests assistance;[185] or narcotics trafficking is involved.[186] It may not be enforced with regard to crimes taking place before entry into the territorial sea if the vessel is only passing through the territorial sea without entering internal waters.[187] However, these limitations do not operate with regard to foreign ships which leave the state's internal waters and pass into the territorial sea.[188] Foreign government vessels, including warships, are generally immune from the coastal state's criminal jurisdiction under customary international law. In international practice, coastal states normally enforce in the territorial sea only where

1) the offender or victim is neither a passenger nor a crew member,
2) the offence disturbs the peace and order of the coastal state,
3) a person actively sought by the coastal state is aboard the vessel,
4) intervention is directly requested by the Master, or
5) the conduct of the ship directly violates rules of navigation, fishing, or customs.[189]

None of the particulars of the innocent passage regime under international law is made explicit in Canada's *Oceans Act*. However, section 477.2(1) of the *Criminal Code* provides that proceedings in respect of an offence committed by a non-Canadian national and on a foreign vessel

---

184 *UNCLOS*, above note 120, arts. 17–19 and 24.
185 See, for example, *R. v. Frisbee* (1986), 1 W.C.B. (2d) 154 (B.C.S.C.); *R. v. Kharsekin* (1994), 88 C.C.C. (3d) 193 (Nfld. C.A.).
186 *UNCLOS*, above note 120, art. 27(1). This provision actually provides that criminal jurisdiction "should not be exercised" except in exceptional cases. Use of the word "should" rather than "may" or "shall" (except for subsection 5) seems to mean that states are still entitled to exercise criminal jurisdiction at large, but should generally refrain from doing so in the interests of international comity. See R.R. Churchill & A.V. Lowe, *The Law of the Sea*, 3d ed. (Manchester: Manchester University Press, 1999) at 99.
187 *UNCLOS*, above note 120, art. 27(5). See second protocol to the *UN Convention against Transnational Organised Crime*, A/RES/55/25, Annex II, reprinted (2001), 40 I.L.M. 335, arts. 7–9 [*TOC Convention*] for a limited treaty exception to this.
188 *UNCLOS*, ibid., art. 27(2).
189 John Liljedahl, "Transnational and International Crimes: Jurisdictional Issues" in Proshanto Mukherjee *et al.*, eds., *Maritime Violence and Other Security Issues at Sea: Proceedings of the International Symposium Held at the World Maritime University, Malmo, Sweden, 26–30 August 2002* (Malmö: WMU Publications, 2002) 115 at 121.

"in or on the territorial sea of Canada" cannot be continued without the consent of the Attorney General.[190] Formally, this leaves to executive discretion the question of whether enforcing Canadian criminal law in the territorial sea would infringe unacceptably on the innocent passage obligations owed to other states. If the Attorney General determines that continuing a particular criminal proceeding would have this effect or be otherwise undesirable, then he can withhold consent and the proceeding can be discontinued.

Enforcement jurisdiction over offences in the territorial sea or internal waters is provided for in section 477.3(2)(a) of the *Code*. While the enforcement power is not explicitly limited geographically (unlike the power conferred for offences which take place beyond the territorial sea; see Sections B(4)(b)–(e), below in this chapter), Canadian authorities will only be allowed to pursue ships/persons having committed offences in the territorial sea beyond Canadian waters if "hot pursuit" has been commenced. They also may not exercise enforcement jurisdiction in the territorial waters (or territory) of another state.[191]

b) Contiguous Zone

States are entitled to claim limited jurisdiction over a belt of water up to 12 nautical miles outside the 12-mile territorial sea, which is known as the "contiguous zone."[192] In this zone, states may enforce their "customs, fiscal, immigration or sanitary laws and regulations" by either excluding vessels which would violate these laws in the territorial sea if they entered, or by arresting or otherwise enforcing against vessels in the contiguous zone where these ships have violated customs, fiscal, immigration, or sanitary laws in the territorial sea or territory.

In Canada the contiguous zone regime is implemented by sections 10–12 of the *Oceans Act*, which allows enforcement with regard to the *Customs Act*, the *Immigration and Refugee Protection Act*, the *Income Tax Act*, the *Controlled Drugs and Substances Act*, and federal environmental protection legislation. This would also apply to any provisions of the *Criminal Code* which could be characterized as relating to "customs, fiscal, immigration or sanitary" matters.

---

190 Though, curiously, this limitation does not apply to summary conviction offences; *Code*, above note 54, s. 477.2(1.1).

191 See Section D, below in this chapter, and *R. v. Dunphy*, [1996] N.J. No. 100 (S.C.T.D.).

192 *UNCLOS*, above note 120, art. 33.

c) Exclusive Economic Zone

The exclusive economic zone (EEZ) is a *sui generis* regime under *UN-CLOS*[193] that entitles states to certain sovereign rights—but without true sovereignty—over an area that is otherwise considered the high seas.[194] The EEZ is a zone of waters extending up to 200 nautical miles from the baselines of a coastal state,[195] wherein states enjoy sovereign rights to explore, exploit, conserve, and manage natural resources, and to generate economic activities therefrom.[196] States also have jurisdiction over establishment and use of artificial islands, installations, and structures; marine scientific research; and the protection and preservation of the marine environment.[197]

Canada's EEZ and the sovereign rights relating to it are claimed via sections 13–15 of the *Oceans Act*. Paragraph 477.1(1)(a) of the *Criminal Code* provides for jurisdiction over offences under any federal law in the EEZ if the person is in the EEZ "in connection with exploring or exploiting, conserving or managing" natural resources,[198] but limits jurisdiction to nationality and passive personality situations.[199] Enforcement jurisdiction is provided for in section 477.3 of the *Code*; consent of the Attorney General is required for enforcement against foreign ships.[200] An expanded jurisdiction over foreign fishing vessels is conferred under the *Coastal Fisheries Protection Act*,[201] which regulates access to Canadian fishing waters contained within the EEZ.[202] Sections 18.1–18.5 of the Act extend application of Canadian criminal law to waters covered by the UN *Fish Stocks Agreement*,[203] the NAFO Regulatory Area,[204] and other fisheries treaties. The EEZ extends beyond

---

193 *Ibid.*, arts. 55–75.
194 *Ibid.*, art. 58(2).
195 *Ibid.*, art. 57.
196 *Ibid.*, art. 56(1)(a).
197 *Ibid.*, art. 56(1)(b). Enforcement is provided for under art. 73(1).
198 *Code*, above note 54, s. 477.1(1)(a)(i).
199 *Ibid.*, s. 477.1(1)(a)(ii).
200 *Ibid.*, s. 477.3(3).
201 R.S.C. 1985, c. C-33.
202 The law governing fishing zones is, since *UNCLOS*, a sub-regime of the EEZ. Canada maintains a distinction between its EEZ and its fishing zones; see *Oceans Act*, above note 175, s. 16.
203 *Agreement for the Implementation of the Provisions of the United Nations Convention on the Law of the Sea of 10 December 1982 Relating to the Conservation and Management of Straddling Fish Stocks and Highly Migratory Fish Stocks 1995* (1995), 34 I.L.M. 1542.
204 Fisheries and Oceans Canada, "Canada's Enforcement Program in the NAFO Regulatory Area," online: www.dfo-mpo.gc.ca/media/back-fiche/2004/hq-ac21b-eng.htm.

Canada's arctic islands into the Arctic Ocean, and the *Arctic Waters Pollution Prevention Act*[205] emplaces an environmental regulatory regime covering traffic by vessels in the arctic islands and out to 100 nautical miles from the land.

d) Continental Shelf

The continental shelf refers to the seabed and subsoil of underwater areas that are a natural prolongation of a state's land territory which extends at least 200 nautical miles out.[206] States enjoy sovereign rights towards exploring and exploiting the resources in their continental shelves, though without prejudice to the waters and airspace above.[207] State also have complete jurisdiction over any artificial islands, installations, and structures on the continental shelf.[208]

Canada's continental shelf is established under sections 17–21 of the *Oceans Act*. Prescriptive jurisdiction for offences under any federal law is extended by section 477.1(1)(b) of the *Criminal Code* to installations, structures, and safety zones around them, located in or above the continental shelf, assimilating such locations to Canadian territory. Enforcement jurisdiction is provided for in section 477.3 of the *Code*; consent of the Attorney General is required for enforcement against foreign ships.[209]

e) High Seas

"High seas" refers to those maritime areas outside the jurisdiction of any state. The traditional principle of "freedom of the high seas" is now enshrined in *UNCLOS*, article 87 of which lays out a fairly unrestrictive regime of freedoms for both coastal and landlocked states, encompassing freedom of navigation, overflight, fishing, and so on. In terms of jurisdiction, the governing principle is one of nearly exclusive flag state jurisdiction: a state has nearly complete jurisdiction over vessels which are registered under its laws and which fly its flag.[210] This means that states have both the right and the responsibility to subject their flagged vessels to their criminal laws.

Warships and non-commercial government vessels are completely immune from any enforcement jurisdiction which might be exercised by

---

205 R.S.C. 1985, c. A-12.
206 And possibly more; see *UNCLOS*, above note 120, art. 76.
207 *Ibid.*, arts. 77–78.
208 *Ibid.*, art. 80.
209 *Code*, above note 54, s. 477.3(3).
210 *UNCLOS*, above note 120, arts. 90–94.

foreign vessels.[211] Otherwise, there are some exceptions to flag state exclusivity. In the case of collisions, jurisdiction may be exercised by either the flag state or the state of nationality of any person accused of a collision-related offence.[212] Vessels suspected of piracy may be seized by the government ships of any other state, and persons on board arrested,[213] and government ships may approach and board ships suspected of being engaged in piracy or the slave trade, being stateless, and in some cases, of unauthorized broadcasting.[214] UN Security Council resolutions may also authorize enforcement activities against ships that would otherwise be illegal,[215] and flag states can agree to allow foreign exercises of jurisdiction against their vessels under treaty arrangements.[216]

In Canada, section 477.1(1)(c) of the *Code* extends prescriptive jurisdiction for offences under any federal law to any ship registered or licensed under Canadian law.[217] Accordingly, jurisdiction exists over any criminal or federal regulatory offence that takes place aboard a Canadian-flagged vessel, regardless of location. However, the exercise of enforcement jurisdiction is limited. Section 477.3 provides for enforcement against offences committed aboard Canadian-flagged ships outside Canada, including situations where "hot pursuit" has been commenced (see Section C(4)(f), below in this chapter), though in the latter case enforcement may not take place in the territorial sea of another state.[218] This prevents infringement on the sovereign rights of other states over their own territorial seas. Again, consent of the Attorney General is required for enforcement action against foreign ships.[219]

f) Hot Pursuit

Because vessels at sea may move easily in and out of a state's maritime zones in order to avoid exercises of jurisdiction, the international law of the sea developed certain enforcement tools to provide states with some flexibility in enforcement. Foremost among these is the doctrine of "hot pursuit," which is codified by article 111 of *UNCLOS* and supplemented by customary international law.[220] Where a ship is suspect-

---

211 *Ibid.*, arts. 95–96.
212 *Ibid.*, art. 97.
213 *Ibid.*, art. 105.
214 *Ibid.*, art. 110.
215 Kindred & Saunders, above note 5 at 957.
216 Above note 19.
217 See *R. v. Guilbride*, [2004] B.C.J. No. 861, 2004 BCPC 101 at para. 160.
218 *Code*, above note 54, s. 477.3(1)(b).
219 *Ibid.*, s. 477.3(3).
220 See Nicholas Poulantzas, *The Right of Hot Pursuit in International Law*, 2d ed. (The Hague: Martinus Nijhoff, 2002), and the decision of the International

ed to have violated a state's laws or regulations in one of its maritime zones,[221] government vessels or aircraft may (after giving a visual or auditory signal to stop[222]) pursue the ship beyond the state's maritime zones and arrest it in any location short of another state's territorial sea. The chase must be uninterrupted.

This doctrine essentially confers an exceptional right to arrest foreign-flagged vessels on the high seas or in the EEZs of foreign states. Recent practice has seen its extension by way of treaty among like-minded states, with much innovative practice being promoted by the US.[223]

In addition, hot pursuit may begin against a ship where the ship itself is outside the particular maritime zone but has functioned as a "mother ship" to other craft that have committed the offence in the maritime zone.[224] This applies whether the other craft is a boat of the mother ship (called "constructive presence") or a separate vessel whose crew is acting in concert with that of the mother ship (called "extended constructive presence"). This concept of constructive presence is designed to combat the practice of narcotics traffickers to have a "mother" ship hover outside a state's maritime zones and have drugs transported by other vessels and personnel.

In Canada, hot pursuit is not expressly implemented, though section 477.3(1)(b) of the *Code* provides for enforcement "where hot pursuit has been commenced." The courts have therefore adopted the doctrine as a matter of customary international law,[225] sometimes in a progressive manner.[226]

Tribunal for the Law of the Sea in *M/V Saiga (No. 2) Case (Saint Vincent and the Grenadines v. Guinea)*, reprinted (1999), 38 I.L.M. 1323.

221 The law in question must be one which is within the jurisdictional competence of the state at international law; so, for example, for hot pursuit to originate legally from the contiguous zone, the offence must have been one against customs, fiscal, immigration, or sanitary laws.

222 *UNCLOS*, above note 120, art. 111(4).

223 For example, the US has entered into "shiprider" agreements, whereby drug enforcement officials from a foreign state will ride aboard American ships to aid in the enforcement process; see Churchill & Lowe, above note 186 at 220; William Gilmore, "Narcotics Interdiction at Sea: UK–US Cooperation" (1989) 13 Maritime Policy 218; William Gilmore, *Agreement Concerning Co-operation in Suppressing Illicit Maritime and Air Trafficking in Narcotic Drugs and Psychotropic Substances in the Caribbean Area* (London: UK Foreign & Commonwealth Office, 2003).

224 *UNCLOS*, above note 120, art. 111(4).

225 *North v. The King* (1906), 37 S.C.R. 385; *R. v. Macooh*, [1993] 2 S.C.R. 802.

226 *R. v. Sunila and Solayman* (1986), 28 D.L.R. (4th) 450 (N.S.C.A.); *R. v. Rumbault* (1998), 202 N.B.R. (2d) 87 (Q.B.).

5) Jurisdiction in Space

The international law regarding outer space developed primarily in the latter half of the twentieth century as space exploration and the potential for exploitation of resources became more fully realized. The heart of the current international law in this area is the *Outer Space Treaty* of 1967,[227] which establishes that outer space, the moon, and other celestial bodies are "not subject to national appropriation by claim of sovereignty, by means of use or occupation, or by any other means."[228] This treaty essentially treats space as an area of *res communis*, and is widely accepted as having passed into customary international law.[229]

Jurisdiction over criminal activities in space proceeds primarily on the basis of nationality of either individual or vessel.[230] Article VI of the *Outer Space Treaty* makes states responsible both for their national activities in outer space and for supervising commercial activities by their nationals or any other entity appropriately within their jurisdiction. Article VII requires states to maintain a registry of space-going "objects" and provides for jurisdiction over them and their personnel by the state of registry, in a manner similar to flag state jurisdiction over vessels outside the territorial waters of coastal states. The subsequent *Registration Convention*[231] establishes an international registry for space objects and provides that, while only one state may register an object, agreements between states which are partnering on a particular object are to be accepted without prejudice.[232]

Such an agreement exists between the states which are cooperating on the International Space Station (ISS): Canada, the US, Russia, Japan, and the member states of the European Space Agency. The *Agreement Concerning Co-operation on the Civil International Space Station*[233] provides for nationality-based jurisdiction over each partner state's personnel upon the ISS,[234] subject to the jurisdiction of any partner state

---

227 *Treaty on Principles Governing the Activities of States in the Exploration and Use of Outer Space, including the Moon and Other Celestial Bodies* (1967), 610 U.N.T.S. 205, Can. T.S. 1967 No. 19, in force 1967 [*Outer Space Treaty*].

228 *Ibid.*, art. II.

229 John Currie, above note 33 at 325–28.

230 See Lee Seshagiri, "Spaceship Sheriffs and Cosmonaut Cops: Criminal Law in Outer Space" (2005) 28 Dal. L.J. 473 at 481.

231 *Convention on Registration of Objects Launched into Outer Space*, 12 November 1974, 1023 U.N.T.S. 15, in force 15 September 1976 [*Registration Convention*].

232 *Ibid.*, art. II(2).

233 Reproduced as the Schedule to the *Canadian Civil International Space Station Agreement Implementation Act*, S.C. 1999, c. 35.

234 *Ibid.*, art. 22(1).

over serious offences where either the accused's state of origin consents, or the accused's state of origin refuses to provide assurances that
the accused will be subject to prosecution in that state.[235] The crew is
also subject to the Crew Code of Conduct, which bestows certain enforcement powers upon the ISS Commander.[236] As non-nationals of the
partner states begin to access the ISS in the future, further agreements
on criminal jurisdiction will need to be struck.[237]

For Canadian criminal jurisdiction in outer space, see Chapter 8,
Section C.

6) Jurisdiction over the Internet

The issue of criminal jurisdiction over offences on and involving the
Internet is a complex one, and the law in this area is at an extremely
early stage. The essential question is whether the traditional territorial-
ly-based model of jurisdiction is capable of dealing effectively with the
Internet[238] or whether the law can be stretched to accept that "virtual"
places are different from "real" places and require their own *sui generis*
jurisdictional regime.

The legal issues raised are technical and highly discrete. They are
therefore discussed in Chapter 7, Section H.

D. ENFORCEMENT JURISDICTION

The sections above dealt with the competence of states to exercise
jurisdiction prescriptively. In a sense, a state that even legislates in a
manner that exceeds its entitlement to do so at international law is acting illegally and potentially violating the sovereignty of other states.
However, most conflict will emerge only where a state actively makes a
claim to assert its jurisdiction or, more importantly, where it attempts
to enforce its laws extraterritorially. As noted in Section B(3), above in
this chapter, "enforcement jurisdiction" refers to the ability of the state
(usually acting through the executive branch) to actually give effect
to its criminal law, both by way of engaging in investigative activities
and obtaining custody over, and prosecuting, alleged offenders. If the

---

235 *Ibid.*, art. 22(2).
236 Seshagiri, above note 230 at 490–91.
237 *Ibid.* at 500.
238 For this argument, see Jean-Gabriel Castel, "The Internet in Light of Traditional
     Public and Private International Law Principles and Rules Applied in Canada"
     (2001) 39 Can. Y.B. Int'l L. 3.

international law stance on prescriptive jurisdiction is safely described as being permissive, then the concomitant stance on enforcement jurisdiction can only be described as "restrictive." This position stems from both the highly domesticized approach to criminal law and the primacy of state sovereignty in the international legal system.

Since states have plenary jurisdiction over everything within their own territories as a function of sovereignty, then it follows that as a matter of international law, states can enforce their criminal laws on their territories without any restraint except those imposed by the state's own legal or constitutional structure. As regards extraterritorial enforcement, however, the starting point is again the *Lotus* case, where the Permanent Court of International Justice (PCIJ) held that a state:

> may not exercise its power in any form in the territory of another State. In this sense jurisdiction is certainly territorial; it cannot be exercised by a State outside its territory except by virtue of a permissive rule derived from international custom or from a convention.[239]

Accordingly, not only will states not enforce the criminal law of other states,[240] but absent exceptional circumstances, no state may enforce its own criminal law upon the territory of a second state absent some clear legal authorization to do so.[241] This extends to both investigative and personal jurisdiction.[242] So, for example, Canadian police have no legal basis on which to question a witness, execute a search warrant, or arrest a suspect in any country other than Canada. In the foreign country, their actions (particularly coercive ones) would be without legal effect *ab initio*, since all of their power to operate as police officers stems from the sovereignty of Canada—which cannot exist on foreign soil.[243] Thus, if a Canadian police officer attempted to arrest

---

239 *Lotus*, above note 28 at 18–19.

240 See *The Antelope*, 23 U.S. 66, 10 Wheat. 66 at 123 (1825), Marshall C.J.

241 "The general rule that a state's criminal law applies only within its territory is particularly true of the legal procedures enacted to enforce it; the exercise of an enforcement jurisdiction is 'inherently territorial' . . ." (*R. v. Terry*, [1996] 2 S.C.R. 207 at para. 17; see also para. 14). See also *Hape*, above note 5 at paras. 64–65; *Cook*, above note 16 para. 131.

242 Brownlie, above note 40 at 306; Higgins, above note 39 at 70; John Dugard, *International Law: A South African Perspective*, 2d ed. (Kenwyn: Juta, 2000) at 173.

243 This is not to suggest, however, that the actions of a Canadian police officer in a foreign state should necessarily be treated as being void when they are considered in legal proceedings in Canada. For example, suppose an RCMP officer questions a willing witness at a restaurant in Paris. The officer has no coercive powers which can be exercised, but none are needed. Even if the French government is not aware of the officer's presence, it is difficult to say that French

an individual in France, she could be charged with assault or unlawful confinement under French criminal law. Similarly, in *Yerodia*, the Belgian court may have had jurisdiction to lay charges against Yerodia and issue an arrest warrant, but would not have been able to arrest him unless he entered onto Belgian soil.

This being the case, the result is that states must, and do, cooperate in order to be able to exercise their respective enforcement jurisdictions over matters with an international or transnational aspect. A state may choose to exercise its sovereign capacity and grant permission for a foreign state to enforce on its soil,[244] or alternatively, may agree to conduct the enforcement activity on behalf of the foreign state. The most common method of obtaining jurisdiction over the person of the offender is by way of extradition, whereby states agree to apprehend and transmit fugitives between and among each other.[245] This forestalls any need for a state to attempt to exercise its enforcement jurisdiction on the soil of another state, since the extraditing state itself does the enforcement task (arrest) that the requesting state cannot.[246] In terms of investigative jurisdiction, states have increasingly entered into mutual legal assistance treaties, under which one state's prosecuting authorities can

---

sovereignty has been violated; any infringement is nominal, at best. The officer's actions can still be treated as those of a police officer if the witness statement becomes an issue at a Canadian trial, since nothing stops Parliament from extending the officer's police status wherever she goes (e.g., for extending the application of criminal, disciplinary, and employment law) as long as it does not purport to establish powers that would *prima facie* infringe other states' sovereignty. Even after *Hape*, however, these questions remain open, because they do not come before the courts for consideration.

244 For example, in the case stemming from the *Lockerbie* incident, two Libyans were tried for blowing up Pan Am flight 103 and killing its passengers. The prosecution was under Scottish law and before the Scottish High Court of Justiciary, since the plane had exploded over Scotland, but the trial was held in The Hague at Libya's request. The agreement between the UK and the Netherlands permitting this can be found at (1999), 38 I.L.M. 926; and see Chapter 4.

245 Dealt with more fully in Chapter 9, which also surveys the problem of states illegally exercising enforcement jurisdiction by abducting fugitives from the territory of foreign states.

246 In the European Union, this process has been streamlined by the adoption of the "European Arrest Warrant," by which national police forces arrest accused persons on the basis of court orders issued in partner states, without the need for formal extradition requests to be made on an inter-state basis. See European Commission, "European Arrest Warrant Replaces Extradition between EU Member States," online: http://ec.europa.eu/justice_home/fsj/criminal/extradition/fsj_criminal_extradition_en.htm. And see Rob Blekxtoon & Wouter van Ballegooij, *Handbook on the European Arrest Warrant* (The Hague: TMC Asser Press, 2005).

request the other state to gather evidence on its behalf; here again, the foreign police do the "enforcement work" on their own soil.[247]

Increasingly, police forces have recourse to *ad hoc* or regularized arrangements whereby officers from one state are given permission by the authorities of another to enter into the foreign state and conduct enforcement activities—either under their own direction,[248] or as part of a joint operation overseen by the foreign police.[249] In either case, when acting on foreign soil, police officers are subject to, and their actions are governed by, the law of the foreign state.[250] Note that this does not deprive the courts of the officers' home state of scrutinizing any actions by the officers in the foreign state and giving them some legal effect at a domestic trial, since to do so would not interfere with the sovereignty of the foreign state.[251] These matters are dealt with in more detail in Chapter 10.

A state may also enforce its criminal laws outside its territory where to do so does not offend the sovereignty of any other state, and particularly where the mode of enforcement is underpinned by a rule of customary or treaty law. So, for example, Canada has primary (and mostly exclusive) enforcement jurisdiction over ships on the high seas which carry its flag,[252] and the same is true with regard to aircraft that are registered in Canada and are not over another state's territory.[253]

---

247 An interesting cross-section of these principles occurred in *R. v. Dorsay*, 2006 BCCA 117, where pursuant to the *Canada–US Mutual Legal Assistance Treaty*, Can. T.S. 1990 No. 19, an American court compelled testimony from American witnesses at the request of Canadian prosecutors, and applied Canadian evidence law in so doing. This is often provided for under mutual legal assistance treaties; see Chapter 9 for more detail. The main point for present purposes is that the two states must agree for this to happen, for otherwise, the US will not apply Canadian law on its soil.

248 For example, *Cook*, above note 16.

249 For example, *Hape*, above note 5.

250 *Terry*, above note 241 at para. 19; see also *Hape*, *ibid*.

251 See *Cook*, above note 16 at paras. 120–22, Bastarache J. (concurring); *Hape*, *ibid*. For a review of international (particularly European) jurisprudence on this question, see Ralph Wilde, "Triggering State Obligations Extraterritorially: The Spatial Test in Certain Human Rights Treaties" (2007) 40 Israel L. Rev. 503.

252 *UNCLOS*, above note 120, arts. 94–114, with customary force. See Section C(4), above in this chapter.

253 *Tokyo Convention*, above note 53.

E. TREATY-BASED PRESCRIPTIVE AND ENFORCEMENT JURISDICTION: *AUT DEDERE AUT JUDICARE* AND "CONDITIONAL" UNIVERSAL JURISDICTION

The bases for prescriptive jurisdiction described above are all permissive in character. In customary international law, states are *permitted* to exercise criminal jurisdiction consistently with the traditional principles, but unless a particular prohibition has *jus cogens* status, they are not *required* even to establish jurisdiction over the crime itself; and, importantly, even where a state does criminalize certain conduct, there is no obligation to actually assert its jurisdiction over a particular individual and his acts. This is subject only to the exceptional situations where a treaty-based obligation to prosecute particular offenders has crystallized into a customary international law principle, for example, the obligation to prosecute persons accused of grave breaches of the *Geneva Conventions*.

The potential and actual gaps which are left by a system of solely permissive jurisdiction are obvious. In response, the latter part of the twentieth century saw the conclusion of treaties between like-minded states to fill the gaps with regard to particularly pernicious kinds of crime that had such significant transnational effects that they were of international concern. These treaties, now generally called the "suppression conventions,"[254] cover a number of different crimes, ranging from hijacking and other aviation-related terrorism offences,[255] hostage-taking,[256] and terrorist bombing[257] to counterfeiting,[258] attacks on internationally protected persons,[259] torture,[260] organized crime,[261] and narcotics trafficking.[262]

---

254 For a fuller discussion, see Chapter 7.
255 The *Convention for the Suppression of Unlawful Seizure of Aircraft*, 860 U.N.T.S. 105, Can. T.S. 1972 No. 23; *Convention for the Suppression of Unlawful Acts against the Safety of Civil Aviation*, 974 U.N.T.S. 177, Can. T.S. 1973 No. 6.
256 *International Convention against the Taking of Hostages*, 1316 U.N.T.S. 205, Can. T.S. 1986 No. 45.
257 *International Convention for the Suppression of Terrorist Bombings* (1998), 37 I.L.M. 249, Can. T.S. 2002 No. 8 [*Terrorist Bombing Convention*].
258 *International Convention for the Suppression of Counterfeiting Currency*, (1929), 112 L.N.T.S. 371.
259 *Convention on the Prevention and Punishment of Crimes against Internationally Protected Persons, Including Diplomatic Agents*, 1035 U.N.T.S. 167, Can. T.S. 1977 No. 43.
260 *Torture Convention*, above note 99.
261 *TOC Convention*, above note 187.
262 *Narcotics Convention*, above note 18.

The essential and interrelated goals of the suppression conventions are threefold: (1) to ensure that particularly harmful or destructive transnational crimes are criminalized by a network of states, (2) to ensure that as large a number of states as possible will exercise jurisdiction over these crimes, to avoid the problem of states which operate as "safe havens" for offenders, and (3) to provide for cooperation between the interested states, in particular, to allow for sharing of resources and expertise in a way that assists poorer states.

While the treaties vary in subject matter, coverage, and terms, each employs essentially the same set of mechanisms to provide for expanded state jurisdiction over the crimes in question.[263] First, each contracting state is obliged to criminalize particular conduct under its domestic criminal law, that is, it agrees to exercise prescriptive jurisdiction over the particular offence. Second, each state agrees[264] to exercise jurisdiction on the basis of a number of principles beyond territoriality, for example, nationality, passive personality, and protective, as well as over offences on aircraft, ships, and sometimes offshore platforms registered in the state. Third, each treaty provides that where a state apprehends an offender on its territory,[265] it must submit the case for investigation by its prosecutorial authorities, and must prosecute the offender in appropriate circumstances. If the state chooses not to do so, it may (and often must) extradite the offender to another treaty partner state which is willing to prosecute.

The latter obligation is generally known as *aut dedere aut judicare*, "extradite or prosecute."[266] It operates in conjunction with a jurisdictional clause that provides for prosecution even in the absence of any other link with the person or the offence. So, for example, the *Terrorist Bombing Convention* obliges each state party to "take such measures as may be necessary to establish its jurisdiction over the offences . . . in cases where the alleged offender is present in its territory and it does not extradite that person to any of the States Parties which have established their jurisdiction . . . ."[267] This operates in a similar manner to

---

263 For more detailed treatment, see Chapter 7.

264 Or at least "can agree," depending on whether the obligation to exercise a particular ground of jurisdiction is permissive or mandatory.

265 Many treaties provide that the state is actually obliged to apprehend an alleged offender where investigation substantiates both a basis for the allegation and the presence of the person in the state's territory; see, for example, *Terrorist Bombing Convention*, above note 257, art. 7.

266 See, generally, M. Cherif Bassiouni & Edward M. Wise, *Aut Dedere Aut Judicare: The Duty to Extradite or Prosecute in International Law* (Dordrecht: Martinus Nijhoff, 1995).

267 Above note 257, art. 6(4).

universal jurisdiction, and it is common to see it referred to as such in caselaw and literature. However, though often confused, the two bases for jurisdiction are not the same. Recognition of the differences is shown in the various labels which have been applied to the jurisdiction used in conjunction with the *aut dedere* mechanism: "quasi-universal,"[268] "conditional,"[269] "subsidiary,"[270] "cooperative,"[271] as well as "obligatory territorial jurisdiction over persons."[272] The phrase "conditional universal jurisdiction" will be used here.

The combined effect of the *aut dedere aut judicare* obligation and conditional universal jurisdiction is to compel each contracting state to exercise prescriptive jurisdiction on an extraterritorial basis, without any of the traditional kinds of linkage between the state and the offender or the crime. If the state opts not to enforce its jurisdiction via arrest and prosecution, it may (and, again, often must, depending on the wording of the specific treaty) extradite the individual to a state which will enforce it.

There are four key differences between conditional universal jurisdiction and universal jurisdiction proper. First, universal jurisdiction is a principle of customary international law, while conditional universal jurisdiction arises under treaty. Second, as noted in Section C(3)(d), above in this chapter, the exercise of universal jurisdiction is almost exclusively permissive for states, while conditional universal jurisdiction is mandatory upon signing and ratifying a relevant treaty. Third, a state which is legally entitled to exercise universal jurisdiction under customary international law may do so as against the world, while conditional universal jurisdiction operates only as between states which are parties to the treaty. Fourth, universal jurisdiction in its broadest form crystallizes on the exercise of prescriptive jurisdiction, that is, the making of the domestic law that provides for universal jurisdiction, so that states may request the extradition of an offender on the basis that they are legally exercising jurisdiction. Conditional universal jurisdiction, on the other hand, is strictly "custodial"; it crystallizes only when the offender is apprehended on the territory of the contracting state, so the state is not legally entitled to request extradition solely on this ground of jurisdiction alone (though it may do so if it has other links).

---

268 Shaw, above note 13 at 598.
269 Antonio Cassese, "When May Senior State Officials Be Tried for International Crimes?" (2002) 13 E.J.I.L. 853 at 856.
270 Separate opinion of President Guillaume in *Yerodia*, above note 130 at para. 12.
271 Luc Reydams, *Universal Jurisdiction: International and Municipal Legal Perspectives* (Oxford: Oxford University Press, 2003) at 29.
272 Higgins *et al.* separate opinion in *Yerodia*, above note 130 at para. 41.

The manner in which Canada's jurisdictional obligations under the suppression conventions are implemented is dealt with on a subject matter basis, crime by crime, in Chapter 7.

F. JURISDICTION OF INTERNATIONAL COURTS

The foregoing discussion has addressed the criminal jurisdiction of states as is found in their domestic laws, permitted under customary law, and imposed by operation of treaty. The jurisdictional reach of international criminal courts (such as the Yugoslavia and Rwanda tribunals and the International Criminal Court (ICC) and "internationalized" criminal courts (such as the Special Court for Sierra Leone) is similar in some respects, but different enough in scope and effect to justify separate attention. It may be appropriate to speak of it as "international criminal jurisdiction,"[273] or alternatively, "supra-national criminal jurisdiction," since these courts adjudicate upon international crimes, have a jurisdictional reach that stems directly from international law, and operate in some way with legal authority that is delegated by states.

To date, all international and internationalized criminal courts have been created by some international legal instrument, whether a resolution of the United Nations Security Council as with the *ad hoc* tribunals, an agreement between the UN and the host state of the court as with the Sierra Leone court and the United Nations Interim Administration Mission in Kosovo (UNMIK), or a treaty as with the Nuremberg and Tokyo tribunals and the ICC. Each of these founding instruments establishes the jurisdiction of its court and sets limits which are narrow or broad, depending on the purpose for which the court is being set up.[274] The jurisdiction of each such court, then, is strictly limited in accordance with its founding instrument; "the application of the *Lotus* rule . . . , whereby national criminal jurisdiction under any basis is permissible subject only to a contrary binding rule of international law, does not apply . . . ."[275]

Even the type of jurisdiction created may vary on this basis. For example, article 1 of the *Statute of the International Criminal Tribunal for*

---

273 Bantekas & Nash, above note 13 at 93.
274 These courts possess "*competence de la competence*," i.e., they are empowered to determine their own jurisdiction; see *Tadic* (IT-94-1-AR72), Decision on the Defence Motion for Interlocutory Appeal on Jurisdiction, 2 October 1995; *Rome Statute*, above note 19, art. 19.
275 Bantekas & Nash, above note 13 at 96.

the former Yugoslavia (*ICTY Statute*)[276]gave the tribunal jurisdiction over "persons responsible for serious violations of international humanitarian law committed in the territory of the former Yugoslavia since 1991." This article established both the *territorial* jurisdiction of the tribunal (those territories which were within the state of Yugoslavia prior to its breakup) and its *temporal* jurisdiction (prescribed crimes committed since 1991). Articles 2–5 set out the *subject matter* jurisdiction of the tribunal, covering grave breaches of the Geneva Conventions, violations of the laws or customs of war, genocide, and crimes against humanity. The *Rome Statute*, by contrast, gave the ICC subject matter jurisdiction over aggression, genocide, crimes against humanity, and war crimes,[277] but only where committed by a national of a state party to its founding treaty[278] or if the crime takes place on the territory of a state party.[279] Also, it can exercise jurisdiction only over crimes committed after 1 July 2002, the date the *Rome Statute* came into force.[280]

The temporal limitations on the jurisdiction of an international court vary and are specifically prescribed to fulfill the goals the founders of the court are seeking to accomplish. The jurisdiction of the International Criminal Tribunal for Rwanda (ICTR), for example, was limited to the calendar year 1994, which was when the conflict in question took place. By contrast, when states prosecute international crimes, any temporal limitations on their jurisdiction generally come from domestic criminal and/or constitutional law. These will not take the form of "temporal jurisdiction" in the manner formulated in the founding instruments of international courts, but appear as statutes of limitations and prohibitions on applying criminal law retroactively. The domestic law, however, may in turn be shaped by international law obligations. For example, it is generally held that under customary international law, a state cannot impose a statute of limitation on the international crimes of genocide, crimes against humanity, and torture.[281]

It is worth noting that even where a state is an adherent to or subject of an international court, it will not necessarily be constrained by the jurisdictional limits of that court, but may possess wider jurisdictional competence. For example, Canada is party to the *Rome Statute*,

---

276 Annexed to UN Doc. S/RES/827 (1993).

277 *Rome Statute*, above note 19, art. 5.

278 *Ibid.*, art. 12(2)(a).

279 *Ibid.*, art. 12(2)(b). Also, the court can take jurisdiction over any case referred to it by the Security Council: *ibid.*, art. 13(b).

280 *Ibid.*, art. 11.

281 Cassese, 1st ed., above note 129 at 319. Though this may be controversial; see Robert Cryer *et al.*, *An Introduction to International Criminal Law and Procedure* (Cambridge: Cambridge University Press, 2007) at 63–64.

and its obligations thereunder are implemented by the *Crimes Against Humanity and War Crimes Act*.[282] Under the Act, Canada can prosecute offenders whose crimes fall within the limits of the ICC's jurisdiction (i.e., national/territory of state party, act occurs after 1 July 2002). However, the Act's extraterritorial jurisdiction provisions are wider, and Canada can also prosecute nationals of non-party states or those who have committed the prescribed crimes in non-party states, as well as not being limited to acts which occurred prior to the coming into force date of the treaty. Moreover, the Act provides for jurisdiction over the same crimes as those in the *Rome Statute*, but incorporates developing customary international law into its definitions of those crimes, the result being that the Act's definition of "crimes against humanity," for example, may catch a broader range of behaviour than the corresponding crime as it exists in the *Rome Statute*.

The interaction of an international court's jurisdiction with those of domestic courts will also stem from the legal arrangements under which the international court is set up, particularly as regards primacy. The *ad hoc* tribunals, as manifestations of the exercise of the Security Council's Chapter VII powers, have primacy of jurisdiction over that of all states.[283] The ICC's jurisdiction, however, is designed to be "complementary" to that of the state parties to the *Rome Statute*, and it will take jurisdiction only where an appropriate state party is unwilling or unable to do so.[284]

In terms of enforcement jurisdiction, all of the international and internationalized criminal courts must operate indirectly. While each may adjudicate and make orders, none has a dedicated police force or prison system to give effect to these orders. Accordingly, these courts operate by way of state cooperation; state police or military forces must do the coercive work, such as gathering evidence, executing warrants, and arresting (and even imprisoning) fugitives. The kind of cooperation scheme in place will again depend on the legal status of the court. The *ad hoc* tribunals were meant, at least ideally, to have the force of the Security Council behind their orders and were empowered to compel states to cooperate.[285] The ICC must rely on the state parties to en-

---

282 Above note 154. See Chapter 5.
283 *ICTY Statute*, above note 276, s. 9(2); though the jurisdiction may indeed be initially concurrent with that of national courts (s. 9(1)), the tribunal can still assert primacy and require national courts to defer.
284 See the discussion of the ICC in Chapter 4.
285 Though this came with attendant legal and political problems; see Michael Scharf, "The Tools for Enforcing International Criminal Justice in the New Millennium: Lessons from the Yugoslavia Tribunal" (2000) 49 DePaul L. Rev. 925.

force its dictates or else enter into agreements with non-party states to do so—which famously earned it the label "a giant without arms and legs."[286] In most cases, prosecutorial staff of the court may be empowered to conduct certain investigatory activities within the territory of a state, but will do so either as a matter of UN authority or at the sufferance of a state which is bound by a treaty arrangement to allow it.[287]

FURTHER READING

AKEHURST, MICHAEL, "Jurisdiction in International Law" (1972–73) 46 Brit. Y.B. Int'l L. 145

BANTEKAS, ILIAS, & SUSAN NASH, *International Criminal Law*, 3d ed. (New York: Routledge-Cavendish, 2007) c. 4

BLAKESLEY, CHRISTOPHER L., "Extraterritorial Jurisdiction" in M. Cherif Bassiouni, ed., *International Criminal Law*, 2d ed., vol. II (Ardsley, NY: Transnational, 1999) 33

BROWNLIE, IAN, *Principles of Public International Law*, 6th ed. (Oxford: Oxford University Press, 2003) c. 15

CURRIE, JOHN, *Public International Law*, 2d ed. (Toronto: Irwin Law, 2008) c. 8

CURRIE, ROBERT J., & STEVE COUGHLAN, "Extraterritorial Criminal Jurisdiction: Bigger Picture or Smaller Frame?" (2007) 11 Can. Crim. L. Rev. 141

EUROPEAN COMMITTEE ON CRIME PROBLEMS, *Extraterritorial Criminal Jurisdiction* (Strasbourg: Council of Europe, 1990)

GALLANT, KENNETH S., "Jurisdiction to Adjudicate and Jurisdiction to Prescribe in International Criminal Courts" (2003) 48 Villanova L. Rev. 763

KINDRED, HUGH M., & PHILLIP M. SAUNDERS, eds., *International Law: Chiefly as Interpreted and Applied in Canada*, 7th ed. (Toronto: Emond Montgomery, 2006) c. 9

---

286 Antonio Cassese, "On the Current Trends Towards Criminal Prosecution and Punishment of Breaches of International Humanitarian Law" (1998) 9 E.J.I.L. 2 at 13.

287 The Prosecutor of the International Criminal Court is empowered to conduct certain investigative activities on the territory of a state party without the state's permission; see *Rome Statute*, above note 19, arts. 57(3)(d) and 99(4).

LOWE, VAUGHAN, "Jurisdiction" in Malcolm D. Evans, ed., *International Law* (Oxford: Oxford University Press, 2003) at 329–55

MANN, F.A., "The Doctrine of Jurisdiction in International Law" (1964-I) 111 Rec. des Cours 1

————, "The Doctrine of International Jurisdiction Revisited after Twenty Years" (1984-III) 186 Rec. des Cours 9

RYNGAERT, CEDRIC, *Jurisdiction in International Law* (Oxford: Oxford University Press, 2008)

SHAW, MALCOLM N., *International Law*, 5th ed. (Cambridge: Cambridge University Press, 2003) c. 12

WILLIAMS, SHARON A., & J.-G. CASTEL, *Canadian Criminal Law: International and Transnational Aspects* (Toronto: Butterworths, 1981) cc. 1–7

CHAPTER 3

THE CORE CRIMES

A. INTRODUCTION

This chapter will deal with the four "core" crimes under international law: genocide, crimes against humanity, war crimes, and aggression. These are often labelled international crimes "in the strictest sense" (or *stricto sensu*), as there is direct individual liability under international law for each variety of conduct. The Appeals Chamber of the International Criminal Tribunal for the former Yugoslavia (ICTY) has referred to them as "Universally Condemned Offences," noting that they are "a matter of concern to the international community as a whole."[1] In terms of the analytical framework being used in this book, these are international crimes: the prohibition of each is a *jus cogens* norm under customary international law (or at least is evolving in that direction), and it is generally agreed that states may exercise criminal jurisdiction on a universal basis over each one (with the possible exception of the crime of aggression). Moreover, part of what heightens the opprobrium attached to these crimes is that they are often committed by state officials, whose control over the target populations can increase both the scale of atrocities and the potential for impunity.[2] Accordingly, since

---

1   *Nikolić* (IT-94-2-AR73), Decision on Interlocutory Appeal Concerning Legality of Arrest, 5 June 2003 at paras. 24–25.

2   Professor Schabas opines that this is one reason that the crimes are best referred to as "international" rather than "universally condemned," since other

these are crimes which offend against the interests of the international community as a whole, the statutes of those international tribunals which have had jurisdiction over them have also stripped away immunities based on official status.[3]

Despite this elevated legal status, the history of domestic prosecutions of these crimes is meagre. However, each has been within the subject matter of one or more international criminal tribunals, and the jurisprudence of those bodies (particularly the ICTY and International Criminal Tribunal for Rwanda (ICTR)) has produced the only significant development of the law on each. Accordingly, the caselaw of these tribunals is significant, not just for examining how these crimes are being prosecuted in specific situations, but for assessing the development of the crimes under customary international law,[4] and this caselaw will be given particular attention here. The crime of aggression has a more tentative status but is seeing current development, of which more will be said in Section E, below in this chapter.

B. GENOCIDE

1) History

The term "genocide" was invented by Polish lawyer Raphael Lemkin and first appeared in his study of crimes committed by the Nazis during their occupation of European states.[5] Lemkin combined the words *genos* (ancient Greek for "race" or "tribe") and *caedere* (Latin for "killing") in order to formulate a specific label for the destruction of ethnic, religious, or national groups. While these acts were already essentially prohibited under the laws of armed conflict, Lemkin argued that the international community should specifically condemn the particularly

---

common crimes such as murder and rape are also condemned under virtually every legal system in the world, yet do not have the status of the core crimes; see William Schabas, *The UN International Criminal Tribunals* (Cambridge: Cambridge University Press, 2006) at 155.

3   See, generally, Chapter 11.

4   In *Mugesera v. Canada (Minister of Immigration and Citizenship)*, [2005] 2 S.C.R. 100 [*Mugesera*], the Supreme Court of Canada made extensive reference to the caselaw of the ICTY and ICTR in interpreting the Canadian criminal law on genocide and crimes against humanity, as did the Quebec Superior Court in *R. c. Munyaneza*, 2009 QCCS 2201; see Chapter 5.

5   Raphael Lemkin, *Axis Rule in Occupied Europe: Laws of Occupation, Analysis of Government, Proposals for Redress* (Washington: Carnegie Endowment for World Peace, 1944).

horrific nature of these acts by establishing a convention that would criminalize genocide, whether in peacetime or in war.[6] The prosecutors at Nuremberg used the term to describe Nazi atrocities directed against racial and ethnic groups, and while the International Military Tribunal (IMT) did not provide for genocide as a crime *per se*, it fully described, and convicted some accused persons for, genocidal acts.[7]

Lemkin's call for a specific crime of genocide was taken up by the United Nations following the war. In 1946, General Assembly Resolution 96(I) declared genocide to be "a crime under international law, which the civilized world condemns" and directed the Economic and Social Council to draft a convention. The convention was completed two years later and was adopted unanimously on 9 December 1948.[8] The *International Convention on the Prevention and Punishment of the Crime of Genocide*[9] confirmed the will of the international community to punish genocide, whether it occurred during war or peacetime, a restriction which still operated with regard to crimes against humanity at the time. This was important and remains so, given that acts of genocide are generally committed by state officials or persons acting in concert with them.

In 1951, the International Court of Justice (ICJ) held that the substantive principles underlying the *Genocide Convention* had customary international law status and were "binding on States, even without any conventional obligation."[10] This status certainly extends to the major provisions of the *Genocide Convention* itself, though other parts of the Convention remain controversial. Moreover, the ICJ has subsequently found that the prohibition of genocide is an *erga omnes* obligation for states,[11] and that it is a *jus cogens* principle.[12] Accordingly, states must criminalize genocide within their own national legal frameworks and must act to prevent genocide taking place on their territory, and they may be called to account by other states for failing to do so. In addi-

---

6   *Ibid.* at 92.

7   See William Schabas, *Genocide in International Law: The Crime of Crimes*, 2d ed. (Cambridge: Cambridge University Press, 2009) at 43–48.

8   GA Res. 260(A)(III), 9 December 1948.

9   78 U.N.T.S. 277, Can. T.S. 1949 No. 27 [*Genocide Convention*].

10 *Reservations to the Convention on the Prevention of Genocide (Advisory Opinion)*, [1951] I.C.J. Rep. 15 at 24.

11 *Application of the Convention on the Prevention and Punishment of the Crime of Genocide (Bosnia-Herzegovina v. Yugoslavia)*, Preliminary Objections, Judgment, 11 July 1996, [1996] I.C.J. Rep. 595 at 616.

12 *Case Concerning Armed Activities on the Territory of Congo, Jurisdiction of the Court and Admissibility of the Application (Democratic Republic of Congo v. Rwanda)*, Judgment, 3 February 2006 at para. 64.

tion, in the recent *Serbian Genocide Case*,[13] the ICJ ruled that states are bound themselves not to commit genocide, "through the actions of their organs or persons or groups whose acts are attributable to them,"[14] and will incur international responsibility if they do so.[15]

For a significant period following the adoption of the Convention, however, there were only a few genocide prosecutions. Notable among these was Israel's prosecution and conviction of Adolf Eichmann for "crimes against the Jewish people" which essentially amounted to genocide in accordance with the Convention.[16] However, the crime of genocide was included within the jurisdiction of both the ICTY and ICTR, and those two bodies have produced the only significant body of jurisprudence on the subject. The ICTR Trial Chamber's 1998 decision in *Prosecutor v. Akayesu*[17] was the first international conviction for the crime of genocide, and in a decision soon after, the tribunal memorably referred to it as the "crime of crimes."[18] The *Rome Statute*[19] also contains the crime of genocide, and the state parties have adopted a set of elements, which will be discussed in Section B(7), below in this chapter. There has also been renewed interest in state prosecutions for genocide—an add-on effect of the international prosecutions.[20]

---

13 *Case Concerning the Application of the Convention on the Prevention and Punishment of the Crime of Genocide (Bosnia and Herzegovina v. Serbia and Montenegro)*, Judgment, 26 February 2007 [*Serbian Genocide Case*].

14 *Ibid.* at para. 167.

15 See, generally, *ibid.* at paras. 142–201.

16 Eichmann was prosecuted under Israel's *Nazis and Nazi Collaborators (Punishment) Law 1950*, 57 Sefer Hachukim, 9 August 1950 at 281. This statute contains an offence called "Crimes against the Jewish People" which essentially tracks the *Genocide Convention*. See Chapter 5.

17 *Akayesu* (ICTR-96-4-T), Trial Chamber Judgment, 2 September 1998.

18 *Kambanda* (ICTR-97-23-S), Judgment and Sentence, 4 September 1998 at para. 16; though the Appeals Chamber subsequently disavowed the idea of a hierarchy of international crimes: *Kayishema and Ruzindana* (ICTR-95-1-A), Appeals Chamber Judgment (Reasons), 1 June 2001 at para. 367.

19 *Rome Statute for the International Criminal Court*, UN Doc. A/CONF.183/9; Can. T.S. 2002 No. 13 [*Rome Statute*].

20 See, generally, William Schabas, "National Courts Finally Begin to Prosecute Genocide, the 'Crime of Crimes'" (2003) 1 JICJ 39. See also Holly Jones, "Mexico Appeals Court Says Ex-president Can Be Charged with Genocide," online: http://jurist.law.pitt.edu/paperchase/2006/11/mexico-appeals-court-says-ex-president.php; Jeannie Shawl, "Former Ethiopia Dictator Convicted of Genocide," online: http://jurist.law.pitt.edu/paperchase/2006_12_12_indexarch.php#116593877659782433. And see Chapter 5.

2) Definition and Jurisdiction

The *Genocide Convention* defines the crime as follows:

Article II
In the present Convention, genocide means any of the following acts committed with intent to destroy, in whole or in part, a national, ethnical, racial or religious group, as such:
a)   Killing members of the group;
b)   Causing serious bodily or mental harm to members of the group;
c)   Deliberately inflicting on the group conditions of life calculated to bring about its physical destruction in whole or in part;
d)   Imposing measures intended to prevent births within the group;
e)   Forcibly transferring children of the group to another group.

Article III
The following acts shall be punishable:
a)   Genocide;
b)   Conspiracy to commit genocide;
c)   Direct and public incitement to commit genocide;
d)   Attempt to commit genocide;
e)   Complicity in genocide.

These definitions were incorporated in mostly identical terms into the statutes of both the ICTY[21] and ICTR,[22] as well as (with some variations, discussed in Section B(7), below in this chapter) into the *Rome Statute*,[23] and are thus within the subject matter jurisdiction of each. They certainly constitute the definition of the crime under customary law.

During the first deliberations on the crime of genocide under UN auspices, it had been suggested that there should be universal jurisdiction, since the authors of such acts were most likely to have been within positions of power within the territorial state and not likely to face prosecution there. However, the drafters of the *Genocide Convention* were unable to secure agreement on this point, and thus article 5 contemplates trial only by "a competent tribunal of the State in the territory of which the act was committed, or by such international penal tribunal as may have jurisdiction . . . ." This initial reluctance has now mostly been overcome, and though the matter is not conclusively set-

---

21   *ICTY Statute*, Annexed to UN Doc. S/RES/827 (1993), art. 4.
22   *ICTR Statute*, Annexed to UN Doc. S/RES/955 (1994), art. 2.
23   Above note 19, art. 6.

tled, it is reasonable to state that, under customary international law, states *may* exercise jurisdiction over genocide on a universal basis,[24] though as yet there appears to be no customary international law obligation to do so.

While the statutes of the *ad hoc* tribunals and the International Criminal Court (ICC) provide for subject matter jurisdiction over genocide, their territorial, temporal, and personal jurisdictions are specifically limited. Accordingly, the ICTY can prosecute genocide offences only arising out of the breakup of the former Yugoslavia, and the ICTR those committed only during the events in Rwanda in 1994, either in Rwanda or by Rwandan nationals outside Rwanda.[25] The ICC can for the most part prosecute only genocide that took place after the coming into force of the *Rome Statute* on 1 July 2002, and only acts that either took place on the territory of, or were committed by a national of, a state party.[26]

3) The Mental Element of Genocide: *Dolus Specialis*

Genocide is fairly unique in that, in order to find liability, the prosecution must not only prove that the accused intended to commit a prohibited act, but that in so doing he intended to "destroy, in whole or in part, a national, ethnical, racial or religious group, as such."[27] This "aggravated criminal intention,"[28] which arises from the *chapeau* of article II of the *Genocide Convention*, is referred to as the *dolus specialis* or "special intent" requirement.[29] As Cassese notes, "[I]t logically follows that other categories of mental element are excluded: recklessness . . . and gross negligence."[30] This intention may be proven directly, for example, via an admission or confession, or it may be inferred from

---

24   Ian Brownlie, *Principles of Public International Law*, 6th ed. (Oxford: Oxford University Press, 2003) at 303–5; and Antonio Cassese, *International Criminal Law*, 2d ed. (Oxford: Oxford University Press, 2008) at 338, fn. 4 [Cassese, *ICL*].

25   The various "internationalized" tribunals have similar jurisdictional constraints; see Chapter 4.

26   Though there are exceptions, notably the possibility of Security Council referrals; see Chapter 4.

27   On the words "as such," see Schabas, *Genocide in International Law*, above note 7 at 294–306.

28   Cassese, *ICL*, above note 24 at 137.

29   The two terms are likely interchangeable; see *Stakić* (IT-97-24-T), Trial Chamber Judgment, 31 July 2003 at para. 520. See also *Serbian Genocide Case*, above note 13 at para. 187.

30   Cassese, *ICL*, above note 24 at 137. But see Schabas, *Genocide in International Law*, above note 7 at 268–70.

the factual circumstances of the case, though an ICTY Trial Chamber has stated that this must be "the only reasonable inference available on the evidence."[31]

The intent must be to "destroy" a group, and this has generally been interpreted as referring to physical and/or biological destruction.[32] Even though "cultural" genocide was rejected as a potential ground during the drafting of the *Genocide Convention*, some decisions have flirted with the idea that acts which might qualify as cultural genocide, such as forcible displacement of populations within the context of "ethnic cleansing," could be covered.[33] It does appear that facts indicating destruction of "cultural and religious property and symbols of the targeted group" can be used as evidence of genocidal intent,[34] as can acts of forcible displacement or "ethnic cleansing."[35] The existence of a plan or policy is not a necessary legal ingredient,[36] nor is long meditation,[37] nor prior intent.[38]

The offender must have intended to destroy the group "in whole or in part." While "in whole" is self-explanatory, what "in part" was intended to mean was not clear when the *Genocide Convention* was drafted, and remains uncertain to an extent. The *ad hoc* tribunals have set loose thresholds on the size or nature of the "part" in question, ruling that

---

31   *Brđanin* (IT-99-36-T), Trial Chamber Judgment, 1 September 2004 at para. 970.

32   *Krstić* (IT-98-33-A), Appeals Chamber Judgment, 19 April 2004 at para. 26. This approach was also taken in the *Report of the International Commission of Inquiry on Darfur to the Secretary-General," Pursuant to Security Council Resolution 1564 (2004) of 18 September 2004*, Annex to UN Doc. S/2005/60, 1 February 2005 [*Darfur Commission Report*].

33   *Blagojević et al.* (IT-02-60-T), Trial Chamber Judgment, 17 January 2005 at para. 666. Some domestic courts have also taken the view that the "social concept of destruction" can be included within genocidal intent; see C. Kreß, "The Crime of Genocide under International Law" (2006) 6 Int'l. Crim. L. Rev. 461 at 486.

34   *Krstić* (IT-98-33-T), Trial Chamber Judgment, 2 August 2001 at para. 580. See also *Karadžić and Mladić* (IT-95-5-R61, IT-95-18-R61), Consideration of the Indictment within the Framework of Rule 61 of the Rules of Procedure and Evidence, 11 July 1996 at para. 94.

35   *Serbian Genocide Case*, above note 13 at para. 190; *Brđanin* (IT-99-36-T), Trial Chamber Judgment, 1 September 2004 at paras. 969–91.

36   *Jelisić* (IT-95-10-A), Appeals Chamber Judgment, 5 July 2001 at para. 48; *Simba* (ICTR-01-76-A) Appeals Chamber Judgment, 27 November 2007 at para. 260. But see Section B(7), below in this chapter, regarding the *Elements of the ICC*.

37   *Krstić* (IT-98-33-T), Trial Chamber Judgment, 2 August 2001 at para. 572.

38   *Simba* (ICTR-01-76-A), Appeal Chamber Judgment, 27 November 2007 at para. 266; *Karera* (ICTR-01-74-T), Trial Chamber Judgment and Sentence, 7 December 2007 at para. 534.

it would have to be "substantial"[39] or "significant."[40] In *Krstić* the ICTY Appeals Chamber suggested that the number of persons targeted could be "the starting point, though not in all cases the ending point," noting that this numeric size should be evaluated in relation to "the overall size of the group."[41] In addition, the "targeted portion['s] prominence within the group can be a useful consideration."[42] This interpretation allowed the court to make a finding of genocide as regarded the massacre at Srebrenica, where Bosnian Muslim people were targeted but only men of military age were killed, because the destruction of this sub-group "effectively destroyed the community of Bosnian Muslims in Srebrenica as such . . . ."[43]

The requirement regarding destruction of a group "in part" as regards intent does not limit liability to situations where a substantial or significant part of a group is actually destroyed; a perpetrator can be convicted for an act of genocide against a small group of people, or perhaps even one.[44]

4) Defining the Protected Group

The "group" in question must be "a national, ethnical, racial or religious" one. In delineating the protected groups in this way, the intention of the drafters of the *Genocide Convention* appears to have been to "cover only stable groups into which human beings are born without an (easy) way out,"[45] and genocide against political groups was explicitly excluded. However, the defining of these groups has been controversial. The ICTR's decision in *Akayesu* offered useful definitions: a "national group" is "a collection of people who are perceived to share a legal bond of common citizenship, coupled with reciprocity of rights and duties"; an "ethnic group" is "a group whose members share a common language or culture"; a "racial group" is a group "based on the hereditary physical traits often identified with a geographical region, irrespective of linguistic, cultural, national or religious factors"; and a "religious

---

39 *Jelisić* (IT-95-10-T), Judgment, 10 December 1999 at para. 82; *Serbian Genocide Case*, above note 13 at para. 198.

40 *Stakić* (IT-97-24-T), Trial Chamber Judgment, 31 July 2003 at para. 525; *Krajišnik* (IT-00-39-T), Trial Chamber Judgment, 27 September 2006 at paras. 853–57.

41 *Krstić* (IT-98-33-A), Appeals Chamber Judgment, 19 April 2004 at para. 12.

42 *Ibid.*

43 *Krstić* (IT-98-33-T), Trial Chamber Judgment, 2 August 2001 at para. 597.

44 Contra on the latter point, Cassese, *ICL*, above note 24 at 146.

45 Kreß, above note 33 at 474.

group" is a group "whose members share the same religion, denomination or mode of worship."[46]

However, other parts of the Trial Chamber's decision appeared to break new ground, suggesting that the intention of the drafters of the *Genocide Convention* was "patently to ensure the protection of any stable and permanent group."[47] This was designed to deal with the fact that, within the historical and cultural circumstances of Rwanda, it was doubtful whether the Hutu and Tutsi could truly be said to be distinct on ethnic or racial grounds, and justified the court's ultimate finding that the Tutsi were an ethnic group. This approach has not been subsequently followed, and the ICTY has taken the view that the protection offered by criminalizing genocide is geared towards national minorities and the groups should be defined in that light.[48]

In terms of proving as fact the existence of the group and which category(ies) it falls under, the test appears to be a mixed objective/subjective one, though a fair amount of weight is given to the subjective view of either the victims or the perpetrators — that is, did either the victim or the perpetrator, or both, view the victim as "belonging to a group slated for destruction."[49] However, the preference appears to be to evaluate the question on the basis of both the subjective and the objective evidence in each individual case.[50] The ICJ has held that the group must be defined positively, that is, in a manner based on the characteristics of the group itself, and not negatively (e.g., "the 'non-Serb' population").[51]

5) Acts Constituting Genocide

The list of five acts which constitute genocide is an exhaustive one. In addition to proving the special intent described above, the prosecution must also prove that the act of genocide was itself intentional. Three of

---

46   *Akayesu* (ICTR-96-4-T), Judgment, 2 September 1998 at paras. 512–15.

47   *Ibid.* at para. 516.

48   *Krstić* (IT-98-33-T), Trial Chamber Judgment, 2 August 2001 at paras. 555–56.

49   *Rutaganda* (ICTR-96-3-T), Judgment and Sentence, 6 December 1999 at para. 56. See also *Semanza* (ICTR-97-20-T), Judgment and Sentence, 15 May 2003 at para. 317.

50   *Brđanin* (IT-99-36-T), Trial Chamber Judgment, 1 September 2004 at para. 684. See also on this point *Gacumbitsi* (ICTR-2001-64-A), Appeals Chamber Judgment, 7 July 2006 at paras. 39–40; *Blagojević et al.* (IT-02-60-A), Appeals Chamber Judgment, 9 May 2007 at para. 123; *Seromba* (ICTR-2001-66-I), Trial Chamber Judgment, 13 December 2006 at para. 320; and *Nahimana et al.* (*Media Case*) (ICTR-99-52-A), Appeals Chamber Judgment, 28 November 2007 at paras. 523–25 and 561.

51   *Serbian Genocide Case*, above note 13 at 196.

the acts (killing, causing serious bodily or mental harm, and forcibly transferring children) require proof that the intended result took place, while the other two require proof of intent only.[52]

a) Killing

This means intentionally causing the death of another person. There are two essential elements: the victim must be dead and this death must have been caused by an act or omission of the accused or a subordinate.[53] Only intention, and not premeditation, need be proven,[54] and it may suffice that the accused acted "in reckless disregard of human life."[55] The act or omission need only be a "substantial cause" and not the only cause of the death.[56]

b) Causing Serious Bodily or Mental Harm

Courts evaluating this act have declined to be restrictive in categorizing it and have typically referred to the variety of acts it includes, for example, acts of bodily or mental torture, inhumane or degrading treatment, rape, sexual violence, and persecution.[57] Bodily harm "seriously injures the health, causes disfigurement or causes serious injury to the external, internal organs or senses."[58] Either variety of harm need not be permanent or irremediable, but must be serious[59] and will cause "a grave and long-term disadvantage to a person's ability to lead a normal and constructive life."[60]

c) Deliberately Inflicting Conditions of Life Calculated to Destroy the Group

The indirect means of destruction contemplated under this act include subjection to subsistence diet; systematic expulsion from homes; dep-

---

52 Karim Khan & Rodney Dixon, *Archbold International Criminal Courts*, 2d ed. (London: Sweet & Maxwell, 2005), §§ 13–19.

53 *Akayesu* (ICTR-96-4-T), Trial Chamber Judgment, 2 September 1998 at para. 589.

54 *Kayishema and Ruzindana* (ICTR-95-1-A), Appeals Chamber Judgment, 1 June 2001 at para. 151.

55 *Kordić et al.* (IT-95-14/2-A), Appeals Chamber Judgment, 17 December 2004 at para. 36.

56 *Krnojelac* (IT-97-25-T), Trial Chamber Judgment, 15 March 2002 at paras. 323–24.

57 *Rutaganda* (ICTR-96-3-T), Trial Chamber Judgment, 6 December 1999 at para. 51; *Akayesu* (ICTR-96-4-T), Trial Chamber Judgment, 2 September 1998 at para. 504.

58 *Kayishema and Ruzindana* (ICTR-95-1-T), Judgment and Sentence, 21 May 1999 at para. 109.

59 *Akayesu* (ICTR-96-4-T), Trial Chamber Judgment, 2 September 1998 at para. 502.

60 *Blagojević et al.* (IT-02-60-T), Trial Chamber Judgment, 17 January 2005 at para. 645.

rival of essential medical services; circumstances that could lead to slow death, such as lack of proper housing, clothing, hygiene, and excessive work/physical exertion; and rape.[61] These acts do not have to lead immediately to the deaths of members of the group, but the accused must have been seeking destruction; mere dissolution of the group, by way of deportation, for example, is insufficient.[62]

d) Imposing Measures Intended to Prevent Births

In *Akayesu*, the Trial Chamber found that this act included "sexual mutilation, the practice of sterilization, forced birth control, separation of the sexes, and prohibition of marriages."[63] Rape which is designed to have the mother give birth to a child who "will consequently not belong to its mother's group" is also included as a prohibited measure.[64]

e) Forcibly Transferring Children

This act has not received much in the way of consideration in the caselaw. It is designed to criminalize the intentional transferral of the children of a protected group to another group, in order to accomplish the destruction of the first group. The term "forcible" has been interpreted to mean not only physical force, but also the use of threats or intimidation.[65] In conformity with the UN *Convention on the Rights of the Child*,[66] "children" in this context refers to persons under eighteen years of age, and the *International Criminal Court Elements of Crimes (ICC Elements)* take this approach.[67]

---

61   *Brđanin* (IT-99-36-T), Trial Chamber Judgment, 1 September 2004 at para. 691; *Kayishema and Ruzindana* (ICTR-95-1-T), Judgment and Sentence, 21 May 1999 at paras. 115–16; *Akayesu* ICTR-96-4-T), Trial Chamber Judgment, 2 September 1998 at paras. 503–6.

62   *Stakić* (IT-97-24-T), Trial Chamber Judgment, 31 July 2003 at para. 519. See also *Blagojević et al.* (IT-02-60-T), Trial Chamber Judgment, 17 January 2005 at paras. 641–70; *Simba* (ICTR-01-76-T), Judgment and Sentence, 13 December 2005 at paras. 412–15; *Krajišnik* (IT-00-39-T), Trial Chamber Judgment, 27 September 2006 at paras. 851–60; and *Seromba* (ICTR-2001-66-I), Trial Chamber Judgment, 13 December 2006 at paras. 315–19.

63   *Akayesu* (ICTR-96-4-T), Trial Chamber Judgment, 2 September 1998 at para. 507.

64   *Ibid.* at paras. 507–8; *Musema* (ICTR-96-13-T) Trial Chamber Judgment, 27 January 2000 at para. 158. And see cases cited in note 61.

65   *Akayesu* (ICTR-96-4-T), Trial Chamber Judgment, 2 September 1998 at para. 509.

66   1577 U.N.T.S. 3, Can. T.S. 1992 No. 3.

67   *ICC Elements of Crimes*, UN Doc. PCNICC/2000/1/Add.2 (2000), art. 6(e), Genocide by Forcibly Transferring Children.

6) Inchoate and Incomplete Offences

Article III of the *Genocide Convention* criminalizes conspiracy in, direct and public incitement of, attempt of, and complicity in genocide. These offences have all been available to the international tribunals prosecuting genocide, though some have seen more attention than others. Attempt has not been the subject of any decision by the *ad hoc* tribunals.

In *Musema*, a Trial Chamber of the ICTR reviewed the *travaux préparatoires* of the *Genocide Convention* and concluded that "conspiracy" as used in the Convention was the version of the crime under common law systems.[68] The prosecution must prove that the accused, having the special intent, entered into an agreement with one or more other persons to commit genocide, and "the mere showing of a negotiation in process will not do."[69] However, the existence of the agreement can be inferred from circumstantial evidence, including actions by individuals "acting within a unified framework" or "in an institutional capacity."[70] There is no requirement for genocide to actually have occurred, though such will be useful as evidence of the conspiracy charge. Whether individuals should be convicted for both conspiracy to commit genocide and genocide is unsettled.[71]

Direct and public incitement to commit genocide encompasses the public encouragement or provocation of others to commit genocide, whether by public speeches, written material, "or through any other means of audiovisual communication."[72] "Direct" means that the incitement must be specific and "more than mere vague or indirect suggestion,"[73] while whether the incitement was "public" will be evaluated on the basis of where it took place and whether assistance was selective or limited.[74] There is no requirement that genocide actually have occurred as a result of the incitement,[75] but it must be proven that the accused had the special intent.

---

68 *Musema* (ICTR-96-13-T), Trial Chamber Judgment, 27 January 2000 at paras. 184–98.

69 *Kajelijeli* (ICTR-98-44A-T), Judgment and Sentence, 1 December 2003 at para. 787.

70 *Media Case* (ICTR-99-52-T), Judgment and Sentence, 3 December 2003 at para. 1048.

71 Contra, *Musema* (ICTR-96-13-T), Trial Chamber Judgment, 27 January 2000 at para. 198; Pro, *Niyitegeka* (ICTR-96-14-T), Judgment and Sentence, 16 May 2003 at para. 427.

72 *Akayesu* (ICTR-96-4-T), Trial Chamber Judgment, 2 September 1998 at para. 559.

73 *Ibid.* at para. 557.

74 *Ibid.* at para. 556.

75 *Media Case* (ICTR-99-52-T), Judgment and Sentence, 3 December 2003 at para. 1029. Indeed, as Schabas points out, since genocide actually took place in Rwan-

Complicity in genocide covers various means of participation in the criminal act, other than as the principal perpetrator. After some initial uncertainty stemming from the inclusion of both "complicity" and "aiding and abetting" in the statutes of the *ad hoc* tribunals, it is reasonably settled that the former encompasses the latter.[76] However, complicity covers other kinds of behaviour, such as procuring means to commit genocide and instigation.[77] Genocide must have been committed in order to secure a conviction for complicity,[78] and while special intent must normally be proven, the accused can be convicted for aiding and abetting if she simply knew of the genocidal intent of those committing the acts of genocide.[79]

7) Genocide in the *Rome Statute*

The inclusion of the crime of genocide in the *Rome Statute*[80] was practically a foregone conclusion, though there was an effort among some of the drafters to broaden the conventional definition to include other groups (social, political, etc.), which ultimately was rejected.[81] Article 6 of the *Rome Statute* repeats article II of the *Genocide Convention*. Article III is not expressly included, but liability for incitement, attempt, and complicity are all provided for in article 25(3). However, there is no provision for conspiracy for any of the crimes within the jurisdiction of the *Rome Statute*, and this certainly represents a gap between the customary international law on the crime of genocide and the *Rome Statute*.

---

da, the ICTR has often confused "the inchoate form of incitement with incitement as complicity" (Schabas, *The UN International Criminal Tribunals*, above note 2 at 182).

76   *Krstić* (IT-98-33-A), Appeals Chamber Judgment, 19 April 2004 at para. 139; *Ntakirutimana et al.* (ICTR-96-10-A and ICTR-96-17-A), Appeals Chamber Judgment, 13 December 2004 at paras. 371 and 500. See also *Media Case* (ICTR-99-52-A), Appeals Chamber Judgment, 28 November 2007 at paras. 894–901 and 906–12; *Blagojević et al.* (IT-02-60-T), Trial Chamber Judgment, 17 January 2005 at paras. 679 and 776–82; *Krajišnik* (IT-00-39-T), Trial Chamber Judgment, 27 September 2006 at paras. 864–66.

77   *Archbold*, above note 52 at §§ 13–40.

78   *Blagojević et al.* (IT-02-60-T), Trial Chamber Judgment, 17 January 2005 at para. 638.

79   *Ntakirutimana et al.* (ICTR-96-10-A, ICTR-96-17-A), Appeals Chamber Judgment, 13 December 2004 at paras. 371–500; *Semanza* (ICTR-97-20-A), Appeals Chamber Judgment, 20 May 2005 at para. 316.

80   Above note 19.

81   Mahnoush Arsanjani, "The *Rome Statute for an International Criminal Court*" (1999) 93 A.J.I.L. 22 at 30.

The *ICC Elements* has a somewhat detailed regime which generally reflects the enormous contribution of the *ad hoc* tribunals to the customary international law of genocide. There are some variations and attempts at progressive development, however, most notably the requirement that for each of the prohibited acts, it must have taken place "in the context of a manifest pattern of similar conduct directed against that group or was conduct that could itself effect such destruction." This sets a higher standard than the tribunal jurisprudence, which as noted above, did not require a plan or policy to be in place.[82]

C. CRIMES AGAINST HUMANITY

1) History

The notion of criminal acts so grave and barbaric as to offend the "principles of humanity" is one of some antiquity, and has certainly underpinned the historical development of both the notion of war crimes and the development of international humanitarian law generally.[83] The first modern use of the notion of "crimes against humanity" is generally attributed to a 1915 communication by the three Allied Powers, condemning Turkey's massacre of its ethnic Armenian population.[84] However, individual responsibility for these acts was first established in the *Charter of the IMT*,[85] which directed the tribunal to try persons for

> Crimes against humanity: namely, murder, extermination, enslavement, deportation, and other inhumane acts committed against any civilian population, before or during the war, or persecutions on political, racial or religious grounds, in execution of or in connection with any crime within the jurisdiction of the Tribunal, whether or not in violation of the domestic law of the country where perpetrated.[86]

Read in its historical context, the wording of the crime in the *Charter* discloses solving one international legal problem, finessing another,

---

82   See, generally, Valerie Oosterveld, "The Elements of Genocide" in Roy S. Lee, ed., *The International Criminal Court: Elements of Crime and Rules of Procedure and Evidence* (Ardsley, NY: Transnational, 2001).

83   For a survey, see M. Cherif Bassiouni, "Crimes against Humanity" in M. Cherif Bassiouni, ed., *International Criminal Law*, 3d ed., vol. I (Leiden: Martinus Nijhoff, 2008) 437 at 440–53.

84   *Papers Relating to the Foreign Relations of the United States, 1915, Supplement* (Washington: US Gov't Printing Office, 1928) at 981.

85   82 U.N.T.S. 279.

86   *Ibid.*, art. 6.

and creating a third. The desire to formulate the crime came from the recognition that, while the international law of armed conflict as it existed at the time criminalized offences against civilians in occupied territories, it did not cover offences by governments against their own populations. This was the gap into which many of the Nazi atrocities during the war would have fallen, and which was filled by applying the offence to "any civilian population."

Solving this substantive problem created a further hurdle, as it was strenuously argued at the time (and continues to be to this day) that in criminalizing crimes against humanity, the *Charter* created a new crime, and thus trying offenders in 1945 for acts committed beginning in 1939 offended the principle of *nullem crimen sine lege* in that it was retroactive. The case for this proposition is strong.[87] Various justifications have been proposed, none of which is completely convincing as a matter of strict legal interpretation, but which respond to the intuitive notion that, in the case of the Nazi depredations, the principle of legality should be interpreted in as broad as possible a manner, any necessary formalism giving way to what is almost a natural law view that some acts offend a higher normative order. Professor Cassese aptly describes the view of the *nullem crimen* principle as it existed in 1945 as "a moral maxim designed to yield to superior exigencies whenever it would have been contrary to justice not to hold persons accountable for appalling atrocities."[88] This slight and justifiable finessing has generally won the day,[89] and crimes against humanity are firmly established as a core crime under international law.

The problem created by the *IMT Charter* formulation stemmed from the Allied concern that if the provision was worded too broadly, it might apply to their own activities both on their territories and in their colonies. Accordingly, jurisdiction over crimes against humanity was linked to acts that were related to either of the other two crimes in the *Charter*, that is, war crimes or crimes against peace.[90] The problem was that this excluded liability for offences committed against civilians (or other victims, for that matter) during peacetime, and this require-

---

87   Though it is not absolute, as other courts have accepted the proposition that crimes against humanity existed before 1945 based on the Versailles and Sevres treaties; see the decision of the Australian High Court in *Polyukhovich v. Commonwealth of Australia* (1991), 101 A.L.R. 545, reprinted at (1991), 91 I.L.R. 1.

88   Cassese, *ICL*, above note 24 at 106.

89   In the *Finta* case, [1994] 1 S.C.R. 701, the Supreme Court of Canada accepted a similar argument as it had been put forth by Professor Hans Kelsen; see Chapter 5.

90   Egon Schwelb, "Crimes against Humanity" (1946) 23 Brit. Y.B. Int'l L. 178.

ment for a nexus with armed conflict met a hostile reception almost immediately after the Nuremberg trials were concluded. The most egregious crime against humanity, genocide, was formulated so as to apply whether in war or peacetime,[91] and a number of international instruments abandoned the nexus requirement, including *Control Council Law No. 10*[92] and the 1968 *Convention on the Non-Applicability of Statutory Limitations to War Crimes and Crimes Against Humanity*,[93] as well as the legislation of states. The final strokes were delivered by the ICTY, which has dealt with the fact that the nexus requirement was in its own statute by describing the limitation as "obsolescent"[94] and "purely jurisdictional."[95] The *ICTR Statute*[96] did not contain this limitation, and the *Rome Statute* provisions on crimes against humanity apply whether in war or peacetime.

Crimes against humanity are thus established in both customary international law and as crimes before international tribunals, though the law is in a constant state of evolution. It is this crime, however, which is perhaps most emblematic of the shift from the state-centred paradigm which afforded certain protections to individuals during armed conflicts, to a broader notion of international law as being dedicated to protecting the fundamental human rights of individuals.

2) Definition and Jurisdiction

The Darfur Commission Report described crimes against humanity as "particularly odious offences constituting a serious attack on human dignity or a grave humiliation or degradation of one or more human beings (for instance, murder, extermination, enslavement, deportation or

---

91   William Schabas, *An Introduction to the International Criminal Court*, 3d ed. (Cambridge: Cambridge University Press, 2007) at 99–100.

92   *Punishment of Persons Guilty of War Crimes, Crimes against Peace and against Humanity*, 20 December 1945, 3 Official Gazette Control Council for Germany 50-55 (1946), art. 11(1)(c).

93   GA Res. 2391, UN GAOR, 23d Sess., Supp. No. 18 at 40, UN Doc. A/7218 (1968).

94   *Tadić* (IT-94-1-AR72), Decision on the Defence Motion for Interlocutory Appeal on Jurisdiction, 2 October 1995 at para. 140.

95   *Kunarac et al.* (IT-96-23 and IT-96-23/1-A), Appeals Chamber Judgment, 12 June 2002 at para. 83. The court ruled that the requirement in art. 5 of the *ICTY Statute* that the crime against humanity have been committed "in armed conflict, whether international or internal in character" simply meant that there had to have been an armed conflict ongoing at the time, and the accused's act had to have some geographic and temporal link with that conflict—not a significant hurdle for any of the cases before the ICTY.

96   UN Doc. S/RES/955 (1994), 33 I.L.M. 1598, 1600 (1994).

forcible transfer of population, torture, rape and other forms of sexual violence, persecution, enforced disappearance of persons)."[97] The manner in which crimes against humanity are legally defined continues to oscillate between formulations in domestic criminal laws, the statutes of international criminal tribunals, and customary international law—each of which symbiotically informs the others.

Even the relatively common core of the definition is not as solid as that of the crime of genocide. This is shown by the statutes of the various tribunals having jurisdiction over these crimes, which generally fully adopt the *Genocide Convention* definition of that crime but contain significant variations regarding crimes against humanity. The general trend has been to expand the range of acts covered. The ICTY and ICTR statutes[98] expanded on the *IMT Charter* version of the crime by including rape and imprisonment, while the *Rome Statute* added other "gendered" crimes and the crimes of apartheid and enforced disappearance,[99] and the state parties also adopted a full set of elements for the crimes. As another example, article 5 of the *ICTY Statute* required that the crimes be "directed against any civilian population," while the article 3 of the *ICTR Statute* reads "and as part of a widespread or systematic attack against any civilian population," and moreover, that the attack was "on national, political, ethnic, racial or religious grounds." The *Rome Statute* drafters were able to reach agreement on including the former phrase from the *ICTR Statute*, but the latter "discriminatory intent" requirement was not adopted into article 7.[100]

As with genocide, it is mostly uncontroversial that states may exercise jurisdiction over crimes against humanity on a universal basis, but are not required to do so under customary international law. Similarly, the territorial, temporal, and personal jurisdictions of the *ad hoc* tribunals, the ICC, and the special courts are all limited in accordance with the founding statutes of each.[101]

---

97 *Darfur Commission Report*, above note 32 at para. 178.

98 Arts. 5 and 3, respectively.

99 Above note 19, art. 7. The *Statute of the Special Court for Sierra Leone*, Annexed to UN Doc. S/RES/1315 (2000), contains similar sexual crime provisions.

100 Except insofar as the crime against humanity of persecution requires discriminatory intent; see Section C(5)(h), below in this chapter. As a result of these inconsistencies, the status of any "discriminatory intent" requirement for crimes against humanity under customary international law is uncertain; see Schabas, *The UN International Criminal Tribunals*, above note 2 at 196–98.

101 See Section B(2), above in this chapter.

3) Contextual Elements

a) Civilian Population

The phrase "civilian population" has been interpreted liberally, and reference has been made to the definition of "civilian" in article 50 of *First Protocol to the Geneva Conventions (AP I)*[102] in construing it. The focus is on whether the attack is primarily directed against some portion of a collective, and the requirement "excludes single or isolated acts."[103] The attack need not be targeting the entire population of a state, entity, or territory, but the target population must be "predominantly civilian in nature," although not exclusively so.[104] The population can include military personnel and still be considered "civilian," though the presence of a significant portion of military personnel could cause this status to be lost, depending on the circumstances.[105] Military personnel and members of resistance movements who are wounded or otherwise *hors de combat* or who have laid down arms are considered civilians.[106]

In determining whether the civilian population is the primary target of the attack, the ICTY Appeals Chamber has held that the court should consider

> the means and method used in the course of the attack, the status of the victims, their number, the discriminatory nature of the attack, the nature of the crimes committed in its course, the resistance to the assailants at the time and the extent to which the attacking force may be said to have complied or attempted to comply with the precautionary requirements of the laws of war.[107]

---

102 *Protocol Additional to the Geneva Conventions of 12 August 1949, and relating to the Protection of Victims of International Armed Conflicts (Protocol I)*, 8 June 1977 [AP I].

103 *Bagilishema* (ICTR-95-1A-T), Trial Chamber Judgment, 7 June 2001 at para. 80.

104 *Kordić et al.* (IT-95-14/2-T), Trial Chamber Judgment, 26 February 2001 at para. 180.

105 *Blaškić* (IT-95-14-A), Appeals Chamber Judgment, 29 July 2004 at para. 115.

106 *Akayesu*, (ICTR-96-4-T), Judgment, 2 September 1998 at para. 582; *Naletilić et al.* (IT-98-34-T), Trial Chamber Judgment, 31 March 2003 at para. 235. Though there has of late been some contention on this point: see *Blaškić* (IT-95-14-A), Appeals Chamber Judgment, 29 July 2004; *Kordić et al.* (IT-95-14/2-A), Appeals Chamber Judgment, 17 December 2004 at paras. 95–97; *Martić* (IT-95-11-T), Trial Chamber Judgment, 12 June 2007 at paras. 50–56; *Mrkšić et al.* (IT-95-13/1), Trial Chamber Judgment, 27 September 2007 at paras. 448–64; and *Milosević* (IT-98-29/1), Trial Chamber Judgment, 12 December 2007 at paras. 921–24. See also *AFRC* (SCSL-04-16-T), Trial Chamber Judgment, 20 June 2007 at paras. 216–19; and *CDF* (SCSL-04-14-T), Trial Chamber Judgment, 2 August 2007 at paras. 114–19.

107 *Kunarac et al.* (IT-96-23 and IT-96-23/1-A), Appeals Chamber Judgment, 12 June 2002 at paras. 90–91.

b) Widespread or Systematic Attack

To constitute a crime against humanity, the prohibited act[108] must either be or occur as part of a widespread or systematic attack. The requirement of "attack" is not confined to an armed conflict and under customary international law need not occur as part of one; it is, rather, a course of conduct generally involving violence and mistreatment of civilians.[109] In some cases, such as the crime against humanity of apartheid, it need not involve active violence at all. There must be a nexus between the acts of the accused and the attack,[110] but the accused's acts need not themselves be widespread or systematic,[111] and even a single act connected to the attack may be a crime against humanity. The accused need not be a state official,[112] though this will often be the case.

The "widespread or systematic" requirement certainly exists under customary international law, and the ICTY in fact read this requirement into its own statute.[113] "Widespread" indicates that the attack(s) must have been serious in nature, large scale, and directed against a multiplicity of victims.[114] "Systematic" requires that the attacks have been organized, non-accidental, and following a regular pattern.[115] The

---

108   See Section C(5), below in this chapter.

109   *Akayesu* (ICTR-96-4-T), Trial Chamber Judgment, 2 September 1998 at para. 581; *Naletilić et al.* (IT-98-34-T), Judgment, 31 March 2003 at para. 233.

110   *Akayesu, ibid.* at para. 579; *Tadić* (IT-94-1-A), Appeals Chamber Judgment, 15 July 1999 at para. 251; *Naletilić et al.* (IT-98-34-T), Trial Chamber Judgment, 31 March 2003 at para. 234.

111   *Kordić et al.* (IT-95-14/2-A), Appeals Chamber Judgment, 17 December 2004 at para. 94; *Kunarac et al.* (IT-96-23-T and IT-96-23/1-T), Trial Chamber Judgment, 22 February 2001 at para. 431.

112   *Kayishema and Ruzindana* (ICTR-95-1-T), Trial Chamber Judgment, 21 May 1999 at paras.125–26; *Kupreškić et al.* (IT-95-16-T), Trial Chamber Judgment, 14 January 2000 at para.555; *Blaškić* (IT-95-14-T), Trial Chamber Judgment, 3 March 2000 at para. 205; *Kordić et al.* (IT-95-14/2-T), Trial Chamber Judgment, 26 February 2001 at para. 18; and *Kunarac et al.* (IT-96-23/IT-96-23/1-A), Appeals Chamber Judgment, 12 June 2002 at paras. 83 and 86.

113   *Blaškić* (IT-95-14-A), Appeals Chamber Judgment, 29 July 2004 at para. 98.

114   *Akayesu* (ICTR-96-4-T), Trial Chamber Judgment, 2 September 1998 at para. 580; *Kordić et al.* (IT-95-14/2-A), Appeals Chamber Judgment, 17 December 2004 at para. 94.

115   *Naletilić et al.* (IT-98-34-T), Trial Chamber Judgment, 31 March 2003 at para. 236; *Blaškić* (IT-95-14-A), Appeals Chamber Judgment, 29 July 2004 at para. 98. See also *Kordić et al.* (IT-95-14/2-A), Appeals Chamber Judgment, 17 December 2004 at para. 94; *Semanza* (ICTR-97-20-A), Appeals Chamber Judgment, 20 May 2005 at para. 269; *Seromba* (ICTR-2001-66), Trial Chamber Judgment, 13 December 2006 at paras. 353–60; *Martić* (IT-95-11-T), Trial Chamber Judgment, 12 June 2007 at paras. 50–56; *Milošević* (IT-98-29/1-T), Trial Chamber Judgment, 12 December 2007 at paras. 925–28; for crimes against humanity committed by

courts will also take into account evidence of the use of significant public and private resources; the involvement of high-level state or military personnel; and any plan, policy, or ideology that underlies the attack.[116] It is controversial whether a finding of a plan or policy element on the part of a state or organization is required, or whether such is simply compelling evidence of the widespread or systematic nature of the attack. The *ad hoc* tribunals have generally declined to impose it as having been a requirement at the time of the commission of the crimes within their respective jurisdictions,[117] though as will be seen in Section D(6), below in this chapter, the *Rome Statute* did incorporate it and it has been suggested that customary international law does require it.[118]

4) Mental Element

Not unlike genocide, crimes against humanity have an added mental element; that is, the prosecution must prove both the intent to commit the underlying prohibited act and some further knowledge on the part of the accused related to the circumstances of the attack.[119] If this added mental element cannot be proven, the accused may still be prosecuted for the underlying prohibited act(s), though being common crimes, these are not within the jurisdiction of the international tribunals and would have to be prosecuted under a domestic system.

To be convicted, the accused must have known about the widespread or systematic attack, and that his acts "are part thereof," or are

---

non-state actors on a small scale and the concept of population, see *Limaj et al.* (IT-03-66-T), Trial Chamber Judgment, 30 November 2005 at paras. 180–228; see also *AFRC* (SCSL-04-16-T), Trial Chamber Judgment, 20 June 2007 at para. 215; and *CDF* (SCSL-04-14-T), Trial Chamber Judgment, 2 August 2007 at para. 112, as well as *Lubanga* (ICC-01/04-01/06), Decision on the Confirmation of Charges in the Lubanga Case, 29 January 2007 at para. 320; and *Katanga* (ICC-01/04-01/07-55), Decision on the Evidence and Information provided by the Prosecution for the Issuance of a Warrant of Arrest for Germain Katanga, 5 November 2007 at paras. 32–33.

116 *Kunarac et al.* (IT-96-23 and IT-96-23/1-A), Appeals Chamber Judgment, 12 June 2002 at paras. 95–98.

117 *Blaškić* (IT-95-14-A), Appeals Chamber Judgment, 29 July 2004 at paras. 99–102 and 117–20. In *Mugesera*, above note 4, the Supreme Court of Canada made a similar finding; see Chapter 5.

118 M. Cherif Bassiouni, *Crimes against Humanity in International Criminal Law*, 2d rev. ed. (Dordrecht: Kluwer Law, 1999) at 243–81.

119 As will be seen, the crime against humanity of persecution has as an additional requirement: proof of discriminatory intent; see Section C(5)(h), below in this chapter.

related to the attack.[120] He does not have to know all of the detail of the attack, or be identified with the attack or support it,[121] or have knowledge about any plan or policy underpinning the attack—it is sufficient that he took the chance that his actions would implement the attack.[122] Personal motive is irrelevant.[123] The accused's knowledge need not be proven directly, but can be inferred from the circumstances of the case, including the relevant political and historical background as well as the role of the accused in any organization carrying out the attacks and how well the attacks were known generally.[124]

5) Prohibited Acts

a) Murder

It has generally been held that "murder" means the same as "killing" in the crime of genocide, that is, intentionally causing the death of another person. The *ad hoc* tribunals had wavered at one point on whether an element of premeditation is required, based mostly on the use of the French term *assassinat* in the French language version of their statutes, though the position against that interpretation has been described as "settled" by one ICTY Trial Chamber.[125]

---

120 *Kunarac et al.* (IT-96-23 and IT-96-23/1-A), Appeals Chamber Judgment, 12 June 2002 at paras. 102 and 410; *Tadić* (IT-94-1-A), Appeals Chamber Judgment, 15 July 1999 at para. 271.

121 *Blaškić* (IT-95-14-T), Trial Chamber Judgment, 3 March 2000 at para. 257.

122 *Kunarac et al.* (IT-96-23 and IT-96-23/1-A), Appeals Chamber Judgment, 12 June 2002 at para. 104; *Blaškić* (IT-95-14-T), Trial Chamber Judgment, 3 March 2000 at para. 257. See also *Krnojelac* (IT-97-25-T), Trial Chamber Judgment, 15 March 2002 at para. 59; *Simić* (IT-95-9-T), Trial Chamber Judgment, 17 October 2003 at para. 46; *Stakić* (IT-97-24-T), Trial Chamber Judgment, 31 July 2003 at para. 616; *Vasiljević* (IT-98-32-T), Trial Chamber Judgment, 29 November 2002 at para. 37; *Blaškić* (IT-95-14-A), Appeals Chamber Judgment, 29 July 2004 at para. 126; *Limaj et al.* (IT-03-66-T), Trial Chamber Judgment, 30 November, 2005 at para. 190. For a discussion of the various types of *mens rea* in international criminal law, see *Lubanga* (ICC-01/04-01/06), Decision on the Confirmation of Charges in the Lubanga Case, 29 January 2007 at paras. 349–60.

123 *Tadić* (IT-94-1-A), Appeals Chamber Judgment, 15 July 1999 at para. 255.

124 *Blaškić* (IT-95-14-T), Trial Chamber Judgment, 3 March 2000 at paras. 258–59.

125 *Kordić et al.* (IT-95-14/2-T), Trial Chamber Judgment, 26 February 2001 at paras. 235–36. This has been confirmed by numerous cases since, e.g., *Kordić et al.* (IT-95-14/2-A) Appeals Chamber Judgment, 26 January 2005; *Kvočka et al.* (IT-98-30/1-A), Appeals Chamber Judgment, 28 February 2005; and *Galić* (IT-98-29-A), Appeals Chamber Judgment, 30 November 2006.

b) Extermination

Extermination is essentially the same crime against humanity as murder, except that to make out extermination, the killing must have been directed against a population or "on a mass scale,"[126] and expressly includes "the [subjection] to conditions of life calculated to bring about the destruction of a numerically significant part of the population."[127] It is quite similar to genocide, except that it does not require any specific discriminatory intent, but simply the targeting of a particular population.

c) Enslavement

Outside the scope of crimes against humanity, slavery is a crime under customary international law and has the status of a *jus cogens* prohibition.[128] In the only major decision on slavery as a crime against humanity, the ICTY Appeals Chamber took an expansive view of what acts could constitute slavery; these were not only limited to the traditional concept of "chattel slavery" (i.e., the outright exercise of ownership over a person), but included the exercise of any powers "attaching to the right of ownership, [where] there is some destruction of the juridical personality" of the victim.[129] The court referred to some indicia of enslavement, including "control of someone's movement, control of physical environment, psychological control, measures taken to prevent or deter escape, force, threat of force or coercion, duration, assertion of exclusivity, subjection to cruel treatment or abuse, control of sexuality and forced labour."[130] The *Rome Statute* uses trafficking in women and children as an example,[131] while the *ICC Elements* refers to "purchasing, selling, lending or bartering . . . or by imposing . . . a similar deprivation of liberty."[132]

---

126 *Ntakirutimana et al.* (ICTR-96-10-A and ICTR-96-17-A), Appeals Chamber Judgment, 13 December 2004 at para. 542.

127 *Krstić* (IT-98-33-T), Trial Chamber Judgment, 2 August 2001 at para. 503. See also *Bagilishema* (ICTR-95-1A-T), Trial Chamber Judgment, 7 June 2001; *Brđanin* (IT-99-36-A), Appeals Chamber Judgment, 3 April 2007; *AFRC* (SCSL-04-16-T), Trial Chamber Judgment, 20 June 2007; and *CDF* (SCSL-04-14-T), Trial Chamber Judgment, 2 August 2007.

128 See Chapter 6.

129 *Kunarac et al.* (IT-96-23 and IT-96-23/1-A), Appeals Chamber Judgment, 12 June 2002 at para. 117.

130 *Ibid.* at para. 119. Confirmed by *Krnojelac* (IT-97-25-T), Trial Chamber Judgment, 15 March 2002; *Simić* (IT-95-9-T), Judgment, 17 October 2003; *Galić* (IT-98-29-T), Trial Chamber Judgment, 5 December 2003; *AFRC* (SCSL-04-16-T), Trial Chamber Judgment, 20 June 2007; and *CDF* (SCSL-04-14-T), Trial Chamber Judgment, 2 August 2007.

131 Above note 19, art. 7(2)(c).

132 Above note 67, Crime against Humanity of Sexual Slavery, art. 7(1)(g)-2.

d) Deportation

This crime amounts to "involuntary and unlawful evacuation of individuals from the territory in which they reside."[133] A distinction is usually made between "deportation," which refers to movement of people beyond the borders of one state into another, and "forcible transfer" or "forcible displacement," which would take place within a state. However, either is sufficient to constitute a crime against humanity,[134] and the *Rome Statute* simply refers to displacement of individuals from a place in which they lawfully are present.[135]

e) Imprisonment

The crime against humanity of imprisonment refers to "arbitrary imprisonment, that is to say, the deprivation of liberty of the individual without due process of law."[136] Imprisonment of civilians will be justified in some situations of armed conflict, in accordance with *Geneva Convention IV*.[137]

f) Torture

Like slavery, torture is a crime under international law even outside the scope of crimes against humanity.[138] In defining torture as a crime against humanity, the international caselaw has drawn upon the definitions of torture in the various international instruments on the subject, in particular the *United Nations Convention against Torture (CAT)*.[139] It has been defined as "the [intentional] infliction, by act or omission, of severe pain or suffering, whether physical or mental . . . aim[ed] at obtaining information or a confession, or at punishing, intimidating or coercing the victim or a third person, or at discriminating, on any ground, against the victim or a third person."[140] As can be seen from

---

133 *Krstić* (IT-98-33-T), Trial Chamber Judgment, 2 August 2001 at para. 521.

134 *Krnojelac* (IT-97-25-A), Appeals Chamber Judgment, 17 September 2003 at paras. 222–23. See also *Stakić* (IT-97-24-A), Appeals Chamber Judgment, 22 March 2006; *Simić* (IT-95-9-A), Appeals Chamber Judgment, 28 November 2006.

135 Above note 19, art. 7(2)(d).

136 *Kordić et al.* (IT-95-14/2-A), Appeals Chamber Judgment, 17 December 2004 at para. 116. See also *Simić* (IT-95-9-A), Judgment, 28 November 2006; *Krajišnik* (IT-00-39-T), Trial Chamber Judgment, 27 September 2006; *Martić* (IT-95-11-T), Trial Chamber Judgment, 12 June 2007.

137 *Convention (IV) relative to the Protection of Civilian Persons in Time of War*, Geneva, 12 August 1949 [*GC IV*].

138 See Chapter 6.

139 Can. T.S. 1987 No. 36.

140 *Kunarac et al.* (IT-96-23 & IT-96-23/1-A), Appeals Chamber Judgment, 12 June 2002 at paras. 146–48, confirming trial judgment.

this definition, torture must be aimed at some prohibited purpose, and thus a random, purely sadistic, or gratuitous act of violence would not suffice—though the prohibited purpose need not be the only or dominant purpose.[141] While the *CAT* imposes a condition that torture can be inflicted only by a public official or someone acting in an official capacity, the ICTY has stated that customary international law does not require this limitation for the crime of torture.[142] Rape and other sexual violence can constitute torture, given the level of physical and/or psychological harm done to the victim.[143]

g) Rape

The ICTY Appeals Chamber has endorsed the following definition of rape:

> the sexual penetration, however slight: (a) of the vagina or anus of the victim by the penis of the perpetrator or any other object used by the perpetrator; or (b) of the mouth of the victim by the penis of the perpetrator; (c) by coercion or force or threat of force against the victim or a third person.[144]

This definition also appears in the *ICC Elements*, which describes all of these acts generally as "invasion" of the victim's body, a term specifically intended to be gender neutral. The ICTY Appeals Chamber has also noted that threat or use of force may be evidence of lack of consent, but is not a required element *per se*; the focus is properly on whether the act took place in coercive circumstances.[145]

The *Rome Statute* contains a more expansive list of acts of sexual violence that constitute crimes against humanity in addition to rape: sexual slavery; enforced prostitution; forced pregnancy; enforced sterilization; and "any other form of sexual violence of comparable

---

141 *Kvočka et al.* (IT-98-30/1-T), Trial Chamber Judgment, 2 November 2001 at para. 153.

142 *Kunarac et al.* (IT-96-23 & IT-96-23/1-A), Appeals Chamber Judgment, 12 June 2002 at para. 148. See also *Kvočka et al.* (IT-98-30/1-A), Appeals Chamber Judgment, 28 February 2005; *Brđanin* (IT-99-36-A), Appeals Chamber Judgment, 3 April 2007; *Martić* (IT-95-11-T), Trial Chamber Judgment, 12 June 2007.

143 *Kunarac et al.* (IT-96-23 & IT-96-23/1-A), Appeals Chamber Judgment, 12 June 2002 at paras. 149–51.

144 *Kunarac et al.*, *ibid.* at para. 128; *Kvočka et al.* (IT-98-30/1-A), Appeals Chamber Judgment, 28 February 2005 at para. 395.

145 *Kunarac et al.*, *ibid.* at paras. 127–32. In *Kunarac et al.*, the Appeals Chamber was attempting to reconcile the caselaw of the ICTR (which took a "mechanical" approach to the issue) with that of prior ICTY decisions (which relied on a consent-based approach). The definition in the *Rome Statute* does the same.

gravity."[146] The *ICC Elements* provides explanations of each, and similar crimes appear in the statutes of the Special Court for Sierra Leone, the United Nations Transitional Administration in East Timor (UNTAET) Serious Crimes Panels, and the Iraqi High Tribunal.

h) Persecution

The crime against humanity of persecution originated in the *International Military Tribunal (IMT) Charter*, but has taken on great significance in the jurisprudence of the *ad hoc* tribunals, particularly the ICTY, which has made substantial use of this offence to prosecute acts of "ethnic cleansing." An effective definition was rendered by an ICTY Trial Chamber: "the gross or blatant denial, on discriminatory grounds, of a fundamental right, laid down in international customary or treaty law, reaching the same level of gravity as the other acts prohibited in article 5 [of the *ICTY Statute*]."[147]

Persecution is similar to genocide in that it has an added intent or motive requirement: that the accused intended to discriminate against the victim(s) on political, racial, or religious grounds. The *Rome Statute* expands these grounds to include national, ethnic, cultural, religious, and gender. It must be proven that the accused intended to discriminate in his act or omission,[148] and while there is no requirement that a plan or policy of discrimination be in place,[149] if it is intended to show that such a plan underpinned the discrimination, then the accused must be proven to have known about it and shared its aims.[150] Proving intent is not sufficient by itself, however, and the prosecution must show that discriminatory consequences actually occurred.[151]

The range of denials of fundamental rights that can constitute acts of persecution is quite broad, and all that is required is that "the common element of discrimination in regard to the enjoyment of a basic or fundamental right is present, and persecution does not necessarily require a physical element."[152] The crime was initially targeted at acts of the Nazi regime towards the Jewish population of Germany that effect-

---

146 Above note 19, art. 7(1)(g). Regarding the crimes of sexual slavery and forced marriage, see *AFRC* (SCSL-04-16-T), Trial Chamber Judgment, 20 June 2007.

147 *Kupreškić et al.* (IT-95-16-T), Trial Chamber Judgment, 14 January 2000 at para. 621.

148 *Vasiljević* (IT-98-32-T), Trial Chamber Judgment, 29 November 2002 at para. 248.

149 *Ibid.*

150 *Kordić et al.* (IT-95-14/2-A), Appeals Chamber Judgment, 17 December 2004 at paras. 110–12.

151 *Vasiljević* (IT-98-32-T), Trial Chamber Judgment, 29 November 2002 at para. 245.

152 *Tadić* (IT-94-1-T), Trial Chamber Opinion and Judgment, 7 May 1997 at para. 707.

ively removed Jews from the protection of the law and institutionalized anti-Semitic policy at various levels of government. The jurisprudence of the ICTY has suggested a wide variety of other acts, including harm (both physical and mental), forcible transfer of civilians to camps, economic deprivation, restrictions on family life or access to professions, taking of property, harassment, humiliation, and similar abuse.[153] In a very progressive judgment that drew on international human rights law, the ICTR in *Nahimana* decided that hate speech which incited or directed violence against an ethnic or racial group could constitute persecution, as it was equal in gravity to other crimes against humanity.[154]

i)   Other Inhumane Acts

This is something of a catch-all or residual category of crimes against humanity, which was intended to cover acts that could not be exhaustively enumerated, but which contain a sufficient degree of cruelty to be equal in gravity to the enumerated acts. It appears to cover various kinds of serious physical or mental harm, degrading acts and treatment, forced prostitution and forced disappearance.[155]

6) Crimes Against Humanity in the *Rome Statute*

The drafting of the *Rome Statute* was characterized by a collision between states which had progressive and expansionary views on how the ICC could advance international criminal law norms, and states which took a more cautious approach and in some cases clearly wished to introduce more restrictive elements into the treaty. The very detailed provisions on crimes against humanity in article 7 of the *Rome Statute*, which have been referred to throughout this section, bear the hallmarks

---

153 *Ibid.* at paras. 704–10; *Kvočka et al.* (IT-98-30/1-A), Appeals Chamber Judgment, 28 February 2005 at paras. 324–25. See also *Stakić* (IT-97-24-A), Appeals Chamber Judgment, 22 March 2006; and *Naletilić et al.* (IT-98-34-A), Appeals Chamber Judgment, 3 May 2006.

154 *Nahimana et al.* (ICTR-99-52-T), Trial Chamber Judgment and Sentence, 3 December 2003, confirmed by Appeals Chamber, *Nahimana et al.* (ICTR-99-52-A), Appeals Chamber Judgment, 28 November 2007. The decision of the SCC in *Mugesera*, above note 4, made a similar finding and was referred to in the Appeal Court's judgment in *Media Case* (ICTR-99-52-A), Appeals Chamber Judgment, 28 November 2007.

155 *Kvočka et al.* (IT-98-30/1-T), Trial Chamber Judgment, 2 November 2001 at para. 208. See also *Kordić et al.* (IT-95-14/2-A), Appeals Chamber Judgment, 17 December 2004; and *Galić* (IT-98-29-A), Appeals Chamber Judgment, 30 November 2006. Note that the enforced disappearance of persons is an enumerated crime against humanity in the *Rome Statute*, above note 19.

of this contentiousness. By turns, they reflect codification of customary international law, a more restrictive approach on some points, and a more progressive approach on others.[156]

Progressive elements include the inclusion of apartheid,[157] enforced disappearance of persons[158] and forced pregnancy[159] as prohibited acts, as well as the more expansive list of prohibited discriminatory grounds for the crime of persecution, noted in Section C(5)(h), above in this chapter. Also, the requirement to prove a prohibited purpose to make out the elements of torture was not included. By contrast, the required contextual elements are more restrictive. Article 7(2)(a) defines the required attack on a civilian population as "a course of conduct" that must have been done "pursuant to or in furtherance of a State or organizational policy to commit such an attack," which is more restrictive than customary international law which requires only that the attack be widespread or systematic.[160] The detailed elements of the crime (something the *ad hoc* tribunals' statutes did not have) contain an instruction that, because crimes against humanity are, *inter alia*, "among the most serious crimes of concern to the international community as a whole," they are to be "strictly construed."[161] It has been suggested that this amounts to a warning to the court and a signal that it does not have the latitude in interpretation that the previous international and internationalized courts have had.[162]

D. WAR CRIMES

1) History and Definition

The body of law known as "war crimes" is a complex subset of the larger body of international law (both treaty and customary) that governs

---

156 See, generally, Antonio Cassese, "Crimes Against Humanity," in Antonio Cassese, Paula Gaeta, & John R.W.D. Jones, eds., *The Rome Statute of the International Criminal Court: A Commentary* (Oxford: Oxford University Press, 2002) at 353; M. Boot, C. Hall *et al.*, "Article 7" in Otto Triffterer, ed., *Commentary on the* Rome Statute of the International Criminal Court: *Observers' Notes, Article by Article*, 2d ed. (Portland, OR: Hart, 2008) at 159.

157 Above note 19, arts. 7(1)(j) and 7(2)(h).

158 *Ibid.*, arts. 7(1)(i) and 7(2)(i).

159 *Ibid.*, arts. 7(1)(g) and 7(2)(f).

160 Schabas, *An Introduction to the International Criminal Court*, above note 91 at 102–4.

161 *ICC Elements*, above note 67, Crimes against Humanity, art. 7, Introduction, para. 1.

162 Robert Cryer, *Prosecuting International Crimes: Selectivity and the International Criminal Law Regime* (Cambridge: Cambridge University Press, 2005) at 255.

the conduct of armed conflict—"the law of war" as it is traditionally known, or "international humanitarian law" (IHL), which is the more contemporary term. The general goal of IHL is to, "for humanitarian reasons, limit the right of Parties to a conflict to use the methods and means of warfare of their choice or protect persons and property that are, or may be affected by conflict."[163] The willingness of states, nations, and warring factions to take these goals into account has an ancient pedigree,[164] and as noted in Chapter 1, IHL is likely the oldest form of public international law that still resonates today. Similarly, while it has formally come to the fore only recently, there is a long history of individuals being prosecuted for war crimes; the first war crimes trial is generally believed to have taken place in 1474.[165] IHL also has strong links to, and to some extent overlaps with, both international criminal law and international human rights law.

There is a traditional distinction in IHL between "the law of The Hague," which governs the means and methods by which armed conflicts are conducted, and "the law of Geneva" which is essentially concerned with protecting the victims of war. Hague Law stems from the various conventions struck at peace conferences convened in The Hague in 1899 and 1907, which were primarily directed at the conduct of warfare, though some provisions addressed the protection of prisoners of war. Geneva Law, by contrast, has primarily been the product of efforts by the International Committee of the Red Cross (ICRC) to humanize warfare and protect its innocent victims. Its primary bodies of law are the four *Geneva Conventions* of 1949,[166] which provide for the protection of wounded soldiers (*GC I*), sick and shipwrecked sailors (*GC II*), prisoners of war (*GC III*), and civilians in occupied territories (*GC IV*), as well as *Additional Protocols I and II*,[167] which prescribe additional IHL standards for (*inter alia*) wars of self-determination and internal armed conflicts, respectively. It is Geneva Law which has been the most dynamic and has underpinned the development of war crimes in recent

---

163 Yves Sandoz, Claude Swinarski, & Bruno Zimmerman, eds, *Commentary on the Additional Protocols of 8 June 1977 to the Geneva Conventions of 12 August 1949* (Geneva: International Committee of the Red Cross, 1987) at xxvii [ICRC Commentary].

164 See Leslie C. Green, "International Regulation of Armed Conflicts," in M. Cherif Bassiouni, ed., *International Criminal Law*, 2d ed., vol. I (Ardsley, NY: Transnational, 1999) 355 at 355–63.

165 Georg Schwarzenberger, *International Law as Applied by International Courts and Tribunals: The Law of Armed Conflict*, 3d ed. (London: Stevens & Sons, 1968) vol. II at 462–66.

166 (1950), 75 U.N.T.S. 31, 85, 135, and 287.

167 (1977), 1125 U.N.T.S. 3 and 609.

decades. Given that the dominant focus has come to be on addressing the humanitarian aspects of armed conflict, it has been suggested
that the distinction between the two is increasingly unnecessary.[168] In
any event, since states are much more willing to accept restraints on
how they treat unoffending victims than on how they conduct military
operations, the Law of Geneva is much more developed than the Law
of the Hague.[169]

The key to tracing one's way through the maze of international law
from which the idea of "war crimes" emerges is to remember that a war
crime is not simply a breach of any standard or prohibition contained
in the corpus of IHL. Rather, international law (whether customary
or treaty-based) has to provide that the breach in question has been
criminalized, that is, that it is an offence for which an individual can be
tried, and over which a court may have jurisdiction.[170] Generally speaking, whether the breach has been criminalized relates to the degree of
seriousness that attaches to it under the applicable legal regime. The
first major attempt to codify for the purposes of prosecution was article
6(b) of the *IMT Charter*,[171] which provided for jurisdiction over war
crimes as "namely, violations of the laws or customs of war," and proceeded to give a non-exhaustive list of violations based around murder
and other ill-treatment of civilians and prisoners of war. More specifi-
city was provided by the subsequent work of the ICRC in establishing
the *Geneva Conventions* and their Protocols, which as will be seen, specifically provided for the criminalization of different sets of acts taking
place in any armed conflict, the applicable offences depending on the
status of the armed conflict as "international" or "internal." In turn, the
statutes of the UN tribunals, internationalized tribunals, and the ICC
have all adopted various formulations of both the treaty and customary
law on point, with broader or narrower applicability thresholds.

While the entire body of war crimes law cannot be canvassed here,
it is necessary to outline the major sources of the law and the primary
obligations of states, on the one hand, and substantive offences, on the

---

168 See, for example, Asbjørn Eide, "The Laws of War and Human Rights—Differ-
      ences and Convergences," in Christophe Swinarski, ed., *Studies and Essays on
      International Humanitarian Law and Red Cross Principles in Honour of Jean Pictet*
      (The Hague: Martinus Nijhoff, 1984) 675 at 677–78.

169 William Fenrick, "The Prosecution of War Criminals in Canada" (1989–1990)
      12 Dalhousie L.J. 256 at 259.

170 See, generally, Cassese, *ICL*, above note 24 at 81–86. See also *Tadić* (IT-94-1-
      AR72), Decision on the Defence Motion for Interlocutory Appeal on Jurisdic-
      tion, 2 October 1995 at para. 94.

171 Above note 85.

other, within each of those sources. What has been observed is that there has been an increasing focus on the protection of international human rights reflected in IHL instruments generally, and the law of war crimes in particular.[172]

2) Jurisdictional Requirements

a) Existence of and Nexus to Armed Conflict

Acts prosecuted as war crimes can take place only in the context of an armed conflict. This is a characteristic of traditional IHL and distinguishes war crimes from crimes against humanity or genocide, both of which can take place in peacetime. The ICTY Appeals Chamber authoritatively described "armed conflict" as follows:

> [A]n armed conflict exists whenever there is resort to armed force between States or protracted armed violence between governmental authorities and organized armed groups or between such groups within a State. International humanitarian law applies from the initiation of such armed conflicts and extends beyond the cessation of hostilities until a general conclusion of peace is reached; or in the case of internal conflicts, peaceful settlement is achieved.[173]

Distinguishing between an internal armed conflict and lesser levels of violence (such as terrorist attacks, civil unrest, or criminal violence[174]) involves an assessment of the level of organization of the non-party state(s) involved and whether they have seized territory or have the capacity to do so, as well as how "protracted" the armed violence is.[175]

---

172 On the relationship between IHL and international human rights law, see Mark Freeman & Gibran van Ert, *International Human Rights Law* (Toronto: Irwin Law, 2004) at 124–25; René Provost, *International Human Rights and Humanitarian Law* (Cambridge: Cambridge University Press, 2002). See also *Legal Consequences of the Construction of a Wall in the Occupied Palestinian Territory*, Advisory Opinion, [2004] I.C.J. Rep. 136 at paras. 102–6 [*Palestinian Wall*].

173 *Tadić* (IT-94-1-AR72), Decision on the Defence Motion for Interlocutory Appeal on Jurisdiction, 2 October 1995 at para. 70. And see art. 8(2)(f) of the *Rome Statute*, above note 19.

174 Art. 1(2) of *AP II*, above note 167, speaks to "riots, isolated and sporadic acts of violence and other acts of a similar nature," which are excluded from the definition of armed conflict.

175 *Akayesu* (ICTR-96-4-T), Trial Chamber Judgment, 2 September 1998 at paras. 603 and 619; *Delalić et al.* (IT-96-21-T), Trial Chamber Judgment, 9 October 2001 at para. 182. See also the detailed discussion in *Limaj et al.* (IT-03-66-T), Trial Chamber Judgment, 30 November 2005 at paras. 83–174; as well as *Orić* (IT-03-68-T), Trial Chamber Judgment, 30 June 2006 at para. 254; and *Mrkšić et al.* (IT-95-13/1), Trial Chamber Judgment, 27 September 2007 at paras. 406–8

In terms of geographical application, the charged act does not need to have taken place in or near an actual battle. In international armed conflict, the law applies to the entire territory of an involved state, while in internal armed conflicts it applies to the entire territory which is under the control of one of the parties to the conflict.[176]

There must also be a link or nexus between the crime and the armed conflict, which prevents "ordinary" crimes from being prosecuted as war crimes when they simply happened to take place during a war. The prosecution does not have to prove that the act was committed on behalf of, or to further the interests of, one of the parties;[177] rather, it is sufficient that the act is "shaped by or dependent upon the . . . armed conflict . . . ."[178] In determining whether the nexus exists, the court may take into account whether the accused was a combatant and/ or was acting in the scope of their official duties, whether the victim was a non-combatant or member of the opposing party, and whether the crime furthered the military interests of a party.[179]

b) International versus Internal Armed Conflict

The distinction between whether a particular armed conflict is international or internal in nature is key to any war crimes trial, because it determines what body of international law applies and, depending on

---

and 423–24. See also *AFRC* (SCSL-04-16-T), Trial Chamber Judgment, 20 June 2007 at paras. 243–44; and *CDF* (SCSL-04-14-T), Trial Chamber Judgment, 2 August 2007 at paras. 123–28; as well as *Lubanga* (ICC-01/04-01/06-003), Decision on the Confirmation of Charges in the Lubanga Case, 29 January 2007 at para. 320; and *Katanga* (ICC-01/04-01/07-55), Decision on the Evidence and Information provided by the Prosecution for the Issuance of a Warrant of Arrest for Germain Katanga, 5 November 2007 at para. 29.

176 *Kunarac et al.* (IT-96-23 and IT-96-23/1-A), Appeals Chamber Judgment, 12 June 2002 at para. 57; *Tadić* (IT-94-1-A), Appeals Chamber Judgment, 15 July 1999 at para. 70. See also the *Kordić et al.* (IT-95-14/2-A) Appeals Chamber Judgment, 17 December 2004 at paras. 314–21; the same was said for non-international armed conflicts in *Akayesu* (ICTR-96-4-T), Trial Chamber Judgment, 2 September 1998 at para. 635; as well as in *Rutaganda* (ICTR-96-3-T), Trial Chamber Judgment, 6 December 1999 at paras. 100–1; and *Musema* (ICTR-96-13-T), Trial Chamber Judgment, 27 January 2000 at paras. 282–84; *Vasiljević* (IT-98-32-T), Trial Chamber Judgment, 29 November 2002 at para. 25; *Naletilić et al.* (IT-98-34-T), Trial Chamber Judgment, 31 March 2003 at para. 177; *Semanza* (ICTR-97-20-T), Trial Chamber Judgment, 15 May 2003 at para. 367; and *Halilović* (IT-01-48-T), Trial Chamber Judgment, 16 November 2005 at para. 26.

177 *Tadić* (IT-94-1-T), Trial Chamber Opinion and Judgment, 7 May 1997 at para. 573.

178 *Kunarac et al.* (IT-96-23 and IT-96-23/1-A), Appeals Chamber Judgment, 12 June 2002 at paras. 57–58.

179 *Ibid.* at paras. 58–59.

the makeup of the court, whether the court has subject matter jurisdiction in a particular case. Until the 1990s, it was settled that individual responsibility for war crimes could attach only to conduct during an international armed conflict. Traditionally, there has been a part of IHL that governed what happened in internal armed conflicts, that is, those which take place entirely within the boundaries of one state, such as civil wars. However, states are generally reticent when it comes to allowing international law to reach into their own internal conflicts, particularly when that law is geared towards the prosecution of responsible individuals. Accordingly, even as the *Geneva Convention* regimes developed norms for the protection of various persons during armed conflicts, there was a clear division between the law that applied to international armed conflict and the law that applied to internal armed conflict. Individual criminal responsibility could be found for the former, but not for the latter. There were rules by which states had to abide in internal armed conflicts, and which did provide a basic level of humanitarian protection, as reflected in Common Article 3 of the four *Geneva Conventions* and, eventually, *Second Protocol to the Geneva Conventions (AP II)*. However, responsibility for upholding these rules lay with states and could not be imposed on individuals.

The adoption of the *ICTY Statute* by the Security Council in 1993 seemed to confirm this state of affairs. Articles 2 and 3 of the statute provided for jurisdiction over "Grave Breaches of the *Geneva Conventions* of 1949" and "Violations of the Laws or Customs of War" respectively, but both the Secretary-General of the UN[180] and other distinguished commentators (including the Commission of Experts who had proposed the founding of the tribunal)[181] agreed that these laws applied only to international armed conflicts. However, the political will for extending the notion of war crimes into internal armed conflicts had been growing, and the Security Council flexed its considerable legal might in formulating the *Statute of the ICTR*, article 4 of which founded jurisdiction over Common Article 3 and *AP II*. This very progressive development was furthered by the ICTY Appeal Chamber's surprise ruling in the *Tadić* decision that, in its view, customary international law itself allowed for prosecution of individuals for violations of "the laws or customs of war" as applied to internal armed conflict as well as international.[182] Further authoritative acceptance came with the final-

---

180 *Report of the Secretary General Pursuant to Paragraph 2 of Security Council Resolution 808* (1993), UN Doc. S/25704 at paras. 37–44 [*Report of the Secretary General*].

181 UN Doc. S/1994/674 at para. 42.

182 The reaction to the decision was not so much based on a lack of current acceptance of the desirability of this development, which was generally viewed to be

ization of the *Rome Statute*, where the state parties agreed to the inclusion in article 8(2) of a number of war crimes provisions that applied to internal armed conflicts. Accordingly, it is now clear as a matter of customary international law that there can be individual criminal responsibility for crimes committed during either international or internal armed conflicts, though as explored below, a more limited body of law applies to the latter.

Determining whether an international armed conflict exists is fairly straightforward, since it is by simple definition an armed conflict between two states, including situations where the forces of one belligerent state are occupying the territory of another.[183] An ICTY Trial Chamber relied on the commentary to *GC IV* to define it as "'[a]ny difference arising between two States and leading to the intervention of members of the armed forces,'" and noting that "'[i]t makes no difference how long the conflict lasts, or how much slaughter takes place.'"[184] Article 1(4) of *AP I* effectively extends the definition of international armed conflict to include "armed conflicts in which peoples are fighting against colonial domination and alien occupation and against racist regimes in the exercise of their right to self-determination . . . ."

Internal, or "non-international," armed conflicts take place entirely within the boundaries of one state, the classic example being a civil war, though the massacres in Rwanda were characterized in this way and led to the war crimes law relating to internal armed conflict being incorporated into article 4 of the *ICTR Statute. AP II*, which applies only to internal armed conflict, has a higher threshold in that it applies only to conflicts:

> . . . which take place in the territory of a High Contracting Party between its armed forces and dissident armed forces or other organized armed groups which, under responsible command, exercise such control over a part of its territory as to enable them to carry out sustained and concerted military operations and to implement this Protocol.[185]

---

a salutary one; rather, the more shocking part of the Appeal Chamber's finding was that this was the position in customary international law when the crimes took place, that is, during the breakup of Yugoslavia, which was highly questionable at best.

183 Common Article 2 of the 1949 *Geneva Conventions*, above note 166.

184 *Delalić et al.* (IT-96-21-T), Trial Chamber Sentencing Judgment, 16 November 1998 at para. 208.

185 *AP II*, above note 167, art. 1.

Accordingly, not every internal armed conflict is covered under *AP II*, as not every one of these conflicts will have the requisite degree of intensity.[186]

The complex political situation in the former Yugoslavia underscored the fact that the characterization of a conflict is an essentially factual issue and must be proven by the prosecution, as several accused persons denied that they were acting within the context of an international armed conflict, and thus disputed the application to them of that body of war crimes law. In *Tadić*, the Appeals Chamber held that an internal armed conflict could "become international (or, depending upon the circumstances, be international in character alongside an internal armed conflict) if (i) another State intervenes in that conflict through its troops, or alternatively if (ii) some of the participants in the internal armed conflict act on behalf of that other State."[187] On the latter point, the Appeals Chamber controversially rejected the test put forward by the ICJ in the *Nicaragua Case*, which applied a high standard of "agency" or "effective control."[188] The court preferred the less stringent standard of "overall control" of one of the parties to the conflict by an outside state,[189] which it has gone on to apply in subsequent cases.[190]

3) Mental Element

Somewhat like genocide and crimes against humanity, successfully prosecuting war crimes requires proving an intent component beyond the simple intent to do the proscribed act. The accused must be shown to have been aware of the existence of the armed conflict, though beyond this no special or discriminatory intent or motive need be shown.[191] In addition, some crimes have a specified mental element. For example, the grave breach of "wilful killing" encompasses both intention and recklessness, but excludes negligence. As another example, article 85(3)(b) of *AP I* prohibits "launching an indiscriminate attack affecting the civilian population or civilian objects in the knowledge

---

186 See, generally, Commentary to *Protocol Additional to the Geneva Conventions* of 12 August 1949, and relating to the Protection of Victims of Non-International Armed Conflicts (*Protocol II*), 8 June 1977 at paras. 4463–70.

187 *Tadić* (IT-94-1-A), Appeals Chamber Judgment, 15 July 1999 at para. 84.

188 *Case Concerning Military and Paramilitary Activities in and against Nicaragua (Nicaragua v. United States of America) (Merits)*, [1986] I.C.J. Rep. 14 at para. 115 [*Nicaragua Case*].

189 *Tadić* (IT-94-1-A), Appeals Chamber Judgment, 15 July 1999 at para. 146.

190 *Delalić et al.* (IT-96-21-A), Appeals Chamber Judgment, 20 February 2001 at para. 26. See also *Kordić et al.* (IT-95-14/2-T), Trial Chamber Judgment, 26 February 2001 at paras. 108–46. See also the *Serbian Genocide Case*, above note 13.

191 *Aleksovski* (IT-95-14/1-A), Appeals Chamber Judgment, 24 March 2000 at para. 20.

that such attack will cause excessive loss of life, injury to civilians or damage to civilian objects." Conviction will require proof of both the intent to launch the attack and "knowledge" in the sense of the foreseeability of the result.[192]

4) The *Geneva Conventions* and *Additional Protocols I and II*

a)   Introduction

The *Geneva Conventions* regime is at the core of the substantive portion of war crimes law. The first major post-Nuremberg development in war crimes law came with the conclusion of the four *Geneva Conventions* of 1949, which were developed under the sponsorship of the ICRC. They built on earlier IHL instruments, including the *First Geneva Convention* of 1864[193] and the *Hague Conventions* of 1899 and 1907, but with the more specific goal of providing protection to persons who were not actively involved in armed conflict—wounded soldiers (*GC I*), sick and shipwrecked sailors (*GC II*), prisoners of war (*GC III*), and civilians in occupied territories (*GC IV*). This protection is accomplished in two ways: by prescribing rules for states regarding how their armed forces conduct themselves in international armed conflict, violation of which can lead to responsibility on the part of the states; and by compelling state parties to criminalize and prosecute those who violate a subset of these rules. The four Conventions are widely adhered to[194] and are generally regarded as customary international law. Even insurrectionist groups often declare themselves bound by the *Geneva Conventions*.

The Conventions are lengthy and each codifies a number of prohibitions which were already in place under the laws and customs of war, both treaty-based and customary. The major innovation which they introduced was the obligation on state parties to incorporate repression of war crimes into the fabric of their domestic laws, and cooperate with each other in so doing; in this way, the *Geneva Conventions* were the first modern "suppression conventions."[195] The essential obligations are threefold: (1) each state party must criminalize "grave breaches" (see Section D(4)(b), below in this chapter) of the Conventions in its domestic law and "suppress" all other violations, (2) each must investigate allegations of grave breaches, and (3) each must bring perpetrators before

---

192 Cassese, *ICL*, above note 24 at 93.

193 Which provided protection exclusively for wounded soldiers.

194 There are 194 state parties to each convention; see ICRC, "International Humanitarian Law: Treaties and Documents," online: www.cicr.org/ihl.nsf/CONVPRES?OpenView.

195 See Chapter 7.

its courts "regardless of their nationality," or hand them over to another state party for trial (the *aut dedere aut judicare* mechanism).[196] There is no territorial limit on states' exercise of jurisdiction over perpetrators, and states can prosecute offenders on the basis of universal jurisdiction. In fact, under the GC provisions they are compelled to do so, and the customary status of the Conventions makes this one of the few instances where states not only can, but must prosecute offenders as a matter of customary international law.

As attention to international human rights law became more intense in the decades following the conclusion of the *Geneva Conventions*, and also in the wake of the Vietnam conflict and various wars of liberation, it was recognized that there was willingness among states to update IHL in various ways. In 1977, the two additional Protocols (*AP I* and *AP II*) were concluded, again under the auspices of the ICRC. A major goal of each was to expand state obligations as to the level of humanitarian protection in international and internal armed conflicts, respectively. *AP I*, as noted above, enlarges the definition of international armed conflict to include wars of self-determination of peoples, but more importantly it expands the range of both grave breaches and basic humanitarian protections required. *AP II* was designed to broaden the range of basic humanitarian protections required of states in internal armed conflicts, but was not intended to provide for further individual criminal liability. However, as a result of the *Tadić* decision and subsequent developments as described earlier, parts of *AP II* are now considered to constitute IHL violations of sufficient seriousness to be subject to penal law. Generally speaking, "major parts of both *Protocols* reflect customary law."[197] However, *AP I* has had greater adherence by states, due again to state reluctance to subject internal armed conflicts to the full scrutiny of IHL.[198] *AP II* has played a limited role in the jurisprudence of the *ad hoc* tribunals, which have tended to use it as "a relevant instance of state practice that might be pertinent to a determination that a rule or principle which it contains has become part of customary international law."[199] The most wide-ranging and authorita-

---

196 *GC I*, above note 166, art. 49; *GC II*, above note 166, art. 50; *GC III*, above note 166, art. 129; *GC IV*, above note 137, art. 146.

197 *Kordić et al.* (IT-95-14/2-PT), Decision on Joint Defence Motion to Dismiss for Lack of Jurisdiction based on the Limited Jurisdictional Reach of Articles 2 and 3, 2 March 1999 at para. 30.

198 *AP I* has 167 state parties, while *AP II* has 163; see ICRC, above note 194.

199 Guénaël Mettraux, *International Crimes and the* ad hoc *Tribunals* (Oxford: Oxford University Press, 2005) at 144 [footnotes omitted].

tive study of customary international law of IHL to date was published by the ICRC in 2005.[200]

b)   The Grave Breaches Regime

Each of the *Geneva Conventions* has a particularized group of acts which are defined as "grave breaches" and thus are subject to the prosecutory regime described in Section D(4)(a), above in this chapter when they are committed during international armed conflict.[201] As an initial threshold, grave breaches can be committed only as against "protected persons" (or in some cases protected property), as the *Conventions* themselves were designed to protect certain classes of persons deemed to be the victims of war—"Wounded and Sick Armed Forces in the Field" under *GC I*, "Wounded, Sick and Shipwrecked Members of the Armed Forces at Sea" under *GC II*, "Prisoners of War" under *GC III*,[202] and "Civilian Persons" under *GC IV*.[203] A victim's status as a protected person is a question of fact and must be proven by the prosecution,[204] though in many cases this will easily be ascertained.

Many of the grave breaches are identical or similar across all of the Conventions. Accordingly, it is convenient to describe them in a grouped fashion:[205]

1)   *Wilful killing*

This crime is common across the four Conventions.[206] It obviously does not apply to every intentional or reckless killing in war, but is

---

200   Jean-Marie Henckaerts *et al.*, *Customary International Humanitarian Law, Vol. I: Rules* (Cambridge: Cambridge University Press, 2005) and *Customary International Humanitarian Law, Vol. II: Practice* (Cambridge: Cambridge University Press, 2005).

201   In *Tadić* (IT-94-1-A), Appeals Chamber Judgment, 15 July 1999 at para. 83, the court speculated that changing views among states may be eroding the limitation of the grave breaches regime to international armed conflicts, based in part on an American *amicus* brief. Currently, however, the limitation continues to exist. See Sonja Boelaert-Suominen, "Grave Breaches, Universal Jurisdiction and Internal Armed Conflict: Is Customary Law Moving towards a Uniform Enforcement Mechanism for All Armed Conflicts?" (2000) 5 J. Confl. & Sec. L. 63.

202   "Prisoners of war" is defined in art. 4(a) of *GC III*, above note 166, which definition is supplemented in art. 44(3) of *AP I*, above note 102.

203   Note that *GC IV*, above note 137, has a detailed description of which "civilians" are protected, and excludes protection of persons as against their own governments, as well as nationals of non-party states; see art. 4.

204   *Naletilić et al.* (IT-98-34-T), Trial Chamber Judgment, 31 March 2003 at para. 176.

205   This framework is drawn from UK Ministry of Defence, *The Manual of the Law of Armed Conflict* (Oxford: Oxford University Press, 2005) at ¶16.24.

206   *GC I*, above note 166, art. 50; *GC II*, above note 166, art. 51; *GC III*, above note 166, art. 130; *GC IV*, above note 137, art. 147.

intended to catch acts that would more properly be described as the murder of a protected person.

2) *Torture or inhumane treatment, including biological experiments*
This crime is common across the four Conventions.[207] The elements of torture are the same as those for the crime against humanity of torture.[208] Inhumane treatment is similar in that it causes mental or physical suffering or injury, but to a lower threshold,[209] and there is no requirement to prove that the treatment was for the purpose of extracting information, or indeed for any purpose. An example is the use of protected persons as human shields.[210]

3) *Wilfully causing great suffering or serious injury to body or health*
This crime is common across the four Conventions. It overlaps with that of inhumane treatment, the difference appearing to be that it requires a serious degree of mental/physical injury, and does not include acts that offend only against a person's dignity.[211]

4) *Extensive destruction and appropriation of property, not justified by military necessity and carried out unlawfully and wantonly*
This crime is common across the four Conventions.[212] The contextual elements of the crime are fairly self-descriptive. Central is the type of property protected, which has generally been held to refer to civilian property generally protected by the *Geneva Conventions* (e.g., hospitals and associated facilities), and civilian property protected under article 53 of *GC IV*, (i.e., real and personal property

---

207 *GC I, ibid.*, art. 50; *GC II, ibid.*, art. 51; *GC III, ibid.*, art. 130; *GC IV, ibid.*, art. 147.
208 See Section C(5)(f), above in this chapter.
209 *Naletilić et al.* (IT-98-34-T), Trial Chamber Judgment, 31 March 2003 at para. 246.
210 *Blaškić* (IT-95-14-A), Appeals Chamber Judgment, 29 July 2004 at para. 670.
211 *Kordić et al.* (IT-95-14/2-T), Trial Chamber Judgment, 26 February 2001 at para. 245; *Strugar* (IT-01-42-T), Trial Chamber Judgment, 31 January 2005; *Hadžihasanović et al.* (IT-01-47-T), Trial Chamber Judgment, 15 March 2006; *Orić* (IT-03-68-T), Trial Chamber Judgment, 30 June 2006; *Simić* (IT-95-9-A), Trial Chamber Judgment, 28 November 2006; *Mrkšić et al.* (IT-95-13/1-T), Trial Chamber Judgment, 27 September 2007.
212 See *Kordić et al.* (IT-95-14/2-T), Trial Chamber Judgment, 26 February 2001; *Naletilić et al.* (IT-98-34-T), Trial Chamber Judgment, 31 March 2003; *Brđanin* (IT-99-36-T), Trial Chamber Judgment, 1 September 2004; *Kordić et al.* (IT-95-14/2-A), Appeals Chamber Judgment, 17 December 2004; *Strugar* (IT-01-42-T), Trial Chamber Judgment, 31 January 2005; *Hadžihasanović et al.* (IT-01-47-T), Trial Chamber Judgment, 15 March 2006; *Orić* (IT-03-68-T), Trial Chamber Judgment, 30 June 2006.

belonging to either private persons or the state, when destruction of it was not "absolutely necessary" to military operations).

5) *Compelling a protected person to serve in the forces of a hostile power*
This crime applies to prisoners of war under *GC III*[213] and civilians under *GC IV*.[214] The ICRC's commentary to *GC IV* indicates that the prohibition applies not just to active military service, but more broadly to any work which might assist the enemy.[215] Both prisoners of war (POWs) and civilians can be compelled to work, but only for non-military purposes.[216]

6) *Wilfully depriving a prisoner of war or civilian the rights of a fair and regular trial*
This crime applies to POWs under *GC III*[217] and civilians under *GC IV*.[218] Each Convention provides a set of basic procedural rights for protected persons who face trial, including knowledge of charges, right to counsel, right to question witnesses, right to appeal, and so on. While POWs must generally be tried by military courts,[219] neither they nor civilians can be tried by exceptional courts which do not provide for the basic right provided under the *Conventions*. "The grave breach is committed when any of the constituent elements relating to the concept of a fair and regular trial are missing."[220]

7) *Unlawful deportation or transfer or unlawful confinement*
These are three distinct grave breaches, all of which apply only to civilians under *GC IV*.[221] Unlawful deportation or transfer refers to the forcible movement of people from their residences, either within the borders of a state (transfer) or into another state (deportation). "Evacuation" of civilians is lawful if required for security or safety reasons under article 49 of *GC IV*, though they must be returned to their homes when hostilities in the area are over. The

---

213 Above note 166, art. 130.
214 Above note 137, art. 147.
215 ICRC Commentary to *GC IV*, above note 163 at 254.
216 *GC III*, above note 166, art. 50; *GC IV*, above note 137, art. 40. See *Naletilić et al.* (IT-98-34-T), Trial Chamber Judgment, 31 March 2003; *Simić* (IT-95-9-A), Judgment, 28 November 2006; *Krajišnik* (IT-00-39-T), Trial Chamber Judgment, 27 September 2006.
217 Above note 166, art. 130.
218 Above note 137, art. 147.
219 *GC III*, above note 166, art. 84.
220 *Archbold*, above note 52 at §§ 11–126.
221 Above note 137, art. 147.

prosecution must prove the intent to actually remove the person, "which implies the aim that the person is not returning."[222] Unlawful confinement is essentially the same as its counterpart domestic crime in national legal systems. "Internment" of civilians is a lawful practice if done for security or safety reasons, and if the confinement is periodically judicially or administratively reviewed.[223] However, for internment to be lawful, it must be proven that the interned individual "poses a particular risk to the security of the State."[224]

8) *Taking civilians as hostages*
    This crime applies only to civilians under article 147 of *GC IV*. This grave breach amounts to unlawfully depriving an individual of his liberty, including unlawfully confining him, but with the added element of a threat either to the person's person or to prolong his captivity, as a means of gaining a concession from a third party.[225]

AP I expands the grave breaches regime in two ways. First, article 85(2) provides that grave breaches of the *Conventions* are to be treated as such when committed against combatants, "unlawful combatants,"[226] refugees, the wounded/sick/shipwrecked of an adverse Party, or "medical or religious personnel, medical units or medical transports which are under the control of an adverse Party." Second, it sets up a regime of grave breaches of the Protocol itself, which both supplements and adds to the *Geneva Conventions* grave breaches, and includes:

- unlawful medical experimentation;[227]
- intentional or indiscriminate attacks against civilian targets, or attacks against military targets in the knowledge that the attack will result in "excessive" civilian casualties;[228]
- attacks on non-defended localities or demilitarized zones;[229]
- attacks on persons who are *hors de combat*;[230]

---

222 *Naletilić et al.* (IT-98-34-T), Trial Chamber Judgment, 31 March 2003 at para. 520.

223 *GC IV*, above note 137, arts. 42 & 43.

224 *Delalić et al.* (IT-96-21-A), Appeals Chamber Judgment, 20 February 2001 at para. 322.

225 *Blaškić* (IT-95-14-A), Appeals Chamber Judgment, 29 July 2004 at para. 639. See also *Kordić et al.* (IT-95-14/2-T), Trial Chamber Judgment, 26 February 2001.

226 A term of art which has developed to refer to persons involved in hostilities, but who are not entitled to prisoner-of-war status; see art. 45 of *AP I*, above note 102.

227 *Ibid.*, art. 11.

228 *Ibid.*, arts. 85(3)(a)–(c).

229 *Ibid.*, art. 85(3)(d).

230 *Ibid.*, art. 85(3)(e).

- the "perfidious" use of protected symbols, such as the red cross or red crescent;[231]
- an expanded offence of transfer or deportation of populations;[232]
- unjustifiable delay in the repatriation of POWs or civilians;[233]
- apartheid and similar practices;[234]
- attacks on culturally and historically significant objects;[235] and
- deprivation of a protected person of fair trial rights.[236]

Article 85(5) of *AP I* expressly says that "grave breaches of [the *Geneva Conventions* and *AP I*] shall be regarded as war crimes." While *AP I* is not as widely subscribed to as the *Geneva Conventions*, it is clear that most, if not all, of the supplementary grave breaches it introduced are indeed war crimes under customary international law. This was confirmed by the war crimes provisions of the *Rome Statute*.

c)   Common Article 3 and *AP II*

While the *Geneva Conventions* were intended to apply exclusively to international armed conflicts, there was agreement among state parties to undertake obligations regarding the provision of minimum standards of humanitarian protection in internal armed conflicts. Accordingly, the drafters inserted a detailed provision into article 3 of each of the Conventions (thus, "Common Article 3"), comprised of a set of protections for "persons taking no active part in the hostilities, including members of armed forces who have laid down their arms and those placed *hors de combat* by sickness, wounds, detention, or any other cause[.]"[237] This is a broader definition than the various definitions of "protected persons" under the *Geneva Conventions*.

The following acts are prohibited under Common Article 3:

a)   violence to life and person, in particular murder of all kinds, mutilation, cruel treatment, and torture;

b)   the taking of hostages;

c)   outrages upon personal dignity, in particular humiliating and degrading treatment; and

---

231   *Ibid.*, art. 85(3)(f).
232   *Ibid.*, art. 85(4)(a).
233   *Ibid.*, art. 85(4)(b).
234   *Ibid.*, art. 85(4)(c).
235   *Ibid.*, art. 85(4)(d).
236   *Ibid.*, art. 85(4)(e).
237   See, generally, David E. Elder, "The Historical Background of Common Article 3 of the *Geneva Conventions* of 1949" (1979) 11 Case W. Res. J. Int'l L. 37.

d) the passing of sentences and the carrying out of executions without previous judgement pronounced by a regularly constituted court, affording all the judicial guarantees which are recognized as indispensable by civilized peoples.

There is little doubt of the normative force of this provision, and the ICJ has stated that it represents a codification of customary international law as to the "minimum considerations of humanity."[238] Note again that these provisions were not intended to impose obligations upon individuals and thus allow for individual criminal responsibility, but only to oblige states to emplace these protections on their territory during an internal armed conflict. Nonetheless, as described above, customary international law has moved forward, and most violations of Common Article 3 are now considered to be war crimes. Moreover, the ICTY Appeals Chamber held in the *Čelebići* decision that Common Article 3 must also apply to *international* armed conflicts, since it constituted a minimum set of rules on which the grave breaches regime simply expanded.[239] Nonetheless, the key distinction is that Common Article 3 applies to internal armed conflict, while the grave breaches regime does not.

Both Common Article 3 and *AP II* were designed in such a way as to blur the distinction between Hague and Geneva Law referred to above. *AP II* was intended to update and expand the protections provided by Common Article 3 vis-à-vis internal armed conflicts. As noted above, it applies to a certain kind of internal armed conflict which has reached a high level of intensity, and there is thus a gap between the occasions on which Common Article 3 applies and those where *AP II* applies in its entirety. Nonetheless, there is a great deal of overlap and commonality between the various prohibitions.

Article 4 of *AP II* prohibits the following:

a) violence to the life, health, and physical or mental well-being of persons, in particular murder as well as cruel treatment such as torture, mutilation, or any form of corporal punishment;
b) collective punishments;
c) taking of hostages;
d) acts of terrorism;
e) outrages on personal dignity, in particular humiliating and degrading treatment, rape, enforced prostitution, and any form of indecent assault;

---

238 *Nicaragua Case*, above note 188 at para. 218; see also paras. 255 and 292.
239 *Delalić et al.* (IT-96-21-A), Appeals Chamber Judgment, 20 February 2001 at paras. 140–50.

f)   slavery and the slave trade in all their forms;
g)   pillage; and
h)   threats to commit any of the foregoing acts.

Also, the Protocol prohibits attacks upon civilians[240] and the objects indispensable to their survival (e.g., food supplies),[241] as well as their forced movement;[242] attacks on "works or installations containing dangerous forces" (e.g., a dam which when ruptured would result in civilian injury or damage);[243] and acts of hostility against cultural objects and places of worship.[244]

As it is not certain that all of *AP II* represents customary international law, there has been a bifurcation of prosecution with regard to its prohibitions. Article 3 of the *Statute of the ICTY*[245] gave it jurisdiction over "serious violations of the laws and customs of war," which, after *Tadić*, meant that in adjudicating on charges under *AP II*, it had to ascertain whether the prohibition in question had attained sufficient seriousness that it was deemed to be an offence under customary international law.[246] On the other hand, courts such as the ICTR and the Special Court for Sierra Leone (SCSL) had violations of *AP II* incorporated into their statutes expressly,[247] while the *Rome Statute*[248] contains most of its prohibitions (or updated versions thereof) without naming them as such.

5) Violations of the Laws or Customs of War

As noted earlier, the *Charter of the IMT*[249] gave that tribunal jurisdiction over war crimes as "violations of the laws or customs of war." This was basically intended to cover those parts of Hague Law which had attained sufficient seriousness to be considered crimes, entailing individual responsibility. The primary basis for this body of law is the Regulations annexed to *Hague Convention IV* of 1907,[250] which were

---

240 Above note 167, art. 13.
241 *Ibid.*, art. 14.
242 *Ibid.*, art. 17.
243 *Ibid.*, art. 15.
244 *Ibid.*, art. 16.
245 Annexed to UN Doc. S/RES/827 (1993).
246 *Tadić* (IT-94-1-AR72), Decision on the Defence Motion for Interlocutory Appeal on Jurisdiction, 2 October 1995.
247 Above note 167, arts. 4 and 3, respectively.
248 Above note 19.
249 Above note 85.
250 36 Stat. 2277, in force 26 January 1910.

designed to place limitations on the means by which states and their armies conduct warfare. They accomplish this by prohibiting certain acts and methods of war, such as inhumane treatment of prisoners, use of poisoned weapons, and improper use of flags of truce. The Nuremberg Tribunal recognized that the *Hague Regulations* were not intended to create individual criminal responsibility, but found that the most serious violations of the Regulations had emerged as criminal acts by way of customary international law:

> Many of these prohibitions had been enforced long before the date of the Convention; but since 1907 they have certainly been crimes, punishable as offences against the laws of war; yet the *Hague Convention* nowhere designates such practices as criminal, nor is any sentence prescribed, nor any mention made of a court to try and punish offenders. For many years past, however, military tribunals have tried and punished individuals guilty of violating the rules of land warfare laid down by this Convention.[251]

This, then, is a body of war crimes law of more ancient vintage than the *Geneva Conventions* regime,[252] but which is still a current source of that law as it continues to develop in customary and treaty-based international law. In the recent *Advisory Opinion on the Legal Consequences of the Construction of a Wall in the Occupied Palestinian Territory*, the ICJ held that the Hague Convention has become customary international law.[253] This was also the view of the UN Secretary-General in 1993 when, in reporting on the *ICTY Statute*,[254] stated that article 3 of the Statute (which, like the *IMT Charter*, gave the tribunal jurisdiction over "violations of the law or customs of war") was based on *Hague Convention IV* and its Regulations.[255] Article 3 provides a list of these violations, which includes employment of poisonous weapons; wanton destruction of cities, towns, or villages not justified by military necessity; and bombardment of undefended towns, villages, dwellings or

---

251 *France et al. v. Göering et al.*, reprinted (1947), 41 A.J.I.L. 172 at 218 (Int'l Military Trib.).

252 Though, as noted, the *Additional Protocols* address some of the same subject matter.

253 *Palestinian Wall*, above note 172 at para. 89.

254 Above note 21.

255 *Report of the Secretary-General*, above note 180 at paras. 41–44; though the Appeals Chamber eventually found that art. 3 in fact encompassed *all* serious violations of international humanitarian law other than grave breaches of the *Geneva Conventions*—including, for example, the non-grave breach provisions of the *Geneva Conventions*: *Tadić* (IT-94-1-AR72), Decision on the Defence Motion for Interlocutory Appeal on Jurisdiction, 2 October 1995 at para. 89.

buildings; but this list is clearly indicated to be examples of the kind of offence covered. The *Rome Statute*'s war crimes provisions also include a number of crimes based on the *Hague Convention*, which is further evidence of state practice in this regard. The *Additional Protocols* cover some of the same ranges of conduct as the body of Hague Law crimes, but the customary international law status of the latter means that they would apply even to parties who have not signed the Protocols, and thus to all individual perpetrators.

States thus are obliged to criminalize those parts of the "laws or customs of war" that have attained the status of criminal offences under customary international law, or where the states have entered into treaties that provide for offences. Unlike the grave breaches regime, there is no obligation to actively pursue cases, nor (aside from treaty obligations) any obligation to extradite offenders. States will do this under their domestic criminal laws, their military laws, or a combination of both. The jurisprudence of the *ad hoc* tribunals, however, and particularly the ICTY, has made significant contributions to fleshing out the content of this body of law. Most important, perhaps, was the Appeals Chamber's finding in *Tadić* that individual criminal responsibility could be found for violations of international humanitarian law in both international and internal armed conflicts. This had the effect of applying the laws or customs of war to internal armed conflicts—justified, it would seem, because "[n]o one can doubt the gravity of the acts at issue, nor the interest of the international community in their prohibition."[256]

As a general statement, it is only the most serious breaches of the laws of war which attract criminal liability, even though the violation of any law will entail state responsibility.[257] The following acts are fairly conclusively viewed as Hague Law–based war crimes, which emerge from the *Hague Regulations* and customary international law:[258]

- employing poison or poisoned weapons;
- killing or wounding treacherously individuals belonging to the hostile nation or army;

---

256 *Tadić, ibid.* at para. 129.

257 Ratner provides an apt example: "[I]f the commander of a POW camp failed to keep a record of all disciplinary punishments (a violation of Article 96 of the *Third Geneva Convention*), he would likely not be committing a war crime" (Steven Ratner, "Categories of War Crimes" in Roy Gutman & David Rieff, eds., *Crimes of War: What the Public Should Know* (New York: W.W. Norton, 1999) 374 at 375.

258 Drawn from *The Manual of the Law of Armed Conflict*, above note 205 at ¶¶16.27–16.29.

- killing or wounding an enemy who, having laid down his arms, or having no longer means of defence, has surrendered at discretion;
- declaring that no quarter will be given;
- employing arms, projectiles, or material calculated to cause unnecessary suffering;
- making improper use of a flag of truce, the flag, uniforms, or insignia of the enemy, or the distinctive emblems of the *Geneva Conventions*;
- destroying or seizing enemy property, unless such is imperatively demanded by the necessities of war;
- declaring abolished, suspended, or inadmissible in a court of law the rights and actions of the nationals of a hostile party;
- compelling nationals of a hostile party to take part in operations of war directed against their country;
- pillaging
- punishing spies without proper trials;
- violating the terms of armistice by an individual acting on his own initiative;
- mutilating or other maltreatment of dead bodies;
- looting;
- using a privileged building (e.g., hospitals, churches, schools) for improper purposes, or attacking such buildings or hospital ships/aircraft;
- firing on shipwrecked personnel; and
- using bacteriological methods of warfare.[259]

6) War Crimes in the *Rome Statute*[260]

Perhaps more than the other substantive law provisions in the *Rome Statute*, article 8, which sets out the list of war crimes within the ICC's jurisdiction, is a mixture of progression, codification, retrenchment, and "obsequious[ness] to State sovereignty."[261] Like many other parts of the *Rome Statute*, it reflects the push and pull of the highly political ne-

---

259 Drawing on the *Geneva Protocol for the Prohibition of the Use in War of Asphyxiating, Poisonous or other Gases, and of Bacteriological Methods of Warfare of 1925* (1925), 94 L.N.T.S. 65.

260 Above note 19. See, generally, M. Cottier *et al.*, "Article 8" in Triffterer, ed., above note 156 at 275; Peter Rowe, "War Crimes" in Dominic McGoldrick *et al.*, eds., *The Permanent International Criminal Court: Legal and Policy Issues* (Oxford: Hart, 2004); Herman von Habel & Darryl Robinson, "Crimes within the Jurisdiction of the Court" in Roy Lee, ed., *The Making of the* Rome Statute: *Issues, Negotiations, Results* (The Hague: Kluwer, 1999).

261 Cassese, *ICL*, above note 24 at 97.

gotiations that led to the founding of the court. A noteworthy example is article 8(1), which provides that the court has jurisdiction over war crimes "in particular when committed as part of a plan or policy or as part of a large-scale commission of such crimes." This "non-threshold threshold"[262] is consistent with the role of the ICC as a forum for the prosecution of the most serious and heinous of international crimes, and imports adherence to a level of gravity consistent with that of the other crimes within the court's jurisdiction.[263] It was, however, a compromise to resolve a dispute between the US, which wanted such a threshold as a firm requirement, and the majority of other states which disagreed.[264]

Article 8 contains a detailed list of war crimes drawn from both treaty and customary international law, though it is by no means exhaustive of those bodies of law and has been described as "an incomplete codification of custom."[265] The negotiations leading to the finalization of the article reflected the controversial nature of war crimes and the divergence of state views on how broadly or narrowly the court's war crimes regime was to be formulated. What resulted was a complex formulation of crimes under a "complete code" approach; unlike the ICTY, the ICC will not be able to draw on other sources of IHL to determine its jurisdiction to try offenders, though it will draw on earlier caselaw which has interpreted the specific crimes (or versions thereof) in article 8. Any expansion of the list of crimes will have to be accomplished by way of the cumbersome amendment process set out in the *Rome Statute*. This reflects a much more conservative approach on the part of states than was evident with the provisions on genocide and crimes against humanity, and displays a desire to narrow the potential for state officials to be implicated in war crimes prosecutions. While there are some new crimes and progressive elements added into the mix, on the whole the approach is a static one, and as Professor Schabas suggests,

---

262 von Habel & Robinson, above note 260 at 124.

263 Accord, Schabas, *An Introduction to the International Criminal Court*, above note 91 at 117. This formulation echoes the formulation of war crimes in art. 20 of the 1996 "Draft Code of Crimes against the Peace and Security of Mankind" in *Report of the International Law Commission on the work of its Forty-eighth Session* (6 May–26 July 1996), Supp. No. 10 UN Doc. A/51/10 ["Draft Code"].

264 von Habel & Robinson, above note 260 at 107–8. In practice, the Prosecutor will use her discretion to decline jurisdiction over less serious cases, which are better prosecuted by states that have jurisdiction in any event. See, generally, Chapter 4.

265 Cryer, above note 162 at 268.

"[T]he detailed terms of article 8 may indirectly contribute to impunity in their inability to permit dynamic or evolutive interpretations."[266]

Together, article 8 and the detailed *Elements of the Crimes (ICC Elements)* maintain the requirement that there be armed conflict, and for a nexus between the actions of the accused and the armed conflict. It takes a stricter approach to the nexus than the ICTY, which did not require knowledge of the conflict by the accused. The *ICC Elements* require that the accused "was aware of the factual circumstances that established the existence of an armed conflict," but the accused need not have legally evaluated whether the conflict existed, nor considered its character as international or non-international.[267]

The structure of the war crimes provisions in article 8 do not cleanly adhere to the distinction between Hague Law and Geneva Law, but they do very clearly maintain the line between international and internal armed conflicts, and apply different sets of offences to each. Article 2(a) provides for jurisdiction over grave breaches of the *Geneva Conventions*. Though agreement could not be reached on including grave breaches of *AP I*, many of those grave breaches that have customary status are included in other parts of the article. This is true, for example, of article 2(b), which provides for jurisdiction over "other serious violations of the laws and customs applicable in international armed conflict, within the established framework of international law." The paragraph then lists twenty-six different crimes which are drawn from Hague Law and incorporate mostly customary prohibitions. Subparagraphs 8(2)(b)(i) and (ii) set out prohibitions of attacks against civilians and civilian objects, which reflect article 85(3)(a) of *AP I*, and several other provisions of *AP I* which have attained customary status are included as well. More progressive elements include prohibiting attacks on peacekeeping missions and personnel[268] and attacks which

---

266 Schabas, *An Introduction to the International Criminal Court*, above note 91 at 117. However, it is clear that the development of the law of war crimes has continued in spite of the restrictiveness of the *Rome Statute*; since 2002, two "new" crimes have been added to the arsenal of war crimes, in both cases by criminalizing IHL prohibitions and turning them into ICL crimes. These crimes are causing terror (by the ICTY, although this crime was not specifically in its statute in *Galić* (IT-98-29-T), Trial Chamber Judgment, 5 December 2003; *Blagojević et al.* (IT-02-60-T), Trial Chamber Judgment, 17 January 2004; *Galić* (IT-98-29-A), Appeals Chamber Judgment, 30 November 2006; *Milošević*, IT-98-29/1-T), Trial Chamber Judgment, 12 December 2007) and collective punishments (by the SCSL, which were included in its statute and accepted and further fleshed out in the *CDF* and *RUF* cases.)

267 *ICC Elements*, above note 67, art. 8, War Crimes, Introduction.

268 Above note 102, art. 8(2)(b)(iii).

would cause "widespread, long-term and severe damage to the natural environment."[269] Subparagraph 8(2)(b)(xxii) significantly develops war crimes law as it relates to rape and other forms of sexual assault, a victory for the various women's groups which lobbied for its inclusion, and subparagraph 8(2)(b)(xxvi) criminalizes the recruitment of children into armed forces—the salutary effects of which are being seen in the prosecution of Thomas Lubanga Dyilo of the Democratic Republic of the Congo before the ICC on this very charge.[270]

Paragraphs 8(2)(c) and (e) set out crimes which can be committed in the context of "armed conflicts not of an international character." Here, however, there are two categories: paragraph 8(2)(c) essentially incorporates Common Article 3 of the *Geneva Conventions*, while 8(2)(e) draws primarily on *AP II*. Moreover, paragraph 8(2)(f) makes clear that the more limited range of application of *AP II* is being maintained in the *Rome Statute*, as it loosely reproduces the applicability threshold language from the *Protocol* regarding "protracted armed conflict between governmental authorities and organized armed groups or between such groups," though it does not require control of territory by the organized armed groups. Paragraph 8(2)(e) also includes versions of "gender" crimes[271] and child soldier conscription[272] similar to those in 8(2)(b).

E. AGGRESSION

While in the twentieth century the idea of "aggression" as a crime to which individual responsibility could be attached became prominent, this development was in one way simply an offshoot of one of the largest and most controversial international law norms: the prohibition of the use of force by states against other states.[273] Indeed, one of the sticking points of coming up with an agreeable definition of the *crime* of aggression has been the need to disentangle individual responsibility

269 *Ibid.*, art. 8(2)(b)(iv).
270 *Lubanga* (ICC-01/04-01/06). Developments can be followed online: www.icc-cpi.int/menus/icc/situations%20and%20cases/situations/situation%20icc%200104/related%20cases/icc%200104%20200106/democratic%20republic%20of%20the%20congo?lan=en-GB.
271 Above note 167, art. 8(2)(e)(vi).
272 *Ibid.*, art. 8(2)(e)(vii).
273 See, generally, Hugh Kindred & Phillip Saunders, eds., *International Law: Chiefly as Interpreted and Applied in Canada*, 7th ed. (Toronto: Emond Montgomery, 2006) c. 15.

from aggression as a matter for which states can be responsible, under the doctrine of state responsibility.[274]

The notion of prosecuting individuals for the making of aggressive war was discussed in the aftermath of WW I, as the victorious Allies explored their appetite for prosecuting individuals for breaching various treaties of peace. In the end, this initiative was scuttled by both American antipathy to the idea and the finding of the "Commission on the Responsibility of the Authors of War and on the Enforcement of Penalties" that the making of aggressive war was not a crime.[275] However, there was a revival of the notion in the closing days of WW II, driven in part by intense desire to hold the leaders of the Nazi regime accountable for wartime atrocities, as well as some feeling that war crimes law as existed at the time might not be up to the task.[276] Article 6(a) of the concluded *Charter of the IMT*[277] contained a provision that roughly defined the crime:

> CRIMES AGAINST PEACE: namely planning, preparation, initiation or waging a war of aggression, or a war in violation of international treaties, agreements or assurances, or participation in a Common Plan or Conspiracy for the accomplishment of any of the foregoing.

The Nuremberg Tribunal embraced the legality of the prohibition of aggression, grounding its validity in the *Kellogg-Briand Pact* of 1928.[278] In a famous passage, it pronounced that the making of aggressive war "is not only an international crime; it is the supreme international crime differing only from other war crimes in that it contains within itself the accumulated evil of the whole."[279] Several defendants were convicted for aggression by both the Nuremberg and Tokyo tribunals, and in 1946, the UN General Assembly affirmed the principles of international law that the IMT had recognized,[280] providing some measure of legal weight to the existence of aggression as a crime under customary international law.

---

274 See Oscar Solera, *Defining the Crime of Aggression* (London: Cameron May, 2007).

275 *Report of the Commission to the Preliminary Peace Conference*, reprinted in (1920) 14 A.J.I.L. 95 at 118–20.

276 William Schabas, "The Unfinished Work of Defining Aggression: How Many Times Must the Cannonballs Fly, Before They Are Forever Banned?" in McGoldrick *et al.*, eds., above note 260, 123 at 126–27 [Schabas, "Cannonballs"].

277 Above note 85.

278 Can. T.S. 1929 No. 7.

279 *France et al. v. Göering et al.*, reprinted (1947), 41 A.J.I.L. 172 at 186.

280 UNGA Res. 95(I) (1946).

This was, however, to be one of the high points in the progress of developing the crime, as there was otherwise little post-war political will to pursue the matter, and there have to date been no other trials for aggression before national or international courts. Conditions remained mostly moribund until 1974, when a special committee that in 1954 had been charged with formulating a definition finally reported to the General Assembly. The special committee's definition was adopted in Resolution 3314 (XXIX) of 14 December 1974. The annex to the resolution contained the following definition of aggression: "use of armed force by a State against the sovereignty, territorial integrity or political independence of another State, or in any other manner inconsistent with the *Charter of the United Nations*." It also set out a number of acts which qualify as aggression, including invasion, military occupation, or annexation; bombardment or use of any weapon; blockade of ports/coasts; attack on land, sea, or aerial forces; the use of armed forces which are on the territory of another state by agreement, in violation of that agreement; a state allowing another state to use its territory to initiate aggression against a third state; and sending armed bands, groups irregulars, or mercenaries to accomplish any of the foregoing actions. In 1986, the ICJ ruled that parts of this definition reflect customary international law, particularly the sending of armed bands to attack another state,[281] and it has been convincingly suggested that the definition and list of qualifying acts, at least, do constitute the customary international law crime of aggression.[282] The ILC's 1996 *Draft Code of Crimes against the Peace and Security of Mankind* also contained a definition of aggression. Importantly, it confirmed the Nuremberg finding that the offence is really directed against persons who have sufficient power and authority to put a plan of aggressive war into effect,[283] which was reasonably common ground among the various proposals put forward for the ICC.

When the International Law Commission (ILC) submitted its draft statute for the ICC in 1994,[284] it included the (still undefined) crime of

---

281 *Nicaragua Case*, above note 188 at 103.

282 Cassese, *ICL*, above note 24 at 158. Professor Cassese also notes that the other two "crimes against peace" set out in the *IMT Charter* (i.e., engaging in war in violation of international treaties and conspiracy or planning a war) have not become part of customary international law; *ibid.*

283 "Draft Code," above note 263, Commentary to art. 16. See also the cases and materials cited in Yoram Dinstein, "The Distinctions between War Crimes and Crimes against Peace" in Yoram Dinstein & Mala Tabory, eds., *War Crimes in International Law* (The Hague: Nijhoff, 1996) 1 at 4–6.

284 "Draft Statute for the International Criminal Court" in *Report of the International Law Commission to the General Assembly on the work of its forty-sixth session*, UN Doc. A/CN 4/SER A/1994/Add 1 (Pt. 2).

aggression alongside genocide, crimes against humanity, and war crimes. However, both the question of whether aggression should be included in the *Rome Statute* at all, and if so, how it should be defined, proved to be among the most contentious aspects of the work of the Preparatory Committee[285] and the Rome negotiations.[286] The Rome negotiating text in fact included three different proposals,[287] the second of which was consistent with the elements of the 1974 definition described above, but none attracted sufficient agreement for inclusion. An eleventh-hour compromise resulted in the crime of aggression being included within the court's jurisdiction,[288] but subject to being defined by the Assembly of States Parties at a review seven years from the entry into force of the *Rome Statute*.[289] Work on the definition has since been delegated to a Special Working Group on the Crime of Aggression, which meets regularly and reports to the Annual Assembly of States Parties.[290]

While there are many aspects to the controversy around defining aggression, at its heart is the entanglement of the state and individual responsibility dimensions that it entails, as mentioned earlier. The role that the Security Council is to play has been at the flashpoint of this dilemma; even the three draft proposals before the Rome delegates had to be made "without prejudice to the discussion of the issue of the relationship of the Security Council with the ICC with respect to aggression."[291] Any prosecution for the crime of aggression must, one would think, emerge from a situation where one state has committed an act of aggression that would engage state responsibility.[292] Article 2(4) of the *UN Charter*[293] is the source of the prohibition against the use of force by states, and the Security Council is the body charged with rendering decisions on such matters. However, the highly politicized nature of the Security Council has prevented it from getting into the habit of making declarations of aggression, and in fact it has

---

285 See, for example, *Report of the Preparatory Committee on the Establishment of an International Criminal Court*, UN Doc. A/51/10, vol. I at 18–19, paras. 65–69.

286 von Habel & Robinson, above note 260 at 81–85.

287 *Draft Statute for the International Criminal Court*, UN Doc. A/CONF 183/2/Rev1 at 14–16.

288 *Rome Statute*, above note 19, art. 5(1).

289 *Ibid.*, art. 5(2).

290 Developments can be followed at the ICC website, online: www2.icc-cpi.int/Menus/ASP/Special+Working+Group+on+Aggression/.

291 Schabas, "Cannonballs," above note 276.

292 "Draft Code," commentary to art. 16, above note 263.

293 26 June 1945, 59 Stat. 1031, T.S. 993, 3 Bevans 1153, entered into force 24 October 1945.

done this on only a couple of occasions.[294] Article 5(2) of the *Rome Statute* states that the provision defining aggression and establishing the circumstances under which the ICC can exercise jurisdiction over it "shall be consistent with the relevant provisions of the *Charter of the United Nations*." One interpretation of this phrase that has been put forward is that the Security Council would have to make a determination that an act of aggression had occurred before the court could exercise jurisdiction,[295] and the permanent members of the Security Council preferred this view in Rome.[296] Yet other states are hostile to this idea, both for political reasons and because they are opposed to control over a judicial process being exercised by a political body.

This controversy has been ongoing throughout the deliberations of the Special Working Group, the latest report of which indicates substantial progress on the definition but significant disagreement on the role of the Security Council and when the ICC can assume jurisdiction.[297] In a more general sense, the evils of war being as apparent as they are, it seems unthinkable that the Nuremberg legacy should be undone. And yet in an era when even the legal status of the prohibition on the use of force seems uncertain, the ability to prosecute those who make aggressive war seems as likely to create international friction as it is to address pressing international criminal justice needs. With regard to the ICC, it is accurate to characterize the issue as "a time bomb, capable of transforming the Court and even jeopardising its future."[298]

Among the core international crimes, then, the crime of aggression has perhaps the largest amount of unlocked potential. Whether this is potential for good or for ill remains to be seen.

---

294 SC Res. 387 (1976), where it denounced the South African invasion of Angola; and possibly SC Res. 661 (1990), where it characterized Iraq's invasion of Kuwait similarly.

295 See A. Zimmermann, "Article 5," in Triffterer, ed., above note 156, 129 at 139*ff*; Paula Escarameia, "The ICC and the Security Council on Aggression: Overlapping Competencies?" in Mauro Politi & Giuseppe Nesi, eds., *The International Criminal Court and the Crime of Aggression* (Burlington, VT: Ashgate, 2004) at 133.

296 Including the US, which voted against the *Rome Statute* in part because this aspect of art. 5 was unclear (Leila N. Sadat, *The International Criminal Court and the Transformation of International Law: Justice for the New Millennium* (Ardsley, NY: Transnational, 2002) at 137, n. 38).

297 See *Report of the Special Working Group on the Crime of Aggression* (ICC-ASP/7/SWGCA/2), 20 February 2009, online: www2.icc-cpi.int/iccdocs/asp_docs/ICC-ASP-7-SWGCA-2%20English.pdf. The current draft can be found in Annex I to the Report.

298 Schabas, "Cannonballs," above note 276 at 140.

FURTHER READING

Genocide

AKHAVAN, PAYAM, "Enforcement of the *Genocide Convention*: A Challenge to Civilization" (1995) 8 Harv. Hum. Rts. J. 229

KRESS, CLAUS, "The Crime of Genocide under International Law" (2006) 6 Int'l. Crim. L. Rev. 461

LIPPMAN, M., "Genocide," in M.C. Bassiouni, ed., *International Criminal Law*, 2d ed., vol. I (Ardsley, NY: Transnational, 1999) 589

SCHABAS, WILLIAM, *Genocide in International Law: The Crime of Crimes*, 2d ed. (Cambridge: Cambridge University Press, 2009)

Crimes against Humanity

BASSIOUNI, M. CHERIF, *Crimes against Humanity in International Criminal Law*, 2d rev. ed. (Dordrecht: Kluwer Law International, 1999)

FENRICK, WILLIAM J., "Should Crimes against Humanity Replace War Crimes?" (1999) 37 Columbia J. Transnat'l L. 767

METTRAUX, GUÉNAËL, "Crimes against Humanity in the Jurisprudence of the International Criminal Tribunals for the Former Yugoslavia and for Rwanda" (2002) 43 Harvard Int'l L.J. 237

War Crimes

DINSTEIN, YORAM, & MALA TABORY, *War Crimes in International Law* (The Hague: Martinus Nijhoff, 1996)

HENCKAERTS, JEAN-MARIE *et al.*, *Customary International Humanitarian Law, Vol. I: Rules* (Cambridge: Cambridge University Press, 2005)

————, *Customary International Humanitarian Law, Vol. II: Practice* (Cambridge: Cambridge University Press, 2005)

MCCORMACK, TIMOTHY L.H., & GERRY J. SIMPSON, eds., *The Law of War Crimes: National and International Approaches* (The Hague: Kluwer, 1997)

Aggression

FERENCZ, BENJAMIN, *Defining International Aggression: The Search for World Peace* (Dobbs Ferry, NY: Oceana, 1975)

POLITI, MAURO, & GIUSEPPE NESI, eds., *The International Criminal Court and the Crime of Aggression* (Burlington, VT: Ashgate, 2004)

SCHUSTER, MATTHIAS, "The *Rome Statute* and the Crime of Aggression: A Gordian Knot in Search of a Sword" (2003) 14 Crim. L. Forum 1

SOLERA, OSCAR, *Defining the Crime of Aggression* (London: Cameron May, 2007)

DIRECT ENFORCEMENT AGAINST THE CORE CRIMES: INTERNATIONAL AND INTERNATIONALIZED CRIMINAL COURTS

A. INTRODUCTION

A truly international criminal law (ICL), with justice dispensed by international criminal courts, is undoubtedly one of the most important legal developments of the twentieth century. As noted in the historical survey of international criminal law in Chapter 1, the pre-and early-twentieth-century prototypical ICL proscribed certain acts, but directed the proscriptions towards states in the form of obligations to prevent certain conduct. The idea of an offender being liable under international law *and* being tried before an international court was realized, for all practical purposes,[1] only after WW II, in the form of the Nuremberg and Tokyo tribunals. While the political conditions created by the Cold War put international criminal justice on the back burner for some decades, in the late twentieth century the project was revived and has developed at what can only be viewed as an astonishing pace. The highest point, perhaps, has been the founding of the International Criminal Court (ICC), but the international community has appar-

---

1   The first international criminal prosecution is often said to be that of Peter von Hagenbach, who was tried, convicted, and executed in 1474 for atrocities committed during the occupation of Breisach; see Georg Schwarzenberger, *International Law as Applied by International Courts and Tribunals*, vol. II (London: Stevens & Sons, 1968) c. 39; M. Cherif Bassiouni, "From Versailles to Rwanda in Seventy-Five Years: The Need to Establish a Permanent International Criminal Court" (1997) 10 Harv. Hum. Rts. J. 11.

ently grown so comfortable with the use of criminal tribunals with international aspects that a number have been founded and more are proposed—to the extent that it is not unusual to hear commentators suggesting "tribunal fatigue."[2]

There can be no doubt that international criminal justice is indeed "an idea whose time has come,"[3] and while the other important piece is to create a climate that facilitates domestic prosecutions, there is every reason to believe that international prosecutions will continue to occur. The goal of this chapter is to survey and examine the salient features of the courts which have carried out and continue to carry out this important work. A look at the post–WW II prosecutions will be followed by treatment, in turn, of the United Nations *ad hoc* tribunals (former Yugoslavia and Rwanda), the ICC, and finally what are often referred to as "internationalized" or "hybrid" tribunals.

B. THE NUREMBERG AND TOKYO TRIBUNALS

The seeds for modern international criminal justice were planted just after the conclusion of WW I through efforts by the victorious Allied Powers to continue the vanquishing of Germany, in particular. This would be accomplished by the trials of senior state officials, including the Kaiser of Germany, for breaches of the laws of war, the "laws of humanity," and the making of aggressive war. The "Commission on the Responsibility of the Authors of War and on the Enforcement of Penalties," set up to investigate the causes of the war and to recommend solutions, proposed the creation of an Allied "High Tribunal" to try German war criminals.[4] It also suggested that, while there appeared to be no crime of aggression for which the Kaiser could be held liable, he could nonetheless be tried for the treaty breaches inherent in the beginning of the war. The latter measure, which appeared in article

---

2   Steven Ratner & Jason Abrams, *Accountability for Human Rights Atrocities in International Law: Beyond the Nuremberg Legacy*, 2d ed. (Oxford: Oxford University Press, 2001) at 318; Statement by Judge Fausto Pocar, President, International Criminal Tribunal for the former Yugoslavia to the Security Council on 4 June 2008, online: www.un.org/News/Press/docs/2008/sc9347.doc.htm.

3   William Schabas, "The International Criminal Court: An Idea Whose Time Has Come," John E. Read Memorial Lecture, delivered at Dalhousie University, 27 November 2007 (copy on file).

4   *Report of the Commission to the Preliminary Peace Conference*, reprinted in (1920) 14 A.J.I.L. 95.

227 of the *Treaty of Versailles*,[5] was foiled by the refusal of the government of the Netherlands (to which the Kaiser had fled) to extradite him. As for the crime of aggression, which was contemplated in articles 228 and 229 of the *Treaty of Versailles*, prosecution was abandoned, and the only prosecutions that ultimately took place were carried out by German courts, with questionable results.[6] An attempt to prosecute Turkish war crimes perpetrators[7] was thwarted by the 1923 *Treaty of Lausanne*,[8] which imposed a general amnesty. Later, in 1937, a League of Nations treaty for the formation of an international criminal court to try terrorist offences was concluded, but did not come into force for lack of state support.[9]

Nonetheless, the idea of international war crimes trials was re-invigorated when the world was faced with the problem of how to deal with the incredible monstrosities of the Nazi regime and acts committed during the Japanese occupation of parts of Asia. This was in no small part because the US, which had resisted many aspects of the Commission's proposals in 1920, was in 1945 an enthusiastic proponent of holding war crimes trials. American Justice Robert Jackson, who later became the US Chief Prosecutor at Nuremberg, took an active leadership role in convincing other Allied leaders (notably Winston Churchill) that fair and public trials would be preferable to summary execution of Nazi leaders, not least to legitimize the process in the eyes of the world and leave a fulsome historical record that would challenge future complacency. Accordingly, the UK, France, the US, and the Soviet Union met in London in 1945 and concluded the *London Agreement* of 8 August 1945 which established the *Charter for the International Military Tribunal* (*IMT Charter*).[10] The *IMT Charter* provided that individuals would be tried for "war crimes," "crimes against hu-

---

5   112 B.F.S.P. 1 (1919).

6   The so-called Leipzig trials, held by Germany (with some Allied input as to who would be tried) from 1921–23, tried a relatively small number of offenders and imposed light sentences. For a contemporary account, see Claud Mullins, *The Leipzig Trials: An Account of the Criminals' Trials and a Study of German Mentality* (London: H.F. & G. Witherby, 1921).

7   The initial peace treaty between the Allies and Turkey, the *Treaty of Sèvres*, provided for the establishment of an international war crimes tribunal and an *ad hoc* court to deal with the Armenian massacre (reprinted at (1921), 15 A.J.I.L. 179, arts. 227 and 230).

8   *Treaty of Lausanne between Principal Allied and Associated Powers and Turkey* (1923), 28 L.N.T.S. 11.

9   See Vespasian Pella, "Towards an International Criminal Court" (1950) 44 A.J.I.L. 37.

10   82 U.N.T.S. 279.

manity," and "crimes against peace," the latter of which was an updated version of "the making of aggressive war" proposals from the 1920s.[11]

The trial of the major Nazi war criminals—Hermann Göering, Rudolf Hess, and Alfred Rosenberg, among others—as well as a half-dozen indicted "criminal organizations," took place over ten months between 1945 and 1946. The court was composed of one judge (and one alternate judge) from each of the four *London Agreement* states, presided over by UK Lord Justice Geoffrey Lawrence. In the court's final judgment,[12] rendered in 1946, nineteen of the individual defendants were convicted and three of the indicted organizations were declared criminal organizations under article 9 of the *IMT Charter*, while three individual defendants and three organizations were acquitted and exonerated, respectively. A full dozen of the convicted individuals were sentenced to death, the rest to various terms of imprisonment. Perhaps equally weighty, however, were the tribunal's statements on international criminal law, which established principles that underpin current international criminal justice initiatives, and generally have had significant impact ever since.

Most importantly, the tribunal ruled that, contrary to the historical Westphalian construct of international law, individuals had legal obligations under international law and could be held liable for breaches of those obligations. It famously stated, "That international law imposes duties and liabilities upon individuals as well as upon states has long been recognized. Crimes against international law are committed by men, not by abstract entities, and only by punishing individuals who commit such crimes can the provisions of international law be enforced."[13] It also validated article 7 of the *IMT Charter*, which purported to strip away any immunity from prosecution or mitigation of sentence that extended from the perpetrator being a state official. The principle of state immunity,

> which under certain circumstances, protects the representatives of a State, cannot be applied to acts which are condemned as criminal by international law . . . . [T]he very essence of the Charter is that individuals have international duties which transcend the national obligations of obedience imposed by the individual state.[14]

Finally, the tribunal engaged in extensive fact-finding regarding Germany's acts of aggression towards other states, and ruled that ag-

---

11   These crimes are discussed in more detail in Chapter 3.
12   *France et al. v. Göering et al.*, reprinted in (1947), 41 A.J.I.L. 172 [*Göering*].
13   *Ibid.* at 220–21.
14   *Ibid.* at 221.

gression was indeed a crime under both customary and treaty-based international law, relying in particular on breaches of the *Kellogg-Briand Pact*[15] of 1928 to ground this finding. "[T]o initiate a war of aggression," it ruled, ". . . is the supreme international crime."[16]

In January 1946, the major Allied Powers issued the "Potsdam Declaration," which declared their determination to conduct trials of high-ranking Japanese officials for crimes committed during the occupation of parts of Asia. The International Military Tribunal for the Far East (IMTFE) was set up pursuant to the *Tokyo Charter*,[17] an executive order issued by General Douglas MacArthur, the Supreme Commander of the Allied forces in Japan. The *Tokyo Charter* was similar to the *IMT Charter* and provided for prosecution of the same crimes,[18] as well as some additional available charges of murder attendant upon wartime activities. The two-and-a-half-year trial of twenty-eight defendants was heard by a bench of eleven judges, including Judges Pal and Jaranilla of the post-war independent states of India and the Philippines, respectively. The bench was presided over by Judge Sir William Webb of Australia, and Justice E. Stuart McDougall of Canada also served as a judge. The remaining judges were from China, France, New Zealand, the Netherlands, the UK, the US, and the USSR, all states to which Japan had surrendered.

In the tribunal's ultimate judgment, all of the defendants who remained at the end of the trial[19] were convicted of at least some of the charges against them, and seven were sentenced to death. In terms of the legal basis for the judgment, the tribunal adopted the findings of the Nuremberg IMT nearly in their entirety, including the controversial finding that aggression existed as a crime at the relevant times and did not violate the *nullum crimen* principle.[20] The decision spent some significant time on the crime of conspiracy to commit aggression, and found (by way of the "joint enterprise" doctrine)[21] that there had, be-

---

15   (1928), 94 L.N.T.S. 57.

16   *Göering*, above note 12 at 186.

17   (1946), 4 Bevans 20.

18   Though art. 6(b) of the *IMT Charter*, above note 10, included a non-exhaustive list of acts constituting war crimes, while art. 5 of the *Tokyo Charter*, *ibid.*, simply declared as criminal "violations of the laws or customs of war." Also, the *Tokyo Charter*'s definition of crimes against humanity (art. 5(c)) did not include religion as one of the grounds of persecution, as did art. 6(c) of the *IMT Charter*.

19   Two having died in custody and one declared unfit to stand trial.

20   Though the Nuremberg IMT had also found that, in any event, the prohibition on *ex-post facto* crimes was not firmly established as an international law norm at the relevant time (*Göering*, above note 12 at 217).

21   Neil Boister, "Aggression at the Tokyo War Crimes Trial", ISRCL Conference Proceedings 2007, online: www.isrcl.org/Papers/2007/Boister.pdf.

ginning in 1931, been a long-term and overarching conspiracy in the Japanese government to conquer the whole of East Asia—the kind of finding the Nuremberg IMT had rejected. The IMTFE also developed the principle of command responsibility, which did not play a significant role in the IMT's findings.

While the development of international criminal law has surpassed, or in some circumstances deviated from, the findings at Nuremberg, its role as the antecedent of twenty-first century international criminal justice and the foundation of the moral legacy underpinning this project is unimpeachable.[22] There are certainly criticisms, with varying degrees of validity, including the political optics of having a court set up by the major victorious powers in the war to try the losers and having the judges and prosecutors drawn from these countries. The findings by both tribunals that the crimes of both aggression and crimes against humanity were not *ex post facto* have been attacked.[23] Moreover, some of the German conduct that could have been the subject of indictments (such as saturation bombing and some aspects of the submarine warfare) was selectively passed over due to Allied wartime practices that were uncomfortably within the range of the criminalized conduct. However, on the whole, the historical record bears out that the trials were conducted fairly, with the defendants having access to a reasonable assortment of procedural protections under article 16 of the *IMT Charter*.[24] Moreover, one cannot deny the salutary precedential value of a system that, for the first time, imposed criminal liability on high-ranking individuals by a court that, in historical perspective, represented the aspirations of the international community.

The IMTFE, by contrast, has fared more poorly through the historical lens, often cited as one of the most prominent examples of "victor's justice."[25] The trial process has been viewed as particularly flawed, stemming at least in part from poor leadership by Judge Webb. The judges' findings of fact regarding the operations and dynamics of the Japanese government were, at best, crude and may have reflected a de-

---

22   See Matthew Lippman, "Nuremberg: Forty-Five Years Later" (1991) 7 Conn. J. Int'l L. 1; M. Cherif Bassiouni, "The Nuremberg Legacy" in M. Cherif Bassiouni, ed., *International Criminal Law*, 2d ed. (Ardsley, NY: Transnational, 1999) vol. 3 at 195.

23   See Chapter 3, and Bernard V.A. Röling & Antonio Cassese, *The Tokyo Trial and Beyond* (Cambridge: Polity, 1993) at 3–5. See also Jonathan A. Bush, "'The Supreme . . . Crime' and its Origins: The Lost Legislative History of the Crime of Aggressive War" (2002) 102 Colum. L. Rev. 2324.

24   Above note 10.

25   See Richard Minear, *Victor's Justice: The Tokyo War Crimes Trial* (Princeton: Princeton University Press, 1971).

gree of predetermination of some issues. In particular, it is generally agreed that the finding of the overarching conspiracy of aggression among the defendants was largely without basis.[26] There is no doubt that many of the convictions were properly made and consistent with the pressing need for accountability in the post-war period. However, it is most likely to be regarded with the kind of dubiousness that Professor Bassiouni expressed when he wrote, "Tokyo . . . was a precedent that legal history can only consider with a view not to repeat it."[27]

C. THE UNITED NATIONS *AD HOC* TRIBUNALS

1) The International Criminal Tribunal for the former Yugoslavia (ICTY)

a) Creation and History

The bloody dissolution of the former eastern bloc state of Yugoslavia in the early 1990s has been well-documented. Secessionist impulses among populations divided among ethnic and religious lines, which had been quiescent during the Cold War, spurred a series of political developments that devolved into armed conflict, the establishment of modern-day concentration camps, "ethnic cleansing," and mass atrocities, sexual and otherwise. As the full extent of the conflict became known, public commentary began to suggest that the Nuremberg precedent be rejuvenated and that international war crimes trials be held.[28] Both the Conference for Security and Cooperation in Europe (CSCE) and the United Nations took up this challenge and began conducting investigations with an eye towards prosecution. In particular, the UN Security Council convened a "Commission of Experts,"[29] and these personnel engaged in extensive fact-finding in the former Yugoslavia.[30] In an interim

---

26   See, for example, Marius B. Jansen, *The Making of Modern Japan* (Cambridge, MA: Belknap Press of Harvard University Press, 2000) at 673.

27   M. Cherif Bassiouni, "Nuremberg Forty Years After" (1986) Proc. A.S.I.L. 64. Though Professor Boister points out that "Bassiouni's comment . . . is an invitation not to ignore the trial but to learn from its mistakes" (Boister, above note 21 at 1).

28   See M. Klarin, "Nuremberg Now" *Borba* (16 May 1991), reprinted (in English translation) in *The Path to the Hague: Selected Documents on the Origin of the ICTY* (The Hague: ICTY, 1996) at 43–45.

29   Pursuant to SC Res. 780 (1992).

30   See M. Cherif Bassiouni, "The United Nations Commission of Experts Established Pursuant to Security Council Resolution 780" (1994) 88 A.J.I.L. 784;

report,[31] the Commission called for the creation of a war crimes tribunal, echoing debates which had been going on in the UN, and towards which the United States, in particular, was favourably disposed.

With proposals in hand from various states, including Canada[32] and several NGOs, the UN Secretary-General prepared a report[33] proposing that the Security Council proceed to establish a criminal tribunal by way of a resolution. Appended to the report was a draft statute for the tribunal,[34] which the Security Council adopted without changes.[35] Despite support for the initiative among many states, it was controversial whether the Security Council was competent, as an exercise of its powers, to enforce peace and security under Chapter VII of the *UN Charter*,[36] to set up a court—not least because of the compulsory nature of the tribunal's jurisdiction and what is now called the "vertical" relationship between the tribunal and states, which compels the latter to cooperate with the former. The Preamble of Resolution 827 was bullish on this point, laying out that "as an *ad hoc* measure by the Council," the creation of the tribunal would act to combat and end the crimes being committed, "ensure such violations are halted and effectively redressed," and "contribute to the restoration and maintenance of peace." This was in marked contrast to the Nuremberg precedent, which had been based on "an essentially retributive premise" and operated as a function of the vanquishing of the Axis regimes.[37] The ICTY has consistently justified its missions by underscoring the link between the prosecution of atrocious crimes and the maintenance of international peace and security.[38]

The legal challenge to the Council's bringing the tribunal into being came immediately, as part of preliminary motions in the prosecution of the first offender, Dusko Tadić. Tadić, a low-level Bosnian Serb thug who had been transferred to the tribunal by Germany in 1995,

---

William J. Fenrick, "In the Field with UNCOE: Investigating Atrocities in the Territory of Former Yugoslavia" (1994) 34 RIDMDG 33.

31   UN Doc. S/25272, 10 February 1993 at para. 74.

32   UN Doc. S/25594, 13 April 1993.

33   UN Doc. S/25704 (1993).

34   See, generally, Larry Johnson, "Ten Years Later: Reflections on the Drafting" (2004) 2 JICJ 368.

35   SC Res. 827 (1993).

36   Can T.S. 1945 No. 7.

37   William Schabas, *The UN International Criminal Tribunals: The Former Yugoslavia, Rwanda and Sierra Leone* (Cambridge: Cambridge University Press, 2006) at 8 [Schabas, *UN Tribunals*].

38   See, for example, *Nikolić* (IT-94-2-AR73), Decision on Interlocutory Appeal Concerning Legality of Arrest, Appeals Chamber, 5 June 2003.

was the first to be prosecuted essentially because the still under-resourced tribunal had only a few relatively unimportant individuals in custody and little cooperation in obtaining more, but was compelled to move forward with its work. However, Tadić provided the tribunal with its first, and ultimately one of its most significant, challenges by contesting its jurisdiction to try him on the basis that the Security Council was not competent to set up the court. A cautious finding by the Trial Chamber[39] that it did not have the authority to determine the legality of its own creation was overruled by the Appeals Chamber, which ruled[40] that it did have both the power to review Security Council actions and *compétence de la compétence*. It went on to determine that the Security Council had legally created the tribunal as a valid exercise of its Chapter VII powers, specifically under article 41 of the *UN Charter*, which authorized "measures not involving the use of armed force."[41]

The formal end of the war in the former Yugoslavia in 1995, the conclusion of the *Dayton Agreement*,[42] and increased willingness by North Atlantic Treaty Organization (NATO) forces to arrest indictees, all spurred on the galvanization of the tribunal's work, and the tribunal has had an extremely productive tenure thereafter. A significant event was the indictment of former Serbian dictator Slobodan Milošević by Prosecutor Louise Arbour (later a Justice of the Supreme Court of Canada) — the first criminal indictment of a sitting head of state. Milošević, a former lawyer who opted to defend himself, denied that the tribunal had any jurisdiction over him and characterized his prosecution as a political attempt by the West to cover up its own complicity in the breakup of Yugoslavia. His generally obstructive behaviour, along with the determination of the Trial Chamber to ensure that his trial was perceived to be fair, caused the trial itself to drag out over two-and-a-half years, until Milošević passed away in 2006.[43] The tribunal has also

---

39   *Tadić* (IT-94-1-T), Decision on the Defence Motion on Jurisdiction, Trial Chamber, 10 August 1995.

40   *Tadić* (IT-94-1-AR72), Decision on the Defence Motion for Interlocutory Appeal on Jurisdiction, Appeals Chamber, 2 October 1995.

41   See, generally, Colin Warbrick, "The International Criminal Tribunal for Yugoslavia: The Decision of the Appeals Chamber on the Interlocutory Appeal on Jurisdiction in the *Tadić* Case" (1996) 45 I.C.L.Q. 691.

42   Also known as the *Dayton Peace Accords*, this 1995 agreement between the Republic of Bosnia and Herzegovina, the Republic of Croatia, and the Federal Republic of Yugoslavia brought the main part of the Yugoslavia conflict to an end. The agreement and associated documents can be found online: www1.umn.edu/humanrts/icty/dayton/daytonaccord.html.

43   See, generally, Tom Dannenbaum, "The Milošević Trial" (2008) 33 Yale J. Int'l L. 513; M. Scharf, "The Legacy of the Milošević Trial" (2003) 37 New Eng. L. Rev.

had a major impact on international criminal law jurisprudence, as it (along with the International Criminal Tribunal for Rwanda (ICTR)) has put flesh on the bones of the Nuremberg precedent and established a significant body of caselaw dealing with international crimes. It also developed important new legal tools for dealing with prosecutions of these crimes, which have gone on to be accepted by states and to pervade both national and international practice. The most prominent example is the concept of "joint criminal enterprise," which was first set out by the Appeals Chamber in the *Tadić* appeal.[44] This principle of liability allows individuals to be convicted of crimes where they participate with others in criminal activities having a crime as a common purpose, and that purpose is carried out, even if the individual in question does not participate in the actual commission of the crime or has no knowledge of its commission.[45]

As of March 2009, the tribunal had completed proceedings in the cases of 117 accused persons: ten were acquitted, fifty-eight were convicted and sentenced, and thirteen were transferred to a national jurisdiction which was willing to try them,[46] including new special war crimes chambers created in Bosnia and Herzegovina, Croatia, and the Republic of Serbia.[47] The transfer of individual accused persons to national courts, accomplished under Rule 11 *bis* of the *Rules of Procedure and Evidence*,[48] is a major component of the Security Council's "completion strategy" for the tribunal.[49] In Resolution 1503, the Security Council obliged the Prosecutor to finish investigations by 2004, and

---

915. Another event of some significance was the Prosecutor's decision to commission a preliminary assessment of whether the NATO bombing of Kosovo in 1999 should be investigated by the ICTY. The report of the committee established for this purpose (reprinted at (2000) 38 I.L.M. 1257), which concluded that no investigation was warranted, was controversial; see various articles in (2001) 12 E.J.I.L. See also William J. Fenrick, "The Law Applicable to Targeting and Proportionality after Operation Allied Force" (2000) 3 Y.B. Int'l Human L. 53.

44 *Tadić* (IT-94-1-A), Judgment, 15 July 1999 at para. 220.

45 See, generally, Steven Powles, "Joint Criminal Enterprise: Criminal Liability by Prosecutorial Ingenuity and Judicial Creativity?" (2004) 2 JICJ 606; Kai Ambos, "Joint Criminal Enterprise and Command Responsibility" (2007) 5 JICJ 159.

46 See "Key Figures of ICTY Cases" on the Tribunal's website: www.icty.org/sections/TheCases/KeyFigures.

47 See Section E(6), below in this chapter.

48 Online: www.icty.org/sid/136 [*RPE*].

49 See Dominic Raab, "Evaluating the ICTY and Its Completion Strategy" (2005) 3 JICJ 82; Fausto Pocar, "Completion or Continuation Strategy? Appraising Problems and Possible Developments in Building the Legacy of the ICTY" (2008) 6 JICJ 655.

the tribunal itself to finish trials by 2008 and appeals by 2010. Another measure to support this timeline was the appointment of judges *ad litem* to the tribunal, in order to increase the trial capacity.[50] The Prosecution managed to complete investigations in 2005, but it is currently unclear as to whether the tribunal will be able to adhere to its other deadlines. The chances of accomplishing the major goals the Prosecutor initially set were recently enhanced when the government of Serbia captured and surrendered to the tribunal former Bosnian Serb President Radovan Karadzic, one of the "most-wanted" indictees.[51]

b) Structure

The ICTY is a "subsidiary organ" of the UN Security Council, pursuant to articles 7(2), 8, and 29 of the *UN Charter*,[52] and is located in The Hague. Its three organs are the Chambers, the Office of the Prosecutor, and the Registry. The Trial Chambers generally sit in panels of three judges, while the Appeals Chamber (of which the President of the Tribunal is an *ex officio* member) sits in panels of either three or five. The Office of the Prosecutor has gone from having a skeleton staff and few resources in 1994 to a large professional and support staff with significant funding from the UN. The Prosecutor is charged with "investigating and prosecuting" and is independent of any influence from the Chambers, any national government, or "any other source."[53] The operating[54] Prosecutors to date have been Sir Richard Goldstone of South Africa, Louise Arbour of Canada, Carla del Ponte of Switzerland, and Serge Brammertz of Belgium. The Registry is responsible for the administrative management of the court and provides administrative support to both the Prosecution and the Chambers. It handles tribunal media communications and outreach, and is also in charge of security, victim services, and the detention unit.

---

50   Canadian law professor Sharon A. Williams served as a judge *ad litem* at the tribunal and former Justice Canada official Kimberly Prost is currently a judge *ad litem*. Also, Justice Jules Deschênes served as judge of the Appeals Chamber from 1993–1997.

51   "Radovan Karadzic, Europe's Most Wanted Man, Arrested for War Crimes" *The Guardian* (22 July 2008), online: www.guardian.co.uk/world/2008/jul/22/war-crimes.internationalcrime. For an early comment, see **Göran** Sluiter, "Karadzic On Trial: Two Procedural Problems" (2008) 6 JICJ 617.

52   Above note 36.

53   *ICTY Statute*, UN Doc. S/25704, art. 16.

54   The first Prosecutor appointed by the Security Council was Venezuelan Ramon Escovar, who resigned the post as of the time he was scheduled to take it up.

c) Jurisdiction

Article 1 of the *ICTY Statute*[55] indicates that the tribunal was set up to prosecute "serious violations of international humanitarian law."[56] Yet the ICTY's subject matter jurisdiction is broader than what is normally understood to be the content of international humanitarian law. Articles provide for jurisdiction over grave breaches of the *Geneva Conventions*[57] of 1949, violations of the laws or customs of war, genocide, and crimes against humanity.[58] In one of the most progressive findings in modern international criminal law, the tribunal decided in the *Tadić* appeal that article 3's conferral of jurisdiction over violations of the laws or customs of war allowed for prosecution where the offences were committed in an internal armed conflict, rather than just in international armed conflicts as had been understood at the time of the *Statute*'s drafting.[59]

Regarding other heads of jurisdiction, the ICTY has jurisdiction over the above-referenced crimes where committed anywhere on the territory of the former Yugoslavia (territorial jurisdiction)[60] if committed after 1 January 1991 (temporal jurisdiction).[61] In terms of "personal jurisdiction," jurisdiction may be exercised only over "natural persons,"[62] which excludes liability for corporate bodies or other organizations. Also noteworthy is article 9(1) of the *ICTY Statute*, which states that the tribunal has concurrent jurisdiction with national courts over the crimes under its purview, but that it has "primacy" over such courts. The effect of this is that the tribunal may usurp the jurisdiction of the courts of any state which are trying a perpetrator whose crimes fall under the ICTY's jurisdiction and try the perpetrator itself.[63] While in its origin this provision seems to have been geared towards ensuring that states did not attempt to shelter accused persons,[64] it has effectively been shelved as the tribunal moves through its completion strategy

---

55   Above note 53.

56   See also S/RES/827 (1993) at para. 2.

57   (1950), 75 U.N.T.S. 31, 85, 135, and 287.

58   *ICTY Statute*, above note 53, arts. 2–5.

59   See Christopher Greenwood, "International Humanitarian Law and the *Tadić* Case" (1996) 7 E.J.I.L. 265.

60   *ICTY Statute*, above note 53, art. 8.

61   *Ibid.*, arts. 1 and 8. It was the fact that the temporal jurisdiction is open-ended that permitted consideration of NATO's bombing of Kosovo in 1999 (see above note 43).

62   *ICTY Statute*, above note 53, art. 6.

63   The test for the propriety of deferral is in Rule 9 of the *RPE*, above note 48.

64   Schabas, *UN Tribunals*, above note 37 at 126.

and is currently more interested in actively encouraging states to take jurisdiction over offenders.

2) The International Criminal Tribunal for Rwanda (ICTR)

a) Creation and History

Accounts[65] of the horrific atrocities that took place in the African country of Rwanda during 1994 generally begin with the deaths of the Presidents of Rwanda and Burundi in a suspicious plane crash on 6 April 1994. Those deaths, immediately suspected to be assassinations, took place against the backdrop of ethnic conflict between the minority Tutsi and majority Hutu populations of Rwanda that had been going on since the country's independence from Belgium in 1962. A UN peacekeeping force had been in Rwanda since August 1993 to assist in the transition to a governmental power-sharing arrangement between the two groups after a war from 1990–93. The death of President Habyarimana, however, spurred on the work of radical Hutus who, in cooperation with government officials, began a campaign of "extermination" of Tutsi and moderate Hutus that resulted in the deaths of approximately 800,000 people and countless acts of barbarity and sexual violence.

The UN Security Council viewed itself as essentially powerless to stop the butchery, and the peacekeepers were not permitted to engage in the conflict and were mostly withdrawn.[66] The Council did, however, issue a series of resolutions[67] deploring the violence—which it eventually identified as appearing to be genocide[68]—and signalling the possibility of using an international criminal law mechanism to deal with perpetrators. In June 1994 it established a three-person commission of experts to investigate the massacres, similar to what had been done in Yugoslavia.[69] In its September 1994 preliminary report, the commission recommended[70] that the jurisdiction of the ICTY be

---

65   See, generally, Philip Gourevitch, *We Wish to Inform You That Tomorrow We Will Be Killed with Our Families* (New York: Farrar, Straus & Giroux, 1998).

66   For an account by the Canadian head of the UN peacekeeping mission, see Romeo Dallaire, *Shake Hands with the Devil: The Failure of Humanity in Rwanda* (New York: Carroll & Graf, 2005).

67   UN Doc. S/RES/918 (1994), UN Doc. S/RES/925 (1994). See also UN Doc. S/PRST/1994/21.

68   UN Doc. S/RES/925 (1994).

69   See L. Sunga, "The Commission of Experts on Rwanda and the Creation of the International Criminal Tribunal for Rwanda" (1995) 16 H.R.L.J. 121.

70   UN Doc. S/1994/1125.

expanded so as to allow it to hear cases arising from the Rwandan conflict, and by this time the government of Rwanda had itself requested
that the Security Council set up a tribunal.[71] A revised proposal for
an independent court with its own trial chambers, but which shared
a prosecutor and an appeals chamber with the ICTY, was eventually
accepted and passed by the Security Council. This was in spite of the
fact that the government of Rwanda, which happened to be sitting as a
non-permanent member of the Council at the time, eventually opposed
the proposal on numerous grounds. These included the fact that the
tribunal's temporal jurisdiction would be limited to 1994, rather than
encompassing events leading back to 1990 as the Rwandan government
had proposed, and the fact that the proposed statute did not include the
death penalty. In the end, Rwanda's was the only vote against the establishment of the tribunal, which was accomplished in November 1994.[72]
However, friction between the government of Rwanda and both the UN
and the tribunal has continued to dog the ICTR's efforts.

It took some time for the ICTR to get up and running, despite its
integration with the ICTY, and it was mid-1995 before the seat of the
court was established at Arusha, Tanzania (to the consternation of
the government of Rwanda) and the Trial Chamber judges were appointed. From an operational point of view, the ICTR has travelled a
much rougher path than the ICTY. Its set-up and initial prosecutions
were hamstrung by lack of sufficient funding, and though this slowly
improved, trials have continued to proceed at a slow pace. By 1996–97,
it had become clear that some administrative problems were due to
mismanagement, incompetence, and even corruption, and an investigation by the UN Office of Internal Oversight Services resulted in the re-
signations of both the Registrar and the Deputy Prosecutor. Unethical
defence lawyers were at one point splitting legal aid funds with their
clients;[73] and ethical defence lawyers have complained that the fair trial
rights of defendants are compromised by translation problems,[74] inability to meet with clients, and problematic evidentiary rulings.[75] For

---

71   UN Doc. S/1994/1115.
72   UN Doc. S/RES/955 (1994) [*ICTR Statute*].
73   Schabas, *UN Tribunals*, above note 37 at 30.
74   Due in part to the fact that the tribunal's "working languages" are English and
     French (*ICTR Statute*, above note 72, art. 31), but proceedings must be trans-
     lated into Kinyarwanda.
75   David Paciocco, "Defending Rwandans Accused before the ICTR: A Venture Full
     of Pitfalls and Lessons for the International Criminal Law" in Hélène Dumont
     & Anne-Marie Boisvert, eds., *The Highway to the International Criminal Court:
     All Roads Lead to Rome* (Montreal: Éditions Thémis, 2004) at 97.

their part, the Chambers have tried to manage the proceedings fairly, and at one point the Appeals Chamber even ordered the case against a prominent *génocidaire*, Jean-Bosco Barayagwiza, dismissed, and ordered his release, because of the inordinate length of his pretrial detention.[76] This move damaged relations between the tribunal and the government of Rwanda, which promptly suspended its cooperation and thus made access to witnesses and evidence impossible. Having heard further factual submissions from the Prosecutor, a reconstituted Appeals Chamber reversed the decision[77] and instead gave Barayagwiza a reduction in his ultimate sentence—a finding which has not escaped critical comment.[78]

On the other hand, the ICTR has enjoyed some remarkable successes. This is particularly true with regards to one of the most important missions of international criminal justice: bringing to trial and convicting the political and military leaders who masterminded atrocities. The tribunal has obtained custody over and tried many of the major Rwandan figures who presided over the genocide, and most recently convicted Colonel Théoneste Bagosora, who was Director of Cabinet in the Rwandan Ministry of Defence.[79] Indeed, the ICTR has been a major mover in the development of international caselaw on genocide, starting with the guilty plea of former Prime Minister Jean Kambanda in 1998, which provided a fairly decisive finding that genocide had actually occurred in Rwanda.[80] This was followed by the first-ever international conviction for genocide, in the case of Jean-Paul Akeyesu.[81] *Akayesu* was a landmark decision, not just for the fact that it was an application of the *Genocide Convention*,[82] but for the robust view of genocide taken by the tribunal, as well as for the findings (that have

---

76 *Barayagwiza* (ICTR-97-19-AR72), Decision, Appeals Chamber, 3 November 1999.

77 *Barayagwiza* (ICTR-97-19-AR72), Decision (Prosecutor's Request for Review or Reconsideration), Appeals Chamber, 31 March 2000.

78 See William Schabas, "*Barayagwiza v. Prosecutor*: Commentary" in André Klip & Göran Sluiter, eds., *Annotated Leading Cases of International Criminal Tribunals: The International Criminal Tribunal for Rwanda 2000–2001*, vol. 6 (Antwerp: Intersentia, 2003) 261.

79 *Bagosora et al.* ("*Military I Trial*"), (ICTR-98-41-T), Decision, Trial Chamber, 18 December 2008.

80 The ICTR now takes judicial notice that genocide occurred in Rwanda in 1994, though not without controversy; see Ralph Mamiya, "Taking Judicial Notice of Genocide? The Problematic Law and Policy of the Karemera Decision" (2007) 25 Wis. Int'l L.J. 1.

81 *Akayesu* (ICTR-96-4-T), Judgment, Trial Chamber, 2 September 1998.

82 78 U.N.T.S. 277, entered into force 12 January 1951.

subsequently been built upon by both tribunals as well as the *Rome Statute*[83]) that genocide can be committed by way of rape and other sexual violence. Indeed, development of the law on the latter topic is generally viewed as one of the foremost contributions of the ICTR to international criminal law jurisprudence.[84]

As of March 2009, the ICTR had completed the cases of thirty-five accused persons. It has convicted nineteen individuals, acquitted five, transferred proceedings to national jurisdictions in two cases (both to France), and had the remaining cases dismissed for various reasons, including withdrawal of charges and death of the accused. There were twenty-three people on trial and eight awaiting trial.[85] It has tried and convicted many of the ringleaders of the genocide, and its record in so doing is likely superior to that of the ICTY. Like the ICTY, it is set to wind down under the Security Council's "completion strategy"[86] and has slowly begun the process of transferring some cases to other states;[87] none have been transferred to Rwanda even though this had been contemplated, due in no small part to continuing concerns on the part of the ICTR regarding fair trials and the possibility of accused persons facing the death penalty or life imprisonment in solitary confinement.[88]

---

83   *Rome Statute of the International Criminal Court*, 2187 U.N.T.S. 3, reprinted at (1998) 37 I.L.M. 1999, entered into force 1 July 2002, online: www.icc-cpi.int/library/about/officialjournal/Rome_Statute_English.pdf [*Rome Statute*].

84   See Sherie Russell-Brown, "Rape as an Act of Genocide" (2003) 21 Berkeley J. Int'l L. 350.

85   See "Status of ICTR Detainees," online: http://69.94.11.53/ENGLISH/factsheets/detainee.htm.

86   See Erik Møse, "The ICTR's Completion Strategy: Challenges and Possible Solutions" (2008) 6 JICJ 667.

87   An application to transfer one case to Norway was refused by the tribunal, essentially because Norway had not formally implemented the crime of genocide into its domestic law (*Bagaragaza* (ICTR-05-86-AR11 *bis*), Decision on Rule 11 *bis* Appeal, Appeals Chamber, 30 August 2006). Bagaragaza was then transferred to the Netherlands, but the Trial Chamber revoked that transfer when the Dutch courts ruled that they did not have jurisdiction over a similarly situated defendant (see *Bagaragaza* (ICTR-05-86-11 *bis*), Decision on Prosecutor's Extremely Urgent Motion for Revocation of the Referral to the Kingdom of the Netherlands Pursuant to Rule 11 *bis* (F) and (G), Trial Chamber, 17 August 2007).

88   See, for example, *Munyakazi* (ICTR-97-36-R11 *bis*), Decision on the Prosecution's Appeal against Decision on the Referral under Rule 11 *bis*, Appeals Chamber, 8 October 2008, which is the latest in a series of cases denying transfer applications.

b) Structure

Like the ICTY, the ICTR is a "subsidiary organ" of the UN Security Council, pursuant to articles 7(2), 8, and 29 of the *UN Charter*.[89] It is located not in Rwanda itself, but in Arusha, Tanzania, a decision which was based on the devastation of Rwanda and the need to have the tribunal sit in a country with at least functioning infrastructure.[90] It has the same three organs—Chambers, Prosecutor, and Registry—as the ICTY. Initially the ICTR shared both an Appeals Chamber and Prosecutor with the ICTY, but in 2003, a separate prosecutor for the ICTR (Gambian judge and lawyer Hassan Bubacar Jallow) was appointed, and the new Office of the Prosecutor set up in Kigali, Rwanda. The Trial Chambers (two initially, three since 1998) sit in panels of three judges each, and as with the ICTY, there recently have been *ad litem* judges appointed to speed up the progress of prosecutions towards the completion date. Two judges from the ICTR were appointed in 2000 to sit as the ICTR Appeals Chamber, which is based out of the Hague but conducts court proceedings in Arusha.

c) Jurisdiction

In terms of subject matter jurisdiction, the ICTR shares with the ICTY jurisdiction over genocide and crimes against humanity.[91] There are some variations in the jurisdictional reach over these crimes; in particular, while the ICTY may prosecute persons only for crimes against humanity when committed in armed conflict, the ICTR may pursue them whenever committed as part of a widespread or systematic attack against any civilian population. Additionally, the ICTR's jurisdiction over war crimes is limited to violations of Common Article 3 of the *Geneva Conventions*[92] and of *Additional Protocol II (AP II)*,[93] which confines it to war crimes committed in non-international armed conflict.

---

89   Above note 36.

90   The location of the tribunal has received criticism as having made it too remote from the people of Rwanda to properly administer justice to and about them; see José Alvarez, "Crimes of Hate/Crimes of State: Lessons from Rwanda" (1999) 24 Yale J. Int'l L. 365. It has also made for logistical difficulties with such practicalities as getting witnesses out of Rwanda and before the tribunal. The UN Secretary-General has acknowledged the desirability of having such tribunals located in the state with which they are dealing, which facilitates the role of victims and aids in national reconciliation and rebuilding; see *The Rule of Law and Transitional Justice in Conflict and Post-Conflict Societies: Report of the Secretary-General*, UN Doc. S/2004/616.

91   *ICTR Statute*, above note 72, arts. 2 & 3.

92   Above note 57.

93   *Second Protocol to the Geneva Conventions* (1977), 1125 U.N.T.S. 609, art. 4.

As to other heads of jurisdiction, under article 1 of the *ICTR Statute*,[94] the tribunal may prosecute crimes committed within the territory of Rwanda, as well as those committed by Rwandan citizens "in the territory of neighbouring states"—resulting in the exercise of both territorial and nationality-based jurisdiction. The latter part of the article was geared towards crimes committed by Hutu extremists, who continued to rape and murder after they had been driven from power, particularly in refugee camps along Rwanda's borders.[95] Temporally, jurisdiction is limited to acts committed during the calendar year of 1994, which covers the bulk of the active part of the conflict as well as "the planning stage of the crimes."[96] In terms of personal jurisdiction, like the ICTY, the ICTR's jurisdiction is limited to "natural persons."[97] The ICTR also has primacy over the national courts of all states in the same manner as the ICTY.

D. THE INTERNATIONAL CRIMINAL COURT (ICC)

1) Creation and History

The conclusion of the *Rome Statute*[98] is fairly viewed as one of the most momentous international law events in modern history[99] and arguably the most important since the *UN Charter*. The earliest modern proposal for such a court was that of Gustav Monnier, one of the founders of the

---

94   Above note 72.

95   See Jaana Karhihlo, "The Establishment of the International Tribunal for Rwanda" (1995) 64 Nordic J. Int'l L. 683 at 698.

96   *Report of the Secretary-General pursuant to Paragraph 5 of Security Council Resolution 955 (1994)*, UN Doc. S/1995/134 at para. 14.

97   *ICTR Statute*, above note 72, art. 5.

98   Above note 83. Official website: www.icc-cpi.int.

99   Similarly momentous is the legal literature relating to the court, for which "voluminous" is a pale descriptor. Any simple research effort will reveal that virtually every aspect of the court and its still mostly prospective work has been examined and dissected from different angles. Some of the most authoritative works are Antonio Cassese *et al.*, eds., *The* Rome Statute of the International Criminal Court: *A Commentary* (Oxford: Oxford University Press, 2002), 2 vols.; Otto Triffterer, ed., *The* Rome Statute of the International Criminal Court: *Observers' Notes, Article by Article*, 2d ed. (Oxford: Hart, 2008); Roy Lee, ed., *The International Criminal Court: The Making of the* Rome Statute, *Issues, Negotiations, Results* (The Hague: Kluwer, 1999); Dominic McGoldrick *et al.*, eds., *The Permanent International Criminal Court: Legal and Policy Issues* (Oxford: Hart, 2004).

International Committee of the Red Cross (ICRC), who in 1872 suggested a tribunal that would prosecute individuals for crimes of war, independently of national courts.[100] The initial groundwork for a standing international criminal court was not laid until the twentieth century, however, by the preparatory work towards the *Genocide Convention*.[101] A statute for a court had been included for consideration in the early drafting of the Convention, but could not attract the political will to create it at that time.[102] However, article VI of the Convention set out that genocide would be tried by a competent national court "or by such international penal tribunal as may have jurisdiction with respect to those Contracting Parties which shall have accepted its jurisdiction."

When it adopted the Convention in 1948, the General Assembly also tasked the International Law Commission (ILC) with producing a draft statute for an international criminal court, a job to be carried out along with its work on the "Nuremberg Principles"[103] and the *Draft Code of Crimes against the Peace and Security of Mankind*.[104] Special ILC committees working on the statute reported to the General Assembly with drafts in 1952[105] and 1954,[106] but finalization was put off until the politically delicate task of defining the crime of aggression within the context of the Draft Code could be completed.[107] The latter job was not completed until 1974, and in the meantime, Cold-War tensions made for disagreement on the need for and structure of a court, which poleaxed the entire effort for decades.

It was in the twilight of the Cold War, in fact, that the court was unexpectedly put back on the international agenda. Trinidad and Tobago, leading a group of like-minded states who wished for an independent international court to prosecute major narcotics producers and traffickers, proposed a General Assembly resolution directing the ILC to

---

100 Cristopher Keith Hall, "The First Proposal for a Permanent International Criminal Court" (1998) 322 Int'l Rev. Red Cross 57.

101 Above note 82.

102 William Schabas, *Genocide in International Law: The Crime of Crimes*, 2d ed. (Cambridge: Cambridge University Press, 2009) c. 2.

103 Completed in 1950 ([1950] 2 Y.B. Int'l L. Comm'n at para. 97). The principles can be found online: http://untreaty.un.org/ilc/texts/instruments/english/draft%20articles/7_1_1950.pdf.

104 Completed in 1996. (GAOR, 51st Sess. Supp. No. 10, UN Doc. A/51/10 (1996)), See Lyal S. Sunga, *The Emerging System of International Criminal Law: Developments in Codification and Implementation* (The Hague: Klewer, 1997).

105 UN Doc. A/2135 (1952).

106 UN Doc. A/2645 (1954).

107 GA Res. 897 (IX) (1954).

produce a new draft statute. The resulting resolution[108] led to the ILC (under the able leadership of Special Rapporteur James Crawford) producing a draft statute by 1994.[109] This draft contained an expansive subject matter jurisdiction for a court, providing for prosecution of genocide, war crimes, crimes against humanity, and aggression, but also for the "treaty crimes" of grave breaches of the *Geneva Conventions* and *Additional Protocol I (AP I)*,[110] the offences in the multilateral terrorism treaties, the 1988 UN *Vienna Narcotics Convention*,[111] and the *Apartheid Convention*.[112] It also provided for automatic jurisdiction only over the crime of genocide, when a state ratified the statute; the parties would have to "opt-in" for the court to have jurisdiction over other crimes vis-à-vis these states. The draft further limited the referral of cases to the UN Security Council or state parties without any independent ability for the Prosecutor in so doing, and generally envisioned a substantial role for the UN Security Council in controlling the court's seizing itself of cases.

There was sufficient enthusiasm for the ILC draft that the General Assembly established an *ad hoc* committee to continue the work, which met two times in 1995. While the ILC's 1994 draft was the starting point for the discussions, negotiations quickly went in different directions on several important matters. In particular, a preference emerged for the crimes within the subject matter jurisdiction of a court to be fully codified, as opposed to the statutes of the *ad hoc* tribunals, which simply enumerated the crimes; and moreover, that a full panoply of procedural protections should be similarly codified. Centrally, while the ILC draft had proposed a court with primacy over states, it was proposed that a new system of "complementarity" be instituted, which would see the court take jurisdiction over a matter only where states were unwilling or unable to do so.[113] These developments carried through to the next stage, five meetings of a Preparatory Committee (PrepCom) that heard submissions from both states and non-governmental organiza-

---

108 GA Res. 44/89.
109 UN Doc. A/49/10 (1994). See James Crawford, "The ILC Adopts a Statute for an International Criminal Court" (1995) 89 A.J.I.L. 404.
110 *Protocol Additional to the Geneva Conventions of 12 August 1949, and relating to the Protection of Victims of International Armed Conflicts (Protocol I)*, 8 June 1977 [*AP I*].
111 *United Nations Convention against Illicit Traffic in Narcotic Drugs and Psychotropic Substances*, Can T.S. 1990 No. 42.
112 *Convention on the Suppression and Punishment of the Crime of Apartheid (1973)*, 1015 U.N.T.S. 243.
113 See Report of the *Ad Hoc* Committee on the Establishment of an International Criminal Court, UN Doc. A/50/22.

tions (NGOs). By the final PrepCom session in January 1998, a draft for
a new statute was reasonably complete, though it departed markedly
from the ILC draft and still contained many points on which there was
disagreement.[114]

This new draft served as the basis for a final negotiation conference,
which was held in Rome over the course of several weeks in June–July
1998. The conference, chaired by Canadian diplomat Philippe Kirsch,
was an interesting and ultimately dramatic exercise in diplomatic negotiation.[115] Negotiations were presided over by a Bureau, which ran the
conference and supervised the work of a number of working groups on
various subject matters. A great deal of the negotiation that took place,
both within the Bureau and the working groups, was informal, and
great efforts were made to attain consensus, or at least general agreement, on all matters. A number of interest groups emerged, the activities
of which pulled the negotiating process in various directions. These
included the "Like-Minded Caucus," a group of approximately sixty
states which was pushing for a strong court with inherent jurisdiction
that would be independent from the Security Council; a group of the
permanent members of the Security Council, led by the US, which was
pushing in essentially the opposite direction; and such groups as the
previously-existing Non-Aligned Movement (NAM) from the UNGA
and groups of states representing regional or ethnic dynamics. Among
the most contentious issues were whether the court was to exercise an
inherent universal jurisdiction, as was favoured by many of the NGOs
which participated very effectively, if informally, in the background;[116]
and the respective power of the Prosecutor and the Security Council in
cases, and whether the former should or could be independent from the
latter. The increasingly tense negotiations ultimately came down to a
vote, on 17 July 1998, on a final "package deal" put together by Kirsch,
which saw 120 votes in favour, 21 abstentions, and 7 votes against what
was ultimately entitled the *Rome Statute for the International Criminal
Court*.[117] The US, which had been a powerful and fairly positive force

---

114 See M. Cherif Bassiouni, "Observations concerning the 1997–98 Preparatory
Committee's Work" (1997) 25 Denv. J. Int'l Law & Pol'y 397.

115 See, generally, Philippe Kirsch & John Holmes, "The Rome Conference on an
International Criminal Court: The Negotiating Process" (1999) 93 A.J.I.L. 2;
Philippe Kirsch & Valerie Oosterveld, "Negotiating an Institution for the 21st
Century: Multilateral Diplomacy and the International Criminal Court" (2001)
46 McGill L.J. 1141.

116 See Marlies Glasius, *The International Criminal Court: A Global Civil Society
Achievement* (New York: Routledge, 2006).

117 Above note 83.

in the Rome negotiations, voted against the adoption of the Statute, but did sign the treaty along with 138 other states by the end of the formal signature process in December 2000.

The finalization of the *Rome Statute* was viewed as a true instance of victory snatched from the jaws of defeat, as there had been great skepticism over whether states could agree on a framework for such a court. Initial developments also proceeded at a relatively breakneck pace. Article 121 provided that the Statute would not come into effect until the sixtieth day following the sixtieth ratification by a state,[118] and this occurred on 1 July 2002. The first Assembly of States Parties (ASP)[119] met in September 2002 and adopted three items which had been formulated by a Preparatory Commission established at the Diplomatic Conference in 1998: the *Elements of Crimes*, the *Rules of Procedure and Evidence*, and the *Agreement on Privileges and Immunities of the Court*.[120] By February 2003, the ASP had elected the first judges, including Philippe Kirsch as President of the court. Notably, over a third of the judges were women, and the geographical representation was wide. In April 2003, the Prosecutor, Argentinean Luis Moreno-Ocampo, was appointed and he was sworn in on 16 June 2003.

Matters began to move more slowly as Prosecutor Ocampo pursued his mandate. In a 2003 policy paper,[121] Ocampo set out a twofold vision of the role of the court. First, it should adhere closely to the spirit, as well as the letter, of the requirement of complementarity in article 17 of the *Rome Statute*, and investigate matters "only where there is a clear case of failure to act by the State or States concerned."[122] The goal was to encourage states as the most logical purveyors of international criminal justice. Second, the court would focus its energy on "those who bear

---

118 Regarding ratification of a treaty, see Chapter 1. Canada ratified the *Rome Statute* on 7 July 2000.

119 The ASP is provided for under art. 112 of the *Rome Statute*, above note 83. As the court's own website notes, the ASP is "the management oversight and legislative body of the International Criminal Court. It is composed of representatives of the States that have ratified and acceded to the *Rome Statute*." It has a Bureau and a permanent Secretariat, which facilitate the ASP in its most important functions: adopting normative texts and the setting of budgets and hiring of judges and prosecutors. See online: www.icc-cpi.int/Menus/ASP/ASP+Homepage.htm.

120 These and other important ICC documents can be found in the "Official Journal of the International Criminal Court," a resource on the court's website, online: www2.icc-cpi.int/Menus/ICC/Legal+Texts+and+Tools/.

121 Online: www.icc-cpi.int/Menus/ICC/Structure+of+the+Court/Office+of+the+Prosecutor/Policies+and+Strategies/Paper+on+some+policy+issues+before+the+Office+of+the+Prosecutor.htm.

122 *Ibid.* at 5.

the greatest responsibility, such as the leaders of the State or organization allegedly responsible for . . . crimes,"[123] leaving the pursuit of lesser criminals to the states themselves. This strategy was meant to reflect what had been anticipated in Rome as a robust use of the Prosecutor's *proprio motu* powers to initiate investigations. It was overtaken, however, as the court received its first referrals of cases from state parties to the *Rome Statute*. While state referrals were clearly anticipated under article 14 of the treaty,[124] what was unanticipated was that the states in question—Uganda (2003), the Democratic Republic of the Congo (DRC) (2004), and the Central African Republic (2004)—would refer matters occurring on their own territories. The fourth case, that of the Darfur situation in the Sudan, was referred to the court by the Security Council of the UN in 2005 after years of inaction by the Sudanese government in failing to prosecute ongoing and horrendous crimes in Darfur. In each case, the office of the Prosecutor moved at a fairly slow and careful pace in completing investigations and initiating prosecutions, a pace which has come in for criticism.[125]

There is little doubt that each of these cases is well within the ICC's general mandate, as there is amassed credible evidence of atrocities taking place within each of the states involved. However, each situation came to the court, not unexpectedly, with difficult practical and/or political elements that appear to have dissipated somewhat the initial prosecution strategy. Tension between the Prosecutor and the court has also been an ongoing issue. In Uganda, the government referred the situation in the northern part of the country to the ICC, essentially as a gambit in its battle with a rebel group called the Lord's Resistance Army (LRA), and as a means to force LRA leaders, particularly Joseph Kony, to the bargaining table. This was apparently successful and led to some reduction in the crimes being committed. However, a standoff of sorts developed whereby the LRA sought immunity from execution of

---

123 *Ibid.* at 7.
124 See Section D(4)(a), below in this chapter.
125 For example, Antonio Cassese, "Is the ICC Still Having Teething Problems?" (2006) 4 JICJ 434. Regarding the eighteen months taken to apply for arrest warrants in the Uganda situation, Professor Schabas comments, perhaps hyperbolically, "Using NGO reports and information in the public domain, a young law student with internet access could probably have drafted the arrest warrants in January 2004, days after the referral" (William Schabas, *An Introduction to the International Criminal Court*, 3d ed. (Cambridge: Cambridge University Press, 2007) at 56). For other criticism of the Prosecutor's investigation methods, see Heikelina Verrijn Stuart, "The ICC in Trouble" (2008) 6 JICJ 409.

the ICC arrest warrants in exchange for concessions towards peace.[126] This is quite apart from the fact that pro-government forces have also been implicated in the ongoing crimes, which will further complicate the ICC's ability to investigate and prosecute.

The situation in Darfur has also had a troubled history, starting with battles between the Prosecutor and the court over the Prosecutor's initial insistence that the investigation would have to be done primarily from outside the Sudan, because the security situation made it too dangerous to take action on the territory.[127] When there were still no indictments in July 2006, over a year after the situation had been referred, the court itself sought opinions from outside *amici curiae*, Antonio Cassese and UN Human Rights High Commissioner Louise Arbour, both of whom opined that the situation did permit investigation and expressly disagreed with the Prosecutor's assessment of the facts on the ground.[128] The Prosecutor has since moved the case forward in a way that appears to be putting the initial prosecutorial strategy back on track, and in May 2007, the court issued arrest warrants for Ahmad Harun, the Sudan's sitting Minister of State for Humanitarian Affairs, and Ali Kushayb, the alleged leader of the Janjaweed militia. In March 2009, the court issued a warrant for Omar Al-Bashir, the sitting President of Sudan, setting off a storm of controversy and prompting Al-Bashir to withdraw Sudan's cooperation with the court and to expel humanitarian aid agencies.[129] As of this writing, the Security Council member states, which referred the case in a momentary fit of unity on the work of the ICC, are now significantly divided as to whether the indictment of a sitting president was either legal[130] or tactically sound,

---

126 As of this writing, it had been suggested by the Ugandan government that it would ask the ICC to defer prosecution to Uganda if Kony and his confederates would sign the "Final Peace Agreement." See Kasaija Phillip Apuuli, "The ICC's Possible Deferral of the LRA Case to Uganda" (2008) 6 JICJ 801.

127 Sixth Diplomatic Briefing of the International Criminal Court, Compilation of Statements, 23 March 2006.

128 *Situation in Darfur, Sudan* (ICC-02/05), Observations on Issues Concerning the Protection of Victims and the Preservation of Evidence in the Proceedings on Darfur Pending Before the ICC, 25 August 2006; *Situation in Darfur, Sudan* (ICC-02/05), Observations of the United Nations High Commissioner for Human Rights Invited in Application of Rule 103 of the *Rules of Procedure and Evidence*, 10 October 2006.

129 See various editorial comments in (2008) 6:5 JICJ

130 Regarding state immunity to criminal jurisdiction, see Chapter 11. There is little actual question about the legality of the indictment of Al-Bashir, as the matter is properly within the ICC's jurisdiction under the referral from the Security Council, and art. 27 of the *Rome Statute*, above note 83, strips state officials of any relevant immunity they might otherwise have enjoyed.

as the indictment was supported by the US, the UK, and France but criticized by Russia and China,[131] as well as by the African Union.[132]

The DRC situation produced the ICC's first indictment, that, in March 2006, of Congolese warlord Thomas Lubanga Dyilo, who has been charged with the war crime of conscripting child soldiers during 2002–2003. Lubanga was in the custody of the Congolese government at the time and was immediately surrendered to the ICC. There were literally years of delays in bringing him to trial, including the hearing of a motion by Lubanga that the court should decline to exercise jurisdiction over him because of the length of his detention in DRC and his treatment there. He argued this motion unsuccessfully all the way to the Appeals Chamber of the court.[133] At one stage the court had stayed the prosecution altogether because of the Prosecutor's failure to disclose potentially relevant evidence to the accused.[134] The case was put back on track in November 2008, but when the trial began in January 2009, it immediately began to run into problems, as the Prosecution's first witness, an alleged child soldier, substantially recanted his testimony.[135]

Problems also cropped up in the only case pending from the situation in the Central African Republic, that of Jean-Pierre Bemba Gombo, a rebel leader charged with crimes against humanity and war crimes. In a March 2009 decision, Pre-Trial Chamber III adjourned the hearing to confirm the charges against Gombo, essentially sending the indictment back to the Prosecutor because the evidence referred to appeared to the court to disclose different crimes than those charged.[136]

The ICC has also had one constant thorn in its side nearly from its inception: hostility from the government of the United States. At the Rome Conference the American delegate was among a small number who voted against the adoption of the *Rome Statute*, but the Clinton administration was mostly receptive to the ICC's mission and signed the treaty on 31 December 2000. However, the Bush administration

---

131 See "Warrant Issued for Sudan's Leader" *BBC News* (4 March 2009), online: http://news.bbc.co.uk/2/hi/africa/7923102.stm.

132 Online: www.france24.com/en/20090329-al-bashir-qatar-before-start-arab-summit-icc-doha-sudanese.

133 *Lubanga*, Case No. ICC-01/04-01/06 (OA 4), Judgment, Appeals Chamber, 14 December 2006.

134 *Lubanga*, Case No. ICC-01/04-01/06 (OA 13), Judgment, Appeals Chamber, 21 October 2008.

135 David Carter, "Chaos Reigns at International Criminal Court Trial of Thomas Lubanga" *The Times* (29 January 2009), online: www.timesonline.co.uk/tol/news/world/africa/article5606892.ece.

136 *Gombo*, Case No. ICC-01/05-01/08, Decision, Pre-Trial Ch. III, 3 March 2009.

which followed was openly hostile towards the court, and in 2002 took the extraordinary step of "unsigning" the *Rome Statute* by expressing to the United Nations Secretariat's Treaty Depository that it did not intend to become a party to the treaty. American resistance to the ICC traces a number of lines, not least of which are discomfort both with multilateral mechanisms generally and the notion of giving up jurisdiction of US courts over American nationals specifically. A particular concern was that the court would be "politicized" in the sense that prosecutions of Americans would be used as a means of retaliating against perceived slights arising from US foreign policy. Most pressing, perhaps, is the fact that the court produced by the Rome Conference was not in a subservient position to the Security Council, an outcome against which American diplomats had worked at the conference.[137]

The Bush government took a number of steps to undermine the authority of the ICC, including the negotiation of more than 100 treaties (under article 98(2)) with states that would prevent the surrender of any US national to the court;[138] pressuring the Security Council to immunize UN peacekeepers from the ICC's jurisdiction;[139] and passing what is colloquially known as the "Hague Invasion Act,"[140] which, among other items, authorizes the use of military force to rescue any Americans who are in the ICC's custody. As the court became better established and the number of ratifying states increased, however, the American position appeared to soften. In 2005, the US refrained from vetoing the referral of the situation in Darfur to the court, and the pursuit of "article 98(2) treaties" had petered out by 2006. Even the Bush administration began to acknowledge the importance of the ICC to international criminal justice, an overall mission that the US had always supported, and early signs from the new Obama administration are that there will be further reconsideration of the American position towards the court,[141] though a re-signing of the *Rome Statute* still seems far from imminent.

---

137 See William Schabas, "United States Hostility to the International Criminal Court: It's All about the Security Council" (2004) 15 E.J.I.L. 701.

138 These were negotiated allegedly pursuant to art. 98(2) of the *Rome Statute*, above note 83; see David Scheffer, "Article 98(2) of the *Rome Statute*: America's Original Intent" (2005) 3 JICJ 333.

139 UN Doc. S/RES/1422 (2002); UN Doc. S/RES/1497 (2003). See Salvatore Zappala, "Are Some Peacekeepers Better Than Others? UN Security Council Resolution 1497 (2003) and the ICC" (2003) 1 JICJ 671.

140 *American Servicemembers' Protection Act of 2002*, Pub. L. No. 107-206, 116 Stat. 820 tit. II (2002).

141 See D. Kraus, "Goodbye Nethercutt Amendment & the BIA Campaign," Citizens for Global Solutions, online: http://globalsolutions.org/blog/2009/03/goodbye_nethercutt_bia_campaign.

That the ICC flourished in the face of American opposition is per-haps emblematic of the first seven years of the court's existence; after all, this was an institution that few thought would even be agreed on at Rome, let alone come into existence and begin to operate as quickly as it did. The ICC has been the subject of much criticism, some unfair, some necessary to sustain the validity of its mission. Given its less-than-universal membership, lack of support from large and powerful states, and active efforts to undermine it, the ICC operates in a pre-carious political environment. The Prosecutor's methods have been questioned, as has the lack of alacrity with which he has pursued his cases. The active cases are politically delicate, both Uganda and Darfur demonstrating the clear potential for the court to be a political football when it necessarily becomes enmeshed in international peace and se-curity matters. And yet, in defiance of all expectation, this is a working court which is actively prosecuting individuals who are alleged to have been involved in some of the most atrocious crimes known to human-ity. There have been indictments—including that of a sitting head of state—and pretrial motions, and a trial is under way. The ICC cannot be all things to all stakeholders, and perhaps expectations are inflated in terms of how large a role it can actually play in the international criminal justice system. The only reasonable current forecast, however, is that its role will continue to be a significant one.

2) Structure

The ICC is an international organization,[142] created by the states which are party to it. It is located in The Hague, though it has opened field offices in various African countries. The court works closely with the United Nations and is subject to the directives of the Security Council in some instances,[143] but is nonetheless independent of the UN; article 2 of the *Rome Statute* states that the court "shall be brought into a re-lationship with the United Nations through an agreement," and in Oc-tober 2004, a *Relationship Agreement* was concluded by the President of the court and the Secretary-General of the UN.[144] The Agreement provides for various forms of cooperation between the ICC and the UN, including judicial assistance, information exchange, and more mun-dane and administrative matters such as mutual observer status.

---

142 See, generally, Kenneth Gallant, "The International Criminal Court in the Sys-tem of States and International Organizations" (2003) 16 Leiden J. Int'l L. 553.
143 See Section D(4)(d), below in this chapter.
144 ICC-ASP/3/Res.1 (2004).

Unlike the *ad hoc* tribunals, the ICC has four organs: the Presidency, Chambers, Office of the Prosecutor, and Registry. The Presidency is made up of the President and two Vice-Presidents, all judges of the court who serve a number of administrative functions, including distributing the workload of the court. Canadian Philippe Kirsch was elected as the first President of the court and presided over the initial matters until the end of his term in early 2009. The Chambers is made up of eighteen judges in total (including the judges of the Presidency), who are distributed between three Divisions: Appeals Division, Trial Division, and Pre-Trial Division. The judges are elected by the Assembly of States Parties from a slate of candidates who are put forward by member states,[145] and each judge must have significant acumen in either international law (particularly international humanitarian or human rights law) or criminal law.[146]

The Office of the Prosecutor is a separate and independent arm of the court, charged under article 42 of the *Rome Statute* with receiving referrals and information on crimes, conducting investigations, and conducting prosecutions. Along with Prosecutor Ocampo, two Deputy Prosecutors have been elected who are responsible for investigations and prosecutions, respectively. The Prosecutor is independent from the rest of the court in the sense of being empowered to exercise prosecutorial discretion and to direct his office administratively, and he cannot seek or act on any instructions from any external source. However, his ability to exercise his *proprio motu* powers and commence a matter on his own initiative is subject to supervision by a Pre-Trial Chamber of the court.[147] The Registry is the administrative arm of the ICC, with responsibilities for administrative support for court activities as well as matters concerning victims and witnesses. The role contemplated for victims is one of the more unique and innovative features of the ICC, in contrast to other international tribunals. Not only does the Registry have a special division for dealing with victims, but under the *Rome Statute* and the *Rules of Procedure and Evidence* (*RPE*),[148] victims are given the right to participate in proceedings, are subject to the court's protection, and are the beneficiaries of a Trust Fund to compensate them for their injuries.[149]

---

145 The most recent elections were held in early 2009, when a number of judges were replaced.

146 *Rome Statute*, above note 83, art. 39(1).

147 *Ibid.*, art. 15.

148 International Criminal Court, *Rules of Procedure and Evidence*, UN Doc. PC-NICC/2000/1/Add.1 (2000).

149 On the ICC regime regarding victims, see Schabas, *Introduction*, above note 125, c. 10; Carsten Stahn *et al.*, "Participation of Victims in the Pre-Trial Proceedings

3) Jurisdiction

a) Subject Matter Jurisdiction

As noted in Section D(1), above in this chapter, the ICC has jurisdiction over the four "core crimes": genocide, crimes against humanity, war crimes, and aggression.[150] These are dealt with in detail in Chapter 3. The three crimes which are currently operative (genocide, crimes against humanity, and war crimes)[151] are defined in some detail in articles 6–8 of the *Rome Statute*. Due to a preference among the negotiating states in Rome to constrain judicial discretion regarding the interpretation of the crimes themselves—a reaction to, *inter alia*, the perceived judicial activism of the *ad hoc* tribunals in developing the customary law regarding these crimes—the crimes are further defined by the *Elements of Crimes (ICC Elements)*,[152] which operate as a subsidiary source of law for the court.

The definitions of the crimes in the *Rome Statute* are drawn from customary international law, though they are conservative in some respects and progressive in others. They have certainly been influential in shaping the treatment of the core crimes by both international[153] and national courts.[154] As the ICTY has remarked, while these definitions are by no means the four corners of custom, they are safely taken as "an authoritative expression of the legal views of a great number of states."[155]

As noted in Section D(1), above in this chapter, the original motivation behind the new push for a permanent ICC was a Caribbean desire to have a court which could punish narcotics traffickers, and these states expressed their annoyance when narcotics trafficking was

---

of the ICC" (2006) 4 JICJ 219.

150 *Rome Statute*, above note 83, art. 5.

151 The definition of the crime of aggression is currently before the Assembly of States parties; see Chapter 3.

152 UN Doc. PCNICC/2000/1/Add.2 (2000).

153 For example, *Hadžihasanović* (IT-01-47-AR72), Decision on Interlocutory Appeal Challenging Jurisdiction in Relation to Command Responsibility, Trial Chamber, 16 July 2003 at para. 53.

154 For example, *Mugesera v. Canada (Minister of Citizenship and Immigration)*, [2005] 2 S.C.R. 100. And legislatures, as well: ss. 4(4) and 6(4) of Canada's *Crimes Against Humanity and War Crimes Act*, S.C. 2000, c. 24 provide a presumption that the crimes described in arts. 6, 7, and 8(2) of the *Rome Statute*, above note 83, were "crimes according to customary international law" as of 17 July 1998. See Chapter 5 for more detail.

155 *Furundžija* (IT-95-17/1-T), Judgment, Trial Chamber, 10 December 1998 at para. 227.

excluded from the court's subject matter jurisdiction.[156] However, despite serious consideration of whether both narcotics and terrorism should be included, no consensus emerged in Rome that such crimes were worthy of inclusion in the *Rome Statute*. It was perceived that the greater need for the ICC was to combat international impunity for the core crimes, and suggested that current transnational cooperation was going to be the most efficient and effective way of dealing with transnational crimes.[157] However, the Final Act of the Rome Conference contained a resolution that the Review Conference (currently scheduled to be held in Kampala, Uganda, in 2010) consider the addition of drug trafficking and terrorism to the court's subject matter jurisdiction.[158]

Article 70 of the *Rome Statute* gives the court jurisdiction over "offences against the administration of justice," such as perjury, interference with witnesses, and corrupting/bribing officials of the court. Article 71 provides that the court may "sanction" persons who disrupt proceedings or refuse to comply with its directions. This is a fairly narrow selection from the range of powers that courts generally have in order to control their own processes,[159] but whether the court has any inherent jurisdiction or powers beyond these is debatable. The Appeals Chamber in the *Lubanga* case opined that the *Rome Statute* does not give the court the powers to remedy "abuse of process" as such, since this is a common law doctrine that is largely unknown to civilian traditions and thus could not be read into the Statute.[160]

b)   Territorial Jurisdiction

Article 12(2)(a) of the *Rome Statute* provides that the court has jurisdiction over crimes which take place "on the territory" of a state party. This is explicitly extended to crimes committed on board a vessel or aircraft which are registered in a party state, which are typical and uncontroversial extensions of territorial jurisdiction. At international law, a state's territory is generally held to include territorial waters and subadjacent airspace, so it would not be a far stretch for the court to make such a finding in an appropriate case.

---

156 See Neil Boister, "The Exclusion of Treaty Crimes from the Jurisdiction of the Proposed International Criminal Court: Law, Pragmatism, Politics" (1998) 3 J. Armed Conflict L. 27 at 29.

157 *Ibid.*; Patrick Robinson, "The Missing Crimes" in Cassese *et al.*, eds., *The* Rome Statute, above note 99.

158 UN Doc. A/CONF.183/C.1/L.76/Add.14 at 8.

159 See also Regulation 29 of the *Regulations of the Court*, ICC-BD/01-01-04 (2004).

160 *Lubanga*, Case No. ICC-01/04-01/06 (OA4), Decision, Appeals Chamber, 14 December 2006.

By contrast, there is no specific indication whether the phrase "on the territory" was intended to incorporate the concept of "qualified territorial jurisdiction," that is, where a state may assume jurisdiction over an offence that was committed in part on its territory or where the effects of the offence were felt in its territory. As set out in Chapter 2, the parameters of this jurisdictional principle are uncertain, though its core is mostly uncontroversial. Determining whether the ICC can exert jurisdiction over such a case will require an exercise of interpretation. On the one hand, the import of the qualified territoriality principle arguably is that states are permitted to exercise jurisdiction over these offences on the basis that if enough of the offence touches the state's territory, then the offence is deemed to have taken place on the state's territory.[161] On the other hand, some of the suppression conventions explicitly anticipate and set out this basis for jurisdiction, so on a strict treaty law interpretation of article 12(2)(a), it could be argued that the silence of the provision means that the negotiating states intended to exclude it.

Article 12(3) provides that the court will have jurisdiction over crimes committed on a non-party state's territory where that state has made an *ad hoc* acceptance of the court's jurisdiction. Also, under article 13(b), the court will have jurisdiction over crimes committed in any state where the Security Council has referred the matter to the court, and thus the Council may effectively designate any state's territory to be within the jurisdiction of the ICC when acting under its Chapter VII powers.

c) Personal Jurisdiction

The *Rome Statute* permits exercise over "natural persons,"[162] thus excluding corporations and other "legal persons." It permits nationality-based jurisdiction over these individuals. Article 12(2)(b) provides that the ICC may exercise jurisdiction over a crime where it is alleged to have been committed by a person who is a national of a state party. Article 12(3) further provides that the court may exercise jurisdiction over a crime where the accused is a national of a non-party state, provided that the state formally provides *ad hoc* acceptance of the court's jurisdiction. As with territorial jurisdiction, the Security Council may also refer a case to the court that implicates the nationals of a non-party state and brings them within the ICC's jurisdiction.

---

161 This is the Canadian position; see Chapter 8.
162 *Rome Statute*, above note 83, art. 25(1).

The debates about the acceptable scope of the ICC's jurisdiction were wide-ranging in Rome, but nationality jurisdiction was an uncontroversial basis from the start, given that, like territoriality, it is one of the most widely accepted bases for jurisdiction among states.[163] In determining any questions regarding nationality, it would seem that the standard international law regarding nationality will apply.[164]

The age at which alleged perpetrators can be prosecuted by the court was a matter of some controversy in Rome, and the solution was to make this a jurisdictional matter and bypass debates around the accepted age at which criminal responsibility can accrue in national or international law.[165] Accordingly, article 26 provides that the court may exercise jurisdiction over an alleged offender only where that person was eighteen or older at the time of the commission of the offence.

The Statute also deals with immunities that may attach to individuals, particularly articles 27 and 98. These are discussed in detail in Chapter 11.

d) Non-party States

As indicated under Sections D(3)(b) and (c), above in this chapter, any non-party state may make an *ad hoc* acceptance of the ICC's jurisdiction under article 12(3).[166] Such an acceptance essentially brings the state within the court's usual regime as regards the particular situation in question, and in fact has an additional impediment in that the acceptance of jurisdiction does not in itself constitute a referral of a matter to the court. Accordingly, a party state would have to refer the matter or the Prosecutor would have to initiate an investigation under his *proprio motu* power. Otherwise, the Prosecutorial machinery moves in the same fashion as it would normally, and the accepting state would be compelled to cooperate with the court under Part 9 of the *Rome Statute*. In response to American concerns, a provision was inserted into the *RPE* to prevent non-party states from accepting jurisdiction over crimes alleged to have been committed by political opponents but shielding other perpetrators to which they are more sympathetic; an ac-

---

163 See Chapter 2.

164 See, generally, Hugh Kindred & Phillip Saunders, eds., *International Law: Chiefly as Interpreted and Applied in Canada*, 7th ed. (Toronto: Emond Montgomery, 2006) c. 8.

165 Per Saland, "International Criminal Law Principles" in Lee, ed., *The International Criminal Court*, above note 99, 189 at 200–2.

166 See Carsten Stahn, "Why Some Doors May Be Closed Already: Second Thoughts on a 'Case-by-Case' Treatment of Article 12(3) Declarations" (2006) 75 Nordic J. Int'l L. 243.

ceptance is with regard to a "situation" and includes all crimes relevant to the situation.[167] To date, article 12(3) has been invoked by Uganda (at least implicitly) to cover a two-month lapse in time between the coming into force of the Statute generally on 1 July 2002 and its coming into force for Uganda on 1 September 2002, and by Côte d'Ivoire, where the Prosecutor is monitoring the situation but has not yet opened a formal investigation.

A contentious issue regarding non-party states is the question of whether the ICC can exercise jurisdiction over a national of a non-party state where the crime was committed on the territory of a party state—referred to in Rome as the "state consent" issue. It has been suggested that such a situation would effectively allow the states which are party to the *Rome Statute* to impinge on, or impose obligations on, non-party states. This suggestion has played some role in US opposition to the ICC. The response given has typically been that states may delegate to the ICC an exercise of jurisdiction that they themselves would be able to exercise under international law, and therefore, since a state could exercise territorial jurisdiction over a crime committed by a national of another state, so may the court. This problem, which has generated significant debate and literature,[168] has yet to be resolved.

e)   Temporal Jurisdiction

Article 11(1) of the *Rome Statute*[169] provides that the court shall have jurisdiction "only with respect to crimes committed after the entry into force of this Statute." Accordingly, for the most part, the court has jurisdiction only over crimes committed after 1 July 2002, the date on which the *Rome Statute* came into force. Article 24 underscores this in providing that no person shall be criminally liable for conduct which occurred prior to the entry into force of the Statute. Where a state becomes party to the Statute after 1 July 2002, article 11(2) gives the court jurisdiction over crimes committed after the date of entry into force for that state. Where a state makes an *ad hoc* acceptance of the court's jurisdiction under article 12(3), it may extend the court's temporal jurisdiction as far back as 1 July 2002. Uganda used this mechanism when, in

167 UN Doc. PCNICC/2000/1/Add.1 (2000), r. 44(2) [*RPE*].

168 See, for example, Jordan Paust, "The Reach of ICC Jurisdiction over Non-Signatory Nationals" (2000) 33 Vand. J. Transnat'l L. 1; Michael Scharf, "The ICC's Jurisdiction over the Nationals of Non-Party States: A Critique of the U.S. Position" (2001) 64 Law & Contemp. Probs. 98; Madeline Morris, "High Crimes and Misconceptions: The ICC and Non-Party States" (2000) 64 Law & Contemp. Probs. 131.

169 Above note 83.

2004, it acceded to the court's jurisdiction over crimes committed back to that date.[170]

4) "Triggering" Proceedings before the Court

While having jurisdiction over a matter is obviously a precursor for any activity by the court, the ICC is unlike the UN *ad hoc* tribunals and other international courts in that the Prosecutor does not simply proceed to select cases for prosecution. Rather, a case must be brought before the court by way of formal processes set out in the *Rome Statute*, often called the "trigger mechanisms." Article 13 provides three methods by which the court's jurisdiction can be "exercised": (a) referral from a state party, (b) referral from the Security Council acting under Chapter VII, and (c) the Prosecutor initiating an investigation on his own (*proprio motu*). These will be considered in turn.

a)   State Party Referral

Article 13(a) provides that a state party may refer a "situation in which one or more . . . crimes appears to have been committed" in accordance with article 14, which itself simply repeats this language and adds that the referring state can request the Prosecutor to investigate the matter. Choosing the words "referral" and "situation" was deliberate during the Rome negotiations; these terms replaced the words "complaint" and "case," which had been used in earlier drafts, in part to avoid the perception of the court being used by one state to target particular individuals or groups.[171] It was foreseen, however, that states could use the mechanism to flag for the court crimes which were taking place in other states. What was not foreseen was that this provision would have much use, or indeed that it would ground three of the first four cases before the court.

Remarkably, these three cases (Uganda, DRC, and the Central African Republic) were all referred to the court by the states themselves, a practice now known as "self-referral," which took most observers by surprise.[172] It has since become clear that the Prosecutor had played a role in obtaining these self-referrals by way of a policy which encour-

---

170   See *Situation in Uganda* (ICC-02/04-53), Warrant of Arrest for Joseph Kony Issued on 8 July 2005 As Amended on 27 September 2005 at para. 32.

171   Philippe Kirsch & Darryl Robinson, "Referral by States Parties" in Cassese *et al.*, eds., *The* Rome Statute, above note 99, 619 at 623.

172   Mohamed El Zeidy, "The Ugandan Government Triggers the First Test of the Complementarity Principle: An Assessment of the First State's Party Referral to the ICC" (2005) 5 Int'l Crim. L. Rev. 83; Paola Gaeta, "Is the Practice of

aged it "as a first step in triggering the jurisdiction of the court."[173] The practice certainly has much to recommend it, given that it has put three very serious cases before the court in a relatively non-contentious manner, and it has been endorsed by Pre-Trial Chamber I[174] and the pre-judicial writings of a current judge of the ICC.[175] Concerns have been raised that states will use this mode of referral as a way of targeting rebel or opposing political groups, and indeed this was clearly the case with the government of Uganda, which explicitly referred to the court the activities of the LRA. In that case, the Prosecutor responded that the "situation" in question included all relevant crimes within northern Uganda regardless of by whom they were committed,[176] but clearly if the Prosecutor is going to continue to encourage self-referrals, he will be walking a tightrope with states that wish to use the court for their own political ends—particularly given the likelihood that state governments will be fully cooperative when their enemies are under the scrutiny of the ICC, but less so when the focus turns to them.[177] Professor Schabas has criticized the practice on numerous grounds: that it is outside the scope of article 13;[178] that it allows states to effectively "jump the queue" by positioning themselves squarely within the Prosecutor's line of sight instead of having to be assessed as part of a *proprio motu* review; and that it allows states to deflect the overall goal of the complementarity regime in the *Rome Statute*, which is to have states prosecute their own situations wherever possible.[179]

b)   Referral by the Security Council

The Security Council is the organ of the United Nations which has "primary responsibility for the maintenance of international peace and security."[180] Under the provisions of Chapter VII of the *Charter of the*

'Self-Referrals' a Sound Start for the ICC?" (2004) 2 JICJ 949 [Gaeta, "Practice of 'Self-Referrals'"].

173 ICC, Office of the Prosecutor, *Report on the Activities Performed During the First Three Years (2003–2006)* (12 September 2006), Ref-RP20060906-OTP.

174 *Lubanga* (ICC-01/04-01/06-8), Decision on the Prosecutor's Application for a Warrant of Arrest, 10 February 2006 at para. 35.

175 Claus Kress, "'Self-Referrals' and 'Waivers of Complementarity': Some Considerations in Law & Policy" (2004) 2 JICJ 944.

176 Presidency Decision Assigning the Situation in Uganda to Pre-Trial Chamber II, 5 July 2004, attachment: Letter of the Prosecutor (17 June 2004), ICC-02/04-1.

177 Gaeta, "Practice of 'Self-Referrals,'"above note 172 at 952.

178 William Schabas, "First Prosecutions at the International Criminal Court" (2006) 27 H.R.L.J. 25 at 32.

179 Schabas, *Introduction*, above note 125 at 148–51.

180 *UN Charter*, above note 36, art. 24.

United Nations,[181] the Security Council is empowered both to take measures and to require measures on the part of states where, in the view of the Council, international peace and security are threatened. Both of these actions would otherwise impinge on the sovereignty of states if attempted by states or other international organizations. The Council is the enforcement arm of the international community, though because its permanent members (the US, the UK, France, China, and Russia) each has a veto over any activities that may be undertaken, it has become highly politicized. Most relevant here, it was the Security Council which created the *ad hoc* tribunals for the former Yugoslavia and for Rwanda as an exercise of its Chapter VII powers, moves which were central to the development of modern international criminal justice.

Article 13(b) of the *Rome Statute*[182] empowers the ICC to take jurisdiction over a matter where it is referred to the Prosecutor by the Council, acting under its Chapter VII powers. It is not clear whether such a referral has to comply with the requirements for admissibility, particularly complementarity,[183] considered in Section D(5)(a), below in this chapter. Nonetheless, this mechanism provides a useful means for the international community as a whole to attempt to impose accountability for mass crimes in a state where the court would otherwise not have jurisdiction, such as where the state is a non-party to the *Rome Statute*. This was precisely the case in Darfur, Sudan, where the Security Council, after intense negotiations, issued Resolution 1593, which referred "the situation in Darfur since 1 July 2002 to the Prosecutor" and ordered the government of Darfur to cooperate with the court.[184] As with many Security Council resolutions, this was a politically sensitive matter, particularly so because, as was made clear in the Report of the International Commission of Inquiry that the Council had earlier appointed to examine the situation, powerful persons in the government were implicated in the atrocities.[185] However, the Council was convinced that the power of the Council and court combined might compel the various players involved to submit to investigation and prosecutions. As noted above, current indications are that this strategy

---

181 *Ibid.*

182 Above note 83.

183 Though the Prosecutor has taken the view that he must do so, even though art. 18 only contemplates admissibility challenges for state party referrals or a *proprio motu* investigation by the Prosecutor. See Schabas, *Introduction*, above note 125 at 173–74.

184 UN Doc. S/RES/1593 (2005).

185 *Report of the International Commission of Inquiry on Darfur to the United Nations Secretary-General*, UN Doc. S/2005/60 at paras. 630–39.

may have backfired, as the ICC's indictment of the Sudanese president has provoked significant resistance by that government to the court's activities.

c) Prosecutor's *Proprio Motu* Powers

Under article 13(c) of the *Rome Statute*,[186] the ICC will have jurisdiction over a situation where the Prosecutor has initiated an investigation into it *proprio motu* (on his own motion). The Prosecutor's powers for so doing are set out in article 15 of the *Rome Statute*. The idea of a Prosecutor whose discretion is not entirely controlled by state parties or the Security Council was hotly contested at the Rome conference, and it was opposed by many major powers, including the US and China. The refrain was a familiar one of fear that a too-independent Prosecutor could seize ideological reins and drag the court into highly politicized prosecutions. However, article 15 discloses a system of close supervision of the Prosecutor's *proprio motu* powers by the court itself, in particular that a Pre-Trial Chamber must authorize the Prosecutor to open an investigation into a matter. As will be seen in Sections D(5)(a) and (b), below in this chapter, he is also constrained by the complementarity requirement and the gravity threshold, making the scenario of a politicized prosecutor run amok a rather unlikely one.[187]

d) Deferral by the Security Council

A bar to the exercise of jurisdiction by the court is contained in article 16, which provides that the Security Council can, in a Chapter VII resolution, request the court to defer an investigation or prosecution, whether ongoing or prospective, and the court must abide by that request. The request extends for only twelve months, though it may be renewed by the Security Council thereafter.

This provision, too, originated from a significant dispute at the Rome conference regarding the interaction between the Council and the court.[188] It was foreseen by some delegations, primarily the permanent five members of the Council, that the court's activities could act to undermine the Council's own efforts in a situation where international peace and security interests were engaged. A sensitive and precarious peace or ceasefire negotiation, the argument went, could be jeopardized by the ICC attempting to prosecute some of the major players or

---

186 Above note 83.

187 See Allison M. Danner, "Enhancing the Legitimacy and Accountability of Prosecutorial Discretion at the ICC" (2003) 97 A.J.I.L. 510.

188 See Lionel Yee, "The ICC and the Security Council: Articles 13(b) and 16" in Lee, ed., *The International Criminal Court*, above note 99 at 143.

their allies. On the other side were a substantial number of states who rejected any possibility for the Council to interfere with the work of the court, because of the potential for maintaining the kind of impunity that the court was designed to attack. Justice, it was said, was being subordinated to peace. In the end, article 16 was agreed on, in no small part because it requires an affirmative act of the Security Council rather than operating as a presumption as the 1994 ILC draft had envisioned.

Thus far, the deferral mechanism has been invoked only in formalized ways, where the US sought to immunize peacekeepers from the jurisdiction of the court in any cases which did arise out of UN missions;[189] some of the relevant resolutions[190] have since lapsed, while other analogous ones[191] are still in place.

5) Admissibility

The provisions in the *Rome Statute* regarding admissibility of cases make up the third piece in the complex process of getting a case before the ICC. The triggering mechanisms are the functional means of getting a matter on the court's radar, and the jurisdiction provisions allow the court to assess whether it *can* hear a case. The question of admissibility effectively allows the court to determine whether it *should* take a particular case. While this might sound like a policy decision—and indeed there are political components mixed in—it is a heavily legalistic issue that uses some novel treaty machinery.

a) Complementarity
Complementarity is the major innovative feature that makes the *Rome Statute* unique and, at least prospectively, underpins the ICC's major role in international criminal justice.[192] It stems from the 1994 draft of the ILC, and while the actual provision evolved a great deal from that draft, the central theme remained intact. It was never seriously con-

---

189 Neha Jain, "A Separate Law for Peacekeepers: The Clash between the Security Council and the ICC" (2005) 16 E.J.I.L. 239.

190 SC Res. 1422 (2002).

191 SC Res. 1497 (2003) and 1593 (2005).

192 See John Holmes, "Complementarity: National Courts versus the ICC" in Cassese *et al.*, eds., *The* Rome Statute, above note 99, 667 at 675 and "The Principle of Complementarity" in Lee, ed., above note 99 at 41; M. Benzing, "The Complementarity Regime of the ICC: International Criminal Justice between State Sovereignty and the Fight against Impunity" (2003) 7 Max Planck Yearbook of United Nations Law 591; Jann Kleffner, *Complementarity in the* Rome Statute *and National Criminal Jurisdictions* (Oxford: Oxford University Press, 2008).

templated that a standing international criminal court would have the resources to try all of the cases that could come within its jurisdiction. Indeed, it is far more efficient and effective to have states themselves prosecute instances of atrocities over which they have or can establish jurisdiction. The *Rome Statute* was designed to encourage states to be the main venues for prosecution of these crimes, a design which is apparent as early as paragraph 6 of the Preamble, which reminds states of their "responsibility" to prosecute. It has become almost axiomatic to say that the best International Criminal Court is one that would have no cases.

The core idea of complementarity is that the ICC is essentially intended to be a "fallback" court, which will prosecute only where there is some good reason that no state is doing so. However, the court itself is given the power to decide whether a particular domestic prosecution is appropriate, and while states may challenge the court's findings in this regard, they are ultimately obliged to defer to the court's decisions. These features distinguish the ICC from previous models of international criminal justice, often described as the "vertical" (a court which has primacy of jurisdiction over states, like the ICTY and ICTR) and the "horizontal" (i.e., states operate as sovereign equals, cooperating with each other in taking jurisdiction over crimes).[193] The relationship between the ICC and states is better described as "lateral," where the two operate in a parallel manner and the court has neither primacy over nor complete subservience to state courts. It is lateral, then, "in the sense of a lateral pass on the rugby pitch, where the player best-placed to pursue the objective is handed the ball, but with more of a compulsory flavour."[194] The relationship also, however, contains the contentiousness and difficult political wrangling which gave birth to the court in Rome and which will continue to characterize its activities.[195]

Article 17(1) of the *Rome Statute*[196] provides a presumption that a case is inadmissible if a state is investigating or prosecuting, or has investigated and decided not to prosecute, unless the court finds that the state was "unwilling or unable genuinely" to investigate or prosecute.

---

193 See Antonio Cassese, *International Criminal Law*, 2d ed. (Oxford: Oxford University Press, 2008) at 346–49; B. Swart, "International Cooperation and Judicial Assistance—General Problems" in Cassese *et al.*, eds., *The* Rome Statute, above note 99 at 1592–1605.

194 Robert Currie, "Abducted Fugitives before the International Criminal Court: Problems and Prospects" (2007) 18 Crim. L.F. 349 at 379.

195 A. Caesius, "The Statute of the ICC: Some Preliminary Reflections" (1999) 10 E.J.I.L. 144 at 145.

196 Above note 83.

The rationale is to have the court defer to state proceedings so long as they take the form of a true criminal investigation and/or prosecution; to prevent states from shielding perpetrators from prosecution by bringing sham proceedings; and to allow a state to give way to the court if its justice system is not up to the task, as in a failed state or one devastated by armed conflict.

To determine unwillingness, article 17(2) directs the court to consider whether

(a) The proceedings were or are being undertaken or the national decision was made for the purpose of shielding the person concerned from criminal responsibility for crimes within the jurisdiction of the Court referred to in article 5;

(b) There has been an unjustified delay in the proceedings which in the circumstances is inconsistent with an intent to bring the person concerned to justice;

(c) The proceedings were not or are not being conducted independently or impartially, and they were or are being conducted in a manner which, in the circumstances, is inconsistent with an intent to bring the person concerned to justice.

As has been commented, "the first criterion gives the Court the difficult task of assessing the motives of the national authorities (whether judicial, executive or legislative); the second two more clearly allow inferences to be drawn from objective factors."[197]

The first four cases before the court have not provided much grist for the mill of "unwillingness." Uganda, DRC, and Central African Republic are all self-referrals and, as would have been expected, no major issues regarding willingness have arisen. The major point of interest has been the extent to which, if at all, the court must consider admissibility in these situations, which are now being called "uncontested admissibility," and the Pre-Trial Chambers have floated different views on the matter.[198] The situation in Darfur has, as noted above, been contentious, and it is expected that Sudan will challenge admissibility of the case[199] on the basis of assertions it has made that it is dealing with

---

197 Robert Cryer *et al.*, *An Introduction to International Criminal Law and Procedure* (Cambridge: Cambridge University Press, 2007) at 128.

198 See *Lubanga* (ICC-01/04-01/06-8), Decision on the Prosecutor's Application for a Warrant of Arrest, 10 February 2006; *Situation in Uganda* (ICC-02/04-53), Warrant of Arrest for Joseph Kony Issued on 8 July 2005 as amended on 27 September 2005.

199 Such challenge would be under art. 19(2) of the *Rome Statute*, above note 83, which also allows challenges by an accused or person subject to an arrest war-

the impugned criminal conduct through its own courts. Another issue which is expected to arise is whether a state which has gone through some form of national reconciliation or a restorative justice process (such as South Africa's Truth and Reconciliation Commission) will be deemed "unwilling" under article 17(2), particularly if amnesties of any kind were granted to perpetrators.[200]

As regards inability, article 17(3) of the *Rome Statute* states

> In order to determine inability in a particular case, the Court shall consider whether, due to a total or substantial collapse or unavailability of its national judicial system, the State is unable to obtain the accused or the necessary evidence and testimony or otherwise unable to carry out its proceedings.

Both Uganda[201] and DRC[202] invoked inability in their self-referrals, as well as essentially waiving the issue of unwillingness. With regard to Uganda, Pre-Trial Chamber II considered the issue closed as a result, while Pre-Trial Chamber I examined the issue and found that DRC was not unable, though this was not conclusive for its decision to issue the arrest warrant.[203] It is not clear at present which approach will prevail.

b) Gravity

Article 17(1)(d) of the *Rome Statute*[204] provides another important admissibility requirement, that of "gravity."[205] It states that the court may find a case inadmissible when "it is not of sufficient gravity to justify further action by the Court." This provision reflects a functional acknowledgement of the reality—foreseen as early as the 1994 ILC draft and arguably as far back as Nuremberg—that the ICC would need to

---

rant, by a state with jurisdiction that claims it is prosecuting, or by any other state from which acceptance of jurisdiction is required under art. 12.

200 See Darryl Robinson, "Serving the Interests of Justice: Amnesties, Truth Commissions and the International Criminal Court" (2003) 14 E.J.I.L. 481; Jennifer Llewellyn, "A Comment on the Complementary Jurisdiction of the International Criminal Court: Adding Insult to Injury in Transitional Contexts?" (2001) 24 Dal. L.J. 192.

201 *Situation in Uganda* (ICC-02/04-53), Warrant of Arrest for Joseph Kony Issued on 8 July 2005 as amended on 27 September 2005 at paras. 33 and 37.

202 Letter from President Joseph Kabila to the ICC, 21 March 2004, ICC-01/04-01/06-32-AnxA1.

203 *Lubanga* (ICC-01/04-01/06-8), Decision on the Prosecutor's Application for a Warrant of Arrest, 10 February 2006 at para. 36.

204 Above note 83.

205 See Ray Murphy, "Gravity Issues and the International Criminal Court" (2006) 17 Crim. L.F. 281.

have the discretion to choose among cases that it might pursue and select those which were the most "grave" or serious. In his letter responding to requests to investigate crimes which took place during the invasion of Iraq, the Prosecutor noted that the definition of war crimes in article 8(1) of the *Rome Statute* contains what he referred to as "a specific gravity threshold" in its use of the words "in particular when committed as part of a plan or policy or as part of a large-scale commission of such crimes." He found that this definition, combined with his office's general policy of also considering the number of victims in a given situation, led to a conclusion that the case of Iraq was insufficiently grave to attract the court's attention.[206]

In his 2003 policy paper, the Prosecutor indicated his view that under the *Rome Statute*, "the Prosecutor should focus its investigative and prosecutorial resources on those who bear the greatest responsibility, such as the leaders of the State or organization allegedly responsible for those crimes."[207] In its decision on the *Lubanga* arrest warrant, Pre-Trial Chamber I endorsed this point of view, noting that the focus on such leaders was justified because these persons are "the ones who can most effectively prevent or stop the commission of those crimes," which in turn underpinned the idea that the court's primary purpose in prosecuting was prevention of such crimes, rather than retribution.[208] The Pre-Trial Chamber further held that to pass the gravity threshold, the crimes themselves must also be either systematic or large-scale, and subject to the consideration of the "social alarm" that the conduct caused in the international community.[209] The Chamber also confirmed that while gravity was an appropriate shaper of ICC prosecutorial policy, in the end it was not a matter of prosecutorial discretion but a mandatory requirement, and any case not of sufficient gravity was inadmissible.

c)   "Interests of Justice"

Articles 53(1)(c) and (2)(c) of the *Rome Statute*[210] indicate that in determining whether to initiate an investigation, the Prosecutor shall consider whether the investigation would "serve the interests of justice." The phrase "the interests of justice" is used throughout the *Rome Statute* and the ICC's *RPE*, but with no definition or explication. In

---

206 Online: www.icc-cpi.int/NR/rdonlyres/04D143C8-19FB-466C-AB77-4CDB2F-DEBEF7/143682/OTP_letter_to_senders_re_Iraq_9_February_2006.pdf.
207 Above note 121.
208 *Lubanga* (ICC-01/04-01/06-8), Decision on the Prosecutor's Application for a Warrant of Arrest, 10 February 2006 at paras. 48–53.
209 *Ibid*. at para. 46.
210 Above note 83.

September 2007, the Office of the Prosecutor released a policy paper[211] indicating the current Prosecutor's perspective. It noted that while the requirements of jurisdiction and admissibility must be satisfied before undertaking an investigation, this is not the case for the "interests of justice" requirement:

> The *interests of justice* test is a potential *countervailing* consideration that might produce a reason *not* to proceed even where the first two are satisfied. This difference is important: the Prosecutor is not required to establish that an investigation or prosecution is in the interests of justice. Rather, he shall proceed with investigation unless there are specific circumstances which provide substantial reasons to believe it is not in the interests of justice to do so at that time.[212]

It was noted that the *Rome Statute* requires the consideration of certain explicit factors (gravity of crime, interests of victims, and the particular circumstances of the accused) as well as other possible factors in a given case (including whether "other justice mechanisms" are operating in a given state, or whether there are peace processes under way).[213]

d) *Ne Bis In Idem*

Article 20 of the *Rome Statute* sets out the principle of *ne bis in idem*, often called "double jeopardy." This provision is at once a part of the larger panoply of human rights protections for accused persons that are set out in the *Rome Statute* and a bar to admissibility for certain cases. It provides that no person can be tried before the ICC for any conduct for which the person has already been tried or convicted by the court;[214] and that no person can be tried by any other court for one of the crimes in the ICC's jurisdiction where that person has already been convicted or acquitted by the ICC.[215] Importantly, it also provides that the ICC cannot prosecute an individual who has already been tried by a national court for alleged crimes unless the domestic proceedings were for the purpose of shielding the person from prosecution by the ICC, or were otherwise not conducted independently or impartially and "were inconsistent with an intent to bring the person concerned to justice."[216]

---

211 "Policy Paper on the Interests of Justice," online: www.icc-cpi.int/NR/ rdonlyres/772C95C9-F54D-4321-BF09-73422BB23528/143640/ICCOTPInterest-sOfJustice.pdf.

212 *Ibid.* at 2–3.

213 *Ibid.* at 4–9.

214 Above note 83, art. 20(1).

215 *Ibid.*, art. 20(2).

216 *Ibid.*, art. 20(3).

Article 20(2) leaves open the question of whether a case would be admissible if an accused person had already been prosecuted for the underlying conduct of one of the offences within the ICC's jurisdiction, for example, murder as a form of genocide or sexual assault in a crimes-against-humanity context.[217] Also, while not explicit, it has been opined that if an individual is granted a pardon or amnesty for a crime after a domestic prosecution which was genuine, then the case is inadmissible and the ICC is barred from prosecuting.[218]

E. INTERNATIONALIZED COURTS

This section will briefly examine the various "special" courts that have been set up to deal with crimes arising from various events particular to certain states or regions. They are referred to as "internationalized" because with each there is some particular combination of national and international law and jurisdiction at play.[219] At best, they represent a continuing expression of solidarity by the international community to prosecute the worst of criminals and record the worst of crimes; at worst, they represent institutionalized *"ad hockery"* that both diffuses prosecutorial resources in an inefficient and expensive manner and fails to address the underlying causes of conflict. Despite claims of "tribunal fatigue" in the international criminal justice community, however, it is clear that internationalized models of prosecution are a popular and portable tool and are likely to see continued use for some time to come.[220]

---

217 Schabas, *Introduction*, above note 125 at 192–93.

218 Holmes, "The Principle of Complementarity," above note 192 at 76–77.

219 Not dealt with here is the arrangement which was reached between the Security Council, the UK, Libya, and the Netherlands to allow a prosecution of two Libyan nationals for the Lockerbie bombing. The Scottish High Court of Justiciary had jurisdiction because the offence had occurred over Scottish territory, and the court sat in the Netherlands (in 2000–2002) but applied Scottish criminal law. See André Klip & Mark Mackarel, "The Lockerbie Trial—A Scottish Court in the Netherlands" (1999) 70 Rev. I.D.P. 777. For the appeal judgment in the case, see *Al-Megrahi v. H.M. Advocate*, Appeal No. C104/01, Opinion in Appeal against Conviction, 14 March 2002.

220 Plans are underway for a special court to be set up in Kenya to prosecute crimes committed during a period of violence after general elections in 2007. See the report by Human Rights Watch, online: www.hrw.org/en/news/2009/03/24/kenya-swiftly-enact-special-tribunal.

1) The Special Court for Sierra Leone[221]

a) Creation and History

The mission of the Special Court for Sierra Leone (SCSL) was made necessary by a protracted armed conflict that began in 1991 between the forces of the governing party All People's Congress (APC) and the rebel group Revolutionary United Front (RUF). As one author describes the scope of the conflict, "[N]early everybody in Sierra Leone lost family members, lost limbs and/or had their homes and livelihoods destroyed, not only as an indirect consequence of legitimate fighting, but also as a direct result of methods of war that deliberately targeted the civilian population."[222] A brokered power-sharing deal between the groups, the 1999 *Lomé Peace Agreement*,[223] set up a Truth and Reconciliation Commission and gave hope that a domestic solution could be reached. These hopes were dashed for the short term by renewed fighting, and in 2000, Sierra Leone President Kabbah (having been reinstalled by West African UN peacekeepers) formally requested that the Security Council create an international tribunal to prosecute members of the RUF.[224] In Resolution 1315, the Security Council took an approach that was both broader and more narrow than that requested by President Kabbah: broader in the sense that it directed the Secretary-General to negotiate a treaty to establish a special court that could try offences by the major perpetrators in the conflict, regardless of which side of the political fence they came from;[225] but more narrow in the sense that it rejected the option of an *ad hoc* tribunal similar to the ICTY and ICTR. This approach was based in part on "tribunal fatigue" and the lack of will among the UN collective to fund another *ad hoc* tribunal, but it was also hoped that "a treaty-based court enjoying the consent and support of the host State would enjoy greater legitimacy, raise fewer legal concerns, and function more effectively."[226] The negotiations culminated in the conclusion of an agreement on the establishment of the Special Court, with the statute appearing as an annex to the agreement. Sierra

---

221 The SCSL's website is online: www.sc-sl.org.
222 Alison Smith, "Sierra Leone: The Intersection of Law, Policy, and Practice" in Cesare Romano *et al.*, eds., *Internationalized Criminal Courts: Sierra Leone, East Timor, Kosovo and Cambodia* (Oxford: Oxford University Press, 2004) 125 at 127.
223 *Peace Agreement between the Government of Sierra Leone and the Revolutionary United Front of Sierra Leone*, 7 July 1999, online: www.unhcr.org/refworld/docid/3ae6b5064.html.
224 UN Doc. S/2000/786, annex.
225 UN Doc. S/RES/1315 (2000).
226 James Miglin, "From Immunity to Impunity: Charles Taylor and the Special Court for Sierra Leone" (2007) 16 Dal. J. Leg. Stud. 21 at 25.

Leone passed legislation to incorporate the treaty shortly thereafter,[227] and the SCSL has been in operation since that time.

The Special Court has gone about prosecuting "those most responsible" with reasonable vigour, though its early indictments of RUF leaders Foday Sankoh and Sam Bockarie were frustrated by the death of the two men.[228] Two complete trials and appeals have been held, resulting in the conviction of the five accused for various crimes against humanity and war crimes.[229] A third trial ended in the conviction of the three accused by the Trial Chamber in February 2009.[230] The Special Court's most prominent prosecution is against Charles Ghankay Taylor, the former President of Liberia, who is alleged to have financed the RUF and AFRC during the conflict in an effort to destabilize Sierra Leone. He has been charged with various war crimes and crimes against humanity[231] on the basis of both individual criminal responsibility and command responsibility for his leadership role. Due to security concerns, his trial is being held before a panel of the SCSL that is sitting in The Hague, pursuant to Security Council Resolution 1688.[232] As of November 2008, the trial had heard testimony from over 80 prosecution witnesses, including hair-raising accounts of Taylor forcing his soldiers to engage in cannibalism.[233] In terms of its completion strategy, the court expects the Taylor trial to be finished by 2009, and any

---

227 *Special Court Agreement (2000) Ratification Act*, Supp. to Sierra Leone Official Gazette Vol. CXXX No. II, 7 March 2002.

228 A third indictee, Armed Forces Revolutionary Council (AFRC)leader Johnny Paul Koroma, is currently missing and thought to be dead, though the court's indictment has not been withdrawn; online: www.sc-sl.org/CASES/JohnnyPaul-Koroma/tabid/188/Default.aspx.

229 *Fofana and Kondewa*, Case No. SCSL-04-14-A-829, Appeals Chamber, Decision of 28 May 2008; *Brima, Kamara and Kanu*, Case No. SCSL-04-16-A, Appeals Chamber, Decision of 22 February 2008.

230 *Sesay, Kallon and Gbao*, Case No. SCSL-04-15-T-619, Trial Chamber, Decision of 25 February 2009.

231 See *Taylor*, Case No. SCSL-03-01-T, Prosecution's Second Amended Indictment, online: www.sc-sl.org/LinkClick.aspx?fileticket=lrn0bAAMvYM%3d&tabid=107.

232 S/RES/1688 (2006), 16 June 2006. The trial is taking place at facilities provided by the ICC.

233 Taylor's son, Charles "Chuckie" Taylor Jr., was recently convicted by an American federal court (exercising custodial universal jurisdiction over extraterritorial torture) in Florida for crimes of torture he committed during the conflict; see John Couwels, "Ex-Liberian President's Son Convicted of Torture," online: www.cnn.com/2008/CRIME/10/30/taylor.torture.verdict/index.html.

appeal decisions to be issued by 2010, which will complete the court's mandate.[234]

b) Structure

In his initial report proposing a draft statute for the SCSL, UN Secretary-General Kofi Annan famously described the court as "a treaty-based *sui generis* court of mixed jurisdiction and composition."[235] Unlike the ICTY and ICTR, it is not a subsidiary organ of the UN and has not been imposed on the international community by way of an exercise of the Security Council's Chapter VII powers. Nor is it a court of the domestic Sierra Leonean legal system, though it has Sierra Leonean judges and has jurisdiction over some of that state's criminal law offences. Rather, it is a stand-alone court which was created by an agreement between the UN and the government of Sierra Leone. Its statute cannot be amended by Security Council Resolution, but only via an agreement between the UN and Sierra Leone.[236] It is funded not out of general UN coffers, as with the *ad hoc* tribunals, but by voluntary contributions from member states. In a preliminary motion in the *Taylor* case, the court itself determined that, for substantive and procedural law purposes, it is an "international" court.[237]

The SCSL sits in Freetown, Sierra Leone. It has the same three organs—Chambers, Prosecutor, and Registry—as do the ICTY and ICTR. The court had first one, and now two Trial Chambers, which sit with three judges, as well as an Appeals Chamber of five judges. At each level, a majority of judges are "international," appointed by the Secretary-General of the UN, who draws on nominations offered by various member states (particularly West African ones), while the remaining one and two judges, respectively, are appointed by the government of Sierra Leone. The Prosecutor is appointed by the Secretary-General for a term of three years,[238] while the Deputy Prosecutor is appointed by

---

234 SCSL, *Fifth Annual Report of the President of the Special Court, 2007–2008*, online: www.sc-sl.org/LinkClick.aspx?fileticket=hopZSuXjicg%3d&tabid=176 at 37.

235 *Report of the Secretary-General on the Establishment of a Special Court for Sierra Leone*, UN Doc. S/2000/915 at para. 9.

236 *Agreement between the United Nations and the Government of Sierra Leone on the Establishment of a Special Court for Sierra Leone*, UN Doc. S/1999/836, 16 January 2002, art. 22 [*SCSL Agreement*].

237 *Taylor*, Case No. SCSL-03-01-I-059, Appeals Chamber Decision on Immunity Motion, 31 May 2004. The decision went specifically to Taylor's defence of state immunity. See Miglin, "From Immunity to Impunity," above note 226; Micaela Frulli, "The Question of Charles Taylor's Immunity" (2004) 2 JICJ 1118.

238 *SCSL Statute*, art. 3(1), reprinted on the court's official website: www.sc-sl.org/LinkClick.aspx?fileticket=uClnd1MJeEw%3d&tabid=176.

the government of Sierra Leone.[239] The current Prosecutor, American Stephen Rapp, is the third SCSL Prosecutor, having succeeded British lawyer Desmond de Silva. Perhaps reflecting the UN experience with the ICTR, the agreement creating the SCSL also created a "Management Committee" to advise the UN Secretary-General regarding financial and policy directions for the court, "including questions of efficiency."[240]

c) Jurisdiction

The subject matter jurisdiction of the SCSL is only over crimes against humanity and war crimes, including in article 4 a partial list of "other serious violations of international humanitarian law" that is less developed than that in the *Rome Statute*. While article 3 of the court's Statute establishes jurisdiction only over offences committed in non-international armed conflicts, the Appeals Chamber of the court has overridden this limitation and allowed prosecution of crimes arising from international armed conflicts.[241] As the killings and atrocities which took place in Sierra Leone were on political grounds and not motivated by racial or ethnic animus, the crime of genocide is not included. The Statute does provide for jurisdiction over crimes under Sierra Leonean law, specifically the abuse of girls and the "wanton destruction of property."[242]

In terms of personal jurisdiction, article 1 of the *SCSL Statute* states that the court is to prosecute "persons who bear the greatest responsibility for serious violations of international humanitarian law and Sierra Leonean law." The court has confirmed that this is a jurisdictional requirement and not simply prosecutorial guidance as the UN Secretary-General had suggested earlier.[243] The Statute also provides for the prosecution of juvenile offenders between fifteen and eighteen years of age[244] and in some circumstances peacekeepers and associated personnel, though such prosecutions are presumptively to be done by the sending state.[245] The court's territorial jurisdiction is limited to the territory of Sierra Leone, while its temporal jurisdiction is open-ended,

---

239　*Ibid.*, art. 3(2).
240　*SCSL Agreement*, above note 236, art. 7.
241　*Fofana* (SCSL-04-14-PT101), Decision on Preliminary Motion on Lack of Jurisdiction—Nature of Armed Conflict, Appeals Chamber, 25 May 2004.
242　*SCSL Statute*, above note 238, art. 5.
243　*Fofana* (SCSL-04-14-PT), Decision on the Preliminary Defence Motion on the Lack of Personal Jurisdiction Filed on Behalf of the Accused Fofana, Trial Chamber, 3 March 2004 at paras. 27 and 39.
244　*SCSL Statute*, above note 238, art. 7.
245　*Ibid.*, arts. 1(2) & (3).

allowing prosecution for crimes "since 30 November 1996." The SCSL has concurrent jurisdiction with, but primacy over, the courts of Sierra Leone.[246]

2) Cambodia Extraordinary Chambers

The Extraordinary Chambers in the Courts of Cambodia (ECCC) was set up by the United Nations and the government of Cambodia to prosecute senior leaders of the Khmer Rouge, whose murderous rule of the country (then known as Democratic Kampuchea) from 1975–1979 led to the deaths of over one million people.[247] The tribunal was established in 2004 after a five-year and unhappy negotiation process between the United Nations and the government of Cambodia, which saw talks break down more than once.[248] The court began its work in June 2007 and indicted its first defendant, Kaing Guek Eva (alias "Duch") in July of that year. Duch went on trial in March 2009, and the court has indicted other prominent Khmer Rouge figures, including Nuon Chea, a.k.a. "Brother Number Two," ex–foreign minister Ieng Sary, and ex-president Khiev Samphan.

Unlike the SCSL, the ECCC has aptly been described as "an internationalized or hybrid tribunal in which the national side predominates."[249] It was created by way of a treaty between Cambodia and the UN[250] under which the court is formally part of the Cambodian domestic system, which is based in civil law. Its trial and appeal chambers are presided over by a mixture of domestic and international judges, but the domestic judges are in the majority. The same is true of the investigating judges and prosecutors. In all cases the officials are appointed by the Cambodian government, though the United Nations provides a list of nominees from which the international judges are drawn. Concerns have been expressed from the beginning about the fairness and impartiality which could be expected from the ECCC, given the potential for political influence and perceived problems with

---

246 *Ibid.*, art. 8.
247 The website of the ECCC can be found online: www.eccc.gov.kh/english/default.aspx.
248 See Craig Etcheson, "The Politics of Genocide Justice in Cambodia" in Romano *et al.*, eds., above note 222 at 181.
249 Cedric Ryngaert, "The Doctrine of Abuse of Process: A Comment on the Cambodia Tribunal's Decisions in the Case against Duch (2007)" (2008) 21 Leiden J. Int'l L. 719 at 719.
250 Signed in Pnom Penh on 6 June 2003, online: www.eccc.gov.kh/english/cabinet/agreement/5/Agreement_between_UN_and_RGC.pdf.

procedural fairness.[251] The adoption of the court's *Internal Rules* allayed these concerns somewhat, given their modelling on the ICC's *RPE*,[252] and an early decision on the procedural fairness implications of Duch's detention did likewise.[253]

The ECCC's temporal jurisdiction is limited to the 1975–79 period of the Cambodian "Killing Fields," and its limited mission is to try the major Khmer Rouge leaders "and those most responsible" for crimes during that period.[254] The distinction between the political leaders and "those most responsible" is deliberate, apparently to ensure the prosecution of Duch, who was an infamous figure during the period but not a senior leader.[255] Nonetheless, it is expected that the number of individuals tried will not be large and that the court will wrap up proceedings within three years. The court's subject matter jurisdiction includes genocide, crimes against humanity, and grave breaches of the *Geneva Conventions*, as well as crimes under Cambodian law.

3) Special Tribunal for Lebanon

The Special Tribunal for Lebanon (STL)[256] came about in the wake of the assassination of former Lebanese Prime Minister Rafiq Hariri and twenty-two others in February 2005, during what was suspected to be Syrian-inspired unrest in Lebanon. Lebanon requested the Security Council to "establish a tribunal of an international character" to try those responsible,[257] and an agreement to set up the STL was reached on 30 May 2007.[258] The *Statute of the Special Tribunal*[259] came into force in June 2007. The STL, still in a ramping-up period as of this writing, is a stand-alone international tribunal similar to the SCSL, which will sit in The Hague. While the government of Lebanon and the Secretary-General of the UN are bound under the treaty establishing the tribunal

---

251 Suzannah Linton, "Safeguarding the Independence and Impartiality of the Cambodian Extraordinary Chamber" (2006) 4 JICJ 327.

252 Guido Acquaviva, "New Paths in International Criminal Justice? The *Internal Rules* of the Cambodian Extraordinary Chambers" (2008) 6 JICJ 129. The third revision of the *Internal Rules* came into force in March 2009.

253 Ryngaert, above note 249 at 726.

254 *SCSL Agreement*, above note 236, art. 1.

255 Héleyn Uñac & Steven Liang, "Delivering Justice for the Crimes of Democratic Kampuchea" in John Ciorciari, ed., *The Khmer Rouge Tribunal* (Pnom Penh: Documentation Centre of Cambodia, 2006) 133 at 143.

256 The STL website can be found online: www.stl-tsl.org/.

257 SC Res. 1664 (2006).

258 SC Res. 1757 (2007).

259 Annexed to S/RES/1757 (2007).

to consult on the membership of the court, it will have a majority of international judges.[260] The Chief Prosecutor is Canadian Daniel Belle-mare, a former prosecutor and the head of the International Independent Investigation Commission which initially investigated the Hariri murder.[261]

The STL's jurisdiction is limited to the Hariri assassination and any other crimes of sufficient gravity which are found to have been related to that assassination, and which were committed in the period from 1 October 2004 to 12 December 2005. Its subject matter jurisdiction includes no international crimes, despite efforts at the Security Council to have crimes against humanity included, but rather a number of domestic Lebanese crimes. The list includes terrorism as an offence, however, which has raised speculation that the STL's work might help to pave the way for the prosecution of terrorist crimes by other international criminal tribunals in the future.[262] Unusually, the Statute allows for trials *in absentia*, which gives the STL more of a civilian character than other tribunals.

4) East Timor

In 1999, the Security Council set up the United Nations Transnational Administration in East Timor (UNTAET) in order to assist with the transition of East Timor into fully sovereign status after it voted for independence from Indonesia, which had forcibly annexed it in 1975. The period around the vote had seen sustained violence and atrocities. As part of an overall effort to rebuild the country's system for administration of justice, UNTAET set up "Serious Crimes Panels" in the District Court of the capital city, Dili, along with a Court of Appeal. These courts had jurisdiction over genocide, crimes against humanity, and war crimes, as well as some serious domestic offences, which occurred from 1 January to 25 October 1999. The courts were mixed panels with international judges in the majority, as was the case with the prosecutors.

The Serious Crimes Panels were plagued with problems from the start, including insufficient cooperation from the government of Indonesia, lack of staff and resources, failure to have all of the judicial

---

260 *SCSL Statute*, above note 238, art. 8. On 24 March 2009, Antonio Cassese, former President of the ICTY, was appointed as the STL's first president, see online: www.un.org/apps/news/story.asp?NewsID=30286&Cr=lebanon&Cr1=tribunal.

261 See James Stewart, "The UN Commission of Inquiry on Lebanon: A Legal Appraisal" (2007) 5 JICJ 1039.

262 See Nidal Jurdi, "The Subject-Matter Jurisdiction of the STL" (2007) 5 JICJ 1125.

positions filled at any one time, a diffuse prosecution strategy,[263] and questionable decisions in law by the Court of Appeal.[264] The UN continued to support the Serious Crimes Panels after elections in 2002, but these were phased out in 2005, and power over the target crimes transferred to local courts.

5) Kosovo

As with East Timor, the United Nations was involved in administering governmental functions for the territory of Kosovo, where Serbian ethnic cleansing against Kosovar Albanians had, in 1999, drawn NATO bombing strikes that completed the decimation of local infrastructure. Part of the UN's mandate was the maintenance of civil law and order,[265] which required some new structures for the administration of criminal justice, and dealing with the late-1990s events. The United Nations Interim Administration Mission in Kosovo (UNMIK) rejected an early proposal to set up a War and Ethnic Crimes Court in favour of "internationalizing" the municipal courts with international judges and prosecutors, as a means of providing appropriate judicial resources and to ensure impartiality in the courts. Operating under Regulation 64 of the *UNMIK Regulations*,[266] internationalized panels and prosecutors under UN auspices have presided over serious and prominent cases. As the new domestic Kosovar legislation came online by 2003–2004, these panels have been able to adjudge cases under modern definitions of the core crimes, rather than the older Yugoslavian law that had been applied of necessity before that.[267]

---

263 See S. de Bertodano, "East Timor: Trials and Tribulations" in Romano *et al.*, eds., above note 222 at 79.

264 *Armando dos Santos*, Case No. 16/2001, Decision of 15 July 2003 (UNTAET Serious Crimes Panel).

265 SC Res. 1244 (1999) at para. 11.

266 UNMIK/REG/2000/64 (15 December 2000).

267 The accused is tried under whichever version of the law and procedure is most beneficial to him. See, generally, M. Bohlander, "Kosovo: The Legal Framework of the Prosecution and Courts" in Kai Ambos & Muhammad al-Shādhilī Uthmān, eds., *New Approaches in International Criminal Justice: Kosovo, East Timor, Sierra Leone and Cambodia* (Freiburg: Edition Luscrim, 2003).

6) Former Yugoslavia: Bosnia and Herzegovina War Crimes Chamber and Serbian War Crimes Chamber

As noted earlier in this chapter, the ICTY has embarked on its "completion strategy," part of which is geared towards the referral of cases to local courts in the states that emerged from the breakup of the former Yugoslavia, a particularly useful strategy for lower-level accuseds.[268] In cooperation with the Security Council and the ICTY, the Federation of Bosnia and Herzegovina established its War Crimes Chamber of the State Court in Sarajevo in 2005. It applies the core crimes (genocide, crimes against humanity, and war crimes) as enshrined in new domestic criminal law and procedure, limited to events which took place in Bosnia. International judges and prosecutors have been provided to preside over and prosecute cases, though the plan is to phase these elements out. The Chamber has received several referrals from the ICTY, though observer reports indicate that overall progress has been limited.[269] The Republic of Serbia has established its own War Crimes Chamber in the Belgrade District Court, and while it received international assistance in setting up the new court, it is entirely a creature of the local government.[270] Its jurisdiction is extraterritorial in the sense that it extends throughout the territory of the former Yugoslavia, and it, too, has received referrals from the ICTY.

7) Iraqi High Tribunal

The Iraqi High Tribunal (IHT)[271] was established by an act of the Iraqi Transitional National Assembly in 2005.[272] The goal was to create a court which could preside over prosecutions of former dictator Sad-

---

268 This is done under r. 11 *bis* of the ICTY *RPE*, above note 167.

269 See Human Rights Watch, *Still Waiting: Bringing Justice for War Crimes, Crimes Against Humanity and Genocide in Bosnia and Herzegovina's Cantonal and District Courts* (2008), online: www.hrw.org/en/reports/2008/07/09/still-waiting-0.

270 See Mark Ellis, "Coming to Terms with Its Past: Serbia's New Court for the Prosecution of War Crimes" (2004) 22 Berkeley J. Int'l L. 165.

271 Official website online: www.iraq-iht.org.

272 An English translation of the *Iraqi High Criminal Court Law*, Law No. (10) 2005, reprinted online: http://law.case.edu/saddamtrial/documents/IST_statute_official_english.pdf. This domestic legislation followed on the heels of a similar instrument enacted by the Interim Governing Council, which had been established by the Coalition forces after the fall of Saddam Hussein's Ba'athist regime—the overall political legitimacy of which was considered highly questionable. See Ilias Bantekas, "The Iraqi Special Tribunal for Crimes against Humanity" (2005) 54 I.C.L.Q. 237.

dam Hussein, among others, for crimes committed during the reign of the Ba'athist regime from 1968 to 2003. The tribunal's jurisdiction extends over the territory of Iraq and any of the relevant crimes committed elsewhere by Iraqi nationals or residents. It is very much an Iraqi court, though the international elements are significant. The core international crimes (genocide, crimes against humanity, war crimes) are within its jurisdiction, based closely on the definitions in the *Rome Statute*, along with several Iraqi offences involving abuse of governmental power.[273] The judges and prosecutors are all Iraqi nationals, as international judges can be appointed only in limited circumstances[274] (though international defence lawyers and advisors are permitted to be involved). The tribunal is also being supported by the coalition states in both financial and practical terms.

The first matter heard by the IHT was, unsurprisingly, the prosecution of Saddam Hussein and others for crimes against humanity committed in the town of Dujail in 1992.[275] The Trial Chamber's decision in November 2006 was upheld by the Appeals Chamber, and Saddam was executed soon thereafter. The trial of the four defendants was reportedly marred by serious procedural and legal problems; one observer of the trial noted "deep dysfunction" within the IHT and commented,

> The serious procedural flaws in the Dujail trial undermined the credibility of the Trial Chamber's verdict and sentence, and the implementation of death sentences after an unfair trial is a violation of the right to life. The hope that the trial might have served as a model of impartial justice for the 'new Iraq' by upholding international human rights law and enforcing international criminal law, was unfulfilled.[276]

Since the *Dujail* trial, the IHT has also completed trials and appeals in the *Anfal* case, dealing with the mass execution of up to 100,000 Iraqi Kurds in 1988, and another relating to the crushing of a Shiite rebellion in 1991. In the result of the latter, the notorious cousin of Saddam Hussein, Ali Hassan al-Majid ("Chemical Ali"), was sentenced to death.

---

273 *Iraqi High Criminal Court Law*, ibid., arts. 11–14.
274 *Ibid.*, arts. 4(3) and 28.
275 See Michael Scharf & Gregory McNeal, *Saddam on Trial: Understanding and Debating the Iraqi High Tribunal* (Durham, NC: Carolina Academic Press, 2006). English translations of all of the IHT's decisions can be found online: http://law.case.edu/grotian-moment-blog/index.asp.
276 Nehal Bhuta, "Fatal Errors: The Trial and Appeal Judgments in the *Dujail* Case" (2008) 6 JICJ 39 at 41.

FURTHER READING

BROOMHALL, BRUCE, *International Justice and the International Criminal Court: Between Sovereignty and the Rule of Law* (Oxford: Oxford University Press, 2003)

DICKINSON, LAURA A., "The Promise of Hybrid Courts" (2003) 97 A.J.I.L. 295

KUOSMANEN, TUO, *Bringing Justice Closer: Hybrid Courts in Post-Conflict Societies* (Helsinki: Erik Castrén Institute of International Law and Human Rights, University of Helsinki, 2007)

METTRAUX, GUÉNAËL, ed., *Perspectives on the Nuremberg Trial* (Oxford: Oxford University Press, 2008)

RÖLING, B.V.A., & ANTONIO CASSESE, *The Tokyo Trial and Beyond* (Cambridge: Polity, 1993)

ROMANO, CESARE, ANDRÉ NOLLKAEMPER, & JANN KLEFFNER, eds., *Internationalized Criminal Courts: Sierra Leone, East Timor, Kosovo and Cambodia* (Oxford: Oxford University Press, 2004)

SANDS, PHILIPPE, ed., *From Nuremberg to the Hague: The Future of International Criminal Justice* (Cambridge: Cambridge University Press, 2003)

SCHABAS, WILLIAM, *An Introduction to the International Criminal Court*, 3d ed. (Cambridge: Cambridge University Press, 2007)

———, *The UN International Criminal Tribunals: The Former Yugoslavia, Rwanda and Sierra Leone* (Cambridge: Cambridge University Press, 2006)

SIMPSON, GERRY, *Law, War and Crime: War Crimes Trials and the Reinvention of International Law* (Cambridge: Polity, 2007)

TAYLOR, TELFORD, *The Anatomy of the Nuremberg Trials* (New York: Knopf, 1992)

TRIFFTERER, OTTO, ed., *The Rome Statute of the International Criminal Court: Observers' Notes, Article by Article*, 2d ed. (Oxford: Hart, 2008)

CHAPTER 5

INDIRECT ENFORCEMENT: NATIONAL PROSECUTION OF THE CORE CRIMES

A. INTRODUCTION

As discussed in Chapter 1, there are two enforcement models which can be used to combat international crimes: the *direct enforcement* model, which refers to the prosecution of perpetrators before international courts that are set up expressly to try international law crimes; and the *indirect enforcement* model, which refers to the prosecution of international crimes before the domestic courts of states. Direct enforcement in the modern day has its roots in the Nuremberg and Tokyo tribunals, and has seen rapid development since the establishment of the *ad hoc* tribunals in the early 1990s and the International Criminal Court (ICC) and internationalized courts thereafter. However, as has been explored in more detail in Chapters 3 and 4, these courts are exceptional; to the extent that the core crimes saw any significant amount of prosecution prior to the late twentieth century, these prosecutions were carried out by state courts. That said, it has often been the case more in law than in practice, since there has traditionally not been a great deal of willingness on the part of states to prosecute such offenders. This has changed in the last twenty or so years, owing in no small part to the success of the direct enforcement regime.

This chapter will survey the prosecution of the core crimes by national courts, with an emphasis on the Canadian context. A mostly historical introduction will be followed by analysis of the primary Canadian legislative instrument, the *Crimes Against Humanity and War Crimes Act*

(*CAH Act*),[1] as well as other legislative schemes that allow Canada to involve itself in enforcement activities against the core crimes.

1) Overview: The Post-war World

The work of the Nuremberg and Tokyo tribunals perhaps represented the peak of post-war willingness to pursue and prosecute perpetrators of the core crimes, but there was a great deal of political and legal will to use criminal justice to address some of the horrors of that conflict. At the international level, international criminal justice mechanisms were among the earliest tasks the fledgling United Nations set for itself, and the first several years after its founding saw the affirmation of the Nuremberg principles by the General Assembly, the drafting and conclusion of the *Genocide Convention*,[2] and the beginning of work on the *Draft Code of Crimes against the Peace and Security of Mankind*.[3] The work of the International Committee of the Red Cross (ICRC) culminated in the conclusion in 1949 of the *Geneva Conventions*.[4] Moreover, in the immediate aftermath of the war, there were thousands of war crimes trials, many held by the victorious allies within the European countries they were occupying (as well as in Japan and Singapore), while others were held by war-torn countries themselves: the UK, France, Denmark, Finland, Belgium, the Netherlands, the USSR, and China. The governments of both East and West Germany prosecuted Nazi war criminals for decades.

However, it is debatable how much justice was actually dispensed. Many of the post-war trials were exercises in symbolism, and parole and commutations of sentence were in common usage.[5] Many Italian war criminals were never prosecuted,[6] nor did the Allied Powers ever provide for their extradition to face trial elsewhere. Moreover, as the Western world sought to move forward and strengthen the apparatuses of peace and stability, interest in pursuing the perpetrators of the core crimes waned even as violent conflicts continued to flare. This

---

1   S.C. 2000, c. 24, online: http://laws.justice.gc.ca/en/showtdm/cs/C-45.9 [*CAH Act*].
2   78 U.N.T.S. 277, entered into force 12 January 1951.
3   GAOR, 51st Sess. Supp. No. 10, UN Doc. A/51/10 (1996).
4   (1950), 75 U.N.T.S. 31, 85, 135, and 287.
5   See, generally, Frank M. Buscher, *The U.S. War Crimes Trial Program in Germany, 1946–1955* (New York: Greenwood Press, 1989); Anthony P.V. Rogers, "War Crimes Trials Under the Royal Warrant: British Practice, 1945–1949" (1990) 39 I.C.L.Q. 780.
6   See Pier Paolo Rivello, "The Prosecution of War Crimes Committed by Nazi Forces in Italy" (2005) 3 JICJ 422.

was exacerbated by the onset of the Cold War, where mutual suspicion and lack of willingness to tolerate inquiries into matters of internal affairs sapped the motivation for political and legal cooperation to actively combat and prosecute these crimes. Developments were modest; the UN *Convention on the Non-Applicability of Statutes of Limitation to War Crimes and Crimes against Humanity*,[7] for example, attracted only a lukewarm reception. While the *Geneva Conventions* were ratified by many states, there was little if any active use of the *aut dedere* mechanism, and "few states adapted their legislation in such a way that traditional barriers to such prosecutions would be removed."[8] While there was no lack of perpetrators—Josef Stalin, Idi Amin, Pol Pot, perhaps even Henry Kissinger[9]—the star appeared to have set on the cause of international criminal justice.

The few domestic trials for international crimes that were held beyond the immediate aftermath of the war were noteworthy.[10] Perhaps the most famous was the trial in Israel of Adolf Eichmann, a prominent Nazi military commander and head of the Jewish Office of the German Gestapo during WW II, who was primarily responsible for the "Final Solution."[11] Eichmann was abducted from his home in Argentina in May 1960 by individuals who were later revealed to have been Israeli

---

7 The *Convention* was adopted in UNGA Res. 2391 (XXIII), 26 November 1968. The adoption of the resolution was passed by a vote of fifty-eight in favour, seven against, with thirty-six states (including Canada) abstaining. Canada is still not a party to this *Convention*. It is debatable whether the non-applicability of statutes of limitations to these crimes has achieved customary international law status; see Robert Cryer *et al.*, *An Introduction to International Criminal Law and Procedure* (Cambridge: Cambridge University Press, 2007) at 64–66. However, art. 29 of the *Rome Statute*, below note 23, expressly prohibits the application of limitations, which makes the matter mostly academic for many states.

8 Christine van den Wyngaert, "War Crimes, Genocide and Crimes Against Humanity—Are States Taking National Prosecutions Seriously?" in M. Cherif Bassiouni, ed., *International Criminal Law*, 2d ed. (Ardsley, NY: Transnational, 1999), vol. 3, 227 at 230.

9 See Christopher Hitchens, *The Trial of Henry Kissinger* (New York: Verso, 2001).

10 Aside from the *Eichmann* case, reviewed here, see also *Fédération Nationale des Déportés et Internés Résistants et Patriotes et Autres c. Barbie* (1985), English translation published in (1988), 78 I.L.R. 125 (Fr. Ct. Cass. Crim.); *Public Prosecutor v. Menten* (1981), 75 I.L.R. 331 (Neth. Sup. Ct.); *Polyukhovich v. Commonwealth of Australia* (1991), 101 A.L.R. 545 (H.C.A.).

11 *The Attorney-General of the Government of Israel v. Eichmann* (1968), 36 I.L.R. 18 (Israel Dist. Ct., 1961) (*Eichmann* (Dist. Ct.)) and (1968), 36 I.L.R. 277 (Israel Sup. Ct., 1962) (*Eichmann* (Sup. Ct.)). See, generally, L.C. Green, "The *Eichmann* Case" (1960) 23 Mod. L. Rev. 507; J.E.S. Fawcett, "The *Eichmann* Case" (1962) 38 Brit. Y.B. Int'l L. 181; Hannah Arendt, *Eichmann in Jerusalem: A Report on the Banality of Evil*, revised and enlarged ed. (New York: Penguin, 1992).

agents, and smuggled into Israel to face trial for his WW II activities. The abduction itself sparked an international incident between Israel and Argentina, which was ultimately resolved by way of a UN Security Council resolution,[12] and Eichmann was eventually convicted by the Israeli District Court of Jerusalem for crimes against the Jewish people, crimes against humanity, and war crimes.[13] The lower court decision was upheld by the Israeli Supreme Court and Eichmann was executed by hanging.

That Eichmann was criminally responsible for the crimes he was alleged to have committed was not really in doubt, and the major procedural issue that needed to be resolved was whether the Israeli courts had prescriptive jurisdiction to prosecute in the first place. The primary jurisdictional stumbling blocks were threefold: (1) the state of Israel did not exist at the time that Eichmann committed his crimes, which undermined its jurisdictional connection to the case; (2) Israel had not been a signatory to the *International Military Tribunal Charter* (*IMT Charter*);[14] and (3) with particular reference to the crime of genocide (or "Crimes against the Jewish People" in the applicable Israeli legislation), the *Genocide Convention* provided for jurisdiction only in the territorial state or an international criminal tribunal with jurisdiction—so Israel had no legal claim at international law to assert jurisdiction over this crime.

The District Court judgment attempted to bridge these difficulties by rather vaguely combining three jurisdictional principles: universal, passive personality, and protective. On the latter two grounds, the court pointed to the obvious connection between the Jewish victims of the Holocaust and the State of Israel, which "needs no explanation."[15] It ruled that in light of this connection, and in light of the fact that Israel had been founded to protect and sustain the Jewish people of the world, "an effective link (and not necessarily identity) between the State of

---

12   The issue of abducted fugitives, and this aspect of the *Eichmann* case in particular, are discussed in more detail in Chapter 9.

13   See above note 11. Specifically, Eichmann was prosecuted under Israel's *Nazis and Nazi Collaborators (Punishment) Law 1950*, 57 Sefer Hachukim, 9 August 1950 at 281. This statute has definitions of war crimes and crimes against humanity which generally comported with the *IMT Charter*, below note 14; "Crimes against the Jewish People" mirrors the provisions of the *Genocide Convention*, above note 2, but is specifically directed to acts committed "with the intent to destroy the Jewish people, in whole or in part." See, generally, Jonathan Wenig, "Enforcing the Lessons of History: Israel Judges the Holocaust" in Timothy L.H. McCormack & Gerry J. Simpson, eds., *The Law of War Crimes: National and International Approaches* (Boston: Kluwer, 1997) 103 at 105–7.

14   (1951), 82 U.N.T.S. 279.

15   *Eichmann* (Dist. Ct.), above note 11 at para. 34.

Israel and the Jewish people"[16] was sufficient to ground jurisdiction under both of these principles. As many subsequent commentators have noted, this was more of a political argument than a statement of law, for there was no basis in international law for founding jurisdiction on the basis of, at best, quasi-nationality of the victim, nor the protection of the interests of a state which had not existed at the relevant time.[17]

More convincing was the court's invocation of the principle of universality, and the Supreme Court's judgment on the appeal emphasized this principle as the strongest case, treating passive personality and protective jurisdiction as supplementary bases:

> Not only do all the crimes attributed to the appellant bear an international character, but their harmful and murderous effects were so embracing and widespread as to shake the international community to its very foundations. The State of Israel therefore was entitled, pursuant to the principle of universal jurisdiction and in the capacity of a guardian of international law and as an agent for its enforcement, to try the appellant.[18]

This case was also strengthened by the fact that neither Argentina, Eichmann's late state of residency, nor Germany, the territorial state, had expressed any willingness to try Eichmann for his crimes, and Germany had in fact been fairly explicit in its approval of Israel conducting the trial.[19]

There has been considerable scholarship suggesting that the *Eichmann* case was a show trial of sorts, allowing Israel to prosecute one individual for all of the murderous persecution associated with the Nazi regime,[20] though opinions are mixed as to whether in this particular case such an event was understandable and even warranted.[21] Legally speaking, while the convictions on war crimes and crimes against humanity were arguably well-founded, there was no real basis in law for Israel to try Eichmann for genocide since the extraterritorial reach of Israel's laws was not recognized under international law as it existed at the time. The mangling of the protective and passive personality prin-

---

16   *Ibid.* at para. 33.
17   See, for example, Green, above note 11 at 512; Fawcett, above note 11 at 191–92.
18   *Eichmann* (Sup. Ct.), above note 11 at 304.
19   Wenig, above note 13 at 114.
20   Arendt, above note 11 at 245; H. Heazlett, "*Eichmann*—International Law?" (1962) 24 U. Pitt. L. Rev. 116.
21   See Georg Schwarzenberger, "The *Eichmann* Judgment: An Essay in Censorial Jurisprudence" (1962) 15 Curr. Legal Probs. 248. See also Karl Jaspers, "Who Should Have Tried Eichmann?" (2006) 4 JICJ 853.

ciples undermined somewhat the legitimacy of the prosecution. On the other hand, no state protested the prosecution, and on the whole it has had the salutary effect of serving as a state practice-based, powerful affirmation of the exercise of universal jurisdiction over international crimes, particularly the crime of genocide. Moreover, quite apart from legal considerations, Israel's moral authority to try Eichmann for crimes against the Jewish people is really not open to dispute.

Eichmann was the exception rather than the rule, however, and those few prosecutions of international crimes that occurred focused on WW II–era perpetrators, even as international criminals and their odious acts proliferated. Significant change emerged in the late 1980s and early 1990s, as the end of the Cold War proved to be a harbinger of change for international criminal justice as much as for social, political, and economic conditions. With the (perhaps relative) unlocking of the Security Council as a meaningful actor, as well as the general swing towards democracy and the protection of human rights as matters of international interest, the will of states to combat impunity for the perpetrators of international crimes was re-energized in a manner not seen since the immediate post–WW II era. The creation of the UN *ad hoc* tribunals by the Security Council, the conclusion of the International Law Commission's (ILC) *Draft Code of Crimes against the Peace and Security of Mankind*,[22] and the unexpected and stunning conclusion of the *Rome Statute*[23] made the mid- to late-1990s very much a turning point.[24] The extent to which this was true for direct enforcement mechanisms has been explored in earlier chapters, but one of the more lasting legacies has been a renewed interest among states in the domestic prosecution of international crimes. States are, after all, the fora with the most well-developed legal systems and permanent criminal justice apparatuses. In the case of territorial states or states of nationality, they are also likely to be the most efficient forum for a trial since all participants are more likely to speak the same language, evidence and witnesses will be more readily available, and so on.

There was a renewed interest in prosecuting WW II criminals starting in the late 1980s and continuing throughout the 1990s, though

---

22   Above note 3.

23   2187 U.N.T.S. 3, entered into force 1 July 2002.

24   John McManus, "A New Era of Accountability through Domestic Enforcement of International Law" in Hélène Dumont & Anne-Marie Boisvert, eds., *The Highway to the International Court: All Roads Lead to Rome* (Montreal: Éditions Thémis, 2004) 503 at 506.

some of the prosecutions did not result in convictions.[25] However, the conclusion of the *Rome Statute* and its coming into force in 2002 has galvanized many states into action, since all state parties to the ICC must incorporate the core crimes, at least, into their domestic law.[26] The changes to domestic legislation have been accompanied by a great deal more enthusiasm on the part of states for utilizing universal jurisdiction as a basis on which to investigate and prosecute cases, and the last decade has witnessed an ever-increasing number of states doing just that.[27] Germany[28] and Denmark,[29] for example, have convicted individuals for genocide and war crimes during the Yugoslav conflict, while in 2001, Belgium convicted the infamous "Butare Four" of genocide in Rwanda.[30] Nor have such prosecutions been limited to the core crimes: famously, Spain initiated a prosecution against Augusto Pinochet for, *inter alia*, the crime of torture, which was only prevented by the refusal of the British government to extradite Pinochet because of his mental

---

25   Such as the *Polyukhovich* case, above note 10, and the four 1990s Canadian prosecutions; see Section B(4), below in this chapter. A more recent and successful British prosecution of a war criminal, based on the principle of universal jurisdiction, was *R. v. Sawoniuk*, [2000] 2 Cr. App. R. 220 (C.A.).

26   See University of Nottingham, Human Rights Law Centre, "Database of National Implementing Legislation," online: www.nottingham.ac.uk/law/hrlc/international-criminal-justice-unit/implementation-database.php. For reviews of the ICC implementation regimes of a number of states (including Canada), see Morten Bergsmo *et al.*, eds., *Importing Core International Crimes into National Criminal Law* (Oslo: Forum for International Criminal and Humanitarian Law, 2007); Matthias Neuner, ed., *National Legislation Incorporating International Crimes: Approaches of Civil and Common Law Countries* (Berlin: BWV, 2003).

27   For a recent, thorough, and wide-ranging survey of domestic prosecutions, see Joseph Rikhof, "Fewer Places to Hide? The Impact of Domestic War Crimes Prosecutions on International Impunity" (2008), online: www.isrcl.org (select "Conference Papers") [Rikhof, "Fewer Places to Hide"]. See also the Journal of International Criminal Justice, recent volumes of which have been dedicated to closely tracking developments in this area, and to A.H. Butler, "The Growing Support for Universal Jurisdiction in National Legislation" in Stephen Macedo, ed., *Universal Jurisdiction: National Courts and the Prosecution of Serious Crimes under International Law* (Philadelphia: University of Pennsylvania Press, 2004) 67.

28   Recounted in Ruth van-Saan, "The German Federal Supreme Court and the Prosecution of International Crimes Committed in the Former Yugoslavia" (2005) 3 JICJ 381.

29   See online: www.trial-ch.org/en/trial-watch/profile/db/legal-procedures/refik_saric_517.html.

30   See Luc Reydams, "Belgium's First Application of Universal Jurisdiction: the *Butare Four* Case" (2003) 1 JICJ 428.

unfitness to stand trial.[31] Senegal was unsuccessful in an attempt to use universal jurisdiction to prosecute former Chadian dictator Hissène Habré for torture during his time in power,[32] but under pressure from the African Union[33] and the European Union,[34] Senegal amended its laws in 2008 to allow the prosecution to take place.[35]

As discussed in Chapter 2, the parameters of when universal jurisdiction can be utilized are still controversial, and there is some diversity of practice among states. Belgium has been one of the most aggressive states in this regard. Its initial 1993 statute conferred broad universal jurisdiction on its courts, permitting the initiation of proceedings without any link to the perpetrator or the crime—and regardless of whether a more closely linked state was investigating or had been approached to do so—and not requiring the presence of the perpetrator in Belgium. Investigations under this law were controversial. The issuing of an arrest warrant for Abdulaye Yerodia Ndombasi, the sitting foreign minister of the Democratic Republic of the Congo (DRC), by a Belgian court sparked a claim by the DRC before the International Court of Justice (ICJ).[36] An indictment of former Israeli Prime Minister

31   R. v. Bow Street Magistrate, ex parte Pinochet (No. 3), [2000] 1 A.C. 147 (H.L.).
      See Richard J. Wilson, "Prosecuting Pinochet: International Crimes in Spanish
      Domestic Law" (1999) 21 Hum. Rts. Q. 927.

32   Guengueng and others v. Habré (2002), A.H.R.L.R. 183 (Senegal Cour de Cass.
      2001). See Stephen Marks, "The Hissène Habré Case: The Law and Politics of
      Universal Jurisdiction" in S. Macedo, ed., above note 27 at 131.

33   Decision on the Hissène Habré case and the African Union, DOC. ASSEMBLY/AU/3
      (VII) adopted at the Seventh Ordinary Session of the Assembly of the African
      Union, 1–2 July 2006, Banjul, The Gambia.

34   Human Rights Watch, Press Release, "Senegal: EU Parliament Calls for Support of Hissène Habré Trial" (26 April 2007), online: http://hrw.org/english/
      docs/2007/04/26/senega15779.htm.

35   At the time of writing, the case was in a sort of abeyance. The government of
      Senegal has stated that it will not try Habré until promised funding from the
      international community is received. In the meantime, Belgium had earlier
      indicted Habré and has brought a case against Senegal before the International
      Court of Justice (ICJ), demanding that Senegal either extradite or prosecute
      him. For an account, see Human Rights Watch, "The Case against Hissène
      Habré, an 'African Pinochet,'" online: www.hrw.org/en/news/2009/02/11/case-
      against-hiss-ne-habr-african-pinochet.

36   Case Concerning the Arrest Warrant of 11 April 2000 (Congo v. Belgium), [2002]
      I.C.J. Rep. 3. The case was ultimately resolved by a ruling of the court that
      Belgium's action had violated Yerodia's immunity as a sitting foreign minister.
      Some members of the court dealt with the universal jurisdiction issue in separate opinions, wherein was demonstrated some division of opinion on the Belgian statute; see the joint separate concurring reasons of Higgins J, Kooijmans J,
      and Buergenthal J, and the dissenting opinion of van den Wyngaert J.

Ariel Sharon was invalidated by the Court of Appeals on the basis that he enjoyed head of state immunity, and that any law suspending that principle could not operate *in absentia*.[37] Investigations into other world leaders, including Fidel Castro and US President George Bush, generated a great deal of negative political pressure from NATO countries, particularly the US, and the law was amended to more modest proportions in August 2003.[38]

Spain's *Organic Law No. 6/1985*[39] also has a broad and aggressive approach to universal jurisdiction. In 2005, proceedings under this law produced one of the first convictions for crimes against humanity based on universality since *Eichmann*, in the case of former Argentinian military officer Adolfo Scilingo.[40] The broad universality of the Spanish law had been debated in various proceedings before the Spanish courts, but in its ruling in the *Guatemalan Generals Case*,[41] the Spanish Constitutional Tribunal confirmed its view that universality is limited only insofar as the presence of the accused is required for trial (but not for initiating proceedings), and that prosecution is precluded if the territorial state is actively and effectively investigating or prosecuting the case.[42]

Accordingly, progress is being made on the two most important legislative tools for combating the core crimes: laws that criminalize the criminal acts themselves, and laws that allow for the exercise of universal jurisdiction over their commission. The practical aspects of initiating and conducting investigations are also being put in place, for example, through the creation of special war crimes investigation units by Canada, Denmark, Ethiopia, Norway, the Netherlands, and the UK. There are also plans for international cooperation between these entities.[43] Granted, these legislative and policing mechanisms will hardly

---

37   *H.S.A. et al. v. S.A. et al. (Decision Related to the Indictment of Ariel Sharon, Amos Yaron, and Others)*, 12 February 2003, reprinted (2003), 42 I.L.M. 596 (Belg. Cour de Cass.).

38   For an overview, see Damien Vandermeersch, "Prosecuting International Crimes in Belgium" (2005) 3 JICJ 400.

39   Also, art. 23.4 of *Organic Law 6/1985* of 1 July 1985 gives Spanish judges and tribunals jurisdiction over acts committed by Spanish nationals or foreigners outside Spain that are categorized as acts of terrorism under Spanish law.

40   See "Symposium: The *Scilingo* Case and its Implications" (2005) 3 JICJ 1074.

41   *Menchu Tumn and Others*, Sentencia 237/2005, Judgment, 26 September 2005 (Sala Segunda).

42   See, generally, Hervé Ascensio, "The Spanish Constitutional Tribunal's Decision in *Guatemalan Generals*: Unconditional Universality is Back" (2006) 4 JICJ 586.

43   See Joseph Rikhof, "War Crimes Law, as Applied in Canada" in Richard D. Wiggers & Ann. L. Griffiths, eds., *Canada and International Humanitarian Law: Peacekeeping and War Crimes in the Modern Era* (Halifax: Centre for Foreign Policy Studies, Dalhousie University, 2002) 121.

be enough without there being sufficient political will among the community of states to actively involve themselves in seeking out and prosecuting the perpetrators. The prosecution of international crimes is a massive undertaking, and governments must be willing to expend the significant resources to do so as well as to make good faith efforts to cooperate with other states, via extradition and mutual legal assistance. However, the cases mentioned above, among others, speak to the existence of the required resolve among many states and provide evidence that it is picking up steam. As was discussed in Chapter 4, Section D(5) (a), the *Rome Statute*, which had 139 signatories and 108 parties as of 4 June 2009,[44] operates via "complementarity," which contemplates the court prosecuting only in a situation where states are unwilling or unable genuinely to do so. As has been commented, the best international criminal court would be one that would see no use whatsoever;[45] while this is unlikely in the near to medium term, all signs are pointing towards continued expansion of international criminal justice and the concomitant shrinking of the possibility of impunity for perpetrators. Moreover, the sketchy history of domestic prosecution of international crimes shows that there will likely always be a place for adjudication of international crimes by international courts, whether as a more well-resourced alternative to underdeveloped legal systems, as a place of common or neutral ground for particularly contentious cases,[46] or as the most profound vehicle for declaring the will and intent of the international community to pursue and mete out justice to *hosti humanii generis*, the "enemies of humanity," wherever they may be.

B. CANADA, 1945–1999

1) Post–WW II Developments

It has been remarked that Canada's record of prosecuting perpetrators of core crimes after WW II was "less than distinguished"[47] and

---

44   See online: www.iccnow.org.

45   Iain Cameron, "Jurisdiction and Admissibility Issues under the *ICC Statute*" in Dominic McGoldrick *et al.*, eds., *The Permanent International Criminal Court: Legal and Policy Issues* (Oxford: Hart, 2004) 65 at 86.

46   Consider the Charles Taylor trial, which is being held in the Special Court for Sierra Leone in The Hague, due to security concerns; see Chapter 4, Section (E)(1)(a).

47   Christopher Amerasinghe, "The Canadian Experience" in M. Cherif Bassiouni, ed., *International Criminal Law*, 2d ed. (Ardsley, NY: Transnational, 1999), vol. 3, 243 at 243.

that Canada was not alone among Western countries in this regard.[48] The immediate post-war period was the most active, and the 1946 *War Crimes Act*[49] was the first war crimes legislation brought into effect. This Act defined "war crimes" as "violation[s] of the laws or usages of war committed during any war in which Canada has been or may be engaged at any time after the ninth day of September 1939,"[50] and was essentially designed to facilitate military trials for war crimes under military law.[51] Canadian War Crimes Investigation Units were active in Europe and Asia after the war, and over 170 cases were investigated. Four war crimes trials were held under the *War Crimes Act*, before Canadian military tribunals in Aurich, Germany, in 1945–46. The most prominent of these[52] was that of S.S. Brigadeführer Kurt Meyer,[53] who was convicted of having incited and counselled his troops to deny quarter to Allied soldiers, and was held responsible for the killing of POWs. There were also several trials of escaped POWs in Alberta,[54] under the *Geneva Convention* of 1929.[55]

By 1948, however, Canada had joined in a British-led disengagement from prosecuting war criminals. Once Canadian troops were decommissioned, responsibility for the trials of twenty-eight further accused persons was transferred to the British authorities.[56] On 13 July 1948, the British Commonwealth Relations Office sent a now-infamous secret telegram to the seven British dominions, including Canada, suggesting

---

48 Jules Deschênes, *Commission of Inquiry on War Criminals: Report* (Ottawa: Minister of Supply and Services, 1986) [Deschênes Commission Report].

49 S.C. 1946, c. 73. This *Act* was designed to re-enact the *War Crimes Regulations* of 30 August 1945 (P.C. 5831), which had been made pursuant to the *War Measures Act*, R.S.C. 1927, c. 206.

50 *War Crimes Act*, *ibid.*, s. 2(f).

51 As Fenrick notes, this legislation has never been repealed, though it has disappeared from the federal statutory restatements, and must be viewed as obsolete as it would never withstand *Charter* scrutiny (William J. Fenrick, "The Prosecution of War Criminals in Canada" (1989–90) 12 Dal. L.J. 256 at 291).

52 Though see also the cases of *Johann Neitz, Jung and Schumacher*, and *Holzer, Wiegel and Ossenbach*, cited in Amerasinghe, above note 47 at 246. See also Patrick Brode, *Casual Slaughters and Accidental Judgments: Canadian War Crimes Prosecutions 1944–1948* (Toronto: University of Toronto Press for Osgoode Society, 1997).

53 *The Abbaye Ardenne Case: Trial of S.S. Brigadeführer Kurt Meyer* (1945), 4 L.R.T.W.C. 97 (Can. Military Ct.). See Howard Margolian, *Conduct Unbecoming: The Story of the Murder of Canadian Prisoners of War in Normandy* (Toronto: University of Toronto Press, 1998).

54 *R. v. Shindler* (1944), 3 W.W.R. 125 (Alta. Police Ct.); *R. v. Brosig*, [1945] O.R. 240 (C.A.); *R. v. Kaehler & Stolski* (1945), 83 C.C.C. 353 (Alta S.C.A.D.).

55 *International Convention relative to the Treatment of Prisoners of War*, 12 August 1949, 75 U.N.T.S. 135.

56 Deschênes Commission Report, above note 48 at 26.

that no new war crimes trials should be commenced after 31 August 1948, even should alleged war criminals be apprehended subsequently. This was justified in the following terms:

> In our view, punishment of war criminals is more a matter of discouraging future generations than of meting out retribution to every guilty individual. Moreover, in view of future political developments in Germany envisaged by recent tripartite talks, we are convinced that it is now necessary to dispose of the past as soon as possible.[57]

Canada acceded to this plan and to the secrecy surrounding it, and as the Deschênes Commission later noted, the RCMP first ignored and later actively discouraged the possibility of apprehending and prosecuting war criminals.[58]

In 1965, Canada ratified the *Geneva Conventions* of 1949 and implemented them via the *Geneva Conventions Act*.[59] However, while section 3 of the Act criminalized grave breaches of the Conventions, it did so only for those offences which would have been crimes if committed in Canada, which had the effect of narrowing the range of prosecutable grave breaches. Moreover, though it did provide for universal jurisdiction over grave breaches, it was prospective and did not extend to acts committed in WW II. At international law, Canada enjoyed universal jurisdiction to prosecute WW II criminals, but lacked any domestic legislation to give effect to it. Though a fuller universal jurisdiction over grave breaches was instituted through Canada's ratification of the *Additional Protocols to the Geneva Conventions*[60] (and the subsequent legislative amendment to implement the changes),[61] to date no one has ever been prosecuted under the *Geneva Conventions Act*. As regards the other core crimes, only the offence of incitement to genocide was added to the *Criminal Code* after Canada's ratification of the *Genocide Convention* in 1949, despite the clear obligation in the Convention (and later, in customary law) to criminalize acts of genocide. Until 1987, an offence of crimes against humanity was nowhere to be seen in Canadian law.

The "shelving"[62] of the Nuremberg legacy in Canada continued for nearly forty years. However, in 1980, Robert Kaplan became Solicitor

---

57 *Ibid.* at 27.
58 *Ibid.* at 28–29.
59 R.S.C. 1985, c. G-3.
60 (1977), 1125 U.N.T.S. 3 and 609.
61 S.C. 1990, c. 14, s. 2.
62 See Sharon A. Williams, "Laudable Principles Lacking Application: The Prosecution of War Criminals in Canada" in McCormack & Simpson, eds., above note 13, 151 at 152.

General of Canada and, reflecting growing public concern about Canada becoming a haven for war criminals, began the institution of a "new approach" within the RCMP, for which he was the responsible minister.[63] Kaplan, who only two years earlier as a Member of Parliament had introduced a private member's bill towards prosecuting war criminals, created an interdepartmental committee within the Canadian government to begin inquiries into the presence of war criminals in Canada, and also opened cooperative channels with the US Office of Special Investigations and receptive European states.[64]

The latter effort paid off quickly in the form of an extradition request by West Germany for Helmut Rauca. Rauca, a German who had held Canadian citizenship since 1956, was accused of having aided, abetted, and participated in the murder of over 11,000 people in Lithuania during the German occupation of that country in 1941, and had been under indictment for five counts of murder in Germany since 1961. In a ruling[65] upheld by the Ontario Court of Appeal,[66] the judge committed Rauca for extradition to Germany. These were not truly war crimes, in a sense, as Rauca had been charged with offences under the German penal code and not with the Nuremberg crimes, and Rauca argued that he should be tried in Canada; nonetheless, Germany was the obvious forum in which to prosecute Rauca—particularly because, as the Court of Appeal pointed out, Canada could not prosecute him for war crimes under either the *War Crimes Act*[67] or the *Geneva Conventions Act*.[68] Rauca died in prison in Germany awaiting trial. For the next quarter century, no other alleged WW II war criminals were extradited, in no small part because Canada had no extradition treaties with important territorial states, such as the USSR, but also because of Cold War suspicion about the quality of justice in communist states.[69] This continued until 2007, when former German SS member Michael Seifert was extradited to Italy, after dismissal of his appeal against the extradition order by the British Columbia Court of Appeal.[70]

63   Deschênes Commission Report, above note 48 at 29.
64   *Ibid.*
65   *Federal Republic of Germany v. Rauca* (1982), 38 O.R. (2d) 705 (H.C.J.).
66   *Federal Republic of Germany v. Rauca* (1983), 41 O.R. (2d) 225 (C.A.).
67   Above note 49.
68   *Federal Republic of Germany v. Rauca*, above note 66 at 245.
69   Amerasinghe, above note 47 at 251–52.
70   *Italy v. Seifert*, 2007 BCCA 407, leave to appeal to S.C.C. refused, [2007] S.C.C.A. No. 503. Seifert had been convicted *in absentia* in Italy in 2000 for a number of murders that took place in 1944–45.

2) The Deschênes Commission Report

The *Rauca* case increased public awareness and concern about war criminals who had taken refuge in Canada, and Jewish groups in particular intensified their lobbying efforts to prompt government action.[71] In response, in February 1985, the federal government appointed[72] Justice Jules Deschênes to head a Royal Commission of Inquiry which would investigate the presence of any war criminals in Canada and make recommendations as to how they could be brought to justice. The Commission investigated over 800 cases, hearing from witnesses and intervening public-interest groups. Its final report was released on 30 December 1986 in two parts:[73] Part I, which reported its findings and recommendations, and Part II, which was confidential and released only to the government, and identified 29 cases which were recommended for action by the RCMP and the federal Department of Justice.

The Commission made a number of recommendations, which were essentially grouped around three key themes. The preferred option for dealing with war criminals was extradition to states which were willing to prosecute, most likely those which had territorial jurisdiction over the crimes in question, and it was proposed that the extradition treaties (in particular that with Israel) and domestic law be updated and revised to accommodate this. The second option would be prosecution of war criminals in Canada. The Commission acknowledged that the existing legislative framework made such prosecution unworkable, and recommended amendments to the *Criminal Code* to add war crimes and crimes against humanity. The last in the Commission's order of preference was to ensure that Canadian citizenship and immigration law could better accommodate both screening potential immigrants for war criminals, and denaturalization and deportation of immigrants and citizens who were discovered to be war criminals. Notably, the Commission deemed the latter option a relatively poor third choice, since it meant simply transferring the criminals rather than ensuring that justice was meted out.[74]

The Commission functionally rounded out these three themes with a recommendation that the RCMP and federal Department of Justice continue with the investigations the Commission itself had started. It

---

71   See David Matas, *Justice Delayed: Nazi War Criminals in Canada* (Toronto: Summerhill, 1987).

72   Order-in-Council No. 1985-348.

73   Above note 48.

74   *Ibid.* at 86.

also recommended that a specialized team of lawyers, historians, and police officers be created to further pursue this agenda.

3) Response to Deschênes: The 1987 *Criminal Code* Amendments

The federal government reacted swiftly to the findings of the Deschênes Commission, and in 1987, it created the Crimes against Humanity and War Crimes Section of the Department of Justice, as well as the War Crimes and Special Investigations Section of the RCMP.[75] These sections were given a specific mandate to "investigate and where the evidence warrants to recommend prosecution, denaturalization or deportation proceedings," with a priority on dealing with WW II crimes first.[76] The federal Department of Justice also negotiated a series of Memoranda of Understanding and exchanges of Diplomatic Notes with the various European countries that had been occupied by Nazi Germany, as well as with West Germany itself and Israel, which provided for various modes of cooperation in the gathering of evidence, taking of witness statements and testimony, and other investigation techniques. This forerunner of modern mutual legal assistance mechanisms,[77] albeit in a manner limited to WW II prosecutions, was something of an early Cold War thaw.[78]

In contrast to what the Deschênes Commission had recommended, however, the government of Canada took the stance that prosecution in Canada would be the preferred option. It brought in the *Act to amend the Criminal Code, the Immigration Act, 1976 and the Citizenship Act*[79] in September 1987. The *Criminal Code* amendments[80] created expansive definitions of war crimes and crimes against humanity, which were linked to customary and conventional international law,[81] as well as providing for jurisdiction over the offences on the nationality, protective, passive personality, and quasi-universal principles.[82] The new

---

75   See Justice Canada, "History of the War Crimes Program," online: www.justice.gc.ca/eng/pi/wc-cg/hist.html.

76   Crimes against Humanity and War Crimes Section, Department of Justice, Canada, *Progress Report on the Investigation of War Crimes in Canada* (1993) at 13, cited in Williams, above note 62 at 154.

77   See Chapter 9.

78   For details, see Amerasinghe, above note 47 at 255–56.

79   S.C. 1987, c. 37.

80   *Criminal Code*, R.S.C. 1985, c. C-46, ss. 7(3.71)–(3.77), subsequently repealed.

81   *Ibid.*, s. 7(3.76).

82   *Ibid.*, ss. 7(3.71)(a) & (b).

scheme also removed any temporal barriers on prosecutions, allowing for prosecution of persons who had committed the prescribed crimes at any time. While this had the appearance of retroactive legislation, the intent was simply to provide Canada with retrospective jurisdiction over acts which were crimes under international law when they were committed, even though Canada did not have legislation implementing the crimes in place at the time—in conformity with section 11(g) of the *Canadian Charter of Rights and Freedoms (Charter)*,[83] which provides that the principle of legality is not offended if the crime for which an individual is prosecuted existed under international law at the time of its commission.

The jurisdictional scheme was, however, quite complicated. The universal jurisdiction provision was custody-based and operated only where Canada could have exerted universal jurisdiction "on the basis of the person's presence in Canada" at the relevant time.[84] As Professor Williams pointed out, this threw into question whether WW II crimes against humanity could be prosecuted under universality at all under the legislation, since it was not at all clear during the war or before the International Military Tribunal (IMT) that such universality was available.[85] Moreover, the crimes were subject to prosecution only if they would have constituted "an offence against the laws of Canada in force at the time of the act or omission."[86] For pre-1987 cases, this requirement meant that prosecutors had to try international crimes by way of the underlying "common crime" acts in Canadian law, excepting the narrow range of grave breaches in the *Geneva Conventions Act* for post-1965 war crimes—"in hind sight, [a] rather simplistic or naïve approach."[87]

The *Act to amend the Criminal Code, the Immigration Act, 1976 and the Citizenship Act* did have more effective provisions for denying entry and citizenship to persons found to have been involved in war crimes or crimes against humanity, as well as for denaturalization and deportation, which ultimately have resulted in an exponentially greater number of "successful" cases, in the sense of bringing some legal consequences to bear on core crime perpetrators.[88] However, no changes were made to the *Extradition Act*.

---

83 Part I of the *Constitution Act 1982* (U.K.), 1982, c. 11.
84 Above note 80, s. 7(3.71)(b).
85 Williams, above note 62 at 162.
86 Above note 80, s. 7(3.71).
87 McManus, above note 24 at 526.
88 See Section D, below in this chapter.

4) The *Finta* Case and Its Fallout

Spurred on by the new investigational and legislative impetus, the Justice War Crimes Section and the RCMP picked up where the Deschênes Commission's work had left off, and commenced investigations into numerous cases of alleged WW II criminals. In the end, only four cases were submitted for prosecution, and none resulted in a conviction.[89] Only one of the four, *R. v. Finta*,[90] went ahead with a full trial and resulted in a final appeal judgment from the Supreme Court of Canada, which acquitted the defendant.

Hungarian-Canadian Imre Finta was alleged to have been a senior officer of the Hungarian *Gendarmerie*, a paramilitary security force that was involved in the internment and deportation to concentration camps of Hungarian Jews in Szeged, Hungary, in 1944. He was charged with the kidnapping, illegal confinement, robbery, and manslaughter of 8,617 Jews, as both war crimes and crimes against humanity, and on the basis that he either committed or, as a commander, had procured, aided, or abetted those who had performed the acts.[91] His eight-month trial before judge and jury ended in an acquittal, and Crown appeals on several legal points were dismissed by split panels of both the Ontario Court of Appeal and the Supreme Court of Canada.

The Supreme Court's ruling in *Finta* was extremely controversial and attracted a great deal of critical comment.[92] A significant procedural point which divided the majority[93] from the minority[94] was the characterization of the new provisions of section 7,[95] under which the

---

89   Aside from *Finta*, the other three were *R. v. Reistetter* (unreported, 1991, Ont. Ct. Gen. Div., Court File No. RE 185/90), stayed because of death/illness of key witnesses; *R. v. Pawlowski* (1992), 13 C.R. (4th) 228 (Ont. Ct. Gen. Div.), quashed 20 C.R. (4th) 233 (Ont. C.A.), leave to appeal to S.C.C. refused (1993), 25 C.R. (4th) 67n, stayed due to Court refusal to order commission evidence in USSR; and *R. v. Grujicic*, [1994] O.J. No. 2280 (Gen. Div.), stayed because of illness of the defendant.

90   (1989), 61 D.L.R. (4th) 85 (Ont. H.C.J.); (1992), 14 C.R. (4th) 1 (Ont. C.A.), aff'd [1994] 1 S.C.R. 701.

91   He had, in fact, been tried and convicted *in absentia* in Hungary after the war (*Re Finta*, Szeged, People's Court, Case No. 221/1947/10).

92   See Irwin Cotler, "War Crimes and the *Finta* Case" (1995) 6 Sup. Ct. L. Rev. (2d) 577 and "*R. v. Finta*" (1996) 90 A.J.I.L. 460; Randolph L. Braham, "Canada and the Perpetrators of the Holocaust: The Case of *Regina v. Finta*" (1995) 9 Holocaust & Genocide Studies 293.

93   Made up of Cory J, writing for himself, Lamer C.J., and Gonthier and Major JJ.

94   Made up of La Forest J, writing for himself, and L'Heureux-Dubé and McLachlin JJ.

95   See above note 79.

prosecution was brought. Justice Cory held that the provisions were offence-creating, in that they were formulations of new crimes under Canadian law, while La Forest J. for the minority found that the provisions were simply intended to create jurisdiction over offences that were already crimes in Canada at the relevant time. This dispute was not in itself significant, though the minority decision was consistent with the express language of the statute. However, the majority's approach compelled it to insert international law contextual elements into the offences — specifically, to impose an additional *mens rea* element beyond the intent required to be proven for the underlying offence. Justice Cory ruled that because of the seriousness of war crimes and crimes against humanity, it was not sufficient that the accused committed the underlying act intentionally, but it must also be proven that "the accused was aware of or wilfully blind to the facts and circumstances which would bring his acts within the definition of a crime against humanity [or war crime]."[96] With regard to crimes against humanity, the majority imposed the further requirement that the acts "were based on discrimination against or the persecution of an identifiable group of people."[97] Justice Cory also ruled that a subjective test was appropriate for the mental element.[98] Justice La Forest disagreed with these propositions, which he correctly identified as being mostly inconsistent with both international law and the legislative intent behind the new provisions.[99]

The majority also made a controversial ruling on the application of the defences of superior orders and "mistake of fact." The operative question for each defence, respectively, is whether the accused had no moral choice but to obey the orders, and whether the facts gave rise to an "air of reality" that the orders given were lawful. The majority ruled that it was open to the judge, in deciding whether to put the defences to the jury, to consider various factual circumstances put into evidence by the accused, including an assortment of anti-Semitic propaganda and the apparent state sanctioning of confiscations of property. As Amerasinghe has commented, the effect of this ruling was that "the accused was permitted to rely on state-sponsored racism and persecution as a defence to the commission of war crimes and crimes against humanity, contrary to the principles of international law."[100]

---

96 Above note 90 at 820 (S.C.R.) for war crimes.
97 *Ibid.* at 813 (S.C.R.).
98 *Ibid.* at 816.
99 See *ibid.* at 755–65.
100 Amerasinghe, above note 47 at 268.

The Court also made rulings on Finta's various *Charter* challenges to the legislation. In particular, Finta had argued that the new provisions violated section 11(g) of the *Charter*,[101] which provides that no one can be found guilty of any crime "unless, at the time of the act or omission, it constituted an offence under Canadian law or international law or was criminal according to the general principles of law recognized by the community of nations." Justice Cory, having found that the provisions did indeed create new Canadian law, turned to the debate over whether crimes against humanity framed in the *IMT Charter*[102] was also retroactive. He adopted the views of Professors Georg Schwarzenberger and Hans Kelsen that the Nuremberg laws were indeed retroactive, but only insofar as they provided for *individual* responsibility for acts which were already illegal (and subject to state responsibility) under international law. Accordingly, the majority was willing to find that the offences were not retroactive in a manner that offended section 11(g).

The *Finta* rulings essentially gutted the entire "prosecutions" limb of the government of Canada's strategy to pursue war criminals. It was clear that if the Crown was going to be required to prove an impossibly high mental standard, and the accused was to be permitted to plead "I believed the hate propaganda"[103] as a defence, it was unlikely that any prosecutions would be successful. The government fell back on the immigration and citizenship mechanisms which had accompanied the new criminal provisions, and shifted its focus to exclusion, denaturalization, and deportation.[104] In 1996, it created a new Modern War Crimes Section within the Department of Citizenship and Immigration Canada (CIC). While, as the Deschênes Commission had suggested, this was in some sense a secondary remedy, it was one that met with a significant measure of success in terms of keeping perpetrators of the core crimes out of Canada,[105] and in some cases deporting them to states where they could face justice.[106] As described in further detail in Section D, below in this chapter, immigration-based measures continue to be an important part of Canada's policy of combating international crime.

---

101 Above note 83.
102 Above note 14.
103 McManus, above note 24 at 526.
104 Cotler, above note 92 at 460 (A.J.I.L.).
105 See Joseph Rikhof, "The Exclusion Clauses: The First Hundred Cases in the Federal Court" (1996) 34 Imm. L.R. (2d) 137.
106 For example, *Canada (Secretary of State) v. Lutjens* (1991), 46 F.T.R. 267 (T.D.). Lutjens was deported to the Netherlands, where he was imprisoned for a 1948 conviction stemming from WW II.

C. THE *CRIMES AGAINST HUMANITY AND WAR CRIMES ACT, 2000*

1) Introduction

The abject failure of the *Finta* prosecution sent the government back to the drawing board in terms of being able to prosecute and convict perpetrators of the core crimes. By the mid-1990s, however, it was clear that the cause of international criminal justice was gaining steam. The establishment of the *ad hoc* tribunals and the incipient founding of the ICC—an effort where Canada was playing a significant leadership role—were powerful indicators that a revamping of the country's prosecutorial and cooperative capacity was necessary, both to continue the hunt for WW II war criminals and to deal with "fresh" international crime as it continued to emerge. In 1997, a review of the War Crimes Program was undertaken, and in 1998, the government overhauled the program in order to devote more resources to it generally, but in particular to facilitate prosecutions and to coordinate activities between the Department of Justice, RCMP and CIC branches.

Currently, the Crimes against Humanity and War Crimes Program[107] (usually called the "War Crimes Program") is a centrally coordinated partnership between Justice Canada, the RCMP, the Canadian Border Services Agency (CBSA), and the CIC. There is a formal division of its activities between the "WW II Program" and the "Modern War Crimes Program," though functionally the policy, legislative, and investigative apparatus is the same. The mandate of the War Crimes Program is to ensure that "Canada is not and will not become a safe haven for persons involved in war crimes, crimes against humanity or other reprehensible acts regardless of when or where they occurred."[108] To this end, the involved government agencies pursue a multi-pronged strategy of "using the most appropriate of seven complementary tools: criminal prosecution, extradition to other countries, transfer to the international tribunals or . . . International Criminal Court, revocation of citizenship, denial of access to Canada, denial of refugee protection and deportation."[109]

---

107 The official website for the program is online: www.justice.gc.ca/eng/pi/wc-cg/ index.html. The program issues annual reports, the most recent of which was for 2006–2007, and is available online: http://cbsa-asfc.gc.ca/security-securite/ wc-cg/wc-cg2007-eng.html [War Crimes Program Annual Report 2006–2007].
108 Official website, *ibid*.
109 Joseph Rikhof, "Canada and War Criminals: The Policy, The Program and The Results" (Paper presented to ICC-International Criminal Court: Implementation

The rest of this section will be devoted to analysis of prosecution of core crimes under the *Crimes Against Humanity and War Crimes Act*,[110] while citizenship and immigration-based mechanisms will be reviewed briefly thereafter in Section D, below in this chapter. Extradition and surrender of fugitives, as well as the provision of mutual legal assistance to other states, is dealt with in Chapters 9 and 10.

2) The Act

The government of Canada brought into force *An Act respecting genocide, crimes against humanity and war crimes and to implement the Rome Statute of the International Criminal Court, and to make consequential amendments to other Acts*[111] on 23 October 2000.[112] The Act had been introduced in Parliament on 10 December 1999, the fifty-first anniversary of the Universal Declaration of Human Rights.[113] This timing was deliberate on the government's part, as a means of underscoring Canada's commitment to ending impunity for such mass human rights violations as the core crimes entail.[114] As can be gathered from the long title, a primary purpose of the Act was to implement Canada's obligations under the *Rome Statute*.[115] Canada ratified the *Rome Statute* on 7 July 2000, one week after the Act received royal assent, and was the fourteenth state (and the first in the Commonwealth) to do so. The Act repealed, *inter alia*, the 1987 amendments to the *Criminal Code* under which the *Finta* prosecution had been commenced, and as will be seen, it contains several legislative responses to the majority's decision in that case. Accordingly, the Act is designed not just to facilitate ICC prosecutions, but also to re-energize Canada's ability to prosecute core crimes committed both domestically and abroad.

a) Jurisdiction

As the titles within the Act indicate, jurisdiction over the enumerated offences (genocide, crimes against humanity, war crimes, and breach

---

in Central and Eastern Europe conference, Bucharest, 9–11 May 2003) (copy on file with author).

110 Above note 1.

111 *Ibid.*

112 SI/2000-95, C. Gaz. 2000.II.2418.

113 A/RES/217, 10 December 1948

114 M. Rosenberg, "Canadian Legislation against Crimes against Humanity and War Crimes" in International Centre for Criminal Law Reform and Criminal Justice Policy, *The Changing Face of International Criminal Law: Selected Papers* (Vancouver: ICCLR & CJP, 2002) 229 at 231–32.

115 Above note 23.

of command/superior responsibility) is divided into two distinct regimes: "Offences Within Canada" (territorial, sections 4 and 5) and "Offences Outside Canada" (extraterritorial, sections 6–8). The overall purpose of the territorial provisions is, of course, to facilitate the prosecution of persons committing these crimes in Canada, and to fulfill Canada's obligation under the *Rome Statute* to exercise territorial jurisdiction over the offences. However, given the unlikelihood of that occurring, the more distinct purpose is to "facilitate surrender of suspects to the [ICC], in that it addresses the double criminality requirement of Canadian extradition legislation by making the core crimes of the *Rome Statute* punishable in Canada."[116] The substantive provisions criminalize both committed and inchoate (conspiracy, attempt, accessory after the fact, counselling) offences that take place in Canada.[117] It is prospective in temporal scope, so perpetrators can be tried for these crimes only if committed in Canada after the coming into force of the Act. That said, nothing prohibits Canadian prosecutors from trying such persons under the domestic law crimes that underpin the international offences, for example, to prosecute an act of genocide by way of killing as an ordinary murder. Indeed, beyond the symbolic value of prosecuting such conduct as a core crime, it is probably more desirable to use the domestic provisions, since these are not temporally limited and provide a less complicated way to obtain a conviction.

The provisions on extraterritorial jurisdiction are mostly unchanged from the 1987 *Criminal Code* amendments. Section 8 provides that anyone committing the crimes is liable if, at the time the offence is committed: the perpetrator is a Canadian national or employed by the government in a civilian or military capacity, or a national or employee of a state engaged in an armed conflict against Canada (an expanded version of the nationality principle);[118] or the victim is a national of Canada or of a state allied with Canada in an armed conflict (passive personality principle).[119] In these cases, then, Canada could request the perpetrator's extradition even if she were not present in Canada.

The Act also provides for the limited "custodial" universal jurisdiction that is typical of Canadian provisions of this sort, that the perpe-

---

116 William Schabas, "Canadian Implementing Legislation for the *Rome Statute*" (2000) 3 Y.B. Int'l Human. L. 337 at 339. This is, for Canada to be able to extradite a fugitive to face a crime, the crime for which the fugitive is being extradited must also be a crime in Canada; on this, the requirement of "double criminality" in extradition, see Chapter 9.

117 Above note 1, ss. 4(1.1) and 5(2.1).

118 *Ibid.*, ss. 8(a)(i) & (ii).

119 *Ibid.*, s. 8(a)(iii).

trator may be prosecuted if, "after the time the offence is alleged to have been committed, the person is present in Canada."[120] Consistent with Canada's general approach to extraterritorial jurisdiction,[121] this provision does not push the envelope as far as the possible scope of universal jurisdiction under international law; it appears to contemplate Canada exercising universal jurisdiction where it can apprehend the offender on Canadian soil, but, for example, would not allow an extradition request to be made.[122] However, it does not appear to bar the government from *initiating* an investigation against an individual, and even submitting charges against her, in anticipation that she may arrive in Canada at some point and cause the prosecution to crystallize. That said, it is more likely that the government will focus its scarce resources on persons who are actually in Canada, and this was indeed the case with the first prosecution initiated under the *CAH Act*.[123]

Temporally, section 6(1) of the Act indicates that this extraterritorial jurisdiction may be exercised for crimes committed "either before or after the coming into force of this section," which removes the limitation found in section 4 regarding territorial crimes. This potentially raises the possibility that the accused could be prosecuted under a current formulation of a crime, even though that current formulation would not have reflected the law in place at the time the crime was committed. This would offend the principle of legality, specifically that aspect of the principle prohibiting the retroactive application of crim-

---

120 *Ibid.*, s. 8(b). In the first prosecution under the Act, *R. c. Munyaneza*, 2009 QCCS 2201, Denis J. referred generally to these provisions and stated that prosecution was possible in Canada if the accused "resides here" (para. 65). While the accused in that case did reside in Canada, this is a narrower characterization than the wording of the sections would suggest—an accused person could be arrested literally as he steps off of the plane at a Canadian airport.

121 See, generally, Chapter 8.

122 An exception here would be the grave breaches provisions of the *Geneva Conventions*, which do contemplate a full-blown universal jurisdiction as between the contracting parties. These provisions have likely passed into customary international law, and, accordingly, Canada could exercise the fullest universal jurisdiction over such offenders by requesting extradition of an alleged perpetrator even where Canada had no other jurisdictional link to the crime. Ironically enough, given the limiting provision in s. 8 of the *CAH Act*, above note 1, the individual could not be prosecuted for the grave breaches *qua* war crimes under the Act, but would have to be prosecuted under the *Geneva Conventions Act*—which indeed is contemplated by s. 3 of that Act (above note 59).

123 *Munyaneza*, above note 120. The *Munyaneza* case is discussed in greater detail in Section C(3), below in this chapter, though relevant findings in the case will be referred to as the law is discussed in the current section.

inal law.[124] To avoid this, the extraterritorial crimes are defined in such a way that the accused can only be tried where the act in question "at the time and in the place of its commission, constitutes a crime against humanity [or war crime or act of genocide] according to customary international law or conventional international law or by virtue of its being criminal according to the general principles of law recognized by the community of nations."[125]

This renders the provision "retrospective" in nature as opposed to retroactive, since it "attaches new procedural or jurisdictional consequences to an act that was already criminal at the time of its commission."[126] This is certainly consistent with section 11(g) of the *Charter*, particularly given the questionably robust approach to legality taken by the majority in *Finta*.[127]

This provision also does not contain the requirement, found in the 1987 provisions, that Canada must have been entitled to exercise universal jurisdiction over the offender at the time of the commission of the offence. At least in regards to WW II offences, this could spark a defence argument that the exercise of jurisdiction is illegal, since, for example, there would likely not have been universal jurisdiction over crimes against humanity during and immediately after the war. However, even if the legality of exercising jurisdiction in such a case would be questionable under international law, the clear Parliamentary intent is for the legislation to operate in this manner, which defeats any international law to the contrary.[128] It is highly unlikely that any state would mount a claim against Canada on this point, and the advancing age of most WW II war crimes suspects renders the matter increasingly moot.

b) Crimes

One main goal of the Act, of course, is to create domestic versions of the core crimes that are prosecutable in Canadian courts. Accordingly, there are definitions of genocide, crimes against humanity, and war crimes, as well as command/superior responsibility for all of these.

---

124 Concerning which see Antonio Cassese, *International Criminal Law*, 2d ed. (Oxford: Oxford University Press, 2008) at 43–47.
125 Above note 1, s. 6(3). In *Munyaneza* (above note 120), Denis J. made specific findings on this point as regarded all of the crimes with which the accused had been charged (genocide, paras. 72 and 75; crimes against humanity, para. 112; war crimes, paras. 133–35). He relied in part on findings of the ICTR in so doing.
126 Darryl Robinson, "Implementing International Crimes in National Law: The Canadian Approach" in Neuner, ed., above note 26 at 53–54.
127 Above note 90.
128 See Chapter 1.

There is no mention of the crime of aggression, which will presumably be added if the ICC Assembly of States Parties (ASP) is able to come up with a definition that can be included in the *Rome Statute*.[129]

The Act eschews the 1987 approach of linking the international definitions of the core crimes to their underlying Canadian domestic offences. In this way it partly affirms one of Cory J.'s rulings in *Finta*—to obtain a conviction the prosecution will be required to prove that the accused committed the proscribed *international* offence, with all of its attached mental, physical, and contextual elements. Notably, however, the definitions do not resemble those in the *Rome Statute*, nor do they incorporate any of the ICC *Elements of Crimes* (*ICC Elements*).[130] There are two definitions of each crime for the territorial and extra-territorial provisions respectively, and each definition, after setting out a general description of the particular criminal act,[131] contains a phrase that incorporates the international law definition of the offence. For genocide and crimes against humanity, the phrase reads "that, at the time and in the place of its commission, constitutes [genocide, a crime against humanity] according to customary international law or conventional international law or by virtue of its being criminal according to the general principles of law recognized by the community of nations, whether or not it constitutes a contravention of the law in force at the time and in the place of its commission."[132] For war crimes, the middle part of the phrase is varied slightly to read "that, at the time and in the place of its commission, constitutes a war crime according to customary international law or conventional international law applicable to armed conflicts . . . ."[133]

The clear intent of these definitions is twofold: to adhere to the principle of legality (and section 11(g) of the *Charter*[134]) by ensuring that accused persons are prosecuted according to the international offence as it existed at the time it was committed; and to allow the definitions of the crimes in the Act to evolve along with the applicable international law. On the latter point, some interpretive tools are pro-

---

129 See Chapter 3.

130 UN Doc. PCNICC/2000/1/Add.2 (2000).

131 Robinson refers to these general descriptions as "touchstones" and suggests that they are provided because a simple reference to customary or conventional international law might have been found to be void for vagueness under the *Charter*, an approach which had already been approved in *Finta* (Robinson, above note 126 at 50).

132 Above note 1, ss. 4(1.1)(3) and 6(1.1)(3).

133 *Ibid.*

134 Above note 83.

vided to the courts for their construction of the applicable international law offence. Section 4(4) states, "For greater certainty, crimes described in Articles 6 and 7 and paragraph 2 of Article 8 of the *Rome Statute* are, as of July 17, 1998, crimes according to customary international law. This does not limit or prejudice in any way the application of existing or developing rules of international law." Section 6(4), regarding extra-territorial crimes, repeats this but adds to the conclusion of the first sentence the following: ". . . and may be crimes according to customary international law before that date." For both territorial and extraterritorial offences, this provides that the *Rome Statute* definitions of the crimes are something of a minimum baseline for courts to draw on in constructing a definition in a particular case, and speak to the authoritative power of the *Rome Statute* definitions of the crimes. However, there is no exclusivity attached to the *Rome Statute* definitions, and Canada is not boxed in by those definitions in its ability to prosecute core crimes.

This flexibility is eminently desirable. There are a number of crimes which did not attract consensus at the Rome Conference which are nonetheless developing or emergent in both customary and treaty law that binds Canada,[135] or will be so in the future. The legislative drafters wisely avoided freezing the definitions in time by simply adopting *holus bolus* the *Rome Statute* versions. Having a flexible definition of a domestic crime that is capable of evolution along with the international law that underpins it will save legislative time and energy, since it dispenses with the need for ongoing legislative amendment that would otherwise be necessary.[136] It also guards against any violation of the principle of legality, since "a perpetrator will be judged according to international law as it existed at the time and in the place of the commission of the crime . . . [the domestic definitions] are by definition precisely co-extensive with the applicable international law."[137]

Further to the principle of legality, the other interpretive tool provided is in section 6(5), which provides, again "for greater certainty," that crimes against humanity were part of customary international law or were criminal under general principles of international law prior to "(a) the *Agreement for the prosecution and punishment of the major war criminals of the European Axis*, signed at London on August 8, 1945; and (b) the Proclamation by the Supreme Commander for the Allied Powers, dated January 19, 1946." This provision is clearly designed to clean

---

135 For example, the use of chemical weapons; see Robinson, above note 126 at 49.

136 See also Rikhof, "Fewer Places to Hide," above note 27.

137 Robinson, above note 126 at 50.

up any lingering doubt arising from Cory J.'s findings in *Finta* regarding whether crimes against humanity were criminal under customary international law during WW II, and forestalling any defence attempts to argue the legality issue on this point—which would amount to re-litigating the Nuremberg precedent. The majority reasoning in *Finta* is dispensed with, and the question of legality is firmly answered in the affirmative.

On the other hand, the way in which the definitions of the crimes are structured means that in each case, the trial judge must determine as a matter of law what the state of the applicable customary and/or conventional international criminal law was at the time (and in the case of treaties, in the place[138]) the offence was committed. With regard to offences committed before 1998, this will sometimes require a great deal of effort; for example, in a case where war crimes in an internal armed conflict are alleged, the court (and the parties) would have to be able to establish with certainty the point in time at which such a crime was even known to the law, since as canvassed in Chapter 3, this is a fairly recent development and has remained controversial ever since.[139] And a fair bit of effort will also be required in the future, since the definitions of crimes may get broader or narrower depending on the future practice of states and the caselaw of international criminal tribunals. Moreover, it must be recalled that the ICC was founded by treaty and its definitions simply reflect what consensus could be reached among the parties. To be sure, the agreement by the large number of signatory states on the offences is compelling evidence that the offences themselves were criminalized under customary international law in 1998. However, the *Rome Statute* is not exactly a helpful yardstick in some ways, since its definitions of the core crimes all contain elements which are generally regarded as being both more restrictive and less restrictive than the applicable customary international law, and courts will have to resist the temptation to simply "jump on" a *Rome Statute* definition, where those more questionable elements are involved.

There can be no question that having domestic criminal trial judges utilize and apply international criminal law (particularly in customary form) effectively will be no mean feat. Canadian courts' wrestling matches with international law do not, generally speaking, read in a

---

138 Though each definition includes the phrase "whether or not it constitutes a contravention of the law in force at the time and in the place of its commission." This prevents an accused from pleading that her conduct was in accordance with local law in the case of a state which has not lived up to its international law obligations to criminalize the core crimes.

139 See Chapter 3, Section (C)(2).

very sparkling manner. There is little doubt that both the courts and the parties will continue to have recourse to the regrettable practice[140] of having international law scholars provide what can only loosely be described as "expert opinion" on the state of international law on given points, though given the considerable expertise and acumen among the members of the War Crimes Section, the Crown will have less need to avail itself of this resource.

However, there is much room for optimism in this regard. Pursuant to the federal government's post-*Finta* decision to expend its core crime combattance resources on immigration and citizenship options, the Federal Court of Canada has developed a reasonably strong jurisprudence on international crimes, and the superior court justices who hear cases under the *CAH Act* will have that caselaw upon which to draw. Moreover, the status of *international* caselaw regarding these crimes has changed significantly since the *Finta* case was prosecuted, and Canada's courts now have the extremely influential judgments of the International Criminal Tribunal for the former Yugoslavia (ICTY) and the International Criminal Tribunal for Rwanda (ICTR) to assist in their assessments of the state of customary international law on a given occasion. On an ongoing basis, they also will be able to draw upon the caselaw of the ICC and the internationalized courts. This, indeed, has been one of the generally salutary effects of the *ad hoc* tribunals: the active engagement with, and refinement of, international criminal law in a manner that can actually be utilized for prosecutions in domestic courts.

This point is effectively demonstrated by the recent decision of the Supreme Court of Canada in *Mugesera v. Canada (Minister of Citizenship and Immigration)*.[141] Mugesera was a Rwandan national who fought a decade-long court battle against the efforts of Canadian immigration authorities to deport him. At issue was a 1992 speech made by Mugesera in Rwanda, which the government alleged constituted, *inter alia*, incitement to genocide and the crime against humanity of persecution. A ruling by the immigration adjudicator that Mugesera had indeed committed all of the alleged crimes was upheld (in various part) on appeal by the then–Immigration Appeal Division and the Federal

---

140   Regrettable because, strictly speaking, international law is the law of Canada, and courts are meant to take judicial notice of it and apply it as they would purely domestic law. To be sure, parties whose cases have complex international law issues should be advised by international law experts, but international law (unlike foreign domestic law) is not an appropriate topic for an expert opinion witness. See, generally, Gibran van Ert, "The Admissibility of International Legal Evidence" (2005) 84 Can. Bar Rev. 31.

141   [2005] 2 S.C.R. 100, 2005 SCC 40 [*Mugesera*].

Court, Trial Division, but overturned by the Federal Court of Appeal. The case reached the Supreme Court of Canada in late 2004.

As it had to apply the law that was in place at the time of Mugesera's alleged crimes—that is, the 1987 *Criminal Code* amendments, which incorporated customary and conventional international law—the task before the Court was to reconstruct the state of customary international law and how it existed in Canada at that time. This is a similar exercise to what a trial court would have to do in a prosecution under the *CAH Act*.[142] The Court ultimately found that Mugesera had committed both incitement to genocide and the crime against humanity of persecution, though it found that he had not committed the crime against humanity of incitement to murder.[143] In making its findings,[144] the Court made liberal use of the caselaw of the *ad hoc* tribunals; in particular, with regard to crimes against humanity, it "wholeheartedly embraced" this jurisprudence.[145] The Court was explicit in recognizing that the domestic law on these offences should be interpreted in a manner that is consistent with Canada's international law obligations,[146] and further, that the caselaw of the ICTY and ICTR constituted "a unique body of authority" which, while not binding, should definitely be persuasive in light of "the expertise of these tribunals and the authority in respect of customary international law with which they are vested . . . ."[147] In fact, the Court relied on the caselaw of the *ad hoc* tribunals to overturn some of its own findings in *Finta*, including the controversial ruling that a discriminatory intent is required to convict for *all* crimes against humanity and not just that of persecution.[148]

The Court's use of the jurisprudence of the ICTY and ICTR will likely be seen as providing moral support for the important work those bodies have done, as well as ensuring convergence and uniformity between international and domestic treatment of genocide and crimes against humanity. In general terms, *Mugesera* greatly advances Canadian law on the core crimes, and will have a constructive effect in terms of the government's ability to successfully prosecute offenders. This was demonstrat-

---

142 Indeed, this is what Denis, J. had to do in the *Munyaneza* case (above note 120), which also involved alleged international crimes during the Rwandan genocide.

143 This was due to the fact that at Canadian and international law, the incited murders had to have taken place, a fact which was not proven as against Mugesera.

144 Some of which are set out in more detail in this Section, below.

145 Joseph Rikhof, "Hate Speech and International Criminal Law: The *Mugesera* Decision by the Supreme Court of Canada" (2005) 3 JICJ 1121 at 1126 [Rikhof, "Hate Speech"].

146 *Mugesera*, above note 141 at para. 82.

147 *Ibid.* at para. 126.

148 *Ibid.* at paras. 142–44.

ed in the 2009 decision of the Quebec Superior Court in *Munyaneza*,[149] where the court relied extensively upon the jurisprudence of the *ad hoc* tribunals in determining the law as it applied in Rwanda in 1994, as well as upon the *Finta* and the *Mugesera* cases.

The sections below briefly review some of the distinct matters raised by the definitions of crimes as laid out in the Act, including the findings in *Mugesera* and *Munyaneza*. It is clear that, based on the definitional scheme set up by the Act, reference to the treaty-based or customary international law on each crime will be necessary to fully flesh out the crimes, and reference should be made to Chapter 3 in this regard.

i)   *Genocide and Advocating/Incitement to Genocide*

Genocide is defined in sections 4(3) and 6(3) as

> an act or omission committed with intent to destroy, in whole or in part, an identifiable group of persons, as such, that at the time and in the place of its commission, constitutes genocide according to customary international law or conventional international law or by virtue of its being criminal according to the general principles of law recognized by the community of nations.

This definition is generally commensurate with the *Genocide Convention*[150] definition, which is reproduced in the *Rome Statute* and is described in more detail in Chapter 3. As with all of the crimes in the Act, the definition incorporates international law by reference so as to allow the Canadian definition to evolve along with the international law.

However, even the first part of the definition contains some potentially broadening elements. For example, the inclusion of the word "omission" departs from customary law, which is as yet confined to the five positive acts set out in the *Genocide Convention*. Similarly, the reference to intent to destroy "an identifiable group of persons" is much more general than the *Genocide Convention* and *Rome Statute* versions, which confine genocide to being committed only against "a national, ethnical, racial or religious group."[151] Accordingly, expansion in the international law of genocide to include, for example, acts of cultural genocide or ethnic cleansing can be expressly accommodated by the wording of the Act, though a court would have to be persuaded that the law has changed in this way in order for a conviction to be possible.[152]

---

149 Above note 120.
150 Above note 2.
151 *Genocide Convention, ibid.*, art. 2; *Rome Statute*, above note 23, art. 6.
152 Schabas, above note 116 at 341.

In *Munyaneza*, the accused had been charged with committing genocide by both killing and causing serious bodily or mental harm to Tutsi during the Rwandan genocide. The court constructed an uncontroversial definition of genocide, relying heavily on the *Genocide Convention*, the *ad hoc* tribunal jurisprudence, the *Mugesera* case, and even the decision of the International Court of Justice (ICJ) in the *Serbian Genocide Case*.[153] Justice Denis spoke to the specific intent requirement,[154] noting that the intent must have been "to physically destroy the targeted group, not only its national, linguistic, religious or cultural identity,"[155] and that the intent must be to destroy the group in "substantial part," meaning "a high proportion of the group, or the most prominent members of the community, the effect of which on the whole group is significant."[156] With regard to the proscribed act of intentional killing, Denis J. was careful to note the distinction between that international offence and the Canadian crime of murder, though noting that "the difference is rather slim" between the two.[157] With regard to the proscribed act of causing serious bodily or mental harm, the court accepted the *ad hoc* tribunals' jurisprudence that the following constituted such acts: physical or mental torture, inhumane or degrading treatment, rape, sexual violence, and persecution.[158] He further accepted that

1) the harm may be physical or mental;
2) the physical harm need not be permanent or irreversible, but must be likely to prevent the victim from living a normal life over a relatively long period;
3) the mental harm must go beyond slight or temporary deterioration of mental faculties; and
4) the harm must be so serious that it threatens to destroy the targeted group in whole or in part.[159]

---

153 *Case Concerning the Application of the Convention on the Prevention and Punishment of the Crime of Genocide (Bosnia and Herzegovina v. Serbia and Montenegro)*, Judgment, 26 February 2007 [*Serbian Genocide Case*].

154 *Munyaneza*, above note 120 at paras. 79 and 97.

155 *Ibid.* at para. 98, citing *Semanza* (ICTR-97-20-T), Judgment, 15 May 2003 at para. 315.

156 *Ibid.* at para. 103, citing art. 2 of the *Genocide Convention* and *Krstic* (IT-98-33-A), Appeal Judgment, 19 April 2004 at paras. 8 and 12.

157 *Ibid.* at paras. 82–83.

158 *Ibid.* at para. 84.

159 *Ibid.* at para. 87, citing *Kajelijeli* (ICTR-98-44A-T), Judgment, 1 December 2003 at paras. 814–15.

He also set out the law regarding serious bodily or mental harm and inhumane or degrading treatment in some detail.[160]

At issue in *Mugesera* was the international offence of incitement to genocide. It should first be noted that the *Criminal Code* contains an offence of "advocating genocide" in section 318.[161] Its wording is somewhat similar to the customary international law offence of "direct and public incitement to commit genocide." However, section 318 was not brought in as a means of implementing Canada's international law obligations regarding the crime of genocide, but rather as part of a package of legislative amendments designed to deal with hate propaganda,[162] and it was not clear that it was meant to be a domestic version of the international crime. There have been no Canadian prosecutions under the section. Nonetheless, it was one of the crimes alleged against Léon Mugesera by the Minister of Citizenship and Immigration, and in *Mugesera*, the Supreme Court of Canada took the opportunity to flesh out the section and to firmly equate it to the corresponding international offence. It will therefore, in the future, act as something of an adjunct to the *CAH Act*, since the latter legislation does not contain such an offence. This was clearly deliberate on the part of Parliament, as section 318 was amended[163] well after the *CAH Act* had come into force.[164]

In *Mugesera*, the Supreme Court was quite explicit that the *Genocide Convention* and the relevant principles of customary international law, as well as tribunal caselaw interpreting them, were "highly relevant to the analysis" of the elements of the offence of advocating genocide.[165] It linked the domestic offence directly to the international offence of incitement to genocide — in fact, using the two phrases interchangeably — and relied heavily on the jurisprudence of the ICTR. The Court

---

160 *Munyaneza, ibid.* at paras. 91–96.

161 Above note 80.

162 Canada, Department of Justice, *Report to the Minister of Justice of the Special Committee on Hate Propaganda in Canada* (Ottawa: Queen's Printer, 1966).

163 S.C. 2004, c. 14. This amendment, in fact, broadened the number of protected groups for domestic purposes, as it included "sexual orientation" as one of the criteria by which an "identifiable group" can be distinguished (s. 318(4)). This is not commensurate with the international offence, but is an example of state practice towards the broadening of the definition that, if it is accepted by sufficient numbers of other states, could become part of the definition in the future.

164 Though there does seem to be significant overlap; while the *CAH Act* does not *expressly* contain this offence, as analyzed in further detail in Section C(2)(d), below in this chapter, s. 22 of the *Criminal Code* does apply to the Act, and this section provides for "incitement" as a mode of participation in any offence. Accordingly, the Act is properly read as containing the offence of incitement to genocide.

165 *Mugesera*, above note 141 at para. 82.

began by noting that incitement to genocide is an inchoate offence, as distinguished from complicity in an offence that actually occurred, and thus "remains a crime regardless of whether it has the effect it is intended to have."[166] Accordingly, proof of incitement to genocide does not require proof that genocide took place.[167]

The Court found that the criminal act (*actus reus*) requirement of incitement to genocide is that the act of incitement must be direct and public. Noting that Mugesera's speech had been delivered in public, the Court considered the directness requirement, which it found requires that the act specifically provoked another to engage in a physical act, and was not vague, obscure, or accomplished by way of innuendo. Directness should be evaluated in light of the audience, its cultural/linguistic context, and what its members could have been expected to understand the words to mean.[168] As to the mental element (*mens rea*), the Court held that what was required was an intent to directly prompt or provoke another to commit genocide, as well as the "specific intent" to commit genocide. Intent, it noted, can be inferred from the circumstances, including whether genocide was indeed inflicted upon the group targeted by the alleged inciter.[169]

ii) Crimes against Humanity

Crimes against humanity are defined in sections 4(3) and 6(3) as

> murder, extermination, enslavement, deportation, imprisonment, torture, sexual violence, persecution or any other inhumane act that is committed against any civilian population or any identifiable group and that, at the time and in the place of its commission, constitutes a crime against humanity according to customary international law or conventional international law or by virtue of its being criminal according to the general principles of law recognized by the community of nations.

The list of enumerated acts at the outset of the definition is generally commensurate with the international law on point, although missing from the list are disappearance of persons and apartheid, which are both listed in section 7 of the *Rome Statute*.[170] If Robinson[171] is correct, the lists of acts in sections 4(3) and 6(3) are simply intended to be a

---

166 *Ibid.* at para. 85.
167 *Ibid.* at paras. 84–85.
168 *Ibid.* at para. 87.
169 *Ibid.* at paras. 88–89.
170 Above note 23.
171 Above note 126.

"touchstone" set of examples and the court would simply have recourse to international law, including but not limited to the *Rome Statute* definition, in order to determine the full scope of the enumerated acts. Therefore, the legislative intent behind this particular list would be read as not excluding any enumerated acts which may exist at customary or conventional international law. This argument would certainly be supported by reference to sections 4(4) and 6(4), deeming the *Rome Statute* provisions to have customary international law status, as well as the inclusion of the *Rome Statute* provisions themselves in an appendix to the Act.[172] A defence argument to the contrary, however, can certainly be foreseen.

In *Mugesera*, the individual had been alleged to have committed two crimes against humanity: counselling of murder and persecution. The Supreme Court endeavoured to construct a definition of crimes against humanity, noting specifically that while there were some slight differences between the definition in the *CAH Act* and that in the 1987 *Criminal Code* provisions, these were not material to the discussion.[173] It found that the *actus reus* of a crime against humanity was threefold: (1) one of the underlying offences or "proscribed acts" had been committed, (2) that it was committed as part of a widespread or systematic attack, and (3) that the attack was directed against any civilian population or any identifiable group of persons. The *mens rea* of a crime against humanity was that the person committing the proscribed act knew of the attack and knew or took the risk that his act comprised a part of that attack.[174]

With regard to the first requirement of the *actus reus*, the Court held that the prosecution had to prove both the *actus reus* and the *mens rea* of the underlying offence: "For instance, where the accused is charged with murder as a crime against humanity, the accused must (1) have caused the death of another person, and (2) have intended to cause the person's death or to inflict grievous bodily harm that he or she knew was likely to result in death."[175] With regard to the counsel-

---

172 Robert Hage, "Implementing the *Rome Statute*: Canada's Experience" in Roy S. Lee, ed., *States' Responses to Issues Arising from the ICC Statute: Constitutional Sovereignty, Judicial Cooperation and Criminal Law* (Ardsley, NY: Transnational, 2005) 47 at 51.

173 *Mugesera*, above note 141 at para. 118.

174 *Ibid.* at para. 119. In enumerating the elements of the offence in this way, the Court appeared to dispense with what amounted to a "throw-away" line by Cory J. in *Finta*, to the effect that to constitute a crime against humanity, "the alleged acts must show an added degree of inhumanity" (paras. 123 and 125–26).

175 *Ibid.* at para. 130.

ling of murder, the Court noted that section 3.77 of the *Code*[176] had provided that "counselling" of a proscribed criminal act was sufficient to ground conviction even if the criminal act was not committed. However, while "counselling" was not known to the international law on crimes against humanity, the equivalent offence was "instigating" a proscribed act, which required that the crime instigated must actually have been committed. Accordingly, the crime of "counselling" was narrowed correspondingly.[177]

As to the underlying offence of persecution, the *actus reus* was the "gross or blatant denial, on discriminatory grounds, of a fundamental right, laid down in international customary or treaty law, reaching the same level of gravity as the other [underlying offences]."[178] With regard to Mugesera's speech, the Court considered the *ad hoc* tribunal jurisprudence on whether hate speech could constitute persecution, and held that it could where the hate speech itself reached the requisite level of gravity, such as where the speech "openly advocates extreme violence (such as murder or extermination) against the target group, but it may not be limited to such instances."[179] Unlike counselling, whether any acts of violence actually took place as a result of the hate speech is irrelevant.[180] The *mens rea* of persecution is a *discriminatory* intent to deny the right, that is, the intention to commit the persecutory acts and to do so with the intention of discriminating.[181] However, the Court held that it was only the crime against humanity of persecution that had this added requirement of discriminatory intent, and explicitly overruled its earlier finding in *Finta* that all crimes against humanity had this requirement.[182]

The second element of the *actus reus* of crimes against humanity, the Court held, is whether the underlying offence is committed "as part of a widespread or systematic attack."[183] It defined "attack" as the commission of acts of violence, which may (but does not have to) include

---

176   Above note 80.
177   *Mugesera*, above note 141 at paras. 133–36.
178   *Ibid.* at para. 141, citing *Kupreškić*, Case No. IT-95-16-T, Trial Chamber II, 14 January 2000 at para. 621.
179   *Mugesera*, *ibid.* at para. 147.
180   *Ibid.*
181   *Ibid.* at paras. 142 and 145.
182   *Ibid.* at paras. 143–44.
183   *Ibid.* at paras. 151 and 170. The Court implicitly acknowledged the debate regarding whether the requirement was "widespread *and* systematic" or "widespread *or* systematic" by adopting ICTY findings on the latter point; see para. 156 [emphasis added].

armed conflict.[184] "Widespread attack" was held to mean "massive, frequent, large scale action, carried out collectively with considerable seriousness and directed against a multiplicity of victims."[185] "Systematic" was held to mean organized, following a regular pattern, and "involving substantial public or private resources."[186] Only the attack itself must be widespread/systematic, "not the act of the accused."[187] The Court acknowledged the debate regarding whether there is a requirement in customary international law that the attack be carried out pursuant to a government or organizational policy or plan. It answered this question in the negative, but noted that such a requirement is present in the *Rome Statute* and explicitly did "not discount the possibility that customary international law may evolve over time so as to incorporate a policy requirement."[188] It also ruled that "as part of" a systematic attack means that the act "must further the attack or clearly fit the pattern of the attack, but it need not comprise an essential or officially sanctioned part of it."[189]

The third element of the *actus reus* of crimes against humanity, the Court held, is whether the attack was "directed against any civilian population or any identifiable group."[190] "Directed against any civilian population" means a civilian population must be the primary (not a collateral) target of the attack. An example of a civilian population is a particular national, ethnic, or religious group. The presence of non-civilians in the group does not affect its civilian status, "as long as it remains largely civilian in nature."[191]

The *mens rea* of crimes against humanity, the Court ruled, requires that the accused "must have knowledge of the attack and must know that his or her acts comprise part of it *or* take the risk that his or her acts will comprise part of it."[192] Once the accused's knowledge of the attack is made out, his or her personal motive is irrelevant.[193]

Generally speaking, *Mugesera* is a very noteworthy case. It provides a model for domestic prosecution of crimes against humanity, indicating that courts should employ the international law regarding

---

184 *Ibid.* at para. 153.
185 *Ibid.* at para. 154.
186 *Ibid.* at para. 155.
187 *Ibid.* at para. 156.
188 *Ibid.* at para. 158.
189 *Ibid.* at paras. 164–68.
190 *Ibid.* at paras. 151 and 170.
191 *Ibid.* at paras. 161–62.
192 *Ibid.* at para. 173.
193 *Ibid.* at para. 174. Again, as noted above, the Crown must also prove the *mens rea* of the underlying offence; see *ibid.* at paras. 119 and 130.

the underlying offences (e.g., murder, torture) rather than the domestic versions. In *Munyaneza*, Denis J. tracked the rulings on the applicable law from *Mugesera* fairly closely.[194] Moreover, as Joseph Rikhof has commented, the Court contributes to the development of an international norm against hate speech in that it finds that one act or event can constitute both incitement to genocide and a crime against humanity, and by setting a threshold of advocacy of extreme violence in order for hate speech to constitute a crime against humanity.[195]

However, since *Mugesera* dealt with only two particular crimes against humanity that occurred in 1992, there are obviously many other legal questions that will require answers in cases that come before Canadian courts.[196] The Supreme Court itself pointed to the imposition of a "policy or plan" requirement by the *Rome Statute* and the potential that customary law may eventually incorporate this requirement.[197] Other issues the courts may have to investigate include: (1) whether a particular prohibited act was part of the law on crimes against humanity at the time of its commission, and what its elements were; (2) whether at the time of commission there was a requirement that crimes against humanity be linked to a war or armed conflict, since it is arguable[198] that this was required as late as the 1990s; and (3) whether the contemplation of an attack against "any identifiable group" in the *CAH Act* definition has any meaning at a given time, since crimes against humanity have thus far been limited to situations of attacks on "civilian populations."

iii) War Crimes
War crime is defined in sections 4(3) and 6(3) as

> an act or omission committed during an armed conflict that, at the time and in the place of its commission, constitutes a war crime according to customary international law or conventional international law applicable to armed conflicts.

This definition is the sparsest of the three core crimes definitions in the Act, where even its "touchstone" *chapeau* contains only the axiomatic requirement that a war crime must take place during an armed

---

194 *Munyaneza*, above note 120 at paras. 108–28.
195 Rikhof, "Hate Speech," above note 145 at 1130–31.
196 On this topic, see Madeleine J. Schwarz, "Prosecuting Crimes against Humanity in Canada: What Must be Proved" (2002) 46 Crim. L.Q. 40, though some of the questions raised were answered in *Mugesera*.
197 *Mugesera*, above note 141 at para. 158.
198 Schwarz, above note 196 at 54–60.

conflict. As with the other crimes, the courts will be called upon to determine whether a particular act constituted a war crime at the time and in the place of its commission, and what the content of the particular offence was (or is) under international law, both treaty-based and customary. Where the prosecution is for extraterritorial crimes that took place in the past, this will require close attention to the developments in war crimes law over time, for example, what the requirements were at a given time for a conflict to constitute an "armed conflict," or whether international law provided for liability for war crimes in internal armed conflicts.[199] The contentious status of the *Additional Protocols to the Geneva Conventions*[200] will require courts to take note of whether either Protocol applied in whole to a particular conflict, and/or what parts of these instruments reflected customary international law at a given time and place where the *Protocol* was not in force.

In *Munyaneza*, none of these obstacles arose, Denis J. being content to adopt the findings of the *ad hoc* tribunals (especially the ICTR) as to the fact that a non-international armed conflict was occurring in Rwanda in 1994,[201] that the *Geneva Conventions* and the *Second Protocol to the Geneva Conventions (AP II)* applied,[202] what the elements of the war crime of pillage were,[203] and the definition of a "protected person" under the treaties.[204] He also relied on the findings of the ICTR in *Semanza*[205] to the effect that "the prosecution must demonstrate that: (a) the armed conflict in Rwanda was non-international; (b) the victims were not taking part in hostilities at the time of the alleged violation; (c) there was a nexus between the accused's alleged crimes and the conflict."[206]

The provisions of the *CAH Act* deeming the *Rome Statute* offences to be customary international law as of 1998 and, in the case of extraterritorial offences, providing that they may have had customary status before that time, means that there will be an interplay between domestic Canadian prosecutions and the *Rome Statute*'s war crimes provisions. However, the *Rome Statute* provisions are in many ways a narrow and selective version of the broader panoply of war crimes law. Accordingly,

---

199 See Chapter 3.

200 Above note 60.

201 *Munyaneza*, above note 120 at para. 148; it appears that the accused conceded this point.

202 *Ibid.* at paras. 132–35.

203 *Ibid.* at paras. 143–46.

204 *Ibid.* at paras. 153–54.

205 Above note 154.

206 *Munyaneza*, above note 120 at para. 138.

Canadian prosecutions can be more broadly based in terms of the applicable law, though in such cases prosecutors likely will be called upon to demonstrate that the *Rome Statute* provisions do not encompass all of the customary international law of war crimes. Moreover, while the *Rome Statute* versions of the crimes are given customary international law status, it is not at all clear that this includes the detailed *Elements of the Crimes*.[207]

The *CAH Act* appears designed to be the primary vehicle for war crimes prosecutions, but the *Geneva Conventions Act* has not been repealed and can serve as a supplemental source of law. That Act also provides the advantage of permitting the exercise of universal jurisdiction over grave breaches on a basis which is legal under international law, since despite the jurisdictional provisions of the *CAH Act*, Canada has not, at all times since WW II, been legally entitled to assert universal jurisdiction over all war crimes.

c)   Command/Superior Responsibility

Sections 5(1) & (2) and 7(1) & (2) of the *CAH Act* create offences called "Breach of responsibility by military commander" ("command responsibility") and "Breach of responsibility by a superior" ("superior responsibility"). "Military commander" is broadly defined to include "a person who commands police with a degree of authority and control comparable to a military commander,"[208] while "superior" is defined as "a person in authority, other than a military commander."[209] The provisions essentially provide that a commander or superior commits an indictable offence where she fails to properly exercise control over person(s) under her command or authority, and this failure results in the person(s) committing one of the core crimes. Liability accrues only if the commander/superior knows or should have known that the offence is about to be committed[210] and fails to take measures to prevent or repress the offence or further commissions of it.[211]

Under international law, command responsibility and superior responsibility are modes of liability or complicity in criminal offences.[212] Under the *Rome Statute*,[213] these are provided for in article 28, and the Canadian provisions roughly correspond, with some changes or addi-

---

207 Above note 130.
208 Above note 1, ss. 5(6) and 7(6).
209 *Ibid.*
210 *Ibid.*, ss. 5(1)(b) and 2(b), 7(1)(b) and 2(b).
211 *Ibid.*, ss. 5(1)(c) and 2(d), 7(1)(c) and 2(d).
212 See, generally, Chapter 4.
213 Above note 23.

tions to the applicable wording, to this provision. However, the *CAH Act* creates new offences of command and superior responsibility, basically on a criminal negligence standard. This approach was taken because of the requirement, imposed by the Supreme Court of Canada under section 7 of the *Charter*,[214] that a conviction for an offence with any significant stigma requires proof of a subjective intention to carry out the act.[215] Genocide, in particular, which requires proof of "special intent," but also war crimes and crimes against humanity — serious stigmatizing offences — and Canadian constitutional law would not permit conviction for committing them on the basis of someone failing to prevent subordinates from actually committing the crime. The solution was to create these specialized, stand-alone criminal negligence offences,[216] which are nonetheless of equal gravity to the core crime offences in the sense that they carry the possibility of a life sentence.[217] They do implement Canada's obligations under article 28 of the *Rome Statute*, but do not correspond exactly and could enable a defence argument that there is not, in fact, double criminality between them — in which case Canada would not be able to surrender a fugitive to the court for prosecution.[218]

d) Liability, Complicity, and Inchoate Offences

The Act provides that "every person who conspires or attempts to commit, is an accessory after the fact in relation to, or counsels in relation to" one of the enumerated crimes (including command/superior responsibility) may be prosecuted for an indictable offence.[219] No definitions are given for any of these offences; however, section 2(2) of the Act states that, "[u]nless otherwise provided, words and expressions used in this Act have the same meaning as in the *Criminal Code*." Moreover, section 34(2) of the federal *Interpretation Act*[220] provides that "All the provisions of the *Criminal Code* relating to indictable offences apply to indictable offences created by an enactment . . . except to the extent that the enactment otherwise provides."

What does this tell us about liability for offences under the Act? The use of the word "offence," combined with section 34(2) of the *In-*

---

214 Above note 83.
215 *R. v. Vaillancourt*, [1987] 2 S.C.R. 636.
216 Robinson, above note 126 at 52–53.
217 Above note 1, ss. 5(3) and 7(4).
218 Schabas, above note 116 at 342.
219 Above note 1, ss. 4(1.1), 5(2.1), 6(1.1), and 7(2.1).
220 R.S.C. 1985, c. I-21.

terpretation Act, appears to render applicable section 21 of the *Code*,[221] which provides that everyone is party to an offence who commits, aids, or abets it, as well as providing "common intention" liability. The same logic means that sections 22 and 464 (counselling), sections 23 and 463 (accessory after the fact), and sections 24 and 463 (attempts) all apply, as well as section 465 on conspiracy.[222] The question that will confront courts trying to apply the Act is the extent to which the *Mugesera* approach can and should be followed, that is, to what extent should the *domestic* law on these modes of liability and inchoate offences be modified to incorporate the *international* law on point?

The obvious answer is that the usual tools of legislative interpretation should apply; Parliament should be presumed not to have legislated in contravention of international law unless intention to that effect is express or clearly implied. While there is no international law of aiding and abetting murder to speak of, there is, for example, international law regarding the aiding and abetting of genocide, and the latter should be taken into account when assessing liability for that crime. The *Charter* will provide appropriate constitutional limits, though to the extent this prevents Canada from prosecuting an offender, it may be deemed by the ICC to be an instance of "inability" to prosecute and thus a situation where the court will take jurisdiction over the case and demand the surrender of the individual. The courts do have a resource in the considerable core crime jurisprudence of the Federal Courts in the immigration and refugee context, which have made detailed consideration of many of the principles of international criminal liability and made extensive use of international caselaw in so doing.[223]

Yet this will no doubt be a difficult exercise at times, particularly where the courts are called upon to reconcile conflicts, inconsistencies, or ambiguities as between the domestic criminal law and international law. Canadian courts are, of course, far more comfortable with the domestic law regarding when a person is a party to an offence and when inchoate offences are committed, and may be resistant to international

---

221 Above note 80.

222 The conspiracy provision in fact goes beyond the *Rome Statute*, which does not contain a provision regarding common law conspiracy, though conspiracy as an inchoate offence is certainly not unknown to international criminal law; for example, conspiracy to commit crimes against peace was contained in the *IMT Charter*, above note 14, and conspiring to commit genocide is provided for under art. III of the *Genocide Convention*, above note 2.

223 See, generally, Joseph Rikhof, "Complicity in International Criminal Law and Canadian Refugee Law" (2006) 4 JICJ 702. Though caution must be exercised in transferring findings from the civil context to the criminal context.

law standards which are different from, though not inconsistent with, the domestic versions. For example, there has been debate in the jurisprudence of the *ad hoc* tribunals about whether there is a distinction to be made between complicity in genocide and aiding and abetting genocide, and the extent to which the two overlap.[224] It is difficult to assess how this would play out domestically. Another difficulty arises with the principle of joint criminal enterprise as a mode of liability, which is provided for in article 25(3) of the *Rome Statute*.[225] Formally speaking, this mode of liability is available under section 21(2) of the *Code*,[226] which makes an individual a party to an offence on the basis of a "common intention" to commit the offence whether or not the individual actually participated. However, similarly to "command/superior responsibility" - dealt with in Section C(2)(c), above in this chapter, Canadian courts have ruled that a person cannot be convicted for a serious offence, like murder, unless there is actual subjective intent to commit the offence, pursuant to section 7 of the *Charter*.[227] The core crimes certainly rise to this level of seriousness, and it would appear that joint criminal enterprise (JCE) may not be available to prosecutors in Canada. There are also inconsistencies between the Act and the *Code*; for example, in the Act, counselling is a distinct inchoate offence, but under section 22 of the *Code*, a person who counsels is a party to the offence if the offence is committed, while under section 464, counselling an offence that is not committed is an inchoate offence.

e) Procedure and Defences

The Act provides that persons accused of committing one of the offences outside Canada may be tried anywhere in Canada, in the same way as if the crime had been committed in that jurisdiction, and incorporates the *Code* provisions regarding presence of the accused at trial and exceptions (such as absconding defendants).[228] The consent of the Attorney General of Canada or his deputy is required for the prosecution of any offence under the Act, while the Attorney General alone can approve prosecution for the offence of "Bribery of judges and officials" under section 18 of the Act, and the prosecutions can be conducted only by the Public Prosecution Service of Canada.[229] Consent of the Attorney General is

---

224 *Ibid.* at 705.
225 Above note 23.
226 Above note 80.
227 *R. v. Logan*, [1990] 2 S.C.R. 731; *R. v. Kirkness*, [1990] 3 S.C.R. 74; *R. v. Laliberty* (1997), 117 C.C.C. (3d) 97 (Ont. C.A.).
228 Above note 1, ss. 9(1) & (2).
229 *Ibid.*, ss. 9(3) & (4).

typically required for prosecution of extraterritorial offences, as is the case under section 7 of the *Code*. The imposition of this requirement for *territorial* commission of the core crimes is somewhat unique, but is explained by the fact that the government is obliged under the *Rome Statute* to maintain control over whether a prosecution is going ahead or will be handed over to the ICC in appropriate circumstances.[230]

The Act specifically provides that the applicable rules of evidence and procedure are those which are in force at the time of the proceedings.[231] One issue which has been identified is the operation of evidentiary burdens. Canadian evidence law shares with the *Rome Statute* the presumption of innocence and the requirement that the prosecution's case be proven beyond a reasonable doubt. The imposition of the legal burden on the prosecution, then, means that the accused must simply raise a reasonable doubt as to guilt in order to be acquitted. However, the *Code* and the common law impose evidentiary burdens on the accused for some defences; while many, such as self-defence or provocation, require only the leading of some evidence that provides an "air of reality" to the defence, others, such as the defence of mental disorder, actually shift the burden of proof to the accused and she must prove the defence on the balance of probabilities.[232] Professor Schabas has noted that this law is inconsistent with article 67(1)(i) of the *Rome Statute*, which gives the accused the right "not to have imposed on him or her any reversal of the burden of proof or any onus of rebuttal," and has suggested that there is a potential conflict between that provision and section 11 of the Act.[233] However, it seems clear that the *Rome Statute* provision applies only to proceedings before the ICC itself. Section 10 of the Act clearly imposes the Canadian evidence and procedural law of the day on any trial under the Act; and in any event the onus reversals (which have all been *Charter*-tested) are most likely compliant with international human rights standards.

The imposition of the current Canadian evidence law and criminal procedure seems rather obvious, but is perhaps necessary as a tool of clarification because, as with the offences, under section 11 the applicable justifications, excuses, and defences available to an accused in a given case are for the most part those which would have been "available under the laws of Canada or under international law at the

---

230 It has also been suggested that this provides a "safeguard against frivolous prosecutions" (Hage, above note 172 at 52).

231 Above note 1, s. 10.

232 *Criminal Code*, above note 80, s. 16(3).

233 William Schabas, "Canadian Implementing Legislation for the *Rome Statute*: Jurisdiction and Defences" in Neuner, ed., above note 26, 35 at 41.

time of the alleged offence or at the time of the proceedings."[234] This is a very defence-friendly provision which allows the accused to benefit from any defences which have developed in either international law[235] or domestic law between the time of the commission of the offence and the time of trial. The first occurrence of the word "or" appears to have a disjunctive effect, meaning that even a defence which is not known to, or expressly excluded by, Canadian law is available to the accused if it exists in international law; or alternatively, if the international law version of a defence is broader than the Canadian version, this provision appears to implement the international law version of the defence, which the accused can then plead instead of the narrower domestic version.

Section 11 is made subject to sections 12 to 14 of the Act and section 607(6) of the *Criminal Code*.[236] Section 12 deals with the special defences of *autrefois acquit* (accused not liable because has been previously lawfully acquitted of the offence), *autrefois convict* (accused not liable because has been previously lawfully convicted of the offence), and pardon (accused not liable because has been previously pardoned for offence), which in international law are subsumed under the *ne bis in idem* principle. Section 12(1) appears to extend the domestic versions of the defences (in section 607 of the *Code*) to situations where the accused has been acquitted, convicted, or pardoned in/by another state (or by an international tribunal) for the offence with which she is charged under the Act. Section 12(2) provides that these defences are not available if the foreign proceedings "were for the purpose of shielding the person from criminal responsibility" or if they were not independent and impartial in accordance with the norms of due process under international law, and were "inconsistent with an intent to bring the person to justice." Section 607(6) of the *Code*, which is expressly made applicable, provides that an accused may not plead *autrefois convict* if she has been convicted by another state *in absentia* and did not receive the punishment rendered by the foreign court.

There may be a *lacuna* in this provision, as section 12(2) does not appear to cover a situation where the court proceedings produced a valid conviction but the person was pardoned by the government for reasons, probably political, inconsistent with "an intent to bring the person to justice." However, asking a court to invalidate the pardon for the purpose of a Canadian prosecution would require the court to ad-

---

234 Above note 1, s. 11.
235 Including, but not limited to, the defences set out in arts. 31–33 of the *Rome Statute*.
236 Above note 80.

judicate upon the exercise of executive powers by another state, which Canadian courts have traditionally been reluctant to do.[237]

Sections 13 and 14 of the Act both contain legislative responses to certain rulings in the *Finta* case. Section 13 provides it is no defence to the core crimes and the command/superior responsibility offences that, in committing the offence, the accused was acting "in obedience to or in conformity with the law in force at the time and in the place of its commission." Though this is not explicit, this clearly applies only to the *domestic* law, since the entire substantive law scheme of the Act is founded on charging the accused under the *international* law that was in force at the time of the offence. This provision disallows the defence of "obedience to *de facto* law" set out in section 15 of the *Code*, and also removes the ambiguity the Court in *Finta* found in a similar provision contained in the 1987 *Code* amendments.[238]

Section 14 provides for the defence of superior orders and mostly mirrors the wording of the defence in article 33 of the *Rome Statute*. Section (3) contains a response to the Supreme Court's controversial ruling in *Finta* that the accused was permitted to adduce evidence that he believed Nazi propaganda about Jews, towards his defences of superior orders and mistake of fact.[239] The Act provides the following limitation:

> [A]n accused cannot base their defence under subsection (1) on a belief that an order was lawful if the belief was based on information about a civilian population or an identifiable group of persons that encouraged, was likely to encourage or attempted to justify the commission of inhumane acts or omissions against the population or group.

It will be reasonably clear that the phrase "inhumane acts or omissions" covers all acts of genocide and crimes against humanity, as well as most, if not all, war crimes.

f)   Other Provisions

Section 15 of the Act enacts sentencing regimes for the core crimes, all of which attract up to life sentences but with varying eligibility for parole depending on whether the crime involved premeditated killing or intentional killing. Normal eligibility for parole applies to crimes

---

237   See *Argentina (Republic) v. Mellino*, [1987] 1 S.C.R. 536 at para. 36; *Canada (Justice) v. Khadr*, 2008 SCC 28 at para. 21.

238   *Finta*, above note 90 at 829 (S.C.C.).

239   See Section B(4), above in this chapter.

which do not involve intentional killing.[240] In sections 16–23, the Act implements article 70 of the *Rome Statute* by creating a number of what are labelled "Offences Against the Administration of Justice," all of which are indictable offences but which carry varying sentences depending on the gravity of the offence. The offences are in fact all geared towards the administration of justice of the ICC itself, and proscribe obstruction of the work of the court and its officials, bribery of judges and officials, perjury, the giving of contradictory evidence, and so on. Sections 25 and 26 extend jurisdiction for these offences, as well as for retaliation against witnesses and their families, over Canadian nationals who commit the offences outside Canada.

The Act also creates a "Crimes Against Humanity Fund," into which will be paid all money obtained through enforcement of ICC orders for reparation or forfeiture, or fines levied by the court, as well as any proceeds of crime, fines under that regime, and donations.[241] Section 30(2) allows the Attorney General (at his discretion) to make payments out of the fund to the ICC itself or its victim trust fund, or to victims of crimes (and their families) which are prosecuted under either the *Rome Statute* or the Act.

The Act also contains a number of consequential amendments, geared primarily towards engaging the Canadian *Criminal Code* scheme on proceeds of crime for crimes under the Act, and facilitating Canada's cooperation with the ICC itself by way of surrender of fugitives and the provision of mutual legal assistance. The latter provisions are discussed in Chapter 9.

3) The *Munyaneza* Case[242]

The first person to be charged with offences under the Act was Désiré Munyaneza, a Rwandan national who was arrested in Toronto on 19 October 2005.[243] A refugee claim launched by Munyaneza in 1997 was rejected on the basis of information that he was linked to the Rwan-

---

240 Above note 1, s. 15(1)(d).

241 *Ibid.*, ss. 30 & 31.

242 The NGO Trial Watch is closely tracking the *Munyaneza* case. Their coverage (including links to external media reports) can be found online: www.trial-ch.org/en/trial-watch/profile/db/facts/desire_munyaneza_423.html. See also Groupe de Réflexion en droit Pénal International et Humanitaire, Munyaneza Trial Monitoring Project, online: www.grepih.uqam.ca/.

243 "Rwandan Charged under Canadian War-Crimes Law" *The Globe and Mail* (20 October 2005).

dan genocide in 1994.[244] A five-year investigation by the War Crimes Section, which included witness interviews in Rwanda, Europe, and Canada, provided sufficient confirmatory information such that he was charged with two counts each of genocide and crimes against humanity, as well as three counts of war crimes. He was alleged to have committed murder, psychological terror, and sexual and physical violence against Tutsis in the town of Butare.

In January–February 2007, prior to the commencement of Munyaneza's trial before the Quebec Superior Court in Montreal, Justice André Denis, the trial judge, and Crown and defence lawyers conducted a "rogatory commission" in Rwanda, where they took testimony from fourteen witnesses who were unwilling or unable to attend the trial in Canada. The trial began on 26 March 2007, hearing from an additional sixteen prosecution witnesses before the prosecution's case closed, including retired Canadian General Romeo Dallaire. At a request from the accused, additional rogatory commissions took testimony from defence witnesses in France, Rwanda, and Tanzania, followed by an additional twelve defence witnesses when the trial resumed in Montreal. The evidence of both the Crown's witnesses, and to some extent those of the defence, painted the horrific tale of a small but odious part of the Rwandan atrocities, detailing killing, maiming, rape, and atrocities of practically endless variety.[245]

Justice Denis rendered his decision on 22 May 2009. Munyaneza was convicted on all seven counts with which he had been charged, at the end of an exhaustively detailed 201-page judgment that set out the applicable law, gave a brief historical account of the Rwandan genocide, and reviewed in some detail the testimony of the witnesses (most of whom were granted anonymity by the judge) and the judge's credibility findings on each. This being the first successful Canadian prosecution of the core crimes since the adoption of the *Rome Statute* and the *CAH Act*, one might venture that Justice Denis was aware he was writing for the world as well as for the Canadian legal community; the decision is replete with explanations of basic principles of Canadian criminal law, evidence law and procedure, the *Charter*, the Act, and the relevant history. Yet it is clear that the decision seeks to uphold one of the most important goals of international criminal justice: the creation of a his-

---

244 The immigration panel's decision appears to be unreported, but is referred to in *Munyaneza v. Canada (Minister of Citizenship and Immigration)*, [2002] F.C.J. No. 1628 (T.D.), which denied an application to reopen his hearing on the basis of new evidence.

245 I. Slabad, "Canada Unveils Universal Jurisdiction" *International Justice Tribune* (2 April 2007) at 1–2.

torical record so that the story of the victims can be told, and will not be forgotten. The judgment can be read almost as a narrative, describing in as much detail as possible[246] the events that took place and the respective roles of many perpetrators other that Munyaneza himself. In his conclusion, Denis J. was moved to comment, "The proof shows that no Rwandan came out unscathed from the events of spring 1994 . . . . Nearly fifteen years after the genocide, Rwandans are afraid. They distrust one another. They are silent and most do not want to, or cannot, talk about the genocide. Their wound is immense, still present, unbearable and indelible, for both victims and executioners."[247]

In terms of the law, as noted above, Justice Denis essentially followed the methodological model set out in *Mugesera*, using international treaties (including the *Rome Statute*) and the jurisprudence of the *ad hoc* tribunals to reach his findings as to what the international criminal law was at any given point, and then applying it. Because that process was channeled through the provisions of the *CAH Act*, which directly implements the international law offences as they existed at the time of the alleged crimes, the court was able to avoid the methodological problem in *Mugesera*—namely that the Supreme Court simply relied upon the tribunal jurisprudence as "the law" without making its own express findings as to what the customary law on point was and recognizing that law as being incorporated into the common law of Canada.

Yet the unquestioning reliance upon, and essentially judicial notice of, the tribunal jurisprudence creates its own problems in the judgment. For example, in reviewing the law of war crimes, Justice Denis notes that both the *Geneva Conventions*[248] and the *Additional Protocols*[249] applied to Rwanda during the time of the genocide. He then comments, "As for customary international law, Article 4 of the *ICTR Statute*,[250] regarding non-international armed conflicts, provides that it applied on Rwandan territory in 1994 and that the list of war crimes included killing, outrages upon personal dignity, rape and pillage."[251] In support of this proposition is cited paragraph 616 of the ICTR's decision in *Akayesu*.[252] Yet the paragraph in question is part of a discussion regarding

---

246 Some of the evidence of the Crown's witnesses was reviewed in more detail in a sealed appendix, due to concerns that the details might allow anonymous witnesses to be identified; see above note 120 at para. 231.

247 *Ibid.* at paras. 2090–93.

248 Above note 4.

249 Above note 60.

250 Annex to UN Doc. S/RES/955 (1994).

251 *Munyaneza*, above note 120 at para. 135.

252 *Akayesu* (ICTR-96-4-T), Trial Chamber Judgment, 2 September 1998.

whether, in 1994, customary international law provided for individual criminal responsibility for the treaty provisions referred to in article 4 of the *ICTR Statute* (itself simply a jurisdiction-conferring provision in the Statute), or whether these provisions simply created state responsibility. In finding the former, the tribunal was saying that the acts contained in article 4 were criminalized as a matter of custom at the relevant time, but that was a finding based on a survey of the applicable law and state practice;[253] accordingly, this is a finding by the tribunal itself that is being relied upon, and not something set out in article 4 of the *ICTR Statute*. While this might seem trivial, it is indicative of the fact that, in places, the use of the international law sources by the court is not very rigorous, and various instruments and legal principles appear as *non sequiturs* in some parts of the judgment. For example, the judge remarks that the Assembly of States Parties to the International Criminal Court (ASP) adopted the *ICC Elements*[254] (which he refers to as "regulations"), "that assist the Tribunal in interpreting and determining genocide, crimes against humanity and war crimes."[255] Yet no further mention is made of the *ICC Elements*. Also, in several places, the court appears to take judicial notice of material taken from the ICRC website, including a finding on the status of ratifications of the *Genocide Convention*,[256] which underpins a ruling that the *Genocide Convention* applied to Rwanda in 1994,[257] and there is also some seemingly outdated comments on the *Rome Statute*.[258] The *Geneva Conventions* and *Additional Protocols* are even cited to the website.[259] Again, while not serious in terms of any inaccuracy of the findings, these rulings are inconsistent with evidentiary rules regarding judicial notice, the admission of unproven hearsay evidence, and proof of questions of fact relating to the status of treaties.

Yet on the whole, the judgment is fairly deft in terms of engaging with the appropriate international law issues which were at play in the case, avoiding confusion and digressions with admirable efficiency. On first reading, the problems are methodological but not substantial, and some may be due to translation problems, as the authoritative version of the judgment is in French. The salutary effect of having a Canadian

---

253 That had been carried out by the ICTY Appeals Chamber in *Tadić*, (IT-94-1-AR72), Decision on the Defence Motion for Interlocutory Appeal on Jurisdiction, 2 October 1995.

254 Above note 130.

255 *Munyaneza*, above note 120 at para. 86.

256 Above note 2.

257 Above note 120 at paras. 72–73.

258 *Ibid.* at para. 61, quoting the ICRC website as saying, in part, "The ICC *will be* established in the Hague and *will have* jurisdiction . . . ." [emphasis added].

259 *Ibid.* at para. 132.

conviction of a Rwandan *génocidaire*, under the principle of universal jurisdiction, cannot be doubted. Moreover, on the whole, this judgment and the others that will hopefully follow will begin the long task of accomplishing a goal to which this text hopes to make a modest contribution: having criminal lawyers and international lawyers speak the same language, through an appropriate synthesis of international criminal law (ICL) and domestic criminal law.

D. IMMIGRATION-BASED MECHANISMS

As noted above, the most successful Canadian efforts to deal with perpetrators of the core crimes have been in the realm of immigration and refugee law, rather than criminal prosecutions. The 2006–2007 report of the War Crimes Program noted that by the end of the 2006–2007 fiscal year, over 33,000 cases had been heard and settled, and this resulted in 3,721 people who were found to have been complicit in war crimes or crimes against humanity being prevented from entering Canada, while 595 people were expelled.[260] This is the use of ICL as a shield, rather than a sword; persons discovered in Canada about whom there is good reason to believe that they committed international crimes are excluded from the country, either by way of denaturalization and deportation, or refusal of immigration and refugee claims (and often deportation in these instances as well). While this means that some consequences attach to the illegal conduct of such persons, they do not face Canada's criminal justice system and are not explicitly deported to a location where they might face trial, such as would be the case if Canada was fulfilling an extradition request for the person. Justice Canada officials have explained that within the context of the War Crimes Program, criminal trials are "a last resort," due to the extreme expense associated with a full-blown criminal investigation and trial.[261] This perspective is also compounded by the difficulty associated with assembling sufficient evidence to prove guilt to a criminal standard, in the context of crimes that often took place far from Canada, sometimes many years ago, and where many of the victims have been dispersed around the world. It also likely reflects the fact that these legal mechanisms are deemed to be a better way to deal with lower-level perpetrators, with prosecution reserved for more important

---

260 War Crimes Program Annual Report 2006–2007, above note 107, Appendix 3.
261 Thierry Cruvellier, "Immigration First, Justice Second" *International Justice Tribune* (2 April 2007) at 2.

figures. Still, criticism has been leveled at the War Crimes Program for not focusing enough on prosecution, since the goals of combating impunity and depriving perpetrators of safe haven cannot ultimately be accomplished by immigration mechanisms.[262]

1) Exclusion from Immigration

The Canadian immigration legal regime, which is embodied in the *Immigration and Refugee Protection Act (IRPA)*,[263] contains measures to exclude individuals from Canada where there are reasonable grounds to believe that they have committed or been complicit in the core crimes. Section 35 of *IRPA* provides

> (1) A permanent resident or a foreign national is inadmissible on grounds of violating human or international rights for:
>
> (a) committing an act outside Canada that constitutes an offence referred to in sections 4 to 7 of the *Crimes Against Humanity and War Crimes Act*;
>
> (b) being a prescribed senior official in the service of a government that, in the opinion of the Minister, engages or has engaged in terrorism, systematic or gross human rights violations, or genocide, a war crime or a crime against humanity within the meaning of subsections 6(3) to (5) of the *Crimes Against Humanity and War Crimes Act*[.]

Inadmissibility on this basis does not require a finding of guilt or formal conviction, but an assessment on the lower standard of "reasonable grounds to believe." As is explicit in the wording of the section, it applies both to permanent residents and to foreign nationals; the latter, for example, could be applying for a visa to enter Canada and be refused admissibility in the literal sense. A person already in Canada who is found to be inadmissible will normally be subject to deportation or other removal proceedings, while a person outside Canada about whom the finding is rendered will be barred from entering Canada. No appeal is available from the determination of inadmissibility,[264] but judicial review is available. Moreover, persons excluded under paragraph (a) of section 35(1) have no recourse by way of application to the Minister to overcome the

---

262 The government is clearly alive to this point, as Jane Stoyles, Director of the Canadian Centre for International Justice, is quoted to this effect in the War Crimes Program Annual Report 2006–2007, above note 107.

263 S.C. 2001, c. 27, as amended [*IRPA*]. For a detailed overview of the immigration and citizenship modalities surveyed here, see Lorne Waldman, *Immigration Law and Practice*, 2d ed. (Markham, ON: LexisNexis Canada, 2005).

264 *IRPA, ibid.*, s. 64(1).

finding, though persons excluded under paragraph (b) may obtain special dispensation from the Minister if they are able to make a case that "their presence in Canada would not be detrimental to the national interest."[265]

The Federal Courts, which have jurisdiction over immigration matters, have established a substantial jurisprudence to the effect that a person is inadmissible if they have actually committed a core crime, or if they are somehow complicit in the commission of the crime. *Mugesera*, considered in greater detail in Section C(2)(b), above in this chapter, is the leading case on the former ground of inadmissibility.

Under section 35(1)(b) individuals are also inadmissible if they are prescribed senior officials in a government that has engaged in the core crimes. The prescribed positions are set out in section 16 of the *Immigration and Refugee Protection Regulations*,[266] and generally encompass senior government officials, bureaucrats, diplomats, and members of the judiciary. The decision as to whether a particular governmental regime should be designated as one involved in core crimes is a political one left solely to the Minister's discretion, though it is taken in consultation with other Ministries, notably Foreign Affairs. A number of regimes have been so designated, including the Marxist government of Afghanistan in 1978–92, the Taliban regime in Afghanistan during 1996–2001, various regimes in Haiti, and governments under which atrocities were committed in both the former Yugoslavia and Rwanda.[267] A number of recent court decisions have dealt with high-ranking members of the Afghan military[268] and secret police.[269]

2) Exclusion from Refugee Status

While the entire point of both international and refugee law is to ensure that persons who have refugee status be given protection by allowing them to stay in a state to which they flee, the legal regime recognizes that some persons are undeserving of this protection based on their having committed, *inter alia*, core crimes. Article 1F of the *Refugee Convention*[270] provides,

---

265 *Ibid.*, s. 35(2).
266 S.O.R./2002-227.
267 War Crimes Program Annual Report 2006–2007, above note 107, Appendix 4.
268 *Holway v. Canada (Minister of Citizenship and Immigration)*, [2006] F.C.J. No. 386 (T.D.).
269 *Hamidi v. Canada (Minister of Citizenship and Immigration)*, [2006] F.C.J. No. 402 (T.D.).
270 *Convention on the Status of Refugees* (1969), Can. T.S. No. 6, as amended by the *Protocol Relating to the Status of Refugees* (1969), Can. T.S. No. 29; art. 1F of the *Convention* is reproduced as a schedule to *IRPA*.

The provisions of this Convention shall not apply to any person with respect to whom there are serious reasons for considering that:

(a) he has committed a crime against peace, a war crime, or a crime against humanity, as defined in the international instruments drawn up to make provision in respect of such crimes[.]

The Federal Court of Appeal described the impact of this provision in domestic law as follows: "When the tables are turned on persecutors, who suddenly become the persecuted, they cannot claim refugee status. International criminals, on all sides of the conflicts, are rightly unable to claim refugee status."[271] Article 1F(a) was clearly drafted to reflect the crimes as laid out in the *IMT Charter*,[272] but Canadian courts have accepted that the crime of genocide is a crime against humanity for this purpose.[273]

The Immigration and Refugee Board is empowered to make a decision that a person should be excluded from refugee status by invoking article 1F(a).[274] The Board must find, on a "serious grounds to believe" standard, a nexus between the person and the crime committed. This can be found on the basis of active commission of the crime; being an accomplice; being complicit, for example, aiding and abetting; or being a member of a "limited brutal purpose" terrorist organization which commits such crimes while the individual is a member.[275] Persons excluded on this basis are ineligible for referral to the Refugee Protection Division[276] and from the "pre-removal risk assessment" process.[277] They are usually removed from Canada,[278] though they may apply for a "stay of removal," which requires a balancing of the gravity of the acts they have committed and any danger they present to Canada's security against their need for protection.[279]

---

271 *Sivakumar v. Canada (Minister of Citizenship and Immigration)*, [1994] 1 F.C. 433 (C.A.).

272 Above note 14.

273 See, for example, *Wajid v. Canada (Minister of Citizenship and Immigration)* (2000), 185 F.T.R. 308 at para. 6 (T.D.).

274 *IRPA*, above note 263, ss. 95–98.

275 Waldman, above note 263 at §8.534. On the latter ground of membership in a limited brutal purpose organization, see the recent decision of the Federal Court of Appeal in *Zazai v. Canada (Minister of Citizenship and Immigration)* (2005), 50 Imm. L.R. (3d) 107, 2005 FCA 303.

276 *IRPA*, above note 263, s. 101(1)(f).

277 *Ibid.*, s. 112(3)(a).

278 On the removal process generally, see Martin Jones & Sasha Baglay, *Refugee Law* (Toronto: Irwin Law, 2007) c. 12.

279 *IRPA*, above note 263, s. 113(d)(ii).

3) Loss of Citizenship

An individual's status as a citizen of Canada is governed by the *Citizenship Act*,[280] section 10 of which provides that a person's citizenship may be revoked if the person has obtained or retained citizenship "by false representation or fraud or by knowingly concealing material circumstances." The Minister of Citizenship and Immigration initiates revocation by providing notice to the individual, alleging that he obtained his status in Canada through fraud in that he did not reveal his connection to the alleged core crimes when he applied to come to Canada. The individual can surrender his status and leave, or ask that the matter be referred to the Federal Court, which can hear a trial on the matter. The Federal Court determines whether fraud was indeed committed, a decision which cannot be appealed.[281] If fraud is found, the Minister then decides whether to recommend to the Governor in Council that the individual's status be revoked. If such a recommendation is made, the individual has the right to respond to the Minister's report in writing. The Governor in Council then makes its decision, which is subject to judicial review. The *Citizenship Act* also provides that a person shall not be granted citizenship while the person is under investigation by the RCMP, Justice Canada, or the Canadian Security Intelligence Service (CSIS) relating to offences under the *CAH Act*, or if that person has been charged with, is on trial for, or has been convicted of any such offences.[282]

The use of "denaturalization" or revocation of citizenship has been a tool for exclusion of war criminals from Canada that has been used with success by the government. In particular, several suspected Nazi war criminals were denaturalized (or at least recommended for denaturalization by the Minister) on the basis that they obtained their Canadian citizenship by way of concealing or misrepresenting material facts when applying for citizenship, and one was subsequently deported.[283]

---

280 R.S.C. 1985, c. C-29.
281 *Ibid.*, s. 18. This finding was made regarding Michael Seifert, whose extradition was mentioned in Section B(1), above in this chapter; see *Canada (Minister of Citizenship and Immigration) v. Seifert*, 2007 FC 1165.
282 *Citizenship Act, ibid.*, s. 22.
283 See, for example, *Lutjens*, above note 106 (deported); *Canada (Minister of Citizenship and Immigration) v. Katriuk*, [1999] F.C.J. No. 90 (T.D.); *Canada (Minister of Citizenship and Immigration) v. Odynsky*, [2001] F.C.J. No. 286 (T.D.). See also Justice Canada, News Release, "Citizenship of Individuals Revoked" (24 May 2007), online: www.justice.gc.ca/eng/news-nouv/nr-cp/2007/doc_32018. html, and highlights of other cases in the War Crimes Program Annual Report 2006–2007, above note 107.

FURTHER READING

AMERASINGHE, CHRISTOPHER A., "The Canadian Experience," in M. Cherif. Bassiouni, ed., *International Criminal Law*, 2d ed. (Ardsley, NY: Transnational, 1999), vol. 2 at 243

COTLER, IRWIN, "War Crimes Law and the *Finta* Case" (1995) 6 Sup. Ct. L. Rev. (2d) 577

DESCHÊNES, JULES, *Commission of Inquiry on War Criminals: Report*, Part I (Ottawa: Minister of Supply and Services, 1986)

FENRICK, WILLIAM J., "The Prosecution of War Criminals in Canada" (1989–90) 12 Dal. L.J. 256

GREEN, LESLIE C., "Canadian Law, War Crimes and Crimes against Humanity" (1988) 59 Brit. Y.B. Int'l L. 217

MCMANUS, JOHN, "A New Era of Accountability Through Domestic Enforcement of International Law" in Hélène Dumont & Anne-Marie Boisvert, eds., *The Highway to the International Court: All Roads Lead to Rome* (Montreal: Éditions Thémis, 2004) 503

RIKHOF, JOSEPH, "War Crimes Law, as Applied in Canada" in Richard D. Wiggers & Ann. L. Griffiths, eds., *Canada and International Humanitarian Law: Peacekeeping and War Crimes in the Modern Era* (Halifax: Centre for Foreign Policy Studies, Dalhousie University, 2002) 121

SCHABAS, WILLIAM A., "Canadian Implementing Legislation for the *Rome Statute*" (2000) 3 Y.B. Int'l Human. L. 337

SCHWARZ, MADELINE J., "Prosecuting Crimes against Humanity in Canada: What Must Be Proved" (2002) 46 Crim. L.Q. 40

WILLIAMS, SHARON A., "Laudable Principles Lacking Application: The Prosecution of War Criminals in Canada" in Timothy L.H. McCormack & Gerry J. Simpson, eds., *The Law of War Crimes: National and International Approaches* (Boston: Kluwer, 1997) 151

CHAPTER 6

OTHER INTERNATIONAL CRIMES

A. INTRODUCTION

As outlined in Chapter 1, the methodology being employed in this book distinguishes international crimes from transnational crimes and divides the former into two subcategories. The first, international crimes in the strict sense (*stricto sensu*), contains those crimes for which there is individual liability under international law itself, and which are deemed by the international community to "shock the conscience of humanity" to a sufficient extent that international courts are given jurisdiction to prosecute them. The second subcategory, called here simply "other international crimes," contains a distinct subset of criminal acts which are deemed by states to be sufficiently odious that all states may (and sometimes must) prosecute them under their domestic criminal law systems—even extending to the use of the principle of universal jurisdiction. Some of them bear some of the trappings of international crimes *stricto sensu* some of the time; the prohibitions of torture and slavery, for example, are both *jus cogens* norms for which there is a broad consensus that universal jurisdiction is available. Moreover, torture, apartheid, and slavery all appear as the base offences for war crimes or crimes against humanity (and sometimes both) under both treaty and customary international law instruments.

As noted earlier in Section C(2) in Chapter 1, the first four crimes dealt with in this chapter—torture, piracy, apartheid, and slavery—have not attracted the status of the core crimes, but are deemed to be sufficiently egregious to justify prosecution of the perpetrators wherever they may go, so as to ensure they can find no safe haven. The fifth, terrorism, bears consideration within this framework because of both its currency as a matter of international concern and the complexity of its current status under international law. It is also dealt with as a transnational crime of international concern in Chapter 7.

B. TORTURE

1) History and Definition

The international law concerning the practice of torture can be said to have three distinct but interrelated streams: torture as a violation of human rights; torture as an underlying offence to an international crime *stricto sensu*, that is, war crimes and crimes against humanity; and torture as a discrete or stand-alone crime. The second of these categories is dealt with in Chapter 3, and it is the latter body of law that is surveyed here.[1]

The prohibition of torture emerged as a *jus cogens* norm in the twentieth century, and as such the prohibition is absolute and may not be derogated from even in times of emergency or crisis, national or international.[2] Torture has a long history as a practice used by both state officials and private parties, usually in order to fulfill certain goals, such as punishment or the obtaining of information or evidence for use in court proceedings.[3] However, the revulsion of the international community grew rapidly in the post–WW II years, and in 1975, the United Nations General Assembly (UNGA) unanimously adopted a resolution condemning torture as "an offence to human dignity and . . . a denial of the purposes of the Charter of the United Nations and as a violation of the human rights and fundamental freedoms proclaimed in the *Universal Declaration of Human Rights*."[4] This status was given its most import-

---

1   For torture under international human rights law, see Mark Freeman & Gibran van Ert, *International Human Rights Law* (Toronto: Irwin Law, 2004) at 90–92 and 277–83.

2   Though in the current anti-terrorism climate, the possibility of an exception for torture in order to prevent terrorism is occasionally mooted; see Paola Gaeta, "May Necessity Be Available As a Defence against Torture in the Interrogation of Suspected Terrorists?" (2004) 2 JICJ 762.

3   See John Langbein, *Torture and the Law of Proof* (Chicago: University of Chicago Press, 1977).

4   *Declaration on the Protection of All Persons from Being Subjected to Torture and Other Cruel, Inhuman or Degrading Treatment or Punishment*, GA Res. 3452

ant boost by the 1984 United Nations *Convention against Torture and other Cruel, Inhuman and Degrading Treatment or Punishment (CAT)*,[5] which is one of the most widely-adhered-to transnational crime conventions.[6] In assessing the status of the norm in the *Suresh*[7] case, the Supreme Court of Canada was able to point to the fact that torture is prohibited under numerous international treaties or instruments, and to the fact that "no state has ever legalized torture or admitted to its deliberate practice and that governments accused of practising torture regularly deny their involvement, placing responsibility on individual state agents or groups outside the government's control."[8] As the Court noted in *Filartiga*, "the torturer has become, like the pirate or slave trader before him, *hostis humani generis*, an enemy of all mankind."[9]

There is a powerful case for classifying torture as an international crime. While it is not an international crime *stricto sensu*, it is the subject of several international treaty regimes, the *CAT* being only the most global in scope.[10] These regimes differ from most other suppression conventions in that there is no requirement, and indeed little anticipation, that the acts of torture themselves will be transnational in scope; rather, it is the will of states to accept the responsibility to prohibit and punish the torturer that is internationalized. When committed within certain prescribed circumstances, torture is both a crime against humanity and a war crime.[11] The most commonly accepted definition of

---

(XXX), UNGAOR, 30th Sess., Supp. No. 34, UN Doc. A/10034 (1975) at 91, art. 2 [*Declaration on Torture*].

5   (1984), 1465 U.N.T.S. 85, Can. T.S. 1987 No. 36 [*CAT*].

6   As of June 2009, the *CAT* has 146 state parties; online: www2.ohchr.org/english/law/cat.htm.

7   *Suresh v. Canada (Minister of Citizenship and Immigration)*, [2002] 1 S.C.R. 3 [*Suresh*].

8   *Ibid.* at para. 63. One need only look to the controversy swirling around the treatment of detainees in the US Guantanamo Bay internment camp to take note of the fact that the debate has all been around whether this treatment qualified as torture — the US administration has not seriously argued that torture is not unlawful. See Karen Greenberg & Joshua Dretel, *The Torture Papers: The Road to Abu Ghraib* (New York: Cambridge University Press, 2005); Philippe Sands, *Torture Team: Rumsfeld's Memo and the Betrayal of American Values* (New York: Palgrave Macmillan, 2008).

9   *Filartiga v. Pena-Irala*, 630 F.2d 876 at 980 (2d Cir. 1980). See also *A(FC) and others (FC) v. Secretary of State for the Home Department*, [2004] UKHL 56 at para. 9, Lord Bingham.

10 See also, for example, the *Inter-American Convention to Prevent and Punish Torture*, OAS Treaty Ser. No. 67 (9 December 1985); the *European Convention for the Prevention of Torture and Inhuman or Degrading Treatment or Punishment* (26 November 1987), reprinted (1988) 27 I.L.M. 1152.

11 See Chapter 3.

the crime, that of the *CAT*, requires that it be committed by a public official of some kind, bringing it within the bailiwick of the most heinous crimes in international law. As explored in more detail in Section B(2), below in this chapter, it is broadly accepted that states may exercise universal jurisdiction over torture. Moreover, while the precise contours are difficult to discern, there is little doubt that torture is a crime under customary international law, and a great deal of the *CAT* itself can be said to have attained customary international law status. Because prohibiting torture is a *jus cogens* norm, states cannot derogate from it, and they have a concurrent obligation under the *International Covenant on Civil and Political Rights (ICCPR)*.[12] States will incur state responsibility not only if they fail to criminalize and punish torture, but also if their officials engage in torture.[13] Accordingly, the international community has decreed that the torturer shall have no safe haven; "no legal loopholes have been left."[14]

2) Jurisdiction over Torture

Recognition of torture as one of the most heinous and serious crimes in law has led to efforts to cast the jurisdictional net as widely as possible in order to allow states to prosecute alleged torturers on as wide a basis as possible. Article 5 of the *CAT* obliges states to take jurisdiction over torture offences which take place on their territories, ships, or registered aircraft, as well as over torture where committed by their nationals.[15] States may take jurisdiction over torture on the basis of the passive personality principle. In addition, under articles 5(2) and 7(1), states must exercise custodial universal jurisdiction and either prosecute or extradite[16] an alleged offender found on the state's territory. Under a convention which has 146 state parties, this is a powerful prosecutorial network. However, it is undercut as always by political concerns, to wit: will a state actually have the political will to prosecute another state's officials or former officials when they travel to that state's territory?[17] More controversial is whether a state party to

---

12   Can. T.S. 1976 No. 47.

13   *Furundžija* (IT-95-17/1-T), Judgment, 10 December 1998 at para. 153.

14   *Ibid.* at para. 146.

15   *CAT*, above note 5, arts. 5(1)(a) & (b).

16   On the *aut dedere aut judicare* obligation, see Chapter 7.

17   A related issue is the immunity of state officials for their actions in office. As discussed in Chapter 11, even former state officials are "functionally" immune from prosecution for their "official" acts, conducted as part of their position. However, as will be seen in Section B(5), below in this chapter, the definition

the *CAT* may exercise custodial universal jurisdiction over an offender where neither the state where the torture occurred nor the state of the offender's nationality is party to the treaty.[18]

An answer to the latter problem would be a general entitlement under customary international law for states to exercise full-fledged universal jurisdiction over alleged torturers. This question was at issue in the *Pinochet*[19]case, where Spain sought to have former Chilean dictator Augusto Pinochet extradited from the UK to face charges in Spain for torture, *inter alia*, beginning in the early 1970s. Lord Millet found (and Chile, appearing before the court, had conceded) that the prohibition on torture had certainly attained *jus cogens* status by 1973. Lord Millet reasoned that a *jus cogens* crime must attract universal jurisdiction,[20] and thus Pinochet could be extradited for prosecution on the full range of crimes. A majority of the Lords disagreed, finding instead that Pinochet could be extradited only for torture that allegedly occurred after 1988, the year that the UK had ratified the *CAT* and became bound by its custodial universal jurisdiction obligation. Since that judgment, a broad consensus has emerged that torture is subject to universal jurisdiction,[21] certainly when it is committed on some kind of large scale, and likely even for isolated acts.[22] Whether states are actually required to establish this jurisdiction or are only permitted to do so is less clear, though the better view is probably that this requirement has not yet crystallized as a principle of customary international law.

---

of torture under the *CAT* presupposes the involvement of state officials of some kind, and thus the *Convention* itself must have removed any such immunity for torture. This appeared to be the position of the House of Lords in the *Pinochet* case, below note 19, and was recently affirmed in *Jones v. Ministry of Interior Al-Mamlaka Al-Arabiya AS Saudiya (the Kingdom of Saudi Arabia) and others*, [2006] UKHL 26 at paras. 19, 80, & 81.

18 Favouring this position, see Nigel Rodley & Matt Pollard, "Criminalisation of Torture: State Obligations under the United Nations *Convention against Torture and other Cruel, Inhuman and Degrading Treatment or Punishment*" (2006) 2 Eur. H.R.L. Rev. 115, n. 17.

19 *R. v. Bow Street Magistrate, ex parte Pinochet (No. 3)*, [1999] 2 All E.R. 97 (H.L.).

20 See M. Cherif Bassiouni, "International Crimes: *Jus Cogens* and *Obligatio Erga Omnes*" (1996) 59 Law & Contemp. Probs. 63.

21 *Princeton Principles on Universal Jurisdiction* (Princeton, NJ: Princeton University Program in Law and Public Affairs, 2001), Principle 2(1).

22 Lord Millet had accepted this qualification as well. See also *Furundžija*, above note 13 at para. 156; Antonio Cassese, *International Criminal Law*, 2d ed. (Oxford: Oxford University Press, 2008) at 151; Ian Brownlie, *Principles of Public International Law*, 6th ed. (Oxford: Oxford University Press, 2003) at 304.

3) Mental Elements

In article 1(1) of the *CAT*, and in customary international law, the required mental element is intention, and thus lesser mental thresholds such as criminal negligence are not part of the international law definition of the offence.[23] The article 1(1) definition of torture also requires that it be inflicted

> For such purposes as obtaining from him or a third person information or a confession, punishing him for an act he or a third person has committed or is suspected of having committed, or intimidating or coercing him or a third person, or for any reason based on discrimination of any kind[.]

This list of purposes provides examples only and is not exhaustive. How far out from this list of purposes a particular act can extend and still be called torture is controversial. There are some suggestions that torture can be inflicted for a broader range of purposes than those in the *CAT*,[24] an approach supported by the definition in article 3 of the *Inter-American Torture Convention*,[25] which sets out a list of possible purposes and concludes with the phrase "or any other purpose." The International Criminal Tribunal for the former Yugoslavia (ICTY) has dealt inconclusively with the possibility that humiliation of the victim may be among the possible purposes;[26] though it seems that the use of rape for a wide variety of purposes constitutes torture.[27] The ICTY has also suggested that the prohibited purpose need not be the only or primary purpose for liability to accrue, but rather just must be some part of the accused's intention.[28]

---

23   Cassese, *ibid.* at 152.

24   See, for example, *Delalić and Others (Čelebići Case)* (IT-96-21), Judgment, 16 November 1998 at para. 470; *Kunarac et al.* (IT-96-23-T and IT-96-23/1-T), Trial Chamber Judgment, 22 February 2001 at para. 486; *Furundžija* , above note 13 at para. 162.

25   (1985) OAS Treaty Series No. 67, Treaty No. A-51. Canada has not signed this treaty.

26   In favour of that position, see *Furundžija*, above note 13 at para. 162; *contra*, *Krnojelac* (IT-97-25-T), Trial Chamber Judgment, 15 March 2002 at para. 186.

27   *Aydin v. Turkey* (1998), 25 E.H.R.R. 251 at paras. 82–84; *Fernando and Racquel Meiji v. Peru*, Decision (1 March 1996), Annual Report of the Inter-American Commission on Human Rights, Report No. 5/96, Case No. 10970 at 182–88. *Furundžija*, *ibid.* at paras. 162–63 and 267.

28   *Čelebići*, above note 24 at para. 470; *Kvočka* (IT-98-30/1), Judgment, 2 November 2001 at para. 153; *Kunarac et al.* (IT-96-23 and IT-96-23/1-A), Appeals Chamber Judgment, 12 June 2002 at para. 155.

It is not clear whether the purpose requirement is contained within the customary law relating to torture. The *Rome Statute*[29] imposes the requirement for the war crime of torture, but not for torture as a crime against humanity.

4) Acts Constituting Torture

There is no closed list of acts which constitute torture, nor is it in anyone's interest to make one since the horrific quality of acts perpetrated by humans upon each other is limited only by the imagination. The essential point is qualitative: whether the act in question causes "severe pain or suffering, whether physical or mental," per article 1(1) of the *CAT*.[30] The severity criterion is significant, for it is this which distinguishes torture from "cruel, inhuman or degrading treatment or punishment," which is also criminalized by article 16 of the *CAT* and customary law; indeed, the former is often described as an "aggravated or deliberate form" of the latter.[31] Obviously, a wide variety of acts can cause pain or suffering severe enough to be called torture, including physical violence; infliction of intense pain or bodily mutilation; sexual violence[32]; solitary confinement; or acts such as the deprivation of food, sleep, or medical care, if the act "can be shown to pursue one of the prohibited purposes of torture and to have caused the victim severe pain or suffering."[33] It is broadly accepted that certain omissions can be serious enough to constitute torture, such as failure to provide a prisoner with sustenance, if the other elements are present.[34]

Whether the treatment causes the victim pain or suffering severe enough to constitute torture appears to rest on a mixed objective/subjective test,[35] and treatment that does not reach this threshold will nonetheless be considered "cruel, inhuman or degrading treatment or

---

29   2187 U.N.T.S. 3, entered into force 1 July 2002 [*Rome Statute*].

30   Note that the *Inter-American Torture Convention*, above note 25, does not require a particular threshold of pain and suffering, and requires none at all if the intention is "to obliterate the personality of the victim or to diminish his physical or mental capacities" (art. 3).

31   *Declaration on Torture*, above note 4, art. 1(2).

32   *Kunarac et al.* (IT-96-23 and IT-96-23/1-A), Appeals Chamber Judgment, 12 June 2002 at para. 150; *Čelebići*, above note 24 at para. 489.

33   *Krnojelac*, above note 26 at para. 183.

34   Maxime Tardu, "The United Nations *Convention against Torture and Other Cruel, Inhuman or Degrading Treatment or Punishment*" (1987) 56 Nordic J. Int'l L. 303 at 304; *Čelebići*, above note 24 at para. 468.

35   See Manfred Nowak, *U.N. Covenant on Civil and Political Rights: CCPR Commentary* (Arlington, VA: N.P. Engel, 1993) at 130; Ilias Bantekas & Susan Nash,

punishment" if it is sufficiently adverse. The European Court of Human Rights has found the latter to include "intense physical and mental suffering" and "acute psychiatric disturbances during interrogation"[36] and degrading treatment that instills in detainees "feelings of fear, anguish and inferiority capable of humiliating and debasing them and possibly breaking their physical or moral resistance."[37] The lines between torture; cruel, inhuman, and degrading punishment; and adverse treatment that is not criminal, are hotly contested, not least because of positions taken by the US regarding the treatment of detainees in the "War on Terror."[38] Certain longstanding techniques of interrogation of prisoners, such as subjection to noise and sleep deprivation, are more commonly being viewed as torture by some courts.[39]

As expressed in article 1 of the *CAT*, pain or suffering "arising only from, inherent in or incidental to lawful sanctions" is not included within the definition of torture. At issue has been whether, by "lawful," the treaty means under domestic law or under international law, though the strongest position is the latter—that is, the domestic law must be in compliance with international law.[40] The Committee against Torture[41] has taken the position that various forms of corporal punishment, which violate international law, are also violations under the *CAT*. As Rodley and Pollard point out, this qualification must at least prevent criminal or state responsibility for the inevitable "mental anguish resulting from the very fact of incarceration," since holding otherwise would defeat the very purpose of that particular sanction.[42]

International Criminal Law, 3d ed. (London: Routledge-Cavendish, 2007) at 164, nn. 54 & 55.

36   *Ireland v. United Kingdom* (1978), 25 E.C.H.R. (Ser. A.) 66 at para. 167.

37   *Ibid.*

38   See Craig Forcese, "New Geography of Abuse—The Contested Scope of U.S. Cruel, Inhuman and Degrading Treatment Obligations" (2006) 24 Berkeley J. Int'l L. 908.

39   Nigel Rodley, "The Definition(s) of Torture in International Law" (2002) 55 Curr. Legal Probs. 467 at 476–77.

40   See Chris Ingelse, *The UN Committee against Torture: An Assessment* (The Hague: Kluwer Academic, 2001) at 212–16; Report of the UN Special Rapporteur on Torture, UN Doc. E/CN.4/1988/17 at para. 42.

41   The Committee against Torture was established under Part II of the *CAT* to monitor measures taken by member states to implement their obligations under the treaty. It is also empowered to hear matters referred to it by individual complainants against party states. The Committee has emerged as an important source of interpretation of the *CAT*. Its web page can be found online: www2. ohchr.org/english/bodies/cat/index.htm.

42   Rodley & Pollard, above note 18 at 121.

5) The Public Official Requirement[43]

The definition of torture in article 1(1) of the *CAT* requires that the act "be inflicted by or at the instigation of or with the consent or acquiescence of a public official or other person acting in an official capacity." This reflects interplay between international human rights law and international criminal law,[44] given that there is a special abhorrence attached to torture that is committed at the behest of the state. However, international criminal law courts have increasingly found this limitation to be untenable when dealing with crimes committed in armed conflicts or widespread attacks. Accordingly, the limitation is increasingly stripped away from war crimes and crimes against humanity,[45] which allows liability for torture to attach to members of guerrilla groups, and so on.

6) Other State Obligations

Aside from simply criminalizing torture[46] and actively preventing its occurrence in state territory,[47] states have other important obligations under the *CAT*. Article 3 obliges states to refrain from expelling, returning, or extraditing an individual "to another State where there are substantial grounds for believing that he would be in danger of being subjected to torture"—usually referred to as the *non-refoulement* obligation. In making this determination, states must take into account "all relevant considerations," including violations of human rights in the destination state.[48]

State parties must also ensure that alleged victims of torture have the right to complain and have their complaints investigated,[49] and that their legal system permits victims to obtain redress and compensation.[50]

---

43 See Paola Gaeta, "When is the Involvement of State Officials a Requirement for the Crime of Torture?" (2008) 6 JICJ 183.

44 See Chapter 1.

45 *Kunarac et al.* (IT-96-23-T and IT-96-23/1-T), Trial Chamber Judgment, 22 February 2001 at paras. 387–91; *Rome Statute*, above note 29, art. 7(2)(e).

46 The Committee against Torture has held consistently in recent years that states must create a distinct offence of torture under their criminal laws, and may not simply rely on criminal offences which cover acts that constitute torture. See, for example, the Committee's report on Canada, CAT/C/CR/34/CAN, 7 July 2005, para. 3(a); Ingelse, above note 40 at 222 and 340.

47 *CAT*, above note 5, art. 2(1).

48 *Ibid.*, art. 3(2).

49 *Ibid.*, art. 13.

50 *Ibid.*, art. 14.

278   INTERNATIONAL AND TRANSNATIONAL CRIMINAL LAW

States must also ensure that any statements taken by torture cannot be led in evidence in any proceedings, "except against a person accused of torture as evidence that the statement was made."[51] This would include not only statements extracted by torture on the state party's territory, but anywhere in the world.[52]

7) Torture in Canadian Law

Canada signed the *CAT* in 1985 and ratified it in 1987. Torture is criminalized by section 269.1 of the *Criminal Code*[53] as an indictable offence punishable by imprisonment not exceeding fourteen years. The offence largely mirrors the *CAT* definition of torture: the perpetrator must be an official "or every person acting at the instigation of or with the consent or acquiescence of an official."[54] "Official" is defined as a peace officer, public officer, or member of the Canadian forces, as well as any person in a foreign state who would exercise the same powers as these Canadian officials, "whether the person exercises powers in Canada or outside Canada."[55] "Torture" is defined as an intentional act or, expressly, an omission, which inflicts severe pain or suffering, whether physical or mental, upon a person for "a purpose." A non-exclusive list of purposes includes extraction of information or a statement, punishment, intimidation, coercion, or "for any reason based on discrimination of any kind," and excludes the results of lawful sanctions.[56] The prosecution must therefore prove both specific intent and an ulterior purpose to sustain conviction.[57]

Section 269.1(3) removes the defence of superior orders and prevents the accused from invoking war or public emergency as a justification, implementing articles 2(3) and (2) of the *CAT*, respectively. Section 269.1(4) implements article 15 of the *CAT*, providing that statements obtained as a result of torture are inadmissible in any proceedings over which Parliament has jurisdiction, except as evidence of torture.

Implementing article 5 of the *CAT*, extraterritorial jurisdiction over torture, is established under section 7(3.7) of the *Criminal Code*, which

---

51   *Ibid.*, art. 15.
52   See "Article 15" in Manfred Nowak & Elizabeth McArthur, *The United Nations Convention against Torture: A Commentary* (Oxford: Oxford University Press, 2008) 503.
53   R.S.C. 1985, c. C-46.
54   *Ibid.*, s. 269.1(1).
55   *Ibid.*, s. 269.1(2).
56   *Ibid.*
57   *R. c. Rainville*, [2001] J.Q. no 947 at paras. 66–75 (C.Q.).

asserts jurisdiction over torture on flag ships and registered aircraft, as well as on the nationality and passive personality principles. The *Code* also provides for custodial universal jurisdiction, establishing jurisdiction where the perpetrator is present in Canada after the commission of the offence even though none of the other prescribed links to Canada are present.

Perhaps unsurprisingly, the caselaw regarding prosecution of Canadians for torture, or of tortures committed in Canada, is scanty.[58] Canada reports regularly to the Committee against Torture, as it is required to under the *CAT*, and publishes these reports and the Committee's responses.[59] Controversy has tended to centre around Canada's adherence to the *non-refoulement* obligation. In the extradition setting, the Supreme Court of Canada ruled in the 1987 case of *Canada v. Schmidt*[60] that section 7 of the *Charter*[61] prohibited the extradition of individuals to face treatment in foreign states that would "shock the conscience" of Canadians, and La Forest J. invoked torture as the prime example of treatment that should preclude extradition.[62] However, in the *Suresh* case,[63] the Supreme Court again dealt with the issue of *refoulement* to face torture, this time in the immigration/refugee setting. Suresh, a Sri Lankan refugee claimant, was facing deportation to his home state as a result of Canadian investigators having amassed evidence suggesting that he was a fundraiser for the Tamil Tigers, a terrorist organization. Suresh provided evidence that he would, in fact, be tortured by the government if he was deported. The question facing the Court was whether, under the *Charter*, individuals could be deported to face torture.

In a unanimous judgment, the Court ruled that a proper application of section 7 of the *Charter* meant that an individual could not be deported to face "a substantial risk" of torture, "barring extraordinary circumstances" which it declined to define.[64] The test under section

---

58   For a review, see Donald Macdougall, "Torture in Canadian Criminal Law" (2003) 24 C.R. (6th) 74, especially 88–90.
59   Online: www.pch.gc.ca/pgm/pdp-hrp/docs/torture/torture-eng.pdf.
60   [1987] 1 S.C.R. 500 [*Schmidt*].
61   *Canadian Charter of Rights and Freedoms*, Part I of the *Constitution Act, 1982* (being Schedule B to the *Canada Act 1982* (U.K.), 1982, c. 11.
62   *Schmidt*, above note 60 at 522.
63   Above note 7.
64   *Suresh, ibid.* at paras. 76–77. The Court was applying the same methodology it had used in *United States of America v. Burns*, [2001] 1 S.C.R. 283, where it had ruled that individuals could not be extradited to face the death penalty, unless there were exceptional circumstances. See Robert J. Currie, "*Charter* Without Borders? The Supreme Court of Canada, Transnational Crime and Constitutional Rights and Freedoms" (2004) 27 Dal. L.J. 235.

7 was whether the rendition of the individual would "shock the conscience" of the Canadian public, and while torture would usually meet this test, the Court was prepared to contemplate situations where it would not. The Court's decision was problematic in that, though it engaged in a survey of the international law regarding torture and noted its status as a *jus cogens* prohibition under customary international law, it failed to pay sufficient attention to Canada's specific international law obligations regarding torture or to consider their implementation in the legislative scheme regarding deportation in the immigration/refugee context. While it is likely that states cannot deport (*refoule*) individuals to face torture as a matter of customary international law, Canada is specifically bound by article 3 of the *CAT* not to do so. Accordingly, the "extraordinary circumstances" loophole appears to empower the government to violate a significant norm of treaty and customary international law—a ruling which, incidentally, flew in the face of La Forest J.'s dictum in *Schmidt* that torture was the paradigmatic fate which would always "shock the conscience."[65]

The Court displayed an improved methodology for analyzing Canadian domestic law in accord with proper implementation of international law obligations in *R. v. Hape*,[66] a case which dealt with the extraterritorial application of the *Charter*. Both of these streams of law are in the midst of significant development currently.[67] Recently, there has been both extreme public controversy[68] and litigation regarding the role of Canadian soldiers serving in Afghanistan who, under an agreement between the governments of Canada and Afghanistan, have turned over Afghans and others whom they detain to the Afghani police. There is credible evidence that these detainees have been subjected to torture by the Afghan officials, and thus Canadian state actors have been implicated in possible rendition to face torture. A case before the Federal Court of Canada, wherein intervenors applied to have this practice declared unconstitutional (specifically involving an extraterritorial application of the *Charter* to the actions of the Canadian military officials, *inter alia*), was unsuccessful.[69]

---

65   *Schmidt*, above note 60 at 522.

66   [2007] 2 S.C.R. 292, 2007 SCC 26. But see John Currie, "Weaving a Tangled Web: *Hape* and the Obfuscation of Canadian Reception Law" (2007) 45 Can. Y.B.Int'l Law 55.

67   See Chapter 10.

68   Most recently, see Josh Wingrove, "Canadians Cleared in Detainee Probe" *The Globe and Mail* (10 June 2009) A12.

69   *Amnesty International Canada v. Canada (Canadian Forces)*, 2008 FC 336, aff'd 2008 FCA 401, leave to appeal to S.C.C. refused, [2009] SCCA No. 63.

C. PIRACY

1) History and Definition

The very word "piracy" conjures literary images and swashbuckling folk songs in the Western mind, but until the twentieth century, the law of nations treated the pirate as the most pre-eminent criminal scourge to be found on Earth, the first true *hostis humani generis* (enemy of humankind).[70] Both the practice of piracy and its condemnation and attempted suppression by governments are matters of ancient origin, and one finds references to the evils of piracy in Greek, Roman, and early European texts.[71] Thus, we see in Gentilli,

> Pirates are common enemies, and they are attacked with impunity by all, because they are without the pale of the law. They are scorners of the law of nations; hence they can find no protection in that law. They ought to be crushed by us . . . and by all men. This is a warfare shared by all nations.[72]

By the time of the great seafaring states and their domination of the oceans, especially by the British navy, there was a crime of piracy under international law (or "piracy *jure gentium*") that at least encompassed violent ship-to-ship attacks. This international consensus combined emergent agreement among states that the freedom of the high seas was a necessary common good, with a collective interest in suppressing activities that damaged the fledgling global economy, as well as revulsion over the murderousness and violence of pirate attacks.[73] The difficulty was in arriving at a definition of piracy under international law, because state practice, and statutes and caselaw from the seventeenth to the early twentieth centuries display differing view-

---

70   *In re Piracy jure gentium*, [1934] A.C. 586 (J.C.P.C.); *Turkey v. France* [*The S.S. Lotus*] (1927), P.C.I.J. (Ser. A) No. 10, dissenting opinion of Moore J. at 70. The first attribution of this status to pirates is generally accorded to Cicero; see Marcus Cicero, *DeOfficiis*, Book III, c. 29, cited in Jacob Sundberg, "The Crime of Piracy" in M. Cherif Bassiouni, ed., *International Criminal Law*, 3d ed. (Leiden: Martinus Nijhoff, 2008) vol. 1, 799 at 799.

71   See Alfred Rubin, *The Law of Piracy*, 2d ed. (Irvington-on-Hudson, NY: Transnational, 1998) c. 1; Gerhard Mueller & Freda Adler, *Outlaws of the Ocean: The Complete Book of Contemporary Crime on the High Seas* (New York: Hearst Marine Books, 1985).

72   Alberico Gentilli, *De Iure Belli Libri Tres*, trans. by John Rolfe (Buffalo, NY: W.S. Hein, 1995) at 423.

73   See Patricia Birnie, "Piracy Past, Present and Future" (1987) 11 Marine Policy 163.

points on a number of important issues, including (1) whether piracy could be committed only on the high seas or within states' territorial waters; (2) whether piracy covered acts solely for personal gain, particularly robbery, or whether other motives (including political goals) were covered;[74] (3) whether acts by a state's warships were covered, and whether this depended on the existence of a state of belligerency between the two or more states involved;[75] and (4) whether acts of mutiny or internal seizure constituted piracy. There was no clear line between state laws that implemented the customary international law of piracy and those which exceeded that scope — particularly in that some of the latter purported to be the former.

Significant strides towards formulating a reasonably universally accepted definition of piracy were made by reports generated by the League of Nations[76] and the Harvard Research team.[77] The Harvard Draft was influential on the International Law Commission (ILC)'s drafting of the 1958 *Convention on the High Seas*,[78] and the definition contained in article 14 of that treaty was acceptable enough that it was reincorporated into article 101 of *United Nations Convention on the Law of the Sea (UNCLOS)*[79] in 1982. That definition is as follows:

> Piracy consists of any of the following acts:
> (a) any illegal acts of violence or detention, or any act of depredation, committed for private ends by the crew or the passengers of a private ship or a private aircraft, and directed:
>   (i) on the high seas, against another ship or aircraft, or against persons or property on board such ship or aircraft;
>   (ii) against a ship, aircraft, persons or property in a place outside the jurisdiction of any State;

---

74   See *United States v. Cargo of the Brig Malek Adhel*, 43 U.S. 210 (1844). A particular difficulty was whether foreign political "insurgents" were exempt from piracy charges; see *The Ambrose Light*, 25 F. 408 (S.D.N.Y. 1885); Sharon Williams & Jean-Gabriel Castel, *Canadian Criminal Law: International and Transnational Aspects* (Toronto: Butterworths, 1981) at 254–57.

75   This was compounded by the fact that pirates were sometimes commissioned as "privateers" to wreak havoc upon a state's enemy as part of otherwise legitimate warfare; see Angus Konstam, *Privateers and Pirates, 1730-1830* (Oxford: Osprey Military, 2001) .

76   Reprinted (1926) 20 A.J.I.L. (Spec. Supp.) 223.

77   Harvard Research in International Law, "Draft Convention on Piracy with Comments" (1932) 26 A.J.I.L. (Supp.) 749.

78   450 U.N.T.S. 11; Canada is not a party to the *High Seas Convention*, though it is a party to the *UNCLOS*.

79   UN Doc. A/CONF.62/122, reprinted (1982), 21 I.L.M. 1261 [*UNCLOS*].

(b)   any act of voluntary participation in the operation of a ship or of an aircraft with knowledge of facts making it a pirate ship or aircraft;

(c)   any act of inciting or of intentionally facilitating an act described in subparagraph (a) or (b).

While it has been suggested that there is still a gap between the customary international law definition of piracy and the treaty definition,[80] the latter has itself achieved customary status and certainly represents the current understanding of piracy *jure gentium*.[81]

The crime of piracy, then, is more than "robbery upon the sea," as it had been traditionally framed.[82] While it is clearly intentional acts that are caught by the definition, the historical requirement of *animus furundi*, usually defined as "intent to rob,"[83] does not apply, and a wider variety of acts for "private ends," that is, personal gain or motivation, are contemplated. Given the broadness of the terms "acts of violence, detention or . . . act of depradation," a large number of familiar crimes must, when taking place at sea, constitute piracy: physical assaults of all sorts (including sexual), robbery and theft, and even property damage. The definition is vague, which, as Rubin suggests, "[leaves] no explanation of how sense is to be made of a purported definition of a 'crime' that rests on an undefined and unreferenced concept of prior 'illegality': Illegal under what law? By whose determination?"[84] There are clearly gaps to be filled in by the municipal law of the state where the trial is taking place, which in turn will present a methodological challenge for judges. For example, what is an illegal act of detention? Any domestic judge could find such crimes in the state's own laws, and yet there must be some international overlay on the treaty definition. Should the judge inquire whether a particular crime constitutes illegal "detention" for the purpose of the definition because it is mirrored in major criminal law systems throughout the world, akin to a "general principle of law" under article 38 of the *Rome Statute*?[85] This matters because, as outlined below, universal jurisdiction over piracy applies

---

80   See Birnie, above note 73; Malvina Halberstam, "Terrorism on the High Seas: The *Achille Lauro*, Piracy and the IMO *Convention on Maritime Safety*" (1988) 82 A.J.I.L. 269.

81   Accord, Bantekas & Nash, above note 35 at 178.

82   *United States v. Smith*, 18 U.S. (5 Wheat.) 153 (1820).

83   *Rex v. Dawson* (1696), 13 St. Tr. 451.

84   Rubin, above note 71 at 366–67. For Professor Rubin's detailed analysis of various interpretive difficulties arising from the drafting of the treaty definition, see Alfred Rubin, "Is Piracy Illegal?" (1976) 70 A.J.I.L. 92.

85   Above note 29.

only to the definition of piracy *jure gentium*: "to the extent that national proscriptions of piracy exceed international law, jurisdiction to enforce them cannot be based on the universality principle."[86]

As well, the definition's parameters have been pared down from past versions of the crime. Piracy can be committed only on the high seas, which has certain jurisdictional implications outlined in Section C(2), below in this chapter. It can be committed only by a private ship or aircraft against another ship or aircraft,[87] and piratical acts committed by personnel of military or state ships would engage only the law of state responsibility—unless the crew of such a vessel has mutinied and taken control and commenced piracy, at which point they are assimilated to "regular" pirates.[88] Importantly, stemming initially from a deliberate decision in the Harvard Draft process,[89] the treaty definition of piracy excludes political or politically motivated acts. To some extent this reflects the ongoing debate and dissension about a definition of terrorism, and was a practical move designed to provide a widely acceptable treaty definition. Nonetheless, maritime terrorism continues to be a major problem,[90] and international treaty efforts (such as the 1988 *Convention for the Suppression of Unlawful Acts against the Safety of Maritime Navigation*)[91] are surveyed in Chapter 7.

Perhaps some of the definitional problems relating to piracy would be of only academic interest if the crime itself was essentially extinct, as appeared to be the case in the late nineteenth century. Yet the opposite is true in the modern day. A newer spate of pirate attacks on international shipping began in the late 1970s and has continued since, particularly along the coasts of West Africa and South America, the

---

86   Hugh Kindred & Phillip Saunders, eds., *International Law: Chiefly as Interpreted and Applied in Canada*, 7th ed. (Toronto: Emond Montgomery, 2006) at 958.

87   Accordingly, mutiny and "internal seizures" do not constitute piracy, though they may be criminalized under domestic laws.

88   *UNCLOS*, above note 79, art. 102.

89   Barry Dubner, "Human Rights and Environmental Disaster—Two Problems that Defy the 'Norms' of the International Law of Sea Piracy" (1997) 23 Syracuse J. Int'l L. & Com. 1 at 19.

90   In particular, it became clear after the *Achille Lauro* incident that the existing law dealing with piracy was insufficient to deal with maritime terrorism. In 1985, Palestinian terrorists hijacked the *Achille Lauro*, an Italian cruise ship, and killed one of its American passengers as part of an effort to convince the Israeli government to release prisoners. This sort of maritime hijacking was not criminalized under existing international law, and a like-minded group of states very quickly moved to conclude the 1988 *Convention for the Suppression of Unlawful Acts against the Safety of Maritime Navigation* (1988), 1678 U.N.T.S. 221, Can. T.S. 1993 No. 10 [*SUA Convention*]. See Halberstam, above note 80.

91   *Ibid.*

Strait of Malacca,[92] and the South China Sea.[93] In 2008, pirate attacks against commercial vessels became so frequent that the Security Council issued an extraordinary series of resolutions authorizing cooperating states to, *inter alia*, enter Somali territorial waters and use "all necessary means" to deal with them,[94] and ultimately to enter onto Somali territory for this purpose.[95] The International Maritime Organization (IMO) continues to document these disturbing incidents and urge states to further cooperate to suppress them.[96]

2) Jurisdiction over Piracy

It was well established from an early time that states could assert universal jurisdiction over pirates, which stemmed logically from the pirate's status as enemy of humankind.[97] It is this factor, in combination with the universal condemnation of the practice of piracy among all states, that qualifies it as an "international crime" for the purposes of this book. Indeed, there has been a dominant stream of thought which holds that universal criminal jurisdiction over piracy is the only cognizable international law attaching to it. In fact, it was the view of the writers of the Harvard Draft that piracy was not an international crime, and that the recognized need among states to cooperate in the curtailment of piracy led to the establishment of universal jurisdiction as the only necessary rule.[98] In any event, it is now clear under *UNCLOS* (and as a matter of customary international law) that states have a duty to cooperate in repressing piracy *jure gentium*,[99] and that both prescriptive and enforcement jurisdiction are available on a universal basis over piracy, regardless of the flag state of the pirate ship[100] or the nationality of the perpetrators or victims. A state may board and seize any pirate ship or airplane on/above the high seas (or outside the territory of any state), and arrest the personnel and seize the property on board.[101] The

---

92 See Nihan Unlu, "Protecting the Straits of Malacca and Singapore Against Piracy and Terrorism" (2006) 21 Int'l J. Marine & Coastal L. 539.

93 International Maritime Organization, *Focus on IMO* (January 2000) at 2–4.

94 S/Res. 1816 (2 June 2008).

95 S/Res. 1851 (16 December 2008).

96 See anti-piracy resources on the general IMO website, online: www.imo.org.

97 See the dissent of Moore J. in *The S.S. Lotus*, above note 70 at 70.

98 Above note 77 at 760. For a skeptical view, see Eugene Kontorovich, "The Piracy Analogy: Modern Universal Jurisdiction's Hollow Foundation" (2004) 45 Harv. Int'l L.J. 183.

99 *UNCLOS*, above note 79, art. 100.

100 See *ibid.*, arts. 103–4.

101 *Ibid.*, art. 105.

courts of the seizing state can prosecute[102] and convict the perpetrators and dispose of the vessel, aircraft, or property. The seizure of the ship or aircraft can be carried out only by clearly identifiable military or government ships or aircraft.[103]

3) Piracy in Canadian Law

Canada has always been a maritime state, and the culture and folklore of the east and west coasts are filled with references to pirates.[104] Canada has long criminalized piracy *jure gentium*,[105] but the history books note that the last full-blown piracy trial in Canada was in 1844.[106] Nonetheless, the crime itself remains on the books, as it must in order to ensure Canada complies with its obligations under the *UNCLOS*.

Section 74(1) of the *Criminal Code*[107] provides the crime of piracy, stating simply, "Everyone commits piracy who does any act that, by the law of nations, is piracy." Subsection (2) rather inelegantly combines the establishment of piracy *jure gentium* as an indictable offence with a

---

102   The US recently embarked on its first piracy prosecution under universal jurisdiction in over a century: see H. Yusuf, "Accused Somali Arrives in US to Face Piracy Charges" *The Christian Science Monitor* (21 April 2009), online: www.csmonitor.com/2009/0421/p99s01-duts.html. In 2008–2009, Canadian ships were involved in the suppression of Somali pirates in the Gulf of Aden, but they simply detained, disarmed, and then released the pirates. Various Canadian military personnel and government officials were repeatedly quoted as stating that Canadian forces were not arresting the pirates because Canada "lacks jurisdiction under international law" to prosecute them (for example, Paul Koring, "Ottawa's Piracy Policy Flouts Law, Experts Say" *The Globe and Mail* (1 May 2009) A14; *CBC News*, "HMCS Winnipeg Helps Thwart 2 Pirate Attacks" (22 May 2009). The government's insistence on this patently incorrect statement is puzzling, though it seems in part geared towards supporting international efforts to have Kenya prosecute Somali pirates.

103   *UNCLOS*, above note 79, art. 107.

104   See, for example, Archibald MacMechan, *Sagas of the Sea* (London: J.M. Dent & Sons, 1929).

105   *Criminal Code, 1892*, S.C. 1892, c. 29, s. 127.

106   Indeed, the historical accounts appear to indicate that this case, involving the mutinous crew of the barque *Saladin*, is illustrative of the bleed-over between piracy under the law of nations and domestic criminal laws. It appears that the mutineers were initially charged with piracy but ultimately were convicted of murder, likely because mutiny was judged not to form part of piracy *jure gentium*; see George Jones *et al.*, *Trial of Jones, Hazelton, Anderson and Trevaskiss Alias Johnson for Piracy and Murder on Board Barque Saladin* (1844; repr., Halifax: Petheric Press, 1967); and D. Howell, "The Saladin Trial: A Last Hurrah for Admiralty Sessions" (1995) 5 The Northern Mariner 1.

107   Above note 53.

provision that liability may be found whether the crime is committed "while in or out of Canada," thus implementing universal jurisdiction. The device used, then, is to incorporate by reference the international law regarding piracy, and thus implement it into Canadian law.[108] The use of the phrase "law of nations" is antiquated, since the current approach is to make specific reference, at least, to either specific treaties to which Canada is a party[109] or to customary international law.[110] The section must refer to Canada's obligations under the *UNCLOS*, referred to above, which are also binding obligations under customary international law;[111] and, to the extent there is any further content to piracy as an international crime under general customary international law, it must implement that law as well. The section seems unlikely to see any testing in the near future.

Section 75 of the *Code*[112] is entitled "Piratical Acts" and provides for the following offences: (a) stealing a Canadian ship; (b) stealing or, without lawful authority, throwing overboard, damaging, or destroying any part of the cargo, fittings, or supplies of a Canadian ship; (c) mutiny; or (d) counselling anyone to do any of the previous three crimes. These offences obviously cover attacks on ships, which are highly criminal but which do not come under the definition of piracy *jure gentium*.[113] There is no extraterritorial jurisdiction provided for these acts, and they can thus generally be prosecuted only where they have taken place in Canadian ports, internal waters, or on the territorial sea.[114] Mutiny, or in the language of the section, "mutinous acts," oddly does not seem to be defined in the *Code*, which would leave the courts with the options of trying to find some meaning in common law cases or looking to international law sources like the 1988 *Convention on the Suppression of Unlawful Acts against the Safety of Maritime Navigation*.[115]

---

108 This is similar to the method used to implement the crimes of genocide, crimes against humanity, and war crimes under the *Crimes Against Humanity and War Crimes Act*, S.C. 2000, c. 24 [*CAH Act*]; see Chapter 5.

109 See, for example, s. 7 of the *Code*, above note 53, which implements Canada's extraterritorial jurisdiction obligations under a number of the suppression conventions, or the definition of "terrorist activity" in s. 83.01(1).

110 As under the *CAH Act*, above note 108, ss. 4(3) and 6(3).

111 Though note that taking extraterritorial enforcement actions against pirates under both *UNCLOS* and customary international law is permissive, rather than required.

112 Above note 53.

113 For an inconclusive prosecution under s. 75, *ibid.*, see *R. v. Heckman* (1902), 5 C.C.C. 242 (N.S.T.D.).

114 Though see s. 477.1 of the *Code*, *ibid.* and Chapter 8.

115 *SUA Convention*, above note 90.

D. SLAVERY

1) History and Definition

The practice of owning persons as property, as well as trading in them, is ancient and pervasive in world history. Where slavery and slavery-related practices have flourished, its effects have been as far-reaching as they were malign, leaving the lives of generations of families and sometimes entire cultures in tatters. However, it was only by the late nineteenth century that slavery became recognized by the international community of states for the odious blight on humanity that it represents. While there was some significant lag time between the time when the utter immorality of slavery was recognized[116] and the actual abolition of the very profitable slave trade engaged in by the major European powers and the US,[117] it was generally recognized by the late nineteenth century that slavery was an international crime. As with the crime of torture, there is a certain amount of legal mapping between the freedom from slavery as a treaty and customary international human rights norm,[118] and slavery as a crime, and both are sometimes placed within a category of international crimes which constitute "crimes against fundamental human rights."[119] In any event, the prohibition on slavery has since developed into a *jus cogens* norm[120] and one which, as the International Court of Justice (ICJ) has held, constitutes an obligation *erga omnes*, that is, enforceable by all states.[121] Slavery and some forms of forced or compulsory labour[122] are universally regarded as criminal, both as a matter of customary international law and as a general principle of international law.[123]

---

116 See, for example, *Sommersett v. Stewart* (1772), 98 E.R. 499 (K.B.).

117 See Ethan Nadelmann, "Global Prohibition Regimes: The Evolution of Norms in International Society" (1990) 44 International Organisation 479; N. Umozurike, "The African Slave Trade and the Attitudes of International Law towards It" (1971) 16 How. L.J. 334.

118 *Universal Declaration of Human Rights*, G.A. Res. 217 A(III), U.N. Doc. A/810 at 71 (1948), art. 4; *ICCPR*, above note 12, art. 8.

119 For example, Bassiouni, ed., *International Criminal Law*, above note 70, c. 5.

120 Theodor Meron, *Human Rights and Humanitarian Norms as Customary Law* (New York: Oxford University Press, 1989) at 20.

121 *Barcelona Traction Light and Power House Co. Ltd. (Belgium v. Spain)*, [1970] I.C.J. Rep. 3, Second Phase at 32.

122 See the International Labour Organization's 1930 *Forced Labour Convention (ILO No. 29)*, 39 U.N.T.S. 55, art. 2(1) of which certainly has attained customary status; and the 1957 *Abolition of Forced Labour Convention (ILO No. 105)*, Can. T.S. 1960 No. 21.

123 M. Cherif Bassiouni, "Enslavement: Slavery, Slave-Related Practices, and Trafficking in Persons for Sexual Exploitation," in Bassiouni, ed., above note 70, 535 at 538–39.

While there is a large number of treaties that underpin the evolution and crystallization of slavery as an international crime,[124] the primary instruments are the 1926 League of Nations *Slavery Convention*,[125] the 1953 *Protocol Amending the Slavery Convention*[126] (which effectively brought the *Slavery Convention* into the UN system), and the 1956 *Supplementary Convention on the Abolition of Slavery, the Slave Trade, and Institutions and Practices Similar to Slavery*.[127] Together, these instruments set out the governing norms regarding what is often referred to as "classic" or "chattel" slavery, that is, slavery in its most traditional context of persons owning and trading in other persons. "Slavery" is defined as "the status or condition of a person over whom any or all of the powers attaching to the right of ownership are exercised."[128] The "slave trade" is defined as

> . . . all acts involved in the capture, acquisition or disposal of a person with intent to reduce him to slavery; all acts involved in the acquisition of a slave with a view to selling or exchanging him; all acts of disposal by sale or exchange of a person acquired with a view to being sold or exchanged; and, in general, every act of trade or transport in slaves [by whatever means of conveyance].[129]

States are required to criminalize both (1) acts of enslavement or inducing enslavement of another person (including attempt, being an accessory, or being party to a conspiracy to do so)[130] and (2) conveying, attempting to convey, or being accessory to the conveyance of slaves from one country to another.[131]

It became clear relatively soon after the conclusion of the *Slavery Convention* that, despite the apparent broadness of the definition of slavery, it did not necessarily catch some slavery-like activities that were (and are, in some regions) still pervasive. As Professors Bantekas

---

124 For an exhaustive list, see M. Cherif Bassiouni, "Enslavement as an International Crime" (1991) 23 N.Y.U. Int'l L. & Pol. 445.

125 Can. T.S. 1928 No. 5 [*Slavery Convention*].

126 Can. T.S. 1953 No. 26.

127 Can. T.S. 1963 No. 7 [*Supplementary Slavery Convention*].

128 *Slavery Convention*, above note 125, art. 1(1); *Supplementary Slavery Convention, ibid.*, art. 7(a).

129 *Slavery Convention, ibid.*, art. 1(2); *Supplementary Slavery Convention, ibid.*, art. 7(c) (bracketed text added in *Supplementary Slavery Convention* definition).

130 *Slavery Convention, ibid.*, art. 6; *Supplementary Slavery Convention, ibid.*, art. 6(1). While this obligation has certainly passed into customary law for the most part, given that some legal systems do not recognize criminal liability for conspiracy, it is doubtful whether that particular crime has customary status.

131 *Supplementary Slavery Convention, ibid.*, art. 3(1).

and Nash note, "[E]xtreme poverty compounded by lack of social and administrative structures soon revealed a different facet of slavery; one where the individual was forced to submit to exploitation or risk extinction."[132] Accordingly, the *Supplementary Slavery Convention* obliged states to suppress and end some specifically recognized forms of this practice: debt bondage, serfdom, "bride-price,"[133] and the transfer of children for exploitation or forced labour.[134]

Even with this more expansive view of what sorts of acts constitute slavery, and while the slave trade in its historical sense has essentially been abolished since the late nineteenth century, significant gaps remain. Both the criminal and human rights customary international law norms regarding slavery are often assailed by critics as being merely aspirational, primarily because of lack of enforcement of either the underlying treaties or the customary international law norms. States could take action[135] against other states to end such practices, but they do not. Even "chattel" slavery continues to persist in many areas of the world, particularly Africa and South Asia, as do debt bondage and various forms of forced child labour.[136] Moreover, the older prohibitions of slavery do not sufficiently provide for the criminalization of contemporary forms of slavery-like treatment, in particular, human trafficking (most often leading to involuntary prostitution) and the exploitation of children. This has led to various treaty efforts to address these practices, the most notable of which are surveyed in Chapter 7.

Nonetheless, there is little doubt of the normative power of the prohibition of slavery. Not only has the UN Working Group on Contemporary Forms of Slavery characterized all forms of slavery as crimes against humanity,[137] but the *Rome Statute* adopted the classic definition of "chattel slavery" in setting out slavery as a crime against human-

---

132 Bantekas & Nash, above note 35 at 154.

133 That is, the transfer of a woman by family or husband for consideration, without her consent, or the disinheritance of a woman from her husband's property.

134 *Supplementary Slavery Convention*, above note 127, arts. 1(a)–(d).

135 That is, states which are parties to the relevant treaties could bring proceedings against breaching states before the ICJ, as the treaties themselves have little in the way of dispute-resolution mechanisms; and/or claims could be made before the ICJ that states had violated the customary norms (whether or not they were parties to the treaties) due to the *erga omnes* status of the norms, as mentioned above in this section.

136 See online: www.antislavery.org.

137 UN Doc E/CN4/Sub2/1997/13 (11 July 1997) at para. 80. Though this statement is dubious in its broadness, given the current definition of crimes against humanity under customary international law; see Chapter 3.

ity.[138] Slavery and forced labour are also war crimes under customary international law,[139] though they are not within the definitions of war crimes in the *Rome Statute*.

2) Jurisdiction over Slavery

It has long been accepted that slavery is one of the few international crimes over which there is unqualified universal jurisdiction under customary international law.[140] This is more a measure of the opprobrium with which slavery is viewed by the international community than an active law enforcement measure, since there are very few, if any, slavery prosecutions based on universality on the books. The persistence of slavery-type practices in some locations is treated as more of a regional problem or a target for aid and assistance, than a crime. Nonetheless, those engaging in slavery or the slave trade can face trial before the courts of any state willing to make the effort, even in the absence of any other ties to the perpetrator or the acts.

In terms of enforcement jurisdiction over slavery, the use of ships and aircraft as the primary transport modes of slavery led to the development of a number of norms. The *Supplementary Slavery Convention* obligated states to take "all effective measures" to prevent their registered ships and aircraft from engaging in the slave trade, to punish those guilty of such acts, and to ensure that their ports, airfields and coasts were not used for this purpose.[141] Article 4 of the same *Convention* states, "Any slave who takes refuge on board any vessel of a State Party to this *Convention* shall ipso facto be free."[142] Article 99 of the *UNCLOS*[143] similarly obliges states to prevent the use of its ships and aircraft in the slave trade and punish the perpetrators, and expands on article 4 of the *Supplementary Slavery Convention* by providing that a slave who "tak[es] refuge on board any ship, whatever its flag, shall *ipso facto* be free." Article 110(1)(b) further provides the ability to use warships to board and inspect any ship on the high seas where there are reasonable grounds to believe it is engaged in the slave trade. However,

---

138 See ICC *Elements of Crimes*, U.N. Doc. PCNICC/2000/1/Add.2 (2000), art. 7(1)(c), "Crime against humanity of enslavement," the explanatory footnote to which notes that this crime would include the trafficking of persons.

139 *Krnojelac* (IT-97-25-T), Trial Chamber Judgment, 15 March 2002 at paras. 350–60; *Naletelić* (IT-98-34), Trial Chamber Judgment, 31 March 2003 at paras. 250–61.

140 *Princeton Principles*, above note 21, Principle 2(1).

141 *Supplementary Slavery Convention*, above note 127, art. 3(2).

142 *Ibid.*, art. 4.

143 Above note 79.

unlike the broad interception, arrest, and prosecution rights associated with pirate vessels, all that the boarding authorities may do is report the incident to the flag state of the ship, which alone has jurisdiction to order the seizure of the ship and prosecute the crew for engaging in the slave trade. The flag state can, of course, request the warship's state of origin to detain and arrest the slavers.

3) Slavery in Canadian Law

Surprisingly, there seems to be no criminal prohibition of slavery in Canadian law. There are, of course, criminal prohibitions of a number of acts which slavery might involve, for example, assault in its various forms, procuring of prostitution, kidnapping, and forcible confinement. In addition, the newer offences regarding trafficking in persons[144] would also catch some of the behaviour involved in slavery. However, while slavery has long been abolished in Canada, and any law allowing it would naturally never survive a *Charter* challenge, it does not appear to be the subject of a codified crime (other than the specific prohibitions of enslavement as a war crime[145] and as a crime against humanity[146]). This is a rather odd legislative oversight, and it arguably puts Canada out of compliance with the *jus cogens* norm binding all states to criminally prohibit slavery. One might posit that, under the adoptionist approach to customary international law,[147] this norm must form part of the common law of Canada even if it is not explicitly implemented. However, this runs into the problem identified in Chapter 1, section 9 of the *Criminal Code*[148] states that there are no common law crimes, and thus to be a crime in Canada, slavery must be legislated. While it hardly seems like a practical problem in current times, this lacuna could cause problems if, for example, another state wished to prosecute an individual resident in Canada for slavery and Canada was asked to extradite him. Since Canada has no crime of slavery on the books, the extradition could be impaired by lack of "double criminality," that is, that under most extradition treaties the crime for which the fugitive is sought must be a crime in both states.[149]

---

144 Section 279.01 of the *Criminal Code*, above note 53, and ss. 118–21 of the *Immigration and Refugee Protection Act*, S.C. 2001, c. 27.

145 *CAH Act*, above note 108, ss. 4(3), (4) and 6(3), (4); *Geneva Conventions Act*, R.S.C. 1985, c. G-3, s. 4(2)(f).

146 *CAH Act*, ibid.

147 See Chapter 1.

148 Above note 53.

149 Though this is a complex question, the answer to which might vary from treaty to treaty. As to extradition and the double criminality principle, see Chapter 9.

E. APARTHEID

Apartheid is another crime which has become internationalized because it represents a heinous attack on fundamental human rights. It refers, of course, to the former colonialist and racist regime that dominated the state of South Africa from 1948 until 1994, and specifically to the government policy of institutionalized racism and oppression during that time.[150] However, while initial efforts to criminalize apartheid were definitively aimed at South Africa, the international law prohibition on the practice of apartheid has developed beyond that particular historical context and continues to have relevance — evidenced by its inclusion as an enumerated crime against humanity in article 7 of the *Rome Statute*.[151]

Opposition by states to the massive human rights violations that the South African apartheid regime represented spurred on the development of an international criminal law norm that germinated and took hold relatively quickly. The first was the 1968 *Convention on Non-Applicability of Statutory Limitations to War Crimes and Crimes against Humanity*,[152] which expressly referred to "eviction by armed attack or occupation and inhuman acts resulting from the policy of apartheid" as a crime against humanity. The next, and most important development, was the 1973 *International Convention on the Suppression and Punishment of the Crime of Apartheid*,[153] sparked by proposals from the USSR and Guinea and negotiated under the auspices of the United Nations General Assembly (UNGA). This treaty established a suppression convention for the crime of apartheid modelled, to some extent, on the *Genocide Convention*.[154] Article 1, like the *Statutory Limitations Convention*, declares apartheid to be a crime against humanity and indicates the intention that both individuals and organizations or institutions

---

150 See, generally, P. Eric Louw, *The Rise, Fall and Legacy of Apartheid* (Westport, CT: Praeger, 2004).

151 Above note 29. See M. Boot & C. Hall, "Article 7" in Otto Triffterer, ed., *Commentary on the* Rome Statute *of the International Criminal Court: Observers' Notes, Article by Article*, 2d ed. (Baden-Baden: Nomos, 2008). The definition of apartheid in the *Rome Statute* is somewhat narrower than the customary international law definition.

152 GA Res. 2391, UN GAOR, 23d Sess., Supp. No. 18, at 40, UN Doc. A/7218 (1968), entered into force 11 November 1970.

153 (1973), 1015 U.N.T.S. 244 [*Apartheid Convention*].

154 78 U.N.T.S. 277, entered into force 12 January 1951. For a detailed analysis, see Roger Clark, "Apartheid" in M. Cherif Bassiouni, ed., above note 70 at 599.

can be liable.[155] Article 2 sets out the definition of the crime, including specifically "similar policies and practices of racial segregation and discrimination as practiced in South Africa," and then sets out a list of "inhuman acts" which constitute apartheid when "committed for the purpose of establishing and maintaining domination by one racial group of persons over any other racial group of persons and systematically oppressing them." The odd wording of the provision seems to suggest that a wider variety of acts than those enumerated may be sufficient for prosecution, but this is not clear.

Given that prosecution by the state in whose territory the crime took place would be unlikely or difficult, the drafters of the *Apartheid Convention* saw the need for broader prescriptive jurisdiction. Accordingly, article 5 confers jurisdiction on any state party to the Convention which apprehends an accused—an exercise of custodial universal jurisdiction. Similar to the *Genocide Convention*, it also anticipates the founding of an "international penal tribunal" with jurisdiction over the crime, and provides for jurisdiction by that body "with respect to those states which will have accepted its jurisdiction."

Soon after the finalization of the *Apartheid Convention*, the Security Council of the UN condemned apartheid as "a crime against the conscience and dignity of mankind,"[156] and by 1984 had confirmed its view that apartheid was a crime against humanity.[157] It has not been seriously contested by any significant number of states in the years following the finalization of the convention that apartheid is indeed a crime against humanity, and thus a crime under customary international law. The convention itself has been in force since 18 July 1976 and currently has 107 parties.[158] While ratification of neither the *Apartheid Convention* nor the *Statutory Limitations Convention* was universal, states voting against adoption or refusing to ratify expressed little discomfort with treating apartheid as a crime against humanity.[159] It is not clear whether, as a matter of customary international law, states may exercise full universal jurisdiction over the crime. However, the available

---

155 This was similar to the approach that had been taken at Nuremberg, as the *Charter of the International Military Tribunal*, 82 U.N.T.S. 279, provided for the prosecution of organizations such as the Gestapo and SS.

156 S/Res. 392 (1976).

157 S/Res. 556 (1984).

158 Online: http://treaties.un.org/Pages/ViewDetails.aspx?src=UNTSONLINE&tabi d=2&mtdsg_no=IV-7&chapter=4&lang=en.

159 For discussion of this point, see Ronald Slye, "Apartheid as a Crime against Humanity: A Submission to the South African Truth and Reconciliation Commission" (1998–1999) 20 Mich. J. Int'l L. 267.

evidence points strongly to nearly universal condemnation of apartheid as a crime which offends the conscience of humanity. Given its status as a crime against humanity, and that it is uncontroversial that universal jurisdiction may be exercised over crimes against humanity, then universal jurisdiction would seem to pertain as a matter of logic, if not state practice.

Canada is not a party to the *Apartheid Convention*, but has criminalized apartheid within the context of the newer provisions criminalizing crimes against humanity.[160]

F. TERRORISM AS AN INTERNATIONAL CRIME?

Terrorism is one of the most frightening, vexing, and pressing transnational problems of our times, and the exercises of defining terrorism and determining the nature and scope of legal responses to it have become even more difficult as a result. Since the 9/11 attacks, the "global war on terror" has become a recognizable catchphrase, at once reflecting the desire of Western states (primarily, and understandably, the US) to combat terrorism, but also raising concern that governments will capitalize upon this law and order climate to classify their political opponents as "terrorists" and thus suppress them — with the impunity that comes from being seen as participating in the anti-terrorism crusade. Nonetheless, the collective interest in suppressing terrorism is obvious and, in the twenty-first century, urgent. The UNGA has recently reaffirmed that

> acts, methods and practices of terrorism in all its forms and manifestations are activities aimed at the destruction of human rights, fundamental freedoms and democracy, threatening territorial integrity, security of States and destabilizing legitimately constituted Governments, and that the international community should take the necessary steps to enhance cooperation to prevent and combat terrorism.[161]

The Security Council has declared that international terrorism is a threat to international peace and security, justifying measures under its Chapter VII powers.[162] Moreover, the international community has

---

160 *CAH Act*, above note 108, ss. 4(3), (4) and 6(3), (4).
161 A/RES/60/288 (2006).
162 See S/Res 1368 (2001) and 1373 (2001). The website of the Security Council's Counter-Terrorism Committee can be found online: www.un.org/sc/ctc/index.html.

concluded a significant number of treaties which oblige states to criminalize certain terrorist acts (or at least acts traditionally associated with terrorism), and to extradite or prosecute offenders. These include the 1997 *Terrorist Bombing Convention*,[163] the 2000 *Terrorist Financing Convention*,[164] and the 2005 *Nuclear Terrorism Convention*.[165] These instruments, part of the network of "suppression conventions" that underpin a great deal of transnational crimes of international concern, are reviewed in more detail in Chapter 7.

The biggest problem with formulating a coherent international legal response to terrorism (as the voluminous literature on the subject indicates) is reaching a definition upon which the international community can agree.[166] It is this single but massive controversy which has driven the entire discourse on terrorism in the twentieth and twenty-first centuries. It defeated both the widespread ratification of the League of Nations' effort at drafting a comprehensive terrorism convention in 1937[167] and a five-year effort by a special committee established by the UNGA in the 1970s.[168] It is also bogging down the current effort under way by the UN to draft a comprehensive convention on terrorism.[169] The Security Council's exercise of peace and security powers referenced above proceeded by reference only to the scourge of international terrorism, and did not include a definition. This is not to say that there are no definitions of terrorism, or that terrorism is not being actively prosecuted by states every day, but rather that there is no firm international norm defining who the terrorist is, what his intention or even motivation must be, and what acts combine with this intent/motive to bring the criminal act to the threshold of "terror"—or even where that threshold is.

Nonetheless, most people have an intuitive understanding of what an act of terrorism is, and one can see the general parameters of a defin-

---

163 Can. T.S. 2002 No. 8.

164 Can. T.S. 2002 No. 9.

165 UNGA Res. 59/290, 13 April 2005, UN Doc. A/59/766.

166 See George Fletcher, "The Indefinable Concept of Terrorism" (2006) 4 JICJ 894, and other articles in the same issue.

167 1937 *Convention for the Prevention and Punishment of Terrorism*, 7 International Legislation 862.

168 See UNGA Res. 3034/27 (18 December 1972).

169 This work is being carried out by Ad Hoc Committee established by UNGA Res. 51/210 (17 December 1996) [Draft *Comprehensive Convention on International Terrorism*]. The reports detailing the work of the committee can be found online: www.un.org/law/terrorism/index.html. See also M. Hmoud, "Negotiating the *Draft Comprehensive Convention on International Terrorism*: Major Bones of Contention" (2006) 4 JICJ 1031. See draft convention, UN Doc. A/59/894.

ition within various instruments that have been formulated.[170] Simply put, an act of terrorism is a serious crime committed for a particular purpose, that purpose usually being described loosely as "political" or "to incite terror." In terms of the mental element, it has been suggested that in general terms, terrorism is analogous to the crime of genocide, which requires a special intent in addition to the specific intent for the underlying criminal offence;[171] it is also similar to the *CAT* definition of torture, which requires that acts of physical or mental brutality must be for what is an evolving list of "purposes" in order to constitute torture.[172] As to what that purpose is, there is a certain common ground displayed in article 2(1)(b) of the 2000 *Terrorist Financing Convention*,[173] which describes the purpose as "to intimidate a population, or to compel a Government or an international organization to do or to abstain from doing any act." The draft *Comprehensive Convention on International Terrorism* uses the same formulation,[174] and in *Suresh*, the Supreme Court of Canada adopted this formulation of the definition of terrorism as constituting an acceptable minimum understanding of terrorism under international law.[175]

As to the physical element, it is clear that the act which underlies the act of terrorism must be a serious criminal offence. The *Terrorist Financing Convention* formulation refers to "act[s] intended to cause death or serious bodily injury to a civilian, or to any other person not taking an active part in the hostilities in a situation of armed conflict,"[176] while the draft *Comprehensive Convention on International Terrorism* adds serious damage to public or private property, including public transport or the environment, or any damage to property, places, facilities, or systems which results in major economic loss.[177] It is also becoming

---

170 These would include the terrorism treaties considered in more detail in Chapter 7, along with regional instruments such as the *European Convention on the Suppression of Terrorism* (1977), C.E.T.S. 90; the OAS *Convention to Prevent and Punish Acts of Terrorism Taking the Form of Crimes against Persons and Related Extortion that are of International Significance* (1971) OAS Treaty Series No. 37; Treaty A-49; and the *OAU Convention on the Prevention and Combating of Terrorism*, (1999), online: www.africa-union.org/root/AU/Documents/Treaties/Text/Algiers_convention%20on%20Terrorism.pdf.

171 Robert Cryer *et al.*, *An Introduction to International Criminal Law and Procedure* (Cambridge: Cambridge University Press, 2007) at 290. As to genocide, see Chapter 3.

172 See Section A(3), above in this chapter.

173 Above note 164.

174 Above note 169. And see S/Res. 1566 (2004).

175 *Suresh*, above note 7 at para. 98.

176 Above note 164, art. 2.

177 Above note 169.

common for both treaties and domestic statutes (including Canada's)[178] to refer to the criminal acts prohibited by the major terrorism treaties as accepted "acts" of terrorism.

These definitions, while helpful reference points, do not reflect any kind of consistent agreement among states as to the shape or parameters of terrorism as a crime, much less an understanding of terrorism as a phenomenon.[179] When one surveys the various domestic terrorism statutes and regional instruments, there is a significant diversity of approaches to both mental and physical elements. It appears that while there is definitely a prevailing international consensus that international terrorism is a crime and may, permissively at least, be incorporated into a state's criminal laws, this is a mere shell of a norm that contains within it only sustained disagreement.

One major area of disagreement is colloquially summed up in the phrase "one man's terrorist is another man's freedom fighter,"[180] which reflects a longstanding debate about whether persons who commit violent acts in furtherance of national liberation or self-determination movements should be exempted from charges of terrorism. Expressions of this point of view can be found in several regional anti-terrorism instruments, such as the *OAU Convention*,[181] the *Arab Convention*,[182] and the *OIC Convention*,[183] though in the post-colonial era, some of these are substantially transparent attempts to legitimize the activities of various Palestinian activities against Israel. Certainly a sufficiently organized group engaged in an armed conflict against colonial domination, alien occupation, or a racist regime in exercising its right to self-determination would fall under the 1977 *Additional Protocol I to the Geneva Conventions*,[184] and accordingly is permitted to conduct armed attacks in accordance with international humanitarian law. Other-

---

178 See s. 83.01 of the *Code*, above note 53.

179 Orlova and Moore, referring to the draft *Comprehensive Convention on International Terrorism*, describe that definition as "an operational definition of the conduct of a terrorist act, not a conceptual definition of the phenomenon of 'terrorism'": Alexandra Orlova & James Moore, "'Umbrellas' or 'Building Blocks'?: Defining International Terrorism and Transnational Organized Crime in International Law" (2004–2005) 27 Houston J. Int'l L. 267 at 272.

180 A phrase often attributed to the late, former US President Ronald Reagan.

181 *OAU Convention on the Prevention and Combating of Terrorism*, above note 170, art. 3(1).

182 *Arab Convention on the Suppression of Terrorism*, 22 April 1998, art. 2(a), reprinted (in translation) online: www.unhcr.org/refworld/docid/3de5e4984.html.

183 *Organization of the Islamic Conference Convention to Combat Terrorism*, 1 July 1999, art. 2, reprinted online: www.oicun.org/7/38/.

184 1125 U.N.T.S. 3 (1979). See Chapter 3.

wise, acts of violence—expressly including[185] acts of terrorism—are prohibited only against civilians and non-combatants. Outside of this limited area, however, there is significant hostility to any exemption from "terrorist" status due to a particular group's political motivations, since politics inevitably underlies the terrorist attack. The prevailing view in Western states, certainly, is that certain acts of terrorist violence are never appropriate. This view has some resonance in the larger international community, as evidenced by a strong 1994 UNGA resolution, adopted by consensus, which proclaimed terrorist acts to be "in any circumstances unjustifiable, whatever the considerations of a political, philosophical, ideological, racial, ethnic, religious or other nature which may be invoked to justify them."[186] In addition, the more recent anti-terrorism suppression conventions contain provisions that prohibit state parties from invoking the "political offence exception" as a bar to extradition or the provision of mutual legal assistance with regard to the criminalized terrorist acts.[187] This effort to prevent or at least shrink the existence of "safe haven" states for terrorists is laudatory, but still exists uneasily with the self-determination question.[188]

Can terrorism, then, legitimately be called an international crime? Professor Cassese has mounted a powerful argument in the affirmative.[189] Describing as a "misconception"[190] the idea that there is no generally agreed international definition of terrorism, he opines that the controversy has actually been around whether or not the "national liberation" *exception* is mutually agreeable to states, and not what constitutes terrorism. He further weighs what he views as the substantial convergence between the 1937 League of Nations definition, the description in 1994 UNGA Resolution 49/60 and subsequent resolutions, various regional treaties, the acts covered by the anti-terrorism suppression conventions, the *Terrorist Financing Convention* formulation, and the manner in which the crime is defined in various national laws. He arrives at the following requirements for terrorism to constitute an international crime: (1) the act must be a crime under most national

---

185 *Ibid.*, art. 4(d).

186 *Declaration on Measures to Eliminate International Terrorism* (1994), annexed to UNGA Res. 49/60 of 9 December 1994.

187 For example, the *Terrorist Bombing Convention*, above note 163, art. 11; the *Terrorist Financing Convention*, above note 164, art. 14; the *Nuclear Terrorism Convention*, above note 165, art. 15.

188 Indeed, it was the blurriness of this line which caused terrorism to be eliminated from the ILC's *Draft Code of Offences* in 1996; see Report on the Work of its 48th Session, UN Doc A/51/10, Supp. No. 10 (6 May–26 June 1996).

189 Cassese, above note 22 at 162–75 and 177–78.

190 *Ibid.* at 162.

legal systems; (2) it is transnational, involving two or more states; (3) its purpose must be to coerce a state or international organization to do, or refrain from doing, something; (4) it uses "two possible modalities: either spreading terror among civilians or attacking public or eminent private institutions or their representatives;" and (5) the perpetrator must be motivated by politics, religion, or ideology and not be acting for private ends.[191]

This formulation (while it is based on Cassese's own methodology for determining what constitutes an "international crime") has some appeal. It is buttressed by the fact that many states, including Canada, are currently exercising wide extraterritorial universal jurisdiction over their formulations of terrorism, and some trials have been conducted on these broad jurisdictional grounds. This would tend to provide evidence that it has risen to the status of "international crime" as that term is being used here.[192] However, what is currently lacking is evidence that such exercise of jurisdiction is permitted under customary international law, that is, that a substantial majority of states are not only doing it (state practice) but accept that they are bound to accede to any other state's exercise of this jurisdiction (*opinio juris*). It may be that the increasing state practice on this point will combine with the acquiescence of the international community and elevate this universal jurisdiction to a customary entitlement of states, so perhaps it is only slightly premature to make this claim.

However, on the whole, in my respectful view, Cassese's case is still wanting on the current evidence. To find a customary norm, specifically a criminal law prohibition, in a field where states have expressly disagreed on how to define the crime for treaty purposes, is rather pre-

---

191 *Ibid.* at 177. Professor Cassese's proposed definition changed markedly between the first and second editions of his book; in the first edition, the definition included requirements that the acts are carried out with the support, toleration, or acquiescence of a state, and that the acts threaten international peace and security (see Antonio Cassese, *International Criminal Law* (Oxford: Oxford University Press, 2003) at 120–31).

192 It should be noted that terrorism is certainly an international crime when viewed as a war crime, as acts of terrorism or spreading terror are specifically prohibited under art. 33(1) of *Geneva IV* (1950), 75 U.N.T.S. 287; art. 51(2) of *Protocol I*, above note 184; arts. 4(2)(d) and 13(2) of *Protocol II*, Can. T.S. 1991 No. 2; and probably under customary international humanitarian law. See *Galić* (IT-98-29-T), Judgment, 5 December 2003. It is not included in the ICC definition of war crimes. An act of terrorism that otherwise met the requirements of crimes against humanity would, logically, also be an international crime; though for the view that this can be stretched too far, see William Schabas, "Is Terrorism a Crime against Humanity?" (2002) 8 International Peacekeeping: The Yearbook of International Peace Operations 255.

carious methodology. This leans towards the danger that such an international law description as Cassese has provided would be too vague to provide the legal underpinning of a prosecution before many national legal systems, or even under customary or treaty-based international human rights law.

With the foregoing background set out as a large caveat, the approach of this book is to treat terrorism as a transnational crime of international concern, and the various terrorism treaties are considered individually in Chapter 7, along with Canada's response to the post-9/11 trends. The discussion of other international law measures to deal with non-state actors, along with the problem of whether one can be at "war" with a highly disparate and un-unified criminal practice, and what the implications of that are, are left to other sources.[193]

FURTHER READING

Torture

EVANS, MALCOLM, "Getting to Grips with Torture" (2002) 51 I.C.L.Q. 365

INGELSE, CHRIS, *The UN Committee against Torture: An Assessment* (The Hague: Kluwer Academic, 2001)

RODLEY, SIR NIGEL, & MATT POLLARD, "Criminalisation of Torture: State Obligations under the United Nations *Convention against Torture and other Cruel, Inhuman and Degrading Treatment or Punishment*" (2006) 2 Eur. H.R.L. Rev. 115

WENDLAND, LENE, *A Handbook on State Obligations under the UN Convention against Torture* (Geneva: Association for the Prevention of Torture: Geneva, 2002)

Piracy

BIRNIE, PATRICIA B., "Piracy Past, Present and Future" (1987) 11 Marine Policy 163

JOHNSON, D.H., "Piracy in Modern International Law" (1957) 43 Grotius Soc. Transactions 63

---

193 See William Schabas, "Punishment of Non-state Actors in Non-international Armed Conflict" in Andrea Bianchi, ed., *Non-State Actors and International Law* (Aldershot, UK: Ashgate, 2009); Marco Sassoli, "The Use and Abuse of the Laws of War in the 'War on Terror'" (2004) 22 L. & Inequality 195.

NOYES, JOHN, "An Introduction to the International Law of Piracy" (1990) 21 Cal. W. Int'l L.J. 105

RUBIN, ALFRED P., *The Law of Piracy*, 2d ed. (Irvington-on-Hudson, NY: Transnational, 1998)

Slavery
RASSAM, A. YASMINE, "Contemporary Forms of Slavery and the Evolution of the Prohibition of Slavery and the Slave Trade under Customary International Law" (1999) 39 Va. J. Int'l L. 303

REDMAN, RENEE C., "The League of Nations and the Right to be Free from Enslavement: The First Human Right to Be Recognized as Customary International Law" (1994) 70 Chicago-Kent L. Rev. 759

WEISSBRODT, DAVID, & ANTI-SLAVERY INTERNATIONAL, *Abolishing Slavery and Its Contemporary Forms* (New York: United Nations, 2002)

Apartheid
CLARK, ROGER, "Apartheid" in M. Cherif Bassiouni, ed., *International Criminal Law*, 3d ed., vol. 1 (Leiden: Martinus Nijhoff, 2008) 643

SLYE, RONALD, "Apartheid as a Crime against Humanity: A Submission to the South African Truth and Reconciliation Commission" (1999) 20 Mich. J. Int'l L. 267

Terrorism
CASSESE, ANTONIO, "Terrorism as an International Crime" in Andrea Bianchi, ed., *Enforcing International Law Norms against Terrorism* (Oxford: Hart, 2004) 213

GUILLAUME, GILBERT, "Terrorism and International Law" (2004) 53 I.C.L.Q. 537

HIGGINS, ROSALYN, & MAURICE FLORY, *Terrorism and International Law* (London: Routledge, 1997)

TRANSNATIONAL CRIMES OF INTERNATIONAL CONCERN

A. INTRODUCTION

As discussed in Chapter 1, greater analytical clarity is to be found if the concept of "international criminal law" is broken out from the related but mostly separate normative regime embodied in "transnational criminal law." To be sure, both are subdivisions of public international law and have in common both international law sources—custom, treaty, state practice, soft law, and so on—and an interface between international law and domestic law. States are the primary movers in both regimes, though in both, modern developments in human rights law have pushed the individual further towards being the subject rather than simply the object of the law. The ultimate goal of each is to prosecute crimes and punish offenders, and states are engaged in cooperative efforts to accomplish this.

However, transnational crime and the legal principles and norms which underpin it have characteristics distinct from international crime *stricto sensu*. "International crime," it will be recalled, refers to conduct which is prohibited under international law itself, and it is international law (primarily customary) that provides for individual liability. Enforcement against perpetrators is carried out by the international community itself—either directly (by way of trial before international courts applying international law) or indirectly (by way of states being permitted to exercise jurisdiction, often universal jurisdiction, to try perpetrators before their own courts, applying international law as it has been implemented in that state's law). By contrast, the term "transnational crime" emerged from the criminology discipline and has been adopted for use by both law and policy makers at the state and international level, particularly in the work of the United Nations and certain bodies of the European Union.[1] In its most general sense, it refers to domestic or "common" crimes that affect or engage the interests of more than one state when they are committed. As soon as more than one state is engaged, so too is international law, and states often utilize international law instruments and principles in order to cooperate and coordinate their efforts at combating the particular crimes. Transnational criminal law, then, covers "the indirect suppression by international law through domestic penal law of criminal activities that have actual or potential trans-boundary effects."[2] Enforcement is always indirect; states use transnational criminal law to facilitate the prosecution of domestic crimes before their domestic courts.

The specific focus of this chapter is transnational crimes of international concern. Under this typology, mutual state interest in suppressing certain kinds of transnational crime[3] is sufficiently pressing that states are moved to create treaties that both oblige the parties to suppress the particular crime and to cooperate with each other in so doing. As noted in Chapter 1, these are not crimes under international law, though there is international law dealing with these crimes. The overall goal is to coordinate the efforts of states in prosecuting transnational crimes, but the prosecutions themselves are still conducted under each state's domestic criminal laws.

There is no direct liability under international law for transnational crimes of international concern, though some prohibitions may eventually attain the status of "international crime" under customary international law. This occurs because the particular "treaty crime" itself

---

1   Bassiouni and Vetere suggest that the term was coined around 1975 by Professor Gerhard O.W. Mueller in the latter's role as Executive Secretary of the Fifth United Nations Congress on the Prevention of Crime and the Treatment of Offenders in Geneva (see M. Cherif Bassiouni & Eduardo Vetere, *Organized Crime: A Compilation of U.N. Documents 1975–1998* (Ardsley, NY: Transnational, 1998) at xxxi, n. 19). See also Gerhard O.W. Mueller, "Transnational Crime: Definitions and Concepts" in Phil Williams & Dimitri Vlassis, eds., *Combating Transnational Crime* (London: Frank Cass, 2001).

2   Neil Boister, "'Transnational Criminal Law'?" (2003) 14 E.J.I.L. 953 at 955.

3   As Andreas and Nadelmann have observed, states are motivated not only by political and economic interests, but by "moralizing impulses" and "emotional considerations"; see Peter Andreas & Ethan Nadelmann, *Policing the Globe: Criminalization and Crime Control in International Relations* (Oxford: Oxford University Press, 2006) at vii and 228.

becomes universalized among states (i.e., all states have a duty under customary international law to prohibit the individual crime) and evolves to a point where states may exercise universal jurisdiction to prosecute it (e.g., torture), or even where states have an obligation to act-ively suppress the crime and may cede jurisdiction to an international court for trial (e.g., grave breaches of the *Geneva Conventions*).[4]

Section B, below in this chapter, will discuss the important charac-teristics of these treaties, usually referred to as the "suppression con-ventions." The sections that follow will canvass the most important of the suppression regimes that are extant today and review Canada's engagement with each. There are a large number of crimes which are likely suitable for inclusion in this category, since there are many dif-ferent treaty regimes which could qualify. Moreover, Canada has been an active participant in international efforts to suppress transnational crime,[5] and there is a large amount of potentially applicable Canadian law. Accordingly, some selectivity is called for, and the crimes to be dealt with are those which are most significant.[6]

B. THE SUPPRESSION CONVENTIONS

1) History and Development

The suppression conventions are those treaties, usually multilateral, which are concluded between states in order to coordinate crime sup-pression efforts between them. The offences concerned are sometimes called "treaty crimes,"[7] though as will be seen, this phrase is a better

---

4   (1950), 75 U.N.T.S. 31, 85, 135, and 287.

5   See Doug Breithaupt, "The Effect of International Conventional Criminal Law on Domestic Legislative Initiatives Since 1990" in Oonagh Fitzgerald, ed., *The Globalized Rule of Law: Relationships between International and Domestic Law* (Toronto: Irwin Law, 2006) 573.

6   Not dealt with here is the *International Convention for the Protection of All Persons from Enforced Disappearance*, a treaty adopted by the UN Human Rights Council in 2006 (UNGA Res. 61/177, 20 December 2006). The text of the treaty and its status can be found online: www2.ohchr.org/english/law/disappearance-convention.htm. As of June 2009 it had 81 signatories but only 10 parties. And see Susan McCrory, "The *International Convention for the Protection of All Persons from Enforced Disappearance*" (2007) 7 Hum. Rts. L. Rev. 545.

7   This phrase was used during the negotiations towards the formulation of the *Rome Statute*, 2187 U.N.T.S. 3, entered into force 1 July 2002; see Official Rec-ords, Vol. II, Summary Records of the Meetings of the Committee of the Whole, UN DOC. A.Conf.183/13 at 172, para. 37. See also Patrick Robinson, "The Mis-sing Crimes" in Antonio Cassese et al., eds., *The Rome Statute of the Internation-*

shorthand name than it is an accurate descriptor. As discussed in Chapter 2, these treaties have three basic goals: (1) to ensure that particularly harmful or destructive crimes are criminalized by a network of states; (2) to ensure that as large a number of states as possible will exercise jurisdiction over these crimes, in order to obviate the problem of states which operate as "safe havens" for offenders; and (3) to provide for cooperation between the interested states, in particular allowing for sharing of resources and expertise in a way that assists poorer states. On a broader and more political level, as Ethan Nadelmann points out, some states engage in the creation of suppression conventions in order to export their values about undesirable behaviour as far into the international sphere as possible, and to encourage other states to adopt a similar perspective and enact crimes which prohibit these behaviours.[8]

Given state chauvinism regarding criminal law, historically there was little effort to try to coordinate prohibition, jurisdiction, and enforcement on anything approaching a general level. Rather, states have been moved to cooperate on matters of mutual concern on a piecemeal, reactionary basis which responded to the perceived problems of the day. For example, perhaps the earliest instrument analogous to a suppression convention was the obligation imposed by Rome on the Kingdoms of Cyprus, Alexandria, Egypt, Cyrene, and Syria to prevent the harbouring of pirates.[9] The abolition of the slave trade in the nineteenth century was accomplished in part by treaties requiring states to prohibit and punish its associated activities. Similarly, a spate of terrorist attacks in the late 1960s and early 1970s moved large numbers of states to enter into treaties that suppressed various terrorist acts, resulting in a group of widely subscribed international treaties that is now over a dozen strong.

What has been observable, however, is increasing willingness on the part of states to expand the areas within and levels on which they cooperate, as well as a resulting increase over time in the sophistication and complexity of the treaties. For example, the four *Geneva Conventions*[10] were fairly blunt instruments in that they were declaratory of conduct which was to be considered either state obligations or (in the

---

al Criminal Court: A Commentary, vol. 1 (Oxford: Oxford University Press, 2002) at 497.

8   Ethan Nadelmann, "Global Prohibition Regimes: The Evolution of Norms in International Society" (1990) 44 International Organization 479 at 480.

9   *The Cnidos Text* (1974) 64 Journal of Roman Studies 195–220, cited in Neil Boister, "Treaty-based Crimes" in Antonio Cassese, ed., *The Oxford Companion to International Criminal Justice* (Oxford: Oxford University Press, 2009) at 540.

10   Above note 4.

case of grave breaches) individually criminal, and they required states to prosecute offenders or extradite them to another state. The 1963 *Tokyo Aircraft Convention* simply contemplated, but did not oblige, states to extradite offenders between and among themselves.[11] By contrast, the various 1970s terrorism conventions provided firm jurisdictional bases and *aut dedere* obligations,[12] while the 1988 *Vienna Narcotics Convention*[13] contained provisions on the confiscation and repatriation of the proceeds of crime and laundered money, and contained obligations requiring states to provide mutual legal assistance. Generally speaking, later conventions have built on these various mechanisms, and the treaties themselves have tended to become broader and more intricate in terms of the level of obligation required of states.

2) Central Features

There are a number of central features which the suppression conventions, particularly the more modern ones, have in common. First is the obligation on states to criminalize within their domestic laws the conduct which is the subject matter of the treaty; accordingly, for example, the *Hijacking Convention*[14] requires states to enact a domestic crime of hijacking. This obligation highlights the indirect nature of the enforcement provided for transnational crimes of international concern, as it is the national law that creates individual liability for the offence, while the treaty simply provides for the creation of similar national laws across jurisdictions. The goal is to get around divergent national laws on whether a particular act is criminal (and even if so, what modes of liability are relevant to its commission[15] and what penalties attach) by imposing some level of commonality. The extent to which this is accomplished varies widely across the treaties and subject matter. The older treaties tend to describe the crimes sought to be suppressed quite generally, focusing on the "specific" part of the criminal law and "barely scratch[ing] the surface" on the general part (such as intent, complicity, and availability of inchoate modes of liability).[16] The

---

11   74 U.N.T.S. 219. See art. 16, para. 2.

12   The obligation to extradite or prosecute; see Section B(2), below in this chapter.

13   Can. T.S. 1990 No. 42 [*Vienna Narcotics Convention*].

14   *Convention for the Suppression of Unlawful Seizure of Aircraft*, 860 U.N.T.S. 105, Can. T.S. 1972 No. 23 [*Hijacking Convention*].

15   For example, whether attempt, aiding/abetting, or conspiracy are criminalized under particular states' laws.

16   Roger Clark, "Offenses of International Concern: Multilateral State Treaty Practice in the Forty Years Since Nuremberg" (1988) 57 Nordic J. Int'l L. 49 at 72.

recent trend is towards more detailed treatment of both conduct and fault elements.[17] It is not unusual to see versions of "model" legislation to implement treaty crimes put forward by international organizations, such as the Commonwealth Secretariat or the United Nations Office of Drugs and Crime (UNODC), in order to help achieve consistency and assist under-resourced states.

The second central feature is the requirement that state parties exert jurisdiction over the proscribed offence on a more expansive set of principles than would normally be the case, that is, not just territoriality (in the case of common law states) or the combination of territorial and nationality jurisdiction (as with civilian states). It is not unusual for there to be variance as to whether a particular basis for jurisdiction is mandatory or permissive in a given treaty. For example, article 6 of the *Terrorist Bombings Convention* requires states to establish jurisdiction over offences taking place in their territories and on their flagged vessels or registered aircraft, and committed by their nationals;[18] but it provides that states "may" establish jurisdiction on other bases, such as passive personality, protective, or crimes against embassies or protected officials.[19] The net effect of this kind of variance is that state parties do not have to adopt an entire range of jurisdictional principles with which they are uncomfortable or with which their legal tradition is unfamiliar, but they have consented to and cannot protest the exercise of such jurisdiction by their treaty partners, at least as regards the crimes which are the subject matter of the treaty.[20] The latter goal is also sometimes accomplished by way of a clause which permits states to exercise any principle of jurisdiction consistent with its national law; indeed, the *Terrorist Bombing Convention* contains such a provision in addition to those described above.[21]

The use of expansive bases of jurisdiction is linked to, and facilitates, the third major feature of the suppression conventions, which is the obligation to extradite or prosecute alleged or suspected perpetra-

---

17   Boister, above note 9.

18   (1998) 37 I.L.M. 249, Can. T.S. 2002 No. 8, arts. 6(1)(a)–(c) [*Terrorist Bombings Convention*]; see online: http://untreaty.un.org/cod/terrorism/terrorism_table-updateJanuary2009.pdf.

19   *Ibid.*, arts. 6(2)(a)–(e).

20   These treaties also contribute to the customary international law status of the jurisdictional principles they contain. For example, the passive personality principle is controversial as a "regular" exercise of criminal jurisdiction by states, but its incorporation into virtually all of the terrorism treaties points towards the conclusion that states are on firmer ground under customary international law in claiming such jurisdiction for terrorist offences.

21   Above note 18, art. 6(5).

tors of the treaty crime, usually referred to as *aut dedere aut judicare*.[22] This mechanism is linked to a further exercise of jurisdiction: when a state apprehends an alleged perpetrator of the treaty crime,[23] it must exercise jurisdiction over her even if it has none of the usual links to the crime or to the individual, often called "conditional universal jurisdiction." Under the *aut dedere* obligation, the state is under a duty to at least consider extradition requests from other treaty states, but if it does not extradite the offender then it must submit the case to its own authorities with a view to prosecution.[24]

In operation, the *aut dedere* mechanism expands the number of states which may legally exercise jurisdiction over offenders and obligates them to do so. An important overall goal of the entire scheme is to ensure that there is "double criminality" (i.e., that the conduct is a crime in each state, which is a usual prerequisite for extradition), and indeed many of the treaties expressly require states to make the treaty crime an extradition crime.[25] Many bases for the exercise of jurisdiction are imposed, in order to draw the jurisdictional net as tightly as possible around the offender. States that have custody and do not wish to prosecute have discretion as to which of any competing extradition requests for an offender they will fulfill, though in practice a state with a territorial or some other close link to the offence or offender emerges, and little conflict is generated.[26] Some treaties address this specifically;

---

22 See the detailed treatment of this mechanism in Chapter 2.

23 And in some treaties, the state is obliged to at least investigate the individual when it becomes aware of her presence, e.g., the *Terrorist Bombings Convention*, above note 18, art. 7.

24 Though given that this obligation ultimately depends on the good faith of both the prosecution authorities and the government referring the case to them, it has been argued that it "may ensure little more than a facade of justice" in some cases (Christopher Joyner & Wayne Rothbaum, "Libya and the Aerial Incident at Lockerbie: What Lessons for International Extradition Law?" (1993) 14 Mich. J. Int'l L. 222 at 248).

25 For example, *Hijacking Convention*, above note 14, art. 8; *Convention for the Suppression of Unlawful Acts against the Safety of Civil Aviation*, 974 U.N.T.S. 177, Can. T.S. 1973 No. 6, arts. 7 & 8 [*Montreal Convention*]. Currently 187 parties; online: http://untreaty.un.org/cod/terrorism/terrorism_tableupdateJanuary2009.pdf.

26 For example, in the initial discussions leading to the conclusion of the *UN Convention against Transnational Organized Crime*, 2225 U.N.T.S. 209 [*TOC Convention*] (about which, see Section C, below in this chapter), the Intergovernmental Group of Experts noted the possibility of conflict based on concurrent jurisdiction, but pointed out that this "might not be a negative development, as it would indicate the interest of numerous states to deal with specific problems. In addition, conflicts of jurisdiction were rather rare and were invariably resolved at the practical level by an eventual determination of which jurisdiction would be ultimately exercised on the basis of the chances for successful prosecution and

article 8(4) of the *Torture Convention*, for example, provides "Such offences shall be treated, for the purpose of extradition between States parties, as if they had been committed not only in the place in which they occurred but also in the territories of the States required to establish their jurisdiction [on territorial, nationality, and passive personality bases]."[27] Allegations of non-compliance with treaty obligations will be resolved by recourse to regular treaty law,[28] or more typically by negotiation between the states involved. The negotiation, in turn, is often facilitated by an obligation on the part of the custodial state to notify other state parties which may have a jurisdictional claim,[29] a mechanism which has the combined effect of smoothing out potential jurisdictional conflicts and facilitating the making of extradition requests.

Further, since the *aut dedere* obligation is binding only as between states which are parties to the treaty, the potential exists for conflict with non-party states. For example, suppose a Mexican national commits a treaty crime in Australia and is apprehended in Canada, where Canada and Australia are parties to a treaty with an *aut dedere* obligation, but Mexico is not. Canada could prosecute the offender under the treaty even without any other links, but Mexico as a non-party state could dispute Canada's assertion of jurisdiction over its national. In practice, no such disputes seem to arise, attributable at least in part to the fact that most of the major suppression conventions are widely subscribed to by states.

---

adjudication of the particular case." (Report of a Meeting of the Inter-Sessional Open-Ended Intergovernmental Group of Experts on the Elaboration of a Possible Comprehensive International Convention against Organized Transnational Crime (Warsaw, 2–6 February 1998) UN ESCOR, 7th Sess. at 10, UN Doc. E/CN.15/1998/5 (1998)). That said, it was this kind of conflict relating to the application of the *Montreal Convention*, *ibid.*, that led to a faceoff between the UK and Libya before the International Court of Justice (ICJ), and resulted in the holding of the Lockerbie trial in an independent third state after the intervention of the Security Council (see Chapter 4).

27   *United Nations Convention against Torture and Other Cruel, Inhuman or Degrading Treatment or Punishment* (1984), 1465 U.N.T.S. 85, Can. T.S. 1987 No. 36 [*Torture Convention*]; see also art. 7(5).

28   For example, there is currently a case pending before the ICJ in which Belgium is alleging that Senegal has failed to exercise its obligation to extradite or prosecute under the *Torture Convention*; see ICJ, News Release, 2009/13, "Belgium Institutes Proceedings against Senegal and Requests the Court to Indicate Provisional Measures" (19 February 2009), online: www.icj-cij.org/docket/files/144/15052.pdf. See also *Questions of Interpretation and Application of the 1971 Montreal Convention Arising from the Aerial Incident at Lockerbie (Interim Measures) (Libya v. United States)*, [1992] I.C.J. Rep. 3.

29   For example, the *Terrorist Bombing Convention*, above note 18, art. 7(6), which also obliges the custodial state to indicate whether it intends to exercise jurisdiction over the offender.

As noted above, the more recent treaties have amplified the level of assistance which is required to be rendered between state parties. The 1988 *Vienna Narcotics Convention* was particularly noteworthy in this regard. Article 7 obliges the parties to provide each other with mutual legal assistance "in investigations, prosecutions and judicial proceedings,"[30] and provides a minimum range of types of assistance which must be furnished.[31] Paragraphs 8–19 of the article constitute an operational stand-alone mutual legal assistance treaty for those state parties which did not have a bilateral treaty between them. Some provisions reach rather far into domestic law; as part of its overall mandate to enable international tracing and confiscation of proceeds of crime, the Convention provides that bank secrecy cannot serve as the basis for refusing a mutual legal assistance request.[32] The Convention also has fairly strong provisions regarding the mutual provision of cooperation and training, in particular with regard to police investigations, though consistency with domestic criminal law regimes is accounted for.[33]

For the treaties to have actual effect, of course, they must be implemented or otherwise incorporated into the domestic legal regimes of the party states. Failure to do so will result in breach of the treaty, but more pressingly may deprive a domestic court of its jurisdiction to try the offender.[34] Unimplemented treaty obligations can thus undermine an otherwise solid international cooperative effort to combat certain crimes, since the strength of even a widely ratified suppression convention is illusory if the treaty provisions have no force in domestic law.[35]

3) Human Rights Concerns

The indirect mode of criminal law enforcement embodied in the suppression conventions is state-centric in that it is based on treaty relations between states and, importantly, how those states choose to

---

30 Above note 13, art. 7(1). On mutual legal assistance, generally, see Chapter 9.

31 *Ibid.*, art. 7(2).

32 *Ibid.*, art. 7(5).

33 *Ibid.*, art. 9. See also, for example, the *Terrorist Bombing Convention*, above note 18, arts. 10 and 15.

34 For an example, see *Hissène Habré*, Senegal Supreme Court (20 March 2001), online: www.icrc.org/ihl-nat.nsf/46707c419d6bdfa24125673e00508145/90e26efa 1bb31189c1256b21005549b0!OpenDocument, where the courts of Senegal could not prosecute the accused, the former dictator of Chad, because art. 4 of the *Torture Convention*, above note 27, had not been fully implemented, though Cassese describes the court's reasoning as "specious" (Antonio Cassese, *International Criminal Law*, 2d ed. (Oxford: Oxford University Press, 2008) at 437, n. 3).

35 See Cassese, *ibid.* at 436–37.

implement and administer their treaty obligations. As early as 1974, Professor Bassiouni noted the disconnect between this international penal cooperation regime, on the one hand, and international human rights law, on the other.[36] An individual being investigated and prosecuted will be subjected to the enforcement processes of at least one, but sometimes two or even three states, and can expect only the loosest of unity in terms of the applicable due process standards. State parties to the suppression conventions were determined that their treaty partners should fulfill their obligations to suppress these crimes, but were less concerned over how it was to be done. In particular, the fact that the cooperation system itself was based in inter-state relations meant that the individual could not personally invoke any of the protections embodied in the treaties, especially what grounds existed for the refusal of assistance or any obligatory protections for his human rights. The individual was left to rely upon the protections of the domestic law of the prosecuting state, which might themselves be compromised by the international obligations.[37] Moreover, the extradition and mutual legal assistance obligations were similarly impenetrable to individuals, who could find themselves surrendered to states with questionable human rights records, where they faced the absence of the right to a fair trial, harsh penal conditions, and even the death sentence. States were interested in improving the overall international consistency of the coercive exercise of criminal law, but their arrangements showed little concern for protecting and promoting human rights obligations.[38]

Some decades after Professor Bassiouni's observation, there are indications that transnational criminal law and international human rights law are not completely bound up in separate silos, but the silos themselves have not been thrown down as yet.[39] To be sure, many of the older suppression conventions did provide certain grounds for refusal of assistance, such as double criminality or the "discrimination clause,"[40]

---

36   M. Cherif Bassiouni, "An Appraisal of the Growth and Developing Trends of International Criminal Law" (1974) 45 Rev. Int'l de Droit Penal 405 at 427.

37   For example, courts might use the treaty obligations as support for the limitation of constitutional human rights protections; see Neil Boister, "Human Rights Protection in the Suppression Conventions" (2002) 2 Hum. Rts. L. Rev. 199 at 209.

38   For commentary regarding the narcotics conventions, see Norbert Gilmore, "Drug Use and Human Rights: Privacy, Vulnerability, Disability and Human Rights Infringements" (1996) 12 J. Contemp. Health L. & Pol'y 355 at 356. See also Christopher Blakesley, *Terrorism, Drugs, International Law and the Protection of Human Liberty* (Ardsley, NY: Transnational, 1992).

39   See, generally, Boister, above note 37.

40   See, for example, the *Vienna Narcotics Convention*, above note 13, art. 6(6).

which had an indirect and limited protective effect on individual rights. In the newer treaties, clauses began to appear which were designed to impose some level of human rights protection on inter-state crime suppression efforts. For example, article 14 of the *Terrorist Bombing Convention* expressly invokes international human rights law in a manner that directly inserts it into any prosecution being undertaken regarding the subject crime:

> Any person who is taken into custody or regarding whom any other measures are taken or proceedings are carried out pursuant to this Convention shall be guaranteed fair treatment, including enjoyment of all rights and guarantees in conformity with the law of the State in the territory of which that person is present *and applicable provisions of international law, including international law of human rights* [emphasis added].[41]

Other modern treaties, by contrast, take a much weaker approach to human rights protection. The *United Nations Convention against Transnational Organized Crime* contains a series of weaker provisions that oblige certain accommodation of defence rights[42] and a vague provision regarding fair treatment,[43] but the execution of these protections is essentially left to the domestic law of the party states for substance. As Professor Boister observes, "the elementary point is that many parties to the suppression conventions may implement their obligations under the suppression conventions but may not be subject to effective international human rights obligations."[44] What is lacking is any sense of coherence between the extremely invasive laws and procedures to which states tie themselves under the suppression conventions and the corresponding obligations of states not only to ensure that they, themselves, do not violate individual rights, but that they do not facilitate other states in doing so in the name of crime-fighting.[45] There also does

---

41   Above note 18. See also *International Convention for the Suppression of the Financing of Terrorism*, Can. T.S. 2002 No. 9, art. 17. [*Terrorist Financing Convention*]. Currently 167 parties; see online: http://untreaty.un.org/cod/terrorism/terrorism_tableupdateJanuary2009.pdf.

42   *TOC Convention*, above note 26, arts. 11(3), 18(5), 24(2), and 25.

43   *Ibid.*, art. 16(13).

44   Boister, above note 37 at 218. See also Dorean M. Koenig, "The Criminal Justice System Facing the Challenge of Organized Crime" (1998) 44 Wayne L. Rev. 1351 at 1359–61.

45   States can be held responsible for their participation or role in wrongful acts by another state; see International Law Commission, *Responsibility of States for Internationally Wrongful Acts*, online: http://untreaty.un.org/ilc/texts/instruments/english/draft%20articles/9_6_2001.pdf, c. IV.

not seem to be a great deal of political will among states to actively enforce such obligations under the suppression conventions themselves; one waits in vain for the spate of cases alleging treaty violation by states which fail to properly provide for human rights protections under these treaty articles.

In Canada, the *Charter*[46] imposes a reasonably rigorous set of procedural rights and protections for the investigation and prosecution process as regards any of the treaty crimes that Canada has implemented. However, Canada's cooperation with other states, particularly with respect to the provision of extradition and mutual legal assistance, does engage these issues and is discussed in detail in Chapter 9.

C. TRANSNATIONAL ORGANIZED CRIME

1) Introduction

While the concept of "organized crime" is a familiar one that evokes images of Al Capone and, to the modern mind, the HBO television series *The Sopranos*, the concept of *transnational organized crime* has leapt to the forefront of international criminal cooperation efforts. The phenomenon began to receive serious international attention in the early 1990s, when the end of the Cold War coincided with the beginning of globalization in transport, trade, and communications—all of which, it is now well known, inured to the benefit of those criminals who could seize the moment. This moment was compounded by the presence of "weak" states which could not effectively combat such crime and thus could serve as bases of operation, and by state-level corruption, particularly among former Eastern bloc states, and throughout the developing world.[47] The UN Office on Drugs and Crime (UNODC), engaged on this issue for some time, by 1995 had identified eighteen categories of criminal offences which were having transnational impact by way of "inception, perpetration and/or direct or indirect effects," including money laundering, terrorist activities, corruption/bribery of public officials, and insurance fraud.[48] Canada put transnational or-

---

46   *Canadian Charter of Rights and Freedoms*, Part I of the *Constitution Act, 1982*, being Schedule B to the *Canada Act 1982* (U.K.), 1982, c. 11.

47   Ilias Bantekas & Susan Nash, *International Criminal Law*, 3d ed. (London: Routledge-Cavendish, 2007) at 233.

48   UNODC, Global Programme against Transnational Organized Crime, *Results of a Pilot Survey of Forty Selected Organized Criminal Groups in Sixteen Countries* (Vienna: United Nations, Office on Drugs and Crime, 2002) at 4.

ganized crime on the agenda of the G8 Summit Meeting in Halifax in 1995,[49] and that group of states has continued to work on the issue,[50] as has the Council of Europe.[51] Having seized itself of the matter in 1994,[52] the United Nations General Assembly (UNGA) sponsored state negotiations towards the conclusion of an international convention that would aid states in combating this phenomenon. These negotiations culminated in the 2000 *United Nations Convention against Transnational Organized Crime (TOC Convention)*,[53] accompanied by three Protocols addressing trafficking in persons, illegal trafficking in and transporting of migrants, and illicit manufacturing and trafficking of firearms.[54] This treaty was followed in 2003 by the *United Nations Convention against Corruption.*[55]

---

49 See Foreign Affairs and International Trade Canada, "Transnational Organized Crime," online: www.international.gc.ca/glynberry/crime-transnational. aspx?lang=eng.

50 See G8 Recommendations on Transnational Crime (updated to 20 October 2005), online: www.icclr.law.ubc.ca/Site%20Map/compendium/Compendium/ Declarations/G8%20Recommendations%20on%20Transnational%20Crime%20 2002.doc. See, generally, John Kirton & Radoslava Stefanova, eds., *The G8, the United Nations and Conflict Prevention* (Aldershot, UK: Ashgate, 2004).

51 See Council of Europe, *Organised Crime Situation Report 2005: Focus on the Threat of Economic Crime* (Strasbourg: Dept. of Crime Problems, Directorate General of Legal Affairs, Council of Europe, 2005).

52 UNGA Res. 49/60 (9 December 1994) and 50/186 (20 December 1995). A fuller account of the history of UN involvement in the development of the treaty instruments discussed here, including the important coordinating work of the UN's Commission on Crime Prevention and Criminal Justice, can be found in Dimitri Vlassis, "The *United Nations Convention against Transnational Organized Crime* and its Protocols: A New Era In International Cooperation" in International Centre for Criminal Law Reform and Criminal Justice Policy, *The Changing Face of International Criminal Law: Selected Papers* (Vancouver: ICCLR & CJP, 2002) 75 at 76–88 [ICCLR & CJP].

53 Above note 26.

54 *Protocol against the Illicit Manufacturing of and Trafficking in Firearms, Their Parts and Components and Ammunition*, UN Doc. A/RES/55/255, Annex (8 June 2001), not yet in Can. T.S. [*Firearms Protocol*]. The *Firearms Protocol* has been in force since 2005 and currently has 52 signatories and 79 parties. See online: www. unodc.org/unodc/en/treaties/CTOC/signatures.html. *Protocol against the Smuggling of Migrants by Land, Sea and Air*, UN Doc. A/RES/55/25, Annex III, (not yet in Can. T.S.) [*Smuggling Protocol*]. *Protocol to Prevent, Suppress and Punish Trafficking in Persons, Especially Women and Children*, UN Doc. A/55/383 (2 November 2000), Can. T.S. 2002 No. 25 [*Human Trafficking Protocol*]. The *Human Trafficking Protocol* has been in force since 2003 and currently has 117 signatories and 130 parties; see online: www.unodc.org/unodc/en/treaties/CTOC/signatures.html.

55 Annex to UNGA Res. 58/4 (31 October 2003) [*UNCAC*], online: www.unodc. org/unodc/en/treaties/CAC/index.html.

Key to the approach states have taken to combating transnational organized crime, as well as the various problems and obstacles thereto, has been the recognition that the emphasis is most effectively placed on the "organized" and "transnational" aspects, as opposed to the specific brands of crime. Currently, certain forms of crime can be identified as having the most profound transnational implications: trafficking in narcotics and human beings; smuggling of migrants; money laundering; illicit trade in firearms; various forms of economic crime; and more recently, cyber-crime. Moreover, there has been a disturbing trend of convergence and synergies between transnational terrorist groups and transnational organized crime actors, which is another very current and evolving focus for law and policy makers.[56]

However, the heart of the perceived danger is the perniciousness and widespread effects of crime that is committed by persons who come together into organized groups for criminal purposes, in combination with the challenges to law enforcement which are presented when that crime crosses borders. The kinds of crime which are committed by these groups are dynamic and changing over time, and the perpetrators adapt their skill bases, resources, and techniques depending on opportunity and (generally speaking) profitability.[57] Against this background, the approach taken by the UN and the negotiating states was to draft the *TOC Convention* in such a way as to give policing authorities the kind of flexibility needed to adapt similarly, and focus on the nature of the actors and the seriousness and transnational nature of the criminal activity. More specific prescriptive regimes on particular crimes are solidified by the Protocols and the *Convention against Corruption*. The major features of each will be examined in turn.[58] Importantly, the Protocols are not stand-alone treaties, and states must be party to the *TOC Convention* in order to sign on to the Protocols. Accordingly, both general and specific cooperation regimes will be in place for states which sign a Protocol; for example, the *TOC Convention* itself contains

---

56   Emmanouela Mylonaki, "The Manipulation of Organised Crime by Terrorists: Legal and Factual Perspectives" (2002) 2 Int'l Crim. L. Rev. 213; John Picarelli, "The Turbulent Nexus of Transnational Organized Crime and Terrorism: A Theory of Malevolent International Relations" (2006) 7 Global Crime 1. In July 2009, the G8 leaders expressed concern about this issue; see UNODC, "G8 Warns of Converging Threats," online: www.unodc.org/unodc/en/front-page/2009/July/g8-warns-of-converging-threats.html.

57   See Michael Levi, "The Organization of Serious Crime" in Mike Maguire *et al.*, *The Oxford Handbook of Criminology*, 3d ed. (Oxford: Oxford University Press, 2002).

58   For detailed commentary on the *TOC Convention* and the three *Protocols*, see John D. McClean, *Transnational Organized Crime: A Commentary on the UN Convention and its Protocols* (Oxford: Oxford University Press, 2007).

provisions on extradition, mutual legal assistance, and other forms of inter-state cooperation, while the *Firearms Protocol* contains specific provisions regarding the tracing of firearms.[59]

2) The Organized Crime Offences

a) International Law

The *TOC Convention* is "often referred to as a 'framework' convention, in that it supplies a framework for further administrative, legislative and treaty-making action."[60] Its provisions are intricate and contain a great deal of built-in flexibility for the divergent legal systems of states expected to ratify the Convention. The delicacy of many issues required the concurrent issuing of over 100 "interpretive notes" to the Convention, and both these and a comparison of the Convention and the Protocols demonstrate tension, finessing of issues, and occasional confusion on the nature and scope of some obligations.[61]

The Convention's approach to helping and obliging states to combat transnational crime is based on a bifurcated approach: each state must criminalize certain kinds of crime that often have transnational aspects, regardless of whether they manifest themselves transnationally in that state;[62] and it must cooperate vis-à-vis these crimes and any other "serious" crime, "where the offence is transnational in nature and involves an organized criminal group."[63] Breaking out the three key concepts, an offence is "transnational" if

(a) It is committed in more than one State;

(b) It is committed in one State but a substantial part of its preparation, planning, direction or control takes place in another State;

---

59   See UNODC, *Legislative Guides for the Implementation of the United Nations Convention against Transnational Organized Crime and the Protocols Thereto* (New York: United Nations, 2004), for example, at 253.

60   Roger Clark, "The United Nations Convention against Transnational Organized Crime" (2004) 50 Wayne L. Rev. 161 at 164, n. 12.

61   McClean, above note 58 at 13–15.

62   Above note 26, art. 34. Indeed, the overall point of the Convention and Protocols scheme is to ensure states are able to prosecute these crimes when they are transnational and have involved organized criminal groups, but also to maintain the ability to prosecute them purely as domestic offences, and in such cases not to require the prosecution to prove either transnationality or organized crime involvement (*Legislative Guides* at 333–34). Of course, this varies with the crime approached; the organized crime offences themselves naturally will have a requirement to prove organized criminality. Similarly, migrant smuggling necessarily involves a transnational aspect.

63   *Ibid.*, art. 3(1).

(c) It is committed in one State but involves an organized criminal group that engages in criminal activities in more than one State; or

(d) It is committed in one State but has substantial effects in another State.[64]

This provision, which partly delimits the scope of the Convention, lays out some fairly broad connecting factors between the crime and the state parties (or at least some of them, insofar as the term "State" does not seem to be confined to the parties) which must be present for the Convention to apply. It should not be confused, but should be read together, with the jurisdictional requirements set out in article 15. Here, states are required to assert territorial and flag ship/registered aircraft jurisdiction,[65] and may use the passive personality[66] and expanded nationality[67] principles. These two provisions together cover a great deal of mutually enforcing ground as to where an offence is, or is deemed to be committed, and contains an approach to qualified territoriality which is very *Libman*-like in scope.[68]

An "organized criminal group" is "structured"[69] and contains three or more persons who have acted together to commit either one of the proscribed crimes or a "serious" crime.[70] The aim of the group must be to commit the offences "in order to obtain, directly or indirectly, a financial or other material benefit," and the latter phrase is to be interpreted broadly in order to catch such "benefits" as trading of children among pedophiles or crimes in which the predominant motivation is sexual gratification.[71] "Serious" crime is defined as "conduct constituting an offence punishable by a maximum deprivation of liberty of at least four years or a more serious penalty."[72] As Clark comments:

> This specific-content-free definition of serious crime is fundamental to the way the Convention itself operates. The scope of the Convention's application turns ultimately on the seriousness of the particular activities (judged in a rough and ready way by the penalty) rather than on substantive content. It is left to its Protocols to spell out some

---

64   *Ibid.*, art.3(2).

65   *Ibid.*, art.15(1).

66   *Ibid.*, art. 5(2)(a)

67   *Ibid.*, art. 5(2)(b).

68   McClean, above note 58 at 53–56, referring to *Libman v. The Queen*, [1985] 2 S.C.R. 178 [*Libman*].

69   For the definition of "structured," see above note 26, art. 2(c).

70   *Ibid.*, art. 2(a).

71   See the Interpretive Note on this provision: UN Doc. A/55/383/Add.1, n. 3.

72   Above note 26, art. 2(b).

particular substantive areas (obviously not all) to which the basic obligations of the Convention are to be applied[.][73]

Beyond the open-ended concept of "serious" crime, the *TOC Convention* does require states to criminalize four distinct crimes, liability to be extended both to individuals and to legal persons (e.g., corporations) where the latter is consistent with domestic legal principles.[74] First, article 5 provides for a crime of participation in an organized criminal group. This offence is explicitly separated from "those involving the attempt or completion of the criminal activity,"[75] and liability accrues either from agreement to participate in a serious crime[76] or taking part in an organized criminal group's activities, with the intention to further the group's aims or in the knowledge that the individual's conduct will do so.[77] Liability also attaches to "organizing, directing, aiding, abetting, facilitating or counselling the commission of a serious crime involving an organized criminal group."[78]

Second, article 6 requires the criminalization of the laundering of proceeds of crime,[79] including "the acquisition, possession or use" of proceeds with knowledge of its nature,[80] and various forms of complicity, inchoate offences, and participation.[81] Parties must seek to implement this offence for the widest possible range of predicate offences in their respective laws,[82] and must include as predicate offences all "serious" crimes as defined in the Convention as well as the offences in the Convention itself.[83] When the predicate offence is committed outside a state's jurisdiction, it must be an offence under the laws of both states in order for the proceeds of crime regime to operate.[84] Article 7 requires each state party to "institute a comprehensive domestic regulatory and supervisory regime for banks and non-bank financial institutions and . . . other bodies particularly susceptible to money laundering."[85] It re-

---

73   Clark, above note 60 at 169.
74   Above note 26, art. 10.
75   *Ibid.*, art. 5(a).
76   *Ibid.*, art. 5(1)(a)(i).
77   *Ibid.*, art. 5(1)(a)(ii). As Clark points out, para. (1)(a)(i) is meant to roughly correspond to conspiracy as the concept is known to common law states, while para. (1)(a)(ii) is more in line with civilian concepts (Clark, above note 60 at 170–72).
78   *Ibid.*, art. 5(1)(b).
79   *Ibid.*, art. 6(1)(a).
80   *Ibid.*, art. 6(1)(b)(i).
81   *Ibid.*, art. 6(1)(b)(ii).
82   *Ibid.*, art. 6(2)(a).
83   *Ibid.*, art. 6(2)(b).
84   *Ibid.*, art. 6(2)(c).
85   *Ibid.*, art. 7(1)(a).

quires the states to institute a system of information sharing among national authorities,[86] and calls upon the governments to utilize in so doing "the relevant initiatives of regional, interregional and multilateral organizations against money-laundering."[87]

Third, article 8 requires state parties to criminalize "corruption" of public officials, in the form both of promises, offering, or giving "an undue advantage, for the official himself or herself or another person or entity, in order that the official act or refrain from acting in the exercise of his or her official duties,"[88] and the solicitation or acceptance of such an advantage by the official.[89] Being an accomplice to the offence must also be made criminal,[90] and states are to consider extending the offences to cover corruption of foreign public officials or international civil servants, which dovetails with the *Organisation for Economic Cooperation and Development Convention (OECD Convention)* [91] considered in Section C(6), below in this chapter. These provisions have since been overtaken by the *United Nations Convention against Corruption*,[92] also considered in Section C(6), below in this chapter.

Fourth, article 23 provides recognition of the unique proclivity of organized crime groups to subvert criminal prosecution by way of intimidation of and tampering with witnesses. It requires state parties to criminalize the "use of physical force, threats or intimidation" or bribery in order to interfere in some way with the giving of evidence in a proceeding regarding organized crime offences,[93] or to interfere with the official duties of judges or law enforcement officials.[94] Importantly, this offence is intended to cover all official government proceedings, including the pretrial phase of prosecution.[95] Articles 24 and 25 provide for obligations to protect witnesses and victims.

The *TOC Convention* also contains modern and progressive provisions on various forms of mutual assistance and cooperation. Article 16 sets out a flexible and highly consultative extradition scheme, providing that states which require a treaty in order to effect extradition may

---

86   *Ibid.*, art. 7(1)(b).
87   *Ibid.*, art. 7(4).
88   *Ibid.*, art. 8(1)(a).
89   *Ibid.*, art. 8(1)(b).
90   *Ibid.*, art. 8(3).
91   *Convention on Combating Bribery of Foreign Public Officials in International Business Transactions*, Reprinted (1998) 37 I.L.M. 1 [*OECD Convention*], online: www.oecd.org/daf/nocorruption/convention.
92   Above note 55.
93   Above note 26, art. 23(a).
94   *Ibid.*, art. 23(b).
95   Interpretive Note: UN Doc. A/55/383/Add.1, n. 46.

use the *TOC Convention* itself for this purpose, and otherwise encouraging[96] and requiring[97] state parties to ensure that extradition arrangements are in place between them. Article 17 provides for the transfer of sentenced persons, while article 18 contains a highly detailed and stand-alone mutual legal assistance regime. Interesting elements of the latter include provision for state authorities to transmit information relating to a crime to a state to which they feel it will be useful, without the request of the receiving state;[98] the continuation of the trend towards stripping away bank secrecy and "fiscal matters" as grounds for refusal of requests;[99] and providing that the usual double criminality requirement for providing information can be waived by a requested state at its discretion.[100] Article 21 provides for the transfer of criminal proceedings between state parties.

There is also a set of specialized measures for enhancing investigational cooperation and information sharing, including joint investigations (article 19), special investigative techniques (e.g., controlled delivery and surveillance) (article 20), law enforcement cooperation (article 27), sharing of information and analytical expertise (articles 28 and 29), and the provision of economic development and technical assistance measures in order to assist developing states and states with economies in transition to comply with their obligations and fully participate in the treaty regime (article 30). States are also obligated to maintain and enhance their own internal expertise by way of training programs for law enforcement personnel (article 29) and the creation of national programs and strategies to "promote best practices and policies aimed at the prevention of transnational organized crime."[101]

b) Canadian Implementing Legislation

The Government of Canada has been an active participant in and coordinator of international efforts to address transnational organized crime, including the drafting of the *TOC Convention* and the Protocols.[102] It has also explicitly recognized that the "inter-relationship

---

96 Above note 26, art. 16(17).

97 *Ibid.*, arts. 6(5) & (6).

98 *Ibid.*, art. 8(4).

99 *Ibid.*, arts. 8(8) and (22).

100 *Ibid.*, art. 8(9).

101 *Ibid.*, art. 31.

102 For example, Canada proposed a consolidated text of the *Firearms Protocol* for negotiation at the second session of the Ad Hoc Committee for the Elaboration of the *UN Convention against Transnational Organized Crime* (Vienna, January 1999).

between the national and international agendas is key to effectively combating organized crime now and in the future."[103] Building on the 2000 inter-Ministerial National Agenda on Organized Crime,[104] in 2001 the federal government put in place the Measures to Combat Organized Crime Initiative, which saw program funding allocated between Justice Canada, the RCMP, the Department of the Solicitor General, and the Correctional Service of Canada.[105] Canada actively cooperates with the US in combating organized crime.[106]

As was the case with many states, Canadian criminal law already contained a number of measures similar to those agreed on in the *TOC Convention*, and thus Canadian implementation of the *Convention* itself both predates and postdates the actual conclusion of the treaty.[107] However, the primary legislative initiative was the *Act to amend the Criminal Code (organized crime and law enforcement)*,[108] which was passed in 2001 and made a series of amendments to the *Criminal Code*[109] and other federal statutes. Regarding jurisdiction, it is noteworthy that no amendment was made to section 7 of the *Code*, which is where extraterritorial jurisdiction is generally provided, and it seems that Canada does not use any of the extraterritorial jurisdiction provisions which are provided for in the *TOC Convention*. The definition of "criminal organization" (see below in this section) does provide that the organization itself may have members "in or outside Canada," but the commission of the offences themselves seems to be limited to Canadian territory under section 6(2) of the *Code*, qualified territoriality in accordance with *Libman*,[110] or the special extraterritorial provisions.[111] This is unusual for Canada, which often makes reasonably full use of any extra-

---

103 Policing and Law Enforcement Directorate, Solicitor General Canada, "Canada's National Agenda on Organized Crime" in ICCLR & CJP, above note 52, 137 at 145.

104 See above note 49.

105 For details, see Justice Canada, Evaluation Division, *Measures to Combat Organized Crime: Mid-Term Evaluation: Summary, Recommendations and Management Response* (February 2004), online: www.justice.gc.ca/eng/pi/eval/rep-rap/04/mcoc-mlco/sum-som/sum.pdf.

106 See the *2006 Canada–US Organized Crime Threat Assessment*, jointly authored by the RCMP, the US Drug Enforcement Administration, and the FBI, online: www.publicsafety.gc.ca/prg/le/_fl/2006_Canada-US_OC-TA_en.pdf.

107 See, generally, David Freedman, "The New Law of Criminal Organizations in Canada" (2006) 85 Can. Bar Rev. 171.

108 Bill C-24, online: www2.parl.gc.ca/HousePublications/Publication.aspx?DocId=2330914&Language=e&Mode=1.

109 R.S.C. 1985, c. C-46.

110 Above note 68.

111 For example, s. 477.1 of the *Code*, above note 109. See, generally, Chapter 8.

territorial jurisdiction which is provided for in any of the suppression conventions.[112] The *Code* does provide for the criminal responsibility of legal persons,[113] per article 10 of the *Convention*.

Section 467.1 of the *Code* sets out definitions of "criminal organization" and "serious offence"[114] that are commensurate with the definitions of "organized criminal group" and "serious crime" from the *TOC Convention*, as well as providing for facilitation of,[115] being party to, and counselling the offence.[116] The three subsequent sections implement article 5 of the Convention. Section 467.11 makes it an offence to participate in or contribute to any activity of a criminal organization for the purpose of enhancing the ability of the organization to facilitate or commit an indictable offence.[117] The offence accrues regardless of whether the organization facilitated or committed the offence, the accused's act actually enhanced the organization's ability to do so, the accused knew the specific nature of the offence facilitated/committed by the organization, or the accused knew the identity of anyone in the organization.[118] Section 467.12 makes it an offence to commit an indictable offence for the benefit of/at the direction of/in association with a criminal organization, again regardless of whether the accused knew the identity of any members of the organization. Section 467.13 makes it an offence for a member of a criminal organization to directly or indirectly instruct any person to commit an offence at the direction of, for the benefit of, or in association with the organization, regardless of whether the offence instructed was actually committed, whether the accused instructed a particular person to commit the offence, or

---

112 See Robert J. Currie & Steve Coughlan, "Extraterritorial Criminal Jurisdiction: Bigger Picture or Smaller Frame?" (2007) 11 Can. Crim. L. Rev. 141 at 155–61 and 169–72.

113 Above note 109, s. 2, *cf.* "every one," "person," and "owner," as well as "organization."

114 *Ibid.*, s. 467.1(1)(a). The definition of "serious offence" indicates that the offence must be an indictable offence under any Act of Parliament, punishable by a maximum sentence of five years or more. Oddly, however, the related provisions do not use the phrase, and simply refer to "indictable offence" or in 467.13, "an offence under this or any other Act of Parliament." The seriousness of the crimes is reflected in section 718.2(a)(iv) of the *Code*, which states that "evidence that the offence was committed for the benefit of, at the direction of or in association with a criminal organization" is an aggravating factor for sentencing purposes.

115 *Ibid.*, s. 467.1(2).

116 *Ibid.*, s. 467.1(3).

117 *Ibid.*, s. 467.11(1). This would appear to attach even to lawful activities which would further the unlawful goals of the organization.

118 *Ibid.*, ss. 467(11)(2)(a)–(d).

whether the accused knew the identity of all members of the organization.[119] Sentences for offences under any of these three sections are to
be served consecutively with any other sentence for related offences.[120]

With regard to article 23 of the Convention, section 139(2) of the
Code criminalizes the obstruction of justice "in any manner," while
subsection (3) extends this specifically to jurors and witnesses. Also,
section 423.1 outlaws the intimidation of a justice system participant in
order to impede the execution of his duties. These provisions are probably wide enough to fully capture article 23. Implementation of articles
6, 7, 12, and 14 of the *TOC Convention* regarding proceeds of crime and
suppressing money laundering is subsumed in Canada's broader legislative regime in these areas, which is considered in Section F, below in
this chapter. Implementation of article 8 regarding corruption is considered with regard to the *UN Corruption Convention*[121] and similar instruments in Section C(6), below in this chapter.

Obligations regarding extradition, mutual legal assistance, and
transfer of offenders are implemented by the general statutes that deal
with these mechanisms for all relevant treaties, that is, the *Extradition
Act*,[122] the *Mutual Legal Assistance in Criminal Matters Act*[123] and the
International Transfer of Offenders Act.[124] Similarly, with regard to the
witness protection obligations in article 24 of the *TOC Convention*, Canada has a developed scheme in the *Witness Protection Program Act*.[125]

3) Trafficking in Persons

a) International Law
While slavery in its classical forms has been outlawed by the international
community and virtually abolished,[126] "contemporary forms of slavery"[127]

---

119 This provision has been struck down for vagueness under s. 7 of the *Charter*
by one provincial superior court: *R. v. Accused No. 1* (2005), 35 C.R. (6th) 140
(B.C.S.C.). Its constitutionality was upheld in *R. v. Lindsay* (2004), 70 O.R. (3d)
131 (S.C.J.), *R. v. Smith* (2006), 280 Sask. R. 128 (Q.B.) (declining to follow *R.
v. Accused No. 1*), and *R. v. Terezakis*, 2007 BCCA 384, leave to appeal to S.C.C.
refused, [2007] S.C.C.A. No. 487.
120 Above note 109, s. 467.14.
121 Above note 55.
122 S.C. 1999, c. 18.
123 R.S.C. 1985 (4th Supp.), c. 30.
124 S.C. 2004, c. 21.
125 S.C. 1996, c. 15.
126 See, generally, Chapter 6.
127 A.Yasmine Rassam, "Contemporary Forms of Slavery and the Evolution of the
Prohibition of Slavery and the Slave Trade under Customary International Law"

and related practices remain an utter scourge and ongoing problem for transnational law enforcement. The practice of trafficking in persons, or "human trafficking," has rightly been called "one of the leading criminal enterprises of the early twenty-first century, affecting every country around the globe."[128] The International Labour Organization (ILO) has estimated that at any given time there are approximately 12.3 million people in forced labour, bonded labour, forced child labour, and sexual servitude,[129] and trafficking is undoubtedly a multi-billion dollar business for organized crime groups. It is thought that some 800,000 people are trafficked across state borders per year, of which 80 percent are women and girls and 50 percent are children, and the majority are forced into prostitution and/or sexual slavery of some variety.[130] However, as the UNODC has pointed out, the clandestine nature of the crime, in combination with lack of diligence on the part of many states in acknowledging and suppressing it, makes any estimation methodology questionable—and any estimates probably too modest.[131] Accordingly, particularly over the last decade, the suppression of the trade in human trafficking has become a matter of focus for the international community, which has also recognized the profound human rights dimension to this problem.[132]

(1999) 39 Va. J. Int'l L. 303. See also Fara Gold, "Redefining the Slave Trade: The Current Trends in the International Trafficking of Women" (2003) 11 U. Miami Int'l & Comp. L. Rev. 99.

128 Clare M. Ribando, *Trafficking in Persons: US Policy and Issues for Congress* (Washington, DC: US Congressional Research Service, 2007), online: http://fpc. state.gov/documents/organization/88062.pdf at 2.

129 Online: www.ilo.org/global/Themes/Forced_Labour/lang--en/index.htm.

130 US Department of State, *2007 Trafficking in Persons Report* (Washington: US Department of State, 2007), online: www.state.gov/g/tip/rls/tiprpt/2007/ at 8. And see the latest (2009) report, online: www.state.gov/documents/organization/123357.pdf.

131 UNODC, *Trafficking in Persons: Global Patterns* (Vienna: UNODC, 2006) at 43–45.

132 See GA Res. 58/137 (4 February 2004), UN Doc. A/RES/58/137; Commission of the European Communities, *Communication from the Commission to the European Parliament and the Council: Fighting Trafficking in Human Beings—An Integrated Approach and Proposals for an Action Plan*, COM (2005) 514 final (Brussels, 18.10.2005). See also Ann Jordan, "Human Rights or Wrongs: The Struggle for a Rights-based Response to Trafficking in Human Beings" (2002) 10 Gender and Development 28. For either side of the debate as to whether a crime control model is the best way to deal with the phenomenon of human trafficking, see Elizabeth Bruch, "Models Wanted: The Search for an Effective Response to Human Trafficking" (2004) 40 Stanford J. Int'l L. 1, and LeRoy Potts, "Global Trafficking in Human Beings: Assessing the Success of the United Nations Protocol to Prevent Trafficking in Persons" (2003) 35 Geo. Wash. Int'l L. Rev. 227.

The leading[133] international law instrument on human trafficking is the *Human Trafficking Protocol*.[134] The most significant achievement in overcoming past difficulties in criminalizing this practice[135] was the conclusion of an agreed definition of "trafficking in persons," which appears in article 3(a) of the Protocol:

> "Trafficking in persons" shall mean the recruitment, transportation, transfer, harbouring or receipt of persons, by means of the threat or use of force or other forms of coercion, of abduction, of fraud, of deception, of the abuse of power or of a position of vulnerability or of the giving or receiving of payment or benefits to achieve the consent of a person having control over another person, for the purpose of exploitation. Exploitation shall include, at a minimum, the exploitation of the prostitution of others or other forms of sexual exploitation, forced labour or services, slavery or practices similar to slavery, servitude or the removal of organs[.]

As the UNODC's Legislative Guide notes, this definition has three elements: an action (e.g., recruitment, transportation); a means used to carry out the action (e.g., threat or use of force, coercion, abduction); and the prohibited purpose of exploitation, which is partially defined by reference to specific criminal practices.[136] These three elements are also used as reference points for the shaping of other criminalization obligations. Article 3(b) provides that the consent of the victim to the intended exploitation is irrelevant where any of the means in paragraph 3(a) have been used, while article 3(c) provides that any of the actions, if carried out against children, shall be considered "trafficking" even if none of the means in paragraph 3(a) are used.

Article 4 of the Protocol emphasizes the connection to the *TOC Convention*, providing that the Protocol applies to the criminalization of trafficking where it is "transnational in nature and involve[s] an organized criminal group." Article 5 requires states to criminalize inten-

---

133 See also the *Convention on the Elimination of All Forms of Discrimination against Women*, Can. T.S. 1982 No. 31, art. 6; United Nations *Convention on the Rights of the Child* (1989), 1577 U.N.T.S. 3, art. 11 [*UNCRC*].

134 Above note 54.

135 Specifically, that the *Protocol Amending the International Agreement for the Suppression of the White Slave Traffic*, signed at Paris on 18 May 1904, and the *International Convention for the Suppression of the White Slave Traffic*, signed at Paris on 4 May 1910, U.N.T.S. 30/23, Can. T.S. 1951 No. 32 (4 May 1949), did not contain a definition of trafficking. For a succinct account of earlier efforts to address the problems, see McClean, above note 58 at 15–18.

136 UNODC, *Legislative Guides*, above note 59 at 268.

tional trafficking in persons,[137] as well as attempt,[138] participating as an accomplice,[139] and organizing or directing other persons to commit the offence.[140] The Protocol also contains a provision on information exchange and training between the law enforcement and immigration authorities of party states,[141] as well as specialized provisions regarding the strengthening of border controls and the security of travel and identity documents.[142]

There are both obligatory and permissive provisions in the Protocol that, while consistent with the overall scheme of the TOC "package" are nonetheless quite holistic and progressive. The Protocol is replete with references to the special circumstances of women and children, and acknowledges their particular vulnerability and need for protection, both within the context of trafficking and before the legal systems of the party states.[143] Part II of the Protocol encapsulates a scheme for the assistance and protection of victims of trafficking,[144] while article 9 at least acknowledges "the factors that make persons, especially women and children, vulnerable to trafficking, such as poverty, underdevelopment, and lack of equal opportunity" and requires states to take or strengthen measures that will prevent trafficking and alleviate the conditions that give rise to it.[145]

b) Canadian Implementing Legislation[146]

The government of Canada was active in the negotiations leading to the conclusion of the *Human Trafficking Protocol*, and has taken an interdisciplinary approach to implementing its obligations thereunder. The Interdepartmental Working Group on Trafficking in Persons (IWGTIP) was formed during the Protocol negotiations and is now the central coordinative body for federal policy and programs to combat human

---

137 Above note 134, art. 5(1).
138 *Ibid.*, art. 5(2)(a).
139 *Ibid.*, art. 5(2)(b).
140 *Ibid.*, art. 5(2)(c).
141 *Ibid.*, art. 10.
142 *Ibid.*, arts. 12 & 13.
143 For example, *ibid.*, arts. 6(4) and 9(4).
144 *Ibid.*, arts. 6–8.
145 *Ibid.*, art. 9(4).
146 For background, see Report of the Standing Committee on the Status of Women: *Turning Outrage Into Action to Address Trafficking for the Purpose of Sexual Exploitation in Canada*, February 2007, 39th Parliament, 1st Sess., online: http://cmte.parl.gc.ca/Content/HOC/committee/391/fewo/reports/rp2738918/feworp12/feworp12-e.pdf.

trafficking.[147] Co-chaired by the departments of Justice and Foreign Affairs, the IWGTIP membership also includes fifteen other federal departments, including the Canadian Border Security Service (CBSA), the Canadian International Development Agency (CIDA), the Canadian Security Intelligence Service (CSIS), the RCMP, and Status of Women Canada, and coordinates training of personnel and the kinds of public dialogue and information providing contemplated by the *Protocol*.[148]

Trafficking is criminalized in two legislative schemes. The one most closely related to the *Human Trafficking Protocol* is a set of provisions which were introduced into the *Criminal Code*[149] in 2005.[150] Section 279.01(1) creates an offence of trafficking in persons which is commensurate with article 3(a) of the Protocol, providing for imprisonment for life if the accused kidnaps, commits aggravated assault or aggravated sexual assault, or causes death to the victim during the commission of the offence, or a maximum sentence of fourteen years otherwise. Section 279.01(2) invalidates any consent to any part of the offence, which implements article 3(b) of the Protocol. Section 279.02 makes it an offence to receive any financial or other material benefit from the commission of the trafficking offence in 279.01; this is essentially a proceeds-of-crime offence, linked with article 6 of the *TOC Convention*. Section 279.03 creates an offence of withholding or destroying personal documents relating to travel, identity, or immigration status for the purposes of committing/facilitating the trafficking offence, which has no specific predicate in the Protocol but is consistent with its overall spirit. Section 279.04 creates a broad definition of "exploitation" that easily covers off the definition in article 3(a) of the Protocol.

In terms of jurisdiction, these offences are subject to section 6(2) of the *Code* and are basically territorial in scope, though the *Libman* qualified territorial approach[151] is available and significantly broadens the Crown's ability to prosecute. It certainly enables prosecution of trafficking that is internal to Canada, which is important in order to be able to properly suppress traffickers moving their victims around within the country. Moreover, these offences fall under the definition of "serious offence" in the organized crime provisions of the *Code* (specif-

---

147 Foreign Affairs Canada, "Human Trafficking and Migrant Smuggling," on-line: www.international.gc.ca/crime/human-traf-personne.aspx?menu_id=27&menu=R.

148 Justice Canada, "Trafficking in Persons—IWGTIP," online: www.justice.gc.ca/eng/fs-sv/tp/p4.html#one.

149 Above note 109.

150 S.C. 2005, c. 43.

151 Above note 68.

ically section 467.1(1)(a)), and thus attract additional liability for those offences if committed as part or in facilitation of organized crime activities—which will inevitably be the case with human trafficking., though it may be difficult to prove Also, the definition of "criminal organization" in the latter section provides that the organization itself may have members inside and outside of Canada.

An overlapping human trafficking offence is created by section 118 of the *Immigration and Refugee Protection Act (IRPA)*, which provides, "No person shall knowingly organize the coming into Canada of one or more persons by means of abduction, fraud, deception or use or threat of force or coercion,"[152] while section 119 criminalizes disembarking at sea for the purpose of inducing, aiding, or abetting persons to come into Canada illegally. Contravention of either of these sections exposes the perpetrator to a maximum fine of $1 million, life imprisonment, or both.[153] Section 121 provides that committing the offences "for the benefit of, at the direction of or in association with a criminal organization" is an aggravating factor for sentencing,[154] and provides a definition of criminal organization that is somewhat similar to the *TOC Convention* definition (and the definition in section 467.1 of the *Code*) but omits the purpose requirement.[155]

Section 121 has survived a constitutional challenge on the basis that the inclusion of the terms "fraud and deception" rendered it overly vague under section 7 of the *Charter*.[156] In rejecting this defence argument, MacLean J. utilized the *Human Trafficking Protocol* as an interpretive tool, specifically citing the appearance of the words "fraud" and "deception" in the Protocol definition of trafficking.[157]

There is a curious amount of overlap between the *Code* and *IRPA* provisions. To be sure, the *IRPA* provisions are limited to the organizing of persons to come into Canada and thus are tailored to the immigration and refugee context in that sense. However, under *Libman*, the *Code* provisions are more than broad enough to catch this behaviour, even to the extent that the organizing occurred in another state, since the ar-

---

152 S.C. 2001, c. 27, s. 118(1). Section 118(2) states that "organize" includes "recruitment or transportation and, after their entry into Canada, the receipt or harbouring of those persons."

153 *Ibid.*, s. 120.

154 *Ibid.*, s. 121(1)(b).

155 *Ibid.*, s. 121(2).

156 *R. v. Ng*, 2006 BCPC 111. The accused was eventually acquitted of human trafficking, though he was convicted of human smuggling under s. 117 of *IRPA*: *R. v. Ng*, 2007 BCPC 204.

157 *Ibid.* at para. 10 (2006 BCPC).

rival of the persons in Canada would constitute the required "real and substantial connection."[158] Moreover, it is the *Code* provisions which are clearly designed to implement the *Human Trafficking Protocol*.

Another oddity in the *IRPA* context is section 135 of that Act, which provides,

> An act or omission that would by reason of this Act be punishable as an offence if committed in Canada is, if committed outside Canada, an offence under this Act and may be tried and punished in Canada.

This is a rather remarkable jurisdictional provision, which has the effect of exerting extraterritorial jurisdiction over every offence under *IRPA*. It resembles universal jurisdiction, although the argument could be made that the *IRPA* offences are all tied to Canada's immigration and refugee regime and thus extraterritoriality may be justified as an exercise of the protective principle. The effect on the human trafficking offence is reasonably modest; an individual who, in another country, organizes the trafficking of persons *into Canada* may be prosecuted in Canada for so doing. This level of jurisdiction at an international law level is consistent with the concept of "transnational crime" as defined in the *TOC Convention* (specifically article 3(2)(a)), and as an exercise of *qualified territorial* jurisdiction, it is certainly commensurate with *Libman*. If the extradition arrangement with the foreign state where the offender is located is amenable to extradition for extraterritorial offences, and/or if that state is a party to the *TOC Convention*, then extradition is a viable option. However, all of this could be accomplished under the *Criminal Code* provisions.

4) Smuggling of Migrants

a) International Law

Migration of persons from one state to another is certainly not a new phenomenon, nor is unauthorized or illegal entry by migrants into target states. The Migrant *Smuggling Protocol*[159] to the *TOC Convention* responded to the need of states to deal with a relatively new practice: the for-profit smuggling of migrants by organized criminal groups, as contrasted with any illegal entry or other activities of migrants themselves. Driven by the pressures of globalization, increased poverty,[160] improved transportation and communication technologies, and increasing strin-

---

158 See, generally, Chapter 8.

159 Above note 54.

160 See Report of the Independent Expert on Human Rights and Extreme Poverty, UN Doc. E/CN.4/2003/52 at paras. 30–35.

gency of immigration laws in developed states, the smuggling of people is a fast-growing practice that involves many transnational organized crime groups throughout the world.[161] It occurs via land, sea, and air, and typically involves persons from Asia, Africa, and South America being smuggled into Western Europe or Canada and the US via various routes.[162] There is a great deal of potential overlap between persons who are smuggled and those who are trafficked, since it is all too easy for the former to end up as the latter.

The *Smuggling Protocol*[163] defines "smuggling of migrants" as "the procurement, in order to obtain, directly or indirectly, a financial or other material benefit, of the illegal entry of a person into a State Party of which the person is not a national or a permanent resident."[164] "Illegal entry" is defined as "crossing borders without complying with the necessary requirements for legal entry into the receiving State."[165] States are obliged to criminalize smuggling[166] and producing,[167] procuring, providing, or possessing[168] a fraudulent travel or identity document,[169] or enabling a person to stay in the state illegally.[170] Because migrants are often smuggled by sea, Part II of the *Smuggling Protocol* contains provisions regarding enforcement against vessels suspected of migrant smuggling.[171] These provisions are consistent with the consent-based, exclusive high-seas flag state jurisdiction under the *United Nations Convention on the Law of the Sea (UNCLOS)*[172] and share features with the similar regime under the 1988 *Vienna Narcotics Convention*[173] and the International Maritime Organization (IMO) Interim Measures,[174] including cooperation obligations as between state parties.[175]

---

161 Lenore Richards, "Trafficking in Misery: Human Migrant Smuggling and Organized Crime" (2001) 63:3 Gazette 19.

162 See INTERPOL, "People Smuggling," online: www.interpol.int/Public/THB/PeopleSmuggling/Default.asp.

163 Above note 54.

164 *Ibid.*, art. 3(a).

165 *Ibid.*, art. 3(b).

166 *Ibid.*, art. 6(1)(a).

167 *Ibid.*, art. 6(1)(b)(i).

168 *Ibid.*, art. 6(1)(b)(ii).

169 Defined, *ibid.*, art. 3(c).

170 *Ibid.*, art. 6(1)(c).

171 *Ibid.*, arts. 7–9.

172 1833 U.N.T.S. 3.

173 Above note 13.

174 IMO Doc. MSC/Circ896, Annex. See McClean, above note 58 at 399–401.

175 It is unfortunate that the negotiating parties missed the opportunity to provide within the treaty the consent to board, inspect, and enforce against migrant smuggling ships. On the other hand, as Bantekas and Nash note, "[I]t would

As with the *Human Trafficking Protocol*, protection of victims and the human rights implications of migrant smuggling were a focus of the negotiations, and this can be seen in the text.[176] Article 5 provides that migrants cannot be prosecuted simply for having been smuggled, or for the "identity documents" and "enablement" offences in article 6(1)(b) and (c). The return/repatriation provisions regarding illegal migrants are less generous than the protections accorded to trafficked persons, who were seen by the negotiating states to be more "victimized" than migrants.[177] Otherwise, the *Smuggling Protocol* contains a nearly identical cooperation regime to that of the *Human Trafficking Protocol*.[178]

b) Canadian Implementing Legislation

The government of Canada has been active in investigating human smuggling cases, and has cooperated a great deal with the US authorities.[179] The smuggling offence is implemented by section 117 of *IRPA*, which incorporates by reference the parts of that *Act* dealing with illegal entry (so as to satisfy article 3(b) of the Protocol). The smuggling of fewer than 10 persons is a hybrid offence,[180] while smuggling 10 or more is an indictable offence for which the penalty is a maximum of life imprisonment or fine of $1 million, or both.[181] As with human trafficking under section 118, committing the offence to facilitate organized crime activities is an aggravating factor for sentencing.[182]

The false documents offences are implemented by sections 122 and 123 of *IRPA*. As with human trafficking, jurisdiction over the offences is extended on an extraterritorial basis.[183] Some of the border measures suggested under article 11 of the Protocol appear to be implemented by section 148 of *IRPA*, which sets out obligations of owners/operators of

---

not be inconsistent with the *Protocol* and *UNCLOS* to assimilate a smuggling vessel to a slave vessel, thereby granting the right to any other ship to liberate the migrants, even without the consent of the Flag State" (above note 47 at 238, footnote omitted).

176 See, for example, above note 54, art. 4. See, generally, Tom Obokata, "Smuggling of Human Beings from a Human Rights Perspective: Obligations of Non-State and State Actors under International Human Rights Law" (2005) 17 Int'l J. Refugee L. 394.

177 See Gillian Blackell, "The Protocols on Trafficking in Persons and Smuggling in Migrants" in ICCLR&CJP, above note 52, 105 at 116–17.

178 Above note 54.

179 See, for details, Public Safety Canada, *US-Canada Bi-National Assessment of Trafficking in Persons* (2006), online: www.publicsafety.gc.ca/prg/le/_fl/1666i-en.pdf.

180 Above note 152, s. 117(2)(a).

181 *Ibid.*, s. 117(2)(b).

182 *Ibid.*, s. 121(1)(b).

183 *Ibid.*, s. 135; see Section C(3)(B), above.

vehicles and transportation facilities as regards passengers and their documents. At least with regards to the criminal law and enforcement obligations, Canadian implementation is reasonably fulsome.

5) Illicit Manufacturing of and Trading in Firearms

a) International Law

The international legal regime regarding the illicit manufacturing and trafficking of firearms is best described as a work in progress—albeit one that is the focus of intense activity by states and international organizations, particularly the UN, at the time of writing. This is in part because the proliferation of small arms and light weapons (SALW) contributes to the violence level of states which are in conflict, and makes both conflict resolution and post-conflict reconciliation more difficult. It also contributes to crime problems in states at large, and of late particular concern has been generated about the acquisition of SALW by terrorists.[184] The focus is on the illicit trade in weapons and the various administrative and law enforcement measures which need to be taken to combat it, most notably the marking of weapons, record-keeping, controlling imports/exports, and maintaining the ability to trace weapons. In 2001, the United Nations adopted the Programme of Action to Prevent, Combat, and Eradicate the Illicit Trade in Small Arms and Light Weapons in All Its Aspects[185] as an umbrella initiative under which to continue work on the issue, which work has proceeded apace.[186]

While the *Firearms Protocol*[187] to the *TOC Convention* was the first instrument adopted to deal with this criminal activity at the global level, it was preceded by the 1997 *Inter-American Convention against the Illicit Trafficking and Production of Firearms, Ammunition, Explosives and Other Related Materials*.[188] The Organisation for Security and Co-operation in Europe (OSCE) has also been engaged with the SALW issue

---

184 See, generally, James Hayes, "The United Nations Firearms Protocol" in ICCLR&CLJ, above note 52, 125–145.

185 *Report of the United Nations Conference on the Illicit Trade in Small Arms and Light Weapons in All Its Aspects*, New York, 9–20 July 2001, UN Doc. A/CONF.192/15.

186 See E. Kytömäki & V. Yankey-Wayne, *Implementing the United Nations Programme of Action on Small Arms and Light Weapons: Analysis of the Reports Submitted by States in 2003* (New York: United Nations, 2004); UNGA Res. 60/68 (6 January 2006) and UNGA Res. 60/81 (11 January 2006); Secretary-General's Report to the Security Council on Small Arms, UN Doc. S/2006/109 (17 February 2006). Developments can be followed online: http://disarmament.un.org/cab.

187 Above note 54.

188 AG/RES. 1445 (XXVII-O/97) [*OAS Convention*]; not yet in Can. T.S. See online: www.oas.org/juridico/english/sigs/a-63.html.

for some time,[189] and a group of 40 mostly OECD states have been involved in the "Wassenaar Arrangement" to coordinate export controls on SALW for over a decade.[190] Additionally, the Security Council has issued several resolutions which prohibit the transfer of arms (including SALW) to certain states because of the security implications.[191]

The *Firearms Protocol* is more of a first step in what is foreseen to be a long engagement with the suppression of illicit weapons and the social problems they cause. The import of the *Protocol* is aptly described by the UN Office on Drugs and Crime:

> By ratifying the Protocol, States make a commitment to adopt a series of crime-control measures and implement in their domestic legal order three sets of normative provisions: the first one relates to the establishment of criminal offences related to illegal manufacturing of, and trafficking in, firearms on the basis of the Protocol requirements and definitions; the second to a system of government authorizations or licensing intending to ensure legitimate manufacturing of, and trafficking in, firearms; and the third one to the marking and tracing of firearms.[192]

Most important for present purposes are the criminalization provisions, which basically require states to ensure it is a criminal offence to manufacture and deal in firearms (and their associated components and ammunition) without being properly licensed to do so by the state; administrative measures for regulating firearms are the subject of part II of the Protocol. Accordingly, "illicit manufacturing" is defined as manufacturing firearms from illicitly trafficked parts,[193] unlicensed manufacturing,[194] or manufacturing weapons without marking them.[195] "Illicit trafficking" is defined as the import, export, transfer, or sale otherwise of firearms either without a license to do so from the state or if the firearms are unmarked.[196]

As with all of the Protocol crimes, the goal is to attach liability to these offences when conducted transnationally and in the organized

---

189 See OSCE, *OSCE Document on Small Arms and Light Weapons*, FSC.DOC/1/00 (24 November 2000); *Handbook of Best Practices on Small Arms and Light Weapons* (Vienna: OSCE Secretariat, 2003).

190 See, generally, online: www.wassenaar.org.

191 For example, S/RES/1596 (2005) and previous resolutions cited therein, regarding the Democratic Republic of Congo; S/RES/1572 (2004), regarding Côte d'Ivoire.

192 Online: www.unodc.org/unodc/en/treaties/CTOC/index.html.

193 Above note 54, art. 3(d)(i).

194 *Ibid.*, art. 3(d)(ii).

195 *Ibid.*, art. 3(d)(iii). The marking of firearms is dealt with in art. 8.

196 *Ibid.*, art. 3(e).

crime setting,[197] and the Protocol specifically exempts state-to-state transfer of weapons in the interests of national security.[198] Article 5 requires the criminalization of illicit manufacturing[199] and illicit trafficking[200] of firearms, their parts, components, and ammunition, as well as falsifying, illicitly obliterating, removing, or altering the markings on firearms.[201] Article 6 has a fairly weak obligation for states to have measures in place for confiscation, seizure, and destruction or other disposal of firearms.[202]

b) Canadian Implementing Legislation

Canada's domestic framework for control of SALW is as broad and diffuse as the international law framework surveyed above. Canada has signed but not yet ratified the *Organization of American States Convention* (*OAS Convention*)[203] and the *Firearms Protocol*,[204] though ratification of each is most likely awaiting the coming into force of the *Firearms Marking Regulations*[205] to the *Firearms Act*.[206] Canada is also a participant in both the UN Programme of Action and the Wassenaar Arrangement.

The key pieces of Canadian legislation are:

1) the *Firearms Act* and regulations thereto,[207] which set out the overall regulatory framework with licensing and regulation requirements;
2) the *Criminal Code*,[208] which contains a range of offences including possession,[209] trafficking[210] and illegal import or export,[211] and has search and seizure provisions,[212] and also provides definitions which are incorporated by reference into the *Firearms Act*;
3) the *Export and Import Permits Act*,[213] which provides for the restriction of import and export of various items, including arms and mu-

---

197 *Ibid.*, art. 4(1).
198 *Ibid.*, art. 4(2).
199 *Ibid.*, art. 5(1)(a).
200 *Ibid.*, art. 5(1)(b).
201 *Ibid.*, art. 5(1)(c).
202 *Ibid.*, arts. 6(1) & (2).
203 Above note 188.
204 See online: www.unodc.org/unodc/en/treaties/CTOC/signatures.html.
205 S.O.R./2004-275, which came into force on 1 December 2009 (s. 6).
206 S.C. 1995, c. 39.
207 *Ibid.*
208 Above note 109.
209 *Ibid.*, especially ss. 91, 92, and 95.
210 *Ibid.*, ss. 99–101.
211 *Ibid.*, ss. 103–104.
212 *Ibid.*, ss. 117.02–117.06.
213 R.S.C. 1985, c. E-19.

nitions, as well as for a range of offences for importing or exporting controlled goods without being licensed to do so;[214]

4) the *United Nations Act*,[215] under which the government makes regulations to comply with Security Council resolutions that bar the export of arms and munitions to specified states;[216] and

5) the *Defence Production Act*,[217] which *inter alia* regulates access to certain controlled goods, including firearms, and establishes offences for possession or transfer of them.[218]

6) Corruption

a) International Law

While none would venture that corruption within both the public and private sectors of society is anything new, there has been recent recognition of its destructiveness for harmonious economic relations between and within states, and its distortion of human rights norms and the overall perception of the rule of law among the populaces of states generally.[219] In developing states, corrupt practices can result in the diversion and misappropriation of foreign aid resources. All of this has led to a spate of anti-corruption activity since the 1990s,[220] among states,[221] international[222] and inter-governmental[223] organizations, non-governmental organizations (NGOs),[224] and academic insti-

---

214 *Ibid.*, ss. 13–21.

215 R.S.C. 1985, c. U-2.

216 For example, *United Nations Sudan Regulations*, S.O.R./2004-197. These regulations typically make it an offence to export or otherwise transfer arms to the named state, with jurisdiction on both the territorial and nationality bases.

217 R.S.C. 1985, c. D-1.

218 *Ibid.* See ss. 37, 44, and 45 and the Schedule to s. 35.

219 See World Bank, "Anticorruption," online: http://go.worldbank.org/QYR-WVXVH40.

220 For a recent but US-focused survey, see Margaret Ayres, ed., "Developments in U.S. and International Efforts to Prevent Corruption" (2007) 41 Int'l Lawyer 597. See also Indira Carr, "Fighting Corruption through Regional and International Conventions: A Satisfactory Solution?" (2007) 15 Eur. J. Crime, Crim. L. & Crim Just. 121.

221 See Carr, *ibid.*

222 For example, the United Nations Global Compact, online: www.unglobalcompact.org.

223 For example, the European-based Group of States against Corruption (GRECO), online: www.coe.int/t/dghl/monitoring/greco/default_en.asp.

224 For example, TRACE International, online: www.traceinternational.org; Global Witness, online: www.globalwitness.org; the International Chamber of Commerce, online: www.iccwbo.org/policy/anticorruption/.

tutions.[225] Transparency International, one of the leading NGOs in this area, has defined corruption as follows:

> Corruption is operationally defined as the misuse of entrusted power for private gain. TI further differentiates between "according to rule" corruption and "against the rule" corruption. Facilitation payments, where a bribe is paid to receive preferential treatment for something that the bribe receiver is required to do by law, constitute the former. The latter, on the other hand, is a bribe paid to obtain services the bribe receiver is prohibited from providing.[226]

The first major international treaty initiative was the *1996 Inter-American Convention against Corruption (OAS Convention against Corruption)*,[227] followed closely by the 1998 OECD-sponsored *Convention on Combating Bribery of Foreign Public Officials in International Business Transactions (OECD Convention against Corruption)*,[228] and European[229] and African[230] instruments. The most significant treaty to date has been the 2003 *United Nations Convention against Corruption (UNCAC)*,[231] which currently has 140 signatories and 136 parties.[232] This treaty came about because of a perception after the conclusion of the *TOC Convention* that corruption was within the bailiwick of organized crime, but was such a systemic problem that it demanded a specialized, stand-alone treaty—a means for compelling and assisting states to address the root causes of corruption, for which article 8 of the *TOC Convention* or a further protocol would have been inadequate. While the earlier treaties were primarily geared towards combating corruption in the public sphere (by way of promoting transparency of government operations and information), institutionalizing ethics and

---

225 For example, the Jack and Mae Nathanson Centre on Transnational Human Rights, Crime and Security, online: www.yorku.ca/nathanson/default.htm.

226 Transparency International, "Frequently Asked Questions about Corruption," online: www.transparency.org/news_room/faq/corruption_faq.

227 Reprinted (1996) 35 I.L.M. 724, online: www.oas.org/juridico/english/treaties/ b-58.html [*OAS Convention against Corruption*]. In force 6 March 1997; ratification status online: www.oas.org/juridico/english/Sigs/b-58.html. See, generally, "The Experts Roundtable: A Hemispheric Approach to Combating Corruption" (1999–2000) 15 Am. U. Int'l L. Rev. 759.

228 Above note 91, currently 38 parties.

229 The *Criminal Law Convention on Corruption*, 27 January 1999, Eur. T.S. No. 173, and the *Civil Law Convention on Corruption*, 4 November 1999, Eur. T.S. No. 174.

230 *African Union Convention on Preventing and Combating Corruption*, 12 July 2003, online: www.africa-union.org/Official_documents/Treaties_%20Conventions_ %20Protocols/Convention%20on%20Combating%20Corruption.pdf.

231 Above note 55.

232 See online: www.unodc.org/unodc/en/treaties/CAC/index.html.

conflict of interest avoidance, and suppressing bribery, the *UNCAC* also deals with private sector corruption.

The two major instruments for present purposes are the *OECD Convention* and *UNCAC*. While there is some overlap between the two, an important breakthrough made with the *UNCAC* was agreement to focus on the demand side of corruption (e.g., bribe solicitation, extortion), whereas the *OECD Convention* had addressed only the supply side (i.e., bribery). The *OECD Convention* requires states to criminalize "bribery of foreign public officials," which is defined as

> intentionally to offer, promise or give any undue pecuniary or other advantage, whether directly or through intermediaries, to a foreign public official, for that official or for a third party, in order that the official act or refrain from acting in relation to the performance of official duties, in order to obtain or retain business or other improper advantage in the conduct of international business.[233]

There are also broad definitions of "foreign public official,"[234] "foreign country,"[235] and the scope of acting/refraining to act within the scope of official duties.[236] Legal persons are to be made liable if possible under each state's domestic law.[237] Jurisdiction must be exercised at least on a territorial basis,[238] and any state party which has "jurisdiction to prosecute its nationals for offences committed abroad" is required to do so.[239] Unlike, for example, the *OAS Convention against Corruption*,[240] the *OECD Convention* does not contain an "extradite or prosecute" jurisdictional provision.

The *UNCAC*[241] is similar to the *TOC Convention* and protocols, in that it is broad in scope and evinces an intention to be not only a classic

---

233 Above note 91, art. 1(1).

234 *Ibid.*, art. 1(4)(a).

235 *Ibid.*, art. 1(4)(b).

236 *Ibid.*, art. 1(4)(c).

237 *Ibid.*, art. 2.

238 *Ibid.*, art. 4(1).

239 *Ibid.*, art. 4(2). The Commentary to the *OECD Convention* (online: www.oecd. org/document/1/0,3343,en_2649_37447_2048129_1_1_1_37447,00.html) makes clear that "jurisdiction" (as well as a reference in the article to domestic "principles") refers to the usual decision-making process of states regarding the bases on which they choose to exercise jurisdiction. Thus, a state such as Canada, which does not ordinarily exercise nationality jurisdiction, will still be in compliance with this article if it uses only territoriality; this is, indeed, what Canada does: see Section C(6)(b), below in this chapter.

240 Above note 227, art. V(3).

241 See, generally, Michael Kubiciel, "Core Criminal Law Provisions in the *United Nations Convention against Corruption*" (2009) 9 Int'l Crim. L. Rev. 139.

"suppression convention" but to enhance and promote both cooperation and technical assistance, as well as to institutionalize prevention measures,[242] in part by promoting "integrity, accountability and proper management of public affairs and public property."[243] The state parties are required to, or must consider, criminalizing a wide range of public sector corruption offences, including bribery of national public officials,[244] bribery of foreign public officials and officials of public international organizations,[245] embezzlement, misappropriation or other diversion of property by a public official,[246] trading in influence,[247] and abuse of function and illicit enrichment by public officials.[248] There are permissive articles towards criminalizing bribery and embezzlement in the private sector.[249] Each party must criminalize the laundering of proceeds of corruption crimes[250] and must have a regime in place for the freezing, seizure, and confiscation of proceeds, property, equipment, or other instrumentalities linked to the crimes.[251] There are also mandatory obligations for obstruction of justice offences,[252] and legal persons are to be made liable if possible under each state's domestic law.[253] In terms of jurisdiction, states are required to exert territorial[254] and flag ship/registered aircraft jurisdiction,[255] and may use the passive personality,[256] expanded nationality,[257] and protective[258] principles. There is also an extradite or prosecute obligation.[259]

The *UNCAC* has a substantial set of provisions regarding various forms of mutual assistance,[260] cooperation, and technical assistance[261]

---

242 Above note 55, arts. 5–14.
243 *Ibid.*, art. 1(c).
244 *Ibid.*, art. 15.
245 *Ibid.*, art. 16.
246 *Ibid.*, art. 17.
247 *Ibid.*, art. 18.
248 *Ibid.*, arts. 19 & 20, respectively.
249 *Ibid.*, arts. 21 & 22, respectively.
250 *Ibid.*, art. 23.
251 *Ibid.*, art. 31.
252 *Ibid.*, art. 25.
253 *Ibid.*, art. 26.
254 There is also a specific qualified territoriality jurisdiction accorded to certain inchoate money-laundering offences: *Ibid.*, art. 42(2)(c).
255 *Ibid.*, art. 42(1).
256 *Ibid.*, art. 42(2)(a).
257 *Ibid.*, art. 42(2)(b).
258 *Ibid.*, art. 42(2)(d).
259 *Ibid.*, art. 42(4).
260 *Ibid.*, arts. 43–50.
261 *Ibid.*, arts. 60–62.

which clearly build on the scheme under the *TOC Convention* and *Protocols*. The unique feature of the treaty is the scheme regarding asset recovery,[262] which the *UNODC* described as a "major breakthrough" and a matter of significant concern to developing states whose assets (including aid) are often plundered by corrupt local officials.[263] Article 51 states that the return of assets which have been taken out of a state by way of corruption offences is "a fundamental principle of this Convention," and the asset recovery chapter of the treaty provides both for the return of state assets and for access to the courts of party states by victims of corruption crimes, in order to allow the return of assets taken from them. There are also detailed provisions obliging states to confiscate and return assets upon request of partner states.

b) Canadian Implementing Legislation[264]

Canada has been a participant in various anti-corruption initiatives on the international level and was actively involved in the negotiations leading to the conclusion of the *UNCAC*.[265] Canada is a party to the *OAS* and *OECD Conventions*, and has signed but not ratified the *UNCAC*.

The *OECD Convention* is implemented by the *Corruption of Foreign Public Officials Act (CFPOA)*.[266] The *Act* contains definitions of "foreign public official" and "foreign state" that comport with the *Convention*, and liability of corporations is provided for in the definition of "person."[267] Section 3 of the Act criminalizes the giving of any money or other consideration to a foreign public official as consideration for an act or omission in the course of her duties, or to induce such an act or omission. The offender must intend to obtain or retain an advantage in the course of business.[268] The same section provides exemptions for certain kinds of payments, such as payments that are legally compulsory, go towards the official's expenses, or are paid for licenses, permits, or as service fees, and so on.[269] Section 67.5 of the *Income Tax Act*[270] pro-

---

262 *Ibid.*, arts. 51–59.

263 See *UNCAC*, above note 55.

264 See Lori Ann Wanlin, "The Gap between Promise and Practice in the Global Fight against Corruption" (2006) 6 Asper Rev. Int'l Bus. & Trade L. 209.

265 See Foreign Affairs and International Trade Canada, "Corruption," online: www.dfait-maeci.gc.ca/internationalcrime/corruption-en.asp. This page also contains a number of links to anti-corruption organizations and resources.

266 S.C. 1998, c. 34 [*CFPOA*].

267 *Ibid.*, s. 2.

268 *Ibid.*, s. 3(1).

269 *Ibid.*, ss. 3(3) & (4).

270 R.S.C. 1985 (5th Supp.), c. 1.

vides that payments made in contravention of section 3 of the *CFPOA* are not deductible.

Jurisdiction under the *CFPOA* is territorial, as no explicit grant of extraterritorial jurisdiction is made in the statute. Article 4 of the *OECD Convention* does require jurisdiction over the offence when it is "committed in whole or in part in its territory," and the OECD's commentary to that article states that territoriality "should be interpreted broadly so that an extensive physical connection to the bribery act is not required."[271] In its ongoing review and consultations with the OECD regarding the implementation of the Convention,[272] Canada has maintained that its approach to qualified territoriality under *Libman*[273] provides a sufficiently broad approach.[274] This argument has been challenged by the OECD's reviewers, who have found that the *Libman* approach requires "substantial links" between the offence and Canada and is "in fact much narrower than most parties to the Convention."[275] The reviewers have also criticized Canada's refusal to exert nationality-based jurisdiction, as it is the only state party to the Convention that has not done so.[276] To date there has been only one conviction under the *CFPOA*, which was reached by way of a guilty plea.[277]

Canada ratified the *UNCAC* on 2 October 2007, having earlier made amendments to the *Criminal Code*[278] in order to implement the

---

271 Commentary, above note 239 at para. 25.

272 For background, see Foreign Affairs and International Trade Canada, Sixth Report to Parliament (21 October 2005), online: www.dfait-maeci.gc.ca/foreign_policy/internationalcrime-old/6-report_parliament-en.asp.

273 Above note 68. See, generally, Chapter 8.

274 See OECD, Directorate for Financial and Enterprise Affairs, *Canada: Phase 2: Report on the Application of the Convention on Combating Bribery of Foreign Public Officials in International Business Transactions* (25 March 2004), online: www.oecd.org/dataoecd/20/50/31643002.pdf.

275 See OECD, Directorate for Financial and Enterprise Affairs, *Follow-up Report on the Implementation of the Phase 2 Recommendations* (21 June 2006), online: www.oecd.org/dataoecd/5/6/36984779.pdf at 5. In my view, this is based on a misreading of *Libman*, above note 68, though this misreading seems to have been facilitated by the information provided to the reviewers during Phase 2; see *Phase 2 Report, ibid.* at 32.

276 *Ibid.* As the *Follow-up Report* notes, Canadian officials have responded that nationality jurisdiction is usually only exerted when there is a treaty-based obligation to do so. This is not strictly true, as there are a number of treaties where, like the *OECD Convention*, nationality jurisdiction is permissive, but Canada has made provision for it nonetheless. See, generally, Chapter 8.

277 *R. v. Watts*, [2005] A.J. No. 568 (Q.B.).

278 Above note 109.

Convention.[279] The *Code* now contains two distinct offences related to the bribery of judicial officers[280] and other justice system officials.[281] Section 121 was amended to implement the offences in articles 15 (bribery of national public officials), 18 (trading in influence), and 19 (abuse of functions) of the *UNCAC*.[282] Article 16 (bribery of foreign public officials/officials of international organizations) is implemented by the *CFPOA*, while article 23 (money laundering) is implemented via Canada's general legislation on that topic.[283] The embezzlement crimes, both public (article 17) and private (article 22), seem to be covered by the *Code*'s general theft provisions,[284] while private sector bribery (article 21) is implemented via section 426(1)(a). When it signed the *OAS Convention against Corruption*, Canada submitted a "Statement of Understanding" to the effect that the offence of illicit enrichment in article IX of that Convention "would be contrary to the presumption of innocence guaranteed by Canada's Constitution,"[285] and that it would not implement this offence. Canada is thus unlikely to implement the corresponding offence in article 20 of the *UNCAC* when it ratifies that treaty. The obstruction of justice offences are implemented by the same *Code* provisions covered under the treatment of the *TOC Convention*, described in Section C(2)(b),above in this chapter.

Various amendments were made to section 490 of the *Criminal Code* to implement the *UNCAC* obligations regarding confiscation of proceeds of crime. The asset recovery scheme appears to be implemented by way of the *Mutual Legal Assistance in Criminal Matters Act*,[286] which gives the courts the power to order enforcement in Canada of foreign orders for seizure and forfeiture.[287]

---

279 S.C. 2007, c. 13, in force 31 May 2007.
280 *Ibid.*, s. 119.
281 *Ibid.*, s. 120.
282 *Ibid.*, s. 123 also extends these offences to municipal government officials.
283 See Section F(2), below in this chapter.
284 Above note 109, ss. 322–34.
285 OAS, General Information on the *Inter-American Convention against Corruption*, online: www.oas.org/juridico/english/Sigs/b-58.html. Presumably this is because the offence reverses the onus of proving the source of a "significant increase in assets" onto the accused.
286 Above note 123.
287 *Ibid.*, ss. 9.3 & 9.4.

D. TERRORISM

In the current socio-political climate, the fact that terrorism is a focal point of international legal interest will come as no surprise to the reader. For good or for ill (or some combination of both), the attacks of 11 September 2001 galvanized the international community into increasing the level of cooperation and coordination of terrorism suppression efforts among states. The UN is the most significant player in these efforts, having sponsored and brought into being a number of the prevailing anti-terrorism treaties.[288] In the wake of the 2001 attacks, the Security Council established[289] the Counter-Terrorism Committee (CTC), which monitors member state implementation of both Security Council resolutions and the global terrorism treaties.[290] On 8 September 2006, the UNGA unanimously adopted the United Nations Global Counter-Terrorism Strategy,[291] which set out an ambitious multi-pronged plan to suppress terrorism, deal with its causes and conditions, and promote adherence to human rights norms in so doing. Of particular note here, states were encouraged to become parties to the multilateral terrorism conventions, to implement all Security Council and UNGA resolutions regarding terrorism, and to continue the efforts at reaching agreement on a comprehensive terrorism convention.[292] The UNODC is active in promoting these and other levels of cooperation, and providing technical assistance to states.[293]

The major features and controversies of the current state of international law regarding terrorism are described in Chapter 6. This section will review the major terrorism suppression conventions[294] and

---

288 Andrea Gioia, "The UN Conventions on the Prevention and Suppression of International Terrorism" in Giuseppe Nesi, ed., *International Cooperation in Counter-Terrorism* (Aldershot, UK: Ashgate, 2006) 3.

289 Through SC Res. 1373 (28 September 2001).

290 Online: www.un.org/sc/ctc/.

291 UNGA Res. 60/288 (8 September 2006), online: www.unodc.org/pdf/terrorism/symposium/Symposium-en.pdf (opening statement).

292 *Ibid.* The resolution explicitly notes the connections between terrorism and other forms of transnational crime, and encourages states to become parties to the *TOC Convention* and *Protocols*, the Financial Action Task Force (FATF) Recommendations on Money Laundering and Terrorism Financing, and so on. The continuing work on the comprehensive terrorism convention can be monitored online: www.un.org/law/terrorism/index.html.

293 See UNODC, "Counter-Terrorism," online: www.unodc.org/unodc/en/terrorism/the-role-of-unodc-in-terrorism-prevention.html.

294 See, as well, Reuven Young, "Defining Terrorism: The Evolution of Terrorism as a Legal Concept in International Law and its Influence on Definitions in Domestic Legislation" (2006) 29 B.C. Int'l & Comp. L. Rev. 23.

examine Canada's implementation of each, and will also assess Canada's new transnational terrorism offences. The focus will be on the criminalization aspects, and thus not all of Canada's international commitments that touch on terrorism will be canvassed.[295]

1) Civil Aviation

As the 9/11 attacks tragically illustrated, the use of commercial airplanes as tools of terrorism is a significant danger.[296] However, international law regarding attacks on airplanes and airport facilities has a history that well pre-dates the 2001 incidents.[297] The first major international instrument was the *Convention for the Suppression of Unlawful Seizure of Aircraft* (*Hague Convention*),[298] which was concluded in The Hague in 1970 under the auspices of the International Civil Aviation Organization (ICAO). Concerned essentially with hijacking, this treaty obliged state parties to criminalize the seizure of control of an aircraft in flight, "by force or threat thereof, or by any other form of intimidation" (or attempt or complicity in this act).[299] States must establish jurisdiction over both the proscribed offence and any other act of violence against passengers or crew committed during the offence when the offences occur on board a plane registered in the state, when the plane lands in the state, where a lessee of the plane is connected to the state, or where the state apprehends the offender on its territory.[300] The *Hague Convention* was the first of the modern suppression conventions and displays a prototypical version of the elements which are now common among modern instru-

---

295 For example, the 1963 *Tokyo Convention on Offences and Certain Other Acts Committed on Board Aircraft*, above note 11, is often listed as an anti-terrorism treaty, but is really designed to allocate jurisdiction for crimes committed on aircraft and is examined briefly in Chapter 8. Also, the 1991 *Convention on the Marking of Plastic Explosives for the Purpose of Detection*, Can. T.S. 1998 No. 54, is really a regulatory regime and does not involve significant criminalization.

296 For an argument that they also demonstrate the inadequacy of the current terrorism suppression conventions, see John P. Grant, "Beyond the *Montreal Convention*" (2005) 36 Case W. Res. J. Int'l L. 453.

297 See, generally, Edward McWhinney, *Aerial Piracy and International Terrorism: The Illegal Diversion of Aircraft and International Law*, 2d rev. ed. (Dordrecht: Martinus Nijhoff, 1987); Christopher Joyner & Robert Friedlander, "International Civil Aviation" in M. Cherif Bassiouni, ed., *International Criminal Law*, 2d ed., vol. 1 (Ardsley, NY: Transnational, 1999) at 837.

298 860 U.N.T.S. 105, Can. T.S. 1972 No. 23 [*Hague Convention*]. Currently 183 parties; see online: http://untreaty.un.org/cod/terrorism/terrorism_tableupdate-January2009.pdf.

299 *Ibid.*, art. 1.

300 *Ibid.*, art. 4.

ments: a custodial universal jurisdiction provision,[301] an obligation to apprehend and investigate,[302] an extradite or prosecute obligation,[303] and obligations regarding extradition and mutual legal assistance.[304]

The *Hague Convention* was followed quickly by the *Convention for the Suppression of Unlawful Acts against the Safety of Civil Aviation* (*Montreal Convention*),[305] concluded in Montreal in 1971. The goal of this treaty was to supplement the narrower hijacking crime in the *Hague Convention*, and accordingly it proscribes various violent acts which might damage, destroy, or endanger the safety of an aircraft in flight, including the placing of dangerous devices or substances, destroying or damaging air navigation facilities, or communicating false information.[306] Jurisdiction follows the territorial principle as well as the other bases set out in the *Hague Convention*,[307] and the other features correspond in a similar manner. The *Montreal Convention* was later supplemented by the *Protocol for the Suppression of Unlawful Acts of Violence at Airports Serving International Civil Aviation*, concluded at Montreal in 1988,[308] which extended the provisions of the *Montreal Convention* to cover violent crimes, "using any device, substance or weapon," committed at or against airports and aircraft not in service.[309]

As is typical with the Canadian approach to the suppression conventions, the civil aviation treaties are implemented by combining offence provisions (which automatically have territorial jurisdiction attaching to them) with a jurisdictional provision. Section 76 of the *Criminal Code*[310] criminalizes hijacking, while section 77 provides for a range of offences which endanger the safety of an aircraft or airport. Section 7(2) of the *Code* provides that any of these offences are deemed

---

301 *Ibid.*, art. 4(2).

302 *Ibid.*, art. 6.

303 *Ibid.*, art. 7. It is worth noting as background that this obligation, which appears in virtually every suppression convention, represents a certain compromise; states are not actually obliged to extradite or prosecute in every case, but rather must "submit the case to its competent authorities for the purpose of prosecution." At the Hague negotiations, it was clear that this wording was deliberate, a means of assuaging the fears of states that did not wish to remove prosecutorial discretion completely. See Gillian White, "The *Hague Convention for the Suppression of Unlawful Seizure of Aircraft*" (1971) 6 Rev. Int'l Comm. Jur. 38 at 42.

304 *Ibid.*, arts. 8 and 10.

305 Above note 25.

306 *Ibid.*, art. 1.

307 *Ibid.*, art. 5.

308 1589 U.N.T.S. 474, Can. T.S. 1993 No. 8. Currently 167 parties; online: http://untreaty.un.org/cod/terrorism/terrorism_tableupdateJanuary2009.pdf.

309 *Ibid.*, art. II.

310 Above note 109.

to have been committed in Canada if the perpetrator is present in Canada after the commission of the offence, which covers off both custodial universal jurisdiction and the obligations (in article 4 of the *Montreal Convention* and article 5 of the *Hague Convention*) to establish jurisdiction where the aircraft on board which the offence takes place lands in Canada with the offender still onboard. There are also definitions of "flight," "in flight,"[311] and "in service"[312] which correspond with the Conventions.

2) Maritime Terrorism

While the international law on piracy has been established for centuries,[313] modern international law instruments have been developed to deal with the specific threats posed by terrorist attacks on ships and maritime installations. The first efforts in this area were developed in response to the October 1985 hijacking of the Italian ship *Achille Lauro* by Palestinian terrorists, which resulted in the death of an American passenger. This incident spurred the UNGA to make a resolution asking the International Maritime Organization (IMO) to recommend appropriate action,[314] and the latter organization sponsored negotiations[315] which eventually led to the 1988 conclusion of the *Convention for the Suppression of Unlawful Acts against the Safety of Maritime Navigation (SUA Convention)*[316] and an optional *Protocol for the Suppression of Unlawful Acts Against the Safety of Fixed Platforms Located on the Continental Shelf (SUA Protocol)*.[317]

The *SUA Convention*[318] applies to "ships," defined as "a vessel of any type whatsoever not permanently attached to the sea-bed,"[319] though it excludes military and other governmental non-commercial vessels,[320] and the ship need not be flying the flag of a party state to come under its terms. Article 4 is a rather complex provision regarding geographical

---

311 *Ibid.*, s. 7(8).

312 *Ibid.*, s. 7(9).

313 See, generally, Chapter 6.

314 UNGA Res. 40/61 (9 December 1985).

315 See Malvina Halberstam, "Terrorism on the High Seas: The *Achille Lauro*, Piracy and the IMO *Convention on Maritime Safety*" (1988) 82 A.J.I.L. 269.

316 (1988) 1678 U.N.T.S. 221, Can. T.S. 1993 No. 10 [*SUA Convention*]. As of June 2009, this treaty had 152 parties; see online: www.imo.org (select "Conventions").

317 1678 U.N.T.S. 304, Can. T.S. 1993 No. 9 [*SUA Protocol 1988*].

318 For a detailed review, see Glen Plant, "The *Convention for the Suppression of Unlawful Acts against the Safety of Maritime Navigation*" (1990) 39 I.C.L.Q. 27.

319 Above note 316, art. 1.

320 *Ibid.*, art. 2.

application, and essentially applies the Convention only where there is an international element to the ship's travel.[321] High seas attacks appear to be left to the *UNCLOS* regime. The offences combine the kinds of crimes laid out in the *Hague* and *Montreal Conventions*, transposed onto ships: hijacking, acts of violence against persons, destroying or causing damage to ships and their cargo, placing dangerous devices or substances on ships, destroying or damaging maritime navigational facilities, and communicating false information that endangers maritime navigation.[322] Article 3(1)(g) provides for a specific crime of injuring or killing a person while committing one of the other enumerated offences, though unlike the other offences, there is no requirement that the act is likely to destroy the ship or endanger its safe navigation. Article 3(2)(c) provides for a specific offence for a person to threaten to commit any of the offences under subparagraphs (1)(b), (c), or (e) "aimed at compelling a physical or juridical person to do or refrain from doing any act." This provision is aimed at the common terrorist technique of threatening violent acts unless demands are met. The provision is permissive as to whether the threat must be accompanied by conditions.

Article 6(1) requires a state party to exercise jurisdiction where the ship in question is flagged by that state, where the offence takes place in its territorial sea, or where the offence is committed by a national of the state, and custodial universal jurisdiction is required under article 6(4). Article 6(2) provides permissively for the use of expanded nationality (that is, stateless persons with habitual residence in the state), passive personality, and protective jurisdiction. Article 7 requires the state party to take the offender into custody for prosecution or extradition (where it is "satisfied that the circumstances so warrant"), and article 10 provides for an extradite or prosecute obligation.

The *SUA Protocol* is designed to implement a regime similar to that in the *SUA Convention* to fixed platforms located on the continental shelf, and indeed it incorporates by reference various provisions of the latter, including those dealing with the exercise of jurisdiction, the extradite or prosecute obligation, and cooperation provisions.[323] "Fixed platform" is defined as "an artificial island, installation or structure permanently attached to the sea-bed for the purpose of exploration or exploitation of resources or for other economic purposes"[324] and thus excludes mobile rigs which would be covered by the *SUA Convention*. Due to poor drafting, the remainder of the Protocol refers to the "con-

---

321 Plant, above note 318 at 37–40.
322 Above note 316, arts. 3(1)(a)–(f).
323 Above note 317, art. 1(1).
324 *Ibid.*, art. 1(3).

tinental shelf" rather than the sea-bed, but it is clear that the sea-bed of the continental shelf is the point of reference.[325]

Article 2 provides for a range of offences similar to those in the *SUA Convention*: seizing or exercising control over a fixed platform, acts of violence against a person on a platform if such endangers the platform's safety, destroying or damaging a platform, placing a device/substance which is likely to destroy or threaten the platform, and injuring/killing any person in connection with the other offences.[326] Article 2(2)(c) contains the same offence regarding terrorist-type threats as article 3(2)(c) of the *SUA Convention*. Jurisdiction is also similar to the *SUA Convention*: mandatory territorial (for attacks on or against a platform fixed to the state's continental shelf) and nationality jurisdiction;[327] permissive for stateless persons with habitual residence in the state, passive personality and protective jurisdiction;[328] and mandatory custodial jurisdiction[329] to accompany the *aut dedere aut judicare* obligation.[330]

In October 2005, the IMO's Diplomatic Conference on the Revision of the SUA Treaties adopted protocols to both the *SUA Convention*[331] and the *SUA Protocol*.[332] These new instruments are designed to amplify the anti-terrorism aspects of the *SUA Convention* and *SUA Protocol*, and each adds a range of offences regarding the use and transport of biological, chemical, or nuclear weapons, several of which apply where the perpetrator's intention is to intimidate a population, or to compel a government or international organization to do or abstain from doing any act.[333] They also modify some of the cooperation provisions to bring them into line with more recent suppression conventions. The 2005 protocols are in the early stages of consideration by states, and neither has yet come into force.[334]

---

325 See Commonwealth Secretariat, *Implementation Kits for the International Counter-Terrorism Conventions*, online: www.thecommonwealth.org/Internal/38061/documents/ at 210.

326 Above note 317, art. 2(2).

327 *Ibid.*, art. 3(1).

328 *Ibid.*, art. 3(2).

329 *Ibid.*, art. 3(4).

330 *Ibid.*, art.1(1).

331 *Protocol of 2005 to the Convention for the Suppression of Unlawful Acts against the Safety of Maritime Navigation*, IMO Doc. LEG/CONF.15/21 (1 November 2005).

332 *Protocol of 2005 to the Protocol for the Suppression of Unlawful Acts against the Safety of Fixed Platforms Located on the Continental Shelf*, IMO Doc. LEG/CONF.15/22 (1 November 2005) [*SUA Protocol 2005*].

333 For a summary, see IMO online: www.imo.org/Conventions/mainframe.asp?topic_id=259&doc_id=686#review.

334 For ratification status, see IMO online: www.imo.org/Conventions/mainframe.asp?topic_id=247.

In Canada, section 78.1 of the *Criminal Code*[335] sets out offences against maritime safety, including seizing control of a ship or fixed platform,[336] endangering the safety of a ship or fixed platform,[337] making a false communication that endangers the safe navigation of a ship,[338] or making threats to commit offences in order to compel a person to do or refrain from doing any act.[339] The definitions of "ship" and "fixed platform" accord with those in the *SUA Convention* and *Protocol*.[340] Jurisdictionally, section 7(2.1) establishes jurisdiction over the section 78.1 offences committed outside Canada, utilizing all of the principles set out in the *SUA Convention* and *Protocol* if the offence is committed "against or on board a ship or fixed platform attached to the continental shelf of any state or against or on board a ship navigating or scheduled to navigate beyond the territorial sea of any state." Section 7(2.2) provides for the same range of jurisdiction exercised over the same offences if committed "outside Canada against or on board a fixed platform *not* attached to the continental shelf of any state or against or on board a ship *not* navigating or scheduled to navigate beyond the territorial sea of any state" (emphasis added). The offence is also deemed to have been committed in Canada if the offender is found in the territory of a state, other than the state in which the act or omission was committed, if the state is a party to the *SUA Convention* or *Protocol*.[341] The latter provision allows for the fullest exercise of the *aut dedere aut judicare* obligation by both Canada and its treaty partners, and goes beyond custodial universal jurisdiction to a full-blown (though treaty-based) exercise of extraterritorial jurisdiction.

3) Hostage-Taking

The taking of civilian hostages during time of war has been established as a war crime at least since Nuremberg[342] and is prohibited in the *Geneva Convention* regime.[343] The taking of hostages for the furtherance of terrorist aims (howsoever defined) was well on the anti-terrorism radar by the 1960s, and kidnapping more generally is a common tactic by in-

---

335 Above note 109.
336 *Ibid.*, s. 78(1).
337 *Ibid.*, ss. 78(2)(a)–(d).
338 *Ibid.*, s. 78(3).
339 *Ibid.*, s. 78(4), specifically referring to the offences under ss. 78(2)(a)–(c).
340 *Ibid.*, s. 78(5).
341 *Ibid.*, ss. 7(2.2)(b)(i) & (ii).
342 *IMT Charter*, 82 U.N.T.S. 279, art. 6(b).
343 Specifically, *Geneva Convention IV*, above note 4, art. 34.

surrectionist and organized crime groups in the present day. However, after the abduction and murder of Israeli athletes at the 1972 Munich Olympics, as well as a number of kidnappings of Germany businesspeople, the Federal Republic of Germany successfully pushed for the elaboration of a UN treaty on hostage-taking.[344] The *International Convention against the Taking of Hostages*[345] was completed in December 1979 and is widely adhered to by states.[346] The *Hostages Convention* creates an offence of "hostage-taking," which comprises three distinct elements: (1) seizing or detaining a person; (2) threatening to kill, injure, or continue to detain the person; and (3) doing the above "in order to compel a third party, namely, a State, an international intergovernmental organization, a natural or juridical person, or a group of persons" to do or abstain from doing any act—the latter as "an explicit or implicit condition for the release of the hostage."[347] While the *Hostages Convention* itself was directed at hostage-takers with political motives, the definition of the offence is broad enough to cover acts of common kidnapping. This is subject, however, to article 13, which provides that the *Hostages Convention* does not apply "where the offence is committed within a single state, the hostage and the alleged offender are nationals of that State and the alleged offender is found in the territory of that State." Accordingly, as soon as the offence acquires *any* transnational aspect, the *Hostages Convention* will apply.[348]

Article 6 requires states to exercise enforcement jurisdiction over an alleged offender who is present in its territory (again, where it is "satisfied that the circumstances so warrant"), and also to make a preliminary inquiry into the facts of the case, towards criminal prosecution or extradition. A unique obligation in this Convention is found in article 3, which obliges a state in whose territory hostages are being held to "take all measures it considers appropriate to ease the situation

---

344 For the history and a detailed commentary, see Robert Rosenstock, "*International Convention against the Taking of Hostages*: Another International Community Step against Terrorism" (1980) 9 Denv. J. Int'l L. & Pol. 169 at 172–74. See also Sami Shubber, "The *International Convention against the Taking of Hostages*" (1981) 52 Brit. Y.B. Int'l L. 205.

345 1316 U.N.T.S. 205, Can. T.S. 1986 No. 45 [*Hostages Convention*].

346 Currently 166 parties; see online: http://untreaty.un.org/cod/terrorism/terrorism_tableupdateJanuary2009.pdf.

347 Above note 345, art. 1(1).

348 It has been speculated that even an offence which meets the criteria under art. 13 might still invoke the *Hostages Convention* if it were done towards compulsion of another State or a person in another State (Commonwealth Secretariat, above note 325 at 143, quoting Joseph Lambert, *Terrorism and Hostages in International Law* (Cambridge: Grotius, 1990) at 302–7).

of the hostage, in particular, to secure his release."[349] In terms of jurisdictional principles, article 5 requires mandatory territorial (along with registered ship and registered aircraft),[350] nationality[351] and protective[352] jurisdiction, as well as mandatory custodial universal jurisdiction[353] to allow implementation of the *aut dedere aut judicare* obligation.[354] It is permissive regarding stateless persons ordinarily residing in the state[355] and passive personality.[356]

Article 14 notes that the treaty is not to be "construed as justifying the violation of the territorial integrity or political independence of a State in contravention of the Charter of the United Nations." This is meant to preclude unilateral intervention by one state (likely the state of nationality of the victim) into the territory where the hostage-taking is occurring, and was included in response to the 1976 Entebbe raid by Israel.[357] The citation of the *UN Charter*[358] invokes, *inter alia*, the right of self-defence under article 51, which in the present climate makes for an uncertain scope to the protective power of this particular provision.

In Canada, section 279.1 of the *Criminal Code*[359] provides an offence of hostage-taking, where the perpetrator "(a) confines, imprisons, forcibly seizes or detains [a] person, and (b) in any manner utters, conveys or causes any person to receive a threat that the death of, or bodily harm to, the hostage will be caused or that the confinement, imprisonment or detention will be continued," with intent to force any entity towards any conduct.[360] It is distinct from the ordinary domestic offence of kidnapping and forcible confinement,[361] which of course may not have the compulsion of a third party as a necessary element. Section 7(3.1) of the *Code* exerts jurisdiction for the offence over Canadian ships and aircraft, as well as extraterritorial jurisdiction on the nation-

---

349 States are also obliged to take "all practicable measures" to prevent hostage-taking in the first place (above note 345, art. 4). It is typical for states to refuse to accede to the demands of hostage-takers, though this is sometimes unavoidable; Bantekas & Nash, above note 47 at 206.

350 Above note 345, art. 5(1)(a).

351 *Ibid.*, art. 5(1)(b).

352 *Ibid.*, art. 5(1)(c).

353 *Ibid.*, art. 5(2).

354 *Ibid.*, art. 8.

355 *Ibid.*, art. 5(1)(b).

356 *Ibid.*, art. 5(1)(d).

357 Commonwealth Secretariat, above note 325 at 147.

358 1 U.N.T.S. xvi.

359 Above note 109.

360 *Ibid.*, s. 279.1(1).

361 *Ibid.*, s. 279.

ality (including resident stateless person), protective, passive personality, and custodial universal principles.[362]

4) Internationally Protected Persons

Crimes against government officials, particularly diplomats and heads of state engaged in diplomatic functions abroad, was an early subject of anti-terrorism initiatives. The OAS had concluded a treaty on the kidnapping of diplomats as early as 1971,[363] and the UNGA referred the drafting of a global convention to its Sixth Committee in November 1972.[364] The *Convention on the Prevention and Punishment of Crimes against Internationally Protected Persons, Including Diplomatic Agents*[365] was concluded on 14 December 1973. It is geared towards the protection of two classes of government officials: (1) heads of state, heads of government, or ministers of foreign affairs, as well as their families, whenever they are in foreign states[366] and (2) officials/representatives of states or intergovernmental organizations and their families and property, in such place and time as they are "entitled pursuant to international law to special protection."[367] The latter term covers primarily diplomats, but more generally anyone who is entitled to some level of protection and immunity under international law by virtue of the functions they serve, for example, UN officials.[368]

The scheme of the Convention is essentially the same as that of the *Hague* and *Montreal Conventions.*[369] States are obliged to criminalize

---

362 In *R. v. Ribic*, 2008 ONCA 790, the Ontario Court of Appeal upheld the conviction of the accused for taking hostage two UN personnel (one of whom was a Canadian citizen) in Bosnia during the Yugoslav conflict. The defence conceded that the courts were properly exercising jurisdiction under s. 7(3.1) of the *Code* (*ibid.* at para. 3), though it seems that jurisdiction could also have been exerted under s. 7(3) because the hostages were UN personnel; see Sections D(4) and D(5), below in this chapter.

363 *The Convention to Prevent and Punish the Acts of Terrorism Taking the Form of Crimes against Persons and Related Extortion That Are of International Significance*, reprinted (1971) 10 I.L.M. 255.

364 See, generally, Michael Wood, "The *Convention on the Prevention and Punishment of Crimes against Internationally Protected Persons, Including Diplomatic Agents*" (1974) 23 I.C.L.Q. 791.

365 1035 U.N.T.S. 167, Can. T.S. 1977 No. 43 [*Protected Persons Convention*]. Currently 171 parties; see http://untreaty.un.org/cod/terrorism/terrorism_table-updateJanuary2009.pdf.

366 *Ibid.*, art. 1(1)(a).

367 *Ibid.*, art. 1(1)(b).

368 See Wood, above note 364 at 799–802.

369 *Ibid.* at 804–5.

murder, kidnapping, or other attacks upon internationally protected persons,[370] as well as violent attacks on their official premises, private accommodation, or means of transport which are "likely to endanger his person or liberty."[371] Jurisdiction is to be exercised territorially (including registered ship and aircraft),[372] using the nationality principle,[373] and also where the victim "enjoys his status [as an internationally protected person] by virtue of functions which he exercises on behalf of that State."[374] The latter is something of a modified passive personality principle, but clearly extends beyond individuals of the nationality of the state party and covers third-state nationals who are working for the state party. States must also exercise custodial universal jurisdiction[375] in order to comply with the *aut dedere aut judicare* obligation.[376]

In Canada, the *Code* contains a definition of "internationally protected person" that accords with that in the treaty.[377] Section 7(3) extends jurisdiction extraterritorially over a range of offences[378] if they are committed against an internationally protected person or their families or property, by way of ship, aircraft, nationality and custodial universal principles, as well as the quasi-passive personality jurisdiction provided for in the Convention.[379] Section 424 criminalizes threats to commit any of these offences, while section 431 criminalizes attacks on their premises, residences, or means of transport; both of these offences fall within the extraterritorial jurisdiction in section 7(3).

5) UN and Associated Personnel[380]

In the late 1980s and early 1990s the United Nations was deploying peacekeepers to extremely troubled regions where there had been breakdown in the public order, such as Somalia, the former Yugoslavia, and Rwanda. It quickly became apparent that the troops were being exposed to greater levels of danger than had been the case in the past,

---

370 Above note 365, art. 2(1)(a).
371 *Ibid.*, art. 2(1)(b).
372 *Ibid.*, art. 3(1)(a).
373 *Ibid.*, art. 3(1)(b).
374 *Ibid.*, art. 3(1)(c).
375 *Ibid.*, art. 3(2).
376 *Ibid.*, art. 7.
377 Above note 109, s. 2.
378 For example, murder, manslaughter, and assault.
379 Above note 109, s. 7(3).
380 See, generally, Ola Engdahl, *Protection of Personnel in Peace Operations: The Role of the 'Safety Convention' against the Background of General International Law* (Leiden: Martinus Nijhoff, 2007).

evidenced by a significant increase in the number of fatalities due to attacks on UN personnel.[381] The UNGA's Sixth Committee was charged with the elaboration of a new international convention to provide for the protection of UN peacekeepers and personnel involved in peace-keeping operations.[382] It was at least arguable that the *Protected Persons Convention*[383] accomplished this level of protection, given the broadness of the definition of "protected personnel" in that treaty,[384] and it was also proposed that the new treaty could be in the form of a protocol to the *Protected Persons Convention*. However, the ultimate decision was for a separate convention, in part because of the important symbolic value of such an instrument, and also out of a wish not to exclude states which were not parties to the *Protected Persons Convention*.[385] The *Convention on the Safety of United Nations and Associated Personnel*[386] was concluded on 9 December 1994.

The mechanical provisions of the *UN Personnel Convention* are es-sentially built on those of the *Protected Persons Convention*, and so one finds the criminalization of murder, kidnapping, or other attacks, as well as violent attacks upon official premises, private accommodation, and means of transport of UN personnel.[387] While, as is typical, threat to commit these acts is covered, that offence is qualified by the phrase "with the objective of compelling a physical or juridical person to do or refrain from doing any act."[388] The treaty also provides that participa-tion in "organizing or ordering others to commit" an attack on UN per-sonnel is an offence in order to emphasize the collective political will to prosecute the "masterminds" of such attacks.[389] Territorial jurisdiction (accompanied by ship/plane of state registration) is mandatory,[390] as are nationality[391] and custodial universal jurisdiction,[392] and the Conven-

---

381 See Report of the Secretary-General, *An Agenda for Peace*, UN Doc. A/47/277-S/24111 at para. 66 (1992).

382 See Philippe Kirsch, "*Convention on the Safety of United Nations and Associated Personnel*" (1994) 23 Can. Council Int'l L. Proc. 182.

383 Above note 365.

384 Hugh Kindred, "The Protection of Peacekeepers" (1995) 33 Can. Y.B. Int'l Law 257 at 268.

385 M.-Christiane Bourloyannis-Vrailas, "The *Convention on the Safety of United Nations and Associated Personnel*" (1995) 44 I.C.L.Q. 560 at 576.

386 2051 U.N.T.S. 391, Can. T.S. 2002 No. 7 [*UN Personnel Convention*]. In force since 1999.

387 *Ibid.*, arts. 9(1)(a) & (b).

388 *Ibid.*, art. 9(1)(c).

389 Bourloyannis-Vrailas, above note 385 at 577.

390 Above note 386, art. 10(1)(a).

391 *Ibid.*, art. 10(1)(b).

392 *Ibid.*, art. 10(4).

tion is permissive as regards stateless persons habitually resident in the state and the passive personality and protective principles.[393]

More contentious during the negotiations for the *Convention* was what and which "United Nations and Associated Personnel" were going to be covered, and in what situations. Article 1(a) defines "United Nations personnel" as persons engaged by the UN as part of the military, police, or civilian components of a UN operation, as well as other officials and experts of the UN and its specialized agencies who are working on a UN operation in their official capacities. "Associated personnel" includes members of state governments assigned to a UN operation, persons engaged by the UN or specialized agencies, or persons deployed by humanitarian NGOs or agencies in connection with a UN operation.[394] "United Nations operation" itself was defined narrowly, limited to UN-controlled[395] operations for maintaining or restoring international peace and security, or where the Security Council issues a declaration that there is an "exceptional risk to the safety of personnel participating in the operation."[396] The *Convention* expressly does not apply to Chapter VII[397] enforcement actions where the UN personnel are "engaged as combatants against organized armed forces and to which the law of international armed conflict applies."[398]

The *UN Personnel Convention* itself was, of course, no guarantee of safety for the protected persons, and attacks on not only UN but intergovernmental organization (IGO) and NGO staff members continue to be a problem.[399] Of particular concern was the narrow scope of the *Convention*, which basically covered only peacekeeping operations and the work of non-UN agencies that was closely associated with these, but did not cover the kind of post-conflict or "peace-building" operations that have become standard of late.[400] In response, in January 2006 the UNGA adopted an *Optional Protocol to the Convention on the Safety of United Nations and Associated Personnel*,[401] which expanded the scope of the *Convention* to include UN operations for "(a) delivering humani-

---

393 *Ibid.*, art. 10(2).
394 *Ibid.*, art. 1(b).
395 That is, not including a Chapter VII operation authorized by the Security Council but directed by one or more states.
396 Above note 386, art. 1(c).
397 *UN Charter*, above note 358.
398 Above note 386, art. 2(2).
399 See Report of the Secretary-General, UN Doc. A/60/223 (12 August 2005).
400 See "Strengthening Laws against Terrorism and Other Threats," UN Chronicle, 60th General Assembly, Sixth Committee, online: www.un.org/Pubs/chronicle/2005/issue4/0405p22.html.
401 UN Doc. A/RES/60/42 (6 January 2006).

tarian, political or development assistance in peacebuilding; or (b) delivering emergency humanitarian assistance."[402] States are permitted to declare that they will not apply the *Protocol* with respect to emergency humanitarian assistance where the operations are "conducted for the sole purpose of responding to a natural disaster."[403] The *Protocol* is not yet in force.

Canada is a party to the *UN Personnel Convention*, but has not signed the Protocol. Section 2 of the *Criminal Code*[404] contains definitions of "United Nations operation," "United Nations personnel," and "associated personnel" that accord with the Convention. Section 7(3.71) extends extraterritorial jurisdiction over the same range of offences as in section 7(3),[405] described in Section D(4), above in this chapter, on all of the jurisdictional principles contained in the Convention. Section 424.1 criminalizes threats to commit any of these offences (including the "intent to compel" requirement), while section 431 criminalizes attacks on premises, residences, or means of transport; both of these offences fall within the extraterritorial jurisdiction in section 7(3.71).

6) Terrorist Bombings

The use of various kinds of explosives has been a standard tool in the terrorist arsenal, and as noted above, several of the terrorism suppression conventions have provisions dealing with the use of "devices" that were meant to deal with bombs. However, post–Cold War, these acts, which had mostly been contained to incidents occurring within a single state, began increasingly to assume a transnational character. After a spate of terrorist bombings in public places, including the 1996 truck-bombing attack on American military personnel in Dhahran, Saudi Arabia, it became apparent that the lack of a suppression convention to combat this kind of incident was a gap in the international law regime as it existed.[406] Initially proposed by the US and endorsed by the G7/P8

---

402 *Ibid.*, art. II(1).

403 *Ibid.*, art. II(3).

404 Above note 109.

405 Omitting ss. 280–83 of the *Code*, which concern abduction of children, as family members are not protected under the *UN Personnel Convention*.

406 Samuel Witten, "The *International Convention for the Suppression of Terrorist Bombings*" (1998) 92 A.J.I.L. 774 at 774–75. The UNGA established the Ad Hoc Committee on Terrorism in 1996, which gave direction on the drafting of the *Terrorist Bombings Convention*, the *Terrorist Financing Convention*, and the *Nuclear Terrorism Convention* (UNGA Res. 51/210 (17 December 1996), aff'd by UNGA Res. 53/108 (8 December 1998).

states, the *International Convention for the Suppression of Terrorist Bombings*[407] was finalized and adopted by the UNGA in late 1997.[408]

Article 2 of the *Terrorist Bombings Convention* contains the criminalization provisions: states must make it an offence where a person "unlawfully and intentionally delivers, places, discharges or detonates an explosive or other lethal device in, into or against a place of public use, a State or government facility, a public transportation system or an infrastructure facility."[409] Intent must be "to cause death or serious bodily injury," or "to cause extensive destruction of such a place, facility or system, where such destruction results in or is likely to result in major economic loss."[410] Included among the various forms of participation and modes of liability[411] is liability for organizing or directing others to commit the offence[412] or intentionally contributing in any way to the commission of the offence by a group acting with a common purpose[413] — a broad clause that presaged the similar mode of liability under the *TOC Convention*,[414] and was in implicit recognition of the links between organized crime and terrorism. The definitions of the various constituent parts of the offence are similarly broad.[415] In particular, "explosive or other lethal device" is defined to include not only conventional explosives but also devices which release "toxic chemicals, biological agents or toxins or similar substance or radiation or radioactive material,"[416] which would cover, for example, release of toxins into water systems or subways, and "dirty bombs."

Article 4 provides that the Convention does not apply where there are no transnational aspects to the offence, that is, it takes place on the territory of one state, both offender and victim are nationals of that state, the offender is found in that state, and no other state has a jurisdictional claim. Even in this event, however, the provisions regarding mutual assistance and human rights guarantees (articles 10–15) continue to apply. The activities of armed forces during an armed conflict are exempted.[417] As to jurisdiction, article 6 of the *Convention* provides for mandatory territorial, registered ship/aircraft, and nationality juris-

---

407 Above note 18. Currently 161 members.
408 Annex, GA Res. 52/164 (15 December 1997).
409 Above note 18, art. 2(1).
410 *Ibid.*
411 *Ibid.*, arts. 2(2) & (3).
412 *Ibid.*, art. 2(3)(b).
413 *Ibid.*, art. 2(3)(c).
414 Above note 26.
415 Above note 18, art. 1.
416 *Ibid.*, art. 1(3).
417 *Ibid.*, art. 19.

diction, and permissively for passive personality, stateless person ordinarily resident in the state, and protective jurisdiction. There are also more unusual provisions for jurisdiction where the attack is committed against a government aircraft or "against a State or government facility of that State abroad, including an embassy or other diplomatic or consular premises."[418] The latter provision is really a slightly expanded version of the protective principle, but is progressive in the sense that it will reach "extraterritorial government facilities such as tourist centers, economic development offices and military facilities."[419] The *Convention* also provides for custodial universal jurisdiction,[420] in order to facilitate the *aut dedere aut judicare* obligation in article 8.

Building on what was, even at the time, a decrease in popularity of the "political offence exception" for extradition,[421] article 5 of the *Terrorist Bombings Convention* contains a new progressive clause which obliges states to ensure that offences covered by the *Convention* (including, but not limited to, those which "are intended or calculated to provoke a state of terror in the general public or in a group of persons or particular persons") are not subject to defences built on "considerations of a political, philosophical, ideological, racial, ethnic, religious or other similar nature." This represented an important development, incorporating as it did explicit multilateral agreement that particular acts of terrorism are condemnable and worthy of suppression regardless of the motivation of the perpetrators.[422] Another progressive element is the obligation for alleged offenders to receive "fair treatment" in the investigating/prosecuting state, contained in article 14. Unlike other suppression conventions (notably the *TOC Convention*, which was later in time), "fair treatment" is defined as including "applicable provisions of international law, including international law of human rights." To be sure, the level of protection which must be provided is contingent on a determination of what international human rights laws apply to the state in question; but this is nonetheless fairly robust protection.

In Canada, the *Terrorist Bombings Convention* is implemented by sections 431.2 and 7(3.72) of the *Criminal Code*.[423] The former sets out the necessary definitions for the offence (e.g., "explosive or other legal

---

418 *Ibid.*, art. 6(2)(b).
419 Witten, above note 406 at 778, n. 24.
420 Above note 18, art. 6(4).
421 See, generally, Chapter 9.
422 As early as 1994, the UNGA had solemnly reaffirmed their "unequivocal condemnation of all acts, methods and practices of terrorism as criminal and unjustifiable"; see UNGA Res. 49/60, above note 52.
423 Above note 109.

device," "infrastructure facility")[424] and the offence itself,[425] both in a manner which tracks the *Convention* closely. It also implements the exemption of the activities of armed forces during an armed conflict.[426] The latter section extends extraterritorial jurisdiction over the offence on all of the bases provided for in the Convention itself.

7) Terrorist Financing

As has been noted earlier, while the fall of the Eastern Bloc states and the end of the Cold War was something of an enabler for various kinds of both international and transnational crime, it represented partial dis-enablement for many terrorist organizations that had previously been funded by states.[427] This practice began to decline in the early 1990s, and very quickly the international law enforcement community had noted a shift in the patterns and means by which organized terrorist groups funded and armed themselves. The growing links between terrorism and organized crime were obvious,[428] as terrorists allied themselves with organized criminal groups in order to make money, or even dedicated their own personnel and resources to these activities. The arms trade, narcotics trafficking, money laundering, and the smuggling of nuclear material all figured highly in modern terrorist activities,[429] and this continues to be the case. This is a particularly dangerous state of affairs, since the already socially-destructive forces of organized criminal activity can be harnessed to fuel the ideological fires of terrorists, making for a sinister synergy and producing extremely powerful groups, such as the Peruvian Shining Path, Al-Qaeda, and the Taliban.[430] However, terrorism is also funded by private individuals through legitimate means, such as circulating funds through bank accounts and ordinary financial transactions (including the practice of *hawala*); funneling of monies from charities, legitimate or otherwise; and the use of trusts.[431]

---

424 *Ibid.*, s. 431.2(1).
425 *Ibid.*, s. 431.2(2).
426 *Ibid.*, s. 431.2(3).
427 For a solid overview, see Ilias Bantekas, "The International Law of Terrorist Financing" (2003) 97 A.J.I.L. 315.
428 Alex P. Schmid, "The Links between Transnational Organized Crime and Terrorist Crimes" (1996) 2 Transnat'l Organized Crime 40.
429 See Annex, UNGA Res. 49/60, above note 52.
430 See Mylonaki, above note 56.
431 Bantekas, above note 427 at 320–23.

In 2000, as the result of a French initiative, the UNGA adopted the *International Convention for the Suppression of the Financing of Terrorism*.[432] The central obligations under the treaty are threefold: criminalization of acts of terrorist financing; identification, detection, and freezing/seizure of funds used for terrorist financing; and putting in place legal regimes for the prevention of terrorist financing, including stricter regulation of financial institutions, other professions involved in financial transactions, and money-transmission agencies. Article 2 is the offence provision, which obliges states to make it an offence for any person who "by any means, directly or indirectly, unlawfully and willfully, provides or collects funds" with the intention or knowledge that they are to be used for one of two proscribed purposes. The first is "an act which constitutes an offence within the scope of" any of the nine treaties which are listed in the annex to the Convention.[433] These treaties are those which were at the time commonly identified as the "counter-terrorism" treaties[434] and includes those discussed here.[435] The second proscribed purpose is any violent act which is geared towards intimidating a population or compelling a government or international organization to do or refrain from doing any act.[436] States must, within the context of their own legal frameworks, make legal persons liable for the offences and attach some form of serious sanction to such liability, without prejudice to personal liability for the directing mind of the organization.[437] The Convention incorporates some of the broader anti-terrorism tone of the *Terrorist Bombings Convention*, and provides that there can be no defence to prosecution of the offence based in, for example, political or ideological motivations.[438] It also provides that for extradition and mutual legal assistance purposes, the terrorist finan-

---

432 Above note 41. See Alexander Conrad Culley, "The *International Convention for the Suppression of the Financing of Terrorism*: a Legal Tour de Force?" (2007) 29 Dublin U. L.J. 397.

433 *Terrorist Financing Convention, ibid.*, art. 2(1)(a).

434 Though the list of "counter-terrorism treaties" would now include the *Nuclear Terrorism Convention*, below note 471, dealt with in Section D(8), below in this chapter.

435 Article 2(2)(a) provides that upon ratifying the *Terrorist Financing Convention* a state may declare that any of the counter-terrorism treaties to which it is not a party is deemed not to be included within the scope of art. 2(1)(a). If it does not do so, however, it seems that the offence would be included even if the state was not a party to the specific treaty.

436 Above note 41, art. 2(1)(b).

437 *Ibid.*, art. 5. As Bantekas notes, in some states this may include charities and trusts; above note 427 at 324.

438 *Terrorist Financing Convention, ibid.*, art. 6.

cing offence can be considered neither a political offence[439] nor a fiscal offence;[440] the latter provision strips away what has historically been a standard basis for refusing extradition.

The *Terrorist Financing Convention* requires jurisdiction on the territorial, registered ship/aircraft, and nationality principles.[441] Given that financing of terrorism is an "intermediate" act towards a terrorist end, the Convention provides permissively that states may exercise jurisdiction where the financing was "directed towards or resulted in the carrying out of" one of the proscribed offences in article 2(1), either in a state's territory or against one of its nationals,[442] against a state or government facility located abroad,[443] or committed in an attempt to compel the state to do or abstain from doing any act.[444] It also provides permissively for jurisdiction over stateless persons ordinarily resident in a state[445] or where the offence is committed on board a government aircraft.[446] States must exercise custodial universal jurisdiction[447] and comply with the *aut dedere aut judicare* obligation.[448] As with earlier treaties, article 3 provides that the Convention does not apply where there are no transnational aspects to the offence, that is, it takes place on the territory of one state, both offender and victim are nationals of that state, the offender is found in that state, and no other state has a jurisdictional claim. The Convention also has a version of the stronger "fair treatment" provision similar to that in the *Terrorist Bombings Convention*, which incorporates international human rights law.[449]

Like other modern suppression conventions, the *Terrorist Financing Convention* aspires to be somewhat holistic in scope and addresses other aspects of the problem. Article 8 sets out obligations (though couched in terms of "appropriateness" and "in accordance with its domestic legal principles") for each state party to set up domestic laws allowing for identification, detection, forfeiture, and freezing and/or seizure of funds, either as used in the commission of the offences or derived therefrom.[450] States may conclude agreements among them-

---

439 *Ibid.*, art. 14.
440 *Ibid.*, art. 13.
441 *Ibid.*, arts. 7(1)(a)–(c).
442 *Ibid.*, art. 7(2)(a).
443 *Ibid.*, art. 7(2)(b).
444 *Ibid.*, art. 7(2)(c).
445 *Ibid.*, art. 7(2)(d).
446 *Ibid.*, art. 7(2)(e).
447 *Ibid.*, art. 7(4).
448 *Ibid.*, art. 10.
449 *Ibid.*, art. 17.
450 *Ibid.*, arts. 8(1) & (2).

selves for the sharing of forfeited funds[451] and must consider establishing mechanisms for victim restitution using the funds.[452] More teeth are found in article 18, which obliges states to establish mechanisms to prevent terrorist financing, most importantly by way of requiring financial institutions to identify and report suspicious and/or criminal transactions.[453] States are also obliged to regulate money-transmission agencies and "the physical cross-border transportation of cash and bearer negotiable instruments."[454]

Security Council resolutions have also played a major role in the elaboration of the international law of anti-terrorist financing. In 1999, the Council embarked on a series of resolutions which targeted Osama bin Laden and Al-Qaeda, as well as the Taliban regime in Afghanistan which supported them through economic sanctions. Resolution 1267 created a committee of the Security Council (the "1267 Committee") which ultimately would formulate lists of Taliban and Al-Qaeda entities and "associated individuals and entities,"[455] with regard to which states were to freeze assets and prohibit any person from funding them. The 1267 Committee actively maintains this list,[456] and all UN member states are obliged to take the prescribed measures against these persons.

In the immediate wake of the 9/11 attacks, the Security Council adopted Resolution 1373,[457] which essentially imposed a regime very similar to, but potentially more expansive than, that in the *Terrorist Financing Convention* on all UN member states. The resolution contains very robust provisions[458] that in one way make the *Terrorist Financing Convention* redundant, though of course a Security Council Resolution is of indeterminate duration. Resolution 1373 also created the Counter-Terrorism Committee, a subsidiary organ of the Council tasked with monitoring compliance with the resolution.[459] Operationally, a great deal of the law and policy regarding terrorist financing is drawn from anti-money-laundering work, and the authoritative work done in that regard by the Financial Action Task Force (FATF)—particularly its "Special Recommendations on Terrorist Financing"—are the inter-

---

451 *Ibid.*, art. 8(3).
452 *Ibid.*, art. 8(4).
453 *Ibid.*, art. 18(1).
454 *Ibid.*, art. 18(2).
455 See SC Res. 1333 (19 December 2000).
456 Online: www.un.org/sc/committees/1267/pdf/pdflist.pdf.
457 SC Res. 1373 (28 September 2001), reprinted (2001) 40 I.L.M. 1278.
458 The Security Council has, in fact, been accused of exceeding the generally accepted scope of its powers and "legislating" in this area; see Paul Szasz, "The Security Council Starts Legislating" (2002) 96 A.J.I.L. 901.
459 Above note 457, operative para. 6.

national gold standard. This is dealt with in Section F, below in this chapter.

In Canada, the criminalization provisions of the *Terrorist Financing Convention* are implemented by sections 83.02 and 7(3.73) of the *Criminal Code*.[460] Section 83.02 criminalizes the provision or collection of "property" (rather than "funds," the term used in the Convention)[461] for terrorist purposes, in a manner which tracks article 2 of the Convention. Section 7(3.73) establishes jurisdiction over individuals who commit the offence in section 83.02, in accordance with each of the bases set out in article 7 of the Convention. In addition, sections 83.08–83.12 provide for the freezing of property owned or controlled by or on behalf of a terrorist group, and sections 83.13–83.17 provide for the forfeiture and seizure of property either owned by a terrorist group or which is used to carry out a terrorist activity. However, these provisions exist within a larger body of Canadian law regarding terrorist financing that was brought in as part of Canada's omnibus *Anti-Terrorism Act*,[462] the terrorism finance provisions of which respond specifically to Security Council Resolution 1373.[463] Accordingly, the property freezing, forfeiture, and seizure provisions noted above are more broadly cast than would be necessary to implement the *Terrorist Financing Convention*. Similarly, sections 83.03 and 83.04 create offences that are designed to catch any financial dealings or financial support of terrorist groups—again, cast in a manner far broader than the treaty terms, but made to comply with operative paragraph 1 of Resolution 1373.

The other avenue of compliance with the Security Council's various resolutions is by way of domestic regulatory "listing mechanisms," that is, regulatory means of establishing lists of individuals or entities with whom financial dealings are prohibited, on the basis that there are reasonable grounds to believe they are associated with terrorism. There are currently three such lists, all of which are promulgated by regulations to existing federal statutes. The *United Nations Afghanistan Regulations*[464] make it an offence[465] to have any financial dealings with the Taliban, Osama bin Laden, or his associates (including Al-Qaeda),

---

460 Above note 109.
461 The definition of the term "property" in s. 2 of the *Code* is expansive and includes postage stamps.
462 S.C. 2001, c. 41. See Section D(9), below in this chapter.
463 For an overview, see E. Alexandra Dosman, "For the Record: Designating 'Listed Entities' for the Purposes of Terrorist Financing Offences at Canadian Law" (2004) 62 U.T. Fac. L. Rev. 1.
464 S.O.R./99-444, pursuant to the *United Nations Act*, R.S.C. 1985, c. U-2.
465 Both territorial and nationality-based jurisdiction are asserted.

in accordance with the list of associated individuals and entities maintained by the 1267 Committee. The *United Nations Suppression of Terrorism Regulations*[466] create a list of persons and entities known to be associated with terrorism and makes it an offence to have financial dealings with these persons, including fundraising on their behalf, as well as providing for the freezing of their assets. The list itself is provided in a Schedule to the Regulations. The third listing mechanism is in the *Regulations Establishing a List of Entities*[467] which are promulgated under section 83.05(1) of the *Code*. Persons or entities listed under any of these three mechanisms are subject to having their assets frozen, by way of instruction to Canadian financial institutions by the federal Office of the Superintendent of Financial Institutions Canada.[468]

8) Nuclear Terrorism[469]

The threat of nuclear terrorism has long been a matter of concern to states, and this concern increased after the end of the Cold War, when the problems of aging nuclear infrastructure, security weaknesses, and the threat of terrorist use of nuclear weapons became apparent. Nuclear terrorism was the third matter of which the UNGA's 1996 Ad Hoc Committee on Terrorism was seized,[470] and as a result of a Russian initiative the *International Convention for the Suppression of Acts of Nuclear Terrorism*[471] was negotiated and adopted by the UNGA in 2005. The overall format of the Convention is quite similar to that of the *Terrorist Bombings* and *Terrorist Financing Conventions*, but the negotiations were made more controversial by proposals to include the use of nuclear materials by military forces within the scope of the Convention, and by general disagreement about the legality of the use of nuclear weapons.[472] The resulting compromise is reflected in article 4

---

466 S.O.R./2001-360, pursuant to the *United Nations Act*, above note 464.

467 S.O.R./2002-284, pursuant to the *Criminal Code*.

468 That office maintains an up-to-date compilation of the individuals and entities on all three lists, online: www.osfi-bsif.gc.ca/osfi/index_e.aspx?DetailID=525.

469 See, generally, Walter Gehr, "The Universal Legal Framework against Nuclear Terrorism" (2007) 1 Nuclear Law Bulletin 5.

470 Along with terrorist bombing and terrorist financing; see above note 406.

471 UNGA Res. 59/290, 13 April 2005, UN Doc. A/59/766 (not yet in force for Canada) [*Nuclear Terrorism Convention*]. In force 2007; currently 115 signatories and 40 parties; online: http://untreaty.un.org/cod/terrorism/terrorism_table-updateJanuary2009.pdf.

472 See David Fidler, "International *Convention for the Suppression of Acts of Nuclear Terrorism* Enters into Force" *ASIL Insights* (5 July 2007), online: www.asil.org/insights/2007/07/insights070705.html#_ednref1.

of the Convention, which explicitly exempts the activities of armed forces during an armed conflict from the application of the Convention and expressly takes no position on "the legality of use or threat of use of nuclear weapons by States."[473]

The Convention contains carefully worded definitions of "radioactive material," "nuclear material," and "device," the latter of which is defined in such a manner as to catch any nuclear explosive device or other radioactive device that might cause harm.[474] Article 2 is the offence provision, and requires states to criminalize (1) possession of radioactive material or possessing/making a device with the intent to cause injury or property/environmental damage;[475] (2) use of radioactive material or a device, or use of/damage to a nuclear facility which causes or risks the release of radioactive material, accompanied by an intention to cause injury, property damage, or to compel a person, international organization or state to do or refrain from doing any act[476] (or threatening to commit any of these acts[477]); or (3) demanding radioactive material, a device, or a nuclear facility by way of threat or use of force.[478] States are obliged to take steps to prevent and counter such activities and their preparations,[479] and also to protect radioactive material, taking into account International Atomic Energy Agency guidelines.[480]

For the most part, the Convention is very similar to the *Terrorist Financing* and *Terrorist Bombings Conventions*. Jurisdiction is mandatory on the territorial, registered ship/aircraft, and nationality principles,[481] and permissive for passive personality, stateless person usually resident in the state, protective (including the "state or government facility abroad" version), and aboard a government aircraft.[482] States must exercise custodial universal jurisdiction[483] and comply with the *aut dedere aut judicare* obligation.[484] As with earlier treaties, article 3 provides that the Convention does not apply where there are no transnational aspects to the offence, that is, it takes place on the territory of one

---

473 Above note 471, art. 4(4).
474 *Ibid.*, art. 1.
475 *Ibid.*, art. 2(1)(a).
476 *Ibid.*, art. 2(1)(b).
477 *Ibid.*, art. 2(2)(a).
478 *Ibid.*, art. 2(2)(b). This provision is oddly worded, but seems designed to criminalize attempts to *obtain* these materials, other than by purchase.
479 *Ibid.*, art. 7(1).
480 *Ibid.*, art. 8.
481 *Ibid.*, art. 9(1).
482 *Ibid.*, art. 9(2).
483 *Ibid.*, art. 9(4).
484 *Ibid.*, art. 11.

state, both offender and victim are nationals of that state, the offender is found in that state, and no other state has a jurisdictional claim. The Convention also has a version of the stronger "fair treatment" provision similar to that in the *Terrorist Bombings* and *Terrorist Financing Conventions*, which incorporates international human rights law.[485] Unique to the Convention is article 18, which imposes duties on states to ensure that the devices, substances, or facilities implicated in an offence are rendered harmless, and provides for their disposition or return in appropriate circumstances.

Canada has signed but has not ratified the *Nuclear Terrorism Convention*. Nonetheless, its criminalization provisions appear to have been implemented; in fact, the offences related to nuclear materials go far beyond what would be required to implement the Convention (though to some extent they are geared to implementing the earlier *Convention on the Physical Protection of Nuclear Material*[486]). Section 7(3.2) of the *Criminal Code*[487] makes it an offence to receive, possess, use, transfer, deliver, alter, transport, dispose of, disperse, or abandon nuclear material,[488] and thereby causing injury or property damage—where the act takes place outside Canada and would be an offence under the *Code* if committed in Canada.[489] In addition, it limits jurisdiction over this extraterritorial offence to the grounds provided for in section 7(3.5), that is, ship, aircraft, nationality, and custodial universal jurisdiction. Sections 7(3.3.) and (3.4) provide similarly with regard to such offences as fraud and robbery, where they are committed with relation to nuclear materials. The level of intention provided for in the Convention likely inheres in the provisions themselves, except for article 2(1)(b)(iii), which, it will be recalled, is the intention to compel a person, state, or international organization to do or to refrain from doing some act. However, arguably, this is caught under section 83.01, which provides a definition of "terrorist activity" that both includes the section 7 offences and provides for liability based on this kind of intentionality. This broader category of "terrorist activity" has some transnational aspects, however, which makes it the subject of the next section.

---

485 *Ibid.*, art. 12.
486 Can. T.S. 1987 No. 35.
487 Above note 109.
488 Which is defined commensurately with the Convention in s. 7(3.6).
489 Since no other provisions of the *Code* incorporate nuclear material in any substantial way, this appears to be designed to incorporate by reference other offences related to causing injury or property damage by way of a substance or device, regardless of the nature of the substance or device.

9) The "New" Terrorism: Part II.1 of the *Criminal Code*

In the wake of the 9/11 attacks, Canada and many other states responded quickly by enacting laws that implemented a more robust and aggressive anti-terrorism posture. In Canada, the federal government introduced the omnibus *Anti-Terrorism Act*,[490] which made amendments to a wide range of legislation, notably the *Criminal Code*, the *Canada Evidence Act*, the *Official Secrets Act* (which became the *Security of Information Act*), the *United Nations Act*, and the *Proceeds of Crime (Money Laundering) Act* (which became the *Proceeds of Crime (Money Laundering) and Terrorist Financing Act*).

The new anti-terrorism regime in Canada is best characterized as a combination of criminal law/investigational measures and powers, and other legislative mechanisms which are geared towards promoting national security. The latter aspects of the regime are beyond the scope of this book and successfully dealt with elsewhere.[491] Nor can the entire span of Canadian anti-terrorism law be surveyed here, including the cogent criticism thereof.[492] However, since it is beyond doubt that terrorism in a general sense is a transnational crime of international concern, this section will focus on the major transnational criminal law aspects, specifically the amendments to the *Criminal Code*,[493] which provided for new offences and an expanded extraterritorial jurisdiction.

Section 83.01(1) provides the relevant definitions for the new Part II.1 of the *Code*, entitled "Terrorism," and central is the definition of "terrorist activity." Subsection (a) of that definition refers to the offences covered under the terrorism suppression conventions reviewed in Section B, above in this chapter,[494] extraterritorial jurisdiction for which is provided under section 7. Subsection (b) then extends the definition of "terrorist activity" to include acts, whether inside or outside of Canada, intentionally causing serious threats to life or safety, substantial property damage, and serious interference with essential services, when those acts are meant to intimidate the public or a government and are

---

490 Above note 462.

491 Craig Forcese, *National Security Law* (Toronto: Irwin Law, 2008).

492 See the various articles in (2005) 51 Crim. L.Q., as well as Ronald Daniels *et al.*, eds., *The Security of Freedom: Essays on Canada's Anti-Terrorism Bill* (Toronto: University of Toronto Press, 2002); David Paciocco, "Constitutional Casualties of September 11: Limiting the Legacy of the *Anti-Terrorism Act*" (2002) 16 Sup. Ct. L. Rev. (2d) 185.

493 Above note 109.

494 There is no reference to the *Nuclear Terrorism Convention*, which Canada has signed but not ratified.

committed for a political, religious, or ideological cause.[495] The rest of Part II.1 includes a number of other, specific terrorism offences, including provision, use, or possession of property for terrorist purposes (sections 83.03–83.04); participation in the activity of a terrorist group (section 83.18); facilitating terrorist activity (section 83.19); committing an indictable offence for the benefit of or in association with a terrorist group (section 83.2); instructing to carry out an activity for a terrorist group (section 83.21); instructing to carry out a terrorist activity (section 83.22); and harbouring or concealing terrorists (section 83.23).

In terms of extraterritorial jurisdiction, section 7(3.74) extends jurisdiction not over "terrorist activity" but over "terrorism offences" committed outside Canada, on the bases of nationality, stateless resident, or permanent residency (the latter only if found in Canada after the offence). "Terrorism offence" is defined in section 2 of the *Code*: it includes "terrorist activity" but also includes all of the specific offences in Part II.1 of the *Code* and indictable offences committed for the benefit of a terrorist group. However, section 7(3.74) specifically excludes from this extension of jurisdiction offences under section 83.02 (financing of terrorism) and those listed in section 83.01(1)(a); that is, it excludes the terrorist activity explicitly covered by treaties and implemented by other *Code* provisions.

Section 7(3.75) gives Canada jurisdiction over "terrorist activity committed outside Canada" on the bases of passive personality, protective, and where the act was intended to compel the government of Canada or a province. The section is limited to conduct that is an indictable offence and is a "terrorist activity" as defined in section 83.01(1)(b), that is, it too deals with terrorism offences *other than* those specifically covered by a treaty.

While this is a complex jurisdictional formula, the net result is this: on the one hand, a set of treaty-based terrorist offences for which extraterritorial jurisdiction is provided in strict accordance with the jurisdictional provisions of the treaties themselves; and on the other hand, a set of Canadian-designed "terrorism offences" for which extraterritorial jurisdiction is asserted without any specific international law basis. The latter is completely out of keeping with Canada's usual practice of asserting extraterritorial jurisdiction only in accordance with treaty

---

495 In *R. v. Khawaja* (*Ruling on Charter Challenge to Certain Provisions of Part II.1 — Criminal Code*), [2006] O.J. No. 4245 (S.C.J.), leave to appeal to S.C.C. refused [2006] S.C.C.A. No. 505. Justice Rutherford severed the requirement for a "political, religious or ideological purpose, objective or cause" from the definition of "terrorist activity." Other judges have not followed his ruling; see *United States of America v. Nadarajah*, [2009] O.J. No. 946 at para. 25*ff* (S.C.J.).

obligations to do so, or in accordance with applicable customary international law principles.[496] To be sure, the drafting reflects consideration of the international law implications of these assertions of jurisdiction. The "new terrorism" jurisdiction is, generally speaking, extended over offences which have some connection to Canada—to wit, there is no assertion of custodial universal jurisdiction since there would be no *aut dedere aut judicare* obligation to back it. Accordingly, jurisdiction over extraterritorial "terrorist activity," for example, is limited to attacks on Canadian nationals or other interests.

However, it is not clear whether all of these jurisdictional provisions would be legal at international law, since, as discussed in Chapter 2, simple connection to the forum state is not the be-all and end-all of whether a particular extension of prescriptive jurisdiction is lawful. For example, section 7(3.74) extends nationality-based extraterritorial jurisdiction over the offence of participating in the activity of a terrorist group in section 83.18. Should it seek to have an offender extradited, Canada might run into double criminality problems, depending on whether the treaty partner state has a similar definition of "terrorist group" and a similar participation offence in its own law. However, the extension of jurisdiction is not, by itself, controversial since the nationality principle is well established under customary international law.[497]

On the other hand, section 7(3.75) extends extraterritorial jurisdiction over an act of "caus[ing] a serious risk to the health or safety of the public or any segment of the public"[498] arising from a terrorist act, on the passive personality principle, *inter alia*. Under this scheme, any terrorist bombing in any city in the world would be subject to Canadian criminal jurisdiction—if a Canadian happened to be in the vicinity, and even if he was not injured by the bomb. Are other states, particularly the state in which the bombing occurred, likely to view this as a permissible extension of extraterritorial jurisdiction? Outside the treaty context, passive personality is controversial at the best of times, and the answer is probably in the negative. This is an extreme example, and it is unlikely that Canada would prosecute such an offence, but it effectively demonstrates the jurisdictional overbreadth of these provisions.

The argument might be mounted that the current international climate regarding terrorism has led sufficient numbers of states to acquiesce in more expansive assertions of jurisdiction over terrorist of-

---

496 See, generally, Currie & Coughlan, above note 112, and Chapter 8.
497 This was the basis on which Momin Khawaja was prosecuted (*R. v. Khawaja*, [2008] O.J. No. 4244 (S.C.J.)).
498 In accordance with the definition of "terrorist activity" in s. 83.01(1) of the *Criminal Code*, above note 109, specifically para. (b) of that definition.

fences—to the point that Canada's "new terrorism" is in compliance with *customary* international law. This is highly questionable, particularly in light of the absence of any explicit treaty-based agreement on what constitutes terrorism, let alone on extraterritorial jurisdiction over it. Establishing customary international law norms entails a very high threshold. Canada's extraterritorial jurisdiction provisions have seen little traffic and no international law analysis as yet,[499] so we remain in "wait and see" mode for the moment.

E. DRUG TRAFFICKING

1) International Law[500]

The international community is now decades into a sustained effort to fight what is often called "the drug trade," which includes both the trafficking of illegal substances and the illicit trade in licit drugs.[501] The problem is a complex and multi-layered one. An upward-spiraling increase in the demand for illegal drugs since the early 1970s has ensured that the drug trade has remained a lucrative one for those criminal elements involved in it.[502] Drug abuse is a serious problem that taps, and sometimes overtaxes, the social, economic, and political resources of many states. Drug abusers not only suffer from health problems, but are often moved to other forms of crime to support addiction. The criminals involved on the supply side, virtually always organized crime groups in some form, make massive amounts of profit at what can only be viewed, in the current law enforcement milieu, as manageable risk. These profits, in turn, can have distorting effects on domestic economies, particularly when combined with the corruption and political

---

499 In addition to Rutherford J.'s decision in the trial of Khawaja, above note 497, see *R. c. Namouh*, 2009 QCCQ 9324.

500 See, generally, Bernard Leroy, M. Cherif Bassiouni & Jean-François Thony, "The International Drug Control System" in M. Cherif Bassiouni, ed., *International Criminal Law*, 3d ed., vol. 1 (Leiden: Martinus Nijhoff, 2008) at 855.

501 Neil Boister, "The Historical Development of International Legal Measures to Suppress Drug Trafficking" (1997) 30 Comp. & Int'l L.J.S. Afr. 1.

502 UNODC, *UNDCP Technical Series No. 6: Economic and Social Consequences of Drug Abuse and Illicit Trafficking* (Vienna: UNODC, 1998) at 12, online: www.unodc.org/pdf/technical_series_1998-01-01_1.pdf. The UNODC has only recently (and cautiously) indicated that international demand for drugs may be levelling out; see UNODC, *World Drug Report 2008* (Vienna: UNODC, 2008) at 25, online: www.unodc.org/unodc/en/data-and-analysis/WDR-2008.html.

influence engendered by powerful drug lords in vulnerable states, such as in Bolivia and Colombia in the 1980s.

The international dimensions of the problem are similarly well known. Illicit drugs can be manufactured in one state, smuggled through three more, and trafficked in a fifth. The organized crime groups involved in drug trafficking are increasingly internationalized and avail themselves of jurisdictional gaps to move drugs across borders, often transporting by way of the high seas to avoid territorial entanglement with enforcement authorities. Trafficking routes are "lubricated" by bribery of customs officials and other enforcement personnel. The domination of the trade by such groups became more intense in the early 1990s, as the criminal element exploited the transitional nature of some emerging economies in post–Eastern bloc Europe, in particular. Interestingly, one traditionally thinks of drugs being extracted and manufactured in developing states (e.g., cocaine in South America, heroin from southeastern and southwestern Asia) and shipped off to domestic markets in the developed states of North America and Western Europe. However, it has become clear that there are multiple flows in multiple directions; the precursor chemicals for refining and processing of heroin and cocaine, for example, mostly come from industrialized states and are sent to the source states of the raw elements. European traffickers do a booming business exporting psychotropic substances to many other markets, including Africa.[503] The source states (and transit states) have also seen rises in domestic consumption of drugs and the corresponding problems that go with it.[504]

States (including Canada) have long been engaged in cooperative efforts to deal with the drug trade, as is evidenced by early treaties dealing with suppressing opium abuse[505] and the work of the League of Nations on regulating narcotics[506] and suppressing the trade in them.[507] The fledgling United Nations became immediately involved, and in 1946 it founded the Commission on Narcotic Drugs as an organ of the United Nations Economic and Social Council (ECOSOC) to analyze

---

503 William C. Gilmore, *Dirty Money: The Evolution of International Measures to Counter Money Laundering and the Financing of Terrorism*, 3d ed. (Strasbourg: Council of Europe Publishing, 2004) at 15.

504 For current figures broken down on a geographical basis, see *World Drug Report 2008*, above note 502.

505 *International Opium Convention* (1912), 8 L.N.T.S. 187.

506 *International Convention for Limiting the Manufacture and Regulating the Distribution of Narcotic Drugs*, Can. T.S. 1932 No. 7.

507 *Convention of 1936 for the Suppression of the Illicit Traffic in Dangerous Drugs*, Can. T.S. 1939 No. 12.

and report on world patterns in the drug trade and formulate mechanisms and recommendations to assist states in their efforts to combat drug trafficking. This body is still operational, supported by the United Nations Office on Drug Crime (UNODC) in its role as administrator of the UN International Drug Control Program (UNDCP).[508] The UN generally has been the nerve centre of international drug trafficking suppression efforts,[509] and spearheaded the negotiations which resulted in the major treaties dealt with here. Its work is supplemented by regional inter-state organizations, such as the OAS-sponsored Inter-American Drug Abuse Control Commission (CICAD).[510]

The first of these instruments was the 1961 *Single Convention on Narcotic Drugs*,[511] as modified by the 1972 *Protocol Amending the Single Convention on Narcotic Drugs*.[512] As suggested by the title, the *Single Convention* was designed to replace the various drug control conventions that had been concluded between states. It obliged states to criminalize and control the cultivation and manufacture of several illicit drugs, primarily opium, cannabis, cocaine, and their ingredients, and after the conclusion of the 1972 Protocol states were obliged to actually seize and destroy plants used in production. The latter instrument provided that the offences set out in the *Single Convention*[513] were to be extraditable between parties,[514] and laid out a prototypical *aut dedere aut judicare* provision.[515] However, the main use of the *Single Convention* and its Protocol was regulating the cultivation, manufacture, use, and trade of mostly licit drugs. This is a quality it shared with the 1971 *UN Convention on Psychotropic Substances*,[516] which was designed to deal with emerging kinds of synthetic drugs not covered under the *Single Convention*, such as amphetamines, barbiturates, tranquilizers, antidepressants, and LSD.

By the 1980s, it had become clear that the international drug trade, mostly in illicit substances, was quickly becoming a global problem that threatened to overwhelm the primarily regulatory and mild coopera-

---

508 See "The Commission on Narcotic Drugs," online: www.unodc.org/unodc/en/commissions/CND/index.html.
509 See the historical overview in UNODC, *World Drug Report 2008*, above note 502.
510 Online: www.cicad.oas.org/en/default.asp.
511 Can. T.S. 1964 No. 30 [*Single Convention*].
512 Can. T.S. 1976 No. 48.
513 Article 36 of the *Single Convention*, above note 511, as amended by the 1972 Protocol.
514 *Ibid.*, art. 36(2)(b).
515 *Ibid.*, art. 36(2)(a)(iv).
516 Can. T.S. 1988 No. 35 [*Psychotropic Substances Convention*].

tive stance the previous treaties had put in place.[517] International determination to formulate a comprehensive criminal law and enforcement mechanism to combat this scourge led to the landmark *United Nations Convention against Illicit Traffic in Narcotic Drugs and Psychotropic Substances*,[518] concluded at Vienna in 1988 after four years of negotiations. The *Vienna Narcotics Convention* is widely subscribed to by states and remains the key international instrument around which the fight against drug trafficking revolves. Explicitly designed to supplement and not replace the earlier treaties,[519] the wide-ranging approach of the treaty rests on a number of pillars. It contains now-standard obligations regarding the establishment of offences, potentially wide-ranging jurisdiction over these offences, extradition, mutual legal assistance, and cooperation between state authorities (including a specific article regarding cooperation with transit states[520]). However, the *Vienna Narcotics Convention* was the first global treaty containing obligations regarding the confiscation of proceeds of crime and the criminalization of money laundering.[521] It also contains unique provisions imposing stringent regulatory controls on the precursor substances, materials, and equipment used in the manufacture of illicit drugs. Specifically, parties are required to criminalize the "manufacture, transport or distribution" of these materials where the offender knows "they are to be used in or for the illicit cultivation, production or manufacture of narcotic drugs or psychotropic substances."[522] There are also a set of obligations on states to prevent diversion of precursor substances out of areas of legitimate use (e.g., the scientific and medical sectors), including strict monitoring of exports.[523] As would increasingly become the case with modern suppression conventions, there is recognition in the *Vienna Narcotics Convention* regime that states should act, and cooperate, to address the causes of the crime. In this context, the focus is on reducing demand for illegal drugs and providing social assistance of

---

517 See Jack Donnelly, "The United Nations and the Global Drug Control Regime" in Peter H. Smith, ed., *Drug Policy in the Americas* (Boulder, CO: Westview Press, 1991) 282 at 287.

518 Above note 13. See, generally, United Nations, *Commentary on the* United Nations Convention against Illicit Traffic in Narcotic Drugs and Psychotropic Substances *1988* (New York: UN Publications, 1998) 1-11 [*UN Commentary*].

519 *Vienna Narcotics Convention, ibid.*, art. 25.

520 *Ibid.*, art. 10.

521 See Section F, below in this chapter.

522 Above note 13, art. 3(1)(a)(iv).

523 *Ibid.*, art. 12.

various kinds to addicts, in accordance with guidelines propounded by the UN "and other competent international organizations."[524]

The offence provisions contained in article 3 of the *Vienna Narcotics Convention* are designed to suppress the various kinds of activity which make up the international drug trade. The offences are framed with a certain level of generality. As Boister remarks, "the whole Convention labours under the restrictions contained in article 2(1) which provides that application of the Convention's obligations must be 'in conformity with the fundamental provisions of [states'] respective domestic legislative systems',"[525] which has led to inconsistent levels of criminalization among state parties. As regards the prohibited substances themselves, article 3 integrates the *Vienna Narcotics Convention* with the earlier treaties, while augmenting in places. Article 3(1)(a) sets out the required "standard trafficking offences,"[526] criminalizing production, manufacture, sale, distribution, transport, and so on, of the prohibited substances,[527] as well as the possession/purchase of any substances for any of these purposes;[528] cultivation of opium poppy, coca bush, or cannabis plant for the purpose of producing narcotics;[529] manufacture, transport, or distribution of equipment, materials, or substances which can be used in production or manufacture;[530] and the organizing, management, or financing of any of these.[531] Article 3(1)(b) provides for required money-laundering offences associated with narcotics, and criminalizes conversion or transfer of property derived from the earlier offences,[532] as well as the concealment or disguise of the nature of such property.[533] Article 3(1)(c) provides for, though it does not require, criminalization of acquisition, possession, or use of property, knowing that it was derived from an offence;[534] possession of equipment and precursor substances knowing they are being used or to be used in drug manufacture;[535] publicly inciting/inducing others

---

524 *Ibid.*, art. 14(4).
525 Neil Boister, *Penal Aspects of the UN Drug Conventions* (The Hague: Kluwer Law International, 2001) at 99.
526 *Ibid.*, at 100.
527 Above note 13, art. 3(1)(a)(i).
528 *Ibid.*, art. 3(1)(a)(iii).
529 *Ibid.*, art. 3(1)(a)(ii).
530 *Ibid.*, art. 3(1)(a)(iv).
531 *Ibid.*, art. 3(1)(a)(v).
532 *Ibid.*, art. 3(1)(b)(i).
533 *Ibid.*, art. 3(1)(b)(ii).
534 *Ibid.*, art. 3(1)(c)(i).
535 *Ibid.*, art. 3(1)(c)(ii).

to commit the offences;[536] and various forms of complicity in offences and inchoate offences, including conspiracy.[537] The article also contains a large number of provisions designed to enhance the seriousness of drug offences for the purposes of domestic punishment and sentencing regimes.

Jurisdiction is provided for in article 4 of the Convention, with a mixture of mandatory and permissive grounds. States are obliged to establish jurisdiction on the basis of the territorial principle,[538] as well as on board registered aircraft and flagged vessels.[539] The official commentary to the Convention notes that territoriality as used in this article should be read broadly as encompassing the various forms of qualified territoriality available under customary international law (objective, subjective, and "effects").[540] States may also establish jurisdiction on the basis of nationality/habitual residence[541] and where one of the inchoate offences set out in article 3(1)(c)(iv) is committed outside the state with a view to the commission of an offence in its territory.[542] Article 4(1)(b)(ii) authorizes states to exercise jurisdiction where the state has invoked article 17 of the Convention. The latter provision is designed to combat maritime transport of drugs by allowing states observing suspicious vessels to request the flag state's permission to board and search the vessel, if the ship is exercising freedom of navigation under international law.[543] This is, at best, a weak provision, since nothing prevents any state from requesting permission to board, either under UNCLOS or general international law.

The *aut dedere aut judicare* mechanism, standard in most suppression conventions, is in a somewhat attenuated form in the *Vienna Narcotics Convention*. The extradite or prosecute obligation itself is found in article 6(9), but is linked with article 4(2), which combines obligations regarding the exercise of jurisdiction with grounds for refusal of extradition. Article 4(2)(a) obliges parties to establish jurisdiction over offences where the offender is on the state's territory and it refuses to extradite her because either (1) the offence was committed on the

---

536 *Ibid.*, art. 3(1)(c)(iii).
537 *Ibid.*, art. 3(1)(c)(iv).
538 *Ibid.*, art. 4(1)(a)(i).
539 *Ibid.*, art. 4(1)(a)(ii).
540 *UN Commentary*, above note 518 at 104 and 111–12. Regarding these bases of jurisdiction, see, generally, Chapter 2.
541 Above note 13, art. 4(1)(b)(i).
542 *Ibid.*, art. 4(1)(b)(iii).
543 See William Gilmore, "Drug Trafficking by Sea: The 1988 *United Nations Convention against Illicit Traffic in Narcotic Drugs and Psychotropic Substances*" (1991) 15 Marine Policy 183.

state's territory, or its flagged vessel or registered aircraft, or (2) the offence was committed by one of its nationals. Article 4(2)(b) provides, permissively, that a state may establish jurisdiction where the offender is present in its territory and it does not extradite her to another state party. The net effect is a rejection of a mandatory *aut dedere aut judicare* mechanism, a position which was successfully pushed by mostly common law states at the Vienna Conference.[544]

The Convention contains what were, for the time, some fairly novel provisions regarding inter-state cooperation. In recognition of the need to disable traffickers by removing profits from their operations, article 5 obliges states to enable its competent authorities to confiscate proceeds of the crimes laid out in article 3(1); property derived therefrom; and drugs, materials, equipment, or other instrumentalities used or intended for use in these offences.[545] States must also put in place measures to identify, trace, freeze, or seize these materials for the purpose of confiscation.[546] Importantly, states must respond to requests from other states to take these measures within the territory of the requested state, subject to the latter's domestic law and any treaty obligations.[547] The provision does not require the requested state to send the confiscated proceeds or materials to the requesting state, but state parties are encouraged to conclude agreements to allow for this, as well as for sharing information with other interested party states or intergovernmental bodies specializing in combating the drug trade.[548]

Article 6 of the Convention provides for a fairly standard extradition scheme, where states must include the treaty offences as extraditable offences for the purpose of any extradition treaty to which they are parties.[549] Parties may consider the extradition provisions as an extradition treaty in situations where they are dealing with states that are parties to the Convention but with which they have no existing extradition arrangements.[550] Similarly, article 7 provides for a detailed mutual legal assistance scheme for use by parties, and provides that paragraphs 8–19 of that article *shall* apply as a mutual legal assistance arrangement as between states which have no existing treaties.[551] This

---

544 See Boister, above note 525 at 246–50.
545 Above note 13, arts. 5(1)(a) & (b).
546 *Ibid.*, arts. 5(2) & (3). Article 5(3) emphasizes that states cannot invoke bank secrecy as a reason for refusing to engage in these activities.
547 *Ibid.*, art. 5(4).
548 *Ibid.*, art. 5(5).
549 *Ibid.*, art. 6(2).
550 *Ibid.*, art. 6(3).
551 *Ibid.*, art. 7(7).

was quite progressive for the time, and reflects the fact that the practice of mutual legal assistance was in its infancy and most states were not party to a large number of treaties, if any. Its mandatory character, as well, underscored the international law enforcement community's view of the increasing importance of this mode of criminal law enforcement cooperation. There are also articles dealing with transfer of proceedings,[552] cooperation and training as between national law enforcement personnel,[553] and the inter-state use of "controlled delivery," an investigational technique whereby quantities of illegal or suspect drugs are permitted to pass through borders or states while being monitored by authorities, in an effort to identify the principals, organizers, or financiers behind the operation.[554]

2) Canadian Implementing Legislation

As part of "Canada's Drug Strategy"[555] to counteract the effects that drugs and the drug trade have on Canadians and the international community, Canada has actively participated in international efforts to suppress the drug trade. It is a party to the *Single Convention*[556] and its 1972 Protocol,[557] the *Psychotropic Substances Convention*,[558] and the *Vienna Narcotics Convention*, as well as being active in numerous intergovernmental organizations dedicated to narcotics suppression, such as the OAS-based Inter-American Drug Abuse Control Commission (CICAD).[559] As would be expected, cooperation with the US plays a significant role in Canada's international efforts. A range of law enforcement agencies in each state jointly prepare the "Canada–U.S. Border Drug Threat Assessment" annually.[560]

Canada's implementation of its international obligations is primarily accomplished by way of the *Controlled Drugs and Substances Act*

---

552 *Ibid.*, art. 8.
553 *Ibid.*, art. 9.
554 *Ibid.*, art. 11.
555 Health Canada, *Canada's Drug Strategy* (Ottawa: Office of Alcohol, Drugs and Dependency Issues, Health Canada, 1998). And see the "National Anti-Drug Strategy," online: www.nationalantidrugstrategy.gc.ca/.
556 Above note 511.
557 Above note 512.
558 Above note 516.
559 Above note 510. For more details, see Department of Foreign Affairs and International Trade, "Illicit Drugs," online: www.dfait-maeci.gc.ca/international-crime/drugs-en.asp.
560 Online: www.publicsafety.gc.ca/prg/le/oc/_fl/us-canadian-report-drugs-eng.pdf (last available report is 2007).

(*CDSA*).[561] The *CDSA* has four schedules (I–IV) which list a number of drugs (both licit and illicit) and four which contain precursor materials and substances (V–VIII). The offence provisions in the Act incorporate the schedules by reference. Accordingly, the Act criminalizes possession of drugs (section 4), trafficking and possession of drugs for the purpose of trafficking (section 5), importing/exporting and possession for the purpose of importing/exporting both drugs and precursor materials and substances (section 6), and producing drugs (section 7). Article 3(1)(a)(iv) of the Convention, regarding equipment, materials, and substances is criminalized via section 462.2 of the *Criminal Code*.[562] Complicity and inchoate offences are provided for by incorporation of the relevant parts of the *Criminal Code* under section 3(1) of the *CDSA*. The money-laundering offences are provided for in Canada's money-laundering and proceeds-of-crime legislation, explained below.

The Act contains no explicit provisions regarding jurisdiction, and thus the default must be territorial jurisdiction, as amplified in the qualified territoriality sense by *Libman*.[563] Section 477.1 of the *Code* provides for jurisdiction over offences committed on Canadian-flagged ships, while section 7(1) of the *Code* provides for jurisdiction over offences committed on board Canadian-registered aircraft. Sections 477.1 and 477.3 also seem to be the vehicle by which the jurisdictional option under article 4(1)(b)(ii) (regarding boarding and searching of vessels exercising freedom of navigation) can be exercised. However, those provisions authorize boarding and search on the high seas only in situations where hot pursuit[564] has been commenced, which is not as broad an exercise of this particular treaty provision as could be. The obligations in article 4(2)(a) regard decisions which are made at the executive level, and complying with subparagraph 4(2)(a)(ii) will be easy given that Canada does not refuse to extradite its nationals on the basis of their citizenship, as so some European states. The custodial universal jurisdiction set out in article 4(2)(b), by contrast, is permissive, and for some reason Canada has not implemented it.

The freezing, seizure, and confiscation obligations under the *Vienna Narcotics Convention* are largely implemented under the *CDSA*. Sections 11–13 provide for search, seizure, and detention of controlled substances, precursor substances, offence-related property, and evidence,

---

561 S.C. 1996, c. 19.
562 Above note 109. It is not clear whether art. 3(1)(a)(v) is clearly implemented, though such conduct could be prosecuted as conspiracy to traffic or produce a controlled substance.
563 Above note 68.
564 See Chapter 2.

while restraint and management orders are available as against offence-related property under sections 14–15. Sections 16–23 provide a forfeiture regime for offence-related property. All matters regarding proceeds of crime (including sharing) are dealt with in Section F(2), below in this chapter. The extradition, mutual legal assistance, and transfer of proceedings obligations are implemented via the general legislation on each of those topics.[565]

F. PROCEEDS OF CRIME AND MONEY LAUNDERING

1) International Law

A review of the legal responses to transnational crimes of international concern discussed in Sections C, D, and E, above in this chapter, reveals that, particularly of late, there has been an increased focus on combating the transnational criminal by way of "financial devastation"[566] — that is, removing or at least obstructing the profitability of organized criminal activity. This is a logical means of dealing with forms of crime (such as the narcotics trade, financial crime, or arms smuggling) by which criminals derive astounding profits, conservatively measured in the hundreds of billions of dollars per year.

The primary means of bringing the battle to this end of transnational criminal operations has been to oblige states to put in place two kinds of mechanisms: (1) laws which enable authorities to trace, freeze, seize, and/or confiscate the "proceeds of crime" (whether in the form of money or other property derived from criminal activity) and (2) criminal offences which criminalize the practice of "money laundering."[567] The latter term refers to the conversion of money gained through criminal activity ("dirty money") into legitimate or "clean" money, disguising its origin so as to free it up for subsequent use by the criminal party. Money laundering is accomplished by way of a variety of techniques, often by circulating funds through banks and other kinds of financial institutions and companies.[568] While traditionally

---

565 See Chapter 9.

566 Gilmore, above note 503 at 20.

567 See, generally, Guy Stessens, *Money Laundering* (Cambridge: Cambridge University Press, 2000); Hector L. MacQueen, ed., *Money Laundering* (Edinburgh: University of Edinburgh Press, 1993).

568 William C. Gilmore, one of the major international authorities in the area, describes the three stages of money laundering: "[1] *Placement stage*: where cash

the laundering was carried out by the same criminals who generated the illegal profits in the first place, recent trends indicate that a great deal of it is now done by "professional" launderers who offer it as a service to their criminal clients in return for a healthy percentage as a fee. It has been clear for some time that money laundering is a highly internationalized activity,[569] and in a time of computerized banking transactions that can cycle money through ten different jurisdictions in the space of a second, this is obviously going to continue to be the case. Just as obviously, in the globalized economy, inter-state cooperation is not only the key to combating money laundering but probably the only effective way of doing it.

The international legal and policy regime around proceeds of crime and money laundering has a trait in common with anti-corruption efforts: because the international financial and business communities are directly affected, a great deal of resources has gone into efforts to formulate and coordinate the responses. Accordingly, the array of instruments and institutions is more multi-layered and complex than most. On the purely criminal law side, the 1988 *Vienna Narcotics Convention*[570] was the first modern suppression convention to set out both confiscation measures and money laundering offences—all, as was outlined, in the context of a treaty which obliged states to cooperate in investigation, the provision of mutual legal assistance, and extradition. This model proved to be highly influential, in particular on subsequent European instruments such as the 1990 Council of Europe *Convention on Laundering, Search, Seizure and Confiscation of the Proceeds of Crime.*[571] States quickly embraced the *Vienna Narcotics Convention* approach and, spurred on by the United Nations,[572] began to extend it to other forms

derived directly from criminal activity (for example, from sales of drugs) is first placed either in a financial institution or used to purchase an asset. [2] *Layering stage*: the stage at which there is the first attempt at concealment or disguise of the source of the ownership of the funds. [3] *Integration stage*: the stage at which the money is integrated into the legitimate economic and financial system and is assimilated with all other assets in the system." (Gilmore, above note 503 at 32). See the illustrative diagram provided by the UNODC, online: www.unodc.org/images/odccp/money_laundering_scheme_big.jpg.

569 Margaret Beare & Stephen Schneider, *Tracing of Illicit Funds: Money Laundering in Canada* (Ottawa: Solicitor General of Canada, 1990) at 304.

570 Above note 13. See Section E, above in this chapter.

571 E.T.S. 141. See also Council of Europe Directive 91/308/EEC on prevention of the use of the financial system for the purpose of money laundering, as amended by Directive 2001/97/EC of the European Parliament of the Council of 4 December 2001. For more on European developments, see Bantekas & Nash, above note 47 at 256–61; Gilmore, above note 503, cc. VII & VIII.

572 See GA Res. 49/159 and S-20/4D.

of serious crime.[573] These developments culminated in the inclusion of proceeds and money laundering obligations in both the *TOC Convention*[574] and the *Corruption Convention*.[575] The most important development in the last decade has been the extension of confiscation and anti-money-laundering techniques to the fight against terrorism. The 1999 *Terrorist Financing Convention*[576] obliges states to trace, freeze, and seize monies and resources being used to finance terrorist acts, and post 9/11, this treaty regime has been somewhat overtaken by binding Security Council resolutions[577] under which all states must engage in an expanded range of anti-terrorist financing activities.

The treaty work has been supported by a backbone made up of other international organizations. The UN has played a prominent role, having shepherded in the *Vienna Narcotics Convention*, the *TOC Convention*, and the *Corruption Convention*, and continues major international coordinative efforts.[578] By way of the UNODC and its Anti Money Laundering Unit (AMLU),[579] the UN has formulated model legislation dealing with the major aspects both of domestic confiscation and prosecution of money laundering and inter-state cooperation, for use by both common law[580] and civil law[581] states. It has also circulated the 2003 UN *Model Terrorist Financing Bill*,[582] an instrument designed to help (primarily common law) states to implement the 1999 *Terrorist Financing Convention* and the associated Security Council resolutions.

The other central organization in the field is the Financial Action Task Force (FATF),[583] which has been described as "the single most

---

573 Both the Commonwealth Secretariat and the OAS have propounded model legislation for the guidance of their respective members; see Commonwealth Model Law, online: www.imolin.org/pdf/imolin/Comsecml.pdf; CICAD Model Regulations, online: www.imolin.org/imolin/cicadml.html.

574 Above note 26.

575 Above note 55.

576 Above note 41. See Section D(7), above in the chapter.

577 SC Res. 1368 and 1373.

578 For example, the UN was the founder of the International Money Laundering Information Network (IMoLIN), "an Internet-based network assisting governments, organizations, and individuals in the fight against money laundering" (see IMoLIN online: www.imolin.org/imolin/index.html).

579 Online: www.unodc.org/unodc/en/money-laundering/index.html.

580 See UNODC *Model Money-Laundering, Proceeds of Crime and Terrorist Financing Bill 2003*, online: www.imolin.org/imolin/poctf03.html.

581 See UN/IMF Model legislation on money laundering and financing of terrorism, 1 December 2005, online: www.imolin.org/pdf/imolin/ModelLaw-February2007.pdf.

582 Online: www.imolin.org/imolin/en/tfbill03.html.

583 Online: www.fatf-gafi.org.

important international body in terms of the formulation of anti-money-laundering policy and in the mobilization of global awareness of the complex issues involved in countering this sophisticated form of criminality."[584] Founded by the G7 states, along with the European Commission and eight other interested states in 1989,[585] the FATF is essentially an anti-money-laundering think-tank, policy workshop, and monitor of states. Housed at the OECD offices, it brings together significant international expertise to formulate policy recommendations — targeted both at governments, in terms of criminal law methods of dealing with money laundering, and at the international financial sector, in terms of helping these "target" institutions both to identify and to prevent money laundering from taking place through them. The organization also monitors the compliance of its member states with its policy imperatives,[586] and plays a role in mounting pressure on other states to bring their laws in line with FATF policies by way of its "Non-Cooperative Countries and Territories Initiative."[587]

The primary work of the FATF has been their celebrated "40 Recommendations"[588] on combating money laundering, which are divided into four sections that describe the topics they address:

1) Legal Systems (i.e., criminal offences for money laundering and confiscation);
2) Measures to be Taken by Financial Institutions and Non-Financial Businesses and Professions to Prevent Money Laundering and Terrorist Financing;
3) Institutional and Other Measures Necessary in Systems for Combating Money Laundering and Terrorist Financing; and
4) International Cooperation.

The Recommendations are fairly specific policy goals, which are supplemented by official commentary and "best practices" guides to help with their implementation. In the aftermath of the 9/11 attacks, the

---

584 Gilmore, above note 503 at 89.

585 The FATF now has 34 members, including Canada.

586 As Hubbard *et al.* note, "Canada has been the object of two FATF mutual evaluations. The new *Proceeds of Crime (Money Laundering) and Terrorism Financing Act* reflects the persuasive and real authority of the FATF review process, for the Act is a direct result of FATF reviews" (Robert Hubbard *et al.*, *Money Laundering & Proceeds of Crime* (Toronto: Irwin Law, 2004) at 54).

587 Online: www.fatf-gafi.org/document/51/0,3343,en_32250379_32236992_33916403_1_1_1_1,00.html.

588 These Recommendations were first issued in 1990 and were revised in 1996 and 2003. For a current version, see online: www.fatf-gafi.org/document/28/0,3343,en_32250379_32236930_33658140_1_1_1_1,00.html.

FATF was charged by the G7 and European Union to formulate a set of recommendations to address specifically terrorist financing, and the "9 Special Recommendations on Terrorist Financing" were issued quickly thereafter.[589] These called on states to ratify international treaties regarding terrorist financing and contained specific directions for identifying and confiscating terrorist funds for both governments and the private sector, but also dealt with such cutting-edge issues as the abuse of wire transfers and non-profit organizations by terrorists, as well as such non-Western "alternative remittance" mechanisms as *hawala, hundi*, and *fei-chien*[590] that can allow terrorist financing to go on undetected. While not a treaty, the FATF's Recommendations are nonetheless the international gold standard of anti-money-laundering norms and constitute a form of "soft law" that is far more compelling and widely subscribed to than many treaty regimes.

There are a number of other international organizations that are engaged in influential policy work in this area. Since its creation in 1974 by the governors of the central banks of ten major OECD states, the Basel Committee on Banking Supervision (Basel Committee)[591] has played a major role in the formulation of anti-money-laundering policy globally. This role is a function of the Basel Committee's unique character as a forum for the creation of supervisory and best practices standards for banks, by way of close contact between state central banking authorities.[592] In this role it has released numerous publications dealing with anti-money-laundering techniques for financial institutions, most notably "Prevention of Criminal Use of the Banking System for the Purpose of Money Laundering" (1988), "Core Principles for Effective Banking Supervision" (1997), "Customer Due Diligence for Banks"

---

589 The Special Recommendations initially numbered eight, but a ninth (dealing with cross-border cash movement) was added in 2004. For a current version, see online: www.fatf-gafi.org/document/9/0,3343,en_32250379_32236920_34032073_1_1_1_1,00.html.

590 These are "informal" methods of cash movement and remittance that do not use negotiable instruments and generally are based in networks of acquaintance and/or family. See International Monetary Fund, *Regulatory Frameworks for Hawala and Other Remittance Systems* (Washington: IMF, 2005); INTERPOL, "The Hawala Alternative Remittance System and its Role in Money Laundering," online: www.interpol.int/Public/FinancialCrime/MoneyLaundering/hawala/default.asp.

591 Online: www.bis.org/bcbs/index.htm. The Basel Committee is housed in the Bank for International Settlements in Basel, Switzerland.

592 The Basel Committee is made up of public authorities. The Wolfsberg Group is a group of major global private banks engaged in similar policy-formulation activity, online: www.wolfsberg-principles.com/.

(2001), and "Sharing of Financial Records Between Jurisdictions in Connection with the Fight Against Terrorist Financing" (2002). The Basel Committee is generally credited with the origin of the "know your customer (KYC)" concept, which encourages customer identification among banks as a primary means of detecting and preventing money laundering, and its work has been very influential on the FATF and states generally. Also notable is the Toronto-based Egmont Group,[593] an informal group of national financial intelligence units (FIUs)[594] which is dedicated to developing the roles and functions of these agencies.

2) Canadian Implementing Legislation[595]

Canada is no stranger to the practices and effects associated with money laundering, particularly by way of the illicit narcotics trade and organized crime groups more generally. The money derived from illegal activities and recirculated through both the legitimate and underground economies in Canada likely numbers in the billions of dollars, and Canadian authorities have been actively engaged in investigating and at least attempting to suppress it.[596] Canada is party to the major treaties which contain proceeds of crime and money-laundering obligations, and participates in the FATF, the Caribbean Financial Action Task Force (CFATF), and the Egmont Group, *inter alia*. Canada's legislative history begins with the 1989 implementation of the obligations in the *Vienna Narcotics Convention*[597] and has continued apace since that time as the federal government keeps abreast of international developments, particularly regarding terrorist financing.[598]

---

593 Online: www.egmontgroup.org/.

594 FIUs are the brainchild of the FATF: national authorities or agencies, whether police-based or simply governmental, that are designed to monitor reports of transactions from financial and other institutions, analyze these, and report and act on suspicious transactions. Canada's FIU is FINTRAC (see below in this section).

595 The Canadian legal regime regarding proceeds of crime and money laundering is made up of many groups of complex and disparate laws, both criminal and regulatory. It is effectively surveyed in Hubbard *et al.*, above note 586.

596 See Stephen Schneider, *Money Laundering in Canada: An Analysis of RCMP Cases* (Toronto: Nathanson Centre for the Study of Organized Crime and Corruption, 2004).

597 Above note 13.

598 For a review, see EKOS Research Asociates, *Year Five Evaluation of the National Initiatives to Combat Money Laundering and Interim Evaluation of Measures to Combat Terrorist Financing* (Ottawa: EKOS Research Associates, 2004).

In terms of purely criminal laws, the main offences are contained in sections 462.31 and 354 of the *Criminal Code*.[599] Section 462.31 is contained within Part XII.2 of the *Code*, entitled "Proceeds of Crime." It is a broadly worded prohibition on doing anything with or to any property or proceeds of property, with intent to conceal or convert it, if the accused knows or believes that the proceeds or property derived directly or indirectly from a designated offence,[600] whether in Canada or elsewhere.[601] The provision for the accused's belief as part of the *actus reus* of the crime, separately from the requirement of knowledge, allows for the police to use reverse sting operations that mislead the target into thinking the monies being laundered are proceeds of crime when, in fact, it is "clean" property used for this purpose.[602] Section 354 is an older provision that well predates concern about money laundering, and is broader than section 462.31 in that it is not linked to designated offences. It criminalizes the possession of any property or proceeds of property, where the accused knows that all or part of the property or proceeds was derived directly or indirectly from the commission of an indictable offence in Canada, or an act or omission elsewhere that would constitute an indictable offence if committed in Canada. Given that the criminal act which gave rise to the property involved in both provisions can stem from a criminal act in another state, a transnational aspect is automatically built in to both. There is also an ancillary proceeds of crime offence which acts to implement the transnational aspects of Canada's international law obligations: section 357 of the *Code*, which criminalizes the bringing into Canada of any property derived from crime.[603]

The regime for seizure and forfeiture of proceeds of crime is also contained within Part XII.2 of the *Code*, where it was updated and streamlined by the organized crime amendments.[604] "Proceeds of crime" is defined broadly in section 462.3(1) as "any property, benefit or advantage, within or outside Canada, obtained or derived directly or indirectly" from a designated offence, committed in or outside of Canada. The remainder of Part XII.2 provides for the various required mechanisms:

---

599 Above note 109.
600 Defined in s. 462.3(1) as any indictable offence under any federal act except by way of regulation, or conspiracy to commit, or any inchoate form of these offences.
601 Specifically, where the act or omission from which the property or proceeds derived would have been a designated offence if it had occurred in Canada.
602 See *R. v. Daoust*, 2004 SCC 6.
603 See *R. v. Yue*, [1996] B.C.J. No. 385 (C.A.).
604 Above note 108.

search and seizure (section 462.32), restraint orders (section 462.33), forfeiture upon conviction (section 462.37) including special provisions dealing with organized crime proceeds (section 462.37(2.01)–(2.07)), and forfeiture prior to conviction but upon an information being laid (section 462.38).[605] Forfeiture orders can be issued concerning property located outside Canada (section 462.37(2.1)), though these would have to be enforced by way of a request to the foreign state's government, either on an *ad hoc* basis or under the applicable treaty provisions. A supplementary forfeiture regime specifically targeting "offence-related property" is contained in sections 490.1–490.9 of the *Code*. These provisions are targeted at property which is used in or to facilitate the commission of a crime, as opposed to proceeds thereof, though there is some overlap. They extend to indictable offences under the *Code* or under the *Corruption of Foreign Public Officials Act*,[606] and obviously have some overlap with the proceeds forfeiture provisions. The *Controlled Drugs and Substances Act* (*CDSA*)[607] contains a stand-alone regime of this kind that provides for the forfeiture of offence-related property in drug cases.[608] Similarly, the *Anti-Terrorism Act* inserted seizure and forfeiture provisions into the *Code* regarding terrorist property.[609]

Also of note is the *Seized Property Management Act*,[610] which creates a scheme under which the Seized Property Management Directorate (under the authority of the Minister of Public Works and Government Services) takes possession of and manages property seized or forfeited under the foregoing provisions. In particular, section 11 of the Act empowers the Attorney General to enter into agreements with foreign states for the reciprocal sharing of proceeds or property forfeited, where the foreign state's authorities participated in the investigation that led to the forfeiture. This implements provisions in a number of treaties that concern sharing, though for the most part these are "soft" obligations which only call upon party states to consider this kind of allotment.[611]

---

605 Section 490(9) of the *Code* provides a further avenue for proceeds confiscation, independent of Part XII.2; see Hubbard *et al.*, note 586 at 159–77.

606 Above note 266.

607 Above note 561.

608 *Ibid.*, ss. 6–22. The Supreme Court of Canada recently rendered a badly divided judgment on how to apply the forfeiture provisions regarding real property (ss. 16(1) and 19.1(3)): *R. v. Craig*, 2009 SCC 23.

609 Above note 462, ss. 83.13 & 83.14.

610 S.C. 1993, c. 37.

611 For example, *Vienna Narcotics Convention*, above note 13, art. 5(5)(b)(ii); *TOC Convention*, above note 26, art. 14. Interestingly, the *Rome Statute*, above note 7 contains a "hard" obligation for states to enforce orders of fines or forfeiture by

As explained above, the current international scheme to combat money laundering envisions a regulatory structure that operates in tandem with the criminal law aspects. In order to find the criminal activity for the purpose of prosecution, financial transactions and currency flows must be monitored, and banks and other financial institutions must have both the duty to report suspicious transactions and a means of alerting the authorities. In Canada, this scheme is implemented by way of the *Proceeds of Crime (Money Laundering) and Terrorist Financing Act.*[612] While sometimes described as the means by which Canada can "conform to its international obligations"[613] regarding money laundering, this regime in fact "implements" the non-binding but extremely influential work of the various organizations described above, particularly the FATF. The Act's function is well summarized by section 3:

3. The object of this Act is

(a) to implement specific measures to detect and deter money laundering and the financing of terrorist activities and to facilitate the investigation and prosecution of money laundering offences and terrorist activity financing offences, including

   (i) establishing record keeping and client identification requirements for financial services providers and other persons or entities that engage in businesses, professions or activities that are susceptible to being used for money laundering or the financing of terrorist activities,

   (ii) requiring the reporting of suspicious financial transactions and of cross-border movements of currency and monetary instruments, and

   (iii) establishing an agency that is responsible for dealing with reported and other information;

(b) to respond to the threat posed by organized crime by providing law enforcement officials with the information they need to deprive criminals of the proceeds of their criminal activities, while ensuring that appropriate safeguards are put in place to protect the privacy of persons with respect to personal information about themselves; and

(c) to assist in fulfilling Canada's international commitments to participate in the fight against transnational crime, particularly money laundering, and the fight against terrorist activity.

---

the International Criminal Court, and transfer the property or proceeds to the court (art. 109).

612 S.C. 2000, c. 17, as am. S.C. 2001, cc. 12, 27, 32 and 41, and S.C. 2006, c. 12.

613 Hubbard *et al.*, above note 586 at 253.

Accordingly, the Act is the main instrument by which Canada adheres to the FATF's 40 Recommendations[614] (except the criminal law aspects of that list) and the newer 9 Special Recommendations on Terrorist Financing.[615] It gives rise to three sets of regulations that govern the behaviour of financial service providers and impose such FATF-inspired requirements as the KYC principle, record-keeping, and suspicious transaction monitoring and reporting: the *Proceeds of Crime (Money Laundering) and Terrorist Financing Regulations,*[616] the *Proceeds of Crime (Money Laundering) and Terrorist Financing Suspicious Transaction Reporting Regulations,*[617] and the *Cross-Border Currency and Monetary Instruments Reporting Regulations.*[618] The Act also creates the Financial Transaction and Report Analysis Centre (FINTRAC).[619] FINTRAC is an example of a financial intelligence unit (FIU), an agency at arm's length from law enforcement which functions to collect, analyze, and (in appropriate circumstances) report information that will assist in the detection and prosecution of money laundering. It is also responsible for enforcing the record-keeping and transaction reporting obligations which the Act imposes on financial service providers,[620] and is empowered to exchange information with FIUs in other states.[621]

Additionally, section 74 of the Act creates an offence of failing to comply with the obligation in section 6 of the Act to keep records in accordance with the regulations.

G. "CHILD SEX TOURISM"

1) International Law

The sexual exploitation of children in its various forms is a horrendous enough practice, but since the mid-1990s significant attention has been paid to a particularly pernicious transnational phenomenon, popularly referred to as "child sex tourism."[622] This phrase essentially refers to the

---

614 Above note 588.

615 Above note 589.

616 S.O.R./2002-184.

617 S.O.R./2001-317.

618 S.O.R./2002-412.

619 Above note 612, Part 3.

620 *Ibid.*, ss. 62–64.

621 *Ibid.*, ss. 56–56.2.

622 See, generally, Elizabeth Bevilacqua, "Child Sex Tourism and Child Prostitution in Asia: What Can Be Done to Protect the Rights of Children Abroad under International Law?" (1998–1999) 5 ILSA J. Int'l. & Comp. L. 171.

fact that child prostitution is particularly widespread in certain states which are popular tourist destinations, where local economic conditions combine with under-resourced or corrupt policing to produce havens for foreign pedophiles. This practice has been identified as a particular problem in South Asian states such as Thailand, Cambodia, and Vietnam, but also in other parts of the developing world, including South and Central America and parts of Africa.[623]

There is a substantial body of soft law instruments which evidence, at least formally, a fair amount of political will on the part of states to suppress this activity. UNICEF has been particularly active in this regard, and views the commercial sexual exploitation of children as "one of the worst forms of child labour and a modern form of slavery."[624] In 2001, UNICEF was a co-organizer (along with ECPAT[625], the NGO Group for the Convention on the Rights of the Child,[626] and the Japanese government) of the Second Congress against Commercial Exploitation of Children,[627] held in Yokohama, Japan, which produced the "Yokohama Global Commitment."[628] In this document, states expressed their commitment to cooperate and intensify their efforts towards protecting children from sexual exploitation and abuse, and to take steps both to deal with domestic root causes of the practice and to implement relevant international law instruments that would facilitate this. Of particular importance for present purposes was the affirmation of the development of "new laws to criminalize this phenomenon, including provisions with extra-territorial effect."[629]

In terms of hard international law obligations, several are key. Article 34 of the 1989 United Nations *Convention on the Rights of the Child (UNCRC)*[630] obliges states to "undertake to protect the child from all forms of sexual exploitation and sexual abuse" by way of "all appropriate national, bilateral and multilateral measures." In 2000, a group of states parties to the *UNCRC* concluded the *Optional Protocol to the Convention on the Rights of the Child on the Sale of Children, Child Prostitution*

---

623 See, generally, ECPAT International, an NGO in special consultative status with ECOSOC, online: www.ecpat.net/EI/Programmes_project.asp?groupID=3.

624 UNICEF, "Child Protection Information Sheet: Commercial Sexual Exploitation," online: www.unicef.org/protection/files/Sexual_Exploitation.pdf.

625 End Child Prostitution Child Pornography and Trafficking of Children for Sexual Purposes, online: www.ecpat.net/EI/index.asp.

626 Online: www.crin.org/NGOGroupforCRC/index.asp.

627 The first congress was held in Stockholm, Sweden, in 1996.

628 Reproduced online: www.unicef.org/events/yokohama/outcome.html.

629 *Ibid.*

630 Above note 133.

and Child Pornography.[631] Article 3 of the *CRC Protocol* requires states to criminalize child prostitution and sexual exploitation and the sale and possession of child pornography, as well as the transfer of a child's organs for profit, and engaging children in forced labour. Article 4 deals with jurisdiction, providing for obligatory territorial, registered ship and registered aircraft jurisdiction,[632] and permissively for nationality and passive personality jurisdiction.[633] It also provides for custodial universal jurisdiction, and contains obligatory and standard extradite or prosecute provisions.[634] Article 6 contains obligations regarding the provision of extradition[635] and mutual legal assistance between the parties. Article 7 provides for the seizure and confiscation of assets and proceeds of crime, either at the state's own initiative or at the request of a treaty partner, as well as "measures aimed at closing, on a temporary or definitive basis, premises used to commit such offences."[636]

There is other, more general, treaty law which supplements the very specific obligations in the *CRC Protocol*. The ILO's 1999 *Convention concerning the Prohibition and Immediate Action for the Elimination of the Worst Forms of Child Labour (ILO Convention)*[637] obliges state parties to "take immediate and effective measures to secure the prohibition and elimination of the worst forms of child labour[.]"[638] "The worst forms of child labour" is defined broadly and includes child slavery, trafficking, and "the use, procuring or offering of a child for prostitution, for the production of pornography or for pornographic performance."[639] Also, as explored in more detail in Section C(3), above in this chapter, the *Human Trafficking Protocol*[640] to the *TOC Convention*[641] emphasizes the protection of children as part of the overall scheme regarding human trafficking.

---

631   UN Doc. A/RES/54/263 (2000) [*CRC Protocol*]. This Protocol has 131 state parties; see online: http://treaties.un.org/Pages/ViewDetails.aspx?src=TREATY&mtdsg_no=IV-11-c&chapter=4&lang=en.
632   *Ibid.*, art. 4(1).
633   *Ibid.*, art. 4(2).
634   *Ibid.*, arts. 4(3) and 5.
635   See also *ibid.*, art. 5.
636   *Ibid.*, art. 7(c).
637   *ILO Convention No. C-182*, Can. T.S. 2001 No. 2. This *Convention* has been ratified by 164 states: see online: www.ilo.org/ilolex/cgi-lex/ratifce.pl?C182.
638   *Ibid.*, art. 1.
639   *Ibid.*, art. 3.
640   Above note 54.
641   Above note 26.

2) Canadian Implementing Legislation[642]

Canada was an active participant at the 1996 Stockholm Conference that gave initial impetus to the *CRC Protocol*, and moved far in advance of many other states to follow through on its objectives. The acts which the *CRC Protocol* eventually required to be criminalized were already essentially offences under Canadian law; territorial and qualified territorial commission of these offences were thus caught under the *Criminal Code* and the *Libman*[643] approach. Jurisdiction being the key component, Canada provided for nationality-based jurisdiction over the prescribed offences by way of amendments to the *Criminal Code*.[644] Section 7(4.1) provides for the prosecution of Canadian citizens or permanent residents for offences under a long list essentially dealing with sexual offences against children and child pornography.[645] Canada signed the *Protocol* on 10 November 2001 and ratified it on 14 September 2005.[646] The approach taken also seems to implement the concurrent obligations under the *ILO Convention*.

There has been only one conviction to date under this provision, which was reached by way of a guilty plea.[647] In December 2008, the British Columbia Supreme Court dismissed a constitutional challenge to section 7(4.1) by accused sex tourist Kenneth Klassen.[648] Klassen was charged with having committed sexual offences against children in Colombia, Cambodia, and the Philippines. He challenged the constitutional validity of Canada's exercise of nationality-based jurisdiction over him on various grounds, including an argument that the right to a fair trial under section 7 of the *Charter*[649] required that he be tried in Canada only for offences which took place in Canada, and that a trial in Canada for an extraterritorial offence would infringe the sovereignty of the territorial states. The court dismissed these arguments, noting

---

642 See, generally, Dwight Stewart & Monique Trépanier, "The Prosecution of Child Sex Tourism Offences in Canada" (paper delivered at the 19th Annual Conference of the International Society for the Reform of Criminal Law, Edinburgh, Scotland, 26–30 June 2005), online: www.isrcl.org (select "Conference Papers").

643 Above note 68.

644 S.C. 1997, c. 16, and S.C. 2002, c. 13. See Currie & Coughlan, above note 112 at 161.

645 Specifically, ss 151, 152, 153, 155, or 159, ss. 160(2) & (3), ss 163.1, 170, 171, 173, and 212(4).

646 See above note 631.

647 See Petti Fong, "Pedophile Sex Tourist Gets 10 Years for Assaults" *The Globe and Mail* (3 June 2005) A12; *R. v. Bakker*, [2005] B.C.J. No. 1577 (Prov. Ct. Crim. Div.). See also Currie & Coughlan, above note 112 at 160–61.

648 *R. v. Klassen*, 2008 BCSC 1762.

649 Above note 46.

that nationality-based jurisdiction was both expressly permitted under the *CRC Protocol* and lawful under customary international law, and also held that "a proscription against extraterritorial jurisdiction is not a principle of fundamental justice."[650]

H. CYBERCRIME

1) International Law

Among the trite but true tropes often floated about the impact of globalization in trade, transport, and communications is that the advent of the Internet, and globalized communication generally, has us living in a "borderless world." The legal implications of this have been the object of attention for some time, and it is safe to say that from the point of view of transnational criminal law they are both startling and challenging. In a relatively short period of time, the concept of "cybercrime" has moved from being a figment of science fiction to the object of focused attention by law enforcement officials worldwide.[651] The worldwide inter-connectedness of computer and communications networks pushes the idea of transnational crime to some of its most intense extremes,[652] presenting the spectre and the reality of criminals who are empowered by technology—empowered to evade detection in the mostly unregulated and unmonitored Internet environment, empowered to attack multiple targets in multiple states by way of a single act or series of acts, and empowered to effect these attacks in a way that presents significant jurisdictional difficulties for both apprehension and prosecution. A single person in a house in Canada can cause harm half a world away, by using spybots and botnets to skim money from bank accounts;[653] or by hacking or blocking access to government or commercial websites, causing financial, social, and even physical harm; or by extorting money from companies by threat of electronic sabotage; or by stealing sensitive trade or military information; or by circulating

---

650 Above note 648 at para. 113.
651 Richard W. Downing, "Shoring Up the Weakest Link: What Lawmakers Around the World Need to Consider in Developing Comprehensive Laws to Combat Cybercrime" (2004–05) 43 Colum. J. Transnat'l L. 705.
652 See Ellen S. Podgor, "Cybercrime: National, Transnational or International?" (2004) 50 Wayne L. Rev. 97.
653 Bernard Lagan, "Teenager 'Headed Cyber Crime Network'" *The Times (London)* (1 December 2007) Section "Home News" at 2; "NZ Teen Convicted of Cyber Crime" *BBC News*, online: http://news.bbc.co.uk/2/hi/asia-pacific/7323733.stm.

child pornography. The threat of terrorist attacks, particularly in a time when more and more critical infrastructure is subject to electronic connection to the rest of the world, is real and pressing.[654]

The term "cybercrime" itself is more effective as an explanatory label than as a legal term of art. It is used to describe a number of different types or methods of crime, virtually always involving the use of computers and, more often than not, computer networks. A useful way of classifying cybercrimes is by way of three somewhat overlapping categories:[655]

1) *Computer as tool*: Any number of "ordinary" crimes can be committed by using computers, such as possession and distribution of child pornography, piracy of copyrighted material such as music and software, forgery, stalking, fraud, extortion, and money laundering. This would also include otherwise common crimes which have uniquely electronic bases, such as online auction fraud and Internet luring of children.[656] E-mail, Internet messaging, online chatting, and so on can also be used for the purpose of planning or facilitating the commission of any crime, particularly between criminals who are in different jurisdictions.

2) *Computer as storage device*: Any use of computers as a means of committing or facilitating the commission of a crime means that the computer inevitably stores information that may be relevant to the crime. Digital information may be stored not just on conventional computers but on cell phones, iPods, global positioning system (GPS) devices, and personal digital assistants (PDAs). This gives rise to unique electronic evidence issues, as states must ensure their laws have the capacity for the collection, disclosure, and admission into court of this kind of data.[657]

3) *Computer as target*: Computers, and particularly computer networks, can also be the subject of criminal attacks of various kinds. These can involve theft of some kind, whether of information or money,

---

654 See McAfee Inc., *Virtual Criminology Report: Cybercrime — The Next Wave* (2007), online: www.mcafee.com/us/local_content/reports/mcafee_criminology_report2007_en.pdf.

655 Drawn from Downing, above note 651 at 711–13. See also Scott Charney & Kent Alexander, "Computer Crime" (1996) 45 Emory L.J. 931 at 934, describing computers as "target of the offence," "tool of the offence," and "incidental to the offence;" and Peter Grabosky, "The Global Dimension of Cybercrime" (2004) 6 Global Crime 146 at 146.

656 For a recent Canadian example of the latter, see *R. v. Innes*, 2007 ABPC 237.

657 See, generally, Stephen Mason, ed., *Electronic Evidence: Disclosure, Discovery & Admissibility* (London: LexisNexis Butterworths, 2007).

or the destruction of information or interference with data systems, such as distributed denial-of-service (DDOS) attacks. Such acts can be undertaken for any number of objectives, and while some are reasonably unique to the computer age (such as the circulation of malicious code), many are simply a means of accomplishing more "ordinary" criminal objectives, such as espionage, extortion, terrorism, and vandalism (e.g., defacement of websites).

Given the highly transnational nature of cybercrime, the key legal issue is jurisdiction.[658] The primary question is whether traditional international law notions of jurisdiction, based as they are around the notion of state sovereignty over territory and extraterritoriality as an exception, are up to the challenges posed by cybercrime. This tension is typified in an oft-quoted passage by Johnson and Post:

> The rise of the global computer network is destroying the link between geographical location and: (1) the power of local governments to assert control over online behavior; (2) the effects of online behavior on individuals and things; (3) the legitimacy of the efforts of a local sovereign to enforce rules applicable to global phenomena; and (4) the ability of physical location to give notice of which sets of rules apply.[659]

Jurisdiction is affected in all three of its manifestations: prescriptive, enforcement, and adjudicative. With many cybercrimes it will be very difficult to determine where an offence is actually committed for the purpose of states exercising jurisdiction, since there can easily be territorial differences between where the perpetrator physically acts, where the physical/electronic results of his acts take place, and where the effects are felt. Each of these affected states may assert jurisdiction on a different principle—qualified territoriality, nationality, or protective (especially if the act is one of terrorism). Thus, while states may wish to assert qualified territorial or extraterritorial jurisdiction over cybercrime, this will necessarily set up situations of concurrent prescriptive jurisdiction and at least the potential for conflict between states as a result. And even this set of issues is still founded on real-world territorial versions of what crime entails. The increasing use of such "virtual reality" spaces such as Second Life is actually leading to

---

658 Susan W. Brenner & Bert-Jaap Koops, "Approaches to Cybercrime Jurisdiction" (2004) 4 J. High Tech. L. 1.
659 David R. Johnson & David G. Post, "Law and Borders—The Rise of Law in Cyberspace" (1996) 48 Stanford L. Rev. 1367 at 1370.

"virtual crimes" which are subject, at least nominally, to investigation by police—but who has jurisdiction in cyberspace?[660]

Cybercrime also raises distinct issues for enforcement jurisdiction. Up front at this point is the unevenness with which states are enacting laws prohibiting cybercrimes. Cybercriminals and their tools are nothing if not highly mobile, and as with other forms of serious crime, the lack of international coordination in passing applicable criminal laws could lead to the problem of some states being "computer crime havens."[661] What is criminal in one state may not be criminal in another, which can lead to prosecutorial issues. Typically, for extradition to take place, "double criminality" is required (i.e., the impugned conduct must be criminal in both the requesting state and requested state[662]). Suppose a Canadian sets up, from Canada, an online gambling business from a server in a state where such gambling is legal. Under investigation in Canada, he flees to that state, which will be highly unlikely to extradite him since his conduct is legal according to its laws.

In addition, how are states to sort out potential conflicts regarding enforcement jurisdiction that itself has transnational aspects? Consider the famous case of Gorshkov and Ivanov,[663] two Russian hackers who stole large amounts of personal information, including credit card numbers, from American Internet service providers (ISPs), online banks, and e-commerce dealers. They used this information for various acts of online theft and fraud. FBI investigators enticed the two to travel to Seattle, Washington, using phony job interviews as a pretext, and monitored Gorshkov when he accessed his computer back in Russia, obtaining his login and password information. The investigators then arrested the two and used the information obtained to download the entire contents of Gorshkov's computer remotely. Russian authorities protested this investigation as an intrusion on their sovereignty, but faced US denials on the basis that the agents had never left US soil. The agents were later charged with hacking by the Russian government.[664]

---

660 Consider the recent "Habbo Hotel" case, where in November 2007, Dutch police arrested a teenager for virtual theft. The accused was a user of "Habbo Hotel," a Finnish social network and gaming site, and was alleged to have moved furniture from the virtual room of another user to his own virtual room. The furniture, while virtual, was paid for with real money. Online: www.cbc.ca/technology/story/2007/11/15/virtual-theft.html.

661 Edward Wise, "Computer Crimes and Other Crimes against Information Technology in the U.S." (1993) 64 Int'l Rev. Pen. L. 647 at 668.

662 See Chapter 9.

663 See discussion of case in Brenner & Koops, above note 658 at 21–23. See also online: www.usdoj.gov/criminal/cybercrime/gorshkovconvict.htm.

664 Online: www.theregister.co.uk/2002/08/16/russians_accuse_fbi_agent/.

This case highlights that, even in an age of enhanced and increasing criminal cooperation and mutual assistance between states, sovereignty continues to be jealously guarded. It is a bedrock notion of international and transnational criminal law that states cannot exercise enforcement jurisdiction on the territory of another state.[665] On a traditional international law analysis, computers or servers physically located in one state are wholly within that state's territorial sovereignty, and thus transborder access by foreign law enforcement authorities can only be accomplished legally by way of consent. Yet the argument has been floated that a computer that is networked into an international environment is beyond such territorial exclusivity, and should be available to foreign law enforcement, particularly in situations of urgency. We are, after all, talking about streams of electronic data rather than actual territorial incursions. There have been international discussions and negotiations between states on this very issue for a decade,[666] and yet very little agreement has been reached.[667]

The above points are raised as questions because the state of transnational criminal law relating to cybercrime is in a state of flux. Where there has been some movement towards rationalizing the difficult jurisdictional issues involved, the resort has been to first principles and the traditional customary international law principles of jurisdiction.[668] In particular, as Brenner and Koops have noted, "territoriality still turns out to be a prime factor; apparently, cyberspace is not considered so a-territorial after all."[669] This is illustrated by the first major international suppression convention on the subject, the Council of Europe *Convention on Cybercrime*.[670] The *Cybercrime Convention* was not the first indication of international determination to address combating this kind

---

665 See Chapter 2, Section D.

666 See Henrik W.K. Kaspersen, "Jurisdiction in the Cybercrime Convention" in Bert-Jaap Koops & Susan Brenner, *Cybercrime and Jurisdiction: A Global Survey* (The Hague: TMC Asser Press, 2006) 9 at 19–21.

667 With the exception of art. 32 of the Council of Europe *Convention on Cybercrime* (below note 670); see discussion below in this section.

668 As early as 2001, eminent Canadian international law scholar Jean-Gabriel Castel opined that "public international law principles and rules still provide a solid foundation for determining the jurisdiction of Canada to prescribe law covering activities on the Internet" (Jean-Gabriel Castel, "The Internet in Light of Traditional Public and Private International Law Principles and Rules Applied in Canada" (2001) 39 Can. Y.B. Int'l Law 3 at 64).

669 Bert-Jaap Koops & Susan Brenner, "Cybercrime Jurisdiction—An Introduction" in Koops & Brenner, *Cybercrime and Jurisdiction*, above note 666, 1 at 6.

670 C.E.T.S. No. 185. See, generally, Kaspersen, above note 666; Mike Keyser, "The Council of Europe *Convention on Cybercrime*" (2002–2003) 12 J. Transnat'l L. & Pol'y 287.

of crime, as the G8 states and the OECD had been actively considering the issue since the mid-1990s. The UNGA issued a resolution entitled "Combating the criminal misuse of information technologies" in 2000,[671] and since the 9/11 attacks the security and anti-terrorism aspects of cybercrime have seen increased activity by the UN and other bodies such as the OAS.[672] The OECD's 2002 *Guidelines for the Security of Information Systems and Networks: Towards a Culture of Security*[673] set out nine principles which encourage the creation of a "culture of security" among all participants in global information networks, including risk assessment, embedding of security design, ethical conduct, and the protection of democracy. These guidelines (now a formal recommendation of the OECD Council) have been very influential in both public and private sectors, and formed the basis for a UNGA resolution on "The Creation of a Global Culture of Cyber Security" in December 2002.[674]

The *Cybercrime Convention* was the product of four years of negotiations, drafting, and haggling between the member states of the Council of Europe and a number of non-member states (including Canada) which were invited to join the negotiations and eventually sign the Convention. In force since 2004, the Convention currently has 46 signatories, 26 of which have ratified the Convention—the latter number including the US, which ratified on 29 September 2006.[675] The Convention is fairly ambitious in tone, the Preamble setting out the objectives of harmonizing state criminal policy and legislation regarding cybercrime, fostering international cooperation, protecting fundamental human rights, and shielding privacy and personal data. Chapter I provides necessary definitions for use in the treaty: "computer system," "computer data," "service provider," and "traffic data."[676] All are broad and reasonably flexible definitions, designed to allow for adaptation to developing technologies.

Chapter II, section 1 of the Convention sets out the substantive criminal offences which states must implement. These are divided into four classifications. The first, "Offences against the confidentiality, integrity and availability of computer data and systems," contains offences

---

671 UN Doc. A/RES/55/63.

672 CP/RES.839 (1359/03), 12 March 2003.

673 DSTI/ICCP/REG (2002) 6.

674 A/RES/57/239.

675 Online: http://conventions.coe.int/Treaty/Commun/ChercheSig.asp?NT=185& CM=7&DF=6/15/2009&CL=ENG.

676 Above note 670, art. 1.

of illegal access,[677] illegal interception of data,[678] data interference,[679] system interference[680] and misuse of devices.[681] The second category, "Computer-related offences," contains offences of computer-related forgery[682] and computer-related fraud.[683] The third category, "Content-related offences," contains only offences related to child pornography,[684] while the fourth, "Offences related to infringements of copyright and related rights" provides for the offences described by the title, invoking various international instruments related to intellectual property.[685] Offences in the first three categories are required to be intentional, while the intellectual property offences must be committed "willfully, on a commercial scale and by means of a computer system."[686] States may also reserve the right not to impose criminal liability for the intellectual property offences, "provided that other effective remedies are available."[687] Article 11 requires parties to criminalize aiding and abetting the listed offences, and sets out an optional provision for criminalizing attempt. Parties must also ensure that corporate persons are liable for the offences, though subject to national laws as to whether the liability is criminal, civil, or administrative.[688] As is typical of European treaties, the crime of conspiracy is not provided for.

Jurisdiction is provided for in article 22, and surprisingly, given the transnational subject matter, it is fairly narrow. Parties are required only to establish territorial jurisdiction; flag ship, registered aircraft, and nationality jurisdiction are provided for[689] but optional.[690] The custodial

---

677 Ibid., art. 2.
678 Ibid., art. 3.
679 Ibid., art. 4.
680 Ibid., art. 5.
681 Ibid., art. 6.
682 Ibid., art. 7.
683 Ibid., art. 8.
684 Ibid., art. 9.
685 Ibid., art. 10.
686 Ibid., arts. 10(1) & (2).
687 Ibid., art. 10(3).
688 Ibid., art. 12.
689 Ibid., arts. 22(1)(b)–(d). The exercise of nationality jurisdiction requires double criminality or that the crime took place outside the territorial jurisdiction of any other state (para. d).
690 Ibid., art. 22(2). It has been suggested that this flexibility is required because many states will wish to rely on their laws regarding "common crimes" to implement the Convention's substantive law provisions, but may not wish to extend extraterritorial jurisdiction over these crimes otherwise (Kaspersen, above note 666 at 17).

provision[691] is not "universal" in scope, applying only where the requested state has refused to extradite the offender to another party state on the basis of his nationality. The latter provision is to address the common tendency of European states to refuse extradition of their nationals.

The related *aut dedere* obligation is oddly worded, requiring states to prosecute *only* where extradition has been refused on the basis of the nationality of the offender, or where the requested state deems that it has jurisdiction over the offence.[692] Since the prescriptive jurisdiction that states may exercise might even be limited to territoriality, this would seem to leave rather a large "impunity gap." For example, State A arrests an offender who is wanted for cybercrime by state B. State B is exercising passive personality jurisdiction over the crime. The extradition treaty between the two states allows each to refuse to extradite where it does not exercise this form of jurisdiction over this crime. State A does not exercise passive personality jurisdiction over cybercrime, and thus refuses to extradite on this basis. State A now has custody of the offender, but has no jurisdiction over the offence and cannot prosecute; moreover, it has no obligation to prosecute arising from the treaty.

This would not, of course, affect a situation where the requested party state already exerted extraterritorial jurisdiction over cyber-crimes, but the fact remains that the *Convention* does not require this, and the above situation is a real possibility.[693] Jurisdictional conflicts are to be resolved by way of consultation between the states involved.[694]

Chapter III of the treaty is entitled "International co-operation" and article 23 obliges parties to cooperate "to the widest extent possible" with regard both to "investigations or proceedings" and for the collection of electronic evidence. Article 24 provides a brief but standard set of extradition arrangements for use by the parties, but which mostly rests on the assumption that the parties will already have extradition arrangements in force between them. This is certainly true of the Council of Europe states,[695] though otherwise the treaty itself can serve as an extradition treaty if necessary.[696]

---

691 *Ibid.*, art. 22(3).

692 *Ibid.*, art. 24(6).

693 The official explanatory report confirms this analysis but offers no explanation for the gap. See Council of Europe, Convention on Cybercrime: *Explanatory Report*, online: http://conventions.coe.int/treaty/en/reports/html/185.htm at para. 251.

694 Above note 670, art. 22(5).

695 *European Convention on Extradition* (1957), E.T.S. No. 24. Art. 39 of the *Convention* specifically states that it is designed to supplement treaties between parties, including the various European instruments on extradition and mutual legal assistance.

696 Above note 670, art. 24(3).

Of more interest are the provisions regarding both domestic investigation by party states and inter-state investigative cooperation. Perhaps more than any of the other international suppression conventions, the *Cybercrime Convention* deals with coordinating the exercise of investigative jurisdiction in a detailed manner and goes far beyond standard mutual legal assistance provisions in treaties of this kind. This is due to the fact that the Council of Europe (CoE) states are much more integrated in terms of criminal investigation,[697] and these provisions draw on that history to a great extent. However, it is a much more detailed and far-reaching set of provisions than those familiar to states outside the CoE.

The investigative regime in fact begins prior to Chapter III. Section 2 of Chapter II is concerned with "Procedural law," and articles 16–21 require each state to enact measures to allow for effective investigation of cybercrimes in the form of expedited preservation of stored computer data, expedited preservation and partial disclosure of traffic data, orders for production of any specified computer data held by any person or subscriber information by ISPs, search and seizure of data, real-time collection of traffic data, and interception of content data. These are made subject to "the adequate protection of human rights and liberties" by states, including (but not requiring) any human rights treaty obligations each state has taken on, and incorporating the principle of proportionality.[698] Investigations are to be subject to judicial or other independent supervision, "as appropriate."

The mutual legal assistance provisions are also highly developed. As with extradition, the treaty anticipates the use of existing mutual legal assistance treaties between the parties, but allows the convention to serve as such an agreement if needed[699] and, unlike the extradition provisions, provides a basic procedural framework for mutual legal assistance.[700] Articles 29–34 bring the earlier investigation technique obligations (in articles 16–21, described above in this section) into play: states can request that any other state obtain the preservation of data, disclosure of traffic data, and so on, and disclose it pursuant to a mutual legal assistance request. In recognition of the often time-sensitive nature of cybercrime investigations, including data preservation/destruction issues, article 35 provides for a "24/7 Network" by which state authorities will provide each other with immediate assistance in

---

697 For a survey of EU instruments and practice on cybercrime, see Bantekas & Nash, above note 47 at 269–76.

698 Above note 670, art. 15. For an explanation, see *Explanatory Report*, above note 693 at paras. 145–48.

699 *Cybercrime Convention*, *ibid.*, art. 27(1). And see art. 28 regarding confidentiality.

700 *Ibid.*, arts. 27(2)–(9).

investigations at all times. There is also provision for states to spontaneously transmit information to each other as it is gathered in investigations, "when it considers that the disclosure of such information might assist the receiving party" in various ways.[701]

Article 32 deals with the contentious issue of transborder investigation by state authorities, particularly access to computer data located abroad via computers in the investigating state, on which little agreement could be reached during the treaty negotiations because of competing viewpoints and "lack of concrete experience" on point.[702] The compromise struck was that states could access data extraterritorially where the data is "publicly available (open source)" or if the state obtains the lawful and voluntary consent of a person who is legally entitled to disclose the data.[703] The latter situation is to be contextually determined.[704]

A possible criticism of the *Cybercrime Convention* is one common to suppression conventions generally: it is too heavily geared towards law enforcement and does not pay sufficient attention to human rights protections.[705] In some respects, this was quite deliberate on the part of the drafters of the treaty, and again reflects the heavily European nature of the instrument. For example, the issue of offenders facing multiple prosecutions by several party states for the same conduct (i.e., *ne bis in idem*, or double jeopardy) was intentionally left to be regulated at the level of extradition law, rather than jurisdiction.[706] This makes sense from the point of view of the European party states, all of which are parties to the *European Convention on Human Rights*[707] and the *European Convention on Extradition*,[708] both of which preserve the right against double jeopardy. However, it is not clear that all extradition treaties between all parties (or potential parties) to the Convention will contain such protections. The human rights provisions in the Convention itself are weak, containing no reference to customary international human rights law and only a watery reference to any treaties to which a state may happen to be party.[709] This is a matter of concern if, as has been

---

701 *Ibid.*, art. 26.

702 See *Explanatory Report*, above note 693 at paras. 293–94.

703 Above note 670, art. 32.

704 See *Explanatory Report*, above note 693 at para. 94.

705 Accord, Miriam Miquelon-Weismann, "The *Convention on Cybercrime*: A Harmonized Implementation of International Penal Law: What Prospects for Procedural Due Process?" (2005) 23 J. Marshall J. Computer & Info. L. 329 at 349.

706 Kaspersen, above note 666 at 15–16.

707 (1950), E.T.S. No. 5.

708 Above note 695.

709 Above note 670, art. 15.

proposed, membership in the treaty should be extended globally. Of course, the *Cybercrime Convention* could be modified in this event, but another possible venue for addressing it is the proposed formulation of a UN convention on cybercrime,[710] though this would seem to be duplicative of an otherwise fairly strong effort. In any event, there is little evidence thus far of the level of effectiveness of the *Convention*, though the Council of Europe is closely tracking developments.[711]

The next development on cybercrime was the conclusion in 2003 of the *Additional Protocol to the Convention on Cybercrime*, concerning the criminalization of acts of a racist and xenophobic nature committed through computer systems.[712] It stemmed from recognition that globalized communication and the Internet have allowed racists and xenophobes to circulate their views more widely than ever, and the goal of the treaty was to coordinate both substantive criminal law and international cooperation on point. Addressing these kinds of crimes was discussed during the negotiations leading to the *Cybercrime Convention*, but there was disagreement from several states, which objected to including such crimes in the Convention proper "on freedom of expression grounds."[713] The *Additional Protocol* has been in force since 2006 and to date has been signed by 34 states, including Canada, 14 of which have ratified it.[714]

Article 2(1) of the *Additional Protocol* defines "racist and xenophobic material" broadly, as any material which "advocates, promotes or incites hatred, discrimination or violence, against any individual or group of individuals, based on race, colour, descent or national or ethnic origin, as well as religion if used as a pretext for any of these factors." There follows in articles 3–7 a list of offences relating to various modes of intentionally communicating such ideas by way of a computer system: dissemination; threatening a serious criminal offence (as deter-

---

710 See ECOSOC, Committee on Crime Prevention and Criminal Justice, 11th Sess., 29 January 2002, E/CN.15/2002/8 at 6. There does not appear to have been much progress on this point of late, likely due to significant disagreement between the US and Russia as to its overall desirability; see John Markoff & Andrew Kramer, "US and Russia Differ on a Treaty for Cyberspace" *The New York Times* (28 June 2009) A1.

711 See online: www.coe.int/t/dghl/cooperation/economiccrime/cybercrime.

712 C.E.T.S. No. 189.

713 *Council of Europe, Additional Protocol to the Convention on Cybercrime, concerning the Criminalization of Acts of a Racist and Xenophobic Nature Committed through Computer Systems: Explanatory Report*, online: http://conventions.coe.int/Treaty/en/Reports/Html/189.htm at para. 4.

714 Online: http://conventions.coe.int/Treaty/Commun/ChercheSig.asp?NT=189&CM=7&DF=6/15/2009&CL=ENG.

mined under domestic law); public insult; denial, gross minimization, approval, or justification of genocide or crimes against humanity; or aiding or abetting any of these. These offence provisions are mandatory but, with the exception of the article 4 offence of racist or xenophobic threatening of a person with a serious criminal offence, they are inter-cut with various opportunities for reservations. While the *Explanatory Report*[715] does not address this point specifically, it would seem that these reservations are provided as a means of accommodating states whose approaches to freedom of expression would otherwise make it impossible for them to sign the *Additional Protocol*.

Article 8 links the *Additional Protocol* to the Convention, providing that the latter's article on various matters apply, including corporate liability, the investigative techniques and corresponding human rights protection in articles 14–21, the jurisdictional provision, and the pro-visions on extradition and mutual legal assistance. As with the *TOC Convention*[716] and its Protocols,[717] only states which have signed the Convention may sign the *Additional Protocol*.[718]

2) Canadian Implementation

The government of Canada is engaged on the issue of cybercrime, the harm it causes, and the various kinds of investigational problems it presents. Police forces in various cities now have cybercrime units, as does the RCMP. There is an integrated approach between the federal and provincial governments and international partners to facilitate the online reporting of economic crime, various forms of which are often committed online.[719] There have been many successful prosecutions of crimes in the nature of "computer as tool" described in Section H(1), above in this chapter, such as Internet luring.[720] Police, prosecutors, and courts are becoming quite comfortable in this setting, and in par-ticular there have been various successful investigations and convic-tions in child pornography cases, both domestic[721] and international. The *Canada Evidence Act*, as well as its provincial counterparts, has been amended to provide courts with the means of dealing with the

---

715 Above note 693.
716 Above note 26.
717 Above note 54.
718 Above note 712, art. 9(1).
719 Recol.ca, "Reporting Economic Crime On-Line," online: www.recol.ca.
720 See, for example, *R. v. Innes*, above note 656.
721 See, for example, *R. v. Dabrowski*, 2007 ONCA 619.

admissibility and weight of electronic evidence,[722] and the Crown is equipped to gather and disclose such evidence.[723]

To date, Canada has signed but not ratified both the *Cybercrime Convention* and the *Additional Protocol*. As a result, what is missing from Canadian law thus far is any kind of integrated approach to dealing with cybercrime in its transnational manifestations; police and prosecutors must rely on piecemeal attacks under older legislation, much of which is not specifically designed to deal with cybercrime. This seems to put Canada "behind the times" in terms of its approach, and it certainly lags behind states such as Australia and Indonesia, *inter alia*, which have already implemented omnibus legislation to deal with these phenomena. Indeed, the government's official web page on this topic, while it touts Canada's participation in such efforts as the *Cybercrime Convention* and the G8 and OAS efforts, seems to acknowledge this: "Coordinating an inclusive Canadian position, intended for international distribution, is one of the main challenges of Foreign Affairs and International Trade Canada."[724]

This is not to say that the *Cybercrime Convention* and *Additional Protocol* are totally unimplemented in Canadian law, nor that Canada is ill-equipped to deal with cybercrimes. Many of the basic offences required to be implemented are already in the *Criminal Code*[725] or other legislation, for example, child pornography,[726] uttering threats,[727] public incitement/wilful promotion of hatred,[728] forgery,[729] and fraud.[730] Some offences are reasonably well tailored to the cybercrime context. For example, there is a distinct offence of mischief in relation to data, as well as offences for the unauthorized use of a computer[731] and possession of a device to obtain computer service.[732] While jurisdiction over all of these offences is territorial, the *Libman*[733] approach to qualified territoriality is available to stretch the boundaries and deal with transnational

---

722 *Canada Evidence Act*, R.S.C. 1985, c. C-5, ss. 31.1–31.8.

723 See, generally, Robert J. Currie & Stephen Coughlan, "Canada" in Mason, ed., *Electronic Evidence*, above note 657.

724 Online: www.international.gc.ca/crime/cyber_crime-criminalite.aspx?menu_id=26&menu=R.

725 Above note 109.

726 *Ibid.*, s. 163.1.

727 *Ibid.*, s. 264.1.

728 *Ibid.*, s. 319.

729 *Ibid.*, s. 366.

730 *Ibid.*, s. 380.

731 *Ibid.*, s. 342.1.

732 *Ibid.*, s. 342.2.

733 Above note 68.

offences. Indeed, the Supreme Court of Canada has applied applicable provisions of the *Copyright Act*[734] on this basis.[735] As well, some of the investigative obligations under the *Convention* can be obtained by way of ordinary search warrants, though not all can, and it is quite unclear whether the law authorizes real-time collection of computer data.[736] Yet for the time being, Canada is not equipped with all of the latest legal tools to fully combat, and cooperate in combating, cybercrime. Presumably the *Cybercrime Convention* and *Additional Protocol* will be ratified in the future, at which point the requisite legislative measures will have to be put in place.

FURTHER READING

BOISTER, NEIL, "'Transnational Criminal Law?'" (2003) 14 E.J.I.L. 953

———, *Penal Aspects of the UN Drug Conventions* (The Hague: Kluwer Law International, 2001)

CAO, LAN, "The Transnational and Sub-National in Global Crimes" (2004) 22 Berkeley J. Int'l L. 59

CLARK, ROGER, "Offenses of International Concern: Multilateral State Treaty Practice in the Forty Years since Nuremberg" (1988) 57 Nordic J. Int'l L. 49

ENGDAHL, OLA, *Protection of Personnel in Peace Operations: The Role of the 'Safety Convention' against the Background of General International Law* (Leiden: Martinus Nijhoff, 2007)

GALLAGHER, ANNE, "Human Rights and the New UN Protocols on Trafficking and Migrant Smuggling: A Preliminary Analysis" (2001) 23 Hum. Rts. Q. 975

GILMORE, WILLIAM C., *Dirty Money: The Evolution of International Measures to Counter Money Laundering and the Financing of Terrorism*, 3d ed. (Strasbourg: Council of Europe Publications, 2004)

KIRSCH, PHILIPPE, "The 1988 ICAO and IMO Conferences: An International Consensus Against Terrorism" (1989) 12 Dal. L.J. 5

---

734 R.S.C. 1985, c. C-42, ss. 2 and 27.

735 *Society of Composers, Authors & Music Publishers of Canada v. Canadian Assn. of Internet Providers*, [2004] 2 S.C.R. 427.

736 See Currie & Coughlan in Mason, ed., *Electronic Evidence*, above note 657.

KOOPS, BERT-JAAP, & SUSAN W. BRENNER, *Cybercrime and Jurisdiction: A Global Survey* (The Hague: TMC Asser, 2006)

LAMBERT, JOSEPH J., *Terrorism and Hostages in International Law* (Cambridge: Grotius, 1990)

ORLOVA, ALEXANDRA, & JAMES MOORE, "'Umbrellas' or 'Building Blocks'?: Defining International Terrorism and Transnational Organized Crime in International Law" (2005) 27 Houston J. Int'l L. 267

CHAPTER 8

TRANSNATIONAL CRIMES OF DOMESTIC CONCERN

A. INTRODUCTION: "PURELY" DOMESTIC CRIMES WITH A TRANSNATIONAL ELEMENT

Decades ago, Sir Robert Jennings argued that states should not take jurisdiction over conduct that had "more or less remote repercussions" in the state's territory.[1] With regard to criminal conduct, developments in the last three or four decades indicate that states are taking increasingly broad views on the kinds of "repercussions" that will justify taking jurisdiction over regular, domestic law crimes that have a transnational aspect.

Both the transnational criminal and the transnational crime are real. By now it is trite rhetoric to note that developments in communications and mobility of persons mean that not only will crime and criminals often be beyond purely territorial reach, but that the crimes themselves are "messier" and can sometimes only be said to take place in more than one state. A state often will have an interest in punishing conduct that has some impact on its domestic interests, even if strictly speaking some or all of the elements of the crime in question took place outside that state. From the perspective of Canada, many of the most serious crimes having an impact on Canadians (e.g., drug trafficking;

---

1 Robert Jennings, "Extraterritorial Jurisdiction and the United States Antitrust Laws" (1957) 33 Brit. Y.B. Int'l L. 146 at 159.

money laundering; identity-related crime; cybercrime, including child pornography on the Internet; and terrorism) are increasingly linked with activity conducted in or through countries that lack effective domestic criminal justice regimes, including a lack of capacity to engage in international cooperation with Canada. Criminals and terrorists strategically exploit these countries, which they perceive to be "safe havens," and use them as bases for their criminal and terrorist activities.

Moreover, there is recognition that it is in the mutual interest of states to protect the populations of other states from criminal conduct that may originate domestically but have effects abroad. Some generosity with regard to jurisdiction is required if criminals are to be prevented from using state borders and antiquated notions of sovereignty to create impunity. As Justice Meredith, speaking specifically to conspiracy, opined in the early twentieth century, "the law would be lame if it were powerless to reach conspirators so long as they took care to agree to carry into effect their wrongs beyond the borders of the country in which they conspired to do the wrongs."[2]

The focus of this chapter is transnational crimes of domestic concern. As was outlined in Chapter 1, this label describes offences that are made criminal under the domestic law of a state; have not been the subject of any international law regime, whether by way of customary principles or treaty; and have aspects which touch on the jurisdiction of another state. It is both a broad and a narrow category: broad because it could encompass nearly the entire body of a state's criminal and regulatory law, but narrow because it basically amounts to a few rules which need to be applied when a domestic offence somehow has a transnational feature.

As was outlined in Chapter 2, a state will sometimes assume jurisdiction over offences, the conduct or effects of which occur in more than one state, but where there are sufficient links to the prosecuting state that jurisdiction is nonetheless considered "territorial" under international (and the applicable domestic) law. Section B, below in this chapter, surveys how this concept of *qualified territoriality*[3] is dealt with under Canadian law. Given that nearly any offence may have some aspect that touches on another state, nearly the entire body of Canadian criminal and regulatory offences is potentially subject to jurisdiction on the basis of qualified territoriality. Accordingly, the goal here is not to attempt to address the broad range of crimes that might be susceptible

---

2   *R. v. Bachrack* (1913), 21 C.C.C. 257 at 265 (Ont. C.A.).

3   Also called "extended territoriality"; see, for example, Kate Brookson-Morris, "Conflicts of Criminal Jurisdiction" (2007) 56 I.C.L.Q. 659.

to qualified territoriality, but rather to examine the test and how it is applied. Some queries and suggestions are posed about the international law aspects of the matter, which are currently underdeveloped.

Section C, below in this chapter, focuses on those offences for which Canada exerts *extraterritorial jurisdiction*, that is, offences which take place entirely outside of Canada but are nonetheless made subject to Canadian criminal law. A great majority of extraterritorial offences arise from Canada being party to the various crime suppression treaties and properly qualify as "transnational offences of international concern," and are thus dealt with in detail in Chapter 7. However, Canada does assert extraterritorial jurisdiction over a range of what might be called common domestic offences, employing a number of the customary international law principles of jurisdiction to do so, and these will be explored. The peculiar issue of extraterritorial application of the *Charter*[4] poses discrete problems, and is discussed in Chapter 10. Section D, below in this chapter, examines the problems associated with acts of criminal conspiracy that have extraterritorial aspects.

It will be apparent from the foregoing that this chapter is focused primarily on jurisdiction, specifically *prescriptive jurisdiction* (the ability of a state to make criminal law) and to some extent *judicial jurisdiction* (the ability of courts to determine whether domestic or international law makes them competent to adjudicate a particular case). *Enforcement jurisdiction* (the ability of a state to enforce its criminal law by arresting and prosecuting offenders) is not particularly problematic in this area; where Canadian courts have jurisdiction, either territorial or extraterritorial, over an offence, they will try the offender domestically. If the offender is not present in Canada, jurisdiction over his person will be sought and possibly obtained by way of extradition or other cooperative mechanisms, which are dealt with in Chapter 9.

B. QUALIFIED TERRITORIALITY IN CANADIAN LAW

1) The *Libman* Test

Traditionally, Canada has adhered to its British roots and taken a primarily territorial approach to the administration of criminal law. This

---

4   *Canadian Charter of Rights and Freedoms*, Part I of the *Constitution Act, 1982*, being Schedule B to the *Canada Act 1982* (U.K.), 1982, c. 11.

was embodied in what is now section 6(2) of the *Criminal Code*,[5] which states, "Subject to this Act or any other Act of Parliament, no person shall be convicted . . . of an offence committed outside Canada." As Cory J. noted in *R. v. Finta*, this imports a presumption that "Canadian courts, as a rule, may only prosecute those crimes which have been committed within Canadian territory."[6]

From early days, however, Canadian courts had to deal with cases that involved more than one jurisdiction, and employed a variety of techniques for determining whether particular acts or conduct could be said to have been committed in Canada—with varying degrees of success.[7] In 1985, La Forest J, writing for the Supreme Court of Canada, addressed the issue squarely in his compelling judgment in *Libman v. The Queen*.[8] In that case, the accused had been committed for trial for fraud and conspiracy to commit fraud, and applied to have his committal quashed on the basis that the crimes he was alleged to have committed occurred outside Canada. From a Toronto location, Libman had employed a number of people to sell what were apparently worthless shares in two fictitious mining companies. The sales were made by telephone to US residents, who also received promotional material from Panama and Costa Rica. The purchasers sent their money to offices operated by Libman's associates in Panama and Costa Rica, to which countries Libman would travel to obtain his share of the proceeds; he would then return to Canada with the money and pay his salespeople.[9]

Though not framed this way by the Supreme Court, Libman's argument was essentially that section 5(2) (now 6(2)) of the *Criminal Code* should apply and defeat the charges. Importantly, Libman had been charged with conspiracy under section 423(1)(d)[10] of the *Code*, which covered conspiracies to commit an offence *in* Canada, and not section 423(3),[11] which explicitly covered conspiracies to commit an offence *outside* Canada. The fraud provisions of the time contained no extra-

---

5   R.S.C. 1985, c. C-46 [*Code*].

6   *R. v. Finta*, [1994] 1 S.C.R. 701 at para. 170 [*Finta*]. In dissent, La Forest J. reflected that this provision did not remove the status of a criminal act as "culpable conduct in the eyes of Canadians and the underlying values of Canadian criminal law," but simply precluded prosecution. This implemented the normal preference in favour of the territorial principle of jurisdiction at international law: *ibid*. at para. 40.

7   See the survey of Canadian caselaw in *Libman v. The Queen*, [1985] 2 S.C.R. 178 at paras. 43–59 [*Libman*].

8   *Ibid*.

9   *Ibid*. at paras. 3–5.

10   Now s. 465(1)(d).

11   Now s. 465(3), which came into effect only after some of the transactions were complete; *Libman*, above note 7 at para. 9.

territorial language. The factual question to be answered was whether the alleged acts had occurred in Canada, for if they had not, then Canadian courts had no jurisdiction. The legal question was what factors the courts should use to determine whether a transnational crime could be said to have occurred in Canada.

Writing for the Court, La Forest J. began by noting the primarily territorial nature of criminal jurisdiction, but cited the *Lotus*[12] case for the proposition that "states increasingly exercise jurisdiction over criminal behaviour in other states that has harmful consequences within their own territory or jurisdiction."[13] He then surveyed in detail the historical approaches of both English and Canadian courts and the variety of theories that had been used to determine jurisdictional questions in cases with transnational aspects, noting the state of "doctrinal confusion" that existed.[14] He emphasized, however, that the courts of neither country had felt bound by strict territoriality. Both had demonstrably taken jurisdiction over criminal conduct that had taken place in whole or in part in foreign countries, where it had unlawful or harmful consequences domestically, as well as over offences where the victim and impact were abroad.[15] Section 5(2) of the *Code*, he noted, "does not say that criminal law is confined to Canadian territory; it says rather that no person 'shall be convicted in Canada for an offence committed outside of Canada.'"[16]

Drawing on various aspects of the older cases, as well as on academic writings, La Forest J. then formulated a test to determine when Canada could take criminal jurisdiction over transnational crimes. The most frequently cited passage from the case is as follows:

> I might summarize my approach to the limits of territoriality in this way. As I see it, all that is necessary to make an offence subject to the jurisdiction of our courts is that a significant portion of the activities constituting that offence took place in Canada. As it is put by modern academics, it is sufficient that there be a "real and substantial link" between an offence and this country, a test well known in public and private international law.[17]

However, it appears from the judgment that La Forest J. was proposing a two-part test: first, that there be a "real and substantial link" between

---

12 *SS "Lotus," The Case of the (France v. Turkey)* (1927), P.C.I.J. (Ser. A) No. 9 [*Lotus*].

13 Above note 7 at para. 11.

14 *Ibid.* at para. 17.

15 *Ibid.* at paras. 66–68.

16 *Ibid.* at para. 66.

17 *Ibid.* at para. 74.

Canada and the offence, and second, if a real and substantial link is established, "[o]ne must then consider whether there is anything in those facts that offends international comity,"[18] specifically whether there is "anything in the requirements of international comity that would dictate that this country refrain from exercising its jurisdiction."[19] La Forest J. emphasized that the comity inquiry will shape the connection inquiry,[20] but the latter must clearly precede the former since a state without a real and substantial connection to a matter will not be able to exert territorial jurisdiction, and international comity need not be considered.

Analyzing the facts before the Court in *Libman*, La Forest J. concluded that the links between Canada and the offence were "ample."[21] He agreed with a lower court finding that the preparatory activities that had been put in place in Toronto to perpetrate the frauds would alone support territorial jurisdiction, though he also emphasized the fact that the profits generated were brought to Canada. He further held that the fact that the harm to victims occurred outside Canada made no difference to the analysis.[22] Nothing in relation to international comity would preclude Canada from prosecuting the crime, and in fact La Forest J. suggested that international comity compelled Canada to do so.[23] The committal for both fraud and conspiracy was upheld.

Though the two portions of the test are often mingled, as indeed they were in *Libman* itself, individual attention to each may be helpful.

2) "Real and Substantial Connection"[24]

Again, the purpose of the *Libman* test is to determine whether an offence took place in Canada, and the bulk of that determination lies in ascertaining whether there is a "real and substantial connection." Since this is a test for *territorial* jurisdiction, the connection must be between

---

18   *Ibid*. at para. 71.
19   *Ibid*. at para. 78.
20   "Just what may constitute a real and substantial link in a particular case, I need not explore . . . . The outer limits of the test may, however, well be coterminous with the requirements of international comity[.]" (*Ibid*. at para. 76).
21   *Ibid*..
22   *Ibid*. at paras. 70–72.
23   *Ibid*. at para. 77.
24   There is no particular distinction to be made between "real and substantial links," which is the phrase used in *Libman*, and "real and substantial connection," which is how La Forest J. rephrased the test for application in other contexts (e.g., *Morguard Investments Ltd. v. de Savoye*, [1990] 3 S.C.R. 1077, regarding assumption of jurisdiction in civil matters). The latter phrase is most frequently used now, and will be used here.

some aspects of the crime and the territory of Canada; any offence that took place wholly outside Canada will not be caught by Canadian territorial jurisdiction.[25] The Court was clearly suggesting a generous approach to this question, and *Libman* makes clear that it is not necessary that particular elements of the crime have taken place in Canada, since this was the formal, "mechanical" approach of the past that the Court was specifically rejecting. Rather, the focus was to be on "all relevant facts that take place in Canada" — for example, the fact that the proceeds of the fraud were brought to Canada.[26]

Such relevant facts may, of course, include any formal elements of the crime that took place in Canada. For example, in *Canada (Human Rights Commission) v. Canadian Liberty Net*,[27] the appellants were enjoined from broadcasting a particular "hate message" by a Federal Court injunction. An answering message on their phone line in Canada subsequently referred callers to an American number where a similar message was broadcast, and they were convicted of contempt. On appeal, they contended that the court lacked jurisdiction because, *inter alia*, the injunction sought to restrain conduct outside of Canada. The Supreme Court dismissed this ground of appeal based on *Libman*, Bastarache J. noting for the majority that part of the conduct forming the violation of the order was the advertisement in Canada of the American number, and that this "[did] not even test the outer limits" of real and substantial connection.[28]

Other facts relevant to the connection analysis may be those relating to "the formulation, initiation, or commission of the offence."[29] In *R. v. Vézina*,[30] the Supreme Court held that *Libman* would support jurisdiction over a conspiracy and attempt to defraud, where the scheme was launched in Canada but the victim would be in another state.[31] In

---

25 "Canadian courts may not prosecute an ordinary offence that has occurred in a foreign jurisdiction" (*Finta*, above note 6 at para. 180).

26 *Libman*, above note 7 at para. 71. However, in *R. v. Drakes*, [2005] O.T.C. 577 (S.C.J.), the court found that in a fraud case, mere evidence that the proceeds of an otherwise extraterritorial fraud ended up in Canada was insufficient to constitute a real and substantial connection "absent a scheme devised and initiated in Canada" (para. 61). The court appeared to rely heavily on the fact that in *Libman*, La Forest J. had found the depositing of the proceeds in Canada to be an integral part of the scheme.

27 [1998] 1 S.C.R. 626 [*Canadian Liberty Net*].

28 *Ibid.* at para. 52.

29 *R. v. O.B.* (1997), 99 O.A.C. 313 at para. 12 (C.A.).

30 [1986] 1 S.C.R. 2.

31 *Ibid.* at 20.

general, the analysis should be shaped by the nature of the offence with which the accused has been charged.[32]

In *R. c. Ouellette*,[33] Béliveau J. of the Quebec Superior Court framed "real and substantial connection" in a way that still reflects the current practice of the courts, describing it as a

> . . . test of varying content which is assessed in relation to the circumstances and, in particular, the importance of the elements of the offence linked to Canada, the relevant facts which arose in Canada and the harmful consequences which were caused, or which could have been caused, in Canada.[34]

The application of the "real and substantial connection" portion of the test by lower courts has been occasional and uneven.[35] In *R. v. O.B.*, the accused was a Canadian who took his granddaughter on a trip to the US and allegedly sexually assaulted her there. The lower court found jurisdiction, citing *inter alia* as links the nationality of both offender and victim, that the witnesses and the vehicle were in Canada, and that "any impact on the complainant may produce consequences in this jurisdiction."[36] The Ontario Court of Appeal allowed the accused's appeal on the basis that there was no significant link "with respect to any part of the offence."[37] By contrast, in *R c. Ouellette*,[38] the accused was charged with manslaughter after assaulting the victim while in the Dominican Republic. The victim died from the injuries sustained during the assault after returning home to Canada. Justice Béliveau held that there was a real and substantial connection for the manslaughter charge, based *inter alia* on the fact that the victim had died in Canada and the harmful consequences of the offence occurred in Canada. He

---

32   In *Libman*, in dispensing with the "gist of the offence" approach that some courts had used, La Forest J. emphasized that the offence of fraud consisted both of obtaining goods, money, and so on, and that they have been obtained fraudulently, and similarly for obtaining property by false pretences. He wrote "I see no overriding policy reason that would favour the place of obtaining the goods [as the location of the crime]. There are many cases, it is true, where this is also the place where the impact is felt, but that is not necessarily so" (above note 7 at para. 69).

33   (1998), 126 C.C.C. (3d) 219 (Que. S.C.).

34   *Ibid*. at 229 [translation].

35   In addition to the cases reviewed here, see *R. v. Hammerbeck*, [1993] B.C.J. No. 685 (C.A.) (child abducted from Canada to US); *R. v. Doiron*, [1989] N.B.J. No. 12 (C.A.) (accused imported narcotics into Canada where he "caused" them to be transported over the border by picking up the drugs and leaving them 250 metres from the border for transport by associates).

36   Above note 29 at para. 11.

37   *Ibid*. at para. 12.

38   Above note 33.

emphasized that the death of the victim was an element of the crime of manslaughter, and while it was a "secondary aspect" of the crime, it was the "determinant element" for the jurisdictional inquiry.[39]

In *R. v. Dos Santos*,[40] the court found the accused guilty of "[fishing] in Canadian fisheries waters" for the purposes of the *Coastal Fisheries Protection Act*.[41] The accused was the Master of a ship anchored outside Canada's 200-mile limit, and sent his crew in small boats to drop nets within the 200-mile zone. Justice Barry correctly identified that the issue was not one of extraterritorial jurisdiction but whether the conduct occurred "inside Canadian fishing waters."[42] He ruled that "while the planning and evolution of the offence may have occurred outside the 200-mile limit, the culmination of the offence occurred [inside],"[43] which satisfied the *Libman* test.

The leading lower court application of *Libman* is probably the judgment of Moldaver J.A. in *R. v. Greco*.[44] The accused was alleged to have assaulted the victim while on vacation in Cuba, and was charged with breach of his probation order. He argued that section 6(2) of the *Criminal Code* divested Canadian courts of jurisdiction, since the conduct that formed the breach of the order did not occur in Canada. In upholding lower court determinations that Canada had jurisdiction, Moldaver J. first set forth practical and policy reasons that probation orders issued by Ontario courts should bind probationers both in Canada and abroad.[45] Having ruled that this was so, he briefly addressed the application of the *Libman* test to the facts, finding that section 6(2) did not preclude prosecution of Greco in Ontario, based on the facts that the "treatment, protection and safety of the victim . . . who lives in Canada" had substantial impacts within Canada,[46] that only Canada has any interest in ensuring compliance with orders made by Canadian courts,[47] and that the offence arose out of a breach of a Canadian probation order.[48]

---

39 *Ibid.* at 233. Béliveau J. also cited the accused's interest in being tried in Canada as a relevant factor.
40 (1992), 96 Nfld. & P.E.I.R. 13 (Nfld. S.C.) [*Dos Santos*].
41 R.S.C. 1985, c. C-33.
42 *Dos Santos*, above note 40 at 28.
43 *Ibid.*
44 (2001), 159 C.C.C. (3d) 146 (Ont. C.A.), leave to appeal to S.C.C. refused (2001), 162 C.C.C. (3d) vi [*Greco*].
45 Though this is the source of some of the confusion inherent in the judgment; see Section B(4), below in this chapter.
46 Above note 44 at para. 25 (C.A.).
47 *Ibid.* at paras. 41–42.
48 *Ibid.* at para. 42.

More recently, in *R. v. Larche*,[49] Fish J. of the Supreme Court of Canada conducted a brief *Libman* analysis in the context of sentencing. The accused had been involved in an organized-crime operation, smuggling cannabis from the Quebec Eastern Townships into the US and then bringing the proceeds back to Quebec. He had not been charged in Canada with any of his American activities, as he had also been charged in the US for those activities, and the Crown wished to accommodate that state's extradition request. The questions were whether uncharged acts that were related to an offence, but that occurred in another state, were properly "circumstances of the offence" for the purpose of sentencing, and whether a Canadian sentencing court had the (territorial) jurisdiction to take them into account. The sentencing judge had answered this question in the affirmative.

Justice Fish, for a unanimous Supreme Court, agreed with most of the sentencing judge's findings,[50] noting that the bulk of the US-based facts taken into account "might reasonably be characterized as the missing half of the single criminal enterprise that was the true substratum of the offence."[51] He briefly conducted the first part of the *Libman* analysis and found that most of the implicated US activities had a "real and substantial connection" to Canada, given that they were part of an operation whose elements were "seamlessly connected,"[52] and in fact were analogous to the transnational fraud operation in *Libman* itself.[53] Accordingly, the US activities could be taken into account in the Canadian sentencing, as the Canadian court had territorial (implicitly, qualified territorial) jurisdiction over them.

In the recent case of *R. v. Stucky*,[54] the Ontario Court of Appeal used the *Libman* test in interpreting the jurisdictional scope of section 52 of the federal *Competition Act*.[55] The accused had been engaged in an allegedly fraudulent direct mail business that sold lottery tickets and merchandise to people outside Canada. He was charged under section 52, which prohibits false or misleading representations "to the public,"

---

49   *R. v. Larche*, [2006] 2 S.C.R. 762 [*Larche*].
50   The exception was that Sansfaçon J.C.Q. had taken into account a single instance of possession of proceeds that occurred entirely in Vermont. Justice Fish ruled that since this had taken place "entirely in the United States," there was no territorial jurisdiction over it and thus it could not be taken into account in sentencing (*ibid.* at para. 61).
51   *Ibid.* at para. 14.
52   *Ibid.* at para. 56.
53   *Ibid.* at para. 62.
54   2009 ONCA 151, leave to appeal to the S.C.C. granted, [2009] S.C.C.A. No. 186 [*Stucky*].
55   R.S.C. 1985, c. C-34.

and was acquitted by the trial judge who interpreted the phrase to mean "to the Canadian public." The Court of Appeal ruled this to be in error, finding that "the meaning of 'the public' is not restricted to the Canadian public where there is a real and substantial link or connection between the offence and Canada."[56] Since, at the time of the offence, the accused was in Canada, initiated his alleged misrepresentations in Canada, and received his profits here, "[t]here is a real and substantial connection between the offence alleged and Canada, notwithstanding the fact that the 'public' to whom the representations were made was located outside Canada."[57]

3) International Comity

The *Libman* case is probably most noteworthy for the expansive view of the notion of "international comity" put forth by La Forest J. The term "comity" he defined simply as "no more nor less than 'kindly and considerate behaviour towards others.'"[58] A better definition for this purpose was suggested by Estey J. in *R. v. Spencer*:

> . . . neither a matter of absolute obligation, on the one hand, nor of mere courtesy and good will, upon the other. But it is the recognition which one nation allows within its territory to the legislative, executive or judicial acts of another nation, having due regard both to international duty and convenience and to the rights of its own citizens or of other persons who are under the protection of its laws.[59]

More important, however, was La Forest J.'s recognition that the notion of what comity required had expanded significantly. It included a much more generous and expansive view of territorial criminal jurisdiction than was consistent with Anglo-Canadian tradition, since states no longer so closely guarded their respective administration of criminal law, but in fact were actively cooperating to suppress criminal activity of various sorts. Jurisdictional elasticity was the key to combating modern transnational crime; "In a shrinking world," he memorably opined, "we are all our brothers' keepers."[60] Given this level of active

---

56   *Stucky*, above note 54 at para. 24.

57   *Ibid*. at para. 32.

58   *Libman*, above note 7 at para. 77.

59   [1985] 2 S.C.R. 278 at para. 8, quoting *Hilton v. Guyot*, 159 U.S. 113 (1895) at 163–64. And see Cedric Ryngaert, *Jurisdiction in International Law* (Oxford: Oxford University Press, 2008) at 136–42. The Supreme Court's recent elevation of comity to a principle of statutory interpretation is discussed in Chapter 1.

60   *Libman*, above note 7 at para. 77.

interest in cooperation among states, Canada should take steps to ensure that it not allow itself to be used by sophisticated transnational criminals as a venue for throwing up jurisdictional hurdles to capture and prosecution. A more aggressive approach to territorial criminal jurisdiction would thus serve both domestic public law purposes and be consistent with emerging trends in international law.

Practically, and consistently with the approach to real and substantial connection, Canadian courts since *Libman* have interpreted the requirements of international comity expansively. This portion of the test has been interpreted as requiring the court to ask itself, as part of the jurisdictional inquiry, whether any other state's interests in prosecuting a particular offender are at play, and if so, whether Canada should give way to that state and refrain from asserting territorial jurisdiction. In the cases to date there has been no evidence of any competing claims to jurisdiction by other states, which has made it easy for courts to rule that international comity will not be infringed if Canada prosecutes. In *Greco*, for example, the Court of Appeal found as fact that the Cuban authorities had formally declined any interest in prosecuting, and that Cuba had not registered any protests with the Canadian government over its decision to prosecute Greco. It also noted that there was no evidence that Greco's conduct was illegal under Cuban law, and that Cuba could most likely not have prosecuted a breach of a Canadian probation order under its own law.[61]

Most often courts simply make no finding as to international comity, or make general remarks to the effect that prosecution will not affect it.[62] This is doubtless due to the fact that the Crown will make a number of decisions in the background prior to deciding to bring charges. For example, it may satisfy itself that there is no competing claim prior to embarking on prosecution, even to the point of negotiating with other potential interested states to ensure this. If there is a competing claim, a decision might be made to cede jurisdiction to another state with a greater interest or where practicality dictates, as in cases where the accused is actually within the competing state. It is possible, however, that in the future, a case will come up where the Canadian Crown wishes to prosecute an individual for the same crime for which she is sought by another state. At that point, the courts will have to embark on a more nuanced inquiry as to what "international comity" requires in such situations than has been seen to date.[63]

---

61   *Greco*, above note 44 at paras. 40–41.
62   For example, *R. v. Doiron*, above note 35.
63   For a brief review of the American position (where a similar test of "reasonableness" has been considered), see Jordan Paust *et al.*, *International Criminal Law:*

What will such an inquiry entail? Procedurally, it is likely incumbent upon the Crown to put evidence of the competing claim before the court, both to maintain the Crown's general obligation of balance and fairness in conducting proceedings, and because this is the sort of evidence that is much more easily accessed by the government than by an accused person. The foreign government might also intervene in the Canadian proceedings in order to have its claim determined. The court might consider the following factors:

1) Has the foreign government made an extradition request?[64]
2) Has the foreign government protested the exercise of jurisdiction by Canada and actively expressed an interest in prosecuting?
3) Is there any evidence that the foreign government is seeking prosecution for an improper purpose (e.g., persecutory, discriminatory, political)?
4) Does the foreign state itself have a "real and substantial connection" to the offence, and if so, how does it compare to the Canadian connection?
5) Related to (4), the court may wish to inquire as to the comparative strength of connection to the matter, for both Canada and the foreign state, as a matter of international law. For example, if the foreign state is asserting jurisdiction on a passive personality basis, Canada's territorially based claim would be stronger.[65] As Bastarache J. suggested in *Cook*, where a state "without any, or with a lesser, real and substantial connection to the events in question" applies its laws, this would be inconsistent with international law and would weigh towards declining jurisdiction in favour of the state with the better connection.[66]

Also open to question is whether this kind of inquiry is suited to the courts.[67] International *comity*, after all, is only loosely an issue of international *law*. Certainly in the extradition context, both the Su-

---

Cases and Materials, 3d ed. (Durham, NC: Carolina Academic Press, 2007) at 208–11.

64 In *Larche*, above note 49, Fish J. in *obiter dicta* suggested that an outstanding extradition request from a treaty partner would be relevant (para. 64).

65 For more on the international-law-based test, see Chapter 2, Section C(3)(e).

66 *R. v. Cook*, [1998] 2 S.C.R. 597 at para. 136, though Bastarache J. confusingly identified such a state of affairs as amounting to "impermissible extraterritoriality." A claim to territorial jurisdiction does not become "extraterritorial" simply because it is inferior to a stronger claim by another state, even though the case itself may have "extraterritorial" aspects.

67 See Michael Scharf, "Beyond the Rhetoric of Comparative Interest Balancing" (1987) 50 Law & Contemp. Probs. 95.

preme Court of Canada and Parliament have been clear that matters relating to Canada's international obligations and foreign relations, while nominally justiciable, are best left to determination at the ministerial level (though subject to judicial review). If the Crown can adduce evidence of serious consideration of comity factors, the courts are unlikely to second-guess that. In *Larche*, Fish J. appeared to suggest that where an accused has actually been charged for a transnational offence of the *Libman* variety, that is, where Canada has jurisdiction over the entire crime even though parts of it took place in another state, the court's ability to inquire into comity will be limited: "This choice is made at the executive level, and the appropriate time for comity to be given effect is *before* either jurisdiction presses charges. The comity principle will at that stage favour an agreement as to where the offender ought to be prosecuted for a single transnational offence."[68]

4) *Libman* and Extraterritoriality

Libman is sometimes cited in international law texts to support the emergence of a principle of "real and substantial connection" to justify assertion of jurisdiction at *international* law.[69] However, as will be clear from the foregoing discussion, *Libman* had a more modest goal — to incorporate objective and subjective *territorial* jurisdiction into Canadian jurisprudence.[70] To be sure, it is an extremely enlightened judgment in that it incorporates some consideration of whether international law, or at least international comity, will allow Canada to take jurisdiction.[71] However, when the *Libman* test is answered affirmatively, it means that Canada has territorial jurisdiction over the offence, with all of the international law solidity that attaches to territorial claims.

This point is emphasized here because as cases with both territorial and extraterritorial elements become increasingly common, the courts must deal with the jurisdiction issue more frequently. However, there is sometimes confusion between whether there is territorial jurisdiction over cases with extraterritorial elements and whether there is truly extraterritorial jurisdiction, that is, jurisdiction over matters occurring entirely outside Canadian territory. For the purpose of determining

---

68 *Larche*, above note 49 at para. 67 [emphasis in original].

69 And see the discussion of this test in Chapter 2, Section (C)(3)(e).

70 Neither term actually occurs in the text of the *Libman* decision, and it was not until Bastarache J.'s concurring decision in *Cook*, above note 66, that the international law phraseology appeared in the Court's jurisprudence (para. 135).

71 For reviews of the American approach, which is similar, see Paust *et al.*, above note 63 and Ryngaert, above note 59 at 153–63.

whether Canadian courts have jurisdiction over a crime, *Libman* applies to the former but not to the latter.[72]

This point is sometimes missed. In *SOCAN*,[73] for example, the Supreme Court of Canada was dealing with whether music transmitted via an Internet server located in the US, but received by Internet servers in Canada, was a telecommunication to the public for the purpose of applying the offence provisions of the *Copyright Act*.[74] Justice Binnie, writing for the majority, correctly identified that the *Libman* test applied and considered the issue of "real and substantial connection" to Internet transmissions. However, both the majority and the dissent framed the jurisdictional issue in terms of whether the *Copyright Act* had extraterritorial reach, Binnie J. even invoking the principle of statutory interpretation that presumes against extraterritorial effect at the beginning of his analysis. This suggests that Canada has taken jurisdiction over matters outside its borders, when in fact the case boiled down to whether the telecommunication had sufficient links to Canada such that it could be said to have occurred here.[75] When Parliament wishes the courts to take extraterritorial jurisdiction over persons or conduct completely outside Canadian borders, it must instruct the courts to this effect by making it explicit or necessarily implied in the legislation. Otherwise, territorial jurisdiction—as expanded by the *Libman* criteria—is the default.

Similar confusion is evident in *Greco*, which has been cited for the proposition that "there is no rule of international law depriving a judge of jurisdiction to make a probation order binding on the conduct of a probationer abroad."[76] This interpretation rests on Moldaver J.'s reasoning that, since "there is nothing in the principle of territoriality that prevents Canada from enacting laws enforceable in Canada that govern the conduct of persons outside of its territory,"[77] then a probation order could be interpreted as attaching to an individual even when he went

---

72   See *R. v. Klassen*, 2008 BCSC 1762 at paras. 72–73.

73   *Society of Composers, Authors and Music Publishers of Canada v. Canadian Assn. of Internet Providers*, [2004] 2 S.C.R. 427 at para. 54 [*SOCAN*].

74   R.S.C. 1985, c. C-42.

75   Stephen Coughlan *et al.*, "Global Reach, Local Grasp: Constructing Extraterritorial Jurisdiction in the Age of Globalization" (2007) 6 C.J.L.T. 29 at 42–44. For an example of a court getting into similar trouble by applying *SOCAN*, see *Lawson v. Accusearch Inc.*, 2007 FC 125, with commentary on this aspect of the case by Donna Davis, "Tracking Cross-Border Data Flows: A Comment on *Lawson v. Accusearch, Inc.*" (2007) 6 C.J.L.T. 119.

76   Edward Greenspan & Marc Rosenberg, eds., *Martin's Criminal Code 2009* (Aurora, ON: Canada Law Book, 2008), annotation to s. 6 at 25.

77   *Greco*, above note 44 at para. 17.

outside Canada—despite there being no specific wording to this effect in the *Criminal Code*.[78] Justice Moldaver felt that he had to determine whether the provision applied to conduct that took place outside Canada prior to engaging the *Libman* analysis and determining whether the breach took place in Canada. With respect, this draws the question of jurisdiction too finely. Where a *Criminal Code* provision, such as the probation order in *Greco*, does not expressly bind extraterritorial conduct, then it does not apply to an incident that took place wholly outside Canada. Canadians do not take their criminal law with them outside of Canada unless Parliament says so expressly or by necessary implication. The only inquiry required is whether the conduct can be said factually to have "real and substantial connection" to Canada and thus be construed to have occurred here.

Indeed, *Greco* was likely correctly decided on its facts. The conduct forming the breach of the probation order (i.e., the assault) was not within the jurisdiction of the court, since it took place entirely in Cuba. However, the effects of the breach of the order certainly spilled over into Canada, and since Canada was the only state even remotely interested in enforcing its own probation orders, no international comity considerations arose. The case was therefore resolvable as being properly within Canada's *territorial* jurisdiction, without any need for inquiry into the provision's extraterritorial effect. Justice Moldaver's finding that the probation order did reach the conduct of the perpetrator abroad amounted to finding that the wording of the section necessarily implied extraterritorial effect. However, if that was the case (and, with respect, the ruling is fairly questionable), then no inquiry under *Libman* was necessary.[79]

The Ontario Court of Appeal's decision in *Stucky*[80] is more satisfying from a methodological point of view. Similarly to the *SOCAN* case, the court was analyzing whether an offence provision in a federal regulatory statute (section 52 of the *Competition Act*)[81] could apply to conduct that occurred partially outside Canada—in this case, the fact that misleading and fraudulent representations were alleged to have been made to "the public" of the US. The Court of Appeal found that it did, given that while the victims were in the US, the impugned conduct and the proceeds were in Canada. The court was careful to distinguish

---

78   *Ibid.* at paras. 18–31.
79   The Ontario Court of Appeal recently reaffirmed its *Greco* analysis in *R. v. Rattray*, 2008 ONCA 74. And see *R. v. Stanny*, 2008 ABQB 746.
80   Above note 54.
81   Above note 55.

finding extraterritorial jurisdiction under a statute from applying it in a manner consistent with the principle of qualified territoriality:

> To interpret the phrase "to the public" as being broader than the Canadian public does not violate the presumption against extraterritoriality. In this case, the Act is being applied to the conduct of a person who is in Canada, whose alleged misrepresentations were initiated in Canada, and whose profits were received in Canada. There is a real and substantial connection between the offence alleged and Canada, notwithstanding the fact that the "public" to whom the representations were made was located outside Canada. Applying the real and substantial connection test supports an interpretation of "the public" which includes persons outside Canada while not violating the presumption against extraterritoriality.[82]

In fact, the court carried the analysis even further, ruling that quite apart from the application of the *Libman* test, a proper reading of section 52 under the principles of statutory interpretation revealed legislative intent that the phrase "to the public" not be limited to persons in Canada, in part because of the need to harmonize the Act with Canada–US treaties designed to coordinate enforcement against deceptive marketing practices.[83] However, the court appeared to acknowledge that this analysis could not be sustained if its legality was not supported by a positive finding under the *Libman* test, ultimately holding that "the phrase 'to the public' . . . should be interpreted as meaning 'a group of persons' with whom the accused has a real and substantial connection."[84]

5) Summary

As the Law Reform Commission wrote in 1985:

> As in English legislation, the general rule, that is, the territorial principle, is not stated expressly in Canadian legislation. But it is implicit in the way in which the offence-creating sections of the Criminal Code and of other criminal enactments of Canada are drafted; that is, no mention is made in an offence-creating section as to the locus of the conduct unless the section is to be applicable to conduct outside Canada, and in that event, the section expressly says so.[85]

---

82 Above note 54 at para. 32.
83 *Ibid.* at paras. 42–43.
84 *Ibid.* at para. 57.
85 Law Reform Commission of Canada, Working Paper 37, *Extraterritorial Jurisdiction* (Ottawa: Ministry of Supply and Services, 1984) at 13 [Law Reform Commission Report].

- Under section 6(2) of the *Criminal Code*,[86] no person may be convicted for conduct that, while it is contrary to a section of the *Code*, is committed outside Canada. For any offence provision to apply to conduct committed wholly outside Canada, it must say so expressly or by clear implication. Where this is not the case, Canadian courts cannot assume jurisdiction over offences that take place wholly outside Canada. The Crown bears the burden of proving that an offence was committed in Canada.[87] These same rules apply to federal regulatory legislation which contains offence provisions.[88]

- In the case of conduct that has extraterritorial aspects but is contrary to an offence provision which does not have any extraterritorial application, the *Libman* test must be applied to determine whether there is territorial jurisdiction over the offence. Such conduct will be found to have been committed in Canada if (1) it has a real and substantial connection with Canadian territory and (2) international comity does not require Canada to refrain from assuming jurisdiction.

- The "real and substantial connection" inquiry is broad and requires assessment of all of the facts related to the alleged offence, including but not limited to (1) where some or all of the elements took place; (2) where the offence was initiated; (3) where the offence was prepared or formulated; (4) where harm or injury resulting from the offence occurred, including the location of the victims; or (5) where proceeds of the offence were brought. The inquiry must be shaped by the nature of the offence which is alleged.

- The caselaw regarding the "international comity" inquiry is largely undeveloped. It appears at least to involve assessment of (1) whether any other state has jurisdiction and wishes to prosecute; (2) the strength of that state's jurisdictional connection to the alleged offence; (3) and whether international comity actually weighs towards or away from a prosecution by Canada.

---

86   Above note 5.

87   *R. v. Finta* (1992), 92 D.L.R. (4th) 1 at 102 (Ont. C.A.); Tim Quigley, *Procedure in Canadian Criminal Law*, 2d ed., looseleaf (Toronto: Carswell, 2005), updated to 2009—Release 1 at 3-22.

88   See *Canadian Liberty Net*, above note 27; and *Stucky*, above note 54. In *Stucky*, the Ontario Court of Appeal commented that the *Libman* test "has general application" and "is part of our general law concerning jurisdiction," citing the *SOCAN* case, above note 73 at para. 33). The Supreme Court of Canada had implicitly made this finding as early as *Canadian Liberty Net*. There is no reason, in principle, why the *Libman* test should not apply to provincial regulatory legislation, so long as the "extraterritorial" elements took place in another state. If the extraterritorial elements took place in another province, a separate regime applies: see Quigley, above note 87 at 3-17–3-21.

C. PRESCRIPTIVELY TRANSNATIONAL CRIMES: EXTRATERRITORIAL CRIMINAL JURISDICTION

1) Canada and Extraterritorial Jurisdiction

As surveyed in more detail in Chapter 2, while territorial jurisdiction is the norm for the exercise of criminal jurisdiction by states, international law does permit the exercise of prescriptive jurisdiction on an extraterritorial basis, that is, taking jurisdiction over criminal conduct that occurs entirely outside the state's territory. Traditionally, the starting point has been the Permanent Court of International Justice's proposition in the *Lotus* case[89] that, international law being essentially permissive, states are free to exercise whatever jurisdiction they wish in the absence of a prohibitive rule that prevents it. Since the main "prohibitive rule" is that states cannot exercise jurisdiction where it would interfere with the sovereign rights of other states, exercises of jurisdiction have tended to be based on certain kind of links between the asserting state and either the offender, the criminal act, or the effects of the act. These links are embodied in the "principles" of jurisdiction which are used by states as legal justifications of their exercises of jurisdiction: nationality, passive personality, protection of state interests, and universal.[90]

However, a state's *entitlement* to exercise prescriptive jurisdiction under international law is a separate issue from its *ability* to do so under domestic law. The latter issue is an important one, because the domestic law—usually constitutional—may place limits on extraterritorial jurisdiction which are more restrictive than those of international law. Conversely, as is the case with Canada, the UK, and other Commonwealth countries, the domestic law may in fact permit the state's legislative, executive, or judicial bodies to exceed the state's powers under international law. Therefore, an understanding of the domestic law regarding extension of criminal jurisdiction on an extraterritorial basis underpins any review of transnational crimes of domestic concern.

The competence of the English Parliament to legislate with extraterritorial effect was established as early as the sixteenth century,[91] and in Canada the *Statute of Westminster* established that ". . . the Parlia-

---

89   Above note 12.
90   See Chapter 2, Section C(3).
91   See, generally, Michael Hirst, *Jurisdiction and the Ambit of the Criminal Law* (Oxford: Oxford University Press, 2003) cc. 1 & 2.

ment of a Dominion has full power to make laws having extra-territorial operation."[92] This competence is made even more expansive by the constitutional principle of legislative supremacy, which translates into the ability of Parliament both to legislate in violation of customary international law[93] and to refuse implementation of international treaties entered into by the executive.[94] Accordingly, as a matter of domestic law, Canada (through Parliament and the courts) may extend extraterritorial jurisdiction to virtually any crime that takes place anywhere.

However, this formal competence is tempered in three ways. First, as a matter of statutory interpretation, courts "must presume that legislation is intended to comply with Canada's obligations under international instruments and as a member of the international community,"[95] unless a contrary intention is made manifest. Second, courts generally strive to give some effect to treaties under which Canada has taken on international law obligations, even if there has been no or only partial domestic implementation.[96] Third, any survey of Canadian law will reveal that, as a general rule, Canada tends to act in accordance with its international law obligations.

The latter point is certainly true with regard to criminal jurisdiction. The federal *Interpretation Act*[97] provides that federal laws apply to "the whole of Canada,"[98] though it preserves Parliament's ability to prescribe extraterritorially.[99] The territorial principle set out in section

---

92   *Statute of Westminster, 1931* (U.K.), 22 & 23 George V, c. 4, s. 3. See also *Croft v. Dunphy* (1932), 59 C.C.C. 141 (P.C.).

93   Ronald St. John Macdonald, "The Relationship Between International Law and Domestic Law in Canada" in R. St. J. Macdonald, G.L. Morris, & D.M. Johnston, eds., *Canadian Perspectives on International Law and Organization* (Toronto: University of Toronto Press, 1974); John Currie, *Public International Law*, 2d ed. (Toronto: Irwin Law, 2008) at 228.

94   Currie, *ibid.* at 235–38.

95   *Ordon Estate v. Grail*, [1998] 3 S.C.R. 437 at para. 137.

96   See also Chapter 1. See, generally, Hugh Kindred *et al.*, *International Law: Chiefly as Interpreted and Applied in Canada*, 7th ed. (Toronto: Emond Montgomery, 2006) at 221–44. It has been suggested that there is a "heavy duty" on courts to give effect to unimplemented treaties, in fulfillment of which they should take account of a broad range of legal sources; see Hugh Kindred, "The Use of Unimplemented Treaties in Canada: Practice and Prospects in the Supreme Court" in Chi Carmody *et al.*, eds., *Trilateral Perspectives on International Legal Issues: Conflict and Coherence* (Baltimore, MD: American Society of International Law, 2003).

97   R.S.C. 1985, c. I-21.

98   *Ibid.*, s. 8(1).

99   *Ibid.*, s. 8(3).

6(1) of the *Criminal Code*[100] is made "subject to this Act or any other Act of Parliament." However, the gap between how Canada *could*, as a matter of domestic law, extend criminal jurisdiction to wholly extra-territorial conduct, and the extent to which it *does* do so, is quite wide. The existence of this gap displays a clear policy imperative towards compliance with international law, which both avoids friction in Canada's international relations generally and promotes effective inter-state cooperation in the suppression of criminal matters.

In a recent study,[101] the author and Professor Coughlan suggested that Canada's various extraterritorial extensions of prescriptive criminal jurisdiction[102] can be understood as serving four distinct policy goals: implementing international treaties on specific offences, avoiding lawlessness and territorial gaps, controlling the behaviour of representatives of Canada, and protection of Canadian interests. While there is some interplay and overlap between the policy areas, it is suggested that this framework is a useful analytical tool, not least because it also helps to illustrate the manner in which Canada uses the international law principles of jurisdiction to serve its own objectives in suppressing transnational crime.

Extensions of extraterritorial criminal jurisdiction within this framework are surveyed over the next four sections, followed by consideration of other discrete jurisdictional issues. It should be noted again that, while coverage of relevant *Criminal Code* provisions is fairly complete, no attempt will be made here to cover every extraterritorial provision of every regulatory statute, though some will be used by way of illustration.

In the *Code* itself, a great number of the extraterritorial jurisdiction provisions are found in section 7. Generally speaking, the device used in both section 7 and other extraterritorial jurisdiction-creating provisions (both in the *Code* and in other federal statutes) is to provide that the offence taking place outside Canada is "deemed" to have taken place in Canada for the purpose of prosecution.[103] It is also worth noting two general features of section 7: subsection (6) provides for constructive

---

100 Above note 5.
101 Robert Currie & Stephen Coughlan, "Extraterritorial Criminal Jurisdiction: Bigger Picture or Smaller Frame?" (2007) 11 Can. Crim. L. Rev. 141.
102 The distinction between prescriptive jurisdiction and enforcement jurisdiction is covered in Chapter 2. Though Canada may pass laws or render judgments with extraterritorial effect, entitlement to enforce those laws or judgments is mostly limited to Canadian territory.
103 Provisions relating to venue, as opposed to jurisdiction, are provided for separately: see ss. 7(5), 481.1, and 481.2 of the *Code*, above note 5.

use of the pleas of *autrefois acquit*, *autrefois convict*, and pardon if the offender "has been tried and dealt with outside Canada in respect of" an offence covered in section 7;[104] and subsection (7) provides that the Attorney General must consent to prosecution under the section if the accused is not a Canadian citizen. The latter provision allows for some executive discretion whether to prosecute an offender in cases where another state may have a better jurisdictional claim at international law.

2) Implementing International Treaties

Canada is a signatory to many international treaties, usually called the "suppression conventions," that are dedicated to suppressing specific crimes or crimes in specific kinds of places. Virtually all of these treaties require Canada to exert extraterritorial jurisdiction over offenders, though usually only those who are apprehended in Canada. Accordingly, Canada asserts its jurisdiction on this basis because of international agreement that doing so helps in combating particularly pernicious varieties of crime. Its entitlement and obligation to do so at international law, of course, exists only as between the state parties to the particular treaties, except under those treaties which have passed into customary law, such as the *Torture Convention*.[105] The jurisdictional provisions extending extraterritorial jurisdiction occur for the most part in section 7 of the *Code*, as well as in specialized legislation such as the *Crimes Against Humanity and War Crimes Act*.[106]

Most of the crimes covered by these treaties are properly considered to be transnational crimes of international concern, and both the relevant international law and domestic implementing provisions are surveyed in depth in Chapter 7 on a crime-by-crime basis. With regard to truly international crimes, such as the "core crimes," piracy, and torture, Canada generally has a mixture of obligations under both treaty and customary international law. As to these crimes, the relevant international law and domestic implementing provisions are surveyed in Chapters 3, 5, and 6.

---

104 See also s. 15 of the *Code*, which provides that "no person shall be convicted of an offence in respect of an act or omission in obedience to the laws for the time being made and enforced by persons in *de facto* possession of the sovereign power in and over the place where the act or omission occurs." This could have some application as a double jeopardy defence; while it is unclear whether it is intended to apply extraterritorially, the reference to sovereign power may suggest this.

105 *United Nations Convention against Torture and Other Cruel, Inhuman or Degrading Treatment or Punishment*, (1984) 1465 U.N.T.S. 85 [*Torture Convention*].

106 S.C. 2000, c. 24.

3) Avoiding Lawlessness and Territorial Gaps

As a function of wanting to suppress crime, Canada and like-minded states tend to extend criminal jurisdiction so that it reaches areas that are not within the territory (or other sovereign jurisdiction) of any state. This avoids having areas of lawlessness in the world and allows states to minimize gaps in the international network of enforcement. Accordingly, there is overlap between this category and the previous one, since there is often international agreement that "lawless territories" should not exist. The distinction is that these laws are designed to combat crime that takes place in particular locations, rather than being geared towards the suppression of particular crimes.

The most obvious example of such areas is the high seas, and thus the laws regarding piracy are the earliest examples of crafting jurisdictional regimes that will catch behaviour outside any state's territory. Since all waters outside a state's territorial sea are essentially high seas for the purpose of enforcing criminal law, the international law of the sea contains numerous jurisdictional provisions which allow states to exert criminal jurisdiction over these areas. The law of the sea is supplemented by treaties such as the *Convention for the Suppression of Unlawful Acts against the Safety of Maritime Navigation*[107] and the *Protocol for the Suppression of Unlawful Acts against the Safety of Fixed Platforms Located on the Continental Shelf*.[108]

The Canadian laws which implement this regime are described in Chapter 2, Section C(4). Noteworthy also, however, is the interplay between sections 78.1 and 7(2.2) of the *Code*. The former criminalizes certain attacks and acts of violence on board ships and offshore platforms, while the latter asserts jurisdiction over the section 78.1 offences where they take place on board a fixed platform not attached to the continental shelf of any state or against/on board ships not navigating or scheduled to navigate beyond the territorial sea of any state. Jurisdiction is asserted on several principles, including nationality, passive personality, and protective. This jurisdictional reach appears to exceed that provided for in the relevant treaties.

Outer space is another area that would be lawless in the absence of states' assertion of extraterritorial criminal jurisdiction. As noted in Chapter 2, Section C(5), Canada is a party to the *Outer Space Treaty*,[109]

107 1678 U.N.T.S. 221.
108 1678 U.N.T.S. 304.
109 *Treaty on Principles Governing the Activities of States in the Exploration and Use of Outer Space, including the Moon and Other Celestial Bodies*, Can. T.S. 1967 No. 19, 610 U.N.T.S. 205, in force 1967.

which requires that states regulate the conduct of their nationals, vehicles, and "objects" in outer space. Canada is also a party to the *Agreement Concerning Cooperation on the Civil International Space Station*,[110] which requires it to exercise jurisdiction over its nationals on the International Space Station (ISS).[111] Section 7(2.3) of the *Code* provides for nationality-based jurisdiction over indictable offences committed on the ISS[112] or on "any means of transportation to or from" the ISS.[113] Section 7(2.31) provides for jurisdiction over indictable offences by non-Canadian ISS crew members based on the passive personality principle,[114] or where the conduct "is committed on or in relation to, or damages, a flight element [that is, a part of the ISS] provided by Canada."[115]

The most interesting provision that combats "lawless spaces" is section 477.1(e), which provides for nationality-based jurisdiction over "offence[s] under a federal law, within the meaning of section 2 of the *Oceans Act*,"[116] where the offence is "committed outside the territory of any state." The rest of section 477.1 provides for jurisdiction on basic law of the sea principles; however, paragraph 477.1(e) is of wider application. Section 2 of the *Oceans Act* defines offences as including, *inter alia*, all federal statutes and regulations, and not just the *Criminal Code*. Accordingly, every Canadian effectively takes the entire body of Canadian criminal and federal regulatory law with her into any area that is not within the territory of another state. While seemingly designed to fill any gaps that might occur in maritime areas, this provision is quite broad in scope. It would catch, for instance, any Canadian who engaged in space travel or activity beyond that dealing with the ISS, or any Canadian who committed an offence in Antarctica.

4) Controlling the Behaviour of Representatives of Canada

There are a number of provisions that extend criminal or regulatory jurisdiction over persons abroad who are employed by or are representing Canada in some governmental capacity. Section 7(4) of the *Code* extends jurisdiction over indictable offences which are committed by

---

110 Reproduced as the Schedule to the *Canadian Civil International Space Station Agreement Implementation Act*, S.C. 1999, c. 35, art. 22.

111 *Ibid.*, art. 2(1).

112 Above note 5, s. 7(2.3)(a).

113 *Ibid.*, s. 7(2.3)(b).

114 *Ibid.*, s. 7(2.31)(a).

115 *Ibid.*, s. 7(2.31)(b).

116 S.C. 1996, c. 31.

anyone "while employed as an employee within the meaning of the *Public Service Employment Act* in a place outside Canada,"[117] so long as the conduct is also an offence in the *locus* state. Section 269.1 of the *Code* asserts extraterritorial jurisdiction for torture over "officials," which is defined broadly to include both Canadian peace officers, public officers, or members of the armed forces, and their foreign equivalents.

The provision of the *National Defence Act*[118] dealing with service offences under the *Code of Service Discipline*[119] gives jurisdiction "whether the alleged offence was committed in Canada or outside Canada,"[120] and section 273 of the same Act gives criminal jurisdiction where a person covered by the *Code of Service Discipline* commits an offence "while outside Canada" that would be an offence in Canada.[121] Coverage under the *Code of Service Discipline* is provided for in section 60 of the *National Defence Act*, and includes members of the armed forces and their dependents, foreign nationals seconded to the Canadian armed forces, foreign nationals serving with any Canadian force outside of Canadian territory, and alleged spies. In effect, members of the Canadian military (as well as their dependents and persons accompanying the forces) bring Canadian criminal law with them wherever they go, at least in terms of being liable under it.

To some extent these extensions of jurisdiction are based on the nationality principle, which is otherwise unusual for Canada. The goal, however, is clearly not to control the conduct of Canadian nationals abroad, but rather to apply Canadian criminal law to persons outside Canada who are acting in some way as the "public face" of the country. For the most part, this is uncontroversial under the broader version of the nationality principle that has gained acceptance in recent years.[122] However, section 7(4) of the *Criminal Code* would apply the entire body of indictable offences under Canadian criminal law to foreign nationals in their home states who happened to be employed in some public service capacity by the government of Canada. This would certainly be at the fringes of even the broadest version of either the nationality or

---

117 *Public Service Employment Act*, S.C. 2003, c. 22.

118 *National Defence Act*, R.S.C. 1985, c. N-5.

119 Which regulates the behaviour of "(a) an officer or non-commissioned member of the regular force; (b) an officer or non-commissioned member of the special force" (*ibid.*, s. 60(1)).

120 *Ibid.*, s. 67. To the same effect is s. 39 of the *Royal Canadian Mounted Police Act*, R.S.C. 1985, c. R-10, as regards that organization's "Code of Conduct."

121 *National Defence Act, ibid.*, s. 273.

122 See Robert Jennings & Arthur Watts, *Oppenheim's International Law*, 9th ed. (London: Longmans, 1996) at 1156–57; and see Chapter 2.

protective principles, and as the Law Reform Commission pointed out, extradition might well be refused by the foreign government in such a situation.[123] The torture provisions would be less problematic, given the wide-ranging jurisdictional scope permitted under international law; see Chapter 7.

5) Protection of Canadian Interests

A number of extraterritorial provisions are designed to protect vital national interests of Canada, including but not limited to security,[124] and thus are properly understood as exercises of the protective principle. Section 46 of the *Criminal Code*[125] provides that both high treason and treason may be prosecuted if committed outside of Canada "by a Canadian citizen or a person who owes allegiance to Her Majesty," which combines the protective and nationality principles. Section 57 extends extraterritorial jurisdiction over everyone engaging in offences relating to creation, use, and possession of forged Canadian passports, while section 58 provides similarly for fraudulent use of certificates of citizenship. The *Citizenship Act*[126] provides for jurisdiction over fraud relating to citizenship and various illegal uses of certificates of citizenship that take place outside Canada.[127] Section 135 of the *Immigration and Refugee Protection Act*[128] provides for extraterritorial jurisdiction over all offences found in that statute.

There are several provisions that seek to protect Canada's security extraterritorially, as well. The *Security Offences Act* provides for extraterritorial jurisdiction broadly over "an offence under any law of Can-

---

123 Above note 85 at 70. On the other hand, as Williams and Castel point out, this would allow Canada to prosecute such people in situations where they have diplomatic or other immunity which Canada does not wish to waive; see Sharon A. Williams & Jean-Gabriel Castel, *Canadian Criminal Law: International and Transnational Aspects* (Toronto: Butterworths, 1981) at 86–87.

124 Arguably, the provisions of the *National Defence Act* regarding offences under the *Code of Service Discipline*, discussed in Section C(4), above in this chapter, belong in this category as well, since they protect the essential interest of maintaining order and good discipline in the Canadian forces when they are abroad. Moreover, on the whole these kinds of provisions protect a further "essential interest": that of having Canadian nationals or employees be tried in Canada rather than a foreign legal system. In some cases, exercising extraterritorial jurisdiction would be preferable to seeing the individual tried in foreign courts, or to be permitted to go free.

125 Above note 5.

126 R.S.C. 1985, c. C-29.

127 *Ibid.*, s. 30.

128 S.C. 2001, c. 27.

ada" where the conduct in question constitutes "a threat to the security of Canada."[129] The *Security of Information Act*[130] prescribes a range of offences relating essentially to espionage for foreign powers and, especially since the 2001 terrorism legislation, provision of confidential or sensitive information to terrorists for purposes "prejudicial or injurious to the State." Section 26 extends extraterritorial jurisdiction on the basis of nationality[131] and "extended nationality" (that is, persons owing allegiance to the Crown[132] and persons locally engaged in a Canadian mission outside Canada[133]), but also to any person who commits an offence extraterritorially and is later found in Canada.[134] The latter provision is purely an exercise of protective jurisdiction, even though enforcement options are territorially limited as always.

The extraterritorial offences found in sections 3 and 4 of the *Foreign Enlistment Act*,[135] jurisdiction over which is extended on a nationality basis, are best understood as falling under this category as well.

6) "Non-extraterritorial" Offences

The vast majority of offences in the *Criminal Code*[136] are subject to section 6(2) and are territorial in scope. As explained in the review of *Libman* in Section B(4), above in this chapter, these offences may in some cases have transnational elements or aspects but will nonetheless be found to have been committed in Canada if the *Libman* test is met. A smaller number of offences are explicitly extraterritorial, that is, they are caught by Canadian criminal jurisdiction even though all of the relevant conduct happens outside of Canada. However, there is an odd group of offences in the *Criminal Code* which contain some transnational elements, but which are nonetheless properly understood as territorial offences because the transnational element is irrelevant to the purpose of the offence. For the most part they stem from older versions of the *Code* that predate the modern understanding of both quali-

---

129 R.S.C. 1985, c. S-7, s. 2, which cross-references the definition of "threats to the security of Canada" to s. 2 of the *Canadian Security Intelligence Service Act*, R.S.C. 1985, c. C-23; the latter definition contains the extraterritorial provision.
130 R.S.C. 1985, c. O-5.
131 *Ibid.*, s. 26(1)(a).
132 *Ibid.*, s. 26(1)(b).
133 *Ibid.*, s. 26(1)(c).
134 *Ibid.*, s. 26(1)(d).
135 R.S.C. 1985, c. F-28.
136 Above note 5.

fied territoriality and extraterritorial jurisdiction, and for that reason they are referred to here as being "non-extraterritorial."

An example is section 354 of the *Code*, which criminalizes possession of property obtained from a criminal act in Canada, or from "an act or omission anywhere that, if it had occurred in Canada, would have constituted an offence punishable by indictment." The fact that the theft of property might have occurred outside Canada makes no difference for whether the offence can be proven, since what is caught is the subsequent possession, in Canada, of something illegally obtained. Another example is the offence of bigamy in section 290 of the *Code*, which provides for jurisdiction over any Canadian citizen, resident in Canada, who "leaves Canada with intent" to commit various bigamous acts and carries any of them out. The individual would not be prosecuted until he was present in Canada, at which point his status of being a bigamist crystallizes. The intent of the offence is to prosecute persons in Canada who have gone through two marriages, irrespective of where either marriage took place.[137] Similar analyses can be carried out of the offences of procuring illicit sexual intercourse (section 212(a)), making a false document (section 366), sending an unseaworthy vessel or unsafe aircraft (section 251), gaming in stocks (section 383), and brokers illegally reducing stock (section 384).

Even if one disagrees with a characterization of any of these offences as being essentially non-extraterritorial, it is clear that each offence is set up in such a way that there are significant links to Canada—to the extent that the *Libman* test would be satisfied in every case. Even taking into account the mild potential for concurrent jurisdiction with another state that might exist with, for example, the bigamy provisions, Canada's claim is still primarily territorial.

7) Ships, Aircraft, and Fixed Platforms

As the customary international law of the sea developed, ships were deemed to be subject to the jurisdiction of the state whose flag they flew, usually called the "flag state." This jurisdiction was exclusive in the flag state's waters and on the high seas, though concurrent jurisdiction might be exercised by foreign states where the ship was in the foreign state's waters. While state interest in having extraterritorial jurisdiction over flagged vessels was obvious, the matter was doctrinally uncertain for some time. A theory which dominated into the twen-

---

137   Interestingly, the offence of polygamy in s. 293 of the *Code*, *ibid.*, is not similarly worded.

tieth century was that ships were deemed to be floating "islands" of the flag state's territory, and thus the jurisdiction was territorially based.[138] This was unsatisfactory, since when a ship is within the territorial waters of a foreign state, then that state has concurrent jurisdiction on a territorial basis.

Today ships are usually thought of as having the *nationality* of the state in which they are registered and whose flag they fly.[139] This allows them to exercise the international law rights of their flag states as to freedom of navigation, engaging in fishing, and so on, and also subjects them to the jurisdiction and laws of their flag state.[140] Whether terming this basis for jurisdiction "nationality" is any better than the previous territorial theory is not important. As the European Committee on Crime Problems puts it: "Regardless of whether ships and aircraft are deemed to be national territory, or are considered as such, or are considered as independent entities, all states claim jurisdiction over offences committed on board vessels or aircraft flying the national flag, irrespective of the nationality of the offender."[141] Under the *United Nations Convention on the Law of the Sea* (*UNCLOS*),[142] states are obliged to exercise criminal jurisdiction over their flagged vessels,[143] though in some circumstances foreign states may exercise concurrent jurisdiction on the high seas, for example, collisions.[144]

In Canada, section 477.1(1)(c) of the *Code* extends prescriptive jurisdiction for offences under any federal law to any ship registered or licensed under Canadian law.[145] Accordingly, jurisdiction exists over any criminal or federal regulatory offence that takes place aboard a Canadian-flagged vessel, regardless of the location of the vessel or the nationality of the offender. Section 477.3 provides for enforcement against offences committed aboard Canadian-flagged ships outside Canada, including situations where "hot pursuit" has been commenced,[146] though

---

138 This was the position at the time of the *Lotus* case, above note 12, discussed in Section B(1), above in this chapter. See also *R. v. Oteri*, [1976] 1 W.L.R. 1272 at 1276 (P.C.), Lord Diplock.

139 The rules for nationality of the ship are determined under the domestic laws pertaining to registration of ships.

140 Kindred *et al.*, above note 96 at 539.

141 European Committee on Crime Problems, *Extraterritorial Criminal Jurisdiction* (Strasbourg: European Committee on Crime Problems, 1990) at 12.

142 1833 U.N.T.S. 3.

143 *Ibid.*, art. 94.

144 *Ibid.*, art. 97. See Chapter 2 for more.

145 See *R. v. Guilbride*, [2004] B.C.J. No. 861 at para. 160 (Prov. Ct.).

146 See Chapter 2, Section C(4)(f).

in the latter case enforcement may not take place in the territorial sea of another state.[147]

With regard to the special case of high seas collisions or other navigational incidents, article 97 of *UNCLOS* entitles Canada to take criminal jurisdiction over its flagged ships or over any of its nationals among the crew who are implicated in the offence. Domestically, section 78.1(2)(b) of the *Code* criminalizes destruction or damage to a ship "where that act is likely to endanger the safe navigation of [the] ship." Jurisdiction over a Canadian-flagged ship involved in a collision also comes under section 477.1(1)(c); jurisdiction over a Canadian national aboard a foreign-flagged ship who was implicated in a collision would appear to come under section 477.1(1)(e).

In a similar manner to ships, aircraft also have the "nationality" of the state in which they are registered,[148] and under the 1963 *Tokyo Convention on Offences and Certain Other Acts Occurring on Board Aircraft*,[149] states are obliged to exercise criminal jurisdiction over offences taking place on board their registered aircraft,[150] though that jurisdiction is limited to when the plane is in flight, over the high seas, or otherwise outside the territory of any state.[151] Both of these instruments most likely reflect customary international law.

Section 7(1)(a) of the *Code* provides for jurisdiction over indictable offences where they are committed on or in respect of Canadian-registered aircraft or aircraft leased without crew and operated by a person "qualified to be registered as an owner of an aircraft registered in Canada,"[152] while the aircraft is in flight. Section 7(1)(b) provides similarly for offences on any aircraft in flight, "if the flight terminated in Canada." The definition of "flight" is provided in section 7(8) and corresponds to the regime in the *Tokyo Convention*.

Under articles 60 and 80 of *UNCLOS*, states have complete jurisdiction over any artificial islands, installations, and structures in their exclusive economic zones (EEZ) or on their continental shelves. Section 14 of the *Oceans Act*[153] gives Canada jurisdiction over fixed platforms in the EEZ, and section 477.1(1)(a) of the *Code* extends criminal juris-

---

147 *Code*, above note 5, s. 477.3(1)(b).
148 *Chicago Convention on International Civil Aviation* (1944), 15 U.N.T.S. 295, Can. T.S. 1944 No. 36, art. 17.
149 (1963), 704 U.N.T.S. 219, Can. T.S. 1970 No. 5 [*Tokyo Convention*].
150 *Ibid.*, art. 3.
151 *Ibid.*, art. 1(1).
152 The *Aeronautics Act*, R.S.C. 1985, c. A-2, and regulations thereto provide for registration of aircraft.
153 Above note 116.

diction to persons who are in the zone in connection with natural re-sources contained therein, though only via the nationality and passive personality principles. Section 20 of the *Oceans Act* applies all federal laws to marine installations, structures, or artificial islands attached or connected to the continental shelf, and within safety zones around them, while specific jurisdiction under the *Criminal Code* is provided by section 477.1(b). Various specific offences against fixed platforms[154] are set out in section 78.1 of the *Code*. Extraterritorial jurisdiction over offences on fixed platforms affixed to another state's seabed (or un-attached to any) is a matter of treaty and is dealt with in Chapter 7.

D. CONSPIRACY

The law surrounding inchoate offences is conceptually difficult, and it is not surprising that these offences raise interesting jurisdictional issues which touch on both qualified territorial and extraterritorial jurisdiction. Conspiracy offences[155] are the most prominent of these, both because the transnational aspects are fairly complex and because a specific (and somewhat confusing) jurisdictional regime has been set forth in section 465 of the *Criminal Code*.[156]

---

154 Defined as "an artificial island or a marine installation or structure that is permanently attached to the seabed" in accordance with the above *Criminal Code* sections.

155 For general treatment of the law regarding criminal conspiracy, see Kent Roach, *Criminal Law*, 4th ed. (Toronto: Irwin Law, 2009).

156 No attempt will be made here to canvass the even trickier issues that arise when considering transnational issues associated with other inchoate offences, such as attempt, aiding and abetting, and counselling (though see the Law Reform Commission Report, above note 85; Cedric Ryngaert, "Territorial Jurisdiction over Cross-frontier Offences: Revisiting a Classic Problem of International Criminal Law" (2009) 9 I.C.L.R. 187 at 204–8; and two recent reports by the UK Law Commission, No. 300 (July 2006) and No. 305 (May 2007), both of which are available online: www.lawcom.gov.uk/lc_reports.htm). The con-ceptual difficulties here are profound, given that a major part of the task is to evaluate the potential for territorial jurisdiction claims over offences that are largely lacking an *actus reus*. The *Criminal Code* provisions regarding attempt (s. 24), aiding and abetting (s. 21), and counselling (s. 22) contain no explicit language that extends their scope beyond Canada. Therefore, Canadian courts have only territorial jurisdiction over offences that stem from these provisions, and cases with extraterritorial aspects must be resolved by reference to *Libman*, above note 7. To date, there seem to have been no reported cases where the *Libman* test was applied in these contexts. There is no reason in principle why *Libman* could not be applied to ground jurisdiction over these acts in appropriate

It is first useful to examine section 465(1) and its interrelationship with section 465(3) before moving on to the truly extraterritorial jurisdiction provided under section 465(4).[157] Paragraph 465(1)(a) criminalizes conspiring to commit murder or to cause another person to be murdered, "whether in Canada or not." Paragraph 465(1)(b) provides for the specific crime of "conspir[ing] with anyone to prosecute a person for an alleged offence, knowing that he did not commit that offence." Paragraph 465(1)(c) criminalizes conspiracy to commit any other indictable offence, while paragraph 465(1)(d) criminalizes conspiracy to commit a summary conviction offence. Section 465(3) states as follows: "Every one who, while in Canada, conspires with any one to do anything referred to in subsection (1) in a place outside Canada that is an offence under the laws of that place shall be deemed to have conspired to do that thing in Canada."

A logical reading of the section would proceed as follows: section 465(1)(a)–(d) creates the offence of conspiracy to murder, prosecuting the innocent, all other indictable offences, and all summary conviction offences. Section 465(3) provides that it is an offence to conspire, in Canada, to commit any of these crimes in another state, provided that the conspired offence is also an offence in the other state (a "double criminality" requirement). Section 465(4) provides that it is an offence to conspire, in another state, to commit any of these crimes in Canada. The latter is a truly extraterritorial offence, with no double criminality requirement.

This would be a reasonably simple matter, except that section 465(1)(a) reads "every one who conspires with any one to commit murder or to cause another person to be murdered, *whether in Canada or not*, is guilty of an indictable offence" (emphasis added). Logically, the phrase "whether in Canada or not" refers to the conspiring, and not the murder. However, given section 465(3), this phrase appears to be redundant. Dissenting in *Finta*, La Forest J. appeared to suggest that this provision created an extraterritorial offence of "conspiracy to murder abroad."[158] However, this interpretation would make redundant section 465(4), which covers conspiracy to commit "anything referred to in subsection (1)" — that is, including murder — while the offender is "in a place outside Canada." One might therefore interpret the paragraph as creating a *territorial* offence of conspiracy to commit murder,

---

cases, though the inquiry as to "real and substantial connection" will be highly fact-specific and might require more detailed consideration than it has received in cases regarding regular offences.

157 Section 465(2) was repealed by R.S.C. 1985 (1st Supp.), c. 27, s. 61(3).

158 *R. v. Finta*, above note 6 at 743.

whether the plan is for the murder to take place in Canada or abroad; again, however, this makes section 465(3) redundant with regard to the offence of murder (though not as regards other offences). The only way to truly resolve the problem is to note section 465(3)'s double criminality requirement, that the offence conspired must be against the laws of both Canada and the foreign state. Thus, a conspiracy in Canada to commit murder in another state where murder was not an offence[159] would not be caught by subsection (3), and Canada's jurisdiction to prosecute in that case is saved under paragraph 1(a). This is logically consistent, though unrealistic given that murder is an offence common to every country in the world.

With that in mind, subsection (1) is perhaps best read as making it an offence to conspire, in Canada, to commit any indictable or summary conviction offence in Canada, and also to conspire in Canada to commit murder anywhere in the world. As there is no obvious reason for the insertion of the phrase "whether in Canada or not," it should be regarded as redundant drafting.

Section 465(3), again, makes it an offence to conspire in Canada to engage in certain conduct, where that conduct is both an offence in Canada and "is an offence under the laws of that place." The requirement that the conduct be criminal in both Canada and the foreign state has been described as an effort to avoid interference with the sovereignty of the foreign state,[160] since it might seem irregular to punish persons for conspiring to do things which are not criminal in the place they plan to do them. With regard to some offences, this is logical. For example, it would be overreaching to prosecute someone who conspires in Canada to engage in unlicensed gambling, if their plan is to travel to a state where this is not illegal.

However, in an international legal environment that has been geared for some decades to ensuring that there are no areas of asylum for serious criminal offenders, this "protection" may have too general an application. It seems like bad public policy for Canada to apply a "hands-off" policy to those who wish to, for example, launder money in, commit terrorist offences in, or smuggle narcotics to or from states which are either holdouts in international efforts to combat these scourges, or which simply have underdeveloped legal regimes. Surely it is undesirable for Canada to allow itself to be used as a launching ground for the planning of such offences.

---

159 Or, presumably, in a place outside the territory of any state, though that would be caught by s. 477.1(e) of the *Code*, above note 5.
160 Williams & Castel, above note 123 at 89–90.

In that light, it is interesting that, to all appearances, the *Libman* test arguably has made the double criminality requirement in section 465(3) irrelevant for most practical purposes. In both *R. v. Douglas*[161] and *R. v. Rowbotham*,[162] the Ontario Court of Appeal ruled that where accused persons had conspired in Canada to traffic in narcotics in the US, there was no need for recourse to section 465(3) — the conspiracy had a sufficient "real and substantial connection" to Canada so that there was jurisdiction over the offence in section 465(1)(c).

This interpretation is broad and seems to miss the point of section 465(3). First of all, territorial jurisdiction over a conspiracy is not hard to justify, since the conspiracy is complete before any acts taken in furtherance of it are completed. Paragraphs 465(1)(c) and (d) have no explicit extraterritorial ambit; so, as noted above, and especially in light of sections 465(3) and 465(1)(b), subsections (c) and (d) must simply make it an offence to conspire in Canada to commit an offence in Canada. Section 465(3) imposes an additional requirement: the Crown must prove not only that the acts about which the accused was conspiring would be offences if committed in Canada, but are also against the law in the foreign state. There is a sound policy purpose behind section 465(3) (albeit one that is not so easily justified in some limited circumstances, as noted above in this section). *Douglas* and *Rowbotham* seem to indicate a desire to use *Libman* as a means of subverting this purpose, since by this interpretation any conspiracy in Canada to commit any Canadian offence anywhere would be an offence. In that event, courts would not have to concern themselves with the foreign law question that section 465(3) insists on. In practice this does not seem to be happening, although the purpose is often accomplished by the unnecessarily complicated route of charging the accused under both sections 465(1)(c) and 465(3). Statutory amendment could help to clarify matters.

Section 465(4) says, "Every one who, while in a place outside Canada, conspires with any one to do anything referred to in subsection (1) in Canada shall be deemed to have conspired in Canada to do that thing." The section is oddly worded, and read literally would provide for jurisdiction over a conspiracy outside Canada to engage in a conspiracy inside Canada to commit any offence.[163] More sensibly, this section deems conspiracies to commit an offence in Canada to have occurred in Canada even if the conspiring actually occurred outside the country.

---

161 (1989), 72 C.R. (3d) 309 (Ont. C.A.), aff'd on other grounds, [1991] 1 S.C.R. 301.
162 (1992), 76 C.C.C. (3d) 542 (Ont. C.A.), aff'd [1993] 4 S.C.R. 834.
163 The same could be said of s. 465(3), relative to the wording in that section.

This extends extraterritorial jurisdiction over a criminal conspiracy that takes place anywhere outside Canada, so long as the goal of the conspiracy is to commit an offence in Canada.

In the Anglo-American tradition, courts have long perceived a need to take jurisdiction over foreign conspiracies aimed at harming domestic interests, even prior to there being any explicit legislative direction to do so. The House of Lords ruled in *D.P.P. v. Doot*[164] that a conspiracy in a foreign state to commit offences in England was within the jurisdiction of the English courts, but only if some overt act in furtherance of the conspiracy took place in England.[165] Later cases extended jurisdiction to the foreign conspiracy even where no overt act had occurred in England, on the rationale that such was needed to deal with the new realities of transnational crime and that comity was not offended by so doing.[166] Statutory effect, similar to section 465(4) of the *Code*, was eventually given to this approach.[167] US courts have taken a similar approach,[168] as have other Commonwealth states.[169] Some European states, by contrast, have maintained the requirement for acts furthering the conspiracy to take place in the state in order for jurisdiction to be grounded.[170]

In Canada it is well established that a foreign conspiracy comes within domestic jurisdiction where some acts are done in connection with the conspiracy; indeed, *Libman* is itself authority for this proposition.[171] In the recent case of *United States of America v. Kavaratzis*,[172] Doherty J.A. briefly reviewed several authorities (including *Libman*)[173] and concluded that Canada would take jurisdiction over a conspiracy in a foreign state to violate Canadian narcotics laws if acts done in furtherance of the conspiracy were committed in Canada—even where the person charged with the conspiracy never entered Canada

---

164 [1973] A.C. 807.

165 *Ibid.* at 832–33.

166 *Liangsiriprasert v. Government of the United States of America*, [1991] 1 A.C. 225 at 251C (P.C.) [*Liangsiriprasert*]. See also *R. v. Bow Street Metropolitan Stipendiary Magistrate, Ex parte Pinochet Ugarte (No. 3)*, [1999] 2 All E.R. 97 at para. 125 (H.L.), Lord Hope of Craighead.

167 Section 3(2) of the *Criminal Justice Act 1993* (U.K.), 1993, c. 36.

168 See *United States v. Noriega*, 746 F. Supp. 1506 (S.D. Fla. 1990); *United States v. Wright-Barker*, 784 F.2d 161 (3d Circ. 1986).

169 For a solid overview, see Joshua Blackmore, "The Jurisdictional Problem of Extraterritorial Conspiracy" (2006) 17 Crim. L.F. 71.

170 Ryngaert, above note 156 at 207.

171 See also *R. v. Taylor* (1976), 32 C.C.C. (2d) 409 (Ont. Prov. Ct.).

172 (2006), 209 O.A.C. 180 (C.A.).

173 *Ibid.* at paras. 15–19.

and the acts were committed by co-conspirators. Oddly, His Lordship appeared to ground the finding on *Libman* and made no reference to section 465(4), and thus must have been referring to section 465(1). Accordingly, this would constitute *territorial* jurisdiction over the foreign conspiracy on the basis of "real and substantial connection," the connection residing in the acts of the co-conspirators in Canada. Applying the *Libman* test to such a situation would require considering the interests of international comity, though it is easy to see a case for Canada as the most affected state where some acts furthering the conspiracy have been done in Canada.[174]

On this logic, however, the range of acts covered by section 465(4) must be quite narrow. Since the "domestic" conspiracy provisions would catch a foreign conspiracy with related acts committed in Canada, section 465(4) must be purely extraterritorial and confined to situations in which there is a foreign conspiracy and *no* related acts in Canada. Of course, such an offence could be enforced only if the offender happened to come to Canada, or was extradited here.

This being the case, what is the international law basis for Canada exerting extraterritorial jurisdiction over such a situation? Canada's interest in prosecuting foreign conspiracies aimed at Canada has been described as "obvious,"[175] but unless the accused is a Canadian national, what is not obvious is any well-accepted basis in international law for extending jurisdiction. To be sure, a foreign conspiracy aimed at Canada will engage Canadian interests; in some cases the offence might be of little interest to the *locus* state, for example, a conspiracy to counterfeit Canadian currency. However, non-Canadians conspiring to import narcotics into Canada or commit a terrorist act in Canada might be of more interest to the state in which the conspiracy occurs, and formally, Canada's entitlement to prosecute under international law could be questionable.[176] On the other hand, the practice of at least the common law states reveals that a robust application of the protective principle appears to be emerging on exactly this basis,[177] and without significant protest from other states.

Practically speaking, the state which apprehends the conspirator is likely to prosecute if it has any interest in doing so, and conflicts will be resolvable under any applicable extradition treaties. Even in the

---

174 A similar point was made in *R. v. Guilbride*, above note 145: see paras. 142–45. However, that case was considering the issue of jurisdiction under s. 465(4).

175 Alan Mewett and Morris Manning, *Mewett & Manning on Criminal Law*, 3d ed. (Toronto: Butterworths, 1994) at 338.

176 Accord, Law Reform Commission Report, above note 85 at 117.

177 Blackmore, above note 169.

absence of such treaties, it is still desirable for states to be able to prosecute those who conspire abroad to harm their territorial interests,[178] though it is uncertain whether an *entitlement* to do so has emerged as a principle of customary international law. It seems wisest, as Blackmore has proposed, to proceed with a more expansive view of what the protective principle may entail, supplemented by close attention to international comity and clear statutory language that restrains otherwise controversial conduct.[179]

FURTHER READING

BLACKMORE, JOSHUA D.A., "The Jurisdictional Problem of the Extraterritorial Conspiracy" (2006) 17 Crim. L.F. 71

COUGHLAN, STEVE *et al.*, "Global Reach, Local Grasp: Constructing Extraterritorial Jurisdiction in the Age of Globalization" (2007) 6 C.J.L.T. 29

CURRIE, ROBERT J., & STEVE COUGHLAN, "Extraterritorial Criminal Jurisdiction: Bigger Picture or Smaller Frame?" (2007) 11 Can. Crim. L. Rev. 141

EUROPEAN COMMITTEE ON CRIME PROBLEMS, *Extraterritorial Criminal Jurisdiction* (Strasbourg: Council of Europe, 1990)

LAW REFORM COMMISSION OF CANADA, *Working Paper 37: Extraterritorial Jurisdiction* (Ottawa: Ministry of Supply and Services, 1984)

MORGAN, ED, "Criminal Process, International Law and Extraterritorial Crime" (1988) 38 U.T.L.J. 245

RYNGAERT, CEDRIC, "Territorial Jurisdiction Over Cross-frontier Offences: Revisiting a Classic Problem of International Criminal Law" (2009) 9 Int'l Crim. L. Rev. 187

WILLIAMS, SHARON A., & J.-G.CASTEL, *Canadian Criminal Law: International and Transnational Aspects* (Toronto: Butterworths, 1981) c. 2

---

178 See *Liangsiriprasert*, above note 166.
179 Blackmore, above note 169 at 101. In this respect, perhaps s. 465(4) should have a requirement of approval by the Attorney General before proceeding with charges, as do most other extraterritorial jurisdiction clauses in the *Code*.

ZUCKER, SYMON, "Extraterritoriality and Canadian Criminal Law" (1974–75) 17 Crim. L.Q. 146

INTERNATIONAL CRIMINAL COOPERATION

A. INTRODUCTION

This chapter deals with the primary mechanisms which states use to assist each other in the prosecution of criminal offenders. Those mechanisms are *extradition* and *mutual legal assistance in criminal matters*, and they are discussed in Sections B and D respectively. There is a tendency in older and even contemporary caselaw to refer to all such cooperative mechanisms as "mutual assistance." Because "mutual legal assistance," meaning the treaty-based transmission of evidence between states, has become a term of art, the approach here will be to eschew the older practice and call each mode of cooperation by its usual name.

Extradition and mutual legal assistance between states are necessary because of the overarching legal underpinning of all international and transnational criminal law: the territorial sovereignty of states and the limits on the exercise of enforcement jurisdiction by criminal authorities (for more on this, see Chapter 1, Section D). The importance of international criminal cooperation for dealing with these limits was expressed by La Forest J. in an oft-cited passage from *United States of America v. Cotroni*:

> The investigation, prosecution and suppression of crime for the protection of the citizen and the maintenance of peace and public order is an important goal of all organized societies. The pursuit of that goal cannot realistically be confined within national boundaries.

That has long been the case, but it is increasingly evident today. Modern communications have shrunk the world and made McLuhan's global village a reality. The only respect paid by the international criminal community to national boundaries is when these can serve as a means to frustrate the efforts of law enforcement and judicial authorities.[1]

Accordingly, states have been moved by common interest to enter into agreements whereby each could do the important criminal enforcement work of the others, in situations where proper investigation and prosecution was confounded by "national boundaries."

Of course, there are often situations where sovereignty concerns do interfere with a state's ability or willingness to arrest and prosecute particular offenders, and historically more than one state has been moved to utilize "alternatives" to extradition—that is, to use extra-legal means to obtain custody over the offender. Section C, below in this chapter, deals with the age-old practice of abduction of fugitives, as well as the more recent and controversial practice of "extraordinary rendition." Another problem area is the uneasy interaction between modes of criminal cooperation between states and the human rights obligations which bind states under both treaties and customary international law. The discourse on this area, once referred to as academically "fashionable,"[2] increasingly has become a source of friction between prosecutorial authorities, criminal defence lawyers, and state governments, and shows no sign of becoming less so. Accordingly, these issues deserve their own discrete discussion and are canvassed in Chapter 10.

This chapter and the next, then, deal not with trials of criminals nor the substantive law regarding the crimes they commit, but rather with important procedural mechanisms used by states to facilitate crime suppression. The subject matter is not truly international criminal law (ICL) or even transnational criminal law (TCL), but really a species of transnational criminal procedure. However, the expansion of both ICL and TCL during the last century has significantly increased the importance of this kind of machinery, and it would be inappropriate not to deal with them in some way in this text. Accordingly, the subject matter will be referred to simply as "international criminal cooperation."

---

1   [1989] 1 S.C.R. 1469 at 1485.
2   Christine van den Wyngaert, "Applying the European Convention on Human Rights to Extradition: Opening Pandora's Box?" (1990) 39 I.C.L.Q. 757 at 757.

B. EXTRADITION

1) International Law

a) History

Extradition is the formal rendition of a criminal fugitive from a state that has custody (the requested state) to a state that wishes either to prosecute or, if the fugitive has already been convicted of an offence, to impose a penal sentence (the requesting state). Other (usually immigration-based) means of removing individuals from states, such as deportation and expulsion, are geared towards protecting domestic interests.[3] Extradition, by contrast, is aimed at the facilitation of a foreign state's criminal process, and is thus a sovereign act of cooperation between states. However, there is obviously a sense of mutual self-interest at play among states which enter into extradition agreements, since facilitating the criminal processes of other states serves general crime suppression goals that benefit all. For situations in which extradition is not available, some states have been known to resort to what is often called "irregular rendition," for example, abduction or extraordinary rendition,[4] which can have deleterious effects on inter-state relations. Extradition is thus far preferable, and is in fact one of the oldest forms of inter-state cooperation (criminal or otherwise), extradition-type arrangements being traceable back to ancient Egypt.[5]

International law writers as far back as Grotius have mused about the desirability of a solid international law rule requiring states to extradite fugitives to face foreign criminal proceedings.[6] However, it may safely be stated that there is no general duty under customary international law to surrender fugitives to other states.[7] Accordingly

---

3   The practice of using immigration devices to deport individuals to states where they face criminal proceedings in order to subvert the more stringent extradition laws is often referred to as "disguised extradition"; see *Re Shepherd and Minister of Employment and Immigration* (1989), 70 O.R. (2d) 765 (C.A.).

4   These practices are dealt with in Section C, below in this chapter.

5   Ivan A. Shearer, *Extradition in International Law* (Dobbs Ferry, NY: Oceana Publications, 1971) at 5.

6   This is the origin of the maxim *aut dedere aut judicare* ("extradite or prosecute"); see Hugo Grotius, *De Iure Belli Ac Pacis*, Book II, Chapter XXI, paras. III & IV, trans. by Francis W. Kelsey (Washington, DC: Carnegie Institution, 1925) at 526–29. See also M. Cherif Bassiouni & Edward Wise, *Aut Dedere Aut Judicare: The Duty to Extradite or Prosecute in International Law* (Boston: Martinus Nijhoff, 1995).

7   *United States of America v. McVey* (1992), 77 C.C.C. (3d) 1 at 6–7 (S.C.C.); *United States of America v. Allard* (1991), 64 C.C.C. (3d) 159 at 162 (S.C.C.). There are

extradition operated earlier as a matter of comity between states, and now operates almost exclusively by way of treaties. The treaties are predominantly bilateral, as states tend to be fairly choosy about with whom they will open active arrangements to send individuals to face foreign criminal process. The United Nations has put forward a Model Treaty on Extradition (UN Model Treaty) which provides the basic mechanisms of extradition arrangements (and sometimes choices between several) in order to assist states which are developing extradition treaties.[8] Multilateral extradition arrangements come in two forms. The first is treaties between states which have geographical and/or historical ties that make a multilateral treaty desirable; examples are the Commonwealth, the Organization of American States (OAS), the Organization of African Unity (OAU), and various treaties and instruments between the members of the European Union (EU).[9] The second variety is extradition provisions that can be found in the suppression conventions, such as the *Vienna Narcotics Convention*[10] and the *United Nations Convention against Transnational Organized Crime (TOC Convention)*.[11] As explored in more detail in Chapter 7, the latter treaties all contain *aut dedere aut*

---

two possible exceptions. The first is the obligation to extradite war criminals under the *Geneva Conventions* (1950), 75 U.N.T.S. 31, 85, 135, and 287, since the provisions of those treaties have the force of customary international law. The second is a duty under customary international law to either extradite or prosecute individuals who are alleged to have committed any of the core crimes, that is, war crimes, crimes against humanity, or genocide. The International Law Commission (ILC) has appointed a Special Rapporteur to examine this question, and work is proceeding at the time of writing. The Special Rapporteur's reports and associated documents can be found online: http://untreaty.un.org/ilc/guide/7_6.htm.

8 UN Doc. A/RES/45/117 (1990), as amended UN Doc. A/RES/52/88 (1997) [UN Model Treaty]. The UNODC has published a manual on the treaty, available online: www.unodc.org/pdf/model_treaty_extradition_revised_manual.pdf.

9 On European initiatives, see Ilias Bantekas & Susan Nash, *International Criminal Law*, 3d ed. (New York: Routledge-Cavendish, 2007) at 312–25. Among EU states, the extradition process has been streamlined by the adoption of the "European Arrest Warrant," by which national police forces arrest accused persons on the basis of court orders issued in partner states, without the need for formal extradition requests to be made on an inter-state basis. See European Commission, "European Arrest Warrant Replaces Extradition between EU Member States," online: http://ec.europa.eu/justice_home/fsj/criminal/extradition/fsj_criminal_extradition_en.htm. And see Rob Blekxtoon & Wouter van Ballegooij, *Handbook on the European Arrest Warrant* (The Hague: T.M.C. Aser Press, 2005).

10 *United Nations Convention against Illicit Traffic in Narcotic Drugs and Psychotropic Substances*, Can. T.S. 1990 No. 42 [*Vienna Narcotics Convention*].

11 2225 U.N.T.S. 209.

judicare provisions which oblige state parties to extradite offenders to other party states which are willing to prosecute if the custodial state does not wish to prosecute. The extradition provisions in the treaty act as a fallback for situations where any two states which are party to the suppression convention do not have a bilateral extradition treaty, and thus the suppression convention itself becomes the extradition treaty for this purpose.

Historically, extradition was a completely discretionary and political act on the part of the sitting government, but it now generally involves interaction between the executive and the courts of a given state. Canada, as will be seen, has both a judicial phase and a ministerial phase in its extradition process, though the final decision whether to extradite is a predominantly political (but reviewable) one made by the Minister of Justice, a senior cabinet minister in the government. Extradition regimes as they are employed today had taken form in Europe by the eighteenth century,[12] and most of the modern international law template of extradition features (though still in treaty form) was established by the nineteenth century. Extradition law and practice still continues to shape, and be shaped by, the existence of differing criminal law traditions among states, particularly as regards jurisdiction. For example, most civil law–based European states are constitutionally prohibited from extraditing their nationals; some do not even extradite their residents, leaving extradition available only for "fugitives" in the truest sense. This is what spurred on the broad exercise of nationality-based criminal jurisdiction by these states, as a means to avoid providing safe haven to criminals simply because they were nationals of those states. Common law states such as the UK, the US, and Canada, by contrast, have no such prohibition and generally freely extradite their nationals to states where they are alleged to have committed crimes. Accordingly, no broad use of nationality jurisdiction was needed, which informed the tendency of these states to confine criminal jurisdiction territorially.

b) Principles of Extradition Law

As noted, crime suppression was and is the goal that underpins extradition. It is a process that, as McLachlin J. wrote, "is founded on the concepts of reciprocity, comity and respect for differences in other jurisdictions."[13] From the outset, however, a heavy policy component of extradition law and practice was the state's interest in protecting the in-

---

12 See, generally, Christopher Blakesley, "The Practice of Extradition from Antiquity to Modern France and the United States: A Brief History" (1981) 4 B.C. Int'l & Comp. L.J. 39.

13 *Kindler v. Canada (Minister of Justice)*, [1991] 2 S.C.R. 779 at 844 [*Kindler*].

dividual who had come onto its territory, alleged or convicted criminal though she might be. States traditionally guarded jealously their own criminal jurisdictions, and were reluctant to take any action that might be seen as enforcing the criminal law of another state. Coupled with this was the desire not to become involved in the internal affairs of even a treaty partner state, a concern raised particularly during the eighteenth and nineteenth centuries when individuals were often as likely to be fugitives from difficult political situations as from any criminal activity. These concerns were particularly paramount among common law states, which unlike civilian countries extradited their own nationals to face foreign process. States were, and are, quite careful, even finicky, about the details of the extradition obligations they undertook.

Thus, based on extradition treaties and practice thereunder, a set of international extradition law principles developed. These were designed both to facilitate orderly extradition and protect state interests, and to accord certain protections to the individual in the extradition process—in particular, to ensure as much as reasonably possible that the individual receive fair treatment in the requesting state. The latter mechanisms were truly meant to be protective of the interests of states themselves, and protection accorded to fugitives was more of a knock-on effect.[14] The sufficiency of these principles, and of extradition generally, in light of modern human rights standards has become an issue in the last thirty years, and is dealt with in Chapter 10. What follows is a brief description of the principles of extradition law. It is worth noting that individual extradition treaties have a great variety of features, even idiosyncrasies, which require individualized interpretation. The following discussion is pitched at a high level of generality.

i)   *Double Criminality and Extraditable Offences*[15]
Double criminality, a nearly ubiquitous feature of extradition treaties, requires that a person can be extradited only for acts which are criminal under the laws of both the requesting and requested state. The policy underpinning has been effectively described as follows: "The rule ensures that no State is obliged to extradite a person for an act not

---

14 Though they were often not inconsiderable as a means of indirectly protecting human rights; see William Gilmore, "The Provisions Designed to Protect Fundamental Rights in Extradition and Mutual Legal Assistance Treaties" in Commonwealth Secretariat, *International Co-operation in Criminal Matters: Balancing the Protection of Human Rights with the Needs of Law Enforcement* (London: Commonwealth Secretariat, 2001).

15 See Sharon A. Williams, "The Double Criminality Rule and Extradition" (1991) 15 Nova L. Rev. 581.

recognized as criminal by its own standards, and also serves the principle of reciprocity in that a State is not required to extradite categories of offenders which it, in turn, would never have occasion to demand."[16] For reciprocity, see Section B(1)(b)(ii), below in this chapter. So, for example, Canada would not extradite an individual to face criminal prosecution in one of the many states which criminalize homosexual activity, as this is not an offence in Canada. Historically, this was strictly interpreted as requiring fairly exact correspondence between the particular offence in both requesting and requested state, both as to its name and to the elements of the offence. The more modern trend is to simply focus on whether the particular conduct is criminalized under the laws of both states, without requiring exact matching. This loosening is indicative of the extent to which criminal law is being harmonized between states, but maintains states' ability to decline to aid in foreign prosecutions where it would be against domestic public policy to do so.

A related procedural point is the tendency of states to define, in some way, either the exact crimes or the kinds of crimes for which extradition will be carried out. The historical practice was to take a "listing" or "extradition crimes" approach, which required the contracting states to agree on a list of crimes that were extraditable. As criminal laws have become more complex and change with greater frequency, this kind of arrangement is increasingly unworkable, and many states now use the "eliminative" or "no-list" approach, whereby they agree that offences will be extraditable if they meet a certain level of gravity, usually expressed by the minimum available sentence. Most recently, states have begun to use these mechanisms to extend extradition to offences beyond the purely criminal realm, such as environmental or other regulatory offences.

An interesting issue is whether a requirement of double criminality must be held to also require reciprocal grounds of jurisdiction. This can become an issue when the requesting state is exerting extraterritorial jurisdiction over the offence for which extradition is sought, and the requested state, while it criminalizes the same conduct, does not exert jurisdiction on the same basis.[17] This situation would be particularly problematic if the requesting state's jurisdictional claim is not only one the requested state does not use, but is felt to be illegal. For example,

---

16   Torsten Stein, "Extradition" in Rudolf Bernhardt, ed., *Max Planck Encyclopedia of Public International Law*, vol. 2 (New York: Oxford University Press, 1995) 327 at 329.

17   Gráinne Mullan, "The Concept of Double Criminality in the Context of Extra-Territorial Crimes" [1997] Crim. L.R. 17.

in *Romania (State) v. Cheng*,[18] the fugitives were sought by Romania, *inter alia*, for murders allegedly committed on a ship on the high seas. The extradition judge ruled that the double criminality requirement was not met, as the only jurisdictional claim Romania had was the passive personality principle, which was not valid under international law. This issue can even extend to assessments of whether the requested state exercises qualified territorial jurisdiction in the same manner as the requesting state, so as to determine whether the double criminality requirement is satisfied.[19] In practice, extradition treaties tend to afford the parties the entitlement to decline an extradition request on the basis that they do not utilize the particular (usually extraterritorial) jurisdictional ground in question.

ii) Reciprocity

Traditionally, reciprocity has been the basic operating principle of extradition. Stemming from the close guarding of states' own criminal law and jurisdiction, as well as doubts about "foreign" systems, "states were, and even today are, unwilling to concede advantages to other states unless the concessions proceed on the basis of reciprocity . . . [and] mutual obligations[.]"[20] Accordingly, extradition treaties tend to be structured in such a way that there is fairly complete mutuality of obligation for the state parties. More recently, strict reciprocity requirements are often loosened, in light of the desire to substantively respect foreign states' legal systems and maximize the flexibility which is increasingly necessary for transnational crime suppression. This is particularly the case for states which have close relations and/or complementary legal systems, such as Canada and the US. This is exhibited by treaties which do not contain a reciprocity obligation, or expressly allow for cooperation in the face of juridical differences between the states, for example by way of optional grounds for refusal of extradition. As in all areas of public international law, however, reciprocity remains an important guiding concept.

---

18 (1997), 158 N.S.R. (2d) 13 (S.C.), aff'd (1997), 162 N.S.R. (2d) 395 (C.A.).

19 For example, *United States of America v. Kavaratzis* (2006), 208 C.C.C. (3d) 139 (Ont. C.A.). See also *Re Reyat's Application for a Writ of Habeas Corpus* (22 March 1989), CO/1157/88, MWC (Q.B.D.), as cited in Geoff Gilbert, *Responding to International Crime* (Leiden: Martinus Nijhoff, 2006) at 11–15. And see art. 4(f) of the UN Model Treaty, above note 8.

20 Sharon A. Williams & Jean-Gabriel Castel, *Canadian Criminal Law: International and Transnational Aspects* (Toronto: Butterworths, 1981) at 339.

iii) Specialty and Re-extradition

The principle of specialty (or, as it is often rendered, "speciality") is an important one in extradition law and practice, and as in double criminality, it is incorporated into virtually every extradition instrument. Specialty provides that an extradited individual cannot be tried in the requesting state for any offences except those for which he was extradited. While strictly interpreted in the past, such provisions are now often held to allow for prosecution on different offences than those specified in the request, so long as the new offences arise from the same facts and are also extraditable crimes under the treaty. Specialty provisions are often accompanied by provisions preventing the requesting state from re-extraditing the fugitive to a third state, without the consent of the requested state.

Specialty gives the requested state a certain amount of control over the fugitive's ultimate fate, and is particularly useful in allowing requested states to facilitate prosecutions in states from which, due to doubts about the fairness of the legal system, they might otherwise decline requests. Requesting states, in turn, are compelled to be careful around specialty issues, as violation of specialty is a prime ground for souring of extradition relations. The rule thus supports both the reciprocity and double-criminality principles, protects the fugitive from prosecution for crimes of which he had no notice during extradition, and protects the requested state's process from abuse.[21]

There are several situations where specialty will not operate or will cease operating: the requested state may simply give consent for the fugitive to be tried for other crimes before the requesting state's courts, or the fugitive may himself consent; if the fugitive does not leave the requesting state when given a reasonable chance to do so, or voluntarily returns to that state; or if the fugitive, having left, is re-extradited to the requesting state by a third state.

iv) Evidentiary Requirements

Historically, there have been sharp divisions between common law and civil law states surrounding what information — and specifically what evidence — the requesting state must present as part of an extradition request. The usual approach in common law states is to require the requesting state to provide evidence which makes out a *"prima facie case"* of the fugitive's guilt for extradition to be granted. This generally accords with the threshold that would need to be met by the Crown in order to commit an accused for trial in a purely domestic case. By

---

21   Stein, above note 16 at 330.

contrast, civil law states tend to require more of a formalized request, which includes copies of charging documents and relevant laws, information regarding the offender, and some version of the facts of the case. This is generally supplemented by the ability to make specific evidentiary inquiries where necessary.

This divide has caused difficulty in the past, particularly as regards requests by civil law states to common law states. The *prima facie* case standard requires the submission of some amount of actual evidence to support the extradition requests. Owing to substantial differences in the criminal law systems at play, it has been difficult for civilian states to muster a case cognizable by the common law courts; for example, most civil law systems do not provide for taking evidence, especially documentary evidence, under oath, which is a standard feature of any preliminary proceeding in common law states. This kind of difficulty has caused the failure of many extradition requests. The response has been to adapt common law requirements to impose a less onerous standard on the requesting state; Canada, for example, has brought in changes to allow for the requesting state to file a "Record of the Case," rather than lead evidence at the extradition hearing. This sort of development, while facilitating law enforcement goals, has been criticized as undermining the important protective aspects of the *prima facie* case requirement.[22]

v)   Political Offence Exception[23]

The "political offence exception" refers to the entitlement of a requested state to deny extradition of an offender on the ground that the offence for which the fugitive is being sought is a "political offence," or as it is more commonly phrased an "offence of a political nature." The exception is at once one of the most long-standing principles of extradition law, and probably the most controversial. Some provision of this sort is found in virtually every extradition treaty and in many of the extradition provisions found in the suppression conventions. The UN Model Treaty accords it pride of place as the first mandatory ground for refusal of a request[24] based on its historical importance, and its ubiquity makes it a candidate for the status of customary international law. However, the

---

22   Gilbert, above note 19 at 119–27; AnneW. La Forest, "The Balance between Liberty and Comity in the Evidentiary Requirements Applicable to Extradition Proceedings" (2002) 28 Queen's L.J. 95 [La Forest, "Liberty and Comity"].

23   See, generally, Christine van den Wyngaert, *The Political Offence Exception to Extradition: The Delicate Problem of Balancing the Rights of the Individual and International Public Order* (Boston: Kluwer, 1980).

24   Above note 8, art. 3(a).

actual substance of the exception is extremely contentious, and a wide array of approaches by states and national courts can be observed.

The roots of the exception are philosophical, and it emerged in the century or so following the French Revolution.[25]As Lord Mustill described it in an oft-quoted decision, "during the 19th century those who used violence to challenge despotic regimes often occupied high moral ground, and were welcomed in foreign countries as true patriots and democrats."[26] Enabling a legal refusal of extradition on such grounds allowed requested states to shelter (sometimes) deserving fugitives from the wrong side of civil unrest, to protect emerging democratic and revolutionary ideals in so doing, and to remain detached from political affairs in other states. Its first appearance was in an 1833 Belgian statute, and it soon appeared in all European laws, followed by most other states involved in extradition relations.[27] It is even referred to in the *Universal Declaration of Human Rights.*[28]

The very use of the word "political" has resulted in all such provisions being quite deliberately vague, and determination as to when an offence has a sufficiently political character as to justify refusal has usually been left to the courts or the executive of the requested state. Generally speaking, there are three groups of offences which have attracted scrutiny under this principle, each more controversial than the last. First, states tend to be comfortable with refusing to extradite for "purely" political offences, that is, those which are "directed solely against the political order."[29] This covers a limited range of offences, examples of which are treason, sedition, espionage, and sabotage, and all of which are directed solely at the machinery, political organization, or rights of the state.[30] Second is the more complex group of common crimes (murder, assault, and so on) which are adjudged to have a "predominantly" or disproportionately political character. These might be offences which are incidental to a purely political offence, or which are deemed to attack political interests by way of also attacking private rights. Important, though not determinative, to characterizing these offences as "political" is whether the offender had a political motive in

---

25   Robert Jennings & Arthur Watts, eds., *Oppenheim's International Law*, 9th ed., vol. 1 (Harlow, UK: Longman, 1992) at 962.

26   *T. v. Immigration Officer*, [1996] A.C. 742 at 753 (H.L.).

27   M. Cherif Bassiouni, *International Extradition: United States Law and Practice*, 4th ed. (Dobbs Ferry, NY: Oceana Publications, 2002) at 595.

28   UNGA Res. 217/3 (1948), art. 14(2).

29   Shearer, above note 5 at 181.

30   *Re Giovanni Gatti*, [1947] Ann. Dig. 145 (Fr.).

committing the crime,[31] and the motivation of the requested state in attempting to prosecute.[32]

The third and most contentious group of offences is terrorist crimes. The most contentious aspect, in fact, may be attempting to distinguish terrorist crimes from the former category of "predominantly political crimes," a task made no easier by the lack of an internationally accepted definition of terrorism.[33] It is difficult to reconcile the notion that the commission of certain crimes, particularly crimes of violence, should exempt the perpetrator from extradition simply because he was engaged in some kind of *bona fide* political conflict with a government, with the international community's condemnation of "terrorism"—if that concept can be held to include (at a minimum) an attempt to intimidate a government and a civilian population, for some kind of political goal which is not *bona fide*. The assessment of the political *bona fides* is an extremely difficult one to make. In the post-9/11 era, there has been a definite swing in the international community towards renouncing some crimes as ever being justified on a political basis. This has manifested itself in the practice, which had already been established,[34] of excluding the application of the political offence exception to particular crimes that attract consensus on their status as "terrorism." For example, article 11 of the *Terrorist Bombing Convention* provides,

> None of the offences set forth in article 2 shall be regarded, for the purposes of extradition or mutual legal assistance, as a political offence or as an offence connected with a political offence or as an offence inspired by political motives.[35]

In the end, it may be twenty-first century antipathy to terrorism that puts an end to most of the notion of "political offence" in the extradition context. For, as Lord Mustill observed in *T. v. Immigration Officer* just after the passage quoted above,

> Now, much has changed. The authors of violence are more ruthless, their methods more destructive and undiscriminating; their targets are no longer minister and heads of state but the populace at large.

31   Gilbert, above note 19 at 214–16.
32   *R. v. Governor of Pentonville ex parte Cheng*, [1973] A.C. 931.
33   See Chapter 6, Section E.
34   For example, art. VII of the 1948 *Genocide Convention*, 78 U.N.T.S. 277 provides, "Genocide and the other acts enumerated in art. III shall not be considered as political crimes for the purpose of extradition. The Contracting Parties pledge themselves in such cases to grant extradition in accordance with their laws and treaties in force."
35   *UN Terrorist Bombings Convention* (1998), 37 I.L.M. 249, Can. T.S. 2002 No. 8.

What I regard as the exceptional difficulty of this appeal is that the courts here, as in other legal systems, must struggle to apply a concept which is out of date.[36]

vi) Discrimination

A less blunt and more palatable subset of the political offence exception emerged in the 1957 *European Convention on Extradition*, which provided that extradition could be refused where the requested state reasonably believes that a request has been made "for the purpose of prosecuting or punishing a person on account of his race, religion, nationality or political opinion, or that that person's position may be prejudiced for any of those reasons."[37] This is now a common provision in many extradition treaties, particularly multilateral ones, and obviously has human rights implications—regarding which see Chapter 10. To the extent that consideration of discrimination is permitted to be considered by judges under domestic extradition law,[38] this principle interacts uneasily with the "rule of non-inquiry," examined in Section B(1)(b)(vii), below.

vii) The "Rule of Non-inquiry"

The so-called rule of non-inquiry is a judge-made interpretive tool, which holds that courts in extradition matters should not inquire into any aspects of the requesting state's pursuit of the fugitive, whether that be the motivation for the request, the procedural rights afforded to accused persons, conditions of incarceration, or the conduct of the trial itself. Such matters are best left to the executive, the argument goes, because they involve sensitive issues of comity and reciprocity and because the executive must be presumed to have assured itself that the criminal justice system of the requesting state is satisfactory, in order to open extradition relations. As La Forest J. wrote, any suggestion of deficiency on the part of the requesting state's law or procedure "amounts to a serious adverse reflection . . . on foreign governments to whom Canada has a treaty obligation."[39]

---

36 Above note 26.
37 E.T.S. No. 24 (1957), art. 3(2). See also UN Model Treaty, above note 8, art. 3(b) which sets this ground of refusal out as mandatory and has virtually the same wording.
38 Though, as will be seen below, consideration of this factor would be a ministerial function in Canada.
39 *Argentina (Republic) v. Mellino*, [1987] 1 S.C.R. 536 at 555.

Non-inquiry appears to be a common law doctrine, and the extent to which courts apply it varies from state to state. In the post-*Charter*[40] era, the Supreme Court of Canada has maintained an approach of giving significant weight to the rationale behind the "rule" (though typically without referring to it as such). Indeed, in terms of ensuring the law enforcement flexibility necessary for combating transnational crime, which in turn requires accommodation of foreign legal systems, this rationale still has a place. As La Forest J. wrote in *Canada v. Schmidt*,

> The judicial process in a foreign country must not be subjected to finicky evaluations against the rules governing the legal process in this country. A judicial process is not, for example, fundamentally unjust—indeed it may in its practical workings be as just as ours—because it functions on the basis of an investigatory system without a presumption of innocence or, generally, because its procedural or evidentiary safeguards have none of the rigours of our system.[41]

However, the Court has also consistently spoken to the need for *Charter* rights to be protected within the extradition context, which necessitates some inquiry into "the manner in which the foreign state will deal with the fugitive on surrender, whether that course of conduct is justifiable or not under the law of that country."[42] The approach is one of circumspection, and there is a presumption of respect for the requesting state's system, but the Court has been willing to abrogate the non-inquiry approach to the extent that only its spirit infuses the process. That this stance has developed with regard to the protection of human rights is concomitant with developments internationally, which have seen the undermining of non-inquiry in the interest of human rights protection.[43] This is discussed in more detail in Chapter 10.

viii) Military/Fiscal Offences

A common feature of older extradition treaties is a clause entitling the requested state to refuse to extradite fugitives for offences under military or fiscal laws, or even explicitly excluding such crimes from the

---

40 *Canadian Charter of Rights and Freedoms*, Part I of the *Constitution Act, 1982*, being Schedule B to the *Canada Act 1982* (U.K.), 1982, c. 11.

41 *Canada v. Schmidt*, [1987] 1 S.C.R. 500 at 522–23.

42 *Suresh v. Canada (Minister of Citizenship and Immigration)*, [2002] 1 S.C.R. 3 at para. 56, quoting *Schmidt, ibid.* at 522.

43 See Ivan A. Shearer, "Extradition and Human Rights" (1994) 68 Austl. L.J. 451; Richard J. Wilson, "Toward the Enforcement of Universal Human Rights through Abrogation of the Rule of Non-Inquiry in Extradition" (1997) 3 International Law Students Association J. Int'l. & Comp. L. 751.

treaty altogether. The latter arose from states' distaste for enforcing the fiscal, and primarily taxation, laws of other states because these were too locally flavoured or idiosyncratic. It is mostly of historical interest now, as the increasing weight given to the danger of financial crimes to domestic economies has led to corresponding willingness to extradite for such offences, particularly as extradition has moved out of the traditional "criminal" realm into serious offences which are not strictly criminal but regulatory in nature. As to military offences, to the extent that such a limitation still exists, it tends to be in similar form to the way in which it is phrased in the UN Model Treaty, where a request can be refused "[i]f the offence for which extradition is requested is an offence under military law, which is not also an offence under ordinary criminal law."[44] This kind of refusal is typically justified on the basis that breaches of a state's military code are generally not important enough to merit the energy and expense required for international cooperation, as well as the protection of those who oppose mandatory military service as a matter of conscience.[45]

ix) Double Jeopardy/Ne Bis in Idem

Article 3 of the UN Model Treaty[46] provides—as a mandatory ground of refusal—that extradition shall not be granted "[i]f there has been a final judgment rendered against the person in the requested State in respect of the offence for which the person's extradition is requested." This sort of provision, which is very common to both bilateral and multilateral extradition treaties, embodies the idea of "double jeopardy" or the customary international law principle ne bis in idem: an individual should not be tried twice for the same crime. While there is no consensus that this is a rule of customary international law that binds all states in extradition matters,[47] in practice it is very common.[48] It is more typical, however, for the provision to allow refusal where the previous prosecution was in the requested state, than it is to include situations where it is alleged the fugitive has already been tried in the

---

44 Above note 8, art. 3(c).
45 Gilbert, above note 19 at 185–86.
46 Above note 8.
47 See Antonio Cassese, *International Criminal Law* (Oxford: Oxford University Press, 2003) at 319.
48 For example, it has been a feature of European extradition arrangements since the 1950s and is mandatory under the new European Arrest Warrant; see Harmon van der Wilt, "The European Arrest Warrant and the Principle *ne bis in idem*" in Rob Blekxtoon, ed., *Handbook on the European Arrest Warrant* (The Hague: T.M.C. Asser Press, 2005).

requesting state.[49] It is even less likely to include situations where the accused has been tried and/or convicted by a third state.[50] States will also sometimes incorporate an entitlement to refuse extradition if the fugitive has already been convicted *in absentia* by the requesting state, though extradition will usually be granted if the requesting state agrees to give the fugitive a new trial.

2) Canadian Law

Canada's involvement in international extradition predates Confederation, stemming back to early UK–US treaties such as the *Jay Treaty* of 1794 and the *Webster-Ashburton Treaty* of 1842.[51] The UK was responsible for Canada's extradition arrangements under such imperial treaties until WW II, after which time Canada concluded its own treaties. Canada is currently party to 50 bilateral and 25 multilateral extradition treaties.[52] The first solely Canadian legislation which implemented extradition treaties was the 1877 *Extradition Act*,[53] modelled on earlier British legislation.[54] Even after some 1992 amendments, the 1877 legislation basically continued as the legislative framework in Canada until the passing of the "new" *Extradition Act* in 1999.[55]

The 1999 legislation was enacted in reaction to a perception on the part of the government that Canada's treaty partners found Canadian extradition procedure to be slow, cumbersome, and sometimes impossible to access, particularly where the requesting state did not have a common law system.[56] Accordingly, the legislation was specifically designed

---

49   G. Conway, "*Ne Bis in Idem* in International Law" (2003) 3 Int'l Crim. L. Rev. 217 at 233. See also Christine van den Wyngaert & Guy Stessens, "The International *Non Bis in Idem* Principle: Resolving Some of the Unanswered Questions" (1999) 48 I.C.L.Q. 779.

50   Alexander Poels, "A Need for Transnational *Non Bis in Idem* Protection in International Human Rights Law" (2005) 23 Nethl. Q.H.R. 329 at 334–35.

51   For historical accounts, see Gary Botting, *Extradition between Canada and the United States* (Ardsley, NY: Transnational, 2005) cc. 2–4, and Anne W. La Forest, *La Forest's Extradition to and from Canada*, 3d ed. (Aurora, ON: Canada Law Book, 1991).

52   For full text of the bilateral treaties and relevant excerpts from the multilateral treaties, see Gary Botting, *Canadian Extradition Practice 2009* (Toronto: Butterworths LexisNexis, 2008).

53   S.C. 1877, c. 25.

54   See reasons of La Forest J. in *McVey*, above note 7 at 7.

55   S.C. 1999, c. 18.

56   See, in particular, remarks by Eleni Bakopanos, Parliamentary Secretary to the Minister of Justice and Attorney General of Canada, while introducing Bill C-40, which eventually became the new Act (House of Commons Debates, No. 135 (8 October 1998) at 1605).

to "modernize and streamline Canada's extradition procedure, thereby enabling Canada to more effectively meet its international extradition obligations."[57] The Act is now the means by which all of Canada's international law extradition obligations (both as requesting and requested state) are implemented, replacing a previously separate arrangement by which fugitives were surrendered to other Commonwealth states[58] and adding provisions allowing extradition and surrender to the International Criminal Tribunal for the former Yugoslavia (ICTY), the International Criminal Tribunal for Rwanda (ICTR), and the International Criminal Court (ICC). The new regime maintains the traditional bifurcation of roles between the judiciary, which conducts the court proceeding (the "extradition hearing") that determines whether a factual and legal basis for the extradition request exists, and the Minister of Justice, who makes the ultimately political decision whether the fugitive should be surrendered to the requesting state. However, the procedures of the extradition hearing have been amended to allow for a more flexible approach to requests, particularly as to evidentiary matters, and the role and discretion of the Minister have been expanded. The new scheme has been criticized as unduly restricting the ability of the extradition judge to properly adjudicate upon the cogency and sufficiency of the requesting state's case against the fugitive,[59] and for creating insufficiently controlled Ministerial discretion in the surrender process.[60]

The Act is divided into four parts: Interpretation (Part 1), Extradition from Canada (Part 2), Extradition to Canada (Part 3), and Transitional Provisions (Part 4). Parts 2 and 3 contain the main provisions of the domestic extradition processes and will be discussed here. Essentially, as summarized by Watt J. (as he then was) in *Germany v. Schreiber*,

> The extradition process includes two discrete phases:
> * the judicial phase
> * the ministerial or executive phase
>
> The judicial phase includes court proceedings whose objective it is to decide whether a factual and legal basis for extradition exists. In the end, and only if the judicial phase results in an order of committal, it will be for the Minister to say whether the fugitive will be surrendered.[61]

---

57 Elaine Krivel, Thomas Beveridge, & John Hayward, *A Practical Guide to Canadian Extradition* (Toronto: Carswell, 2002) at 10.
58 The *Fugitive Offenders Act*, R.S.C. 1985, c. F-32 (repealed).
59 La Forest, "Liberty and Comity," above note 22.
60 Gary Botting, "The Supreme Court 'Decodes' the *Extradition Act*: Reading Down the Law in *Ferras* and *Ortega*" (2007) 32 Queen's L.J. 446.
61 [2004] O.J. No. 2310 at para. 7 (S.C.J.).

a) Part 2 of the *Extradition Act*: Canada As Requested State

i) *Authority to Proceed*

The term "extradition agreement" is defined in section 2 of the *Extradition Act* as "an agreement that is in force, to which Canada is a party and that contains a provision respecting the extradition of persons." Accordingly, the Act allows Canada to respond to requests under any of the bilateral or multilateral treaties to which it is party. However, an agreement need not be in place, as section 9 allows the Minister of Justice to designate states or entities as "extradition partners" and cooperate with them as well. The Schedule to the Act designates all Commonwealth states as extradition partners, as well as the ICC, the ICTY, the ICTR, Japan, and Costa Rica. Section 10 provides that Canada can also enter into *ad hoc* extradition agreements with states or entities for the purposes of a particular case.

Section 3 of the Act provides for the "eliminative" or "no-list" approach to double criminality referred to in Section B(1)(b)(i), above in this chapter, stating that "extraditable offences" are generally those for which there is a minimum sentence of two years imprisonment in both the requesting state and Canada (five years in Canada in the case of an *ad hoc* agreement), though this is made subject to any extradition agreement. An example of the latter is the *Canada–US Extradition Treaty*,[62] article 2 of which provides for extradition for offences for which the minimum sentence exceeds one year.

Requests for extradition (or for provisional arrest pending an extradition request) are received by the office of the Minister of Justice,[63] but are practically fielded by specialized staff in the International Assistance Group (IAG) of Justice Canada. These persons are charged with making the Minister's initial determination, which is whether the section 3 criteria regarding extraditable offences are met in the request and whether the offence for which the fugitive is sought is an extraditable one. The corresponding Canadian offence is identified and inserted into an "Authority to Proceed,"[64] which authorizes the Attorney General of Canada (again, represented by staff lawyers) to seek an order of the court[65] committing the fugitive for extradition. The "committal hearing," described in Section B(2)(a)(ii), below in this chapter, is preceded

---

62   *Treaty on Extradition between the Government of Canada and the Government of the United States of America*, Can. T.S. 1976 No. 3, as amended by *Protocol 1*, Can. T.S. 1991 No. 37 and *Protocol 2*, Can. T.S. 2003 No. 11.

63   *Extradition Act*, above note 55, s. 11.

64   *Ibid.*, s. 15.

65   Specifically, a superior court justice (*ibid.*, s. 2).

by necessary procedures, such as the issuing of a summons or arrest warrant for the fugitive,[66] the appearance of the fugitive before a judge for identification, and the adjudication of any interim release application[67] or of the transfer of the person to another place in Canada.[68]

ii) The Judicial Phase

The next phase of the extradition process is also initiated by the Attorney General but presided over by a superior court justice, usually called the "extradition judge." Under section 24 of the Act, when the Crown presents the Authority to Proceed to the extradition judge, she must convene an "extradition hearing," or (as it is more often called) a "committal hearing." The goal of the committal hearing is to allow the extradition judge to determine whether the case put forward by the requesting state is such that it is justifiable to extradite the person to face trial in the foreign state. Traditionally, Canada has adhered to the common law approach which requires a *prima facie* case in order to commit the fugitive; as set out in the foundational case of *United States of America v. Shepherd*,[69] there must be evidence pertinent to each element of the offence such that a reasonable jury, properly instructed, could render a guilty verdict. This is also the test for whether a case should go forward against an accused under Canadian law, and indeed the so-called "*Shepherd* test" has been used for that purpose as well. Section 24(2) of the Act provides that an extradition judge has the same powers as a judge acting under part XVIII of the *Criminal Code*[70] dealing with preliminary inquiries, "with any modification that the circumstances require." However, the Supreme Court of Canada has stated that the role of the extradition judge is not to be equated with that of a judge presiding over a preliminary inquiry, given the differences in purpose and the manner in which the powers are to be exercised.[71]

The most pertinent provisions for the committal hearing are those dealing with the determination to be made by the extradition judge and the rules of evidence that govern the hearing. Section 29(1) of the Act provides,

> **29.** (1) A judge shall order the committal of the person into custody to await surrender if

---

66   *Ibid.*, s. 16.
67   *Ibid.*, ss. 16–21.
68   *Ibid.*, s. 22.
69   [1977] 2 S.C.R. 1067.
70   R.S.C. 1985, c. C-46.
71   *United States of America v. Ferras; United States of America v. Latty*, [2006] 2 S.C.R. 77 at para. 48 [*Ferras*].

(a) in the case of a person sought for prosecution, there is evidence admissible under this Act of conduct that, had it occurred in Canada, would justify committal for trial in Canada on the offence set out in the authority to proceed and the judge is satisfied that the person is the person sought by the extradition partner; and

(b) in the case of a person sought for the imposition or enforcement of a sentence, the judge is satisfied that the conviction was in respect of conduct that corresponds to the offence set out in the authority to proceed and that the person is the person who was convicted.

As the Supreme Court stated in *Ferras*, "this requires the judge to determine two matters: (1) what evidence is admissible under the Act; (2) whether the admissible evidence is sufficient to justify committal."[72] Simply put, the judge will consider the evidence provided by the requesting state and decide whether such a body of evidence would be sufficient to allow the fugitive to be tried before Canada's courts for the corresponding Canadian offences. If so, then the fugitive will be ordered committed for extradition. If not, then the fugitive is ordered discharged.

As to admissibility of the evidence, section 32 of the Act provides that any evidence that satisfies the Canadian rules of evidence is admissible at the hearing. Two exceptions are provided, whereby documentary evidence that would not otherwise be admissible under Canadian law may be admitted if (1) it is presented in the form of a "record of the case"[73] or (2) it is "submitted in conformity with the terms of an extradition agreement."[74] These provisions are important because the requesting state's evidence is often presented in the form of out-of-court statements rather than by actual testimony, particularly as regards witnesses who would be giving direct evidence at trial, and much of it would otherwise offend the hearsay rule. However, any evidence that was gathered in Canada must be admissible under Canadian evidence law, possibly even if it forms part of the requested state's case under sections 32(1)(a) or (b).[75] The fugitive is entitled to lead relevant evidence if the judge considers it reliable.[76]

---

72 *Ferras, ibid.* at para. 36.

73 Above note 55, s. 32(1)(a).

74 *Ibid.*, s. 32(1)(b).

75 *Ibid.*, s. 32(2). The term "possibly" is used here because, at the time of writing, there was significant divergence on this point as between the Ontario and British Columbia Courts of Appeal; see *United States of America v. McDowell* (2004), 183 C.C.C. (3d) 149 (Ont. C.A.), leave to appeal to S.C.C. refused, [2004] S.C.C.A. No. 325, and *United States of America v. Anekwu*, 2008 BCCA 138, leave to appeal to S.C.C. granted, [2008] S.C.C.A. No. 246.

76 *Extradition Act, ibid.*, s. 32(1)(c).

The "record of the case" is an innovation under the new Act, which was geared nominally towards accommodating treaty partners with differing legal, and in particular differing evidentiary, traditions.[77] It is governed by section 33 of the Act, which allows the requesting state to submit a summary of the evidence that is available for the requesting state's prosecution of the fugitive,[78] so long as a judicial or prosecuting authority of the requesting state certifies that the evidence is indeed available for trial, and either is sufficient under that state's law to justify prosecution or was gathered in accordance with that state's law.[79] This is a remarkable tool and a significant departure from traditional Canadian extradition law, as under the record of the case approach, the documents need not be authenticated nor bear any indication of oath or affirmation.[80]

It is important to note that the Supreme Court of Canada has consistently ruled that the *Charter*,[81] specifically section 7's protection against deprivation of liberty not in accordance with the principles of fundamental justice, infuses the entire domestic extradition process.[82] In *Ferras*, the first major constitutional challenge to the new Act, the Supreme Court underscored this point as regards the committal hearing, noting that a "meaningful judicial process" in extradition "involves three related requirements: a separate and independent judicial phase; an impartial judge or magistrate; and a fair and meaningful hearing."[83] Most importantly, the Supreme Court cleared up some significant division in lower court extradition jurisprudence and ruled that sections 29 and 32 of the Act must be read as permitting the extradition judge to refuse committal where the evidence is not shown to be available for trial or is shown to be unreliable. Reading in this discretionary power, the Court held, brought this part of the Act into *Charter* compliance. The fugitive is permitted to challenge the evidence on the basis of availability or reliability,[84] by adducing evidence or making argument,

---

77   Though Botting points out that the US moved to avail itself of this approach fairly quickly, even though it was fully capable of providing the evidence in a recognizable common law format; Botting, *Extradition between Canada and the United States*, above note 51 at 271.

78   Above note 55, s. 33(1)(a).

79   *Ibid.*, s. 33(3)(a).

80   *Ibid.*, ss. 33(4), (5), and 34.

81   Above note 40.

82   *Cotroni*, above note 1 at 1500; *Schmidt*, above note 41 at 515.

83   *Ferras*, above note 71 at para. 22.

84   The Ontario Court of Appeal has recently held that, in order to be excluded, the requesting state's evidence must be shown to be "manifestly unreliable" (*United States of America v. Thomlinson*, [2007] O.J. No. 246 at para. 45 (C.A.), Moldaver

regardless of whether the requesting state's evidence is brought under the "record of the case" approach or in conformity with the applicable treaty. This requires the extradition judge to engage in "limited weighing" of the evidence to determine whether a reasonable jury, properly instructed, could convict on the evidence.[85] Under the "record of the case" approach (section 32(1)(a)), the evidence is presumed to be reliable, and the fugitive has the onus of rebutting this presumption. Under the "conformity with treaty" approach (section 32(1)(b)), the requesting state bears the onus of establishing *prima facie* that the evidence exists and is available for trial at the time of the extradition hearing.[86] The fugitive may then adduce reliable evidence to rebut these facts. The fugitive may also seek to have the requested state's evidence excluded under section 24(2) of the *Charter* if the evidence was gathered in such an abusive manner that allowing it to be adduced would make the committal hearing unfair pursuant to section 7 of the *Charter*.[87]

The extradition judge also has, under section 25 of the Act, a *Charter*-based jurisdiction to police the conduct of the requesting state in the making of the request, so as to ensure the fairness of the hearing. The leading authorities are *United States of America v. Cobb*[88] and two companion cases,[89] released by the Supreme Court of Canada in 2001. In those cases, the Court declined to order the committal of the fugitives because the requesting state had abused the process of Canadian courts by making threats of reprisal against the fugitives if they contested extradition back to the US. The Court held that this remedy was available in any event as a function of the court's abuse of process powers, but explicitly imposed it as a *Charter* remedy under section 7 since it would be inconsistent with the principles of fundamental justice to extradite an individual where the requesting state had abused the process of the court. The fugitives were entitled to lead evidence that related to allegations of the requesting state's questionable conduct, since this was evidence that "bore upon the judicial phase of the extradition process in its entirety . . . ."[90]

J.A.). Regarding disclosure of evidence by the requesting state, see *Germany v. Schreiber*, [2000] O.J. No. 2618 at paras. 79–84 (S.C.J.), aff'd [2006] O.J. No. 789 (C.A.).

85   *Ferras*, above note 71 at para. 54.
86   *Ibid.* at paras. 57–58.
87   *United States of America v. Shulman*, [2001] 1 S.C.R. 616 at para. 56 [*Shulman*].
88   [2001] 1 S.C.R. 587.
89   *Shulman*, above note 87 and *United States of America v. Tsioubris*, [2001] 1 S.C.R. 613. See also *United States of America v. Kwok*, [2001] 1 S.C.R. 532.
90   *Shulman*, *ibid.* at para. 60.

iii) The Ministerial Phase

Once a fugitive has been committed for extradition by the extradition judge, the Minister of Justice must make the final decision as to whether the fugitive will be surrendered to the requesting state. In the recent case of *Lake v. Canada (Minister of Justice)*,[91] LeBel J. summarized and commented on this part of the process:

> After an individual has been committed for extradition, the Minister reviews the case to determine whether the individual should be surrendered to the requesting state. This stage of the process has been characterized as falling "at the extreme legislative end of the *continuum* of administrative decision-making" and is viewed as being largely political in nature: *Idziak v. Canada (Minister of Justice)*, [1992] 3 S.C.R. 631, at p. 659 (emphasis in original). Nevertheless, the Minister's discretion is not absolute. It must be exercised in accordance with the restrictions set out in the *Extradition Act*, as well as with the *Charter*.[92]

Under section 40 the Act, the Minister must make the surrender decision within 90 days of the issuance of the order of committal, and may seek any assurances from the requesting state that he deems appropriate or impose appropriate conditions on the surrender order;[93] the surrender order need not be given until the Minister is assured that the assurances have been given or the conditions agreed to by the requesting state.[94] The committed fugitive is entitled to make submissions to the Minister respecting the surrender decision,[95] and "the Minister must consider them before making his decision."[96] If he decides to surrender the fugitive, the Minister must both give reasons for his decision and respond to the fugitive's submissions.[97] The fugitive may also apply for judicial review of a surrender order to the Court of Appeal of the province in which committal was ordered.[98] This is a form of administrative law review, and the Court of Appeal must evaluate the Minister's decision on a standard of reasonableness.[99]

Sections 44–47 of the Act contain grounds on which the Minister either may or must refuse to order surrender of the fugitive, many of

---

91   2008 SCC 23 [*Lake*].
92   *Ibid.* at para. 22.
93   Above note 55, s. 40(3).
94   *Ibid.*, s. 40(4).
95   *Ibid.*, s. 43(1).
96   *Lake*, above note 91 at para. 25.
97   *Lake, ibid.*
98   Above note 55, s. 57.
99   *Lake*, above note 91 at para. 26.

which are consonant with the principles of extradition law identified above. Indeed, there are a number of parallels between the grounds for refusal and the obligations/entitlements contained within Canada's existing extradition treaties, and accordingly, "the weight of domestic law is brought to bear on matters that were previously left to be determined on a treaty-by-treaty basis."[100] There is a distinction drawn between the grounds of refusal set out in section 44 and those in sections 46–47, in that the latter may be displaced if they conflict with the language (or lack thereof) of an existing extradition treaty.[101]

Subject to the latter qualification, the Minister *must* refuse to order surrender where

- surrender would be "unjust or oppressive having regard to all the relevant circumstances" (section 44(1)(a));
- the extradition request is made for a discriminatory purpose or such a purpose would somehow "prejudice" the person's position (section 44(1)(b));
- the prosecution is statute-barred under the requesting state's law (section 46(1)(a));
- the offence for which extradition is requested is a military offence that is not also an offence under criminal law (section 46(1)(b)); and
- the offence for which extradition is requested is a political offence or an offence of a political character (section 46(1)(c)).[102]

The Minister *may* refuse to order surrender where

- the offence for which extradition is requested is subject to the death penalty in the requesting state (section 44(2));[103]
- "the person would be entitled, if that person were tried in Canada, to be discharged under the laws of Canada because of a previous acquittal or conviction" (essentially a double jeopardy protection) (section 47(a));

---

100 Krivel *et al.*, above note 57 at 340.

101 Above note 55, s. 45. Note that in s. 45(2), with regard to multilateral extradition treaties, the treaty prevails "only to the extent of any inconsistency" between the treaty and the Act. This qualification is not attached to bilateral treaties.

102 This ground is qualified, in s. 46(2), to exclude as grounds for exclusion any offence for which Canada has an obligation under a multilateral extradition treaty to extradite or prosecute, or serious offences such as murder, sexual assault, kidnapping, and extortion.

103 Though the SCC ruled in *United States of America v. Burns* (below note 107) that the Minister must refuse to surrender a fugitive to face the death penalty in all but the most exceptional cases.

- the fugitive was convicted *in absentia* in the requesting state and could not, on surrender, have the case reviewed (section 47(b));
- "the person was less than eighteen years old at the time of the offence and the law that applies to them in the territory over which the extradition partner has jurisdiction is not consistent with the fundamental principles governing the *Youth Criminal Justice Act*" (section 47(c));
- the conduct underpinning the offence for which extradition is requested is the subject of criminal proceedings against the fugitive in Canada (section 47(d));[104] and
- "none of the conduct on which the extradition partner bases its request occurred in the territory over which the extradition partner has jurisdiction," that is, the requesting state is exerting extraterritorial jurisdiction that Canada does not recognize or does not wish to recognize with regard to a particular extradition request (section 47(e)).

As LeBel J. noted in *Lake*, the *Charter* applies to the Ministerial phase of extradition and must be complied with by the Minister. However, assessment of the Minister's decision on *Charter* issues is assessed by the courts on the reduced standard of "reasonableness" rather than "correctness," largely because of the need for fact-finding by the Minister and because his expertise in Canada's international obligations is a foundational aspect of the process and deserves deference by the courts. Nonetheless, there is a necessary interaction between the protection of the fugitive's section 7 *Charter* rights and the grounds for refusal; "Where surrender would be contrary to the principles of fundamental justice, it will also be unjust and oppressive . . . . Where extradition is sought for the purpose of persecuting an individual on the basis of a prohibited ground, ordering surrender would be contrary to the principles of fundamental justice[.]"[105]

The general test for whether surrender will violate the fugitive's section 7 rights is whether surrender would, in the circumstances, "shock the conscience" of the Canadian public.[106] The Supreme Court's most recent exposition of this test occurred in *United States of America v. Burns*,[107] where it ruled that extraditing fugitives to face the death penalty in a foreign state would shock the conscience in all but the most "exceptional cases," the nature of which it refused to define. In *Lake*, the

---

104 This is, in part, a means of implementing Canada's obligation of *aut dedere aut judicare* under many of the multilateral suppression conventions, where Canada is entitled to refuse extradition only if a Canadian investigation or prosecution is under way. See Chapter 7.

105 *Lake*, above note 91 at para. 24 (citations omitted).

106 *Kindler*, above note 13.

107 [2001] 1 S.C.R. 283.

court reaffirmed that the "shocks the conscience" test applies to every surrender order, noting that "[i]n making this assessment, the relevant factors may be specific to the fugitive, such as age or mental condition, or general, such as considerations associated with a particular form of punishment."[108] Fuller explanation of the "shocks the conscience" test and its constitutional implications is provided in Chapter 10.

One distinct *Charter* issue pertaining to surrender relates to section 47(d) of the Act, specifically, whether extradition of a Canadian citizen would violate his right to remain in Canada under section 6 of the *Charter*. This is referred to as the "*Cotroni* issue," pursuant to the 1989 decision of the Supreme Court of Canada in *United States of America v. Cotroni*.[109] In this case, La Forest J. decided, for the Court, that as a matter of common law application of the *Charter*, extradition infringed section 6 of the *Charter*. Given the importance of extradition to the operation of a free and democratic society, the violation can be saved by section 1 — if the prosecutorial authorities "in good faith direct their minds to whether prosecution would be equally effective in Canada, given the existing domestic laws and international co-operative arrangements."[110] The authorities would normally consult with the appropriate authorities in the requesting state and render a decision based on relevant factors, which include,

- in which jurisdiction was the impact of the offence felt or likely to have been felt;
- which jurisdiction has the greater interest in prosecuting the offence;
- which police force played the major role in the development of the case;
- which jurisdiction has laid charges;
- which jurisdiction has the most comprehensive case;
- which jurisdiction is ready to proceed to trial;
- where is the evidence located;
- whether the evidence is mobile;
- the number of accused involved and whether they can be gathered together in one place for trial;
- in which jurisdiction were most of the acts in furtherance of the crime committed;
- the nationality and residence of the accused; and

---

108 Above note 91 at para. 32.
109 Above note 1.
110 *Ibid.* at 1498.

- the severity of the sentence the accused is likely to receive in each jurisdiction.[111]

This analysis is now conducted pursuant to section 47(d) of the Act. The Supreme Court indicated in *Lake* that the *Cotroni* analysis is an exercise of prosecutorial discretion and attracts the powerful degree of deference usually accorded the authorities by the courts to such matters.[112] While the *Cotroni* assessment is usually done by prosecutors, the Minister bears ultimate responsibility for the constitutionality (or not) of its result, that is, whether the fugitive is to be extradited to the requesting state or is to face prosecution in Canada. That said, a survey of the caselaw indicates that fugitives win *Cotroni* challenges very infrequently, at best.

b) Part 3 of the *Extradition Act*: Canada As Requesting State

The section of the Act dealing with extradition requests by Canada to foreign states is relatively brief. Section 78 empowers the Minister of Justice to make a request to a foreign state or "entity" (such as a war crimes tribunal) for the surrender of a fugitive to either face trial or serve a sentence in Canada, so long as Canada has jurisdiction over the relevant offence. Formally, this request is conveyed by diplomatic means, though it will often be to a "Central Authority" designated for this purpose under the extradition treaty. The Minister may also request that the fugitive be provisionally arrested by the requested state or entity.[113] The assembly of any evidence required for the making of the request is accomplished by the relevant authority (such as a provincial Attorney General) making application to a superior court justice for the gathering and/or certification of the evidence. If the requested state agrees to extradite the fugitive, the Minister must authorize an agent of the requested state to bring the fugitive into Canada.[114]

Section 80 legislatively confers the right of specialty[115] upon any person extradited to Canada, subject to the terms of the relevant extra-

---

111 *Ibid.* at 1498–99. See also *United States of America v. Reumayr*, 2003 BCCA 375. A similar mechanism is built into art. 17 *bis* of the *Canada–US Extradition Treaty*, above note 62. However, the treaty does not require that a prosecution have been initiated in the requested state for the consultative process to begin, unlike s. 47(d). See Krivel *et al.*, above note 57 at 372.

112 *Lake*, above note 91 at para. 30.

113 Above note 55, s. 78(2).

114 *Ibid.*, s. 81.

115 See Section B(1)(b)(iii), above in this chapter.

dition treaty.[116] This right is lost if the person has voluntarily left Canada after surrender or does not leave Canada after being afforded the opportunity to do so, or unless the fugitive or the requested state consents to prosecution for another offence.[117] Old case authority under the former Act suggests that where a person waives the protection of the extradition proceedings in the requested state, she loses the protection of specialty as well.[118]

C. "ALTERNATIVES" TO EXTRADITION: ABDUCTION AND EXTRAORDINARY RENDITION

Extradition has always been a response to the fact that the exercise of enforcement jurisdiction by states is territorially limited. To put it more simply, states need extradition arrangements because police from state A cannot enter into state B and arrest the fugitive — this power can only be exercised by state B's police. It is within the power of states A and B to enter into a treaty whereby police from each may arrest fugitives on the other's territory, but in practice states prefer to control policing on their territories and there are not many such agreements.[119]

States sometimes resort to what are politely called "alternatives" to extradition[120] in order to obtain custody over offenders. There are many reasons for this: lack of an extradition treaty with the state where the fugitive is; lack of faith in the extradition procedures of the latter state; frustration with the often slow pace of extradition proceedings; or simply, pressing need to get custody over a particular offender. Historically, it has not been uncommon for states to resort to abducting fugitives from other states, the most prominent example of which is probably still the abduction of Nazi leader Adolf Eichmann from his home in Argentina by Israeli agents. In Israel, Eichmann was tried, convicted, and hanged for his crimes.[121] However, the fact of his abduction sparked

---

116   Regarding challenging a failure to comply with specialty, see *R. v. MacIntosh*, 2008 NSCA 124.

117   Above note 55, s. 80(b).

118   *R. v. Gagnon* (1956), 117 C.C.C. 61 (Que. C.S.P.).

119   Though for European initiatives, see Bantekas & Nash, above note 9 at 414–33.

120   See Satya Bedi, *Extradition: A Treatise on the Laws Relevant to the Fugitive Offenders within and with the Commonwealth Countries* (Buffalo, NY: William S. Hein, 2002) c. 8, "Alternatives to Extradition."

121   *Attorney-General of Israel v. Eichmann* (1968), 36 I.L.R. 18 (Jerusalem Dist. Ct. 1961) [*Eichmann* (Dist. Ct.)], aff'd (1968), 36 I.L.R. 277 (Israel Sup. Ct. 1962).

an international incident between Israel and Argentina—in which the UN Security Council became involved—and also underpinned part of his defence before the Israeli courts. More recently, some states have practised "extraordinary rendition," which has been defined as "the transfer of an individual, without the benefit of a legal proceeding in which the individual can challenge the transfer, to a country where he or she is at risk of torture."[122] Each of these practices raises distinct issues under both international and domestic law.

1) Abduction

The first, and least controversial, issue regarding abduction is that it is illegal under international law. This has been settled since even before the time of the Harvard Research Draft, in which it was acknowledged.[123] A state may not exercise policing or other criminal enforcement powers on the territory of another state without the latter state's permission, as this is an illegal exercise of enforcement jurisdiction.[124] It is illegal because it violates the territorial sovereignty of the target state,[125] and can incur state responsibility for the violating state.[126] As the Security Council noted in its resolution regarding the Eichmann abduction, such acts invite retaliation by the targeted state and they therefore "endanger international peace and security."[127]

It is also reasonably uncontroversial that abduction is illegal because it violates the international human rights law obligations of the abducting state, particularly those dealing with due process and security of person.[128] The major international human rights bodies

---

122 Margaret L. Satterthwaite, "Rendered Meaningless: Extraordinary Rendition and the Rule of Law" (2006–2007) 75 Geo. Wash. L. Rev. 1333 at 1336.

123 Harvard Research in International Law, "Draft Convention on Jurisdiction With Respect to Crime" (1935) 29 A.J.I.L. 435, Special Supplement, Part II at 623–24.

124 See Chapter 2, Section D; see also *S.S. Lotus (France v. Turkey)* (1927) P.C.I.J. (Ser. A.) No. 10 at 18–19.

125 The Security Council held to this effect regarding Israel's abduction of Eichmann: UN Doc. S/4349 (1960), S/RES/138, 1960, in particular para. 2.

126 Note that this would be true even if persons who are not formally state employees conduct the actual abduction, so long as their actions are in some way attributable to the state which receives and prosecutes the fugitive. See Chapter II of the ILC's Articles on State Responsibility.

127 Security Council Resolution, above note 125.

128 For example, *International Covenant on Civil and Political Rights* (1966) 999 U.N.T.S. 171 [ICCPR], art. 9; *European Convention for the Protection of Human Rights and Fundamental Freedoms* (1950) 213 U.N.T.S. 221 [ECHR], art. 5; *American Convention on Human Rights* (1969) O.A.S.T.S. No. 36 [ACHR], art. 7.

have made fairly consistent findings on this point.[129] In *Lopez Burgos v. Uruguay*,[130] for example, the UN Human Rights Committee found a violation of article 9(1) of the *International Covenant on Civil and Political Rights (ICCPR)*,[131] where Uruguayan agents forcibly abducted a Uruguayan refugee from Argentina. In *Bozano v. France*,[132] the European Court of Human Rights found a violation of article 5(1) of the *European Convention for the Protection of Human Rights and Fundamental Freedoms (ECHR)*,[133] where the petitioner was the victim of a disguised extradition, having been seized in France and deported to Switzerland, whereupon he was extradited to Italy. There is some divergence of approach regarding the weight to be given to the violation of state sovereignty, as while the UN Human Rights Committee considers this point irrelevant, the European Court of Human Rights has held that no rights violation is made out if the abduction took place with some consent from the target state.[134] Where a violation has been found, it tends to lead to a remedy of dismissal.

Despite the findings of the human rights bodies, however, their results apply only to those states where such decisions must be given direct effect within the domestic law, and thus they do not state a more widely applicable international law norm. The more complex question is whether, as a matter of state practice, there is a case to be made that it is illegal under customary international law for a state to try an individual who has been abducted or subject to irregular rendition.[135] There

---

129 See, for example, *Stocké v. Federal Republic of Germany* (1989), 95 I.L.R. 328 at 332–33 (Eur. Comm. Hum. Rts.); *Garcia v. Ecuador* (Human Rights Committee), Comm. No. 319/1988, UN Doc. A/47/40 (1994) at 287–90; *Celiberti de Casariego v. Uruguay* UN Doc. CCPR/C/13/D/56/1979, 29 July 1981 (Human Rights Committee).

130 UN Doc. CCPR/C/13/D/52/1979, 29 July 1981 (Human Rights Committee).

131 Above note 128.

132 (95-14-T), (1987), 9 E.H.R.R. 297 (Eur. Ct. Hum. Rts.).

133 Above note 128.

134 Silvia Borelli, "Terrorism and Human Rights: Treatment of Terrorist Suspects and Limits on International Co-operation" (2003) 16 Leiden J. Int'l L. 803 at 807. On the latter, see *Öcalan v. Turkey*, Appl. No. 00046221/99, Merits, Judgment of 12 May 2005 (Eur. Ct. Hum. Rts. Grand Chamber).

135 There is an enormous literature on this question; see, for example, Edwin D. Dickinson, "Jurisdiction Following Seizure or Arrest in Violation of International Law" (1934) 28 A.J.I.L. 231; F.A. Mann, "Reflections on the Prosecution of Persons Abducted in Breach of International Law" in Yoram Dinstein, ed., *International Law at a Time of Perplexity: Essays in Honour of Shabtai Rosenne* (Dordrecht: Martinus Nijhoff, 1989) 407; A. Lowenfeld, "US Law Enforcement Abroad: The Constitution and International Law" (1989) 83 A.J.I.L. 880 (plus follow-up articles at (1990) 84 A.J.I.L. 444, (1990) 84 A.J.I.L. 712 and (1991)

are two streams of caselaw from domestic courts, which demonstrate what may be labeled as the "*mala captus* approach" and the "abuse of process approach." [136] In each approach, courts have attacked the question not as one purely of international law, but rather as a determination of whether the illegal abduction has an impact on whether courts can and/or must decline to assume jurisdiction over the crime. That said, an important aspect of each stream is what weight to give to the violation of state sovereignty stemming from the abduction as part of the exercise of determining whether to exercise jurisdiction.

The *mala captus* stream is so named for its origin in the Roman law maxim *mala captus bene detentus* (literally "wrongly captured, properly detained"). This approach entails that, because the "illegality" involved in the accused's rendition arises from an *international* delict, the domestic court "will assert *in personam* jurisdiction without inquiring into the means by which the presence of the defendant was secured."[137]. This illustrates the central issue: violation of one state's rights by another does not, in and of itself, provide the individual concerned with standing to request a remedy for the violation. She is truly, in this sense, the traditional "object" of the law, rather than its subject. The international law violation must be cognizable and justiciable by the domestic criminal court, on the basis of the domestic law. Under the *mala captus* approach, the domestic judicial forum should not entertain issues related to the legality of capture. This approach was taken by the Israeli District Court in *Eichmann*, where it was held to be "an established rule of law."[138] Another prominent example of *mala captus* was the 1992 case of *United States v. Alvarez-Machain*,[139] where a majority of the US Supreme Court found that that the abduction of a Mexican national by agents retained by the US Drug Enforcement Agency did not provide the individual with a jurisdictional bar to criminal prosecution. The international law violation was a matter to be dealt with by the Executive, and the accused enjoyed no cognizable right which he could assert before the Court. The decision ignited a storm of con-

---

85 A.J.I.L. 655); Abraham Mohit, "The Customary Law of International Abductions: Limits and Boundaries" (2006) 11 Asian Y.B. Int'l L. 123.

136 This terminology is drawn from R.J. Currie, "Abducted Fugitives before the International Criminal Court: Problems and Prospects" (2007) 18 Crim. L.F. 349, where the issue is considered in more detail.

137 M. Cherif Bassiouni, *International Extradition: United States Law and Practice*, 4th ed. (Dobbs Ferry, NY: Oceana, 2002) at 250.

138 *Eichmann* (Dist. Ct.), above note 121 at 59.

139 112 S. Ct. 2188 (1992).

troversy internationally,[140] but certainly represents current practice by the US and other states.[141]

The "abuse of process" stream of practice, by contrast, has as its central tenet the idea that a court has an inherent duty to protect the dignity, legitimacy, and legality of its process, which would be subverted in any case where a criminal accused has been apprehended through illegal activities or abuses of power on the part of the state. Accordingly, where clearly illegal and/or abusive activity by state officials is implicated in the accused's arrest, the court may decline to exercise jurisdiction. This entitlement is usually not framed in mandatory terms, but it does cover a broad array of state behaviour which can provoke the remedy; indeed, "abuse of process" is simply shorthand for a mix of domestic and international legal issues, which have been described as "arrests effected in violation of extradition procedures," "official complicity in the unlawful conduct leading to the presence of the accused before the court," and "egregious conduct on the part of law enforcement authorities amounting to an abuse of the court's process."[142] Violations of state sovereignty, in this matrix, become one of a number of circumstances which may be given weight as part of the court's effort to control its own process and ensure that the state "come[s] to court 'with clean hands' as it were."[143]

The most prominent example of the abuse of process approach is probably that of the House of Lords in *Ex Parte Bennett*,[144] where

---

140 For example, the UN Working Group on Arbitrary Detention stated that "[the] detention of Humberto Alvarez-Machain is declared to be arbitrary, being in contravention of . . . Article 9 of the [ICCPR]" (Report of the Working Group on Arbitrary Detention, UN Commission on Human Rights, 50th Session, UN Doc. E/CN.4/1994/27 (1993) at 139–40). See also Martin Feinrider & Thilo Marauhn, "Kidnapping" in Rudolf Bernhardt, ed., *Encyclopedia of Public International Law*, vol. 3 (Oxford: Elsevier, 1997) 79–84; Mark S. Zaid, "Military Might versus Sovereign Right: The Kidnapping of Dr. Humberto Alvarez-Machain and the Resulting Fallout" (1997) 19 Houston J. Int'l L. 829 at 853–55.

141 It may be worth noting that the charges against Dr. Alvarez-Machain were later dismissed for lack of evidence, the court noting that the indictment was based on "the wildest speculation" (Seth Mydans, "Judge Clears Mexican in Agent's Killing" *New York Times* (15 December 1992) A20).

142 Susan Lamb, "The Powers of Arrest of the International Criminal Tribunal for the Former Yugoslavia" (1999) 70 Brit. Y.B. Int'l L. 167 at 232–37.

143 *State* v. *Ebrahim*, [1991] 2 S. Afr. L.R. 553, in translation at 95 I.L.R. 417 at 442.

144 *R.* v. *Horseferry Road Magistrates' Court, Ex parte Bennett*, [1994] 1 A.C. 42. See V. Lowe, "Circumventing Extradition Procedures is an Abuse of Process" (1993) 52 Cambridge L. J. 371. See also *R.* v. *Hartley*, [1978] 2 N.Z.L.R. 199, 77 I.L.R. 330 (C.A.); *State* v. *Ebrahim*, above note 143; *State* v. *Beahan*, [1992] 1 S.A.C.R. 307 (A) (Zimbabwe).

a New Zealand national was illegally deported from South Africa by way of complicity with British police. The Law Lords ruled the authorities' deliberate flouting of UK–South Africa extradition arrangements, *inter alia*, justified a remedy of dismissal. It was not the subversion of extradition procedures itself that was so offensive to the court; rather, the matter was one of respect for the rule of law, which "demands the courts take cognizance" of state illegality.[145] This generally extends to human rights violations on the part of state authorities. For example, in the US, there is an exception to the *mala captus* doctrine whereby courts may decline jurisdiction in the presence of egregious physical human rights abuses perpetrated upon the fugitive which were brought about by irregular trans-border conduct by US authorities.[146]

More recently, the ICTY became engaged in the problem of abducted fugitives, which it was compelled to address squarely in the case of *Prosecutor v. Dragan Nikolić*.[147] In that case the accused, an indicted war criminal, had been abducted by persons unknown from his home in what was then the Federal Republic of Yugoslavia (FRY) and smuggled across the border into Bosnia and Herzegovina. He was there handed over to UN forces operating in the area, and eventually to the tribunal. Nikolić argued that his abduction had violated both the sovereignty of FRY and his internationally protected human rights, as well as being an abuse of process, and that the only appropriate remedy was dismissal and his return to (the by this time renamed) Serbia and Montenegro. In the course of dismissing this argument, the Appeals Chamber cursorily surveyed national caselaw, finding support for its proposals that national courts found it easier to assume jurisdiction in such cases where the perpetrator was charged with odious crimes such as genocide or crimes against humanity, and particularly where there was no protest by the ostensibly "injured" state. It then emphasized the importance of ensuring accountability for "Universally Condemned Offences,"[148] and held that "jurisdiction should [not] be set aside on the ground that there was a violation of the sovereignty of a State, when

---

145 *Ex parte Bennett, ibid.* at 67, Lord Bridge of Harwich. See also *R. v. Mullen*, [1999] 3 W.L.R. 777 (Crim. Ct. App.).

146 *United States v. Toscanino*, 500 F.2d 267 at 274 (Ct. App. 2d Circ. 1974). See Stephan Wilske and Teresa Schiller, "Jurisdiction over Persons Abducted in Violation of International Law in the Aftermath of *United States v. Alvarez-Machain*" (1998) 5 U. Chicago L. Sch. Roundtable 205 at 208.

147 *Nikolić* (IT-94-2-AR73), Decision on Interlocutory Appeal Concerning Legality of Arrest, 5 June 2003. See James Sloan, "Breaching International Law to Ensure Its Enforcement: The Reliance by the ICTY on Illegal Capture" (2003) 6 Y.B. Int'l Human. L. 319; Currie, "Abducted Fugitives," above note 136.

148 *Nikolić, ibid.* at para. 24.

the violation is brought about by the apprehension of fugitives from international justice, whatever the consequences for the international responsibility of the State or organisation involved."[149] It finally concluded that jurisdiction should be set aside only if there were extremely serious human rights violations involved in the apprehension of the accused, since only this would strike the appropriate balance between protecting human rights and prosecuting heinous offenders.

Nikolić is an interesting decision, not least for the rather startling proposition that prosecuting persons accused of "Universally Condemned Offences" itself has such intense implications for international peace and security that it supersedes the tension and conflict that international abductions can produce. In one swoop, the Appeals Chamber has elevated international human rights law to significant importance in international prosecutions, and also allowed the accused to plead violations of state sovereignty in his defence—even though it declines to give any weight to the latter, and little to the former, in considering jurisdiction. The next significant battleground on this question may be the International Criminal Court (ICC), which has made one limited finding on analogous issues already in the course of the drawn-out proceedings in the *Lubanga* case.[150] Interestingly, the Appeals Chamber declined to view the question of pre-custodial and custodial human rights violations as a matter of jurisdiction, preferring instead to find a potential entitlement of a remedy for the accused under article 21(3) of the *Rome Statute*,[151] which applies international human rights law norms to the court's proceedings. This completely removes from the equation whether violations of state sovereignty are to be given any weight in the exercise—perhaps a perilous decision, given that, unlike the ICTY, the ICC's authority does not extend over all states.[152]

From the foregoing, it is clear that there is no customary international law norm which prohibits states from taking a *mala captus*

---

149 *Ibid.* at para. 26. The court also noted that jurisdiction certainly would not be set aside where individuals acted privately in carrying out the abduction, since there would be no violation of sovereignty (*ibid.*).

150 *Lubanga*, Case No. ICC-01/04-01/06 (OA4), Judgment on the Appeal of Mr. Thomas Lubanga Dyilo against the Decision on the Defence Challenge to the Jurisdiction of the Court pursuant to art. 19(2) of the Statute of 3 October 2006, 14 December 2006. The Extraordinary Chambers in the Courts of Cambodia (about which, generally, see Chapter 4) recently rendered an interlocutory decision on a similar matter; see Cedric Ryngaert, "The Doctrine of Abuse of Process: A Comment on the Cambodia Tribunal's Decisions in the Case against Duch" (2008) 21 Leiden J. Int'l L. 719.

151 2187 U.N.T.S. 3, entered into force 1 July 2002.

152 See Currie, "Abducted Fugitives," above note 136 at 387–93.

approach and trying an abducted or irregularly rendered individual. However, the argument that it is illegal to try an individual where the circumstances of arrest resulted in either serious (if not egregious) human rights violations and/or manifest illegality by state officials, is at least gaining some purchase. So far as Canadian law goes, there is little on point. There are two decisions in which the *mala captus* rule was applied, but both were well before the *Charter.*[153] It is also noteworthy that the government of Canada intervened before the United States Supreme Court (USSC) in *Alvarez* to argue the illegality of the abduction and the side-stepping of the extradition treaty,[154] which seems to indicate there is unlikely to be official sanction of abductions.[155] It is difficult to imagine modern Canadian courts countenancing significant illegality on the part of Canadian police or other officials, and any prosecutorial ambition to try an abducted accused would likely founder under section 7 of the *Charter* and/or the defence of abuse of process. This might differ where the accused was abducted by "parties unknown" and simply handed over to Canadian police, without any involvement of the latter. Since the *Charter* applies only to the actions of Canadian officials, the only remaining argument would be for trial unfairness under section 7. Such circumstances are, however, reasonably unlikely.

2) Extraordinary Rendition

The phrase "extraordinary rendition" is more of a catchphrase than a legal term of art, but as a practice it has received a great deal of attention in recent years from the media, human rights organizations, and, increasingly, governments. As noted above, the phrase refers to the practice on the part of government actors, usually security personnel of some sort, of seizing individuals without any legal process and transporting them secretly to a location where they will face detention, interrogation, and possibly torture. It has been most famously attributed to the US in the aftermath of the 9/11 attacks and as part of the "war on terror," and it is noteworthy that the government acknowledged the

---

153 *R. v. Walton* (1905), 10 C.C.C. 269 (Ont. C.A.); *Re Hartnett and the Queen; Re Hudson and the Queen* (1973), 1 O.R. (2d) 206 (H.C.J.).

154 Canada's *amicus curiae* brief is reproduced at (1992) 31 I.L.M. 919.

155 And see also the *Jaffe* case, where two US bail bondsmen abducted an individual in Canada and took him to Florida for trial, which engendered a dispute between Canada and the US; Wade A. Buser, "The *Jaffe* Case and the Use of International Kidnapping as an Alternative to Extradition" (1984) 14 Ga. J. Int'l & Comp. L. 357.

practice, if not all of its potential legal implications.[156] However, the controversy attracted by extraordinary rendition has tainted other governments—notably the government of Canada over its involvement in the highly publicized Maher Arar affair, where Arar, a Syrian-born Canadian citizen, was illegally rendered by US officials to face torture in Syria based in part on seemingly bogus information supplied by Canadian officials.[157]

The heart of extraordinary rendition is that it is used in a manner that attempts to "wash the hands" of the governments which transfer the individuals, as they are sent either to secret facilities run by the transferring government (so that their law will not apply), or to states where torture is practised under force of law or is tolerated—again in an effort to prevent the actual torture from being conducted under the scrutiny of the transferring state's law.[158] The essential international law issues are twofold. First, extraordinary rendition violates an array of international human rights and/or criminal law norms, both customary and treaty-based.[159] Most disturbingly, this includes the prohibition on torture, as a matter both of *jus cogens* customary international law and under the 1984 UN *Convention against Torture*.[160] Moreover, the violations pertain not just to the conduct of the transporting and torturing states, but potentially also to other states which agree to act as transit points for aircraft on which the individuals are being transported.

The latter point plays into the second issue: the use of secretive techniques, and particularly the use of states' airspace and territories without permission, has had a corrosive effect on international relations. Much of this has stemmed from American use of the airports and territories of European states, in order to transfer individuals both to CIA-run detention facilities in cooperating Eastern European states, and to other loca-

---

156 "President's Remarks on the War on Terror" (6 September 2006), as quoted in Leila N. Sadat, "Extraordinary Rendition, Torture and Other Nightmares from the War on Terror" (2007) 75 Geo. Wash. L. Rev. 1200 at 1200.

157 The 2006 Report of the Maher Arar Commission, presided over by Justice Dennis O'Connor, is archived online: http://epe.lac-bac.gc.ca/100/206/301/pco-bcp/commissions/maher_arar/07-09-13/www.ararcommission.ca/default.htm. The report found that some of the information relayed by Canadian authorities had come from Syria and was likely to have been obtained by torture to begin with.

158 Popular destinations have been Syria, Algeria, and Egypt.

159 David Weissbrodt & Amy Bergquist, "Extraordinary Rendition: A Human Rights Analysis" (2006) 19 Harv. Hum. Rts. J. 123.

160 *Convention against Torture and other Cruel, Inhuman or Degrading Treatment or Punishment*, Can. T.S. 1987 No. 36. See David Weissbrodt & Amy Bergquist, "Extraordinary Rendition and the Torture Convention" (2006) 46 Va. J. Int'l L. 585.

tions such as Egypt. This became a popular media issue in the case of Abu Omar, a terrorism suspect who, in 2005, was subject to extraordinary rendition from Italy by CIA agents without any information being conveyed to Italian authorities. This not only violated Italian sovereignty and engendered protest from Italy and the European Union, but further had the effect of disrupting Italy's own investigation into Omar.[161] This caused the European Parliament to strike the "Temporary Committee on the Alleged Use of European Countries by the CIA for the Transport and Illegal Detention of Prisoners,"[162] whose report explored ten known cases of extraordinary rendition that implicated EU member states, and indicated that in some cases, these states had been complicit. It noted credible evidence that the US had engaged in the practice hundreds of times, and it excoriated a practice which was not only in violation of member states' human rights law, but damaged their own security by hampering local investigations.[163]

Extraordinary rendition is very much a meme of anti-terrorist times. The rhetoric of the "global war on terror" has been used, especially by the US, to justify such actions. The legal case pleaded is sometimes one of self-defence against the new aggressor, the terrorist, though on the whole this is unconvincing.[164] The classic international law statement of the problem is that states which engage in extraordinary rendition are violating international human rights law, in a manner by which an argument that permissible derogation is engaged is not credible. They are also often engaging in illegal exercises of extraterritorial enforcement jurisdiction — to wit, they are violating the sovereignty of other states. This is a practice which undermines decades of incremental development of procedural norms, in favour of authoritarian "disappearance" and the use of Soviet-gulag-style facilities such as Guantanamo Bay. Whether such drastic measures will ultimately be considered to have been justified by the very real threat posed by terrorism remains to be seen. Current indications are to the contrary.

---

161 See Michele Nino, "The Abu Omar Case in Italy and the Effects of CIA Extraordinary Renditions in Europe on Law Enforcement and Intelligence Activities" (2007) 78 Rev. I.D.P. 113.

162 Eur. Parl. Doc. PE 380.593v04-00 4 (16 November 2006).

163 *Ibid.* Amnesty International has since criticized European states for failing to effectively investigate the claims or do more to combat extraordinary rendition; Amnesty International, *State of Denial: Europe's Role in Rendition and Secret Detention* (London: Amnesty International, International Secretariat, 2008).

164 Troy Lavers, "Extraordinary Rendition and the Self Defence Justification: Time to Face the Music" (2007) 16 Mich. St. J. Int'l L. 385.

D. MUTUAL LEGAL ASSISTANCE

1) International Law

Over the last two decades, one international criminal cooperation mechanism that has become increasingly important is the provision of *mutual legal assistance* (MLA) between states in criminal matters, which has been called "the fastest growing business in the criminal justice field."[165] MLA has been simply and practically defined as follows: "the process whereby one State provides assistance to another in the investigation and prosecution of criminal offences," particularly as regards "such unglamourous but highly practical matters" as the provision of evidence (documentary or *viva voce*) for use abroad, the search and seizure of evidence for use in foreign proceedings, the transfer of witnesses for interview or to give testimony, and the service of documents originating in another state.[166]

This kind of inter-state assistance was traditionally carried out by way of a cumbersome diplomatic process known as "letters rogatory," based predominantly on goodwill and international comity rather than legal instruments.[167] Starting with the 1959 *European Convention on Mutual Assistance in Criminal Matters*,[168] the historical practices have been essentially supplanted by a network of treaties, both bilateral and multilateral, through which states can cooperate in transmitting evidence between and among them. The most prominent mutual legal assistance treaty (MLAT) regimes have been between groups of like-minded states which had geographical and/or political features that necessitated cooperation.[169] Accordingly, there are MLATs among the states of the modern-day European Union, the Commonwealth, the African Union, the Organization of American States (OAS), and so on. In addition, there are increasingly sophisticated MLA provisions built into the various anti-crime "suppression conventions,"[170] such as the 1988 *Vienna Narcotics Convention*[171] and the 2000 *United Nations Convention*

---

165 Kimberly Prost, "Breaking Down Barriers: International Cooperation in Combating Transnational Crime," available at the Organization of American States (OAS) website, online: www.oas.org/juridico/mla/mp/resources/prost_en.html.

166 William C. Gilmore, ed., *Mutual Assistance in Criminal and Business Regulatory Matters* (New York: Cambridge University Press, 1995) at xii.

167 For a historical overview, see R.J. Currie, "Peace and Public Order: Mutual Legal Assistance 'The Canadian Way'" (1998) 7 Dal. J. Leg. Stud. 91 at 96–106.

168 (1959) Eur. T.S. No. 30.

169 For historical background, see Currie, "Peace and Public Order," above note 167.

170 Regarding which, see chapter 7.

171 Above note 10.

against Transnational Organized Crime.[172] Many states also conclude bilateral MLATs, and these often see a great deal of traffic; for example, the Canada–US treaty[173] is the basis for the vast majority of Canada's MLA activity. The United Nations has put forward a Model Treaty on Mutual Legal Assistance in Criminal Matters[174] to assist (primarily developing) states to formulate their own.

The ultimate goal of MLATs is to introduce administrative efficiency into the investigation of criminal cases with transnational aspects, by way of treaty obligations. MLA is a creature of international law for simple reasons. Each state has plenary sovereignty over its territory, and the ability to investigate and enforce criminal law in particular is limited to the territory of the state.[175] Accordingly, for example, Canadian police cannot enter the United States to exercise investigative jurisdiction (that is, to gather evidence for a domestic prosecution) and vice versa, as they have no legal authority to do so. Pursuant to an MLAT between states, police and prosecutors can unlock the criminal procedure of another state by making a request for assistance. The authorities of the requested state are thereby empowered to obtain (and in most circumstances compel) evidence which is present in that state, and send it to their counterparts in the requesting state for use in the investigation and prosecution of criminal offences.

While there are variations, each MLAT generally requires a state to designate a "central authority" to both make outgoing requests and receive incoming ones, and each state undertakes to provide the maximum assistance possible to its treaty partner—though typically the treaties are explicit that the request will be executed in accordance with the requested state's law and procedure.[176] MLATs are also similar to extradition treaties in that they contain grounds under which a state may refuse a request for assistance. For example, assistance may be refused if the evidence will be used in a prosecution that is actually for a discriminatory purpose, if the offence is of a political or military

---

172 Above note 11.

173 *Treaty between the Government of Canada and the Government of the United States of America on Mutual Legal Assistance in Criminal Matters*, Can. T.S. 1990 No. 19 [*Canada–US MLAT*].

174 A/RES/45/117 (1990), as amended by UN Doc. A/RES/53/112 (1999). The UNODC has published a manual on the treaty, online: www.unodc.org/pdf/ model_treaty_extradition_revised_manual.pdf.

175 *R. v. Hape*, [2007] 2 S.C.R. 292 at paras. 64–65.

176 This latter point underscores a common source of friction in MLA arrangements, that the requested state may not have the ability to provide the evidence in a form that is useful for the requesting state. For example, the concept of providing evidence under oath is typically unknown in civil law states.

nature, or if assisting would somehow compromise the sovereignty or *ordre public* of the requested state. Unlike extradition treaties, there is often no requirement of double criminality.[177] The grounds for refusal are generally more restrictive in MLATs than in extradition treaties, on the basis that the liberty of the accused person is engaged much less directly. This latter point is a controversial one, and MLA arrangements are commonly criticized for being too firmly within the control of prosecuting authorities and not affording accused persons any meaningful opportunity to gather evidence in the foreign state—thus offending the principle of "equality of arms." In response, some states (such as Australia) have introduced mechanisms for evidence-gathering by the government, at the request of the defence.[178]

MLA is not the only means by which police and/or prosecutors may send evidence to their counterparts in other states. MLATs have mostly overtaken the more traditional methods for transmitting evidence between states,[179] but police in different states still do cooperate with each other on an informal basis by providing intelligence and even evidence where such can be done informally.[180] MLA mechanisms tend to be most important where it is perceived that there is a need to exercise compulsory authority, by way of the requested state's courts, in order to obtain the evidence needed. A legal instrument is then required, for otherwise the requested state's police would be obtaining warrants and seizing evidence regarding crimes over which, for the most part, the requested state's courts would have no jurisdiction. The MLAT provides the necessary legal authority and political legitimacy for so doing. The availability of the treaty mechanisms is also important for the obvious practical reasons, that is, the authorities of the requested state are best suited to do evidence-gathering in that state.

---

177 Though double criminality is sometimes a factor. Contrast, for example, the *Canada–Australia MLAT* (Can. T.S. 1990 No. 2), art. VI(2)(a), where the requested state may refuse the request on this basis, with the *Canada–US MLAT*, above note 173, art. II(3), which excludes such refusal.

178 See Australia's *Mutual Assistance in Criminal Law Matters Act 1987*, s. 39A.

179 That is, the diplomatic sending of letters rogatory and applications under the *Canada Evidence Act*, R.S.C. 1985, c. C-5, s. 46.

180 As do other regulatory agencies, for example, securities regulators. See *Global Securities Corp. v. British Columbia (Securities Commission)*, [2000] 1 S.C.R. 494.

2) Canadian Law

a) The Legislation

As noted in Chapter 1, in order to become law in Canada international treaties must be implemented into the domestic legal framework, which is generally accomplished by statute. Virtually all of Canada's MLA obligations are implemented by way of the *Mutual Legal Assistance in Criminal Matters Act (MLA Act)*.[181]

The term "agreement" is defined in section 2 of the *MLA Act* as "a treaty, convention or other international agreement . . . that contains a provision respecting mutual legal assistance in criminal matters[.]" Accordingly, the Act allows Canada to respond to requests under any of the over 40 bilateral MLATs to which it is party,[182] as well as multilateral treaties such as the *OAS Convention on Mutual Assistance in Criminal Matters*[183] or the *Vienna Narcotics Convention*,[184] and to requests from the ICC, ICTY, and ICTR. Section 6 provides that Canada can also respond to requests from states with which Canada does not have a treaty, or to requests from states with which Canada does have a treaty but where the offence in question is not covered by the treaty. This requires the concluding of an "administrative arrangement" (essentially a one-off treaty) between Canada and the requesting state.[185]

Similarly to extradition proceedings, the Act provides a bifurcation of roles between the executive and the judiciary. Unlike extradition, and as will be examined in more detail in Sections D(2)(b) and (c), below in this chapter, the nature of the judicial function shifts depending on the context in which the Act is being applied, that is, whether Canada is the requesting state or requested state. In terms of the executive role, the federal Minister of Justice is the designated "central authority," responsible both for transmitting requests to other states and for receiving and approving requests from other states. In reality these tasks are handled by Justice Canada's International Assistance Group (IAG). The IAG personnel receive the foreign requests and determine whether fulfilling them is mandated and appropriate under the relevant treaty.

---

181 R.S.C. 1985 (4th Supp.), c. 30, as amended [*MLA Act*]. All statutory references in this section are to the *MLA Act*, unless otherwise indicated. For mutual legal assistance in competition matters, see Part III of the *Competition Act*, R.S.C. 1985, c. C-34.

182 The current number of MLATs can be found at the Foreign Affairs Treaty Information website, online: www.treaty-accord.gc.ca.

183 O.A.S. T.S. 075 (1992).

184 Above note 10.

185 See *Mutual Legal Assistance in Criminal Matters Act, Re (sub nom. Russian Federation v. Pokidyshev)* (1999), 27 C.R. (5th) 316 (Ont. C.A.) [*Pokidyshev*].

They then transmit the requests to a "competent authority," either Justice Canada counsel or provincial prosecutors in the relevant region, who (along with the police) carry out the foreign requests. When an appearance before a Canadian court is required to respond to a foreign request, designated Crown lawyers (usually Justice Canada personnel) appear as counsel.[186]

The Act is divided into three parts: Part I provides the authority and procedure for responding to foreign requests; Part II deals with the admissibility of evidence, in a trial in Canada, which has been provided by way of a request to a foreign state; and Part III sets out rules for various matters relating to witnesses and documents, where Canada has made a request of a foreign state. The focus here will be on Part I, with points on each of the other Parts reviewed briefly thereafter.

b) Part I of the *Mutual Legal Assistance in Criminal Matters Act*: Canada As Requested State

i) Issuing of Search Warrants

The issuance and execution of warrants are governed by sections 10–14 of the Act. It is important to note two things at the outset. First, section 10 provides that the *Criminal Code*[187] applies in respect of a search or seizure under the Act, "with any modifications that the circumstances require." Accordingly, the intent is that the foreign request simply invokes the ordinary, everyday search warrant procedure with which we are familiar, informed as need be by the transnational aspects of the case. Second, the Crown may access not just search warrants under section 487 of the *Code*, but general warrants under section 487.1 as well—the latter being specifically provided for in both sections 11(1) and 13.1 of the Act.

Under section 11, once the "competent authority" has received the approved request and relevant documentation from the IAG, it can apply *ex parte* to the superior court[188] of the province where the evidence may be found for the issuance of a warrant. A judge may issue a warrant authorizing a named officer to execute it where satisfied by statements under oath that there are reasonable grounds to believe that an offence has been committed, evidence of the commission of the offence or information that may reveal the whereabouts of the suspect will be

---

186 See *Canada (Attorney General) v. Fulfillment Solutions Advantage and International Access Inc.*, 2005 BCSC 1764 at paras. 15–28 [*Fulfillment Solutions Advantage*].

187 Above note 70.

188 Above note 181, s. 2(1) defines "judge" as a superior court justice in the relevant province or territory.

found at the relevant site, and it would not be appropriate to apply for an "evidence-gathering order" under section 18(1) of the Act.[189]

The warrant "may be in Form 5 Part XXVII of the *Criminal Code*, varied to suit the case."[190] The judge may apply such conditions as she deems appropriate, and must fix a time and place to consider the execution of the warrant and the executing officer's report thereon.[191] The warrant must contain details of this hearing, including time, place, the fact that an order to send the evidence to the requesting state will be sought, and the entitlement of persons from whom material is seized or who claim to have an interest in the seized material to make representations.[192] The Act also contains a "plain view seizure" provision, which further states that sections 489.1–492 of the *Criminal Code* "apply in respect of any thing seized pursuant to this section."[193]

ii) Challenging the Warrant: The Sending Hearing

Since the evidence seized under an *MLA Act* warrant is destined for use in another jurisdiction, there will, of course, be no Canadian trial at which the execution of the warrant may be considered. While courts have occasionally entertained specific applications to quash search warrants,[194] judicial scrutiny of the warrant, the underlying information, and the execution of the search (as well as various other issues) usually occurs at the hearing convened under section 15 of the Act to consider whether the evidence should be transmitted to the requesting state. This part of the process is generally referred to as the "sending hearing" and is the site of the true battle royale between Crown counsel seeking to fulfill the requesting state's request, and defence counsel attempting to prevent the sending of the evidence abroad.

The judge at the sending hearing is required to hear submissions from the Minister of Justice, the competent authority, the person from whom evidence was seized, and "any person who claims to have an interest in the record or thing seized."[195] The judge may order the ma-

---

189 *Ibid.*, ss. 12(1)(a), (b), & (c). "Evidence-gathering orders" are dealt with in Section D(2)(b)(iii), below in this chapter.
190 *Ibid.*, s. 12(4).
191 *Ibid.*, ss. 12(2) & (3). The officer's report is provided for in s. 14.
192 *Ibid.*, ss. 12(4)(a), (b), & (c).
193 *Ibid.*, s. 13.
194 For example, see *R. v. Budd* (2000), 150 C.C.C. (3d) 108 (Ont. C.A.), leave to appeal to S.C.C. refused, [2001] S.C.C.A. No. 57.
195 Above note 181, s. 15(1). For cases addressing standing, see *United Kingdom v. Ramsden* (1996), 108 C.C.C. (3d) 289 (Ont. C.A.), leave to appeal to S.C.C. refused, [1996] S.C.C.A. No. 443; *Canada (Attorney General) v. China (Republic)* (1996), 113 C.C.C. (3d) 470 (N.S.C.A.) [*Canada v. China*]; *National Cheese &*

terials returned to the person from whom they were seized "where the judge is not satisfied that the warrant was executed according to its terms and conditions or where the judge is satisfied that an order under paragraph (b) [sending the materials to the requesting state] should not be made."[196] "In any other case," the materials are to be sent to the requesting state with any conditions "that the judge considers desirable,"[197] and the Minister must be satisfied that the requesting state has agreed to comply with these conditions before sending.[198]

The leading cases interpret section 15 as providing fairly wide discretion, as well as a broad supervisory jurisdiction, to the sending hearing judge regarding the review of both warrants and their execution. In *R. v. Gladwin*,[199] the Ontario Court of Appeal set out the process for a sending hearing as follows:

> [T]his section imposes a double burden upon the judge called upon to make an order under s. 15(1)(b) of the Act sending the material seized to the foreign state. *He or she is obliged under s. 15(1)(a) to review what has transpired to the date of the return of the application.* Before he can order that the record or thing seized be sent to the foreign state, the reviewing judge must be satisfied, first, that the warrant was executed according to its terms and conditions and, second, that he is satisfied that there is no reason why the order should not be made. The respondent submits, and I agree, that *the inherent nature of this second condition necessarily bestows discretion on the reviewing judge to consider all relevant factors bearing on the application.*
>
> *In both of these instances, the reviewing judge is exercising a jurisdiction akin to that of a trial judge considering the admissibility into evidence of the things seized pursuant to a search warrant.*[200]

Food Co. (Re), [1998] O.J. No. 1988 (C.A.); *Pokidyshev*, above note 185; *A.L.T. Navigation Ltd. v. United States of America*, [2001] N.J. No. 318 (S.C.T.D.); *Sherk v. Canada (Attorney General)*, 2002 BCCA 673; *Fulfillment Solutions Advantage*, above note 186.

196 *MLA Act, ibid.*, s. 15(1)(a). It has been held that s. 490 of the *Criminal Code* (dictating the return of items seized unless a justice is satisfied that "the detention of the thing seized is required for purposes of any investigation . . . ") does not apply to proceedings under the *MLA Act*; *United States of America v. Wilson*, [2002] B.C.J. No. 129 at paras. 123–42 (S.C.) [*Wilson*].

197 *MLA Act, ibid.*, s. 15(1)(b)(i)–(iii); *Canada (Attorney General) v. Sharples*, 2006 BCSC 1768.

198 *MLA Act, ibid.*, s. 16.

199 (1997), 116 C.C.C. (3d) 471 (Ont. C.A.), leave to appeal to S.C.C. refused, [1997] S.C.C.A. No. 325.

200 *Ibid.* at paras. 8–9 [emphasis added].

In *R. v. Budd*,[201] the same court cited the above passage and noted that in deciding whether to send the evidence, the sending judge should consider the conduct of Canadian authorities, including alleged *Charter* violations or abuse of process. However, "the judge will also take into consideration the need to ensure that Canada's international obligations are honoured and to foster co-operation between investigative authorities in different jurisdictions."[202]

These two passages have been heavily cited by subsequent courts, and appear to represent the current judicial consensus on the manner in which a court is to review warrants at the sending hearing. It is settled law that the onus is on the Crown to demonstrate that the warrant was indeed executed in accordance with its terms and conditions, and that a sending order should issue.[203] This presents an interesting contrast with normal procedure, where the onus is on the accused to challenge the warrant or its execution and allege a *Charter* violation.

It is also well established that, in evaluating warrants and their execution, Canadian courts will look to the existing jurisprudence on search warrants and the *Charter* values (specifically section 8) which underpin them. This view is consistent with the Act, which, unlike other federal statutes that contain specific search and seizure provisions,[204] specifically provides for the application of the *Criminal Code* to both search warrants and "other warrants."[205] Whether explicitly or implicitly, the courts have consistently applied the law regarding *Criminal Code* warrants to warrants under the *MLA Act*.[206]

---

201 Above note 194.
202 *Ibid.* at para. 28 [citations omitted].
203 *United States of America v. Sigurdson* (1998), 132 Man. R. (2d) 17 at paras. 21–22 (Q.B.), aff'd (1999), 134 Man. R. (2d) 114 (C.A.); *Wilson*, above note 196 at para. 82; *Germany v. Ebke*, 2001 NWTSC 52 at para. 56; *Canada (Attorney General) v. Hudak*, 2004 BCSC 960 at para. 19 [*Hudak*].
204 Such as the *Income Tax Act*, the *Customs Act*, the *Excise Tax Act*, and the *Fisheries Act*.
205 Above note 181, ss. 10 and 13.1(2).
206 *Ebke*, above note 203 at para. 60; *United States of America v. Future Électronique Inc.* (2000), 151 C.C.C. (3d) 403 at paras. 18–21 (Que. C.A.), leave to appeal to S.C.C. dismissed for mootness, [2001] C.S.C.R. no. 82 [*Future Électronique*]; *United States of America v. Barbarash*, [2002] B.C.J. No. 2803 at para. 13 (S.C. [*Barbarash*]; *Budd*, above note 194 at para. 15. See also *Gladwin*, above note 199, and *Alberta (Attorney General) v. Dawson*, [1999] A.J. No. 809 (Q.B.), leave to appeal refused, [1999] A.J. No. 1332 (C.A.), leave to appeal to S.C.C. refused, [1999] S.C.C.A. No. 570 [*Dawson*]; *Ontario (Commissioner of Competition) v. Falconbridge Ltd.* (2003), 12 C.R. (6th) 243 (Ont. C.A.), leave to appeal to S.C.C. refused, [2003] S.C.C.A. No. 302 [*Falconbridge*]; *United States of America v. Price*, 2007 ONCA 526 [*Price*].

The grounds upon which a warrant or its execution can be challenged are really only limited by the imagination of defence counsel. However, certain issues have attracted a fair bit of scrutiny in the caselaw, including:

- improper participation of a foreign officer in a search, particularly where foreign police are permitted to take copies of documents with them, and thus subverting the whole purpose of the Act and the sending hearing;[207]
- abuse of process by foreign authorities, even when acting in their own jurisdiction;[208]
- facial validity of the warrant, that is, where the warrant on its face does not comply with the Act or with standard search and seizure law;[209]
- problems with sub-facial validity of the warrants, particularly where a great deal of hearsay is relied upon and/or where the information draws on material gleaned from foreign authorities;[210] and
- improper execution of warrants.[211]

An underlying tension that emerges from the caselaw is that courts have been struggling with whether the fact that Canada's transnational crime cooperation obligations are engaged in MLA matters means that the sending judge should be more permissive as to whether standards under Canadian law (particularly the *Charter*) were met, and thus whether the evidence should be sent.[212] The affirmative argument has some merit in some situations—after all, the sending hearing is rough-

---

207 *Mutual Legal Assistance in Criminal Matters Act (Re)*, [1996] O.J. No. 371 at paras. 63–65 (Gen. Div.); *R. v. Rutherford Ltd.* (1995), 101 C.C.C. (3d) 260 at para. 25 (B.C.S.C.); *Ebke*, above note 203; *Canada (Attorney General) v. Schneider*, [2002] B.C.J. No. 1561 (S.C. in Chambers); *United States of America v. Orphanou* (2004), 19 C.R. (6th) 291 (Ont. S.C.J.); *R. v. Budd*, [2004] O.J. No. 3519 (S.C.J.).

208 *United Kingdom v. Wilson-Smith & Co.*, [2002] O.J. No. 5342 (S.C.J.); *Fulfillment Solutions Advantage*, above note 186.

209 *Mutual Legal Assistance in Criminal Matters Act (Re)*, above note 207; *Dawson*, above note 206; *Ebke*, above note 203; *Falconbridge*, above note 206; *Price*, above note 206.

210 *Dawson*, *ibid.*; *Future Électronique*, above note 206; *Barbarash*, above note 206; *United States of America v. Amhaz*, 2002 BCSC 118; *United States of America v. El-Jabsheh*, [2002] B.C.J. No. 1349 (S.C.); *Falconbridge*, above note 206; *Hudak*, above note 203; *Canada (Attorney General) v. Ni-Met Resources Inc.*, [2005] O.J. No. 1169 (C.A.).

211 *Ebke*, above note 203; *Price*, above note 206.

212 For some amplification of this, see the author's (now somewhat dated) article, "Search Warrants under the *Mutual Legal Assistance in Criminal Matters Act*" (2003) 12 C.R. (6th) 275.

ly analogous to a section 24(2) application in a criminal trial, where evidence is often admitted even in the face of *Charter* violations.[213] It is possible to stretch this analogy too far, however, as section 24(2) admission has a constitutional basis, while "sending judges appear to be empowered to send improperly seized evidence on some vague notion of the importance of international comity."[214] The MLATs, after all, explicitly indicate that searches are to be conducted in accordance with the requested state's law, and the Supreme Court of Canada has even framed this as a hard rule.[215] Nonetheless, there are cases where disturbing levels of illegality have been tolerated on this rationale.[216]

iii) Issuing Evidence-Gathering Orders (EGOs)

The evidence-gathering order (EGO) is an investigative device that is unique to the MLA context (though as regards documents, it is similar to a "production order" under section 487.012 of the *Code*). It is a somewhat less intrusive order than a warrant, in that the police do not seize evidence; rather, the EGO requires individuals to attend to give sworn testimony and/or to produce copies of documents, either before a judge or an examiner appointed by the court, or to produce copies of documents alone.[217] The individual can also be compelled to give testimony or produce documents in accordance with the law of the requesting state.[218] An EGO will typically (though not always) be directed at an individual who is not the target of the investigation. It is clearly intended to be the preferred mechanism under the Act since, as noted above, a search warrant should issue only where a judge decides that an EGO would not be appropriate.[219]

As with warrants, under section 17(1), once the "competent authority" has received the approved request and relevant documentation from the IAG, it can apply *ex parte* to the superior court of the province where the evidence may be found for the issuance of an EGO. A judge may issue an EGO where satisfied (though not by "statements under oath," as is the case with warrants) that there are reasonable grounds

---

213 Accord, *Price*, above note 206, Sharpe J.A.

214 R.J. Currie, "*Charter* without Borders? The Supreme Court of Canada, Transnational Crime and Constitutional Rights and Freedoms" (2004) 27 Dal. L.J. 235 at 278.

215 *R. v. Terry*, [1996] 2 S.C.R. 207 at 216.

216 For example, *United States of America v. Maydak*, 2004 BCSC 1550. And see *United States of America v. Black*, [2007] O.J. No. 1304 (S.C.J.).

217 Above note 181, ss. 18(2)(a)–(c).

218 *Ibid.*, s. 18(2)(d). For a case in which this kind of mechanism was applied to a Canadian request made to US authorities, see *R. v. Dorsay*, 2006 BCCA 117.

219 *MLA Act, ibid.*, s. 12(c).

to believe that an offence has been committed and that evidence of the commission of the offence or information that may reveal the whereabouts of the suspect will be found in Canada.[220] The judge may impose conditions deemed desirable,[221] and either the judge or the appointed examiner must produce a report of the results of the execution of the order.[222] The order may be varied on application.[223]

iv)   Challenging the EGO

Generally speaking, the EGO regime has been held to be constitutional[224] and not to require the same safeguards as are required for warrants, given that certain safeguards are already built in.[225] There are essentially three means by which to challenge an EGO. First, targeted individuals (or others with standing) can apply under section 18(6) to set aside the order on the basis that the conditions in section 18(1) have not been met. Arguments that disclosure by the Crown was not sufficient are generally not successful, the courts being convinced that the "reasonable grounds" criterion does not compel or require full *Stinchcombe*-type disclosure.[226] However, "reasonable grounds" is not a paper tiger, either; as Garson J. held in *Sherk v. Canada*:

> [T]he evidence before the authorizing judge must . . . contain sufficient particularity that the authorizing judge can, satisfy himself that there are reasonable grounds to believe the dual requirements of s. 18 are met. It is not sufficient to provide the authorizing judge with an affidavit which screens from the judge a means of assessing the reliability of the evidence as to the commission of the offence and the evidence to be found in Canada. It is the authorizing judge, not

---

220 *Ibid.*, s. 17(2). The EGO is effective throughout Canada (s. 18(4)), and persons required to travel can be reimbursed for travel and living expenses incurred (s. 18(10)).

221 *Ibid.*, s. 18(4), including the sealing of the evidence filed in support of the application; see *United States of America v. Beach* (1999), 132 C.C.C. (3d) 156 (Man. C.A.) [*Beach*].

222 *MLA Act, ibid.*, s. 19.

223 *Ibid.*, s. 18(6).

224 *MacFarlane v. Canada (Attorney General)*, [1995] O.J. No. 4619 (Gen. Div.); *United States of America v. Ross* (1995), 100 C.C.C. (3d) 320 (Que. C.A.) [*Ross*]; *United Kingdom v. Ramsden* (1996), 107 C.C.C. (3d) 104 (Ont. Ct. Gen. Div.) [*Ramsden*].

225 *Falconbridge*, above note 206.

226 *A.L.T. Navigation Ltd. v. United States of America*, [2002] N.J. No. 166 (S.C.T.D.); *Beach*, above note 221; *Sherk v. Canada (Attorney General)*, 2003 BCSC 1216; *Hudak*, above note 203; *Canada (Attorney General) v. Curtis*, 2005 BCSC 516 [*Curtis*].

only the deponent, who must be satisfied of the grounds to issue the order.[227]

Second, section 18(7) anticipates that the individual targeted by the EGO may refuse to answer questions or produce documents on the basis that to do so would violate either "Canadian law of non-disclosure or privilege" or the law of privilege in the requesting state, or would constitute an offence in the requesting state. If the refusal is based on Canadian law, a ruling by a judge is required,[228] and if the objection is overruled, the judge can compel the individual to answer the question or produce the documents, with the backing of a contempt penalty.[229] If the objection is ruled to be valid, that ruling shall be "mentioned in any order that the judge makes under section 20."[230] There is authority to suggest that refusals to answer based on the right to silence under section 7 of the *Charter* will not be valid, but only where the EGO grants the witness use and derivative-use immunity.[231]

If the objection is under the requesting state's law, the objection must be appended to the sending order,[232] though it will be dismissed and the examination or production continued if "a court of the state or entity or a person designated by the state or entity determines that the reasons are not well-founded and the state or entity so advises the Minister."[233]

The final avenue of challenge is by way of the sending hearing under section 20 of the Act, which is similar to the sending hearing for warrants under section 15. The caselaw is much less substantial on this kind of challenge, but it appears that the broad wording of section 20 makes the hearing a fairly open field in terms of what may be argued, and much seems to depend on the facts of the particular case.[234] The Act does not require consideration of the breadth of the EGO or issues as to how it was executed, but courts have thus far been willing to entertain arguments on these points.[235] Failing a challenge to the issuance of the sending order, the person from whom the evidence was seized

---

227 *Sherk, ibid.* at para. 25. See also *Stuckey (Re)*, [1999] B.C.J. No. 2271 (S.C.); *United States of America v. Beach*, [2000] M.J. No. 150 (C.A.).

228 Above note 181, ss. 18(8)(a) and 19(3). For an example of such a ruling, see *Krhanek (Re)*, [2006] B.C.J. No. 1513 (S.C.).

229 *MLA Act, ibid.,* s. 22.

230 *Ibid.,* s. 19(3).

231 *Ross,* above note 224; *Ramsden,* above note 224; *Curtis,* above note 226.

232 Above note 181, s. 19(4).

233 *Ibid.,* s. 20(3).

234 *Pokidyshev,* above note 185.

235 *Canada (Attorney General) v. Foster*, [2006] O.J. No. 4608 (C.A.) [*Foster*].

can apply for the imposition of conditions on the sending order, such as the return of the material to Canada and to what use it may be put by the requesting state.[236]

v) Appeals

Under section 35 of the Act, appeals are available from any decision or order made under the Act, to the provincial courts of appeal. The leave to appeal application must be made within fifteen days, reflecting the expeditious nature of the proceedings. The appeal must be on a point of law alone, and the court of appeal must grant leave. In *Canada (Attorney General) v. Ross*, Southin J.A. of the British Columbia Court of Appeal set out four criteria for leave determination:

1) Is the question raised not settled by authority?
2) Is it of importance generally and, if not of importance generally, is it nonetheless of great importance to a person with serious interests, such as his liberty, at stake?
3) Does the proposition of law put forward have any merit or, to put it another way, does it appear to the judge not to be frivolous?
4) Are there other discretionary considerations, such as prejudice to either the applicant or the requesting state which require to be taken into account?[237]

This framework has been consistently adopted and followed by other Canadian courts.[238]

vi) Costs

Because complying with EGOs, in particular, can be quite onerous, courts have from time to time considered applications for costs to be awarded against the Crown. The small number of cases that have considered the issue[239] have viewed this possibility as a branch of the power to award costs against the Crown in criminal matters generally, and have taken a restrictive approach. There would appear to be a possibility of providing for costs as against the requesting state in an EGO if compliance with the order would be unreasonable;[240] or in a sending

---

236 See, for example, *Stuckey (Re)*, 2000 BCSC 171.

237 [1994] B.C.J. No. 971 at para. 33.

238 *Canada v. China*, above note 195; *Falconbridge*, above note 206; *Ontario (Ministry of the Attorney General) v. Black*, 2007 ONCA 165.

239 *Foster*, above note 235; *Canada (Attorney General) v. Pacific International Securities Inc.*, 2006 BCCA 303.

240 *Foster, ibid.* at paras. 74–75.

order to remedy abuse of process.[241] No such applications have yet been successful.

vii) Other Modalities in Part I of the Act

Sections 9–9.4 of the Act provide for applications to Canadian courts to enforce foreign fines,[242] and orders for restraint, seizure, and forfeiture of property in Canada, the latter being targeted primarily at the proceeds of crime. Sections 22.1–22.4 allow for persons in Canada to give testimony in the foreign state's court by video, while sections 24–25 deal with the transfer of persons detained in Canada to the requested state for live testimony.[243] Sections 30–34 provide for the loaning of exhibits by Canada to a requesting state.

c) Parts II and III of the Act: Canada As Requesting State

i)   The Making of the Request

Requests by Canadian authorities for evidence in foreign states are all fielded through the IAG. The request is an act performed only by the executive, in an exercise of its foreign affairs powers, under the relevant treaty. The Supreme Court of Canada has ruled that section 8 of the *Charter* does not apply to these letters of request, as the request does not constitute a "search" within the meaning of section 8.[244]

ii) Admissibility of Evidence Received

Evidence collected by way of an MLA request is, generally speaking, admissible (or not) according to conventional Canadian evidence law. However, built into sections 36–38 of the Act are provisions which ease the admissibility of foreign records or "things" at trial (particularly to deal with hearsay issues), as well as presumptions of admissibility for documentation which purports to authenticate the records or things. Section 44 provides that, outside use in court, foreign records sent by a requested state are privileged.

In terms of *Charter* exclusion of evidence, the Supreme Court of Canada has been clear that the *Charter* does not apply to the actions of foreign police when they are gathering evidence in their own jurisdictions.[245] However, Canadian courts do have the power to exclude foreign-gathered evidence if admitting it would affect the fairness of the

---

241 *Ibid.* at para. 78. But see *Tele-Mobile Co. v. Ontario*, 2008 SCC 12.
242 See *Zschiegner v. United States of America*, 2001 NSCA 74.
243 For the reciprocal situation, see *MLA Act*, above note 181, ss. 40–42.
244 *Schreiber v. Canada (Attorney General)*, [1998] 1 S.C.R. 841.
245 *R. v. Harrer*, [1995] 3 S.C.R. 562; *Terry*, above note 215; *Hape*, above note 175.

trial, under sections 7 and 11(d) of the *Charter*. The Supreme Court has not been terribly forthcoming with methodology for this type of exclusion, though there is useful lower court authority.[246] This is explained in more detail in Chapter 10.

iii) Foreign Witnesses

Sections 40–42 of the Act, respectively, authorize the Minister to allow persons otherwise inadmissible under the *Immigration and Refugee Protection Act*[247] to enter Canada to give evidence, provide immunity for such persons from criminal or civil proceedings, and obtain an order allowing persons detained abroad to be detained in Canada while they are attending to give effect to a Canadian request.

FURTHER READING

BOTTING, GARY, *Canadian Extradition Law Practice 2009* (Markham, ON: LexisNexis Canada, 2009)

CURRIE, ROBERT J., "Search Warrants under the *Mutual Legal Assistance in Criminal Matters Act*" (2003) 12 C.R. (6th) 276

GILBERT, GEOFF, *Responding to International Crime* (Leiden: Martinus Nijhoff, 2006)

GILMORE, WILLIAM, *Mutual Assistance in Criminal and Business Regulatory Matters* (Cambridge: Cambridge University Press, 1995)

GOLDSTEIN, ROBERT, & NANCY DENNISON, "Mutual Legal Assistance in Canadian Criminal Courts" (2002) 45 Crim. L.Q. 126

KRIVEL, ELAINE, TOM BEVERIDGE, & JOHN HAYWARD, *A Practical Guide to Canadian Extradition* (Toronto: Carswell, 2002)

LA FOREST, ANNE W., *La Forest's Extradition to and from Canada*, 3d ed. (Aurora, ON: Canada Law Book, 1991)

MCCLEAN, DAVID, *International Co-operation in Civil and Criminal Matters* (Oxford: Oxford University Press, 2002)

---

246 See *R. v. Guilbride*, 2003 BCPC 44; *R. v. Mathur*, [2007] O.J. No. 3592 (S.C.J.).
247 S.C. 2001, c. 27.

INTERNATIONAL CRIMINAL COOPERATION, HUMAN RIGHTS, AND THE APPLICATION OF THE *CHARTER*

A. INTRODUCTION

As discussed in the preceding chapter, Canada's international criminal cooperation activities operate at the point of a unique nexus of
international law (both treaty and customary) and domestic laws. The
latter serve two functions: they implement Canada's international law
obligations, but also both empower and control the state in its exercise
of investigational and prosecutorial functions. Historically, in terms of
how these functions operated at the transnational level, they were very
much within the realm of executive discretion, with some limited oversight by the courts. However, the rise of international human rights
law in the latter part of the twentieth century, and in particular the
increasing entrenchments of both substantive and procedural rights for
those facing criminal prosecution, has resulted in increasing scrutiny
of cases which have transnational aspects through the human rights
lens. Particularly since the inception of the *Charter*,[1] Canada, like other
states, has been forced to consider the human rights implications of
its activities and the jurisdictional issues in which they are enmeshed.
For example, should individuals be extradited to foreign states with
poor human rights records? Can Canada lawfully cooperate with such
states, and to what extent? What standards apply to evidence which is

---

1   *Canadian Charter of Rights and Freedoms*, Part I of the *Constitution Act, 1982*, be-
    ing Schedule B to the *Canada Act 1982* (U.K.), 1982, c. 11.

gathered in foreign jurisdictions, and does their scope or applicability differ if Canadian authorities are directly involved? Does the *Charter* apply to any investigational activities that take place outside Canada?

As the final arbiter of these questions, the Supreme Court of Canada has developed what it has identified as "jurisprudence on matters involving Canada's international co-operation in criminal investigations and prosecutions."[2] The fact that there is such a specialized jurisprudence is emblematic of the uncomfortable coexistence of international criminal cooperation and human rights laws, a tension which is in fact being played out throughout the international community. This chapter will survey and analyze these developments,[3] with some effort to assess future directions. Note that the Court's approach has consistently been one of balancing—specifically balancing the protection of human rights by Canadian courts with the need to ensure Canada is able to live up to its international criminal cooperation commitments and "international comity" generally. The result, in many cases, has been a dilution of *Charter* standards in cases of this kind, as the Court seeks to apply the *Charter* differently than it is applied domestically.[4]

B. EXTRADITION, DEPORTATION, AND MUTUAL LEGAL ASSISTANCE

As explored in Chapter 9, extradition was historically a creature of international law and executive discretion. Extradition treaties were instruments that contained binding obligations only as between states, and while there was some judicial oversight of the process, individuals did not have standing before the courts of either the requesting or re-

---

2   *Schreiber v. Canada (Attorney General)*, [1998] 1 S.C.R. 841 at para. 34 [*Schreiber*].

3   While the title of this chapter includes "cooperation," the ambit is also to cover police investigations with extraterritorial aspects, such as cooperative investigations by Canadian and foreign police, and transnational enforcement activities by Canadian authorities generally. While not all such cases are literally "cooperative," there is some element of cooperation in that if Canadian authorities are involved in an investigation anywhere outside Canada, they must be securing some amount of cooperation, even if that means simply the permission of the foreign authorities to be where they are. Otherwise (and particularly if coercive powers are involved), they are likely acting illegally *ab initio*, as it is well established that one state cannot exercise enforcement jurisdiction on the territory of another; see Chapter 2.

4   This theme was developed in greater detail (though pre-*Hape*) in R.J. Currie, "*Charter* without Borders? The Supreme Court of Canada, Transnational Crime and Constitutional Rights and Freedoms" (2004) 27 Dal. L.J. 235.

quested state to invoke any protections they may have enjoyed at international law. This is not to say that there was no protection accorded to the individual in the process. Among common law states, at least, the requesting state was required to put forward a *prima facie* case against the individual in order for him to be committed for extradition. This provided some protection against trial on trumped-up or questionable charges.[5] Also, some of the traditional grounds of refusal in extradition treaties (such as the political offence exception or the non-discrimination clause[6]) tended to provide some protection of human rights in an indirect fashion.[7] However, these latter mechanisms were obligatory only in the sense that the requesting state was bound to accept that, if the requested state had refused extradition on these grounds, the refusal did not breach the extradition treaty. The executive of the requested state was not bound to invoke these grounds and refuse extradition, but was merely legally entitled to do so. For their part, while the courts enjoyed some supervisory powers over the extradition process, they tended to be driven by what is usually referred to as the "rule of non-inquiry" in extradition matters:[8] that courts will not inquire into the rule of law or level of human rights protection in the requesting state, since these are matters best left to the executive in its carrying on of the state's international relations. The courts of the requesting state were, as the Supreme Court of Canada put it, to be "trust[ed] . . . to give the fugitive a fair trial,"[9] *inter alia.*

Most importantly for present purposes, the dominant view was that a state's human rights obligations and its international criminal cooperation obligations were mutually exclusive. Even if the individual was subject to human rights violations in the requesting state, because the requested state was not actually involved in the actual violation of the right(s), it could not be held responsible for a violation of its human rights obligations. This view, which had already been the subject

---

5   See Anne W. La Forest, "The Balance between Liberty and Comity in the Evidentiary Requirements Applicable to Extradition Proceedings" (2002) 28 Queen's L.J. 95.

6   See Chapter 9, Sections B(1)(b)(v) & (vi).

7   See William C. Gilmore, "The Provisions Designed to Protect Fundamental Human Rights in Extradition and Mutual Legal Assistance Treaties" in Commonwealth Secretariat, *International Co-operation in Criminal Matters: Balancing the Protection of Human Rights with the Needs of Law Enforcement* (London: Commonwealth Secretariat, 2001).

8   See Chapter 9, Section B(1)(b)(vii).

9   *Canada v. Schmidt*, [1987] 1 S.C.R. 500 at 524 [*Schmidt*].

of criticism,[10] came under significant attack in the 1990s in a series of remarkable decisions by both international human rights bodies and domestic courts. In a number of decisions, it was found that where individuals were extradited to a state where certain fundamental human rights were threatened, the extraditing state would violate its treaty-based human rights obligations. The most significant of these was the decision of the European Court of Human Rights in *Soering v. United Kingdom*,[11] where the court ruled that "the decision by a Contracting State to extradite a fugitive may give rise to an issue under Article 3 [of the *European Convention on Human Rights*], and hence engage the responsibility of that State under the Convention."[12] Soering, a German national, had appealed the United Kingdom's acquiescence to an extradition request from the United States on murder charges in Virginia, which were subject to the death penalty. The court found that the conditions that would be faced by Soering when on death row in Virginia would constitute "inhuman or degrading treatment or punishment" within the meaning of article 3 of the *Convention*, and thus extradition would breach the United Kingdom's obligation to proscribe such conduct. This, even though the extraditing state was not directly involved in whatever treatment would be faced by the fugitive, but "by reason of its having taken action which has as a direct consequence the exposure of an individual to proscribed ill-treatment."[13] Accordingly, even though complying with its international human rights obligations would obviously have an impact outside that state, this did not amount to extending extraterritorial jurisdiction.[14] What developed under this and other cases was a powerful argument that states will be in violation of their international human rights law obligations (in both their treaty and customary international law forms) when they extradite in-

---

10   Christine van den Wyngaert, "Applying the European Convention on Human Rights to Extradition: Opening Pandora's Box?" (1990) 39 I.C.L.Q. 757.

11   Series A, No. 161 (1989) [*Soering*]. See also the decision of the Supreme Court of the Netherlands in *The Netherlands v. Short*, reprinted in (1990), 29 I.L.M. 1375. Short, an American sergeant stationed in The Netherlands, had killed and dismembered his wife. His extradition was requested by the US under the terms of the NATO Status of Forces Agreement (SOFA). Short faced the death penalty under the US charges, and the Supreme Court found that extraditing him would violate the Netherlands' obligation under *Protocol No. 6* to the *European Convention on Human Rights*, E.T.S. No. 114 (28 April 1983), which prohibits the death penalty.

12   *Soering*, ibid. at para 91.

13   *Ibid.*

14   *Ibid.* at para. 86.

dividuals to face serious human rights violations.[15] The "rule of non-inquiry" has therefore been significantly undermined.

In Canada, the Supreme Court began to grapple with the potential conflict between extradition and human rights protection in the late 1980s. Its jurisprudence has attempted to mitigate the tension between Canada's need to participate in international criminal cooperation efforts, on the one hand, and the protection of the human rights of individuals while they are in Canada, on the other. Early leading cases (authored, as most of the Court's significant extradition cases were, by La Forest J. until his retirement) displayed the themes which animated the Court's balancing exercise. On the one hand, crime suppression is "an important goal of all civilized societies," which requires "effective tools of international cooperation," including extradition.[16] Given the entrenchment of this goal in the long-established extradition process, the *Charter* must necessarily be applied differently to extradition than to other modes of state activity.[17] In particular, the rule of non-inquiry (though La Forest J. generally did not use the phrase) required that the *Charter* not be used to scrutinize foreign legal process too closely, since "[t]he judicial process in a foreign country must not be subjected to finicky evaluations against the rules governing legal process in this country,"[18] and this might in any event result in the application of the *Charter* with objectionable extraterritorial effect.[19]

On the other hand, given the state's involvement, it was clear that the *Charter* must apply to the extradition process itself,[20] and the ap-

---

15   This raises various legal and methodological problems which are mostly beyond the scope of the current discussion. For example, which human rights violations qualify as being sufficiently "serious" for this liability to incur to the extraditing state? In what situations will a refusal to extradite on this "human rights ground" put the requested state in breach of its obligations under the extradition treaty? How is this sort of conflict of international law obligations to be sorted out? For relevant literature on this topic, see John Dugard & Christine van den Wyngaert, "Reconciling Extradition with Human Rights" (1998) 92 A.J.I.L. 187; Sharon Williams, "Human Rights Safeguards and International Cooperation in Extradition: Striking the Balance" (1992) 3 Crim. L.F. 191; N. Jayawickrama, *The Judicial Application of Human Rights Law* (Cambridge: Cambridge University Press, 2002), especially 265–69; Ved Nanda, "Bases for Refusing International Extradition Requests—Capital Punishment and Torture" (2000) 23 Fordham Int'l L.J. 1369; Joanna Harrington, "The Role for Human Rights Obligations in Canadian Extradition Law" (2005) 43 Can. Y.B. Int'l Law 45.
16   *United States v. Cotroni*, [1989] 1 S.C.R. 1469 at 1485.
17   *Ibid.* at 1490–91.
18   *Schmidt*, above note 9 at 522–23.
19   *Ibid.* at 523; *United States of America v. Allard*, [1987] 1 S.C.R. 564 at 571.
20   *Schmidt, ibid.* at 518.

propriate vehicle for that application was section 7 — to wit, Canada had to ensure that the surrender[21] of individuals was consistent with the deprivation of freedom in accordance with the principles of fundamental justice. These principles were to be specifically tailored for the extradition process, however, shaped by "the concepts of reciprocity, comity and respect for differences in other jurisdictions."[22] The heart of the balancing, then, was that courts should be circumspect in assessing Ministerial orders for surrender, overturning them only where "the nature of the criminal procedures or penalties in a foreign country sufficiently shocks the conscience. . . ."[23] The Court later elucidated the "shocks the conscience" test, indicating that it was made out if the fugitive could prove that the treatment in the foreign state would be "simply unacceptable" and

> offends the Canadian sense of what is fair, right and just, bearing in mind the nature of the offence and penalty, the foreign justice system and considerations of comity and security, and according due latitude to the Minister to balance the conflicting considerations.[24]

As to what kind of treatment would meet this threshold, La Forest J. initially offered the example of torture, but noted that the conscience might be shocked in "[s]ituations falling far short of this."[25] In 1991, however, the Court faced the starkest yet test of their balancing exercise, in the companion cases of *Kindler v. Canada (Minister of Justice)*[26] and *Reference Re Ng Extradition*.[27] Kindler was a convicted killer who had escaped custody in Pennsylvania, while Ng was accused of horrific crimes in California, and each faced the death penalty upon extradition. Both were ordered to be surrendered pursuant to US extradition requests, and both had their appeals of the surrender orders dismissed by the Court. Under the Canada–US extradition treaty, the Minister had the ability to seek assurances from the American government that execution would not be carried out,[28] but refused to do so. The Court found that, given the lack of an international law prohibition on the death penalty, this refusal affected the fugitives' liberty and security interests under section

---

21 Section 7 also applies to the judicial phase of extradition; see Chapter 9.
22 *Kindler v. Canada (Minister of Justice)*, [1991] 2 S.C.R. 779 at para. 160 [*Kindler*].
23 *Schmidt*, above note 9 at 522.
24 *Kindler*, above note 22 at para. 176.
25 *Schmidt*, above note 9 at 522.
26 Above note 22.
27 [1991] 2 S.C.R. 858.
28 Can. T.S. 1976 No. 3, as amended by *Protocol 1*, Can. T.S. 1991 No. 37, and *Protocol 2*, Can. T.S. 2000 No. 11, art. 6.

7 but did not ultimately offend the principles of fundamental justice, as applied within the extradition context. These judgments, by the highest appellate court of an abolitionist state, were roundly criticized by both foreign courts[29] and distinguished commentators.[30]

Ten years later, the Court abruptly reversed itself on the specific matter of extradition to face the death penalty. In *United States of America v. Burns*,[31] the two fugitives were wanted on capital charges in Washington State for the bloody slaying of Rafay's family. The Minister ordered their surrender and refused to request assurances that the death penalty would not be imposed. In a unanimous judgment, the Court held that extradition to face the death penalty will, in all but exceptional circumstances (which it declined to define), "shock the conscience of Canadians" and violate a fugitive's rights under section 7. The Minister was constitutionally required to seek assurances, and to decline surrender if they were not forthcoming. The Court justified this shift on the basis that, since *Kindler* and *Ng*, it had become clearer that Canada had adopted the abolition of the death penalty as a principle of fundamental justice, and that on a review of international activity on the question, there was "significant movement towards acceptance internationally" of this principle.[32] This section 7 analysis was repeated several months later in *Suresh v. Canada (Minister of Citizenship and Immigration)*,[33] where the Court assimilated its extradition analysis to deportation under immigration law and ruled that deportation to face torture would almost

---

29 For example, *Pratt v. Attorney General for Jamaica*, [1993] 4 All E.R. 769 (J.C.P.C.). It should be noted that the Supreme Court was not unanimous on these decisions. Particularly noteworthy are the dissenting reasons of Cory J. in *Kindler*, above note 22, where he used both *Soering*, above note 11, and international human rights law generally to hold that the surrender should be invalidated.

30 For example, see William Schabas, *International Human Rights Law and the Canadian Charter*, 2d ed. (Scarborough, ON: Carswell, 1996) at 233.

31 [2001] 1 S.C.R. 283 [*Burns*].

32 *Ibid.* at para. 89. The Court also gave a more thorough explanation of what the "fundamental principles of justice" were in the extradition context, relying for the result in this case on increased concern about wrongful conviction in both Canada and the US; see Currie, "Charter without Borders," above note 4 at 260–65. As Freeman and van Ert point out, neither the Court's use of international law sources nor its constitutional methodology is entirely clear (Mark Freeman & Gibran van Ert, *International Human Rights Law* (Toronto: Irwin Law, 2004) at 253–54).

33 [2002] 1 S.C.R. 3 [*Suresh*]. Suresh was suspected of being a member of the Tamil Tiger terrorist organization and his deportation was ordered on this basis; however, he led a *prima facie* case that he would likely be tortured by that very organization if he was deported back to Sri Lanka, which necessitated judicial review of the deportation order and gave rise to the Supreme Court's decision.

always "shock the conscience" and be unconstitutional. In *Suresh*, however, as in *Burns*, the Court was explicit in not foreclosing the possibility that extradition or deportation to face death or torture could, on some limited facts disclosing pressing governmental objectives, be consistent with the principles of fundamental justice under section 7 (or a justifiable limitation under section 1).[34] This, despite the fact that Canada is obliged under article 3 of the United Nations *Convention against Torture*[35] not to deport individuals to states where they will face torture. *Suresh*, like *Kindler*, has been roundly criticized.[36]

In the meantime, however, the international law developments referred to earlier have come to haunt Canada's extradition and deportation practices. Kindler[37] and Ng[38] both petitioned the UN Human Rights Committee,[39] arguing that by extraditing them Canada had violated their rights under articles 6 (right to life) and 7 (prohibition of cruel, inhuman, or degrading treatment or punishment) of the *International Covenant on Civil and Political Rights (ICCPR)*. The Committee held that in extraditing an individual to face a "real risk" of violations of their human rights in the requesting state, Canada could incur responsibility for violating the *ICCPR*.[40] It determined that Kindler's extradition did not violate the *ICCPR*, as the death penalty was not, *per se*, a violation of the right to life or cruel or unusual treatment, in accordance with article 6(2) of the treaty.[41] Ng's extradition, however, was held to have violated article 6, as the technique of execution by gas asphyxiation that he faced constituted cruel and inhuman treatment and thus violated article 6. Ten years later, the Committee again ruled against

---

34   *Burns*, above note 31 at para. 133; *Suresh*, *ibid.* at para. 78.

35   (1984) 1465 U.N.T.S. 85, Can. T.S. 1987 No. 36.

36   See UN Committee against Torture, *Consideration of Reports Submitted by States Parties under Article 19 of the Convention: Concluding Observations (Canada)*, online: www.pch.gc.ca/pgm/pdp-hrp/docs/cat/105-eng.cfm#a4 at para. 4(a).

37   *Kindler v. Canada* (1993), Comm. No. 470/1991, UN Doc. CCPR/C/48/D/470/1991.

38   *Ng v. Canada* (1993), Comm. No. 469/1991, UN Doc. CCPR/C/49/D/469/1991. See also *Cox v. Canada* (1994), Comm. No. 539/1993, UN Doc. CCPR/C/52/D/539/1993.

39   The UN Human Rights Committee is the supervisory body over whether state parties to the *ICCPR* are complying with their obligations. It is important to note, however, that while the Committee's views are authoritative interpretations of the treaty, these views are issued in the form of non-binding recommendations which are not legally enforceable in Canadian law. For more, see Freeman & van Ert, above note 32, c. 14.

40   *Kindler v. Canada*, above note 37 at para. 13.2.

41   *Ibid.* at para. 15.1.

Canada in the case of Roger Judge,[42] a convicted American murderer who escaped from prison and fled to Canada, from where he was deported in 1998. The Committee found that, by this time, international law developments had moved along sufficiently that an abolitionist state, such as Canada, had an obligation not to expose an individual to a real risk of the death penalty being imposed, whether via deportation or extradition.[43] Accordingly, Canada had violated Judge's right to life under article 6 of the *ICCPR*.

It is clear from the Supreme Court's jurisprudence on the interaction of human rights and international criminal cooperation that in all but the most exceptional circumstances, individuals cannot be extradited or deported from Canada to face either the death penalty or torture in a foreign state. This is because extradition or deportation under these circumstances would be inconsistent with the fundamental principles of justice and violate the individual's rights under section 7 of the *Charter*. It is beyond doubt that there is a great deal that is salutary in the results of these cases, and to some extent the approach is superior to what had been previously employed. Certainly, no one weeps for Kindler, Ng, or Burns. However, there is a great deal which is unclear; for example, which violations of which rights will invoke the protection of section 7 in this manner? There has been only one case since *Burns* in which the courts were willing to overturn a surrender order by applying the "shocks the conscience" test, where the individual had made a compelling case of gross violations of the basic procedural rights of his co-accuseds, compounded by grave misgivings about judicial independence in the requesting state.[44] On the other hand, individuals have been extradited to states with extremely poor human rights records, such as Thailand,[45] when the courts were either satisfied that the Minister was properly relying on credible diplomatic assurances regarding the treatment the individual would face upon extradition, or dissatisfied with the case made by the individual as to that treatment. More pressing, perhaps, is the question of what constitutes the "exceptional circumstances" that the Supreme Court has held will

---

42   *Judge v. Canada* (2003), Comm. No. 829/1998, UN Doc. CCPR/C/78/D/829/1998 [*Judge*].

43   *Ibid.* at para. 10.4.

44   *Canada (Minister of Justice) v. Pacificador* (2002), 60 O.R. (3d) 685 (C.A.), leave to appeal to S.C.C. refused, [2002] S.C.C.A. No. 390.

45   *Thailand v. Saxena*, 2006 BCCA 98, leave to appeal to S.C.C. refused, [2006] S.C.C.A. No. 147; reconsideration denied, 2009 BCCA 223.

justify extradition or deportation even to face death or torture, which has not received any subsequent clarification.[46]

In my view, as it stands, there are two interrelated problems with the Court's approach to these cases: the constitutional methodology and the international law methodology. I have argued elsewhere[47] that the Court's constitutional methodology is, with respect, faulty. It justifies the application of section 7 to the extradition/deportation context by positing that, since the individual will face the actual human rights violation only in the requesting state, the government of Canada is somehow outside the chain of causation of the violation. It suggests that Canada is implicated only in the extradition/deportation *process*, where the fate of the fugitive is relevant but not governing, rather than the treatment of the fugitive himself. Accordingly, while an individual present in Canada and facing death or torture in a foreign country would logically argue that the *Charter* right engaged is section 12's protection against cruel and unusual treatment or punishment,[48] the Court immunizes Canada from the actual right engaged in favour of balancing the fundamental rights under the limitations inherent in section 7. This gives a much wider scope of latitude to the government of the day.

Such latitude, however, justifiable as it might have been in traditional (and pre-*Charter*) extradition matters, has outlived its usefulness. The analytical process which underpins it is flawed. It is simply too difficult to accept that the extradition of the individual by the government of Canada is "too remote from the possible imposition of the penalty complained of to attract the attention of section 12."[49] As the Human Rights Committee remarked in finding Canada liable for breaching its obligations under the *ICCPR* in the *Judge* case, "Canada established the crucial link in the causal chain that would make possible [his] execution."[50] By any sensible legal analysis, sending someone off to meet his doom in a foreign state makes the sending state one of the authors of that doom. By contrast, constraining the state from acting in this way by applying section 12 does not, as the Court has suggested, result in an extraterritorial application of the *Charter*, since

---

46   In *Charkaoui v. Canada (Citizenship and Immigration)*, [2007] 1 S.C.R. 350, the Supreme Court expressly declined to address this issue, which it held was not specifically before it.

47   Currie, "*Charter* without Borders," above note 4.

48   And indeed this has been consistently argued before, and rejected by, the Court, though Cory J. agreed with this logic in dissent in *Kindler*, above note 22 at paras. 108–9.

49   *Kindler, ibid.* at para. 169, McLachlin J.; *Burns*, above note 31 at paras. 50–57.

50   *Judge*, above note 42 at para. 10.6.

if the extradition of an individual to face torture is itself "cruel and unusual treatment or punishment," then (consistently with *Soering*[51]) the
state violates the right if it does so.

The use of section 7 as the analytical focus also exemplifies the
problem with the Court's international law methodology in these
cases—namely, that it is dealing only with the obligations under the
extradition treaties while resolutely refusing to engage with Canada's
international human rights law obligations. The *Charter* itself implements most of Canada's major obligations under the *ICCPR*, yet it is
treated by the Court as if it is a stand-alone constitutional instrument,
devoid of international law context or content. There is now almost
two decades of caselaw and authoritative opinions which extend states'
human rights obligations to the extradition and deportation processes.
This body of law includes findings by an authoritative interpretive body
of the *ICCPR* regarding the relevant human rights treaty to which Canada is a party, and indeed includes findings against Canada on this very
point. Yet the Court (outside dissenting opinions) has never turned
its attention to whether its entire analytical structure which applies
the *Charter* to extradition and deportation is consistent with Canada's
human rights obligations.[52] Thus, while perhaps neither an *Ng* nor a
Judge would happen today, Canada continues to inelegantly dodge its
international human rights law obligations because neither the Court
nor the government will engage with them.

Similar considerations must apply in the context of mutual legal
assistance (MLA), particularly where Canada is the requested state.[53] If
Canada sends evidence to a foreign state for use in the criminal prosecution of an individual, then Canada may in some circumstances be
implicated in any human rights violations that occur. Yet the paucity
of discussion of this point in the international context is mirrored by

---

51   Above note 11.

52   The notion of using "the principles of fundamental justice" as a weighing fac-
      tor in determining whether a right has been violated is, as Freeman and van
      Ert point out, a uniquely Canadian invention which does not emerge from the
      corpus of international human rights law (Freeman & van Ert, above note 32
      at 255). Accordingly, it would provide no defence to a state responsibility claim
      that Canada had violated its human rights obligations.

53   While it is beyond the present scope to explore it, by the same logic this must
      also apply to more informal modes of policing cooperation, particularly police
      officers rendering assistance to foreign police. The RCMP has recently been
      engaged in developing a policy on how to deal with requests for assistance from
      death penalty states or those with poor human rights records; see Jim Bronskill,
      "Info-sharing Gap Stalling Criminal Cases: RCMP Memo" *Canadian Press* (2
      August 2009).

the small amount of consideration it has gathered in caselaw under the *Mutual Legal Assistance in Criminal Matters Act (MLA Act)*.[54]

This is, in and of itself, not terribly surprising. As noted in Chapter 9, there is certainly scope for the reviewing judge in the context of hearings under either of sections 15 or 20 of the *MLA Act* to consider both the conduct of the foreign state and the uses to which the evidence will be put if it is sent.[55] To date, however, there have not been any reported cases where a *Burns*-type situation arose, that is, where the person under investigation requested the court to refuse to send the evidence on account of potential human rights violations (or other state misconduct) in the requesting state. This is likely due to two factors: first, many MLA requests occur prior to the subject of the investigation being charged, so that individual cannot demonstrate that, for example, he will face a capital charge if Canada cooperates. Second, most of the MLA traffic handled in Canada arises under the Canada–US treaty, and aside from capital cases there tends to be little in American prosecutions which has motivated Canadian courts to question the human rights aspects of these matters.[56] Another possibility is that International Assistance Group officials screen out or refuse requests which would engage such concerns, or recommend to treaty partners that requests be modified.

However, as Canada's network of MLA treaties expands, it seems inevitable that a case will come before the courts where the person being investigated is aware of specific criminal charges/penalties that he faces, and attempts to make out a case that he faces human rights violations under the foreign prosecutorial process. When this time arrives, the reviewing courts at the sending hearings will have to wrestle with the methodological problems outlined above, to wit: how is the *Charter* to be applied to MLA practice? In terms of the existing authorities, the obvious analogy is to the "shocks the conscience" test and the corresponding balancing exercise under section 7, and this framework would seem to be the one that is logically applicable. This will entail an exploration of what the "fundamental principles of justice" are in MLA practice, and a tailoring of the test for this particular setting. It will also be a prime opportunity for Canadian courts (and particularly the Supreme Court of Canada) to engage with the issue that has thus far been ignored in extradition jurisprudence: under what circumstances will cooperating with the requesting state violate Canada's international

---

54   R.S.C. 1985 (4th Supp.), c. 30.

55   See *United Kingdom v. Wilson-Smith & Co.*, [2002] O.J. No. 5342 (S.C.J.).

56   Though see the discussion of *Khadr v. Canada (Minister of Justice)*, below note 140, in Section C(3), below in this chapter.

human rights law obligations, and does the *Charter* demand that the court refuse to send the evidence in circumstances where there is a real risk that the prosecution in which it is used will violate the individual's human rights? This inquiry could, in turn, involve a reconsideration of the current section 7 test as I have proposed above. [57] Given that the courts have been willing to tolerate looser procedural (and thus human rights) standards in the MLA setting,[58] however, expectations for developments on this point should probably be modest.

C. ADMISSIBILITY OF EVIDENCE GATHERED IN FOREIGN STATES

1) Evidence Gathered by Foreign Officials

It is axiomatic that, in criminal trials held before Canadian courts, the admissibility of evidence is to be judged by Canadian standards, and thus Canada's law of evidence applies. This is true both of cases that are purely domestic and those which have transnational aspects; so, for example, in a case where the accused is alleged by the Crown to have made a confession to a foreign police officer in a foreign state, the court determines the admissibility of the confession under the regime set out by the Supreme Court of Canada in *R. v. Oickle*[59] and determines whether the confession was voluntarily made.[60] However, there have been cases where accused persons wished to make *Charter* challenges to the admission of evidence gathered in foreign states—either by foreign officials (dealt with in this section), or by Canadian officials acting in the foreign state (see Sections C(2) and (3), below in this chapter). A distinct stream of caselaw has developed on this point, which has centred on two themes: maintaining trial fairness, and not applying the *Charter* in such a way as to give it objectionable extraterritorial effect. The Court itself has framed the balance to be struck as one that "achieve[s] a just

---

57 It is often argued that the provision of mutual legal assistance does not engage the individual's rights as directly as extradition (for example, J. Sheedy, "International Legal Obligations under Human Rights Instruments" in Commonwealth Secretariat, above note 7). To the extent this is so (and I would submit it is faulty at least as regards gross human rights obligations), then the s. 7 analysis might be more appropriate to the MLA context than it is, as I have argued here, to extradition/ deportation.

58 See Chapter 9, Section D(2)(b)(iii).

59 [2000] 2 S.C.R. 3.

60 See *Thomas c. R.*, (2006), 33 C.R. (6th) 336 (Que. C.A.).

accommodation between the interests of the individual and those of the state in providing a fair and workable system of justice."[61]

It is reasonably well settled that the *Charter* does not apply to the actions of foreign officials, though evidence may be excluded if the foreign officials obtained it in such a way that its admission would make the accused's trial unfair. This was first determined by the Supreme Court of Canada in *R. v. Harrer*,[62] where the accused sought to have excluded a statement she had made while under arrest and questioning by American police, because the right-to-counsel warning she was given had not been in accordance with *Charter* standards. The Court held that the *Charter* did not apply to the interrogations, "because the governments mentioned in s. 32(1) were not implicated in these activities"[63] and because doing so would amount to objectionable extraterritorial application of the *Charter*. "[I]t is obvious," wrote La Forest J. for the Court, "that Canada cannot impose its own procedural requirements on other countries."[64] A similar finding was made in *R. v. Terry*,[65] where the accused fled to California after allegedly committing a murder in British Columbia. He was questioned by US police—this time acting on a request from Canadian police—and was advised of his right to counsel in accordance with US procedure, which did not conform to Canadian law. The Supreme Court ruled that the statement Terry gave should not be excluded, McLachlin J. emphasizing "the exclusivity of the foreign state's sovereignty within its territory, where its law alone governs the process of enforcement."[66] Justice McLachlin confirmed the Court's refusal to apply the *Charter* to foreign police even if they were cooperating with Canadian authorities, stating specifically that "any cooperative investigation involving law enforcement agencies of Canada and the United States will be governed by the laws of the jurisdiction in which the activity is undertaken."[67]

There is a strong policy rationale underpinning these judgments. It is highly arguable, and implicit in the Court's approach,[68] that the *Charter* rights typically at stake in a criminal investigation pertain at the time of the actual police activities themselves, for example, the

---

61   *R. v. Harrer*, [1995] 3 S.C.R. 562 at para. 14.
62   *Ibid.*
63   *Ibid.* at para. 12.
64   *Ibid.* at para. 15.
65   [1996] 2 S.C.R. 207.
66   *Ibid.* at para. 19.
67   *Ibid.*
68   See Ed Morgan, "In the Penal Colony: Internationalism and the Canadian Constitution" (1999) 49 U.T.L.J. 447 at 462.

rights to silence and counsel, and to freedom from unreasonable search and seizure. Foreign police officers can conduct these activities only in accordance with their own national laws and procedures, which will inevitably differ in some respects from Canadian standards, and thus applying the *Charter* to them is unworkable. As McLachlin J. wrote in *Harrer*, "it is not reasonable to expect [foreign police] to comply with details of Canadian law. To insist on conformity to Canadian law would be to insist on external application of the *Charter* in preference to local law. It would render prosecution of offences with international aspects difficult if not impossible."[69] Moreover, as Lamer J. pointed out in *Schreiber*, when a person leaves Canada they leave behind Canadian procedural protections and must submit to the law of the state where they have gone.[70] The *locus* of their interactions with the authorities of the foreign state is not within the jurisdiction of Canadian courts.

The Court was clear in both cases, however, as well as in subsequent decisions,[71] that the *Charter* does apply to the trial held in Canada. It thus determined that any evidence gathered by foreign officials could be excluded if its admission would produce significant unfairness in the trial, under sections 7 and 11(d) of the *Charter*. This might happen where the evidence was taken in such a manner as to render it unreliable, where its misleading qualities might outweigh its probative value, or where the conduct of the foreign police was so abusive that admission of the evidence would "irremediably taint the fairness of the trial itself"[72] or would be "an anathema to the Canadian conscience."[73] The degree to which the conduct of the foreign police conforms with or falls below Canadian standards, and indeed whether the foreign police acted in conformity with their own laws, are factors the courts can consider in deciding whether to exclude:[74] "it may be that the law of the foreign jurisdiction has been abused by the authorities . . . rendering it unfair to receive the evidence."[75] In the later case of *Hape*, Lebel J. added the following:

> The circumstances in which the evidence was gathered must be considered in their entirety to determine whether admission of the

---

69   Above note 61 at para. 55.
70   Above note 2 at paras. 23–24. See also *R. v. Hape*, [2007] 2 S.C.R. 292 at para. 99 [*Hape*].
71   *Schreiber*, above note 2; *R. v. Cook*, [1998] 2 S.C.R. 597; *Hape*, ibid.
72   *Harrer*, above note 61 at para. 46.
73   *Ibid.* at para. 51.
74   *Ibid.* at paras. 13–18; *Terry*, above note 65 at para. 25; *Hape*, above note 70 at para. 111.
75   *Harrer*, ibid. at para. 51.

evidence would render a Canadian trial unfair. The way in which the evidence was obtained may make it unreliable, as would be true of conscriptive evidence, for example. The evidence may have been gathered through means, such as torture, that are contrary to fundamental *Charter* values. Such abusive conduct would taint the fairness of any trial in which the evidence was admitted[.][76]

The lower courts have tended to apply the *Harrer/Terry* formula fairly mechanically when they apply it at all, as these cases are usually used by judges to support a finding that the *Charter* does not apply to foreign officials, and the exclusionary formula is mentioned far more often than it is applied. There are only a few cases in which accused persons sought to challenge the admissibility of evidence gathered by foreign police, but these decisions highlight the complexities that are added to a case when there is a transnational element. In *Thomas c. R.*,[77] the Quebec Court of Appeal ruled on the admissibility of a confession made by the accused to police officers in Jamaica, which the Crown sought to adduce in evidence against him. The accused sought to have the confession excluded both as involuntary, under the common law confessions rule, and alternatively pursuant to the *Charter*. Neither the Court nor counsel appeared to be fully prepared to deal with the issues;[78] the court ruled only on the common law voluntariness issue while ignoring the *Terry* argument in any substance, while the accused argued that the Crown's failure to prove that the Jamaican police had complied with that state's law in gathering the confession meant that the statement should be excluded under section 7. The latter argument must be seen as flawed, since the burden would be on the accused to prove any violation of section 7, including the unlawfulness of the foreign police conduct. However, the court failed to engage with it or exercise any methodology to examine the *Charter* claim. This case also highlights the problem that proving violations of foreign law by foreign police will often be extremely difficult for the accused, because access to the foreign police is only by way of the Crown, which is not under an obligation to obtain evidence from the foreign state for use by the accused.[79]

A better methodology can be seen in *R. v. Guilbride*,[80] an admissibility decision in the course of a long and complex narcotics traf-

---

76   *Hape*, above note 70 at para. 109 [citation omitted].
77   Above note 60.
78   See Robert Currie, "Annotation" (2006) 33 C.R. (6th) 336.
79   See *R. v. Mathur*, [2007] O.J. No. 3592 (S.C.J.).
80   [2003] B.C.J. No. 389, 2003 BCPC 44. And see *Mathur, ibid.*

ficking trial involving investigative cooperation between Canadian and Greek authorities. At issue was the installation of a tracking device on the accused's ship, for which the RCMP had received a warrant in Vancouver. When the ship arrived in Crete, RCMP officers sought the assistance of local authorities in Greece, and were told incorrectly that neither local judicial authorization nor the presence of a Greek public prosecutor was required for the installation. Provincial Court Judge Arnold had earlier ruled that this resulted in several significant violations of Greek criminal procedural law by the Greek officials who installed the device,[81] and was requested by the defence to exclude the evidence under section 7 of the *Charter*.

Judge Arnold pointed out that, despite the Supreme Court's decisions in *Harrer* and *Terry*, there was still no test for the admissibility of foreign-gathered evidence nor for the effect that should be given to unlawful conduct by the foreign police.[82] Her Honour then distilled from the then-existing caselaw[83] two useful catalogues of factors. The first was those factors "that assist in evaluating potential trial unfairness":

- the nature of the evidence, including whether it is conscriptive or non-conscriptive;
- whether the evidence collected and the methods employed have resulted in reliable, non-tainted evidence;
- the involvement of Canadian law enforcement officers in its collection, including issues of "good" and "bad" faith;
- whether foreign and/or Canadian police activities were oppressive or abusive in nature;
- whether the evidence was collected in an unfair manner;
- whether other aspects of the investigation exacerbate or minimize the alleged unfairness;
- the probative value to be attached to the evidence; and
- the degree of similarity between the legal system in the foreign country and the Canadian legal system.[84]

The second list was of relevant considerations in addition to those above, regarding "how to approach the admission of foreign-gathered evidence, when the requirements of the domestic law in the foreign

---

81 [2002] B.C.J. No. 1594.
82 *Ibid.* at para. 45.
83 The decision was issued before *Hape*, though *Hape* does not add much to the mix.
84 Above note 80 at para. 70. One might speculate that the last criterion could involve some evaluation of whether the foreign law compares unfavourably to Canadian law as regards fairness—though this would require the judge to walk a rather fine line and avoid the appearance of criticizing the foreign law.

state have subsequently been determined not to have been complied with":

- the nature and extent of the non-compliance with the law of the foreign state;
- whether the violations of foreign law were criminal or penal in nature;
- the efforts made by Canadian law enforcement officials to ensure that foreign requirements were met;
- the activities of the Canadian police to address irregularities in non-compliance with the foreign law; and
- whether the same kind of legal non-compliance, if it occurred in Canada, would be likely to render the evidence inadmissible in the context of *Charter* violation and an analysis pursuant to section 24(2).[85]

Applying these findings,[86] she easily found that the RCMP had demonstrated good faith at all times and that the breaches of Greek law had been inadvertent. Given the seriousness of the crime and the probative value and reliability of the evidence, it was held to be admissible.

In terms of evidence gathered pursuant to a specific request by Canada to the foreign state under the *MLA Act*,[87] one sees few if any reported challenges to the presumed admissibility regime under Part II of the Act. It has also been clear since *Schreiber*[88] that a request by Canada to a foreign state to gather evidence on its behalf does not constitute a "search" within the meaning of section 8 of the *Charter*, and thus the state does not have to obtain a warrant to underpin the request. In that case the Supreme Court did re-emphasize the *Harrer/Terry* holding that while the *Charter* did not apply to the foreign authorities' evidence-gathering, the evidence could be excluded under sections 7 and 11(d) if its admission would make the trial unfair. Those cases which deal with the admissibility of evidence taken pursuant to a Canadian MLA request have tended to be evaluated by way of reference to the *Harrer/Terry* formula.[89]

An interesting recent case is *R. v. Dorsay*.[90] The accused, a Canadian resident of the state of Washington, was being investigated for

---

85   *Ibid.* at para. 71.
86   *Ibid.* at paras. 73–90.
87   See Chapter 9, Section D(2)(c).
88   Above note 2.
89   For example, *R. v. Yashnev*, [1995] O.J. No. 3599 (Gen. Div.), applying *Harrer*, above note 61.
90   (2006), 42 C.R. (6th) 155, 2006 BCCA 117, leave to appeal to S.C.C. refused, [2006] S.C.C.A. No. 374.

the murder of his child and had allegedly admitted his involvement to his psychiatric caregivers in the US. The Vancouver Crown wished to obtain the testimony of the caregivers and made a request under the *Canada–US Mutual Legal Assistance Treaty* (MLAT).[91] As is typical of MLATs, the treaty provides that evidence should be taken in accordance with the law of the requesting state, in order to maintain the integrity of that state's law. However, the applicable US law granted an absolute privilege for psychiatric records, and it was unlikely that the caregivers could be compelled. Therefore, pursuant to the treaty, the Crown asked the American authorities to allow Canadian law — which has no such privilege — to be applied to the giving of testimony, and the US courts assented. The testimony was thus taken in a US courtroom, applying Canadian evidence law. The accused challenged the admissibility of the evidence under section 7 of the *Charter* on the basis that depriving him of the privilege under US law rendered his trial unfair. The trial judge's ruling in favour of the accused was overturned by the Court of Appeal, which ordered a new trial in which the evidence would be admissible.

Dorsay displays a level of flexible cooperation between the police and courts of two states that can definitely enhance inter-jurisdictional investigations. Yet it is troubling that the effect of this cooperation in the Canadian criminal trial was to allow the Crown to subvert both an aspect of American evidence law which protected the accused, and the full effect of the *Charter*. It is difficult to escape the conclusion that the Crown was permitted to pick and choose the application of Canadian law where it suited the prosecution, while using the transnational aspect as a shield against the full power of the *Charter* being applied. While the Supreme Court has been clear that section 7 of the *Charter* does not entitle an accused to the fairest proceedings possible, it has also stated that the *Charter* guarantees are only the bare minimum that should be expected and, one would have thought, discouraged this kind of "race to the bottom" of constitutional standards.

2) Evidence Gathered by Canadian Officials

The foregoing caselaw dealt primarily with situations where foreign officials were exercising investigative jurisdiction in their own states and, as has been seen, the Supreme Court of Canada has essentially relied on two criteria for dealing with such cases: avoiding extraterritorial

---

91   *Treaty between the Government of Canada and the Government of the United States of America on Mutual Legal Assistance in Criminal Matters*, Can. T.S. 1990 No. 19.

application of the *Charter*, and the importance of Canada's international-al criminal cooperation obligations and practices. The situation shifts significantly when, as is happening increasingly frequently, Canadian officials are engaged in investigative activities in foreign states. While there are a number of important legal issues raised by these activities, the reported cases tend to focus on challenges to the admissibility of evidence based on the role or activities undertaken by Canadian police engaged in cooperative investigations with foreign officials, where the resulting criminal trial takes place in Canada. As will be seen, both the legal status of these activities and the implications for admissibility of evidence gathered in this manner are currently extremely unsettled in Canadian law, and the Supreme Court of Canada has been badly divided on these issues for a decade.

It is clear that, even when they are operating in foreign states, the activities of Canadian police officers are not free from judicial—particularly *Charter*-based—scrutiny at the stage of a criminal trial held in Canada. It has been held that violations of a foreign state's law which implicate Canadian officials can affect the entire integrity of the Canadian court's proceedings, and evidence will be excluded on this basis.[92] Beyond that relatively narrow point, however, the water becomes a great deal murkier.

In both *Harrer* and *Terry*, the Court did not foreclose the potential for extraterritorial application of the *Charter*,[93] and La Forest J. had anticipated that this might be possible where it was Canadian police conducting the investigation in the foreign state.[94] This very situation arose soon after in *R. v. Cook*,[95] where Cook had fled to Louisiana after committing a murder in Vancouver. He was detained by police in New Orleans pursuant to an extradition request from Canada, and these officers allowed Canadian RCMP officers to question Cook. During the questioning, the RCMP officers gave a right-to-counsel warning that was seriously defective under *Charter* standards, and at trial Cook sought to have excluded the statements given during the interroga-

---

92 See *R. v. Dunphy* (1996), 140 Nfld. & P.E.I. R. 8 (N.L.S.C.T.D.); *Guilbride*, above note 80 at para. 25. Something resembling the converse was found in *United States of America v. Licht*, 2002 BCSC 1151, where an extradition proceeding initiated by the US was stayed because American authorities had conducted investigations in Canada that were not authorized by Canadian authorities, and thereby breached both Canadian drug and immigration laws.

93 *Harrer*, above note 61 at para. 11; in *Terry*, above note 65, the lack of foreclosure is arguably implicit.

94 *Harrer*, *ibid*.

95 Above note 71.

tion pursuant to section 24(2). The primary question before the Court was whether the *Charter* could be applied at all to the actions of the Canadian police when they were on American soil, and seven of the nine justices answered in the affirmative. Justices Cory and Iacobucci, writing for themselves, Lamer C.J., and Major and Binnie JJ., posited a two-part justification for what they viewed as a permissible extraterritorial application of the *Charter*. First, since the officers were arms of the Canadian state, they were inherently amenable to *Charter* application under section 32, irrespective of their geographical location. The *Charter* could be applied to their actions on the basis of the officers' nationality, which was a well-known and accepted jurisdictional principle under international law. Second, this was an application of the *Charter* to Canadian police, conducting an interrogation pursuant to a Canadian investigation in which the US had no interest other than cooperation, aimed at the ultimate result of a criminal trial in Canada. For Canadian courts to give effect to the *Charter* at a Canadian trial did not produce any "objectionable extraterritorial effect," and thus did not interfere with US sovereignty.[96]

Justice Bastarache, writing for himself and Gonthier J., concurred with the majority's result but took a different approach. He held that whether the *Charter* could apply to the actions of Canadian police operating abroad within a cooperative investigation depended on the role the Canadian police were accorded in the investigation, by the foreign authority. This inquiry would involve

> weighing the relative roles of the Canadian officials and of the foreign officials. When a Canadian officer is invited by the foreign official to exercise some power during an investigation, whether s. 32(1) is engaged will depend on the extent to which the exercise of the power is supervised by the foreign official.[97]

The *Charter* could apply if "the Canadian officials were primarily responsible for obtaining the evidence in a manner which violated the *Charter*[.]"[98] This did not create an objectionable extraterritorial effect for the *Charter* under international law, since the applicable law was the principle of objective territoriality (that is, Canada had a real and substantial connection to the matter, even though it took place in the US), rather than nationality, as the majority had held. Applying objective territoriality in this way would only produce objectionable extraterri-

---

96 *Ibid.* at para. 25.
97 *Ibid.* at para. 126.
98 *Ibid.* at para. 127.

toriality if so doing would "[interfere] with the jurisdictional integrity of the host state," or if the host state had a more real and substantial connection to the matter than Canada.[99] Neither limitation applied in the facts of *Cook*. Justice Bastarache also noted that, practically speaking, all this meant was that if the foreign state's criminal procedure fell below *Charter* standards,

> then the Canadian officials may not take a directing or primary role in the part of the investigation involving those techniques. In essence, they may not exercise, even when invited to do so by the foreign authority, the powers purportedly conferred on them by the foreign investigatory procedures.[100]

Justice L'Heureux-Dubé, writing for herself and McLachlin J. (as she then was), dissented from the majority judgment. In her view, the first question to be asked was whether section 10(b) of the *Charter* was even amenable to being applied to the actions of the police officers when they were operating in a foreign state. Section 32 of the *Charter* provides that the *Charter* applies only to "matters within the authority of Parliament." The investigation in Louisiana was conducted entirely under American sovereignty, and since "it is the foreign government that has legal authority over the mechanics of the investigation,"[101] then the Canadian officers had no attributes of state officials and none of their activities were within the authority of Parliament.

> The principle of respect for the foreign government's sovereignty, clearly articulated in *Terry*, *supra*, means not imposing Canadian standards on a joint investigation on foreign soil, since all officials must respect that country's laws and the procedures of that country's legal system must be followed.[102]

Accordingly, the *Charter* did not apply to the actions of the Canadian police, and exclusion of the evidence was properly considered under the *Harrer/Terry* framework.

There were several problems with the majority's approach in *Cook*. In considering whether Canada could legally apply the *Charter* under the international law principles of jurisdiction, the Court failed to distinguish between prescriptive, enforcement, and adjudicative jurisdiction. The use of the nationality principle to justify applying the *Charter* to the extraterritorial actions of police was unconvincing, as this was

---

99 *Ibid.* at para. 141.
100 *Ibid.* at para. 150.
101 *Ibid.* at para. 94.
102 *Ibid.*

a legal justification for the exercise of prescriptive jurisdiction over the conduct of the offender—while what was being dealt with was police activity in the foreign state (that is, enforcement jurisdiction) and the effect to be given at a domestic trial (that is, adjudicative jurisdiction). This difficult matrix of constitutional law and international jurisdictional principles surfaced again nine years later in *R. v. Hape*,[103] with a startlingly different result. Indeed, like *Cook*, *Hape* has three sets of reasons that, while all concurring in the result, take entirely different approaches to the question. However, the jurisprudential pendulum has swung over to the position held by L'Heureux-Dubé J. in *Cook*, making *Hape* something of a mirror image of the earlier decision.[104]

In *Hape*, the accused was being prosecuted for money laundering under the *Controlled Drugs and Substances Act*.[105] During their investigation, RCMP officers had conducted various activities in the Turks & Caicos Islands, where the accused's investment company was located. These included some searches which were apparently authorized by warrant (though no warrants were entered into evidence), and some perimeter searches which were not. The Canadian officers at all times acted under the authority of local Turks & Caicos police, who asserted their authority in various ways, including presiding over the investigation and preventing the Canadian police from leaving the country with documents. The perimeter searches did not require warrants under Turks & Caicos law, though they would have in Canadian law. Relying on *Cook*, the accused argued that the *Charter* applied to the actions of the Canadian police, that the police had violated section 8 of the *Charter*; and that the evidence seized ought to be excluded as a result.

In a long and wide-ranging judgment, LeBel J. (writing for himself and four others) embarked on an ambitious reformulation both of the interpretation and application of international law in Canada,[106] and specifically the problem of extraterritorial application of the *Char-*

---

103 Above note 70.

104 Professor Roach has ventured that *Hape* amounts to a 5:4 split decision to overturn *Cook*; see Kent Roach, "Editorial: *R. v. Hape* Creates *Charter*-free Zones for Canadian Officials Abroad" (2007) 53 Crim. L.Q. 1. However, as will be seen below in this section, Bastarache J.'s concurring reasons essentially modify his own analytical framework from *Cook*, which was different from the majority's, and thus this set of reasons cannot be taken as overturning *Cook*.

105 S.C. 1996, c. 19.

106 This part of the judgment, while noteworthy, is beyond the scope of this chapter. See, however, Chapter 1, and, for a more detailed treatment, see Gib van Ert, *Using International Law in Canadian Courts*, 2d ed. (Toronto: Irwin Law, 2008). See also John Currie, "Weaving a Tangled Web: *Hape* and the Obfuscation of Canadian Reception Law" (2007) 45 Can. Y.B. Int'l Law 55.

ter. Justice LeBel, after reviewing *Harrer, Terry, Schreiber*, and *Cook*, essentially adopted the main point of L'Heureux-Dubé J.'s dissent in *Cook*: that since section 32 applied the *Charter* only to matters "within the authority of" Parliament and the provincial legislatures, then that section could not apply to anything that happened in another state's territory.[107] The foreign state was sovereign and, as had been established since *Harrer* and *Terry*, its law was the controlling law over any cooperative investigation that happened there. To attempt to apply the *Charter* would be to violate the principle of non-intervention in a foreign state's domestic affairs. He buttressed this interpretation by emphasizing that what the appellant was seeking was no less than to have the *Charter* apply via an exercise of enforcement jurisdiction (specifically "investigative jurisdiction")[108] in the foreign state's territory, and by pointing out the theoretical and practical difficulties that would arise in attempting to apply constitutional law which was meant to constrain state behaviour, within the context of a cooperative police investigation that took place in another state. This was not just an attempt to give *ex post facto* effect to the *Charter* at a Canadian trial, which would be "merely . . . an exercise of extraterritorial adjudicative jurisdiction"[109] and could in any event be carried out by way of the section 7/11(d) formula under *Harrer/Terry*.[110] Rather, "[t]he *Charter*'s primary role is to limit the exercise of government and legislative authority in advance, so that breaches are stopped before they occur."[111] Since the exercise of state authority could only be done in accordance with the foreign state's law, this "strongly intimates that the *Charter* does not apply in the circumstances."[112] He further underscored the need for Canada to participate in cooperative investigations with foreign governments in an era of transnational crime, and noted that applying the *Charter* to investigational activities by Canadian police in foreign states could endanger that cooperation, since it might lead Canadian officers to curtail or even end their involvement in the investigation for fear of breaching the *Charter*. While the foreign cooperative investigation could not be limited by the *Charter*, however, "the principle of comity may give way where the participation of Canadian officers in investigative activities

---

107 *Hape*, above note 70 at paras. 87, 94, and others.
108 *Ibid.* at para. 58, citing Stephen Coughlan *et al.*, "Global Reach, Local Grasp: Constructing Extraterritorial Jurisdiction in the Age of Globalization" (2007) 6 C.J.L.T. 29 at 32.
109 *Hape, ibid.* at para. 91.
110 *Ibid.* at paras. 108–11.
111 *Ibid.* at para. 91.
112 *Ibid.*

sanctioned by foreign law would place Canada in violation of its international obligations in respect of human rights."[113]

Accordingly, LeBel J. proposed a two-stage "balancing methodology" respecting the application of the *Charter* to foreign investigations:[114]

1) *Section 32 stage*: does the *Charter* apply to the foreign conduct? This requires two sub-questions. First, is the conduct at issue that of a Canadian state actor? Police will always satisfy this criterion. Second, if so, is there an exception to the principle of sovereignty that would justify the application of the *Charter* to the extraterritorial activities of the state actor? The court offered the example of a situation in which the foreign state agrees to allow Canadian law to be applied on its territory. "In most cases, there will be no such exception and the *Charter* will not apply."[115]

2) *Trial fairness stage*: using sections 7 and 11(d) of the *Charter*, should the evidence be excluded because its admission would render the trial unfair? This would require the application of the *Terry/Harrer* formula outlined in Section C(1), above in this chapter.

With respect to *Hape* himself, section 8 of the *Charter* did not apply, as "the searches and seizures took place in Turks and Caicos and so were not matters within the authority of Parliament."[116] The actions of both the Canadian investigating police and their Turks & Caicos counterparts were found to be reasonable and not to have undermined the reliability of the evidence. Accordingly, the evidence was not excluded.

Justice Bastarache, writing for himself and Rothstein and Abella JJ., essentially presented a slight re-tooling of the approach taken in his concurring reasons in *Cook*. He took significant issue with some of the main points of the majority's reasons, first noting that section 32 of the *Charter* was designed to define "*who* acts, not *where* they act. In the instant case, the matter is a Canadian criminal investigation

---

113 *Ibid*. at para. 101.
114 *Ibid*. at paras. 102–13.
115 *Ibid*. at para. 113. While the Court did not consider it in any detail, if the foreign state has consented to the application of Canadian law during the investigation, then the *Charter* presumably applies in full and the exclusion of evidence, at least, will be dealt with pursuant to Canadian *Charter* jurisprudence. In this regard, one would think that the s. 24(2) analysis, at least, could incorporate considerations that relate to the transnational aspects of the investigation, for example, under the exclusion regime in *R. v. Grant*, 2009 SCC 32, the Crown could argue certain exigencies relating to the law/procedure in the foreign state as affecting the nature of the *Charter* breach. This is highly speculative at present.
116 *Ibid*. at para. 118.

involving Canadian police acting abroad, which clearly makes it a matter within the authority of Parliament or the provincial legislatures."[117] While agreeing that the central issue was enforcement jurisdiction, he pointed out that as soon as Canadian police were permitted to carry out policing activities on foreign soil, then they were exercising enforcement jurisdiction.[118] Accordingly, Canadian police acting as Canadian police—though under the law of the foreign state—did not produce any objectionable extraterritorial effect by itself, and there was no need to assimilate the Canadian officers to the foreign police just to avoid international law conflicts. Applying the *Charter* extraterritorially did not necessarily create any legal conflict or interference with the sovereignty of the foreign state.

Focusing on the legal rights found in sections 7–14 of the *Charter*, Bastarache J. located the inquiry in the interaction between the fundamental values underpinning the *Charter* and the rights and protections that existed under the foreign law. So long as the Canadian police, in following local procedures, comported themselves with fundamental human rights norms, their actions could withstand scrutiny even if there were gaps between *Charter*-mandated procedure and the local law. Canadian police should essentially follow the local law, and the courts should apply a rebuttable presumption of *Charter* compliance which the accused can overcome only by demonstrating that "those laws or procedures are substantially inconsistent with the fundamental principles emanating from the *Charter*."[119] He noted,

> [D]ifferences resulting from different legal regimes and different approaches adopted in other democratic societies will usually be justified given the international context, the need to fight transnational crime and the need to respect the sovereign authority of other states, coupled with the fact that it is impossible for Canadian officials to follow their own procedures in those circumstances. Flexibility in this case is permitted by s. 1 of the *Charter*. Trivial and technical differences will easily be discarded, more substantial differences between the protections that would be available in Canada and those available in the foreign state will require more in order to be justified.[120]

In his own concurring reasons, Binnie J. held that the case could be resolved via a simple application of the *Cook* criteria. The accused could not demonstrate that applying the *Charter* to the impugned po-

---

117 *Ibid.* at para. 161.
118 *Ibid.* at paras. 151–52.
119 *Ibid.* at para. 174.
120 *Ibid.* at para. 169. See also para. 173.

lice actions would not generate an objectionable extraterritorial effect, since "the record demonstrates that superimposing the Canadian law of search and seizure on top of that of the Turks and Caicos Islands would be unworkable."[121] He agreed with the majority that enforcement jurisdiction was the central issue, but disagreed that *any* extraterritorial effect was necessarily objectionable, pointing out that this overruled *Cook* in the absence of any demonstrable need to do so. He made a number of pointed observations, in particular that "the extent to which, if at all, a constitutional bill of rights follows the flag when state security and police authorities operate outside their home territory" was a serious question being approached by many states, and that a number of cases were making their way through the Canadian courts which were going to require evaluation of the extraterritoriality question in contexts much different from the "routine" kinds of cases such as *Hape*.[122] He rejected LeBel J.'s proposal that international human rights law should become the yardstick for measuring the conduct of Canadian officials on foreign soil, since "the content of such obligations is weaker and their scope more debatable than *Charter* guarantees."[123] He further noted that even though the majority had attempted to leave open a section 24(1) *Charter* remedy for cases where Canadian officials violated the rights of an individual in a foreign state, "the scope of this possible exception is unclear, given the fact that the conduct at issue would necessarily be outside Canada and, according to my colleague, ought not to be judged by the *Charter* standards because 'extraterritorial application of the *Charter* is impossible.'"[124]

3) Other Investigative and Enforcement-Type Actions by State Officials

At the time of writing, the implications of *Hape* are still unclear, and the Supreme Court's dictates have not been applied very often by the lower courts. However, Binnie J.'s signal that the courts would be returning to *Hape*—and that it could cause problems in cases that were not simply about Canadian police engaging in cooperative investigations—bore fruit relatively quickly. In *Re Canadian Security Intelligence Services Act (Canada)*,[125] Blanchard J. of the Federal Court Trial Division dealt with

---

121 *Ibid.* at para. 181.
122 *Ibid.* at para. 184.
123 *Ibid.* at para. 186.
124 *Ibid.* at para. 188.
125 2008 FC 301. This report is of the redacted public reasons released by the court, which were issued after *ex parte* hearings.

an application by the Canadian Security Intelligence Service (CSIS) to have the court issue warrants for investigative activities outside Canada by CSIS agents, pursuant to sections 12 and 21 of the *Canadian Security Intelligence Service Act*.[126] CSIS had targeted various individuals present in Canada whom it suspected of being threats to Canadian security, and sought to be able to intercept communications, gather/record information, and obtain documents as against these individuals if they went to foreign states. It identified certain statutory language which raised the possibility that Parliament had intended such investigations would be conducted outside Canada, and argued that the court thus had jurisdiction to issue the warrants. Moreover, it sought a court ruling that the *Charter* and applicable provisions of the *Criminal Code*[127] applied to the activities of its agents when acting abroad pursuant to these "extraterritorial warrants." It acknowledged that the activities would likely violate the law of the foreign state where they were carried out, and that the Federal Court had no jurisdiction to authorize these activities on foreign soil.[128]

Justice Blanchard applied *Hape* to answer both questions in the negative, ruling first that the statutory language was too ambiguous to conclude that Parliament had authorized CSIS to engage in activities which would violate international law. He seized on the Supreme Court of Canada's adoption of the term "investigative jurisdiction" to characterize the activities which were at play, noting that such jurisdiction could legally be exercised only on a state's territory by that state itself. Since there was no consent being given by any of the target states, Blanchard J. reasoned that by authorizing activities that would "impinge upon the territorial sovereignty of the foreign state," the warrant would purport to allow "activities that are inconsistent with and likely to breach the binding customary principles of territorial sovereign equality and non-intervention, by the comity of nations."[129] Interpreted in such a way as to comport with international law, the statute did not display clear Parliamentary intention to provide the court with the jurisdiction to authorize Canadian officials to travel to foreign countries and violate both the local domestic law and international law.[130] Justice Blanchard gave essentially the same answer to the second question,[131] rejecting an argument by CSIS that *Hape* was distinguishable since it dealt with

---

126 R.S.C. 1985, c. C-23.
127 R.S.C. 1985, c. C-46.
128 Above note 125 at para. 29.
129 *Ibid.* at para. 52.
130 *Ibid.* at para. 55.
131 *Ibid.* at paras. 56–70.

cooperative police investigations rather than security intelligence investigations. Both, he ruled, were clearly aspects of enforcement jurisdiction, which could not be exercised in the foreign state absent that state's consent. Following *Hape*, the *Charter* could not apply, nor did the *Criminal Code* have any express extraterritorial application that would give CSIS what it sought.

Soon after, Justice Mactavish of the Federal Court released her reasons in *Amnesty International Canada v. Canada (Canadian Forces)*,[132] where the applicants had applied for an order that the *Charter* applied to Canadian Forces personnel who, as part of the Canadian mission in Afghanistan, were detaining individuals and handing them over to Afghan authorities. This proceeding had been preceded by significant controversy generated over allegations that detainees handed over by Canadian forces were being tortured and otherwise abused by their Afghan captors. It was clear from the outset that the case would involve an application of *Hape*, and the applicants argued two points: first, that the military context was distinguishable, on both law and facts, from the kind of police cooperation dealt with in *Hape* and called for a different result; and second, that this case fit the exception left open by the Supreme Court of Canada in *Hape*, where a remedy under section 24(1) of the *Charter* might be available if the conduct of Canadian authorities conflicted with international human rights obligations.

Justice Mactavish applied *Hape* to answer both questions in the negative. She found on the facts that, while the government of Afghanistan had agreed to allow Canadian forces to engage in certain activities — even enforcement-type activities — on Afghan soil, it had not consented to the application of Canadian law, including the *Charter*, as would be required to make the *Charter* applicable.[133] Rather, Canada and Afghanistan had agreed that Afghan law and international law, including international human rights and international humanitarian law, would govern the activities of Canadian Forces personnel. Accordingly, the *Charter* could not be applicable on this basis. She further dismissed an argument by the applicants that it was accepted under international law that states were entitled to apply extraterritorial human rights jurisdiction over the acts of their officials in situations where there was "effective military control of the person," finding after a survey of national and international caselaw and commentary that

---

132 2008 FC 336 [*Afghan Detainees*], aff'd 2008 FCA 401, leave to appeal to S.C.C. refused, [2009] S.C.C.A. No. 63. The Federal Court of Appeal restricted its reasons to a review of whether the motions judge had made any errors of law, without any substantial discussion of *Hape* or *Khadr*.

133 *Ibid.* at para. 170 (Fed. Ct.).

this position was too unsettled to merit a different application than that dictated by *Hape*.[134]

As to the section 24(1) argument, the applicants had invoked the "fundamental human rights exception" to the general rule against the extraterritorial application of the *Charter*, which LeBel J. had appeared to leave open in *Hape*. Justice Mactavish found that this position amounted to arguing that the nature of the breach dictated whether *Charter* application was triggered—that is, the *Charter* did not apply to more technical breaches but only to significant breaches—a position she found to be unsound in principle and which would "surely lead to tremendous uncertainty on the part of Canadian state actors 'on the ground' in foreign countries."[135] Moreover, while international human rights law could apply to constrain extraterritorial acts of Canadian state actors, the *Charter* was clearly territorially limited.[136] The exception could apply only where, as LeBel J. had stated, there was "an impact of those activities on *Charter* rights in Canada," which did not apply to the instant case.[137]

In closing, Justice Mactavish expressed some concern with the result in the case, despite its being clearly dictated by *Hape*. She noted that the detainees were not left "in a legal 'no-man's land,' with no legal rights or protections," since Afghan law and international humanitarian law applied, and Canadian forces members could face disciplinary or criminal prosecution for breaches of international law, particularly international humanitarian law (IHL).[138] The court was clearly troubled, however, by the manner in which *Hape* undermined the application of human rights law:

> It is also troubling that while Canada can prosecute members of its military after the fact for mistreating detainees under their control, a constitutional instrument whose primary purpose is, according to the Supreme Court, to limit the exercise of the authority of state actors so that breaches of the Charter are prevented, will not apply to prevent that mistreatment in the first place.[139]

In light of *Hape*, however, the application had to be dismissed.

---

134   *Ibid.* at paras. 214 and 281.
135   *Ibid.* at para. 314.
136   *Ibid.* at paras. 315–18.
137   *Ibid.* at para. 325.
138   *Ibid.* at para. 343.
139   *Ibid.* at para. 340.

The latest stroke was the May 2008 release of the Supreme Court of Canada's decision in *Khadr v. Canada (Minister of Justice)*.[140] The applicant, Omar Khadr, a Canadian citizen, was facing trial before the Military Commission at the US prison in Guantanamo Bay, Cuba, for crimes allegedly committed during the armed conflict in Afghanistan. In 2003, while he was detained at Guantanamo but before charges had been laid, CSIS agents and Department of Foreign Affairs and International Trade Canada (DFAIT) officials had attended at the facility with the permission of American authorities and interrogated him about various topics, including conduct which would eventually be the subject of the charges. They passed summaries of this information on to US authorities. Through other proceedings, Khadr's lawyers had received partial disclosure of these documents, but the copies were heavily redacted, and the Crown refused to disclose the unredacted documents. Khadr's counsel applied to the Federal Court for a *Charter* remedy on the basis that Khadr's right to disclosure under section 7 of the *Charter* had been infringed by the refusal, which impaired his right to full answer and defence before the US court. The question was whether the *Charter* had such extraterritorial reach.

In a decision released just one month before it released its decision on *Hape*, the Federal Court of Appeal[141] overturned the applications judge's denial of the remedy, weaving together several strands of caselaw in so doing. It invoked the *Burns/Suresh* caselaw (described in Section B, above in this chapter) for the proposition that a section 7 remedy was available "if there is a sufficient causal connection between our government's participation and the deprivation [of liberty] ultimately effected."[142] It also cited favourably the decision of the British Columbia Court of Appeal in *Purdy v. Canada (Attorney General)*,[143] where Purdy was facing trial in the US and had received a section 7 remedy in the form of disclosure from the RCMP, because the latter had been engaged in a joint investigation with American police. Applying these authorities, the court noted that the Canadian officials had been "acting independently and were not under instructions of U.S. authorities," and held that their active role in assisting US authorities to make their case against Khadr constituted "a sufficient causal connection between the Canadian government's participation in the foreign investigation and the potential deprivation of life, liberty and security of the person

---

140 2008 SCC 28.

141 *Khadr v. Canada (Minister of Justice)*, [2008] 1 F.C.R. 270.

142 *Ibid.* at para. 30, quoting *Suresh*, above note 33 at para. 54.

143 (2003), 15 C.R. (6th) 211 (B.C.C.A.) [*Purdy*]. See Robert Currie, "Annotation" accompanying the reported case.

which the appellant now faces"[144] to justify a *Charter* remedy. The court then applied the *Cook* criterion of "objectionable extraterritorial effect," finding that no such effect was generated. It invoked *Purdy* again for the proposition that providing disclosure in the circumstances "did not interfere with the sovereign authority of the United States since disclosure does no more than put the individual in the position to offer the evidence obtained to the foreign court."[145] The court ordered the documents be produced for an assessment of which documents should be disclosed, and a hearing of Crown arguments regarding privilege.

In a brief but unanimous judgment, the Supreme Court of Canada dismissed the appeal and, applying *Hape*, found that Khadr was entitled to disclosure.[146] It emphasized that applying the *Charter* to the acts of Canadian officials abroad would normally amount to an unlawful extension of extraterritorial jurisdiction. This conclusion was, however, "based on international law principles against extraterritorial enforcement of domestic laws and the principle of comity which implies acceptance of foreign laws and procedures when Canadian officials are operating abroad."[147] Fastening on the "human rights" exception that LeBel J. had left open in *Hape*, the court noted that, despite its divisions, all judges had been united on the point that international law and comity would give way in any situation where Canadian officials were participating "in activities of a foreign state or its agents that are contrary to Canada's international obligations."[148] Both the conditions of Khadr's detention at Guantanamo and the trial which he faced there had already been ruled illegal by the US Supreme Court[149] in that they violated both US law and the *Geneva Conventions*.[150] Since Canada is a signatory to the *Geneva Conventions*, "[t]he *Charter* bound Canada to the extent that the conduct of Canadian officials involved it in a process that violated Canada's international obligations."[151] The Court was careful to rule that it was simply participation in the illegal process that entitled Khadr to a remedy under section 7, and it was not

---

144 Above note 141 at para. 34.

145 *Ibid.* at para. 36.

146 Though it varied the Court of Appeal's ruling on disclosure somewhat; see Benjamin Berger, "The Reach of Rights in the Security State: Reflections on *Khadr v. Canada (Minister of Justice)*" (2008), 56 C.R. (6th) 268.

147 Above note 140 at para. 17.

148 *Ibid.* at para. 18. This perhaps overstates Binnie J.'s concurring reasons in *Hape*.

149 In *Rasul v. Bush*, 542 U.S. 466 (2004) and *Hamdan v. Rumsfeld*, 126 S. Ct. 2749 (2006).

150 (1950), 75 U.N.T.S. 31, 85, 135, and 287.

151 Above note 140 at para. 26.

necessary to conclude that handing over the fruits of the interviews in this case to U.S. officials constituted a breach of Mr. Khadr's s. 7 rights. It suffices to note that at the time Canada handed over the fruits of the interviews to U.S. officials, it was bound by the *Charter*, because at that point it became a participant in a process that violated Canada's international obligations.[152]

Accordingly, since Khadr's right to liberty was engaged by Canada's participation in the foreign process, disclosure pursuant to section 7 of the *Charter* (and to the applicable law of privilege) was ordered.

The decision in *Khadr* is on one very narrow point, and the Court's unanimous reasons go only as far as they need to; indeed, given the divisions on the court which were apparent in *Hape*, this may be as far as the Court is currently able to go. Moreover, *Khadr* has very unusual facts, in that its determination rests on a finding by the US Supreme Court that the Guantanamo military commission process in place at the relevant time was illegal. For all of these reasons, it is unlikely to have much precedential value.[153]

Enforcing compliance with Canada's international human rights law obligations is obviously laudable, and the result here is unassailable: Canadians should have *Charter* remedies in some form when the Canadian government participates in violations of international human rights. However, two methodological problems are apparent. First, the "human rights exception" from *Hape* was supposed to apply only in situations where the officials' actions had an impact on *Charter* rights *in Canada*.[154] This case does not appear to meet that limitation.

Second, under *Hape*, extraterritorial application is meant to be limited by the sovereignty of the state in which the Canadian officials are acting. Here, the fact that the officials were involved in an illegal process does not make applying the *Charter* any less a violation of US (or possibly Cuban) sovereignty. As Binnie J. pointed out in his separate reasons in *Hape*, it is unclear how one can get a *Charter* remedy in a situation where the *Charter* did not apply.

The Court noted in *Hape* that "[T]he *Charter*'s primary role is to limit the exercise of government and legislative authority in advance, so that breaches are stopped before they occur."[155] However, *Khadr* does not give any more guidance than did *Hape* to Canadian officials as to when they can and cannot participate in a foreign process. When will

---

152 *Ibid.* at para. 27.
153 See *Slahi v. Canada (Minister of Justice)*, 2009 FC 160 for an early application.
154 *Hape*, above note 70 at para. 101.
155 *Ibid.* at para. 91.

it be apparent to them that some aspect of the foreign law which applies to their investigation is contrary to Canada's international human rights obligations? One would like to think it will be obvious in some cases, though if it is so obvious, then Canada should not be cooperating with this state to begin with. Here, it was not a secret that the Guantanamo process was at least questionable under international law, but would that have justified a refusal to cooperate with US officials? This will most always be a difficult call to make.

It is regrettable that the Court did not make any reference to the British Columbia Court of Appeal's decision in *Purdy*[156] or its own decisions in *Burns/Suresh*, which had been central to the Federal Court of Appeal's decision in *Khadr* and could have supported a more developed analytical framework. In the end, all we are left with is that the *Charter* does not apply extraterritorially, except when it does. Determining with any predictability when that will occur will require further clarification from the Court

4) Concluding Observations on *R. v. Hape*[157]

Hape has left the law regarding extraterritorial application of the *Charter* in a very unsettled state. An unusual concatenation of circumstances has brought a veritable flurry of post-*Hape* cases in the short time since the release of the decision. In the most noteworthy of those decisions, *Afghan Detainees*,[158] Mactavish J. was compelled to note the distinct divisions between the irreconcilable approaches taken in the three sets of concurring reasons in *Hape*, and in particular invoked Binnie J.'s reservations about the unnecessary breadth of the majority's approach. She implicitly adopts this point in expressing reservations about the result towards which she was driven by *Hape* in making her decision, though naturally she applies the senior court's dictates.

It is still too early to tell where these matters are headed, but some preliminary observations can be offered.[159] The three sets of reasons in *Hape* indicate serious divisions on the Court—indeed, the Court is not even clear how its reasons in *Hape* are to be read vis-à-vis *Cook*,[160] the former leading case on this point. The majority's reasons indicate that the *Charter* will not be applied to the actions of police officers who are

---

156 Above note 143.
157 Above note 70.
158 Above note 132.
159 Some of these remarks are drawn from Robert Currie, "Annotation" to the *Hape* case, which appears at (2007), 47 C.R. (6th) 96.
160 Above note 95.

operating on the territory of other states, except in the exceptional circumstance of the foreign state's officials actually granting permission for Canadian law to be applied on its territory. While the latter situation is not unheard of,[161] it will not often be a feature of transnational police investigations. Accordingly, the Court has at least invalidated the approach it took to extraterritorial *Charter* application in *Cook*, where section 10 of the *Charter* was given effect on the basis of the nationality of the police officers. The majority reasons are unclear on this point, and the Court's official report of the case indicates its view that *Cook* is being distinguished.[162] However, the *Hape* approach cannot be reconciled with the facts in *Cook*, since in the latter case the Canadian police had been given permission to question the suspect but not to apply Canadian law. Accordingly, it seems that *Cook* has been overruled.

The extraterritorial application of any domestic law, but particularly a constitutional bill of rights, is an extremely complex and challenging subject matter. This is not least because, if domestic law is to be applied extraterritorially, the customary international law principles of jurisdiction are engaged and the interaction between the two must be rationalized. The Court's task here is, to say the least, demanding in an era of increasing law enforcement cooperation between states. More and more, police are engaging in joint or cooperative investigations, a practice which was not contemplated by traditional international law. Historically, states enforced their laws domestically and mostly by way of their own courts. If the offender was in another state, that state's police could arrest and surrender him pursuant to extradition arrangements; this is what extradition was for, to deal with the fact that Canadian police had no jurisdiction to effect arrest in a foreign state. If evidence needed gathering in a foreign state, the Canadian authorities made a request by way of letters rogatory or, more recently, pursuant to a mutual legal assistance treaty or arrangement. The significant split on the Court in *Hape* is emblematic of the fact that a new jurisdictional paradigm is needed under international law to cover this kind of interstate cooperation.

In the absence of such a paradigm emerging, however, the majority in *Hape* made an attempt at rationalization using what law they had. Having set out a salutary and much-needed overhaul of the relationship between international law and Canadian domestic law, the majority reasons then make a series of deliberate choices. These choices drive a

---

161 This sort of permission was actually given in *Dorsay*, above note 90, though in that case it was the American court which was applying Canadian law.

162 [2007] 2 S.C.R. 292.

result that is meant to facilitate an explicit policy rationale: to facilitate international cooperation in combating transnational crime and make it as easy as possible for Canada to participate in that fight.[163] Perhaps inevitably, these choices display some methodological problems, the first of which is the approach taken to section 32 of the *Charter*. The majority decided that the *Charter* does not apply to the activities of Canadian officials in foreign states because anything that happens in the foreign state is under that state's sovereign control, and thus cannot be a "matter within the authority of Parliament." This is a rather dubious interpretation of the phrase "matters within the authority of Parliament," which has always been understood to refer to subject matter and division of powers in sections 91 and 92 of the *Constitution*.[164] Policing and other exercises of enforcement jurisdiction are among the quintessential matters within the authority of the federal Crown, and the *Charter* was obviously intended by the framers to cover these activities. Unlike a regular statute, determining whether the *Charter* has any extraterritorial effect requires reading it together with the law to which it is being applied. Taking a dynamic, contextual approach to interpreting the *Charter*, it is just as valid to reason that, since Canadian law has evolved to allow police to operate outside Canada, the *Charter* must be capable of such evolution and thus amenable to extraterritorial application in appropriate situations. Indeed, this has been the position of the Court since *Harrer*,[165] and attracted the support of the Bastarache minority in *Hape*.

Nonetheless, the majority is convinced that applying the *Charter* extraterritorially to the Canadian police is untenable, since it would result in an exercise of Canadian enforcement/investigative jurisdiction in the foreign state. This, too, is a deliberate choice, and it may be confusing the question of jurisdiction with the question of what law applies to the investigation. Normally, of course, Canadian police cannot exercise any investigational powers in the foreign state. However, as Bastarache J. points out, as soon as the local police or authorities allow them onto foreign soil to act as police (whether it is a "cooperative" investigation or otherwise), then they are being permitted to exercise enforcement jurisdiction. Of course the Canadian police cannot exercise their powers in such a way as to force the Turks & Caicos authorities to set up a different statutory scheme to accommodate them, but that is not the point—they are still exercising enforcement powers. These may be in an attenuated form, because local law applies, and the Can-

---

163 See *Hape*, above note 170 at paras. 96–101.
164 *Constitution Act, 1867* (U.K.), 30 & 31 Vict., c. 3, reprinted in R.S.C. 1985, App. II, No. 5.
165 Above note 61.

adian police can only act within its bounds, but it is still enforcement jurisdiction. This reasoning circumvents the apparition of interference with the sovereignty of the foreign state which so troubles the majority, but there is a deliberate steering away from it.

The Court is *ad idem* that, as a policy goal, we want Canadian police to be participating in transnational investigations. The result the majority reaches, that the *Charter* basically can never be applied extra-territorially, has the advantage of being tidy and easy to apply. *Harrer*[166] and *Terry*[167] are simply extended to cover Canadian police when they are abroad—they are assimilated to the local police and can exercise only the latter's powers, and therefore are immune from *Charter* scrutiny as would pertain at the time they take action. This has a certain appeal. What we do not want is for Canadian police operating in foreign states to be hampered beyond effectiveness by a clash between *Charter* standards and local laws. On the other hand, we also do not want a situation where, simply by putting themselves under the authority of a local official, the Canadian police are immunized completely from *Charter* compliance—which is where the majority position leaves us. This is particularly pressing in cases such as *Khadr*,[168] where no domestic trial is anticipated in which the Canadian officials' actions might be scrutinized, and thus sections 7 and 11(d) do not act as any kind of final gatekeeper, as they do in transnational policing cases which are geared towards a criminal trial in Canada as the final goal. This also highlights the problem flagged by Binnie J. in commenting on the majority's leaving open a potential section 24(1) remedy: once the door has been closed on extraterritorial application of the *Charter*, there is no clear way to access that remedy. So, to use a more serious (if unlikely) example, suppose a Canadian official tortures an individual in another country. Canada owes an obligation under international human rights law not to allow the official to do this[169] and to provide a human rights remedy to that individual. No other state would quarrel with Canadian law restraining the actions of this official—but in light of *Hape*, where is the remedy? Even though Binnie J. signed on to the Court's judgment in *Khadr*, this question remains unanswered.

What appears to trouble the *Hape* majority most about applying the *Charter* to the extraterritorial actions of Canadian police officers is that

---

166 *Ibid..*
167 Above note 65.
168 Above note 140.
169 And this obligation is owed quite apart from Canada's obligation to prosecute the individual, pursuant to the United Nations *Convention against Torture*, above note 35.

its application could interfere with the officers' ability to comply with local laws that apply to the investigation. Nonetheless, not wishing to completely free up Canadian police to become involved in any draconian local practices, a limitation is proposed: where Canada's international human rights obligations are engaged, Canadian police must refuse to undertake any activities that would violate them. This is the final and most problematic choice in *Hape*. How is it that acting in accordance with *Charter* guarantees results in objectionable enforcement jurisdiction, while acting in accordance with international human rights obligations (which may not bind the host state) does not? In both cases, the Canadian police would likely have to refuse to do certain things, which is the kind of interference with the local investigatory standards that the majority sees as the problem to begin with. It is certainly desirable for the police to have some guidance as to what they can and cannot do in foreign states. However, as Bastarache J. points out, the majority's suggestion that Canadian police would have to abstain where the foreign investigational standards would require them to violate Canada's international human rights obligations is essentially no guidance at all—or at least guidance that could be implemented only by having a Crown lawyer staff any cooperative investigation in another state.

Moreover, this underscores a serious international law problem with the majority's position: it blithely invokes Canada's international human rights law obligations as some sort of controlling device but makes a false distinction between those obligations and the *Charter*, treating the latter as if it is some unrelated body of domestic law. The rights most immediately engaged here are the legal rights in sections 7–14 of the *Charter*, but one of the functions of these *Charter* rights that goes unnoticed by the majority in *Hape* is that these rights themselves are the means by which Canada's international human rights law obligations are implemented. This would certainly include the relevant parts of the *ICCPR*, as well as Canada's obligations under customary international human rights law.

This is compounded by the fact that these rights, whether in their domestic or international form, do not exist in a jurisdictional vacuum under international law. The majority in *Hape* does not deal with the fact that there is international law that deals with whether it is legal for states to extend their domestic human rights laws extraterritorially, specifically to cover the enforcement activities of state officials in foreign states. This lacuna in *Hape* is helpfully dealt with by Mactavish J. in *Afghan Detainees*,[170] where the court reviews some international caselaw

---

170 Above note 132.

and commentary on this very issue. Because the Supreme Court was so concerned in *Hape* with ensuring that Canada complied with international law in these situations, it might have done the same. There is a strong case to be made that Canada, like other states, is obliged in some situations to extend its human rights law to the actions of its state officials when they are abroad,[171] though Mactavish J. ultimately ruled that she could not apply any such obligation.[172] If that decision was incorrect, then *Hape* must itself be incorrect insofar as it ruled that Canada's international human rights law obligations cannot be extended extraterritorially. This, at least, may identify the real pressing international law question that arises in these circumstances: how to reconcile Canada's obligation to regulate the extraterritorial actions of its officials that might affect human rights, with its obligation to respect the sovereignty of the foreign states where those officials are acting.

Moreover, in ruling firmly that this "Canadian law" could be applied only on the basis of consent by the foreign state, *Hape* drove the result on the second question in *Afghan Detainees* as well. The applicants had requested a ruling that the *Charter* applied to the actions of the Canadian forces because, as the Supreme Court of Canada had indicated in *Hape*, the *Charter* could apply in circumstances where fundamental human rights of the detainees were at stake. Applying *Hape*'s bar on extraterritorial application of the *Charter*, however, forced Mactavish J. to rule that "it does not follow from the fact that international human rights law obligations may operate to constrain the off-shore activities of Canadian state actors that the *Charter* therefore applies to those activities."[173] This is close to being an absurdity, and one with which Mactavish J. appeared uncomfortable. If Canada has international human rights law obligations that "constrain the off-shore activities of Canadian state actors," and the *Charter* is the means by which our relevant international human rights law obligations are implemented, then the *Charter* must be extended to the offshore activities *ipso facto*. So, for example, if Canada is obliged as a matter of international human

---

171 The European Court of Human Rights, the UN Human Rights Committee, and the Inter-American Commission on Human Rights have all made findings to this effect. The literature on this point is voluminous, but both it and the relevant decisions are canvassed in Ralph Wilde, "Triggering State Obligations Extraterritorially: The Spatial Test in Certain Human Rights Treaties" (2007) 40 Isr. L.R. 503.

172 Above note 132 at para. 264. Justice Mactavish's review of the existing international law authorities referred to *ibid.* is incomplete, but in all fairness, it appears that the full range of relevant law was not argued before her.

173 *Ibid.* at para. 318.

rights law not to transfer the detainees to face torture, then section 7 of the *Charter* (as the implementation of that human rights law obligation) must operate to constrain those actions. This, at least, appears to be the result in *Khadr*,[174] though the methodology is not there to support it.

Is there a way through for *Hape*? On the limited point of Canadian police engaged in investigations (cooperative or otherwise) in foreign states, Binnie J.'s view that the *Cook*[175] approach has been thrown out with the bathwater is compelling. The international law methodology problems in *Cook* notwithstanding, the notion of "objectionable extraterritorial effect" is still salvageable. *Hape* provides the insight that actually requiring the Canadian officers to follow *Charter*-based criminal procedure would produce an objectionable extraterritorial effect, since this would possibly offend the sovereignty of the foreign state. However, there is still nothing objectionable about applying the *Charter* to the actions of Canadian officials at the trial stage, in Canada; this would, in Lebel J.'s words, be "merely . . . an exercise of extraterritorial adjudicative jurisdiction"[176] and not an unlawful exercise of enforcement jurisdiction. The courts can accommodate the fact that the local law applies to the investigation, and must be followed by the Canadian officers to some extent, without throwing the *Charter* out completely. The key is to incorporate this international law requirement into the *Charter* assessment of the police conduct at trial. This could involve, as Bastarache J. suggested in *Hape*, an assessment of the details of the role and level of authority that the Canadian police had in the investigation. Perhaps a better approach, however, is to accept the sovereignty of the foreign state as either a possible limitation on the rights involved (which will usually be sections 7, 8, and 10) under section 1, or as a means of informing the exclusion exercise under section 24(2).[177] This will mean some compromise to the prophylactic nature of *Charter* rights that is preferred in purely domestic jurisprudence, but may be seen to be ne-

---

174 Above note 140.

175 Above note 95.

176 Above note 70 at para. 91.

177 Admittedly, this latter course would involve some restructuring of the current s. 24(2) formula under *Grant*, above note 115. For example, under *Grant*, a self-incriminating statement taken by a police officer from an accused will often be excluded. However, if such a statement is somehow dictated or permitted by local standards, then the exclusion analysis would have to be tempered by this, through recognition that it does not necessarily make the trial unfair. This would be a significant change, but arguably it is no different in effect than *Hape*'s resort to ss. 7/11(d) as the automatic fallback, and has the salutary effect of making the state justify its actions once the accused has proven the violations.

cessary in the transnational context. The specifics of how this sort of application would work can continue to be worked out by the lower courts, in keeping with the traditional common law approach.

As to the application of *Hape* in other contexts, further developments will have to be awaited as all levels of court wrestle its central paradox: that it is impossible for Canada to comply with some of its international law obligations without some recourse to the *Charter*, and yet this is exactly what *Hape* appears to bar. Here, too, there may be some scope for breathing life into *Cook*'s notion of objectionable extraterritorial effect. After all, whether or not Canada is obliged under international law to apply the *Charter* extraterritorially, what is missing from the evidentiary record is any particular objection by other states to Canada doing so, or in particular to giving it effect in a domestic proceeding. Much of the evidentiary review in *Afghan Detainees*[178] was devoted to ascertaining whether Afghanistan had granted Canada consent to apply the *Charter*, but this was because the exercise was dictated by *Hape*. Whether Afghanistan would have objected, or even could validly have objected under international law, was not the subject of any analysis—driven, in no small part, by the Crown's determination that the *Charter* must not apply to the activities of Crown officials outside the country. Perhaps the courts should not be so quick to assume that any exercise of extraterritorial enforcement/investigative jurisdiction will infringe international law; after all, under international law, the extension of extraterritorial jurisdiction is illegal only when it infringes on the sovereignty of other states. Formal consent is not required *ab initio* to extend it. In any event, both *Khadr* and *Afghan Detainees* will continue to provide grist for this mill.

FURTHER READING

CURRIE, ROBERT J., "Human Rights and International Mutual Legal Assistance: Resolving the Tension" (2000) 11 Crim. L.F. 143

———, "*Charter* without Borders? The Supreme Court of Canada, Transnational Crime and Constitutional Rights and Freedoms" (2004) 27 Dal. L.J. 235

DUGARD, JOHN, & CHRISTINE VAN DEN WYNGAERT, "Reconciling Extradition with Human Rights" (1998) 92 A.J.I.L. 187.

---

178 Above note 132.

GANE, CHRISTOPHER H.W., "Human Rights and International Cooperation in Criminal Matters" in Peter J. Cullen & William C. Gilmore, eds., *Crime sans Frontières: International and European Legal Approaches* (Edinburgh: Edinburgh University Press, 1998) 161

MERON, THEODOR, "Extraterritoriality of Human Rights Treaties" (1995) 89 A.J.I.L. 78

WILDE, RALPH, "Legal 'Black Hole'? Extraterritorial State Action and International Treaty Law on Civil and Political Rights" (2004–2005) 26 Mich. J. Int'l L. 739

CHAPTER 11

IMMUNITIES FROM CRIMINAL PROSECUTION

A. INTRODUCTION

While the substantive law concerning individual responsibility for international crimes has increased since the end of WW II, there remain significant bars to the prosecution of state officials for international crimes and transnational crimes of international concern. One bar, which has received considerable attention over the last several years, is immunity.[1]

Immunity from prosecution may be either personal or functional in nature. Personal immunities are time limited and operate to deny a particular court jurisdiction over a particular person while that person is in office. Functional immunities present a permanent bar to adjudi-

---

1 For judicial consideration of immunity in the criminal context in recent years, see, for example, *Case Concerning the Arrest Warrant of 11 April 2000 (Democratic Republic of the Congo v. Belgium)*, [2002] I.C.J. Rep. 3 [*Arrest Warrant*] and *R. v. Bartle and the Commissioner of Police for the Metropolis and Others, Ex Parte Pinochet; R. v. Evans and Another and the Commissioner of Police for the Metropolis and Others, Ex Parte Pinochet* (1999), [1999] UKHL 17, [2000] 1 A.C. 147, [1999] 2 All E.R. 97 [*Pinochet*]. For academic commentary, see, for example, Hazel Fox, *The Law of State Immunity*, 2d ed. (Oxford: Oxford University Press, 2008) [Fox, *State Immunity*, 2d]; Yitiha Simbeye, *Immunity and International Criminal Law* (Aldershot, UK: Ashgate, 2004) [Simbeye]; and Rosanne van Alebeek, *The Immunity of States and Their Officials in International Criminal Law and International Human Rights Law* (Oxford: Oxford University Press, 2008).

cation because they attach to the act rather than the actor.[2] In simple terms, personal immunity protects certain offices, while functional immunity protects certain acts. Because immunity (both personal and functional) is a procedural bar to jurisdiction, it should not be confused with a defence to criminal liability; a defence operates to excuse an otherwise unlawful act, while immunities have no such effect. The only role for immunities is to deny a court the opportunity to exercise its jurisdiction because it is deemed that there are policy reasons which justify doing so.[3]

Three types of immunity from criminal prosecution will receive attention in this chapter.[4] The first is personal immunity or immunity *ratione personae* (also called absolute immunity). This type of immunity attaches only to certain high state offices.[5] The second type of immunity which will be considered is functional immunity, or immunity *ratione materiae*. Immunity *ratione materiae* operates to immunize certain conduct.[6] The final type of immunity which will be examined is a subset of the first—diplomatic immunity. While this is a species of personal immunity, it is governed by its own conventions and so will be considered separately.

---

2   See Robert Cryer *et al.*, *International Criminal Law and Procedure* (Cambridge: Cambridge University Press, 2007) at 423–24 [Cryer].

3   See, for example, Hazel Fox, *The Law of State Immunity* (Oxford: Oxford University Press, 2002) [Fox, *State Immunity*] at 19–20. It should be noted that in relation to functional immunities, it is sometimes asserted that it is a defence rather than a simple jurisdictional bar. This controversy will be discussed further in Section B(3), below in this chapter.

4   This chapter will not consider immunities of states against civil claims for serious human rights breaches amounting to international crimes, nor the worthy issue of whether Canada should adopt legislation similar to the US's *Alien Tort Claims Act*, 28 U.S.C. §1350. But see Christopher K. Hall, "The Duty of States Parties to the *Convention against Torture* to Provide Procedures Permitting Victims to Recover Reparations for Torture Committed Abroad" (2007) 18 E.J.I.L. 921; Lorna McGregor, "Torture and State Immunity: Deflecting Impunity, Distorting Sovereignty" (2007) 18 E.J.I.L. 903; Noah B. Novogrodsky, "Immunity for Torture: Lessons from *Bouzari v. Iran*" (2007) 18 E.J.I.L. 939; Alexander Orakhelashvili, "State Immunity and Hierarchy of Norms: Why the House of Lords Got It Wrong" (2007) 18 E.J.I.L. 955; and Wendy Adams, "In Search of a Defence of the Transnational Human Rights Paradigm: May *Jus Cogens* Norms be Invoked to Create Implied Exceptions in Domestic State Immunity Statutes?" in Craig Scott, ed., *Torture as Tort* (Oxford: Hart, 2001) at 250.

5   See, in general, van Alebeek, above note 1, c. 4. Also see Dapo Akande, "International Law Immunities and the International Criminal Court" (2004) 98 A.J.I.L. 407 at 409–11 [Akande].

6   See, in general, van Alebeek, above note 1, c. 3. See also Akande, *ibid.* at 412–15.

Immunity is a vast topic which, if considered in its entirety, can fill whole textbooks.[7] For this reason, the focus of this chapter will be on certain key questions. The basic rules of personal and functional immunities will be explored. The focus will then turn to the immunities available for the so-called core crimes (for current purposes these are genocide, war crimes, and crimes against humanity) before international courts; this discussion will include the immunities applicable before the International Criminal Court (ICC). Finally, attention will be given to national courts and the immunities available for both core crimes and the treaty crime of torture.[8]

As will become apparent, there is currently some uncertainty surrounding the applicability of immunities. In part this may be attributable to a reconsideration of the rationales which underlie functional immunity in particular.[9] For a number of years, there has been a renewed determination to address the abuses committed by state officials. A key part of this shift towards greater accountability has been the willingness to prosecute officials for their crimes.[10] This new willingness to prosecute has engaged both courts and commentators in a consideration of the reasons for immunity and the law of immunity.

B. IMMUNITY IN INTERNATIONAL LAW

1) General Comments

As suggested above, immunity from prosecution can be a complicated area of international law. While the parameters of diplomatic immunity have been codified in a series of conventions, and are relatively un-

---

7   See, for example, the materials cited, above note 1, and Fox, *State Immunity*, above note 3.

8   Torture will be used to establish an analytical framework for assessing the immunities available for treaty crimes. Due to space limitations, other treaty crimes will not be specifically considered.

9   See, for example, van Alebeek, above note 1, c. 5; Geoffrey Robertson, "Ending Impunity: How International Criminal Law Can Put Tyrants on Trial" (2005) 38 Cornell Int'l L.J. 649. In respect of head-of-state immunity, see David S. Koller, "Immunities of Foreign Ministers: Paragraph 61 of the *Yerodia* Judgment As It Pertains to the Security Council and the International Criminal Court" (2004) 20 Am. U. Int'l L. Rev. 7 at 13 and the references cited therein [Koller]; more generally, see Lee M. Caplan "State Immunity, Human Rights and Jus Cogens; A Critique of the Normative Hierarchy Theory" (2003) 97 A.J.I.L. 741.

10   See Chile Eboe-Osuji, "State Immunity, State Atrocities and Civil Justice in the Modern Era of International Law" (2007) 45 Can. Y.B. Int'l Law 223 at 224.

controversial, there are no similar instruments governing the immunity of state officials more generally.

The *United Nations Convention on the Jurisdictional Immunities of States and Their Property*[11] is the most recent effort to codify the international law of immunity, but it is of little assistance to the question of immunity from criminal prosecution. While not explicitly stated in the text of the *UN Convention on Jurisdictional Immunities*, the Convention was understood to apply only to the question of state immunity from civil process. This is apparent from a review of the Convention articles, which evidence a preoccupation with the sovereign-commercial distinction, a key feature in assessing whether a state is immune from civil process. There is no indication in the articles that the *UN Convention on Jurisdictional Immunities* was intended to address criminal immunities. This reading is confirmed by certain documents related to the Convention. In particular, the Ad Hoc Committee on Jurisdictional Immunities of States and Their Property noted in its 2004 Report the understanding of the Working Group on Jurisdictional Immunities that the Convention would not address immunity from criminal process. The Working Group had suggested that this understanding should be expressed as part of the General Assembly resolution which would accompany the *UN Convention on Jurisdictional Immunities* rather than the Convention itself. The Ad Hoc Committee recommended to the General Assembly that they include this understanding in the resolution.[12] The UN General Assembly accepted this recommendation, and operative paragraph 2 of the resolution accepting the *UN Convention on Jurisdictional Immunities* states that the General Assembly agrees that the *UN Convention on Jurisdictional Immunities* does not address immunity from criminal prosecution.[13]

The International Law Commission (ILC) has recently begun work on the question of the immunity of state officials from criminal prosecution in foreign courts. This work is, however, in its infancy, and it may be some time before the ILC produces a final report. At the time of writing, the Special Rapporteur on the topic, Roman Anatolievich Kolodkin, had delivered a preliminary report. This report details the history of the consideration of the topic by the ILC and the Institute of

---

11   Annex to UNGA Res A/59/38 of 2 December 2004 [*UN Convention on Jurisdictional Immunities*].

12   Ad Hoc Committee on Jurisdictional Immunities of States and Their Property, *Report of the Ad Hoc Committee on Jurisdictional Immunities of States and Their Property* (UN Doc A/59/22, 1–5 March 2004) at paras. 11 and 14.

13   UNGA A/Res/59/38 operative para. 2.

International Law, and outlines the issues which have been proposed for consideration.[14]

It should be noted that while there is no single treaty or set of draft articles governing criminal immunities, the treaties which establish international tribunals for the prosecution of international crimes contain articles dealing with the specific immunities available (or not) before the particular tribunal. In addition, some of the treaties which govern specific international crimes do contain provisions relating to immunities.[15] In the absence of a general treaty governing state practice at the domestic level, what remains is customary law as evidenced by state practice and *opinio juris*.[16]

Prior to examining whether immunities are available either before international courts or domestic courts, it is necessary to understand the types of immunity provided by international law.

2) Immunity *Ratione Personae*

Immunity *ratione personae*, or personal immunity, is an immunity which attaches to certain high government offices. While an individual occupies one of the protected offices, he is personally immune and inviolable; he cannot be subjected to detention, arrest, or prosecution by the authorities of a state (other than his own).[17]

This immunity attaches to a relatively limited class of offices. It has long been accepted that heads of state and diplomats benefit from personal immunity. More recently, it has been held (by the International Court of Justice (ICJ) in the *Arrest Warrant* judgment,[18] see Section D(2)(c), below in this chapter) that foreign ministers also enjoy the benefit of personal immunity. It has also been suggested that heads of government are personally immune.[19]

---

14 Roman Anatolievich Kolodkin, Preliminary Report on Immunity of State Officials from Foreign Criminal Jurisdiction, 29 May 2008, UN Doc. A/CN.4/601 at 4.

15 Among the conspicuous examples of such treaties are the four *Geneva Conventions* of 1949, 1965 Can. T.S. No. 20.

16 See Fox, *State Immunity*, above note 3 at 426.

17 See Antonio Cassese, *International Criminal Law* (Oxford: Oxford University Press, 2003) at 264–67.

18 Above note 1.

19 See, for example, the Institut de droit international 2001 Resolution on Immunities from Jurisdiction and Execution of Heads of State and of Government in International Law, online: www.idi-iil.org/idiE/resolutionsE/2001_van_02_en.PDF.

While the full range of offices to which personal immunity attaches is unclear, the effect of personal immunity is not.[20] While an individual occupies a protected office, he is immune from prosecution for all his acts; no distinction is made between acts that are personal or official, or even acts that were done prior to the person taking office.[21] However, this rule generally appears to apply only as regards prosecution before national courts. There is some practice (and relevant treaty law) which suggests that personal immunities may not be a bar to prosecution before an international tribunal.[22] As will be seen in Section C, below in this chapter, the reasons for the inapplicability of personal immunities before an international tribunal depend on the manner in which the tribunal was established. It is not clear whether the rule has customary status.

Personal immunity, while broad, is comparatively short lived. Because it attaches to the office rather than the individual, once a person leaves that office he ceases to benefit from this immunity and is protected only by the same functional immunity which protects all other state actors.[23]

While in general the law relating to personal immunities is clear, some questions remain. This chapter will explore three questions in particular. The first question, suggested above in this section, is whether personal immunities operate only at the national level, or whether personal immunities also apply against an international tribunal and, if so, to what extent. The second question is who benefits; to which offices do personal immunities attach? Finally, this chapter examines whether personal immunities apply regardless of the alleged crime, or whether exceptions to immunity exist in relation to specific crimes.

3) Immunity *Ratione Materiae*

All state officials, regardless of rank, do enjoy some immunity as a matter of international law. This category of immunity *ratione materiae*,

---

20 Cryer, above note 2 at 436. See also Akande, above note 5 at 411–12, discussing the possible range of offices whose holders are protected by personal immunity.
21 See the decision of the ICJ in *Arrest Warrant*, above note 1.
22 This point will be discussed below in this chapter in relation to the particular international tribunals. Fox, *State Immunity*, above note 3, discusses this point in relation to heads of state at 430–33. See also Chanaka Wickremasinghe, "Immunities Enjoyed by Officials of States and International Organizations" in Malcolm D. Evans, *International Law*, 2d ed (Oxford: Oxford University Press, 2006) c. 13 at 417–18.
23 See Simbeye, above note 1 at 110. Akande, above note 5 at 412–13, notes that current and former officials and persons or bodies acting on behalf of the state may benefit from this immunity.

or functional immunity, applies to a broad class of persons, but to a limited class of acts.[24]

Unlike personal immunities which attach to particular offices, functional immunities operate to immunize certain official acts. For this reason, some commentators have suggested that functional immunity operates more as a substantive defence; the individual is not considered responsible for the impugned acts—instead, the acts are attributable to the state.[25] This type of immunity is, not surprisingly, sometimes confused with the act of state defence.[26] However, functional immunities are, like personal immunities, procedural in nature. They do not relieve an individual from substantive legal responsibility but simply prevent a court from adjudicating.[27] This type of immunity is derived from the traditional rules of international law which attributed actions to the state rather than to the individual; post–WW II developments have altered this traditional rule.[28] The impact of this dismantling will be discussed in more detail throughout this chapter.

In order for immunity *ratione materiae* to apply, two conditions must be met. The first condition is that the individual involved must be a state official; the second condition is that the official must be acting in her official capacity.[29] This latter requirement operates to exclude those acts which were not performed on behalf of the state.[30]

Because state officials are functionally immune in relation to their official acts, and the worst crimes are often purported to be done in an official capacity, international law has evolved to exclude certain acts from the reach of immunity.[31] As will be discussed in more detail in

---

24 See, for example, van Alebeek, above note 1 at 132–35.

25 In his preliminary report on immunity from criminal prosecution, Kolodkin notes that the view that functional immunities operate as a substantive defence is a minority view (above note 14 at para. 65). Cassese appears to be a proponent of the view that functional immunity operates as a substantive defence (see *International Criminal Law*, above note 17 at 264–66). Akande, above note 5 at 413, suggests that functional immunity has both a substantive and procedural aspect. It is a substantive defence because it requires that the act be attributed to the state, not the individual. It is procedural because it prevents a state from circumventing the immunity to which another state is entitled.

26 This appears to be, in effect, what van Alebeek argues in *The Immunity of States and Their Officials*, above note 1, c. 3. For the opposite view, see Fox, *State Immunity*, 2d, above note 1, c. 5.

27 See Cryer, above note 2 at 424. Fox expresses the same view in regards to state immunity: *State Immunity*, 2d, *ibid.* at 33.

28 Koller, above note 9 at 27–28.

29 Cryer, above note 2 at 423, makes this distinction.

30 See *Pinochet*, above note 1, Lord Hope, who clearly makes this distinction.

31 See Cassese, *International Criminal Law*, above note 17 at 267–71.

Sections C and D, below in this chapter, functional immunity is not available for (at the very least) genocide, war crimes, probably crimes against humanity, and the international crime of torture. This is not because (as some have suggested) these crimes are not official acts. Rather, in our view, the denial of immunity reflects a shift in the principles underlying international law which began after WW II.[32] There is now no doubt that immunity is unavailable for certain crimes. This of course raises certain questions: are these exceptions to an otherwise broad principle of immunity or is the law of immunity contracting so that it applies to fewer acts? Or is this simply a function of individual accountability for international crimes?[33]

C. IMMUNITIES BEFORE INTERNATIONAL TRIBUNALS

1) International Military Tribunal: Removal of Personal or Functional Immunity or Both?

Following WW I, there was an abortive attempt by the international community to prosecute certain high-ranking German officials (including the Kaiser) for their roles in the conflict. This attempt was codified in certain clauses of the *Treaty of Versailles*.[34] Such prosecution was also the subject of study by the Commission on the Responsibility of the Authors of the War and on Enforcement of Penalties, which reported to the Peace Conference of 1919.[35] The third issue the Com-

---

32   A judgment which appears to suggest that international crimes are not official acts is the Joint Separate Opinion of Higgins, Koojimans, and Buergenthal JJ. in the *Arrest Warrant* decision, above note 1 at 63. On the post–WW II shift, see Koller, above note 9 at 27–28. When discussing the rule lifting functional immunities for international crimes, Cassese, *International Criminal Law*, above note 17 at 267–71, cites instruments and caselaw which date to or postdate WW II. See also Steffen Wirth, "Immunity for Core Crimes? The ICJ's Judgment in the *Congo v. Belgium* Case" (2002) 13 E.J.I.L. 877 at 884–89, who, in discussing possible exceptions to state immunity in respect of the core crimes, also refers to post–WW II caselaw and international instruments.

33   These questions will be discussed in Sections C & D, below in this chapter.

34   *Treaty of Peace between the Allied and Associated Powers and Germany*, [1920] T.S. No. 4, 10 January 1920. Part VII of the *Treaty* provides for the "arraignment" of the Kaiser (art. 227) as well as a recognition that the Allied Powers could prosecute those accused of war crimes (art. 228).

35   See the Commission on the Responsibility of the Authors of the War and on Enforcement of Penalties, "Report Presented to the Preliminary Peace Conference" reproduced (with some exclusions) in (1920) 14 A.J.I.L. 95.

mission was asked to examine was "[t]he degree of responsibility for these offences attaching to particular members of the enemy forces, including members of the General Staffs, and other individuals, however highly placed."[36] The conclusion of the Commission was expressed as follows:

> [T]he Commission desire to state expressly that in the hierarchy of persons in authority, there is no reason why rank, however exalted, should in any circumstances protect the holder of it from responsibility when that responsibility has been established before a properly constituted tribunal. This extends even to the case of heads of state. An argument has been raised to the contrary based upon the alleged immunity, and in particular the alleged inviolability, of a sovereign state. But this privilege, where it is recognized, is one of practical expedience in municipal law, and is not fundamental.[37]

The Report of the Commission went on to propose the establishment of an international tribunal with the power to prosecute officials, including a head of state (although this with the permission of that state).[38] The American delegation dissented from this position, arguing that there was no precedent for prosecuting a head of state and noting that the acts of the head of state were attributable to the state rather than the individual.[39] The American position was that a head of state was responsible to his own country and that subjecting a head of state to the jurisdiction of another country was incompatible with sovereignty.[40]

No tribunal was established following WW I, and the debate over the criminal liability or immunity of high officials remained more academic than real. However, in the aftermath of WW II, these questions took on practical significance.

Following the end of WW II, the victorious powers drafted the *Charter of the International Military Tribunal (IMT Charter)*[41] and established the IMT to try the major war criminals of the European conflict. A separate International Military Tribunal was established to try individuals accused of crimes in the Far East (IMTFE). It was the proposed creation of the IMT and IMTFE which again raised the issue of whether high officials could be tried for their conduct. The *IMT Charter* purported to answer this question with article 7, which provided, "The

---

36   *Ibid.* at 95.
37   *Ibid.* at 116.
38   *Ibid.* at 122.
39   *Ibid.* at 135.
40   *Ibid.* at 136.
41   82 U.N.T.S. 279 [*IMT Charter*].

official position of the defendants, whether as heads of state or responsible officials in government departments, shall not be considered as freeing them from responsibility or mitigating punishment."[42]

Debate exists over whether the article was intended to remove the personal immunity which protects high officials, or the functional immunity which protects all officials from responsibility for their official acts.[43] This debate cannot easily be resolved by reference to the Nuremberg judgment of the IMT, which simply held,

> The principle of international law, which under certain circumstances protects the representatives of a state, cannot be applied to acts which are condemned as criminal by international law. The authors of these facts cannot shelter themselves behind their official position in order to be freed from punishment in appropriate proceedings. Article 7 of the *Charter* expressly declares:
>
> > "The official position of defendants, whether as Heads of State, or responsible officials in government departments, shall not be considered as freeing them from responsibility, or mitigating punishment."
>
> On the other hand the very essence of the *Charter* is that individuals have international duties which transcend the national obligations of obedience imposed by the individual State. He who violates the laws of war cannot obtain immunity while acting in pursuance of the authority of the State if the State in authorising action moves outside its competence under international law.[44]

---

42   See also the *Charter of the International Military Tribunal for the Far East*, annexed to *Special Proclamation, Establishment of an International Military Tribunal for the Far East*, 19 January 1946, T.I.A.S. No. 1589.

43   Cryer, above note 2 at 428, suggests that in order to remove the procedural immunities attaching to high officials, another mechanism was introduced: trials before an international court. See also van Alebeek, above note 1 at 240–41. This also appears to have been the view taken by Henri Donnedieu de Vabres, "The Nuremberg Trial and the Modern Principles of International Criminal Law" in Guénaël Mettraux, *Perspectives on the Nuremberg Trial* (Oxford: Oxford University Press, 2008) 213 at 214 and 265, but it is not clear whether the author considered the personal immunity removed vis-à-vis only an international tribunal or more broadly. What is clear is that he considered that art. 7 did remove the personal immunity of the high officials. On the other side of the debate, see Geoffrey Robertson, "Ending Impunity: How International Law Can Put Tyrants on Trial" (2005) 38 Cornell Int'l L.J. 649 at 654.

44   Reprinted in (1947) 41 A.J.I.L. 172 at 221.

This statement may easily refer to either the lifting of personal immunity or functional immunity.

Following the judgment of the IMT, the ILC was charged with clarifying the principles which were applied in the judgment.[45] However, this clarification does nothing to help settle the debate as to whether article 7 removed the personal or functional immunities of the defendants. Principle III gave expression to article 7, and its attendant commentary merely repeats the relevant passages of the judgment. The ILC gave no clear indication whether it considered whether article 7 applied to personal or functional immunities.[46]

On balance, the actual effect of article 7 of the *IMT Charter* was probably to remove both personal and functional immunities. The article specifically referenced both heads of state (who had the benefit of personal immunities) and "responsible officials" who had the benefit of functional immunities. At the time of trial, all the accused major war criminals were former officials who could benefit only from functional immunity.[47]

Notably, the IMT did not represent a denial of immunity in respect of all acts. The IMT was solely concerned with prosecuting crimes against peace (aggression), crimes against humanity (including genocide), and war crimes.[48] The IMT did begin the process of denying immunity before international tribunals for those crimes.

2) The *Ad Hoc* Criminal Tribunals

a) General

More recently, the establishment of the *ad hoc* tribunals to prosecute crimes committed in Rwanda and the former Yugoslavia has provided an opportunity to clarify the meaning of article 7 of the *IMT Charter*. In response to the Balkan War, which resulted in the final dissolution of the former Yugoslavia, the UN Security Council requested that the Secretariat of the United Nations prepare a report on the establishment of

---

45   See UNGA Res 94(1), 11 December 1946, UNGA Res 95(1), 11 December 1946.

46   International Law Commission, *Principles of International Law recognized in the Charter of the Nürnberg Tribunal and in the Judgment of the Tribunal, with Commentaries* in the *Yearbook of the International Law Commission*, Documents of the 2d Session including Reports to the General Assembly, 1950 vol. II. (New York: United Nations, 1957) UN Doc A/CN.4/SER.A/1950/Add.1 at 181.

47   Fox, *State Immunity*, 2d, above note 1 at 677, takes the view that if a tribunal considers that the official position of an individual is no defence, it is implicit that it is also no bar to jurisdiction.

48   *IMT Charter*, above note 41, art. 6.

an international criminal tribunal which could prosecute those accused of violating international humanitarian law.[49] In the resulting Report, the UN Secretary-General considered the immunities accorded to state officials by international law. The view of the Secretary-General was that any tribunal created to deal with the conflict would need to apply existing law in order to respect the principle *nullem crimen sine lege.*[50]

In his Report, the Secretary-General noted that many of the states which had provided comments on the future tribunal considered it important to include a provision relating to the criminal responsibility of heads of state and other officials.[51] The proposed article 7.2, which addressed individual criminal liability, was written in terms which were nearly identical to article 7 of the *IMT Charter.*[52] This suggests, although it is not expressly stated, that the UN Secretary-General was of the view that the *IMT Charter* addressed both substantive and procedural immunities.[53] When the International Criminal Tribunal for Rwanda (ICTR) was established, an identical provision was inserted in article 6.2 of its Statute.[54]

Both *ad hoc* tribunals, such as the IMT, have limited jurisdiction; the tribunals are competent to try only war crimes, crimes against humanity, and genocide.[55] The law of immunity as expressed in the *Statutes* and the decisions of the tribunals relates only to those specific crimes. For the International Criminal Tribunal for the former Yugoslavia (ICTY), two important cases when considering personal immunities are *Milosević* and *Karadžić.*[56] For the ICTR, the *Kambanda*[57] decision is of particular interest.

---

49   UN S/RES/808 (1993), 22 February 1993.
50   Report of the Secretary-General Pursuant to Paragraph 2 of Security Council Resolution 808 (1993), UN Doc. S/25704, 3 May 1993 at para 34.
51   *Ibid.* at para 55.
52   The proposed art. 7.2 is found at para. 59 of the Report, *ibid.*
53   Article 7.2 of the *Statute of the ICTY*, below note 55, currently reads, "The official position of any accused person, whether as Head of State or Government or as a responsible Government official, shall not relieve such person of criminal responsibility nor mitigate punishment." While the Statute has been amended, the current art. 7.2 is identical to that proposed by the Secretary-General in his Report.
54   *Statute of the International Criminal Tribunal for Rwanda,* adopted by S/RES/955, UN SCOR, 49th Sess., 3453d mtg. at 3, UN Doc. S/RES/955 (1994), 33 I.L.M. 1598, 1600 (1994) [*Statute of the ICTR*].
55   See the *Statute of the International Criminal Tribunal for the former Yugoslavia,* UN Doc. S/25704 at 36, annex (1993) and S/25704/Add.1 (1993), adopted by Security Council on 25 May 1993, UN Doc. S/RES/827 (1993) [*Statute of the ICTY*], arts. 2–5, and the *Statute of the ICTR, ibid.,* arts. 2–4.
56   *Milosević* (IT-02-54); *Karadžić* (IT-95-5/18-PT 17).
57   Below note 78.

b) *Milosević* (ICTY)

In 1999, Slobodan Milosević, then President of the Federal Republic of Yugoslavia (FRY), was indicted by the Prosecutor for the ICTY for crimes allegedly committed during operations in Kosovo. Subsequent indictments added allegations of crimes committed in Croatia and in Bosnia and Herzegovina. Ultimately, the charges against Milosević included allegations of war crimes, crimes against humanity, and genocide.[58]

Although Milosević was a serving head of state at the time the indictment was issued, no state protested the action taken by the Prosecutor.[59] However, Milosević did not come before the ICTY as a serving head of state; rather, after Milosević suffered electoral defeat, he was arrested and surrendered by the Serbian authorities.

When Milosević was brought before the ICTY, the jurisdiction of the ICTY over Milosević was challenged. The *amicus curiae* appointed in the case argued that the tribunal lacked jurisdiction because of Milosević's status as a former head of state. The Prosecutor, in reply, took the position that article 7 of the *Statute of the International Criminal Tribunal for the former Yugoslavia*,[60] which concerns an individual's official status, reflected customary international law.[61]

In its decision on Preliminary Motions, the Trial Chamber dealt with this argument in short order stating, "There is absolutely no basis for challenging the validity of Article 7, paragraph 2, which at this time reflects a rule of customary international law."[62] According to the Trial Chamber, the customary status of the rule was confirmed by its inclusion in a large number of international instruments (including the *Nuremberg Principles*[63] and the *Genocide Convention*[64]) and by its incorporation into caselaw.[65] What the decision did not make clear was whether article 7.2 removed both functional and personal immunities, nor did it address whether this rule of customary law applied only before international tribunals or was equally applicable before national courts. Given that the indictment was issued while Milosević was a

---

58   The various indictments against Milosević for crimes allegedly committed in Kosovo, Bosnia and Herzegovina, and Croatia are online: www.icty.org/x/cases/slobodan_milosevic/cis/en/cis_milosevic_slobodan.pdf.

59   See Koller, above note 9.

60   Above note 55.

61   *Milosević* (IT-02-54), Decision on Preliminary Motions, 8 November 2001.

62   *Ibid.* at para 28.

63   Below note 95.

64   Below note 188.

65   *Milosević*, above note 61 at paras. 30–33.

serving head of state, it is probable that the tribunal viewed article 7.2 as waiving both personal and functional immunities.

c) *Karadžić* (ICTY)

The more recent decision of the ICTY in its 2008 *Decision on Accused's Second Motion for Inspection and Disclosure: Immunity Issue*[66] in the *Karadžić* proceedings confirms that a former official has no immunity before an international tribunal. The tribunal in that case was concerned with the allegations by Karadžić that Richard Holbrook, as then special envoy of the US to the Balkans, had executed an agreement with Karadžić assuring him that he would not be prosecuted for crimes provided he withdrew from public life.[67] Holbrook has called these assertions lies.[68]

In its decision, the Trial Chamber found that any agreement purporting to grant immunity before an international tribunal for charges of war crimes, crimes against humanity, or genocide would be invalid under international law.[69] Unfortunately, the Trial Chamber did not state its reasons—whether because of the nature of the crimes, the nature of the tribunal, or the nature of immunity. The effect of the decision, however, is clear: regardless of any purported agreement, Karadžić, a former state official, is not entitled to immunity before the ICTY. Although Karadžić appealed, the appeal did not relate to the specific holding on the validity of the immunity agreement, and the Appeals Chamber did not comment on that aspect of the trial court's ruling.[70]

After further applications and disclosure, Karadžić brought another application before the Trial Chamber requesting that the Trial Chamber dismiss the indictment against him for lack of jurisdiction based on the Holbrook Agreement. In the alternative, he asked that the prosecution be dismissed as an abuse of process.[71] The Trial Chamber

---

66   *Karadžić* (IT-95-5/18-PT), Decision on Accused's Second Motion for Inspection and Disclosure: Immunity Issue, 17 December 2008.

67   Hereafter referred to as the "Holbrook Agreement."

68   See BBC news story, online: http://news.bbc.co.uk/2/hi/europe/8140466.stm.

69   *Karadžić*, above note 66 at para 25.

70   *Karadžić* (IT-95-5/18-AR73.1), Decision on Appellant Radovan Karadžić's Appeal concerning Holbrooke Agreement Disclosure, 6 April 2009. See also the comments of the Trial Chamber in its recent Decision (IT-95-5/18-PT) on the accused's Holbrooke Agreement Motion, 8 July 2009.

71   The facts referred to in this section are taken from the summary recited by the Appeals Chamber in its decision on the appeal from this motion, *Karadžić* (IT-95-5/18-AR73.4), 12 October 2009. See especially paras. 3–5.

denied the motion.[72] On 12 October 2009, the Appeals Chamber of the ICTY released its decision on the appeal.[73] The decision was not concerned with the factual existence of the agreement; rather, the question which the Appeals Chamber addressed was, assuming the Holbrook Agreement did exist, could it bind the ICTY. The Appeals Chamber noted that before the Trial Chamber, the parties had agreed that in order for the Holbrook Agreement to be binding it would have to be attributable to the Prosecutor. This would require a finding that either representatives of the Prosecutor or the UN Security Council (UNSC) (as the parent body of the ICTY) were involved in the making of the Holbrook Agreement.[74]

The Appeals Chamber first held that it was not sufficient for representatives of the UNSC to be involved in making the Agreement. Rather, the primary jurisdiction of the ICTY was defined by its Statute, and an amendment to the Statute or derogation from the Statute would require a UNSC resolution. The existence of an agreement was not in itself sufficient to limit the jurisdiction of the tribunal.[75]

The Appeals Chamber went on to agree with the Trial Chamber that even if the Holbrook Agreement had been concluded by the Prosecution, it would not provide a valid basis for discontinuing prosecution. At the time the Agreement was allegedly concluded, there was already an indictment against Karadžić; under the Rules of the ICTY, an indictment can be removed only with consent of the tribunal. The Holbrook Agreement could not override this requirement.[76]

In the course of dismissing arguments based on abuse of process, the Appeals Chamber articulated what was arguably the underlying principle of the decision:

> The Appeals Chamber recalls that one of the fundamental aims of international criminal courts and tribunals is to end impunity and ensure that serious violations of international humanitarian law are prosecuted and punished. Individuals accused of such crimes can have no legitimate expectation of immunity from prosecution. The Appeals Chamber considers that the facts that allegedly gave rise to the Appellant's expectations of impunity do not constitute an exception to this rule. [77]

---

72   *Karadžić* (IT-95-5/18-PT), Decision on The Accused's Holbrooke Agreement. Motion, 8 July 2009.
73   Above note 71.
74   *Ibid.* at para. 8.
75   *Ibid.* at paras. 35–37.
76   *Ibid.* at paras. 40–41.
77   Above note 56 at para. 52 [footnote removed].

This statement is interesting because it suggests that the only source for Karadžić's expectation of immunity was the Holbrook Agreement. It suggests that neither personal nor functional immunity could provide a basis for this expectation.

d) *Kambanda* (ICTR)

The case of Jean Kambanda before the ICTR appears to confirm that at the very least, functional immunities are inapplicable as a result of article 6.2 of the *Statute of the ICTR*.[78] By indictment received 28 October 1997, Kambanda had been charged with five crimes: genocide, conspiracy to commit genocide, direct and public incitement to commit genocide, complicity in genocide, and crimes against humanity.[79] At the time of the Rwandan genocide, Kambanda was the Prime Minister of Rwanda. He left Rwanda about 17 July 1994 and was subsequently arrested by Kenyan authorities on 9 July 1997. He was transferred to the ICTR where, on 1 May 1998, he pleaded guilty to all six charges.[80]

Because Kambanda pleaded guilty, there was no need for the Trial Chamber of the ICTR to opine on any immunities he might possess. However, Kambanda subsequently appealed his conviction and sentence, arguing *inter alia* that his plea of guilty was involuntary and that the sentence imposed was excessive. He did not raise immunity as a ground of appeal. This lack of plea of immunity suggests that even Kambanda accepted that such an argument was meritless.[81]

The *Kambanda* decisions are disappointing because of the non-treatment of immunities. The lack of discussion from the tribunal concerning Kambanda's entitlement (or not) to immunity leaves open the question whether the tribunal considered whether article 6.2 was reflective of customary law (as stated by the UN Secretary-General and the ICTY in *Milosević*),[82] whether all applicable immunities were removed by the UNSC (as certain authors hypothesize),[83] or whether the immunities were inapplicable before the ICTR because Rwanda, a member of the United Nations, had accepted the terms of the *Statute of the ICTR* and, by so doing, itself waived the immunities of its former officials.[84]

---

78   (ICTR-97-23), 4 September 1998.
79   The relevant documents are available online: www.ictr.org.
80   The facts are set out in the decision of the Trial Chamber in *Kambanda* (ICTR 97-23-S), Decision on Judgment and Sentence, 4 September 1998.
81   *Kambanda* (ICTR 97-23-A), Appeals Chamber Judgment, 19 October 2000.
82   See Section C(2)(b) text at note 61.
83   Cryer, above note 2 at 439.
84   See, for example, Akande, above note 5 at 417, who suggests that the ICTY and ICTR statutes are capable of removing immunity of state officials from practical-

It is probable that the ICTR would take the same view of article 6.2 that the ICTY later took of article 7.2; however, this is mere speculation. Absent some judicial comment, all that can be stated with certainty is the obvious: functional immunities are unavailable before the ICTR.

3) Internationalized Tribunals: The Special Court for Sierra Leone

a) General

In addition to the two *ad hoc* international tribunals, there have recently been established a number of *ad hoc* internationalized tribunals. These tribunals are mixed or hybrid tribunals; they are in part competent to apply international law and are in part staffed by international legal experts. And, in part, the tribunals apply domestic law and are staffed by local legal officials. For current purposes,[85] the most important of these internationalized tribunals is the Special Court for Sierra Leone (SCSL), the court which indicted the incumbent Liberian President Charles Taylor for his role in Sierra Leone's civil war. Unlike the Yugoslavia and Rwanda tribunals, which were established by the UN Security Council acting under its Chapter VII powers, the SCSL was established by agreement between the United Nations and Sierra Leone.[86] As with the Yugoslavia and Rwanda tribunals, the *Statute of the Special Court for Sierra Leone* has a provision relating to the immunities available before the court. Article 6.2 of the *Statute of the SCSL* provides, "[t]he official position of any accused persons, whether as Head of State or Government or as a responsible government official, shall not relieve such person of criminal responsibility nor mitigate punishment."[87] This provision is virtually identical to those found in the *Statute of the ICTY* and the *Statute of the ICTR*.

b) Charles Taylor

The meaning and force of this provision, and the law which it embodies, was discussed by the Appeals Chamber of the SCSL in its decision on the immunity of Charles Taylor.[88] After an arrest warrant had been

---

ly all states because those states are parties to the UN and so have indirectly consented to the removal of immunity.

85 See Chapter 4 for more details.

86 The SCSL Agreement is online: www.sc-sl.org/LinkClick.aspx?fileticket=CLk1r MQtCHg%3d&tabid=176.

87 The *Statute of the SCSL* is online: www.sc-sl.org/LinkClick.aspx?fileticket=uCln d1MJeEw%3d&tabid=176.

88 *Taylor* (SCSL-03-01-I-059), Appeals Chamber Decision on Immunity Motion, 31 May 2004.

issued against him, Taylor applied to have the indictment and the arrest warrant set aside on the grounds that as a serving head of state he was immune from the jurisdiction of the tribunal.[89] In part, Taylor argued that as a serving head of state, he was immune from criminal process and, as the SCSL was not established by the UNSC acting under Chapter VII,[90] there was no Chapter VII waiver of immunity. In reply, the Prosecutor argued (in part) that international law permits an international court to try a serving head of state. According to the Prosecutor, the SCSL was such an international court.

For the court, the key issue appeared to be whether it was or was not an international court. The Appeals Chamber determined that the SCSL is an international court, a decision in part dependent on the fact that the court was the product of an agreement between the UN (expressing the will of the international community) and Sierra Leone.[91] Having determined that the SCSL is an international court, the Appeals Chamber turned to the question of the immunities available before the SCSL.

The Appeals Chamber rejected Taylor's claim to immunity, giving essentially four reasons for doing so. First, as noted in the court's reasons for finding that the SCSL was an international court, the UNSC had authorized the UN Secretary-General to conclude an agreement with Sierra Leone for the establishment of the court.[92] In making this observation, the SCSL appeared to be cloaking itself in Chapter VII authority.[93] Second, the *Statute of the SCSL*, which the court was bound to apply unless it conflicted with a peremptory norm of international law, specifically excludes immunity.[94] The Chamber reviewed relevant international practice and noted that as far back as 1950 and the formulation of the *Nuremberg Principles*,[95] it was recognized that official capacity would not bar prosecution before an international tribunal.[96] The court

---

89   In charging Taylor, the Prosecution alleged that he committed his crimes in a private capacity, for private gain (see *ibid.* at para. 5).

90   As suggested in the discussion of *Kambanda* in Section C(2)(d), above in this chapter.

91   Above note 88 at paras. 37–42. See James Miglin, "From Immunity to Impunity: Charles Taylor and the Special Court for Sierra Leone" (2007) 16 Dal. J. Leg. Stud. 21.

92   *Taylor, ibid.*

93   Zsuzsanna Deen-Racsmány, "*Prosecutor v. Taylor*: The Status of the Special Court for Sierra Leone and Its Implications for Immunity" (2005)18 Leiden J. Int'l L. 299 at 301.

94   *Taylor,* above note 88 at para. 43.

95   Published in Report of the International Law Commission Covering its Second Session, 5 June–29 July 1950, Document A/1316 at 11–14.

96   *Taylor,* above note 88 at para. 47.

referred to the long practice of denying immunity before international courts to demonstrate that the provisions of the Statute did not conflict with any peremptory norm of international law.[97] Third, the Appeals Chamber noted that the decision of the ICJ in the *Arrest Warrant* case[98] (discussed in Section D(2)(c), below in this chapter) contained passages suggesting that immunity was not available before certain international courts.[99] And finally, the Appeals Chamber found that immunity was based in the equality of states; because of that equality, one state would not sit in judgment of another. This rationale for immunity was inapplicable before an international court.[100]

The decision of the court concerning Taylor's immunity has been criticized for the reasoning employed by the court.[101] Unlike the *ad hoc* tribunals, the SCSL is not a UN organ and was not established under Chapter VII. This lack of Chapter VII authority has been viewed by some as critical to the question of immunities. While the UNSC is competent to waive the immunities of member states under Chapter VII, there was no such waiver in favour of the SCSL.[102]

---

97 *Ibid.* at paras. 52–53.

98 Above note 1.

99 *Taylor*, above note 88 at para. 50.

100 *Ibid.* at paras. 51–53. In addition to the SCSL, two other courts have recently been established with the assistance of the United Nations. The Extraordinary Chambers in the Courts of Cambodia were established in order to prosecute surviving members of the Khmer Rouge for the crimes committed under Pol Pot. The Agreement between Cambodia and the UN which establishes the Extraordinary Chamber, signed in Phnom Penh on 6 June 2003, online: www. eccc.gov.kh/english/cabinet/agreement/5/Agreement_between_UN_and_RGC. pdf, provides that the crimes within the jurisdiction of the Chamber are genocide, war crimes, and crimes against humanity. In 2007, the Special Tribunal for Lebanon was established to investigate and prosecute those persons allegedly responsible for the bombing which killed former Lebanese Prime Minister Rafiq Hariri in 2005. Under art. 2 of the *Statute for the Special Tribunal for Lebanon*, online: www.stl-tsl.org/sid/49#Statutes, the applicable law is that of Lebanon. Neither statute mentions immunity or the official capacity of the accused. This is likely because the Extraordinary Chambers, although operating with international staff and assistance, is essentially a Cambodian court, not an international tribunal. Cambodian defendants would not be entitled (as a matter of international law) to immunity before Cambodian courts. The lack of reference to official capacity in the *Statute for the Special Tribunal for Lebanon* is probably a function of the fact that the applicable law is Lebanese law. Presumably, if issues of immunity arise, they will be settled according to the provisions found in Lebanese law.

101 See, for example, Deen-Racsmány, above note 93. For a more general critique and discussion, see Cryer, above note 2 at 441–44.

102 Cryer, *ibid.* at 307–13.

However, the SCSL was arguably correct when it held that it was bound to apply the law contained in its own Statute providing there was no conflict with a peremptory norm. The *Statute of the SCSL* specifically excludes claims to immunity and, as this exclusion did not conflict with a peremptory norm, the court had to give effect to article 6.2.[103] This is not to say that the decision of the court was uncontroversial or to deny that it was probably incorrect as a matter of pure international law. It remains the case, however, that as regards the Statute governing the court, the decision was probably correct.

While the practice has been far from explicit, it appears that provisions in the *Statute of the SCSL* similar to those found in the *IMT Charter* have the effect of waiving both personal and functional immunities.

4) The International Criminal Court as a Special Case

a) General

As discussed in detail in Chapter 4, the International Criminal Court (ICC) came into being on 1 July 2002 following the 60th ratification of the *Rome Statute*.[104] The ICC represents a special case in terms of immunity, which stems from the creation of the ICC. Unlike its predecessor tribunals, the ICC was not created following a conflict and is not intended to deal with a geographically or temporally limited situation. It was not created by victor nations following an international armed conflict (as the IMT and IMTFE had been) and it is not a creature of the UNSC's Chapter VII powers. Rather, the ICC is a treaty-based tribunal and is meant to be a permanent international court.

Prior to discussing the specifics of the immunities available under the *Rome Statute*, and the tricky issue of who may claim immunity, it is necessary to review the three types of persons who may find themselves before the ICC.

The ICC has three basic grounds of jurisdiction: territorial jurisdiction, nationality jurisdiction, and jurisdiction conferred by the UNSC through referral. Nationality jurisdiction presents the simplest situation; in those cases, the accused will be a national of a state party, and one set of rules under the *Rome Statute* applies. If the jurisdiction exercised is territorial (the crime was committed on the territory of a state party), there is a possibility that the accused will be a non-party nation-

---

103 This, of course, depends on accepting that art. 6.2 refers to both functional and personal immunities. Cryer takes the opposite view, *ibid.* at 444, stating that the *Statute of the SCSL* refers only to functional immunities.

104 *Rome Statute of the International Criminal Court*, Can. T.S. 2002 No. 13 [*Rome Statute*].

al. In that case, different rules (still under the *Rome Statute*) apply. If an accused comes before the court because a situation has been referred by the UNSC, a third legal regime applies.

The basic rules of immunity which will be applied by the ICC are found in articles 27 and 98 of the *Rome Statute*.

b) Article 27

In terms of immunity, article 27 of the *Rome Statute* clearly removes both functional and personal immunities. Article 27 provides,

> **Irrelevance of official capacity**
>
> 1. This Statute shall apply equally to all persons without any distinction based on official capacity. In particular, official capacity as a Head of State or Government, a member of a Government or parliament, an elected representative or a government official shall in no case exempt a person from criminal responsibility under this Statute, nor shall it, in and of itself, constitute a ground for reduction of sentence.
>
> 2. Immunities or special procedural rules which may attach to the official capacity of a person, whether under national or international law, shall not bar the Court from exercising its jurisdiction over such a person.

According to article 27, no accused who comes before the ICC can claim either functional or personal immunity. The removal of immunity under the *Rome Statute* was done by consent of the parties to the Statute; this is a case of clear waiver of immunities by the parties to the treaty.[105]

However, there remain some concerns about the total inapplicability of immunities before the ICC, because it is possible that a national of a non-party state may find themselves facing trial before the ICC for a crime committed on the territory of a state party.[106] In such a case, article 27 would bar claims to both functional and personal immunities. This inability of a non-party national to claim immunity before the ICC has caused concern to some commentators.[107]

---

105 William A. Schabas, *An Introduction to the International Criminal Court*, 3d ed. (Cambridge: Cambridge University Press, 2007) at 232 [Schabas, *Introduction to the ICC*].

106 See, for example, William A. Schabas, "United States Hostility to the International Criminal Court: It's All About the Security Council" (2004) 15 E.J.I.L. 701 at 710, who notes that one reason provided by the US for "unsigning" the *Rome Statute* was the possibility that it would exercise jurisdiction over citizens of non-party states.

107 See, in particular, Simbeye, above note 1, cc. 4–6.

The mechanism of article 27 is very simple; once an individual accused is before the ICC, immunity cannot be pleaded to bar prosecution. Under the *Rome Statute*, it is irrelevant whether an individual might claim personal or functional immunity, and equally irrelevant whether he is a current or former state official. The *Rome Statute* by its express terms eliminates many of the difficulties which have plagued courts dealing with questions of immunity.

This clarity is only available when an accused is before the ICC. Prior to surrender to the ICC, it is an open question whether immunities are applicable. It is probable that state parties are required by the *Rome Statute* to refuse to give effect to immunity as between themselves even at the national level, at least when detaining an individual at the request of the ICC. This conclusion is arrived at by reading articles 27, 86, 89, and 120 together. As noted, article 27 bars claims of immunity. According to article 86, state parties are obliged to cooperate with the ICC. Under article 89, state parties are required to surrender persons to the ICC, and under article 120, no reservations to the *Rome Statute* are permitted. Parties to the *Rome Statute* are clearly waiving the immunities of their officials before the court.[108]

The question whether an individual may claim immunity in a prosecution before a Canadian court (as opposed to in response to a request to surrender) will be considered below.

A major issue raised by article 27 concerns the immunity of nationals of non-party states to the ICC. As noted above, once a non-party national is before the ICC, she too is unable to claim immunity. This leaves the question whether a non-party national may claim immunity prior to surrender. This question is answered in part by article 98 of the *Rome Statute*.

c) Article 98

Article 98 provides,

> **Cooperation with respect to waiver of immunity and consent to surrender**
>
> 1. The Court may not proceed with a request for surrender or assistance which would require the requested State to act inconsistently with its obligations under international law with respect to the State or diplomatic immunity of a person or property of a third State, unless the Court can first obtain the cooperation of that third State for the waiver of the immunity.

---

108 Cryer, above note 2 at 440. Schabas, *Introduction to the ICC*, above note 105 at 232, also states that by treaty, state parties to the *Rome Statute* have agreed not to invoke the immunity of their officials before the court.

2. The Court may not proceed with a request for surrender which would require the requested State to act inconsistently with its obligations under international agreements pursuant to which the consent of a sending State is required to surrender a person of that State to the Court, unless the Court can first obtain the cooperation of the sending State for the giving of consent for the surrender.

While some commentators have expressed concerns about the effect article 98 will have on article 27,[109] others find no difficulty with the provision and point out that articles 27 and 98 must be read together in order to understand the regime of immunity under the *Rome Statute*; the articles apply at different stages of the proceeding and offer clear rules on the applicability of immunity.[110]

Unlike article 27, which applies after an accused is before the ICC, article 98 applies at the time of a request for surrender. Under article 98, the ICC may request the surrender of an individual only if that request would not require a state to breach an international obligation owed to another state. Effectively, this limitation means that if the request for surrender would require a party to breach the immunity owed to a non-party national, the ICC could not proceed with a request for surrender. The only exception contained in article 98 is agreement by the non-party state. Because immunity is the privilege of the state, not the individual, the state may waive immunity at any time.[111]

As pointed out by Cryer, the protection of article 98 applies only when the accused is a non-party national;[112] the use of the term "third state" in article 98 makes it clear that the recognition of immunity at the surrender stage does not apply to nationals of state parties. The immunity regime created by the *Rome Statute* has been summed up in this way:

> The interplay of Articles 27 and 98(1) therefore creates a regime wherein States Parties agree to relinquish all immunities in relation to ICC requests concerning their own nationals, representatives or officials, while still respecting the existing immunities of States which have not joined the ICC Statute system.[113]

---

109 Simbeye, above note 1 at 136.
110 Cryer, above note 2 at 440. See also Schabas, *Introduction to the ICC*, above note 105 at 74 and 231–32.
111 Schabas, *Introduction to the ICC*, ibid. at 232. See also Cryer, *ibid.* at 441.
112 Cryer, *ibid.* at 440.
113 *Ibid.* It should be noted that not all states are willing to trust the protections contained in the *Rome Statute*. In 2002, the US Congress passed the *American Service-Members' Protection Act of 2001* (*ASPA*), 22 U.S.C. §§ 7421 *et seq.* (2006). Colloquially known as the "Hague Invasion Act," the *ASPA* prohibits US author-

The final question which must be considered is the legal regime which applies when a situation is referred to the ICC by the UN Security Council.

Under article 13(b), the court has jurisdiction over situations which are referred to the ICC by the UNSC acting under Chapter VII. Only one situation, that in the Darfur Region of the Sudan, has so far been referred by the UNSC. The Sudan is not a party to the *Rome Statute* and, as such, has not consented to waive the immunity of its officials. The issue of the interaction between the immunities of state officials and UNSC referrals became very real and relevant in 2009 when the ICC issued an arrest warrant against the Sudanese President Omar al-Bashir.

d) *Bashir*[114]

On 4 March 2009, Pre-Trial Chamber I of the ICC issued an arrest warrant against Sudanese President Omar al-Bashir for five counts of crimes against humanity and two counts of war crimes.[115] The ICC Chief Prosecutor had requested an indictment for genocide, war crimes, and crimes against humanity.[116] Not surprisingly, President Bashir has not turned himself in to the ICC and has instead denounced the indictment as colonialist.[117] In its decision on the arrest warrant, the Pre-Trial Chamber gave some consideration to whether President Bashir's position as head of state could operate as a bar to the jurisdiction of the ICC; the court decided it did not.[118]

---

ities from cooperating with the ICC, prohibits US participation in peacekeeping missions unless the UNSC resolution establishing the peacekeeping mission exempts US forces from the jurisdiction of the ICC, and authorizes the President of the Unites States of America "to use all means necessary and appropriate to bring about the release of any person described in subsection (b) who is being detained or imprisoned by, on behalf of, or at the request of the International Criminal Court."

114 Two recent articles deal specifically with the question of President Bashir's immunity; see Dapo Akande, "The Legal Nature of Security Council Referrals to the ICC and its Impact on Al Bashir's Immunities" (2009) 7 JICJ 333 [Akande, "Bashir's Immunities"] and Paola Gaeta, "Does President Al Bashir Enjoy Immunity from Arrest?" (2009) 7 JICJ 315 [Gaeta].

115 *Al Bashir* (ICC-02/05-01/09), Warrant of Arrest Issued by Pre-Trial Chamber I, 4 March 2009.

116 The Prosecutor has launched an appeal of the decision not to issue a warrant for genocide. Leave to appeal was granted in respect of one of the issues raised by the Prosecutor, ICC-02/05-01/09, 24 June 2009.

117 As reported by the BBC on 5 March 2009, online: http://news.bbc.co.uk/2/hi/africa/7925445.stm.

118 The decision on the arrest warrant bears the same number and date as the arrest warrant itself (above note 115).

The conclusion of the Pre-Trial Chamber was stated at paragraph 41 of its decision in succinct fashion:

> Furthermore, in light of the materials presented by the Prosecution in support of the Prosecution Application, and without prejudice to a further determination of the matter pursuant to article 19 of the Statute, the Chamber considers that the current position of Omar Al Bashir as Head of a state which is not a party to the Statute, has no effect on the Court's jurisdiction over the present case.

The Pre-Trial Chamber gave four reasons for this conclusion:[119] first, that the Preamble to the *Rome Statute* states that one of the purposes of the court is to end impunity;[120] second, that article 27 expressly bars claims of immunity;[121] third, that recourse to legal sources outside the *Rome Statute*, the *Elements of Crimes*, and the *Rules* of the court are to be resorted to only if there is a lacuna in the law contained in those sources;[122] and fourth, that by referring the situation in Darfur to the ICC, the UNSC had accepted that the investigation and prosecution would be carried out in accordance with the ICC's statutory framework.[123]

The UNSC referred the situation in Darfur to the ICC by Resolution 1593 in 2005.[124] In that resolution, the UNSC first determined that the situation in Darfur amounted to a threat to international peace and security. This determination triggers the extensive powers of the UNSC when acting under Chapter VII.[125] The resolution is less clear than one could wish but, read as a whole, it suggests that the Sudanese officials may not claim immunity before the ICC. This would be consonant with the findings in the ICTY caselaw.

The possible immunities of Sudanese officials before the ICC must be considered from two perspectives: that of the Sudan and that of the rest of the international community.[126] In terms of the Sudan, it seems

---

119 On this point, see also Gaeta, above note 114 at 323, who is fairly critical of some of the reasons provided. See also Akande, "Bashir's Immunities," above note 114 at 336, who notes there are in fact two levels to the immunity question: whether Bashir is immune before the court is one question, and whether Bashir is immune in respect of other states which might arrest and surrender him to the court is another.

120 Decision of Pre-Trial Chamber I, above note 115 at para. 42.

121 *Ibid.* at para. 43.

122 *Ibid.* at para. 44.

123 *Ibid.* at para. 45.

124 UN Doc. S/RES/1593 (2005), 31 March 2005.

125 Indeed, the resolution, *ibid.*, expressly states that it is passed under Chapter VII.

126 See, in particular, Akande, "Bashir's Immunities," above note 114.

fairly clear that by referring the situation in Darfur to the ICC, the UNSC has effectively required that the Sudan not raise the immunity of its officials as a bar to prosecution before that court.[127] Paragraph 2 of the operative part of the resolution requires that the Sudan cooperate with the ICC. This cooperation likely (though not expressly) extends to a requirement that the Sudan comply with all the provisions of the *Rome Statute*, including article 59, which governs the arrest of persons upon request of the court, article 89, which governs the surrender of persons to the court, and article 27, which eliminates the availability of immunity before the court. This cooperation may also require that the Sudan waive the immunity of its officials in respect of other states acting on behalf of the court.[128]

From the perspective of states other than the Sudan, it is unclear whether there is a requirement to cooperate with the ICC, and if so, the extent of that requirement. Resolution 1593 urges (although it does not require) all non-party states to the *Rome Statute* to cooperate with the ICC and implicitly recognizes that parties to the *Rome Statute* are obliged to cooperate with the court.[129] The question is how the *UN Charter*[130] and the provisions of Resolution 1593 interact with the *Rome Statute*.

Under article 103 of the *UN Charter*, UN member states must give priority to their *Charter* obligations over all other international obligations.[131] Under article 24 of the *Charter*, the UNSC has "primary responsibility" for the maintenance of international peace and security. As a corollary, UN members have expressly agreed to carry out the decisions of the UNSC (article 25).[132] Under article 39 of the *Charter*, the UNSC may determine that a situation is a threat to international

---

127 Akande, "Bashir's Immunities," *ibid.* at 335, takes the view that the Sudan is obliged to surrender President Bashir to the ICC and is not entitled to invoke his immunity.

128 Schabas, *Introduction to the ICC*, above note 105 at 252, suggests that the obligation on the Sudan to cooperate is an obligation under the *UN Charter* rather than under the *Rome Statute*. See also Akande, "Bashir's Immunities," above note 114 at 345, who suggests that all states, in cooperating with the ICC, are entitled to rely on art. 27 of the ICC as against President Bashir. See further the discussion below in this section.

129 Above note 124 at operative para. 2.

130 1945 Can T.S. No. 7 (24 October 1945).

131 Akande, "Bashir's Immunities," above note 114 at 346–48, explores the application of art. 103 to this situation. In his discussion at 348, he notes the majority view that art. 103 also applies to customary law obligations.

132 On the obligations created by a UNSC decision, see Akande, "Bashir's Immunities," *ibid.* at 341.

peace and security. Following such a determination, the UNSC has binding authority to address the threat. Under article 41 of the *Charter*, the UNSC may order non-forcible measures. It is probably this article which gives the UNSC the authority to refer the situation in Darfur to the ICC.

Once the UNSC has taken a decision under Chapter VII, UN members are bound to carry out those decisions. By referring the Darfur situation to the ICC, the UNSC has decided two things: first, that the ICC has jurisdiction over the situation, and second, that the law which applies to the situation is that contained in the *Rome Statute*.[133] The effect of these decisions is that the Sudan is to be treated as a party to the *Rome Statute* insofar as the situation in Darfur is concerned. If the ICC were to request that a state party to the *Rome Statute* arrest and surrender President Bashir, and that state party were to do so, there would be no breach of any international obligation because the Sudan is to be treated as a party to the Statute.[134] In the case of non-parties to the *Rome Statute*, there is no obligation to cooperate with the ICC.[135] Arguably, by urging all states to cooperate with the ICC, the UNSC has created a situation in which non-party states are permitted but not required to cooperate with the ICC.[136] However, the better view is probably that because the Sudan is required to cooperate fully with the ICC, it is prohibited from frustrating the work of the ICC by raising claims of immunity in favour of its officials, either before the ICC or against a state cooperating with the ICC.[137]

The result of this rather convoluted relationship between the ICC, the UNSC, the law of the *Rome Statute,* and the law of the *UN Charter* is that the Sudan is required to surrender its nationals to the ICC and, once before the court, pleas of immunity are unavailable to Sudanese officials. The situation for other states is far more complicated, but it

---

133 *Ibid.* at 340–42.
134 *Ibid.*
135 Resolution 1593, above note 124. See also Akande, "Bashir's Immunities," *ibid.* at 343–44.
136 Akande, "Bashir's Immunities," *ibid.* at 344–45, doubts this.
137 *Ibid.* at 345. The obligation of other states would be far more clear, and the situation as a whole far more satisfactory, had Resolution 1593 (2005) required that all states cooperate with the ICC. This was the approach taken by the UNSC in relation to the ICTY. UN Doc. S/RES/827 (1993) operative para. 4 states that the UNSC "Decides that all States shall cooperate fully with the International Tribunal and its organs . . . ." A similar provision was included in UN Doc. S/RES/955 (1994), which established the ICTR. Operative para. 2 of that resolution also states that the UNSC "Decides that all States shall cooperate fully with the International Tribunal and its organs . . . ."

appears that state parties to the *Rome Statute* remain bound by that Statute to cooperate with the court while non-parties are permitted to do so.[138]

This interpretation seems to accord with the position of the Chief Prosecutor of the ICC, Luis Moreno-Ocampo. He has opined that state parties to the *Rome Statute* are legally obliged to arrest President Bashir.[139] Ocampo's position is likely based on article 86 of the *Rome Statute*, which obliges state parties to cooperate with the ICC.

5) Conclusions

The above survey suggests that as regards genocide, war crimes, and crimes against humanity, there is sufficient practice to assert with some certainty that neither personal nor functional immunities are available before international tribunals. The same is probably also true of crimes against peace (aggression). Certainly following WW II, the *IMT Charter*[140] made no distinction between crimes against peace and either war crimes or crimes against humanity. More recently, the *Rome Statute* gave that tribunal jurisdiction over aggression, and there is nothing in the Statute which suggests that the official capacity of a person will be treated differently for that crime. Certainly, the view expressed by the UN Secretary-General in his report, the ICTY in the *Milosević* case, and the SCSL in the *Taylor* case would support such a conclusion.

However, this remains uncertain. The non-applicability of immunities before the IMT was not really an issue because, prior to the Nuremberg trial, Germany had surrendered unconditionally to the Allies, and it was within their competence, standing in place of the German government, to exercise territorial jurisdiction.[141] The ICTY and ICTR may be viewed as similarly poor examples of a customary rule, because the waiver of immunity before those tribunals was a valid exercise of the UN Security Council's Chapter VII powers.[142] The parties to the ICC have chosen to waive immunity by consent.[143]

---

138 Though at the time of writing, there is a great deal of resistance from many African states and the African Union to doing so. See, for example, the BBC article "African Union in Rift with Court," online: http://news.bbc.co.uk/2/hi/8133925.stm.

139 See, for example, the report online: http://jurist.law.pitt.edu/paperchase/2009/07/uganda-to-arrest-al-bashir-if-he-enters.php.

140 Above note 41.

141 See Fox, *State Immunity*, above note 3 at 431–32; Cryer, above note 2 at 438.

142 See Fox, *State Immunity*, 2d, above note 1 at 677; Cryer, *ibid.*

143 See Cryer, *ibid.*

Because there has generally been a valid alternative means to waive immunities, some commentators remain of the view that there is no customary rule which renders immunities automatically inoperative before international tribunals.[144] At least as regards personal immunities, it is probably correct that there is no customary rule which renders them automatically inapplicable before international courts. The reason for this is given by Cryer: if such a rule were to exist, article 98 of the *Rome Statute* would be superfluous.[145]

The issue of functional immunities is different. As will be discussed in greater detail in Section D, below in this chapter, functional immunities protect certain acts and, it appears that war crimes, crimes against humanity, genocide, torture, and perhaps other treaty crimes are now excluded from the sphere of protection. Because of this exclusion, there appears to be no basis for asserting that functional immunities remain applicable before international courts unless specifically excluded.

D. IMMUNITY BEFORE DOMESTIC COURTS

1) Introduction

The question of the immunities available before domestic courts is somewhat more complicated than is the issue of immunity before international tribunals. Unlike the international tribunals examined above, domestic courts have jurisdiction not only over the "core crimes" of genocide, crimes against humanity, and war crimes, but also over other international crimes, transnational crimes of both international and domestic concern, and purely domestic crimes. The following discussion will examine the availability of immunity for war crimes, crimes against humanity, and genocide, as well as the international crime of torture.

To further complicate matters, the international law which applies to prosecutions before domestic courts is fairly diffuse. While the *Rome Statute* now contains provisions relating to war crimes, crimes against humanity, and genocide, there remain other treaties which are important because they define and require the criminalization of certain conduct. For this reason, the discussion below will separately focus on war crimes, genocide, crimes against humanity, and torture.

---

144 Cryer, *ibid.* at 438 and 442–43.
145 *Ibid.* at 443.

2) War Crimes

The law relating to war crimes, although recently set out in the *Rome Statute*, is also found in the *Hague* and *Geneva Conventions* as well as in customary law. The most important treaty provisions are found in the four *Geneva Conventions* of 1949.[146]

a) The *Geneva Conventions*

The four *Geneva Conventions* of 1949 are the starting point for a treaty discussion of whether immunities are available for war crimes.[147]

Each of the four *Geneva Conventions* requires that state parties implement certain measures to enforce the obligations under the Conventions; one such measure is the criminalization of grave breaches of the Conventions.

The first *Geneva Convention* concerns the protection of wounded and sick members of the armed forces. Article 49 of the Convention imposes on the parties the obligation to criminalize grave breaches of the Convention:

> The High Contracting Parties undertake to enact any legislation necessary to provide effective penal sanctions for persons committing, or ordering to be committed, any of the grave breaches of the present Convention defined in the following Article.
>
> Each High Contracting Party shall be under the obligation to search for persons alleged to have committed, or to have ordered to be committed, such grave breaches, and shall bring such persons, regardless of their nationality, before its own courts. It may also, if it prefers, and in accordance with the provisions of its own legislation, hand such persons over for trial to another High Contracting Party concerned, provided such High Contracting Party has made out a *prima facie* case.
>
> Each High Contracting Party shall take measures necessary for the suppression of all acts contrary to the provisions of the present Convention other than the grave breaches defined in the following Article.
>
> In all circumstances, the accused persons shall benefit by safeguards of proper trial and defence, which shall not be less favourable than those provided by Article 105 and those following, of the Geneva Convention relative to the Treatment of Prisoners of War of 12 August 1949.

---

146 Above note 15.
147 See, generally, Chapter 3.

Each of the other *Geneva Conventions* contains identical articles.[148]

Two observations may be made about this article. The first is that parties to the Conventions are required to assert jurisdiction over persons who have committed grave breaches of the Convention whether or not those persons are their own nationals. The Convention specifically contemplates, in fact requires, that parties prosecute non-nationals for war crimes. The second observation is that there appears to be no connection required to the crime or to the perpetrator, in order for a state to claim jurisdiction. This interpretation is confirmed by the commentaries.[149]

The effect of the article appears to be that states are required to assert universal jurisdiction over war crimes and to prosecute persons on the basis of universal jurisdiction. This requirement suggests that, at a minimum, a claim of immunity *ratione materiae* is incompatible with the requirements of the Conventions.

State practice, some of which relates to crimes committed during WW II, suggests that such an interpretation is in accordance with customary law. Of particular importance are the decisions (trial and appeal) in the *Eichmann* prosecution because of their detailed discussion of functional immunity.

b)   *Eichmann*

The trial of Adolf Eichmann was an early domestic prosecution for war crimes, crimes against humanity, and crimes which amounted to genocide.[150] Eichmann argued (in part) that he was not guilty of the crimes for which he was charged (crimes against the Jewish people, war crimes, and crimes against humanity) because those crimes were acts of state and the state alone bore responsibility. Although the Israeli courts treated this as the act of state defence, it appears rather to be an assertion of immunity *ratione materiae*.[151]

---

148 *Convention (II) for the Amelioration of the Condition of Wounded, Sick and Shipwrecked Members of Armed Forces at Sea*, Geneva, 12 August 1949, art. 50; *Convention (III) relative to the Treatment of Prisoners of War*, Geneva, 12 August 1949, art. 129; *Convention (IV) relative to the Protection of Civilian Persons in Time of War*, Geneva, 12 August 1949, art. 146.

149 Available online: www.icrc.org/ihl.nsf/WebList?ReadForm&id=365&t=com.

150 *Attorney-General of Israel v. Eichmann* (1968), 36 I.L.R. 18 (Jerusalem Dist. Ct. 1961), aff'd (1968), 36 I.L.R. 277 (Israel Sup. Ct. 1962) [*Eichmann*]. See Chapter 5 for a more detailed discussion.

151 *Eichmann, ibid.* at para. 28 (Jerusalem Dist. Ct.). The full text of the judgment is available online: www.nizkor.org/. Cryer, above note 2 at 433, also seems to take the view that the plea raised by Eichmann was one of functional immunity.

Eichmann had been an official in the Nazi government; his responsibility both before and during WW II was to facilitate first the deportation of Jews from Austria, then from Germany and the Occupied Territories and finally, to arrange the transportation of Jews within Germany and the Occupied Territories to the death camps for extermination.

The Trial Court dealt with the act of state defence along three lines. In the first place, the court referred to the famous dictum of the IMT in the Trial of the Major War Criminals; that "[c]rimes against international law are committed by men, not by abstract entities, and only by punishing individuals who commit such crimes can the provisions of international law be enforced . . . ."[152] (This reference was further supported by recourse to the *IMT Charter* and the *Principles of International Law*[153] adopted by the UNGA.)

Second, the trial court further held that in any event, the principle of equality between the states was inapplicable to Nazi Germany because that state had planned and implemented the "Final Solution"; the court likened Nazi Germany to a gang of criminals. Third, the court noted that there was a system of dual responsibility under international law. As the Trial Court argued, the fact that Germany was responsible as a state for the crimes with which Eichmann was charged "does not detract one iota from the personal responsibility of the Accused for his acts."[154]

On appeal, the Supreme Court of Israel sitting as a Court of Criminal Appeal also addressed the contention that it was not the individual and only the state which bore responsibility for the crimes alleged. While the Supreme Court of Israel upheld the lower court's rejection of the act of state defence, it did so for somewhat different reasons.[155]

The first reason given by the Supreme Court of Israel for rejecting the defence was that it depended on the view that state immunity and the act of state defence were absolute; the Court rejected this, noting that even as far back as the decision in the *Schooner Exchange v. McFaddon* case,[156] Chief Justice Marshall had been careful to state that immunity was based on the implied consent of the state in which a wrongful act occurred.[157]

---

152 (1947), 41 A.J.I.L. 172 at 217.
153 Above note 46.
154 *Eichmann*, above note 151 at para. 28 (Jerusalem Dist. Ct.).
155 The full text of the decision of the Supreme Court of Israel is also available on the Nizkor site, above note 151.
156 11 U.S. (7 Cranch) 116 (1812).
157 *Eichmann*, above note 150 at para. 14(a) (Israel Sup. Ct.).

Second, the Supreme Court of Israel found that there was no basis for the defence when the crime alleged is prohibited by the law of nations; the Court considered that the crimes alleged were "outside the 'sovereign' jurisdiction of the state that ordered or ratified their commission, and therefore those who participated in such acts must personally account for them and cannot seek shelter behind the official character of their task or mission, or behind the 'Laws' of the state by virtue of which they purported to act."[158] To support this finding, the Court noted that even prior to WW II, the act of state defence was not available for war crimes.

The third reason which the Israeli Supreme Court gave for rejecting the act of state defence was that the *IMT Charter*, the judgment of the IMT, and the *Nuremberg Principles* taken together confirmed that there was no basis in international law for the defence.[159] The Court also rejected as a basis for the defence that Eichmann was following the requirements of German law at the time. It first asserted that the orders for the Final Solution were not embodied in law at all and then argued that, in any event, the discriminatory laws of Nazi Germany were not recognized as law by international law.[160]

Other states have also tried officials of foreign states for war crimes. Among the major war crimes cases are the French prosecution of Klaus Barbie and the US prosecution of General Yamashita. Klaus Barbie, the German head of the Gestapo in Lyons, was convicted in France for crimes against humanity for his actions in France during WW II.[161] The US prosecution of General Yamashita, the former Commanding General of the Fourteenth Army Group of the Imperial Japanese Army is particularly interesting. While he was tried and convicted by a US military tribunal, he had applied to the civilian US courts for *habeas corpus* to prevent the trial. The application was ultimately rejected by the US Supreme Court but, what is notable is that General Yamashita did not raise immunity as an argument in support of his motion for *habeas corpus*.[162] Given the lack of reference to immunity in these cases,

---

158 *Ibid.* at para. 14(b).
159 *Ibid.* at para. 14(c).
160 *Ibid.* at para. 14(d).
161 *Fédération Nationale des Déportés et Internés Résistants et Patriotes et Autres c. Barbie* (1985), 78 I.L.R. 125 and (1995), 100 I.L.R. 331 (Fr. Cour de Cassation). In Antonio Cassese, *International Criminal Law*, 2d ed. (Oxford: Oxford University Press, 2008) at 305, n. 5 [Cassese, *International Criminal Law*, 2d], Professor Cassese notes the *Yamashita*, *Eichmann*, and *Barbie* cases (among others) to support his view that international law grants no functional immunity for international crimes, including war crimes, crimes against humanity, and genocide.
162 *In re Yamashita*, 327 U.S. 1 (1946).

and the consequent lack of reference to any authority granted under the *Geneva Conventions*, it is safe to say that the lack of functional immunity for war crimes is a rule of customary international law.[163]

In contrast, it appears that personal immunities do remain applicable against charges of war crimes.

c) *Yerodia*

The International Court of Justice (ICJ) recently affirmed that an individual may raise personal immunity as a bar to jurisdiction in its *Arrest Warrant* decision.[164] That case focused on the immunities of an incumbent minister of foreign affairs. While the key holdings of the ICJ in relation to immunities are admirably clear, they are also, in some respects, controversial. Rather than clarifying the law of immunity from criminal prosecution, the simplicity of the court's holdings has served to obscure the complexity of this area of the law.[165]

For present purposes, three key determinations from the decision are notable. The first is the holding related to the scope of the immunities which a serving foreign minister enjoyed. As will be discussed in greater detail below in this section, the ICJ determined that serving foreign ministers are protected by immunity *ratione personae*. The second holding of importance is the court's determination that international law knows no exception to the immunity *ratione personae* of a high official before national courts. The final aspect of the decision which is of importance here is the listing of situations in which a serving or former foreign minister may be tried for international crimes. Unlike the first two points, this final determination was expressed in *obiter*.

The background to the judgment may be stated relatively briefly. On 11 April 2000, a Belgian investigating judge issued an international arrest warrant for Abdoulaye Yerodia Ndombassi, then minister of foreign affairs for the Democratic Republic of the Congo. The arrest warrant alleged that Yerodia, prior to becoming foreign minister, had committed grave breaches of the *Geneva Conventions* and the *Protocols* thereto as well as crimes against humanity. These acts were violations of Belgium's *Law of 16 June 1993 concerning the Punishment of Grave Breaches of the International Geneva Conventions of 12 August 1949 and of Protocols I and II of 8 June 1977 Additional Thereto*[166] and were subject to

---

163 Cassese, *International Criminal Law*, 2d, above note 161 at 305–8, takes the view that the non-availability of immunity for international crimes is a rule of general international law.

164 Above note 1.

165 Schabas, *Introduction to the ICC*, above note 105 at 232.

166 Official Journal of 05.08.1993 at 17751–55.

universal jurisdiction under Belgian law. Although the arrest warrant had been transmitted to the authorities of the Democratic Republic of the Congo (DRC) and to the International Criminal Police Organization (INTERPOL), no Red Notice had been requested by Belgium or issued by INTERPOL; without the Red Notice, the arrest warrant had no mandatory force.[167]

The DRC protested that this act by Belgium violated the immunity of the DRC's foreign minister and brought an application to the ICJ seeking to have the arrest warrant quashed. By the time the case was heard and judgment given, Yerodia had ceased to be foreign minister.

According to the court, the issue for determination was whether the issuance of an international arrest warrant by Belgium for the arrest of Yerodia "violated the immunities of the then Minister for Foreign Affairs of the Congo.[168] In its analysis of this question, the court began with the premise that incumbent ministers of foreign affairs were protected by absolute personal immunity.[169]

The court managed to reach this conclusion without citing either state practice or *opinio juris* in support of such a holding. Rather, the basis for the conclusion reached was twofold. The first rationale given by the court was that the immunity must be accorded to foreign ministers to enable them to carry out their functions. The second rationale was similar; the court asserted that as is the case of a head of state, head of government, or diplomat, a foreign minister has a representative role.[170] Because of the functions of the foreign minister, it is necessary to recognize that foreign ministers are absolutely immune during their time in office.[171]

The finding by the court that a serving foreign minister enjoyed the benefit of immunity *ratione personae* was by no means a foregone con-

---

167 After Yerodia ceased to hold office, Belgium requested that INTERPOL issue a Red Notice (international wanted persons notice). At the time of the hearing before the ICJ, no Red Notice had yet been issued.

168 *Arrest Warrant*, above note 1 at para. 46.

169 *Ibid.* at para. 51. The court stated, "The Court would observe at the outset that in international law, it is firmly established that, as also diplomatic and consular agents, certain holders of high-ranking office in a State, such as the Head of State, Head of Government and Minister for Foreign Affairs, enjoy immunities from the jurisdiction of other States, both civil and criminal."

170 *Ibid.* at para. 53. Cassese has noted that in the absence of state practice and *opinio juris*, the court used logical inference: Cassese, *International Criminal Law*, above note 17 at 271 and Antonio Cassese, "When May Senior State Officials Be Tried for International Crimes? Some Comments on the *Congo v. Belgium* Case" (2002) 13 E.J.I.L. 853 at 870.

171 *Arrest Warrant*, above note 1 at para. 54.

clusion. A resolution of the Institute of International Law issued prior to the judgment in the *Arrest Warrant* case had declined to recognize that a serving foreign minister was entitled to immunity *ratione personae*. While recognizing the special recognition given to foreign ministers by the *Vienna Convention on the Law of Treaties*,[172] the Institute considered that current international practice had evolved. It noted that in recent years, other ministers had taken on a more representative role (mentioning specifically ministers of finance), and so concluded that the broad immunity *ratione personae* should be confined to heads of state and, in some cases, heads of government.[173]

Working from the premise that incumbent foreign ministers are protected by absolute immunity, the court considered whether there are exceptions to that immunity. After giving brief consideration to international instruments and state practice, the court found that there is no exception to immunity as a matter of customary law.[174] Curiously, in spite of the allegations by Belgium that Yerodia had committed grave breaches of the *Geneva Conventions* and the *Protocols* thereto, the ICJ did not seem to consider it necessary to examine those treaties to determine whether there is a Convention-based exception to the immunity of an incumbent official.

After asserting the absolute nature of the immunity from foreign prosecution enjoyed by an incumbent foreign minister, the ICJ went on, in very brief *obiter*, to state that immunity from prosecution does not mean impunity.[175] At paragraph 61 of its judgment, the court listed the four circumstances in which it considered it possible to prosecute a high official for crimes. According to the ICJ, the four circumstances in which a high official may be prosecuted are,

1) if his own country subjects him to prosecution;
2) if his home country waives immunity before a foreign court;
3) after a high official ceases to hold office, he can be prosecuted for acts committed in a private capacity, or for acts committed while he was not in office; and
4) an incumbent or former foreign minister may be tried before certain international tribunals.

---

172   Can. T.S. 1980 No. 37, 23 May 1969.
173   See the discussion of the Institute's resolution by Lady Hazel Fox, "The Resolution of the Institute of International Law on the Immunities of Heads of State and Government" (2002) 51 I.C.L.Q. 119 at 120.
174   *Arrest Warrant*, above note 1 at para. 58.
175   *Ibid.* at para. 60.

The implication is that the listed situations are the only circumstances in which a serving or former foreign minister may be subject to prosecution. This appears to be the way in which dissenting members of the court understood the paragraph and is perhaps what provoked a stinging rebuke from one of the dissenting judges. In his opinion, Al-Khasawneh J. argued,

> This paragraph (Judgment, para 61) is more notable for the things it does not say than for the things it does: as far as prosecution at home and waiver are concerned, clearly the problem arises when they do not take place. With regard to former high-ranking officials the question of impunity remains with regard to official acts, the fact that most grave crimes are definitionally State acts makes this more than a theoretical lacuna. Lastly with regard to existing international courts their jurisdiction *ration materiae* is limited to the two cases of the former Yugoslavia and Rwanda and the future international court's jurisdiction is limited *ratione temporis* by non-retroactivity as well as by the fact that primary responsibility for prosecution remains with States. The Judgment cannot dispose of the problem of impunity by referral to a prospective international criminal court or existing ones.[176]

Not all the judges of the ICJ agreed with Al-Khasawneh J. that "most grave crimes are definitionally State acts." In their Joint Separate Opinion, Higgens, Kooijmans, and Buergenthal JJ. appeared to take the position that serious international crimes cannot be regarded as state functions.[177] They took this position in spite of noting earlier in their Opinion that the commission of such crimes often involves the use of state apparatus.[178]

Judge *ad hoc* Van den Wyngaert, appointed for the case by Belgium, also dissented from the majority opinion. She opened her dissent by asserting that incumbent foreign ministers who are suspected of war crimes and crimes against humanity enjoy no immunity from criminal process.[179] She stated that two premises underlie the Court's opinion; first that there is a rule of customary law granting absolute immunity to serving foreign ministers, and second, that there is no customary exception to that rule as regards crimes against humanity and war crimes. According to Judge *ad hoc* Van den Wyngaert, both propositions

---

176 Dissenting Opinion of Al-Khasawaneh J., *ibid.* at para 6.
177 Joint Separate Opinion, *ibid.* at para. 85.
178 *Ibid.* at para 79.
179 Dissenting Opinion of Judge *ad hoc* Van den Wyngaert (begins at 137), *ibid.* at para. 1.

are wrong.[180] Her reason for finding that there is no international rule granting absolute immunity to incumbent foreign ministers is simply that there is no evidence of such a rule.[181]

Judge *ad hoc* Van den Wyngaert also criticized the third possibility for prosecution listed at paragraph 61 of the majority decision—that a former minister could be tried for acts committed while out of office or for private acts committed in office. As she points out, the court failed to specify whether crimes against humanity and war crimes are to be considered private acts.[182] As noted above, Judge Al-Khasawneh was clearly of the view that these are public acts. At paragraph 36 of her judgment, Judge *ad hoc* Van den Wyngaert agreed with the assessment of Judge Al-Khasawneh holding that crimes against humanity and war crimes should never be considered private acts. She went on to note that some international crimes (specifically, certain acts of genocide and aggression) require the use of state apparatus and are committed as a part of state policy; for that reason those acts should also not be considered private.[183] According to Judge *ad hoc* Van den Wygaert, immunity should never be permitted for crimes against humanity and war crimes.[184]

The holding by the ICJ that a former minister of foreign affairs will continue to enjoy immunity for official acts has proved to be controversial; in opposition to the findings of the court, some have expressed the view that there can be no functional immunity for official acts when those acts amount to war crimes, crimes against humanity, and genocide.[185]

If the ICJ's decision was intended as a statement that functional immunity subsists for war crimes (the crimes alleged in that case), it must be considered contrary to customary law. The state practice surveyed above is particularly clear that there is no functional immunity in respect of war crimes. Equally, if the court intended to imply (as the Joint Separate Opinion seemed to accept) that war crimes cannot be official acts, this must be viewed with equal scepticism. While it is of course possible that a war crime be committed in a private capacity,[186]

---

180 *Ibid.* at para. 10.
181 *Ibid.* at para. 11.
182 *Ibid.* at para. 36.
183 *Ibid.*
184 *Ibid.*
185 See Wirth, "Immunity for Core Crimes?" above note 32 at 878.
186 For example, Deen-Racsmány, above note 93 at 321, suggests that one way to avoid dealing with the functional immunities of Charles Taylor would be to allege that his acts were committed in a private capacity in order to increase his personal wealth.

it is generally the case that such crimes are committed as part of an official's duties. The nonsense of taking the position that war crimes are always non-official acts was aptly pointed out by Cassese, who noted that if this were accepted, it would mean,

> that the crimes for which Joachim von Ribbentrop (Reich Minister for Foreign Affairs from 1938 to 1945) was sentenced to death, namely crimes against peace, war crimes, and crimes against humanity, should be regarded as "private acts"; or that the crime of having failed "to secure observance of and prevent breaches of the laws of war", for which Mamoro Shigemitsu (Japanese Foreign Minister from 1943 to 1945) was sentenced to seven years' imprisonment, should be considered "private acts."[187]

The holding of the court that personal immunities remain available before national courts has not proven to be as controversial. Taken as a whole, state practice appears to confirm that functional immunities are not available against allegations of war crimes, but personal immunities remain operative before national courts.

3) Genocide

The law relating to charges of genocide appears to be somewhat less settled. As with war crimes, it appears that the law of immunity as it relates to genocide has both a treaty and customary source.

a) The *Genocide Convention*

Article 4 of the *Genocide Convention* of 1948[188] appears to clearly exclude pleas of both functional and personal immunity in relation to the crime of genocide. Article IV states, "Persons committing genocide or any of the other acts enumerated in article III shall be punished, whether they are constitutionally responsible rulers, public officials or private individuals." At first glance, this provision should be sufficient to exclude any claim to immunity; however, this must be assessed having regard to the Convention as a whole. While the *Genocide Convention* requires that parties to the Convention punish the crime of genocide, the only mandatory basis of jurisdiction is territorial.[189] The limited jurisdictional competences raise the question whether article IV was

---

187 Cassese, "Comments on the *Congo v. Belgium* Case," above note 170 at 855.
188 *Genocide Convention*, Can. T.S. 1949 No. 27, 9 December 1948.
189 Article VI: prosecution by an international tribunal is also contemplated.

intended to deny the immunities available at international law, or was simply intended to require states to prosecute their own nationals.

It is submitted that in light of the history which immediately preceded the writing of the *Genocide Convention*, article IV must have been intended to remove the functional and personal immunities of officials before the courts of foreign states. This conclusion is reached by considering the geographic details of the genocide committed during WW II. Unlike the Rwandan genocide of 1994, which was committed largely on the territory of Rwanda by Rwandan citizens, a considerable part of the apparatus built to carry out the Holocaust (or Shoah) was constructed outside Germany's pre–WW II borders.

For example, the six death camps constructed by the Nazis were all located within the territory of pre–WW II Poland. Two of the camps (Chelmno and Auschwitz-Birkenau) were located in an area which had been incorporated into the German Reich. The other four (Treblinka, Sobibor, Maidanek, and Belzec) were located in an area of Poland known as the General Government area. While certainly the commission of genocide was not confined to the territory of Poland, insofar as many of the killings took place on Polish territory, the *Genocide Convention* would have recognized the right of the Polish authorities to try the perpetrators regardless of their nationality or, according to article IV, their official position.[190]

b)   Customary International Law

That the rule contained in article IV of the *Genocide Convention* reflects a general rule of customary international law is fairly uncontroversial. As early as 1951, the ICJ expressed the view that the principles underlying the *Genocide Convention* reflect customary law.[191] It has been suggested that this recognition must be considered as including article IV.[192]

The decision in the *Eichmann* case,[193] discussed in Section D(2)(b), above in this chapter, is an example of state practice which denies the availability of functional immunity for genocide. The non-availability of functional immunity for genocide is not controversial.

---

190 A map of the death camps is reproduced in Rita Steinhardt Botwinick, *A History of the Holocaust*, 2d ed. (Upper Saddle River, NJ: Prentice Hall, 2001) at 193. A more detailed map of the camp system is available on the Yad Vashem website, www.yadvashem.org/.

191 *Reservations to the* Convention on the Prevention and Punishment of the Crime of Genocide, [1951] I.C.J. Rep. 15 at 23 (advisory opinion).

192 Cassese, *International Criminal Law*, above note 17 at 306.

193 Above note 150.

There does remain some lack of certainty as to whether personal immunity can be claimed before a domestic court. Article IV would seem to suggest that such a claim is precluded (and insofar as article IV reflects customary law, immunity must be equally unavailable as a matter of general international law). However, there is little state practice on the issue. In 2007, Spain refused to prosecute Fidel Castro after a complaint was laid alleging that he had committed genocide, terrorism, and torture during the Bay of Pigs invasion.[194] However, in the face of the clear wording of article IV, this decision is probably insufficient to conclude with any certainty that personal immunities remain available before national courts for charges of genocide.

It is probable that, as regards genocide, the clear wording of the Convention (which also reflects customary law) must be interpreted as excluding both personal and functional immunities.

4) Crimes against Humanity

While the presence of applicable conventions and state practice make it reasonably easy to assess the applicability of immunities for war crimes and genocide, the position in relation to crimes against humanity is more difficult to discern. The only instrument which sets out in detail the specific prohibitions underpinning crimes against humanity is the *Rome Statute*.[195] There is nothing like the *Geneva Conventions* or the *Genocide Convention* for this category of offences.

It is probable, based on the fact that courts have not treated crimes against humanity differently from war crimes, that the law in relation to crimes against humanity is the same as that for war crimes. Before a domestic court, personal immunities remain applicable but functional immunities do not. The *Eichmann* decision[196] is probably the key decision supporting this conclusion. However, the lack of clear state practice relating only to crimes against humanity, and the lack of a general treaty similar to the *Geneva Protocols* or the *Genocide Convention*, make any firm statement of the law difficult. The *Rome Statute* does little to help clarify matters. As noted above, it does contain a provision which excludes the application of both personal and functional immunities before the court, but it is far from clear that this exclusion of immunity is intended to apply to the national courts of the state parties to the Statute.

---

194 See the brief article on Jurist Paper Chase, online: http://jurist.law.pitt.edu/ paperchase/2007/12/spain-court-dismisses-bay-of-pigs-war.php.

195 Above note 104.

196 Above note 150.

However, because international law now imposes a direct obligation on individuals to refrain from committing crimes against humanity, it is probable that functional immunity no longer applies.[197] The question of whether personal immunities continue to operate is even less clear.

5) Torture: *Pinochet*

While the law in relation to crimes against humanity is unclear largely because of the lack of state practice, there is emerging practice which relates to treaty crimes and, in particular, the international crime of torture. The major decision concerning the immunity available for torture under the *Convention against Torture*[198] is the House of Lords decision in *Pinochet No 3*.[199]

In 1973, General Augusto Pinochet led a successful coup in Chile, which ousted the left-wing Allende government. Following the coup, Pinochet became Chile's head of state. He remained in office until 11 March 1990 when he resigned. After his resignation, Pinochet continued to enjoy the designation of "Senator for life."

In 1998, while Pinochet was in the UK for medical treatment, Spain issued a request to the UK for Pinochet's extradition.[200] The extradition warrant, as amended, included charges of conspiracy, hostage taking, forced disappearance, genocide, and torture. The counts of genocide were dismissed by the Divisional Court and were not appealed. By the time the warrant reached the second hearing before a panel of the House of Lords, the charges against Pinochet related to conspiracy, torture, and attempted murder.

One of the key issues for the House of Lords was whether Pinochet, as the former Chilean head of state, was immune from criminal process outside of Chile. As Lord Browne-Wilkinson put it:

> [I]f Senator Pinochet is not entitled to immunity in relation to the acts of torture alleged to have occurred after 29 September 1988, it will be the first time so far as counsel have discovered when a local domestic court has refused to afford immunity to a head of state or

---

197 This argument will be considered further, below in Section D(5).

198 Can. T.S. 1987 No. 36.

199 Above note 1.

200 As noted by Wirth, above note 32 at 884, Spain was not the only state which had requested Pinochet's extradition; Belgium, Switzerland, and France had also made requests.

former head of state on the grounds that there can be no immunity against prosecution for certain international crimes.[201]

The decision rendered by the House of Lords is difficult to analyze; each law lord wrote an individual judgment, and it is difficult to tease out a common legal principle. The result was, however, both clear and novel; by a majority of 6:1, the House of Lords denied Senator Pinochet functional immunity for some of the acts of torture contained in the indictment.

Because at the time of the hearing Senator Pinochet was a former head of state, the bulk of the decision relates to the question of functional immunities. However, some of the law lords did express an opinion as to the personal immunities of an incumbent head of state.

Lord Goff of Chieveley provided a clear statement that an incumbent head of state will enjoy immunity from criminal process;[202] he rejected the notion that immunity *ratione personae* was unavailable for the crime of torture.[203] The same principle was expressed by Lord Saville of Newdigate,[204] Lord Millet,[205] and Lord Phillips of Worth Matravers.[206] In fact, none of the law lords suggested that there might be an exception to the personal immunity of a serving head of state as regards the crime of torture.[207]

It must be recalled, however, that this question was not before the law lords. As Lord Millet expressly stated, "This immunity is not in issue in the present case."[208] While the remarks of the law lords regarding the immunity of an incumbent head of state may be dismissed as *obiter*, the majority clearly expressed the view that (at least as regards torture) there is no exception to the personal immunity which protects a serving head of state.

---

201 *Pinochet*, above note 1 at 111 (All E.R.).

202 *Ibid.* at 119.

203 *Ibid.*

204 *Ibid.* at 168.

205 *Ibid.* at 171.

206 *Ibid.* at 181.

207 See Andrea Bianchi, "Immunity versus Human Rights: the Pinochet Case" (1999) 10 E.J.I.L. 237 at 248, who states, "a large majority of the Law Lords agreed that, while current heads of state are immune *ratione personae* from the jurisdiction of foreign courts, both civil and criminal, a plea of immunity *ratione materiae* in criminal proceedings may be of no avail to former heads of state depending on the nature of the crime." See also Fox, *State Immunity*, 2d, above note 1 at 34, and at 250 she states that the lords were unanimous in holding that there was no change to the absolute immunity accorded to a serving head of state.

208 *Pinochet*, above note 1 at 171.

There was far less unity in respect of functional immunities. In the seven opinions delivered, six of the law lords agreed that Senator Pinochet was extraditable in respect of at least some of the offences alleged. All six focused in particular on the allegations of torture and agreed that Senator Pinochet, as a former head of state, was not protected by functional immunity in relation to the crimes he was alleged to have committed while in office. All six also agreed that no claim for functional immunity exists in relation to torture; five of the six tied this holding directly to the *Convention against Torture*, and one did not.[209]

The first judgment by the House of Lords was delivered by Lord Browne-Wilkinson. His judgment has been noted for the less-than-clear reasoning which he employed, a reasoning which left his decision open to very different interpretations.[210]

In discussing whether Senator Pinochet was immune from criminal process, he began with the proposition that, as a matter of international law, a state does not adjudicate on the conduct of a foreign state.[211] Immunity was the rule; the question was whether there was an operative exception to that rule in cases of the international crime of torture. He accepted that at common law, a serving head of state enjoyed absolute immunity;[212] the question was whether Senator Pinochet could assert functional immunity, that is, immunity for official acts carried out in an official capacity, for the crimes with which he was charged.[213] The question which Lord Browne-Wilkinson focused on was whether torture was an official act carried out in an official capacity.[214]

Ultimately, based on the provisions of the *Convention against Torture*, which defined as criminal torture committed by state officials or persons acting in an official capacity, and required the prosecution of persons who commit the international crime of torture, Lord Browne-Wilkinson was satisfied that torture was no longer an official act for which immunity *ratione materiae* could be claimed.[215] The language in

---

209 Lord Goff was the lone dissenter. Lord Phillips was the only member of the majority who did not tie his conclusion on immunity to the provisions of the *Convention against Torture*.

210 See Cryer, above note 2 at 430–32. See also van Alebeek, above note 1 at 229, who describes the reasons for which Lord Browne-Wilkinson denied immunity to Senator Pinochet as "somewhat ambiguous."

211 *Pinochet*, above note 1 at 111.

212 *Ibid.*

213 *Ibid.* at 113.

214 *Ibid.*

215 *Ibid.* at 115 (where Lord Browne-Wilkinson states his conclusion).

which he made this finding is open to at least two possible interpretations.[216]

The first possibility is that Lord Browne-Wilkinson determined that torture committed by a public official within the meaning of the *Convention against Torture* is not an official act.[217] Because the international crime of torture is not an official act, there can be no claim of immunity *ratione materiae* in respect of torture. This type of reasoning, as a matter of the law of immunity, is theoretically possible; immunity *ratione materiae* is available only when two conditions are satisfied: that the person claiming immunity was a state official at the relevant time, and that the act in respect of which immunity is claimed was an official act. It had been conceded that Pinochet, as head of state, was a state official,[218] so the denial of immunity was possible only because the international crime of torture (although committed by a state official) was not an act done in an official capacity.

A second possible reading, based on some of the language used by Lord Browne-Wilkinson, is that he had found that while the international crime of torture was an official act, it was not an act to which functional immunity applied. On that reading, although Pinochet was a state official at the relevant time and the torture was an official act, immunity was not available. Essentially, this position asserts that the international crime of torture falls outside the protective shield of functional immunity.[219]

The reasons of Lord Hope are somewhat easier to follow. On the question of immunity, Lord Hope began with the assumption that the provisions of the UK *State Immunity Act* were reflective of customary law.[220] Under the provisions of the UK Act, the head of state and former head of state were granted immunities similar to those granted to serving and former diplomats. The question for Lord Hope was what the parameters of those immunities were.[221] He rejected the notion that the criminality (or not) of acts had any impact on whether those acts were

---

216 See the discussion of Lord Browne-Wilkinson, *ibid.* at 111–15. See also van Alebeek, above note 1 at 229; Fox, *State Immunity*, above note 3 at 444, takes the view that Lord Browne-Wilkinson had found that international law precluded torture being included in the functions of a head of state. See also Bianchi, above note 207 at notes 32 & 33.

217 Fox and Bianchi, *ibid.*, both state the view that Lord Browne-Wilkinson found that torture was not an act which could be considered a function of a head of state.

218 *Pinochet*, above note 1 at 110.

219 Van Alebeek, above note 1 at 229–30.

220 *Pinochet*, above note 1 at 146.

221 *Ibid.*

official and deserving of immunity. In the opinion of Lord Hope, an assessment of whether the acts were official should focus on whether the acts promoted the interests of the state.[222] Lord Hope considered that there were two exceptions to functional immunity within international law: one exception was for acts committed in a private capacity, the other was for breaches of *jus cogens* norms. However, he considered that it remains uncertain whether the *jus cogens* status of certain crimes necessarily have an impact on the immunities available to a former head of state.[223]

Key to Lord Hope's decision was his interpretation of the *Convention against Torture* to which Spain (the requesting state), Chile (the national state), and the UK (the requested state) were all parties. While noting that the *Convention against Torture* contained no express waiver of immunity, Lord Hope ultimately concluded that following the coming into force of the Convention, immunity could no longer be claimed if the allegations involved systematic or widespread torture. However, the lack of immunity was operative only between parties to the Convention:

> Then there is the Torture Convention of 10 December 1984. Having secured a sufficient number of signatories, it entered into force on 26 June 1987. In my opinion, once the machinery which it provides was put in place to enable jurisdiction over such crimes to be exercised in the courts of a foreign state, it was no longer open to any state which was a signatory to the Convention to invoke the immunity *ratione materiae* in the event of allegations of systematic or widespread torture committed after that date being made in the courts of that state against its officials or any other person acting in an official capacity.[224]

The decision of Lord Hope would strip immunity *ratione materiae* only against the officials of state parties to the *Convention against Torture* and only when the torture alleged amounted to an international crime. The reasons of Lord Hope suggest that he may have been confusing an international crime with a crime against humanity. The decision of Lord Hope would, as a result, recognize a very narrow exception to the immunity of former heads of state.

Lord Hope's decision to deny immunity only in cases of widespread or systematic torture because he considers that only in such cases has an international crime been committed is problematic because he purported to base his decision on the terms of the *Convention against Tor-*

---

222 *Ibid.* at 146–47.
223 *Ibid.* at 147.
224 *Ibid.* at 152.

ture. The Convention clearly defines the international crime of torture, and it does not limit the definition to widespread or systematic acts.[225] This limitation was imported by Lord Hope.

Lord Hutton took yet a different approach to the question of the immunity available to Senator Pinochet. His decision differed from that of Lord Hope in two key respects. First, Lord Hutton considered that there had been no waiver of immunity—rather, the *Convention against Torture* established that acts of torture could no longer be considered functions of a head of state under international law because international law expressly prohibited torture.[226] Second, Lord Hutton asserted that a single act of torture is sufficient to amount to a crime against international law.[227]

Lord Saville also took the position that the continued operation of immunity *ratione materiae* was inconsistent with the *Convention against Torture.*[228] Lord Millet appeared willing to go further than the other law lords in his denial of immunity. Unlike the others, who found that the UK had no extraterritorial jurisdiction over torture until the enactment of the *Criminal Justice Act 1988*[229] specifically provided such jurisdiction, Lord Millet found that the UK had always had extraterritorial jurisdiction over crimes which were subject to universal jurisdiction.[230] However, he proceeded on the basis that the 1988 Act was determinative.[231] As was the case with Lords Hope and Hutton, Lord Millet found that the definition of torture was inconsistent with a claim of immunity *ratione materiae.*[232]

Lord Phillips gave a very different judgment than his peers; unlike the majority of the law lords who began with the proposition that immunity was available unless excluded, Lord Phillips found that there was no rule of international law which required a state to recognize immunity for an international crime.[233] He found that both the existence of extraterritorial jurisdiction and the existence of international crimes were incompatible with immunity *ratione materiae.*[234] As a matter of

---

225 See the *Convention against Torture*, above note 198, art. 1.

226 *Pinochet*, above note 1 at 165.

227 *Ibid.* at 166.

228 *Ibid.* at 167–70.

229 (U.K.), 1988, c. 33.

230 *Pinochet*, above note 1 at 178.

231 *Ibid.*

232 *Ibid.* at 178–79.

233 *Ibid.* at 189–90.

234 *Ibid.* at 190.

domestic law, he argued that the UK *State Immunity Act* accorded immunity only for official visits.[235]

The multiple opinions, and the different reasons given by each law lord, makes analysis of the *Pinochet* opinion difficult.[236] However, in a later judgment, another member of the House of Lords set out his understanding of the rule which emerged from the *Pinochet* decision.

In his judgment in *Jones v. Ministry of the Interior Al-Mamlaka Al-Arabiya AS Saudiya (the Kingdom of Saudi Arabia)*,[237] Lord Bingham of Cornhill provided what may be the most coherent statement of the basis for the decision in *Pinochet*. Lord Bingham stated,

> The essential ratio of the decision, as I understand it, was that international law could not without absurdity require criminal jurisdiction to be assumed and exercised where the *Torture Convention* conditions were satisfied and, at the same time, require immunity to be granted to those properly charged. The *Torture Convention* was the mainspring of the decision, and certain members of the House expressly accepted that the grant of immunity in civil proceedings was unaffected: see p 264 (Lord Hutton), p 278 (Lord Millett) and pp 280, 281, 287 (Lord Phillips of Worth Matravers). It is, I think, difficult to accept that torture cannot be a governmental or official act, since under article 1 of the *Torture Convention* torture must, to qualify as such, be inflicted by or with the connivance of a public official or other person acting in an official capacity. The claimants' argument encounters the difficulty that it is founded on the *Torture Convention*; but to bring themselves within the *Torture Convention* they must show that the torture was (to paraphrase the definition) official; yet they argue that the conduct was not official in order to defeat the claim to immunity.[238]

Two key points are to be taken from this statement. The first is that the decision in *Pinochet* was based on the provisions of the *Convention against Torture*; it was illogical for the Convention to define torture as an official act and to require prosecution of violators on the basis of universal jurisdiction, yet to continue to insist that such individuals be permitted to claim immunity. The second point of importance is Lord Bingham's assertion that the international crime of torture, within the meaning of the Convention, is an official act. This passage makes it very clear that the decision in *Pinochet* was not based on a view that

---

235 *Ibid.* at 191–92.
236 See Fox, *State Immunity*, 2d, above note 1 at 251.
237 [2006] UKHL 26.
238 *Ibid.* at para. 19.

torture is a private act which does not attract immunity. Rather, it is an official act for which immunity is no longer available.

If this is accepted as the fundamental *ratio* of the *Pinochet* decision, it remains problematic in some respects. In the first place, if this is the *ratio*, it is, as was pointed out by Fox, illogical;

> Perhaps the most awkward illogicality of the Lords' decision is the retention of the immunity from criminal proceedings of the serving head of State. In their speeches, the Lords sought to justify this retention by the distinction between immunity *ratione personae* and immunity *ratione materiae*, explaining that the serving head enjoyed a status immunity, whereas the retired head only enjoyed a subject-matter immunity for official acts performed during the time he held office. This immunity for official acts is the immunity of the State and it exists throughout, not being in any way dependent on whether a particular official is in office or not. Consequently if, as seems apparent, the Lords' decision restricts immunity *ratione materiae* to official acts other than the commission of certain international crimes, that same qualification should logically be applicable to the immunity enjoyed by the serving head or indeed by his State.[239]

A second problem with the decision is that, while it is concerned generally with the availability of immunity *ratione materiae*, it very consciously links its denial of immunity to the existence and provisions of the *Convention against Torture*. It is unclear whether the *Pinochet* decision can be used as authority for a denial of immunity *ratione materiae* if there is no convention which contains the two key elements of the *Convention against Torture*: a definition which specifically states that the crime is one committed by state officials and a provision for mandatory universal jurisdiction.[240]

A final comment on the *Pinochet* decision must focus on its suitability as an international legal precedent, rather than a domestic precedent. While each of the law lords made liberal reference to international law, it was ultimately with a view to interpreting the domestic law they were bound to apply; the decision is not necessarily a definitive interpretation of international law itself.[241]

---

239 Fox, *State Immunity*, above note 3 at 447.
240 See van Alebeek, above note 1 at 237.
241 In *Reference re Secession of Quebec*, [1998] 2 S.C.R. 217, the *amicus curiae* objected to the court answering a question of "pure" international law. The argument was that this would require the Court to exceed its jurisdiction and act as an international tribunal. The Supreme Court of Canada responded to this concern by noting that, "In accordance with well accepted principles of

The focus of the House of Lords on the *Convention against Torture* is understandable, but it may have led the House into the error of interpreting the Convention in a vacuum. While Lord Hope specifically cautioned that the Convention must be interpreted against the background of head of state immunity,[242] it is not clear that the House was able to interpret the Convention against the background of international law more generally. The key error was the failure of the House of Lords to distinguish between state responsibility and criminal responsibility.[243]

Classical international law was concerned solely with the responsibility of states for wrongful acts, and individuals had no international legal personality. Immunity *ratione materiae* reflected this lack of international legal personality, removing responsibility to the international plane and requiring reparation from the state for civil or criminal wrongs.[244] By the time the House of Lords was seized with the *Pinochet* case, this classical international model was no longer operative. Instead, modern international law recognizes a system of parallel responsibility.[245] Individuals have some international legal personality and are barred by international law from committing certain acts. International criminal law imposes obligations directly on individuals. There is, in the case of torture for example, a parallel human rights responsibility imposed on states.[246] This parallel responsibility suggests that, at least insofar as international crimes are concerned, the traditional rationale for immunity *ratione materiae* no longer applies. It is perhaps the failure of the House of Lords to engage with this larger issue which resulted in the focus on the *Convention against Torture* and its specific terms.

The failure of the House of Lords to engage with the larger issues of whether immunity *ratione materiae* is at all available when international law imposes an obligation on the individual is not surprising. In the *Pinochet* case, the law lords were specifically concerned with the crime of torture and a Convention to which all the states were parties. There was, in the *Pinochet* case, little need to go beyond the provisions

---

international law, this Court's answer to Question 2 would not purport to bind any other state or international tribunal that might subsequently consider a similar question. The Court nevertheless has jurisdiction to provide an advisory opinion to the Governor in Council in its capacity as a national court on legal questions touching and concerning the future of the Canadian federation." (para. 20).

242　*Pinochet*, above note 1 at 148.

243　Fox, *State Immunity*, above note 3 at 446.

244　*Ibid.*

245　*Ibid.* at 514–15.

246　See the decision of Trial Chamber II in *Furundzija* (IT-95-17/1-T), Judgment, 10 December 1998 at paras. 142–46.

of the *Convention against Torture*. The narrow focus of the House of Lords is also ambiguous; it is not clear whether it is more positive than negative.[247] The negative is obvious; without grappling with the impact of dual responsibility, the law lords accepted that immunity *ratione materiae* was available against allegations of international crimes. The positive is more speculative; because the House of Lords did not examine the rise of the dual responsibility regime and its implications for immunity, it is left to another court, perhaps in a case in which there is no conveniently worded convention, to explore the issue.

The decision of the House of Lords is a useful starting point for a discussion of immunity in relation to international crimes and remains an influential precedent. However, given the reasoning in the House of Lords decision, any court confronted with a foreign state official charged with a treaty crime will have to answer certain questions before concluding that immunity is unavailable. The first question is whether both the prosecuting state and the national state of the defendant are both parties to the relevant treaty. If so, the court must first refer to the provisions of the treaty to determine whether the treaty itself excludes functional immunity either expressly or by necessary implication. If neither state is party to the treaty, or if the treaty does not expressly or impliedly deal with immunities, the court will have to undertake an examination of customary international law in order to determine whether immunity remains available for the particular crime charged.

E. CANADIAN IMPLEMENTATION

1) General Comments

In many ways, the law of immunity in Canada suffers from the same diffusion as the international law of immunity. One key similarity is that, as with international law, Canada's main statute regarding immunity does not apply to criminal proceedings. Section 18 of the *State Immunity Act*[248] provides, "This Act does not apply to criminal proceedings or proceedings in the nature of criminal proceedings."

---

247 Fox, *State Immunity*, 2d, above note 1 at 251, takes the view that the focus of the House of Lords on the *Convention against Torture* as enacted into UK law, combined with the difficulty of isolating a *ratio decidendi*, limits the precedential value of the decision.

248 R.S.C. 1985, c. S-18.

In order to determine whether immunity may be claimed in a criminal proceeding, courts in Canada must look to other statutory instruments. The most comprehensive piece of Canadian legislation for this purpose is the *Crimes Against Humanity and War Crimes Act*, (*CAH Act*).[249] The *CAH Act* was introduced, at least in part, in order to implement Canada's obligations under the *Rome Statute*.[250] Its provisions apply to war crimes, crimes against humanity, and genocide. In addition, Canada has criminalized war crimes in its *Geneva Conventions Act*,[251] and the *Criminal Code*[252] also contains a provision specific to genocide. Each of these statutes will be considered below.

2) War Crimes

The *CAH Act* provides for the criminalization of war crimes both when committed in Canada (section 4(1)(c)) and outside Canada (section 6(1) (c)). The definition of war crime within the Act is extremely broad; a war crime is defined as

> an act or omission committed during an armed conflict that, at the time and in the place of its commission, constitutes a war crime according to customary international law or conventional international law applicable to armed conflicts, whether or not it constitutes a contravention of the law in force at the time and in the place of its commission.

The Act provides for universal jurisdiction over war crimes (section 8(b)), making it possible that a Canadian court will find itself presiding over the trial of a non-national for the crimes enumerated in the Act. Indeed, the first prosecution of an individual under the *CAH Act* was of a Rwandan who was accused of taking part in the genocide of 1994.[253] The very real possibility that a Canadian court will sit in judgment over an individual who is a current or former official of another state makes it necessary to address the possibility of whether a claim to immunity will succeed.

Rather unhelpfully, while the Act provides that all defences which are otherwise available in Canada or under international law are available under the Act (section 11), nowhere in the *CAH Act* are immunities specifically mentioned. This raises the question whether immunities

---

249 S.C. 2000, c. 24.
250 Above note 104. See Chapter 5.
251 R.S.C. 1985, c. G-3.
252 R.S.C. 1985, c. C-46.
253 *R. c. Munyaneza*, 2009 QCCS 2201.

are to be recognized by Canadian courts for charges under the Act. Recall that immunities are not defences; they are procedural bars to jurisdiction. The Act clearly sets out the bases for the jurisdiction of Canadian courts and, absent some statutory directive, it is possible that Canadian courts will refuse to accept a claim of immunity.

A court could nonetheless address the availability of immunity in one of two ways. A court could (erroneously) determine that immunities are defences incorporated by section 11, and based on that assessment, decide whether immunity is available in a particular case. A second possibility stems from the Supreme Court of Canada's holding in R. v. Hape that prohibitive rules of customary international law form part of the common law of Canada.[254] A court, in interpreting the jurisdictional provisions of the CAH Act, should look to the "prohibitive rules" of international law and take into account the interpretive principle that Canadian legislation is presumed to be in accordance with international law. On the basis of these interpretive principles, a court could decide that it must take into account possible claims to immunity in determining whether it has jurisdiction.

The first approach is problematic as a matter of international law. The second is probably acceptable as a matter of both international and Canadian law.

The first approach — determining that immunities are defences — is problematic because (as discussed in Section A, above in this chapter) the immunities provided by international law are merely procedural; they are not substantive defences.

If the second approach were adopted, it would be open to a court to determine that while the CAH Act gives Canadian courts jurisdiction over the specified crimes, in accordance with the directions of LeBel J. in Hape (discussed in Section E(5), below in this chapter), the courts should exercise that jurisdiction in conformity with international law. Under this approach, Canadian courts would be entitled to exercise their jurisdiction provided the defendant was not protected by personal immunity at the time of her appearance before the court.

The situation in relation to a national of a state party to the Rome Statute is a bit more complex. It is possible, based on the wording of article 27 of the Statute, to take the view that the state parties have waived immunity not only before the ICC but also before the domestic courts of member states. Article 27.1 simply provides that official capacity is irrelevant to criminal responsibility under the Statute. As the Statute forms part of Canadian law through the CAH Act, it is possible

---

254 2007 SCC 26, [2007] 2 S.C.R. 292. See Chapter 1.

that a court could decline to accord either personal or functional immunities to the officials of state parties. However, article 27.2 goes on to say that any immunities or special procedural rules which attach to the official capacity of a person are no bar to prosecution before the court. A reading of the article as a whole suggests that it was intended to reflect what appears to be the customary law on the matter; a lack of functional immunity available either before the court or the courts of state parties, but personal immunities remain available at the domestic level and are excluded only before the ICC.[255]

Prior to the enactment of the *CAH Act*, Canadian law had criminalized grave breaches of the *Geneva Conventions*, and the *Additional Protocols*, in the *Geneva Conventions Act*.[256] As in the *CAH Act*, the *Geneva Conventions Act* makes no mention of available immunities to prosecution. Also as in the *CAH Act*, the *Geneva Conventions Act* contemplates the prosecution of non-nationals (see, for example, section 3, which provides that grave breaches are subject to universal jurisdiction, and section 5, which contemplates the prosecution of a "protected person"). In interpreting the provisions of the *Geneva Conventions Act*, a Canadian court should interpret the provisions in conformity with the Conventions.[257] This would provide the same result as that achieved under the *CAH Act*; personal immunities would remain available, but functional immunities would not.

3) Crimes against Humanity

Crimes against humanity have also become crimes under Canadian law through the *CAH Act*. A crime against humanity is defined in sections 4 and 6 in this way:

> "crime against humanity" means murder, extermination, enslavement, deportation, imprisonment, torture, sexual violence, persecution or any other inhumane act or omission that is committed against any civilian population or any identifiable group and that, at the time and in the place of its commission, constitutes a crime against humanity according to customary international law or conventional international law or by virtue of its being criminal according to the

---

255 As Cryer, above note 2 at 440, points out, this does not apply when the ICC requests the surrender of an individual; personal immunities are not available for the purpose of surrender to the ICC.

256 Above note 15.

257 *Pushpanathan v. Canada (Minister of Citizenship and Immigration)*, [1998] 1 S.C.R. 982 at para. 51.

general principles of law recognized by the community of nations, whether or not it constitutes a contravention of the law in force at the time and in the place of its commission.

Like war crimes, crimes against humanity are crimes whether committed inside or outside of Canada. Also like war crimes, they are subject to universal jurisdiction (section 8).

4) Genocide

Like both war crimes and crimes against humanity, the crime of genocide has been implemented into Canadian law through the *Crimes Against Humanity and War Crimes Act*. Section 4(1)(a) governs the crime of genocide when committed in Canada, and section 6(1)(a) criminalizes genocide when committed outside Canada. In respect of both provisions, genocide is described in this way:

> "genocide" means an act or omission committed with intent to destroy, in whole or in part, an identifiable group of persons, as such, that, at the time and in the place of its commission, constitutes genocide according to customary international law or conventional international law or by virtue of its being criminal according to the general principles of law recognized by the community of nations, whether or not it constitutes a contravention of the law in force at the time and in the place of its commission.[258]

In addition to the *CAH Act*, section 318 of the *Criminal Code*[259] makes advocating genocide an offence.

5) Interpretation

While the statutes discussed above tell us what the law is, there remains a need to interpret those statutes (in particular the *CAH Act*, which makes reference to international law). Some guidance on the correct approach to interpreting Canada's war crimes, crimes against humanity, and genocide provisions is found in the decision of the Supreme Court of Canada in *R. v. Hape*.[260] The decision of the five-member majority was written by LeBel J.[261]

---

258 Above note 249, ss. 4(3) and 6(3).
259 Above note 252.
260 Above note 254.
261 Justice Bastarache (for Abella and Rothstein JJ.) wrote a concurring opinion which took a different approach to the issue. Justice Binnie dissented.

The main issue in the case was whether the *Canadian Charter of Rights and Freedoms*[262] applied to a search made (in part by Canadian police officers) in the Turks and Caicos Islands. In determining whether the *Charter* applied to the actions of the RCMP while in the Turks and Caicos, LeBel J, found it useful to first consider the relationship between domestic law and international law.[263]

Justice LeBel began his discussion with the question whether customary international law was a part of Canadian law by adoption, or whether Parliament was required in all cases to enact legislation incorporating international law before it became binding within Canada. Justice LeBel determined that the "adoptionist" approach was correct; the principle was limited only by the enactment of contrary legislation. As LeBel J. put it:

> Despite the Court's silence in some recent cases, the doctrine of adoption has never been rejected in Canada. Indeed, there is a long line of cases in which the Court has either formally accepted it or at least applied it. In my view, following the common law tradition, it appears that the doctrine of adoption operates in Canada such that prohibitive rules of customary international law should be incorporated into domestic law in the absence of conflicting legislation. The automatic incorporation of such rules is justified on the basis that international custom, as the law of nations, is also the law of Canada unless, in a valid exercise of its sovereignty, Canada declares that its law is to the contrary. Parliamentary sovereignty dictates that a legislature may violate international law, but that it must do so expressly. Absent an express derogation, the courts may look to prohibitive rules of customary international law to aid in the interpretation of Canadian law and the development of the common law.[264]

After considering the principles of sovereignty and comity, LeBel J. went on to discuss the longstanding principle of statutory interpretation that Canadian law is presumed to conform to Canada's international legal obligations; laws which are clearly inconsistent with international law are the exception to this rule.[265]

---

262 Part I of the *Constitution Act, 1982*, being Schedule B to the *Canada Act 1982* (U.K.), 1982, c. 11.
263 Above note 254 at para. 34.
264 *Ibid.* at para. 39.
265 *Ibid.* at para. 53. It is worth noting that not all commentators are enamoured of this interpretive approach. See, for example, William Schabas & Stephane Beaulac, *International Human Rights and Canadian Law: Legal Commitment, Implementation and the Charter*, 3d ed. (Toronto: Thomson Carswell, 2007) at

The majority decision in *Hape* thus affirms two important interpretive principles. The first is that courts are entitled to look to the "prohibitive rules" of customary international law to interpret Canadian law. The second is that Canadian law will be presumed to be in conformity with international law. These principles will undoubtedly assist courts which are called upon to determine whether a particular crimes falls within the statutory definitions. It is far less clear that these principles will assist in determining whether, as a matter of Canadian law, a defendant can claim immunity.

While the *Hape* decision reaffirmed the interpretive rule that Canadian law is presumed to be compliant with international law, the case did not need to comment on how to interpret Canadian legislation which implements a specific treaty obligation. This issue was considered by the Court in its earlier decision in *Pushpanathan v. Canada (Minister of Citizenship and Immigration)*. In that case, the Court expressed the correct interpretive approach as follows:

> Since the purpose of the Act incorporating Article 1F(c) is to implement the underlying Convention, the Court must adopt an interpretation consistent with Canada's obligations under the Convention. The wording of the Convention and the rules of treaty interpretation will therefore be applied to determine the meaning of Article 1F(c) in domestic law [citations omitted].[266]

The Canadian legislation which criminalizes war crimes, crimes against humanity, and genocide were all intended to implement Canada's obligations under specific international treaties. In interpreting the legislation, Canadian courts should adopt interpretations which are "consistent with Canada's international obligations." This suggests that when a court is dealing with a statute which implements a specific treaty, a court in interpreting that statute should ensure (as far as possible) an interpretation of the statute which accords with the treaty.

Applying this to an interpretation of the *CAH Act* or the *Geneva Conventions Act* would likely produce a result which accords with inter-

---

94–95, where the authors opine that "[t]he main problem with the presumption of conformity with international law, as with any presumption of intent in statutory interpretation, is the preliminary requirement of ambiguity. Indeed, before courts can trigger the operation of this interpretive tool, there must be a finding that the legislative provision at issue is ambiguous, or is otherwise problematic. Short of fulfilling this precondition, the presumption of conformity with international law cannot become an argument of interpretation, which in turn means that the opportunity to resort to such legal norms is lost."

266 Above note 257 at para. 51.

national law. A court could look to the provisions of the *CAH Act* or *Geneva Conventions Act* which grant jurisdiction to Canadian Courts over the specified crimes, but interpret the grant of jurisdiction in conformity with the "prohibitive rule" of international law which continues the applicability of personal immunities before domestic courts. Such an interpretation would not be incompatible with the terms of the Act and would also not entail twisting international law in order to fit personal immunity within the defence provision of the *CAH Act*. Finally, such an approach would be in conformity with customary international law as discussed in Section D, above in this chapter.

6) Diplomatic Immunity as a Special Case

Diplomatic and consular immunities are a special case under international law, not because of any major differences in the immunities accorded to diplomats and consular officials, but because unlike immunity generally, there are specific treaties establishing the relevant immunities. The two key treaties are the *Vienna Convention on Diplomatic Relations*[267] and the *Vienna Convention on Consular Relations*.[268] Canada is a party to both treaties.

The *Vienna Convention on Diplomatic Relations* sets out the basic rule for immunity in article 29, which states, "The person of a diplomatic agent shall be inviolable. He shall not be liable to any form of arrest or detention. The receiving State shall treat him with due respect and shall take all appropriate steps to prevent any attack on his person, freedom or dignity." Article 31 contains the detailed immunities from criminal jurisdiction.

However, two other provisions of the *Convention on Diplomatic Relations* help to balance the immunity granted to a diplomatic agent. Article 9 preserves the right of the receiving state to declare a diplomatic agent *persona non grata;* if the agent does not leave the receiving state within a reasonable time after such declaration, the receiving state may refuse to recognize them as a diplomatic agent (article 9.2). Article 9 also specifically permits a receiving state to declare a diplomatic agent *persona non grata* before her arrival in the receiving state. Also of importance is article 32, which recognizes the ability of the sending state to waive the immunity of their agents.

The second provision of importance is article 41, which requires diplomatic agents to "respect the laws and regulations of the receiving state."

---

267 Can. T.S. 1966 No. 29, 24 April 1964.
268 Can. T.S. 1974 No. 25, 19 March 1967.

Article 39 specifies that the immunities and privileges start from the time the agent enters the receiving state to take up her post (or if she is already in the receiving state, from the time notification of the posting is given to the minister of foreign affairs of the receiving state). The immunities end either when the agent leaves the country on termination of her posting or after a reasonable period for departure has elapsed.

Article 40 provides that a diplomatic agent is both immune and inviolable when travelling through a third state on her way to or from an appointment or when returning to the agent's own country.

The provisions of the *Vienna Convention on Consular Relations* are similar but do not grant the sweeping protections found in the *Vienna Convention on Diplomatic Relations*. Article 41 establishes the inviolability of consular officers. However, this applies only to arrest and detention preceding trial and does not apply in any event to a "grave crime." Article 43 does preserve the immunity of consular officers in respect of consular functions. Article 45 contains the recognition that the sending state may waive the immunities and privileges of consular officers. Article 53 makes it clear that the immunities apply while the consular officer is in the receiving state and lasts for as long as the officer holds the post. The normal rule is that the immunities come to an end when the officer leaves the receiving state or after a reasonable period for departure has elapsed.

Under article 54, third states through which a consular officer must pass in order to take up or leave her post or to return to the sending state are also required to respect the immunity and inviolability of those officials.

Article 23 permits the receiving state to declare a consular officer *persona non grata*. It also preserves the right of the receiving state to declare an individual unacceptable prior to that person taking up the appointment (article 23.3). As under the *Vienna Convention on Diplomatic Relations*, if an individual who has been declared *non grata* does not leave the territory of the receiving state within a reasonable time, the receiving state may refuse to view that person as a consular official (article 23.2).

Under article 10 of the *Vienna Convention on Consular Relations*, the sending state appoints a consular officer, but the receiving state must admit that officer to the exercise of that person's functions.

Both Conventions have been incorporated into Canadian law through the *Foreign Missions and International Organizations Act*.[269] The

---

269 S.C. 1991, c. 41.

Act goes some way to clarify (as a matter of Canadian law) the meaning of some of the provisions of the Conventions. For example, under Canadian law, "reasonable period" is defined as ten days from either the date on which the individual was declared *persona non grata*, the date on which the individual's functions have come to an end, or, in respect of articles 39.2 and 53.3, on the date specified by the minister of foreign affairs (section 2(2)). Under section 2(4), a grave crime is defined as one created by an Act of Parliament for which an individual may be sentenced for five years or more.

The means of incorporation chosen was to designate in section 3 of the Act which provisions of the *Vienna Convention on Diplomatic Relations* and the *Vienna Convention on Consular Relations* have force of law in Canada. The Conventions are attached as Schedules 1 and 2 to the Act. The provisions which have force of law in Canada include articles 27–40 of the *Vienna Convention on Diplomatic Relations* and articles 41, 43–45 and 53 of the *Vienna Convention on Consular Relations*.

The provisions of the *Foreign Missions and International Organizations Act* which incorporate the immunity provisions of the Conventions make it reasonably clear that as a matter of Canadian law, diplomats remain inviolable. This interpretation accords with the decision of the ICJ in the *Arrest Warrant* case,[270] which confirmed that personal immunities remain operative before national courts.

F. CONCLUSION

While the practice in relation to immunities is complicated, the basic rules can be discerned (although controversies remain). As suggested in Section C, above in this chapter, functional immunity for international crimes and crimes under international law is no longer available either before international tribunals or domestic courts. The imposition of obligations on individuals by international law negates the former rationale for functional immunity, that is, that international law obligations fell solely on the state and any breach was attributable to the state. As regards acts for which international law imposes responsibility directly on individuals, it is probably now the case that functional immunity no longer applies. Certainly, functional immunity is now unavailable at the very least for war crimes, crimes against humanity, genocide, and torture, whether prosecuted before an international tribunal or a domestic court.

---

270 Above note 1.

As regards personal immunities, it seems reasonably well settled that they remain operative before domestic courts. The question whether there is a customary rule which automatically invalidates personal immunities before international tribunals is less settled. It appears that personal immunities must be validly waived, and there is no automatic waiver as a matter of customary law, but there is disagreement on the subject. It is also unclear which state officials benefit from personal immunity. It is settled law that heads of state and of government, ministers of foreign affairs, and diplomats benefit from personal immunity, but it is not clear which other officials also benefit. The decision of the ICJ in the *Arrest Warrant* case leaves the class of offices to which personal immunities attach open to debate.

FURTHER READING

AKANDE, DAPO, "International Law Immunities and the International Criminal Court" (2004) 98 A.J.I.L. 407

CASSESE, ANTONIO, "When May Senior State Officials Be Tried for International Crimes? Some Comments on the *Congo v. Belgium* Case" (2002) 13 E.J.I.L. 853

CRYER, ROBERT et al., *International Criminal Law and Procedure* (Cambridge: Cambridge University Press, 2007) c. 20

FOX, HAZEL, *The Law of State Immunity* (Oxford: Oxford University Press, 2002)

VAN ALEBEEK, ROSANNE, *The Immunity of States and Their Officials in International Criminal Law and International Human Rights Law* (Oxford: Oxford University Press, 2008)

TABLE OF CASES

A(FC) and others (FC) v. Secretary of State for the Home Department,
[2004] UKHL 56 271

A.L.T. Navigation Ltd. v. United States of America (2001), 207 Nfld. &
P.E.I.R. 146, [2001] N.J. No. 318 (S.C.T.D.) 488

A.L.T. Navigation Ltd. v. United States of America (2002), 215 Nfld. &
P.E.I.R. 1, 96 C.R.R. (2d) 155, [2002] N.J. No. 166 (S.C.T.D.)...................... 492

Abbaye Ardenne Case: Trial of S.S. Brigadeführer Kurt Meyer, The
(1945), 4 L.R.T.W.C. 97 (Can. Military Ct.) 224

AFRC (SCSL-04-16-T), Trial Chamber Judgment, 20 June 2007
(Special Court for Sierra Leone).................................. 121, 123, 125, 128, 134

Akayesu (ICTR-96-4-T), Trial Chamber Judgment,
2 September 1998 (Int. Crim. Trib. for
Rwanda) 107, 112, 113, 114, 115, 121, 122, 133, 134, 173, 261

Al Bashir (ICC-02/05-01/09), Leave to Appeal Decision Not To
Issue a Warrant for Genocide, 24 June 2009 (Int'l Crim. Ct.).................... 562

Al Bashir (ICC-02/05-01/09), Warrant of Arrest Issued by
Pre-Trial Chamber I, 4 March 2009 (Int'l Crim. Ct.) 562

Alberta (Attorney General) v. Dawson (1999), 248 A.R. 82, [1999]
A.J. No. 809, 1999 ABQB 518, leave to appeal refused (1999),
250 A.R. 165, [1999] A.J. No. 1332, 1999 ABCA 334, leave to
appeal to S.C.C. refused, [1999] S.C.C.A. No. 570 489

Aleksovski (IT-95-14/1-A), Appeals Chamber Judgment,
24 March 2000 (Int'l Crim. Trib. for the former Yugoslavia) 137

Al-Megrahi v. H.M. Advocate, Appeal No. C104/01, Opinion in Appeal
against Conviction, 14 March 2002 (Scotland Appeal Court,
High Court of Justiciary)... 202

Ambrose Light, The, 25 F. 408 (S.D.N.Y. 1885) 282

Amnesty International Canada v. Canada (Canadian Forces),
[2008] 4 F.C.R. 546, 292 D.L.R. (4th) 127, 2008 FC 336, aff'd
(2008), 305 D.L.R. (4th) 741, 383 N.R. 268, 2008 FCA 401,
leave to appeal to S.C.C. refused, [2009] SCCA No. 63...................... 280, 525

Anglo-Norwegian Fisheries Case, [1951] I.C.J. Rep. 116.................................... 51

Antelope, The, 23 U.S. 66, 10 Wheat. 66 (1825)... 93

Application of the Convention on the Prevention and Punishment of
the Crime of Genocide (Bosnia-Herzegovina v. Yugoslavia),
Preliminary Objections, Judgment, 11 July 1996, [1996]
I.C.J. Rep. 595 106

Argentina (Republic) v. Mellino, [1987] 1 S.C.R. 536, 40 D.L.R.
(4th) 74, [1987] S.C.J. No. 25... 258, 457

Armando dos Santos (Case No. 16/2001), Decision, 15 July 2003
(UNTAET Serious Crimes Panel) 210

Attorney-General of Israel v. Eichmann (1968), 36 I.L.R. 18 (Jerusalem
Dist. Ct. 1961), aff'd (1968), 36 I.L.R. 277 (Israel Sup. Ct.
1962) 7, 70, 73, 107, 216–19, 222, 472–73, 475, 5269–71, 578–79

Aydin v. Turkey (1998), 25 E.H.R.R. 251 (Eur. Ct. Hum. Rts.)..........................274

Bagaragaza (ICTR-05-86-11bis), Decision on Prosecutor's Extremely
Urgent Motion for Revocation of the Referral to the Kingdom
of the Netherlands Pursuant to Rule 11 bis (F) and (G),
Trial Chamber, 17 August 2007 (Int'l Crim. Trib. for Rwanda)..................174

Bagaragaza (ICTR-05-86-AR11bis), Decision on Rule 11 bis Appeal,
Appeals Chamber, 30 August 2006 (Int'l Crim. Trib. for Rwanda) 174

Bagilishema (ICTR-95-1A-T), Trial Chamber Judgment, 7 June 2001
(Int'l Crim. Trib. for Rwanda) 121, 125

Bagosora et al. ("Military I Trial") (ICTR-98-41-T), Decision,
18 December 2008 (Int'l Crim. Trib. For Rwanda) 173

Baker v. Canada (Minister of Citizenship and Immigration), [1999]
2 S.C.R. 817, 174 D.L.R. (4th) 193, [1999] S.C.J. No. 39............................... 32

Barayagwiza (ICTR-97-19-AR72), Decision (Prosecutor's Request
for Review or Reconsideration), 31 March 2000 (Int'l Crim.
Trib. for Rwanda) 26, 173

Barayagwiza (ICTR-97-19-AR72), Decision, 3 November 1999
(Int'l Crim. Trib. for Rwanda) 173

Barcelona Traction Light and Power House Co. Ltd. (Belgium v. Spain),
[1970] I.C.J. Rep. 3..80, 288

Blagojević et al. (IT-02-60-A), Appeals Chamber Judgment, 9 May 2007
(Int'l Crim. Trib. for the former Yugoslavia).................................... 112

Blagojević et al. (IT-02-60-T), Trial Chamber Judgment, 17 January 2005
(Int'l Crim. Trib. for the former Yugoslavia)....................... 113, 114, 116, 151

Blaškić (IT-95-14-A), Appeals Chamber Judgment, 29 July 2004
(Int'l Crim. Trib. for the former Yugoslavia).........121, 122, 123, 124, 141, 143

Blaškić (IT-95-14-T), Trial Chamber Judgment, 3 March 2000
(Int'l Crim. Trib. for the former Yugoslavia)...................................... 122, 124
Bozano v. France (1987), 9 E.H.R.R. 297 (Eur. Ct. Hum. Rts.)...........................474
Brđanin (IT-99-36-A), Appeals Chamber Judgment, 3 April 2007
(Int'l Crim. Trib. for the former Yugoslavia)..................................... 125, 127
Brđanin (IT-99-36-T), Trial Chamber Judgment, 1 September 2004
(Int'l Crim. Trib. for the former Yugoslavia)........................110, 112, 114,141
Brima, Kamara and Kanu, Case No. SCSL-04-16-A, Appeals Chamber,
Decision of 22 February 2008 (Special Court for Sierra Leone) 204
British Columbia Electric Railway Co. Ltd. v. The King, [1946]
A.C. 527 (J.C.P.C.) 55

Canada (Attorney General) v. China (Republic) (1996), 156 N.S.R.
(2d) 297, 113 C.C.C. (3d) 470, [1996] N.S.J. No. 555 (C.A.)......... 487–88, 494
Canada (Attorney General) v. Curtis, [2005] B.C.J. No. 91,
2005 BCSC 516 .... 492, 493
Canada (Attorney General) v. Foster (2006), 274 D.L.R. (4th) 253,
217 O.A.C. 173, [2006] O.J. No. 4608 (C.A.) 493, 494
Canada (Attorney General) v. Fulfillment Solutions Advantage and
International Access Inc. (2005), 204 C.C.C. (3d) 509, [2005]
B.C.J. No. 2794, 2005 BCSC 1764..486, 488, 490
Canada (Attorney General) v. Hudak, [2004] B.C.J. No. 1478,
2004 BCSC 960.. 489, 490, 492
Canada (Attorney General) v. Ni-Met Resources Inc. (2005), 74 O.R.
(3d) 641, 251 D.L.R. (4th) 355, [2005] O.J. No. 1169 (C.A.)...................... 490
Canada (Attorney General) v. Pacific International Securities Inc.
(2006), 268 D.L.R. (4th) 40, 228 B.C.A.C. 99, 2006 BCCA 303 494
Canada (Attorney General) v. Ross (1994), 44 B.C.A.C. 228, [1994]
B.C.J. No. 971 (C.A.) 494
Canada (Attorney General) v. Schneider, [2002] B.C.J. No. 1561,
2002 BCSC 1014 490
Canada (Attorney General) v. Sharples, [2006] B.C.J. No. 3083,
2006 BCSC 1768... 488
Canada (Human Rights Commission) v. Canadian Liberty Net, [1998]
1 S.C.R. 626, 157 D.L.R. (4th) 385, [1998] S.C.J. No. 31......................413, 424
Canada (Justice) v. Khadr, [2008] 2 S.C.R. 125, 293 D.L.R. (4th) 629,
2008 SCC 28... 258
Canada (Minister of Citizenship and Immigration) v. Katriuk (1999),
156 F.T.R. 161, [1999] F.C.J. No. 90 (T.D.) 267
Canada (Minister of Citizenship and Immigration) v. Odynsky (2001),
196 F.T.R. 1, 14 Imm. L.R. (3d) 3, [2001] F.C.J. No. 286 (T.D.).................. 267
Canada (Minister of Citizenship and Immigration) v. Seifert (2007),
318 F.T.R. 1, 54 C.R. (6th) 125, 2007 FC 1165.. 267
Canada (Minister of Justice) v. Pacificador (2002), 60 O.R. (3d) 685,
166 C.C.C. (3d) 321, [2002] O.J. No. 3024 (C.A.), leave to appeal
to S.C.C. refused (2002), 101 C.R.R. (2d) 374, [2002] S.C.C.A. No. 390.... 505

Canada (Secretary of State) v. Lutjens (1991), 46 F.T.R. 267,
    15 Imm. L.R. (2d) 40, [1991] F.C.J. No. 1041 (T.D.) 232, 267
Canada Labour Code, Re, [1992] 2 S.C.R. 50, 91 D.L.R. (4th) 449,
    [1992] S.C.J. No. 49 35
Canada v. Schmidt, [1987] 1 S.C.R. 500, 39 D.L.R. (4th) 18, [1987]
    S.C.J. No. 24 279
Canadian Security Intelligence Services Act (Canada), Re (2007),
    [2008] 4 F.C.R. 230, [2007] F.C.J. No. 1780,
    2008 FC 301 .... 279–80, 458, 465, 499, 501, 502
Case Concerning Armed Activities on the Territory of Congo, Jurisdiction
    of the Court and Admissibility of the Application (Democratic Republic
    of Congo v. Rwanda), Judgment, 3 February 2006 (I.C.J.) 106
Case Concerning Military and Paramilitary Activities in and against
    Nicaragua (Nicaragua v. United States of America), [1986]
    I.C.J. Rep. 14 .... 34, 137, 145, 154
Case Concerning the Application of the Convention on the Prevention
    and Punishment of the Crime of Genocide (Bosnia and Herzegovina v.
    Serbia and Montenegro), Judgment, 26 February 2007 (I.C.J.) 107, 244
Case Concerning the Arrest Warrant of 11 April 2000 (Yerodia Case)
    (Congo v. Belgium), [2002] I.C.J. Rep. 3 .... 71, 74–75, 79, 94, 98, 221,
    539, 543, 544, 546, 557, 572–74, 598, 599
CDF (SCSL-04-14-T), Trial Chamber Judgment, 2 August 2007
    (Special Court for Sierra Leone) 121, 123, 125, 134
Celiberti de Casariego v. Uruguay, UN Doc. CCPR/C/13/D/56/1979,
    29 July 1981 (Human Rights Committee) 474
Certain Criminal Proceedings in France (Republic of the Congo v. France),
    2003, General List No. 129 (I.C.J.) 75
Chapman, Re, [1970] 3 O.R. 344, [1970] 5 C.C.C. 46, [1970]
    O.J. No. 1540 (C.A.) 63
Charkaoui v. Canada (Citizenship and Immigration), [2007] 1 S.C.R. 350,
    276 D.L.R. (4th) 594, 2007 SCC 9 506
Compania Naviera Vascongado v. SS Cristina, [1938] A.C. 485 (H.L.) 59–60
Cox v. Canada (1994), Comm. No. 539/1993, UN Doc.
    CCPR/C/52/D/539/1993 (Human Rights Committee) 504
Croft v. Dunphy, [1932] 3 W.W.R. 696, 59 C.C.C. 141, [1932]
    J.C.J. No. 4 (P.C.) 426

D.P.P. v. Doot, [1973] A.C. 807 (H.L.) 441
Daniels v. White, [1968] S.C.R. 517, 2 D.L.R. (3d) 1, [1968] S.C.J. No. 33 41
Delalić and Others (Čelebići Case) (IT-96-21), Judgment, 16 November 1998
    (Int'l Crim. Trib. for the former Yugoslavia) 274
Delalić et al. (IT-96-21-A), Appeals Chamber Judgment, 20 February 2001
    (Int'l Crim. Trib. for the former Yugoslavia) 137, 143, 145
Delalić et al. (IT-96-21-T), Trial Chamber Sentencing Judgment,
    9 October 2001 (Int'l Crim. Trib. for the former Yugoslavia) 133, 136

Federal Republic of Germany v. Rauca (1982), 38 O.R. (2d) 705,
        141 D.L.R. (3d) 412, [1982] O.J. No. 3470 (H.C.J.), aff'd (1983),
        41 O.R. (2d) 225, 145 D.L.R. (3d) 638, [1983] O.J. No. 2973 (C.A.) 226, 227
Fédération Nationale des Déportés et Internés Résistants et Patriotes
        et Autres c. Barbie (1985), 78 I.L.R. 125 (Fr. Ct. Cass.).................... 7, 216, 571
Fernando and Racquel Meiji v. Peru, Decision (1 March 1996),
        Annual Report of the Inter-American Commission on
        Human Rights, Report No. 5/96, Case No. 10970 274
Filartiga v. Pena-Irala, 630 F.2d 876 (2d Cir. 1980).. 271
Finta, Re, Szeged, Hungary, People's Court, Case No. 221/1947/10 230
Fofana (SCSL-04-14-PT), Decision on the Preliminary Defence Motion
        on the Lack of Personal Jurisdiction Filed on Behalf of the Accused
        Fofana, Trial Chamber, 3 March 2004 (Special Court for
        Sierra Leone)... 206
Fofana (SCSL-04-14-PT101), Decision on Preliminary Motion on
        Lack of Jurisdiction—Nature of Armed Conflict, Appeals Chamber,
        25 May 2004 (Special Court for Sierra Leone) 206
Fofana and Kondewa, Case No. SCSL-04-14-A-829, Appeals Chamber,
        Decision of 28 May 2008 (Special Court for Sierra Leone) 204
Foreign Legations, Re, [1943] S.C.R. 208, [1943] 2 D.L.R. 481,
        [1943] S.C.J. No. 19... 35
France et al. v. Göering et al., reprinted (1947), 41 A.J.I.L. 172,
        22 I.M.T. 203, 13 I.L.R. 203, 1 Trial of the Major War
        Criminals 171 (Int'l Military Trib.)........................... 6, 44, 147, 153, 162, 163
Furundžija (IT-95-17/1-T), Judgment, 10 December 199
        (Int'l Crim. Trib. for the former Yugoslavia)................. 76, 187, 272, 273, 274

Gacumbitsi (ICTR-2001-64-A), Appeals Chamber Judgment,
        7 July 2006 (Int'l Crim. Trib. for Rwanda) 112
Galić (IT-98-29-A), Appeals Chamber Judgment, 30 November 2006
        (Int'l Crim. Trib. for the former Yugoslavia)................................124, 129, 151
Galić (IT-98-29-T) Trial Chamber Judgment, 5 December 2003
        (Int'l Crim. Trib. for the former Yugoslavia)..............................121, 151, 300
Garcia v. Ecuador (Human Rights Committee), Comm. No. 319/1988,
        UN Doc. A/47/40 (1994)...474
Germany v. Ebke (2001), 205 D.L.R. (4th) 123, 158 C.C.C. (3d) 253,
        2001 NWTSC 52.. 489, 490
Germany v. Schreiber (2004), 184 C.C.C. (3d) 367, [2004]
        O.J. No. 2310 (S.C.J.).. 461
Germany v. Schreiber, [2000] O.J. No. 2618 (S.C.J.), aff'd (2006),
        264 D.L.R. (4th) 211, 207 O.A.C. 306, [2006] O.J. No. 789 (C.A.) 466
Giovanni Gatti, Re, [1947] Ann. Dig. 145 (Fr.) 455
Global Securities Corp. v. British Columbia (Securities Commission), [2000] 1
        S.C.R. 494, 185 D.L.R. (4th) 439, 2000 SCC 21 484
Gombo, Case No. ICC-01/05-01/08, Decision, 3 March 2009
        (Int'l Crim. Ct. Pre-Trial Ch. III).. 183

Guatemalan Generals Case, Sentencia 327/2003 (Tribunal Supremo,
Sala de lo Penal), reprinted (2003), 42 I.L.M. 686 .... 75, 222
Guengueng and others v. Habré (2002), A.H.R.L.R. 183
(Senegal Cour de Cass. 2001)..221, 311

H.S.A. et al. v. S.A. et al. (Decision Related to the Indictment of
Ariel Sharon, Amos Yaron, and Others), 12 February 2003,
reprinted (2003), 42 I.L.M. 596 (Belg. Cour de Cass.) 222
Hadžihasanović (IT-01-47-AR72), Decision on Interlocutory Appeal
Challenging Jurisdiction in Relation to Command Responsibility,
16 July 2003 (Int'l Crim. Trib. for the former Yugoslavia) 187
Hadžihasanović et al. (IT-01-47-T), Trial Chamber Judgment,
15 March 2006 (Int'l Crim. Trib. for the former Yugoslavia).....................141
Hamdan v. Rumsfeld, 548 U.S. 557, 126 S. Ct. 2749 (2006) 27, 528
Hamidi v. Canada (Minister of Citizenship and Immigration) (2006),
289 F.T.R. 110, [2006] F.C.J. No. 402, 2006 FC 333 265
Hartnett and the Queen, Re; Re Hudson and the Queen (1973), 1 O.R.
(2d) 206, 14 C.C.C. (2d) 69, [1973] O.J. No. 2153 (H.C.J.)........................ 479
Hilton v. Guyot, 159 U.S. 113 (1895)..417
Hissène Habré, 20 March 2001 (Senegal Sup. Ct.)....................................221, 311
Holway v. Canada (Minister of Citizenship and Immigration), [2006]
F.C.J. No. 386, 2006 FC 309... 265
Hungarian Deserter Case (1959), 28 I.L.R. 343 (Austria Sup. Ct.)................... 77

In re Piracy jure gentium, [1934] A.C. 586 (J.C.P.C.)...................................... 281
In re Urios (1919–22), 1 Annual Digest 107 (Fr. Ct. Cass.) 70
Ireland v. United Kingdom (1978), 25 E.C.H.R. (Ser. A.) 66.............................276
Italy v. Seifert (2007), 246 B.C.A.C. 46, 223 C.C.C. (3d) 301,
2007 BCCA 407, leave to appeal to S.C.C. refused, [2007]
S.C.C.A. No. 503.. 226

Jelisić (IT-95-10-A), Appeals Chamber Judgment, 5 July 2001
(Int'l Crim. Trib. for the former Yugoslavia)...110
Jelisić (IT-95-10-T), Judgment, 10 December 1999 (Int'l Crim. Trib.
for the former Yugoslavia)...111
Jones v. Ministry of the Interior Al-Mamlaka Al-Arabiya AS Saudiya
(the Kingdom of Saudi Arabia), [2006] UKHL 26 .... 273, 586
Joyce v. D.P.P., [1946] A.C. 347 (H.L.) 70
Judge v. Canada (2003), Comm. No. 829/1998, UN Doc.
CCPR/C/78/D/829/1998 (Human Rights Committee) 505–507
Jurisdiction of the Courts of Danzig (1928), P.C.I.J. (Ser. B) No. 15 43

Kajelijeli (ICTR-98-44A-T), Judgment and Sentence, 1 December 2003
(Int'l Crim. Trib. for Rwanda) 115, 244
Kambanda (ICTR 97-23-A), Appeals Chamber Judgment,
19 October 2000 (Int'l Crim. Trib. for Rwanda)..................................... 3, 554

Kambanda (ICTR 97-23-S), Decision on Judgment and Sentence,
    4 September 1998 (Int'l Crim. Trib. for Rwanda) 107, 554
Kambanda, (ICTR-97-23) (Int'l Crim. Trib. for Rwanda) 554
Karadžić (IT-95-5/18-AR73.1), Decision on Appellant Radovan
    Karadžić's Appeal concerning Holbrooke Agreement Disclosure,
    6 April 2009 (Int'l Crim. Trib. for the former Yugoslavia) 552
Karadžić (IT-95-5/18-AR73.4), Appeals Chamber, 12 October 2009
    (Int'l Crim. Trib. for the former Yugoslavia) 552–53
Karadžić (IT-95-5/18-PT), Decision on Accused's Second Motion for
    Inspection and Disclosure: Immunity Issue, 17 December 2008
    (Int'l Crim. Trib. for the former Yugoslavia) 552
Karadžić (IT-95-5/18-PT 17) (Int'l Crim. Trib. for the former Yugoslavia) 550
Karadžić (IT-95-5/18-PT), Decision on the Accused's Holbrooke
    Agreement Motion, 8 July 2009 (Int'l Crim. Trib. for the
    former Yugoslavia) 552–53
Karadžić and Mladić (IT-95-5-R61, IT-95-18-R61), Consideration
    of the Indictment within the Framework of Rule 61 of the Rules
    of Procedure and Evidence, 11 July 1996 (Int'l Crim. Trib. for
    the former Yugoslavia) 110
Karera (ICTR-01-74-T), Trial Chamber Judgment and Sentence,
    7 December 2007 (Int'l Crim. Trib. for Rwanda) 110
Katanga (ICC-01/04-01/07-55), Decision on the Evidence and
    Information provided by the Prosecution for the Issuance of
    a Warrant of Arrest for Germain Katanga, 5 November 2007
    (Int'l Crim. Ct.) 123, 134
Kayishema and Ruzindana (ICTR-95-1-A), Appeals Chamber Judgment
    (Reasons), 1 June 2001 (Int'l Crim. Trib. for Rwanda) 107, 113
Kayishema and Ruzindana (ICTR-95-1-T), Judgment and Sentence,
    21 May 1999 (Int'l Crim. Trib. for Rwanda) 113, 114, 122
Khadr v. Canada (Minister of Justice) (2007), [2008] 1 F.C.R. 270,
    280 D.L.R. (4th) 469, 2007 FCA 182 .... 508, 527, 533, 536
Kindler v. Canada (1993), Comm. No. 470/1991, UN Doc.
    CCPR/C/48/D/470/1991 (Human Rights Committee) 504
Kindler v. Canada (Minister of Justice), [1991] 2 S.C.R. 779,
    84 D.L.R. (4th) 438, [1991] S.C.J. No. 63 .... 449, 469, 502, 503, 506
Kordić et al. (IT-95-14/2-A), Appeals Chamber Judgment,
    17 December 2004 (Int'l Crim. Trib. for the former
    Yugoslavia) 113, 121, 122, 126, 128, 129, 134, 141
Kordić et al. (IT-95-14/2-A) Appeals Chamber Judgment,
    26 January 2005 (Int'l Crim. Trib. for the former Yugoslavia) 124
Kordić et al. (IT-95-14/2-PT), Decision on Joint Defence Motion to
    Dismiss for Lack of Jurisdiction based on the Limited Jurisdictional
    Reach of Articles 2 and 3, 2 March 1999 (Int'l Crim. Trib. for
    the former Yugoslavia) 139

Kordić et al. (IT-95-14/2-T), Trial Chamber Judgment, 26 February 2001
(Int'l Crim. Trib. for the former Yugoslavia)......... 121, 122, 124, 137, 141, 143
Krajišnik (IT-00-39-T), Trial Chamber Judgment, 27 September 2006
(Int'l Crim. Trib. for the former Yugoslavia)................111, 114, 116, 126, 142
Krhanek (Re) (2006), 56 B.C.L.R. (4th) 390, [2006] B.C.J. No. 1513,
2006 BCSC 956... 493
Krnojelac (IT-97-25-A), Appeals Chamber Judgment, 17 September
2003 (Int'l Crim. Trib. for the former Yugoslavia) 126
Krnojelac (IT-97-25-T), Trial Chamber Judgment, 15 March 2002 (Int'l
Crim. Trib. for the former Yugoslavia) 113, 114, 124, 125, 274, 275, 291
Krstić (IT-98-33-A), Appeals Chamber Judgment, 19 April 2004
(Int'l Crim. Trib. for the former Yugoslavia)........................ 110, 111, 116, 244
Krstić (IT-98-33-T), Trial Chamber Judgment, 2 August 2001
(Int'l Crim. Trib. for the former Yugoslavia)................ 110, 111, 112, 125, 126
Kunarac et al. (IT-96-23 and IT-96-23/1-A), Appeals Chamber
Judgment, 12 June 2002 (Int'l Crim. Trib. for the former
Yugoslavia) 119, 121, 122, 123–24, 125, 126, 127, 134, 274, 275
Kunarac et al. (IT-96-23-T and IT-96-23/1-T), Trial Chamber Judgment,
22 February 2001 (Int'l Crim. Trib. for the former
Yugoslavia) 38, 122, 274, 277
Kupreškić et al. (IT-95-16-T), Trial Chamber Judgment, 14 January
2000 (Int'l Crim. Trib. for the former Yugoslavia) 38, 122, 128, 178
Kvočka et al. (IT-98-30/1-A), Appeals Chamber Judgment, 28 February
2005 (Int'l Crim. Trib. for the former Yugoslavia) 124, 127, 129
Kvočka et al. (IT-98-30/1-T), Trial Chamber Judgment, 2 November
2001 (Int'l Crim. Trib. for the former Yugoslavia)...................... 127, 129, 274

Lake v. Canada (Minister of Justice), [2008] 1 S.C.R. 761,
292 D.L.R. (4th) 193, 2008 SCC 23...467, 469, 471
Lawson v. Accusearch Inc., [2007] 4 F.C.R. 314, 308 F.T.R. 186,
2007 FC 125 421
Legality of the Threat or Use of Nuclear Weapons, [1996] I.C.J. Rep. 226 77
Liangsiriprasert v. Government of the United States of America,
[1991] 1 A.C. 225 (P.C.)... 441, 443
Libman v. The Queen, [1985] 2 S.C.R. 178, 21 D.L.R. (4th) 174,
[1985] S.C.J. No. 56 ....16, 41, 49, 65, 81, 318, 322, 328–30, 341, 378, 410,
412–18, 420, 431
Limaj et al. (IT-03-66-T), Trial Chamber Judgment, 30 November
2005 (Int'l Crim. Trib. for the former Yugoslavia) 123, 124, 134
Lopez Burgos v. Uruguay, UN Doc. CCPR/C/13/D/52/1979,
29 July 1981 (Human Rights Committee)...474
Lubanga (ICC-01/04-01/06), Decision on the Confirmation of Charges
in the Lubanga Case, 29 January 2007 (Int'l Crim. Ct.)............. 123, 124, 134
Lubanga (ICC-01/04-01/06-8), Decision on the Prosecutor's
Application for a Warrant of Arrest, 10 February 2006
(Int'l Crim. Ct.)...193, 198, 199, 200

Lubanga, Case No. ICC-01/04-01/06 (OA 13), Appeals Chamber,
  Judgment, 21 October 2008 (Int'l Crim. Ct.).. 183
Lubanga, Case No. ICC-01/04-01/06 (OA 4), Appeals Chamber,
  Judgment, 14 December 2006 (Int'l Crim. Ct.) 183, 188, 478

M/V Saiga (No. 2) Case (Saint Vincent and the Grenadines v. Guinea),
  reprinted (1999), 38 I.L.M. 1323 (Int'l Trib. for the Law of the Sea) 89–90
MacFarlane v. Canada (Attorney General), [1995] O.J. No. 4619
  (Gen. Div.) 492
Macleod v. Attorney-General for New South Wales, [1891] A.C. 455 (P.C.) 48
Martić (IT-95-11-T), Trial Chamber Judgment, 12 June 2007
  (Int'l Crim. Trib. for the former Yugoslavia).......................121, 122, 126, 127
Media Case (ICTR-96-11-A), Appeals Chamber Judgment,
  28 November 2007 (Int'l Crim. Trib. for Rwanda) 112, 116, 129
Media Case (ICTR-99-52-T), Judgment and Sentence, 3 December 2003
  (Int'l Crim. Trib. for Rwanda) 115, 129
Menchu Tumn and Others, Sentencia 237/2005, Judgment,
  26 September 2005 (Spain Constitutional Trib. Sala Segunda) 222
Milosević (IT-02-54), Decision on Preliminary Motions,
  8 November 2001 (Int'l Crim. Trib. for the former Yugoslavia)................. 551
Milosević (IT-98-29/1), Trial Chamber Judgment, 12 December
  2007 (Int'l Crim. Trib. for the former Yugoslavia) 121, 122–23, 151
Morguard Investments Ltd. v. de Savoye, [1990] 3 S.C.R. 1077,
  76 D.L.R. (4th) 256, [1990] S.C.J. No. 135 412
Mrkšić et al. (IT-95-13/1), Trial Chamber Judgment, 27 September
  2007 (Int'l Crim. Trib. for the former Yugoslavia) 121, 133–34, 141
Mugesera v. Canada (Minister of Citizenship and Immigration),
  [2005] 2 S.C.R. 100, 254 D.L.R. (4th) 200, 2005 SCC 40.......36, 39, 105, 123,
  129, 187, 241–45, 247, 250, 254, 261, 265
Munyakazi (ICTR-97-36-R11bis), Decision on the Prosecution's Appeal
  against Decision on the Referral under Rule 11bis, Appeals Chamber,
  8 October 2008 (Int'l Crim. Trib. for Rwanda)..174
Munyaneza v. Canada (Minister of Citizenship and Immigration),
  [2002] F.C.J. No. 1628, 2002 FCT 1203 260
Musema (ICTR-96-13-T), Trial Chamber Judgment, 27 January 2000
  (Int'l Crim. Trib. for Rwanda) 114, 115, 134
Mutual Legal Assistance in Criminal Matters Act (Re), [1996]
  O.J. No. 371 (Gen. Div.) 490
Mutual Legal Assistance in Criminal Matters Act, Re (sub nom.
  Russian Federation v. Pokidyshev) (1999), 178 D.L.R. (4th) 91,
  27 C.R. (5th) 316, [1999] O.J. No. 3292 (C.A.)............................. 485, 488, 493

Nahimana et al. (ICTR-99-52-T), Trial Chamber Judgment and Sentence,
  3 December 2003, confirmed by Appeals Chamber, Nahimana et al.
  (ICTR-99-52-A), Appeals Chamber Judgment, 28 November 2007
  (Int'l Crim. Trib. for Rwanda) 112, 116, 129

Naletilić et al. (IT-98-34-A), Appeals Chamber Judgment, 3 May 2006
   (Int'l Crim. Trib. for the former Yugoslavia)................................. 129
Naletilić et al. (IT-98-34-T), Trial Chamber Judgment, 31 March 2003 (Int'l
   Crim. Trib. for the former Yugoslavia) 121, 122, 164, 140, 141, 142, 143
National Cheese & Food Co. (Re) (1998), 110 O.A.C. 151, [1998]
   O.J. No. 1988 (C.A.)... 487–88
Netherlands v. Short, The, reprinted in (1990), 29 I.L.M. 1375
   (Neth. Sup. Ct.)... 500
Ng v. Canada (1993), Comm. No. 469/1991, UN Doc.
   CCPR/C/49/D/469/1991 (Human Rights Committee)............................... 504
Nikolić (IT-94-2-AR73), Decision on Interlocutory Appeal
   Concerning Legality of Arrest, Appeals Chamber, 5 June
   2003 (Int'l Crim. Trib. for the former Yugoslavia) 26, 104, 166, 477–78
Niyitegeka (ICTR-96-14-T), Judgment and Sentence, 16 May 2003
   (Int'l Crim. Trib. for Rwanda) 115
North v. The King (1906), 37 S.C.R. 385, 26 C.L.T. 380, [1906] S.C.J. No. 16 90
Ntakirutimana et al. (ICTR-96-10-A and ICTR-96-17-A), Appeals
   Chamber Judgment, 13 December 2004 (Int'l Crim. Trib. for
   Rwanda)..116, 125

Öcalan v. Turkey, Appl. No. 00046221/99, Merits, Judgment of
   12 May 2005 (Eur. Ct. Hum. Rts. Grand Chamber)....................................474
Ohlendorf and Others, In Re (1948), 15 I.L.R. 656 (US Military Trib.) 6
Ontario (Commissioner of Competition) v. Falconbridge Ltd. (2003),
   225 D.L.R. (4th) 1, 12 C.R. (6th) 243, [2003] O.J. No. 1563
   (C.A.), leave to appeal to S.C.C. refused, [2003]
   S.C.C.A. No. 302...................................... 489, 490, 492, 494
Ontario (Ministry of the Attorney General) v. Black (2007),
   84 O.R. (3d) 481, [2007] O.J. No. 886, 2007 ONCA 165 494
Ordon Estate v. Grail, [1998] 3 S.C.R. 437, 166 D.L.R. (4th) 193,
   [1998] S.C.J. No. 84 33
Orić (IT-03-68-T), Trial Chamber Judgment, 30 June 2006
   (Int'l Crim. Trib. for the former Yugoslavia)......................................133, 141

Piracy Jure Gentium, Re, [1934] A.C. 586 72
Polyukhovich v. Commonwealth of Australia (1991), 172 C.L.R. 501,
   101 A.L.R. 545, 91 I.L.R. 1, [1991] HCA 32.................................... 118
Pratt v. Attorney General for Jamaica, [1993] 4 All E.R. 769 (J.C.P.C.)............. 503
Public Prosecutor v. Antoni (1960), 32 I.L.R. 140 (Sweden Ct. App.) 66
Public Prosecutor v. Menten (1981), 75 I.L.R. 331 (Neth. Sup. Ct.) 216
Pushpanathan v. Canada (Minister of Citizenship and Immigration),
   [1998] 1 S.C.R. 982, 160 D.L.R. (4th) 193, [1998] S.C.J. No. 46......... 592, 595

Questions of Interpretation and Application of the 1971 Montreal
   Convention Arising from the Aerial Incident at Lockerbie
   (Interim Measures) (Libya v. United States), [1992] I.C.J. Rep. 3................310

R. c. Munyaneza, [2009] R.J.Q. 1432, [2009] Q.J. No. 4913,
2009 QCCS 2201, leave to appeal granted, [2009]
J.Q. no 6465, 2009 QCCA 1279 .... 10, 74, 105, 236, 237, 242–245,
250, 251, 259, 261, 262, 590

R. c. Namouh, [2009] J.Q. no 10496, 2009 QCCQ 9324 370

R. c. Ouellette (1998), 126 C.C.C. (3d) 219, [1998] J.Q. no 2902 (S.C.) 414

R. c. Rainville, [2001] J.Q. no 947 (C.Q.) 278

R. v. Accused No. 1 (2005), 35 C.R. (6th) 140, 134 C.R.R. (2d) 274,
2005 BCSC 1727 324

R. v. Bachrack (1913), 28 O.L.R. 32, 21 C.C.C. 257, [1913] O.J. No. 31
(C.A.) 408

R. v. Bakker, [2005] B.C.J. No. 1577, 2005 BCPC 289 391

R. v. Bartle and the Commissioner of Police for the Metropolis and
Others, Ex Parte Pinochet; R. v. Evans and Another and the
Commissioner of Police for the Metropolis and Others, Ex Parte
Pinochet (1999), [2000] 1 A.C. 147, [1999] 2 All E.R. 97, [1999]
UKHL 17 .... 2, 76, 221, 272–73, 441, 539, 545, 580–83, 585–86, 588

R. v. *Bow Street Metropolitan Stipendiary Magistrate, Ex parte Pinochet Ugarte
(No. 3). See R. v. Bartle and the Commissioner of Police for the Metropolis
and Others, Ex Parte Pinochet; R. v. Evans and Another and the Commissioner
of Police for the Metropolis and Others, Ex Parte Pinochet*

R. v. Brosig, [1945] O.R. 240, [1945] 2 D.L.R. 232, [1945]
O.J. No. 503 (C.A.) 224

R. v. Budd (2000), 138 O.A.C. 116, 150 C.C.C. (3d) 108, [2000]
O.J. No. 4649 (C.A.), leave to appeal to S.C.C. refused, [2001]
S.C.C.A. No. 57 ....487, 489

R. v. Budd, [2004] O.T.C. 763, [2004] O.J. No. 3519 (S.C.J.) 490

R. v. Cook, [1998] 2 S.C.R. 597, 164 D.L.R. (4th) 1, [1998]
S.C.J. No. 68 .... 53, 80, 93, 95, 419, 420, 511, 516–18, 519

R. v. Craig, [2009] 1 S.C.R. 762, 306 D.L.R. (4th) 577, 2009 SCC 23 386

R. v. Dabrowski (2007), 86 O.R. (3d) 721, 229 O.A.C. 20, 2007 ONCA 619 403

R. v. Daoust, [2004] 1 S.C.R. 217, 235 D.L.R. (4th) 216, 2004 SCC 6 385

R. v. Doiron (1989), 93 N.B.R. (2d) 444, [1989] N.B.J. No. 12 (C.A.) 414, 418

R. v. Dorsay (2006), 223 B.C.A.C. 192, 209 C.C.C. (3d) 184, 42 C.R.
(6th) 155, 2006 BCCA 117, leave to appeal to S.C.C. refused,
[2006] S.C.C.A. No. 374 .... 95, 491, 514, 531

R. v. Dos Santos (1992), 96 Nfld. & P.E.I.R. 13, [1992] N.J. No. 34
(S.C.T.D.) 64, 415, 465

R. v. Douglas (1989), 47 O.A.C. 31, 72 C.R. (3d) 309, [1989]
O.J. No. 1664 (C.A.), aff'd on other grounds [1991] 1 S.C.R. 301,
3 C.R. (4th) 246, [1991] S.C.J. No. 16 440

R. v. Drakes, [2005] O.T.C. 577, [2005] O.J. No. 2863 (S.C.J.) 413

R. v. Dunphy (1996), 140 Nfld. & P.E.I.R. 8, [1996] N.J. No. 100
(S.C.T.D.) 86, 515

R. v. Finta (1989), 69 O.R. (2d) 557, 61 D.L.R. (4th) 85, [1989]
O.J. No. 1041 (H.C.J.), (1992), 92 D.L.R. (4th) 1, 14 C.R. (4th) 1,
[1992] O.J. No. 823 (C.A.), aff'd [1994] 1 S.C.R. 701, 112 D.L.R.
(4th) 513, [1994] S.C.J. No. 26 .... 38, 42, 230, 410, 413, 424, 438
R. v. Frisbee (1986), 1 W.C.B. (2d) 154 (B.C.S.C.) 85
R. v. Gagnon (1956), 117 C.C.C. 61, 25 C.R. 38 (Que. C.S.P.) 472
R. v. Gladwin (1997), 101 O.A.C. 116, 116 C.C.C. (3d) 471, [1997]
O.J. No. 2479 (C.A.), leave to appeal to S.C:C. refused, [1997]
S.C.C.A. No. 325 .... 488, 489
R. v. Governor of Pentonville ex parte Cheng, [1973] A.C. 931 (H.L.).............. 456
R. v. Grant (2009), 309 D.L.R. (4th) 1, 391 N.R. 1, 2009 SCC 32 .... 521, 536
R. v. Greco (2001), 155 O.A.C. 316, 159 C.C.C. (3d) 146, [2001] O.J. No. 4147
(C.A.), leave to appeal to S.C.C. refused (2001), 162 C.C.C.
(3d) vi 415, 418, 421, 422
R. v. Grujicic, [1994] O.J. No. 2280 (Gen. Div.) 230
R. v. Guilbride, [2002] B.C.J. No. 1594, 2002 BCPC 254 513
R. v. Guilbride, [2003] B.C.J. No. 389, 2003 BCPC 44 .... 496, 512, 516
R. v. Guilbride, [2004] B.C.J. No. 861, 2004 BCPC 101 .... 89, 435, 442
R. v. Hammerbeck (1993), 26 B.C.A.C. 1, 45 R.F.L. (3d) 265,
[1993] B.C.J. No. 685 (C.A.) 414
R. v. Hape, [2007] 2 S.C.R. 292, 280 D.L.R. (4th) 385,
2007 SCC 26 .... 17, 33, 35, 36, 40, 41, 51, 53, 54, 56, 80, 93–94, 95,
280, 483, 495, 511–12, 513, 519, 520–23, 525–29, 530–37, 591, 593, 595
R. v. Harrer, [1995] 3 S.C.R. 562, 128 D.L.R. (4th) 98, [1995]
S.C.J. No. 81 .... 495, 510, 511, 514, 516, 532
R. v. Hartley, [1978] 2 N.Z.L.R. 199, 77 I.L.R. 330 (C.A.) 476
R. v. Heckman (1902), 5 C.C.C. 242 (N.S.T.D.) 287
R. v. Horseferry Road Magistrates' Court, Ex parte Bennett, [1994]
1 A.C. 42 (H.L.) 476
R. v. Innes (2007), 423 A.R. 14, [2007] A.J. No. 964, 2007 ABPC 237.............. 393
R. v. Kaehler & Stolski, [1945] 3 D.L.R. 272, 83 C.C.C. 353, [1945]
A.J. No. 55 (S.C.A.D.) 224
R. v. Kharsekin (1994), 88 C.C.C. (3d) 193 (Nfld. C.A.) 85
R. v. Khawaja (2006), 214 C.C.C. (3d) 399, 42 C.R. (6th) 348, [2006]
O.J. No. 4245 (S.C.J.), leave to appeal to S.C.C. refused, [2006]
S.C.C.A. No. 505, supplementary reasons (2008), 238 C.C.C.
(3d) 114, [2008] O.J. No. 4244 (S.C.J.) 368, 369, 370
R. v. Kirkness, [1990] 3 S.C.R. 74, 1 C.R. (4th) 91, [1990] S.C.J. No. 119 255
R. v. Klassen (2008), 240 C.C.C. (3d) 328, 63 C.R. (6th) 373,
2008 BCSC 1762 .... 67, 80, 391, 421
R. v. Laliberty (1997), 102 O.A.C. 51, 117 C.C.C. (3d) 97, [1997]
O.J. No. 2808 (C.A.)... 255
R. v. Larche, [2006] 2 S.C.R. 762, 273 D.L.R. (4th) 577,
2006 SCC 56 .... 65, 416, 419, 420
R. v. Lindsay (2004), 70 O.R. (3d) 131, 182 C.C.C. (3d) 301, [2004]
O.J. No. 845 (S.C.J.) 324

R. v. Logan, [1990] 2 S.C.R. 731, 73 D.L.R. (4th) 40, [1990] S.C.J. No. 89 255
R. v. MacIntosh (2008), 272 N.S.R. (2d) 286, 241 C.C.C. (3d) 553,
    2008 NSCA 124 472
R. v. Macooh, [1993] 2 S.C.R. 802, 105 D.L.R. (4th) 96, [1993] S.C.J. No. 28 90
R. v. Mathur (2007), 162 C.R.R. (2d) 23, [2007] O.J. No. 3592 (S.C.J.) 496, 512
R. v. Mullen, [1999] 3 W.L.R. 777 (Crim. Ct. App.) 477
R. v. Neumann, 1949 (3) SA 1238 (Sup. Cr. Ct. Transvaal) 70
R. v. Ng (2006), 140 C.R.R. (2d) 224, [2006] B.C.J. No. 774,
    2006 BCPC 111; [2007] B.C.J. No. 1388, 2007 BCPC 204 329
R. v. O.B. (1997), 99 O.A.C. 313, 116 C.C.C. (3d) 189, [1997]
    O.J. No. 1850 (C.A.) 413
R. v. Oickle, [2000] 2 S.C.R. 3, 190 D.L.R. (4th) 257, 2000 SCC 38 509
R. v. Oteri, [1976] 1 W.L.R. 1272 (P.C.) 435
R. v. Pawlowski (1992), 13 C.R. (4th) 228, [1992] O.J. No. 562
    (Gen. Div.), quashed (1993), 12 O.R. (3d) 709, 20 C.R. (4th) 233,
    [1993] O.J. No. 554 (C.A.), leave to appeal to S.C.C. refused,
    [1993] 3 S.C.R. viii, 25 C.R. (4th) 67n, [1993] S.C.C.A. No. 187 230
R. v. Rattray (2008), 233 O.A.C. 6, 229 C.C.C. (3d) 496, 2008 ONCA 74 422
R. v. Reistetter (1991), Court File No. RE 185/90 (Ont. Ct. Gen. Div.) 230
R. v. Reyat (1993), 24 B.C.A.C. 161, 20 C.R. (4th) 149, [1993]
    B.C.J. No. 622 (C.A.) 63
R. v. Ribic (2008), 238 C.C.C. (3d) 225, 63 C.R. (6th) 70, 2008 ONCA 790 352
R. v. Rowbotham (1992), 60 O.A.C. 75, 76 C.C.C. (3d) 542, [1992]
    O.J. No. 2141 (C.A.), aff'd (1992), [1993] 4 S.C.R. 834,
    85 C.C.C. (3d) 575, [1993] S.C.J. No. 136 440
R. v. Rumbault (1998), 202 N.B.R. (2d) 87, 127 C.C.C. (3d) 138,
    [1998] N.B.J. No. 265 (Q.B.) 90
R. v. Rutherford Ltd. (1995), 101 C.C.C. (3d) 260, [1995] B.C.J.
    No. 1953 (S.C.) 490
R. v. Saunders (2005), 232 N.S.R. (2d) 249, [2005] N.S.J. No. 171,
    2005 NSPC 13 51
R. v. Sawoniuk, [2000] 2 Cr. App. R. 220 (C.A.) 220
R. v. Shindler (1944), 3 W.W.R. 125 (Alta. Police Ct.) 224
R. v. Smith (2006), 280 Sask. R. 128, [2006] S.J. No. 184, 2006 SKQB 132 324
R. v. Spencer, [1985] 2 S.C.R. 278, 21 D.L.R. (4th) 756,
    [1985] S.C.J. No. 60 .... 40, 417
R. v. Stanny, [2008] A.J. No. 1395, 2008 ABQB 746 422
R. v. Stucky (2009), 303 D.L.R. (4th) 1, 56 B.L.R. (4th) 1,
    2009 ONCA 151, leave to appeal to S.C.C. granted,
    [2009] S.C.C.A. No. 186 .... 416, 417, 424
R. v. Sunila and Solayman (1986), 71 N.S.R. (2d) 300, 28 D.L.R.
    (4th) 450, [1986] N.S.J. No. 76 (C.A.) 90
R. v. Taylor (1976), 32 C.C.C. (2d) 409, [1976] O.J. No. 2458 (Prov. Ct.) 171
R. v. Terezakis, 2007 BCCA 384, 223 C.C.C. (3d) 344, 2007 BCCA 384,
    leave to appeal to S.C.C. refused, [2007] S.C.C.A. No. 487 324

R. v. Terry, [1996] 2 S.C.R. 207, 135 D.L.R. (4th) 214, [1996]
S.C.J. No. 62 ....93, 95, 491, 495, 510, 511, 516
R. v. Vaillancourt, [1987] 2 S.C.R. 636, 47 D.L.R. (4th) 399, [1987]
S.C.J. No. 83 253
R. v. Van Rassel, [1990] 1 S.C.R. 225, 53 C.C.C. (3d) 353, [1990]
S.C.J. No. 11 38
R. v. Vézina, [1986] 1 S.C.R. 2, 25 D.L.R. (4th) 82, [1986] S.C.J. No. 2 413
R. v. Walton (1905), 11 O.L.R. 94, 10 C.C.C. 269, [1905] O.J. No. 18 (C.A.)..... 479
R. v. Watts, [2005] A.J. No. 568 (Q.B.) 341
R. v. Yashnev, [1995] O.J. No. 3599 (Gen. Div.)..514
R. v. Yue (1996), 71 B.C.A.C. 157, [1996] B.C.J. No. 385 (C.A.)......................... 385
R. v. Zingre, [1981] 2 S.C.R. 392, 127 D.L.R. (3d) 223, [1981] S.C.J. No. 89 41
Rasul v. Bush, 542 U.S. 466 (2004) 27, 528
Reference Re Ng Extradition, [1991] 2 S.C.R. 858, 84 D.L.R. (4th) 498,
[1991] S.C.J. No. 64... 27
Reference re Secession of Quebec, [1998] 2 S.C.R. 217, 161 D.L.R.
(4th) 385, [1998] S.C.J. No. 61 587–88
Regina and Palacios, Re (1984), 45 O.R. (2d) 269, 7 D.L.R. (4th) 112,
[1984] O.J. No. 3104 (C.A.) 35
Reservations to the Convention on the Prevention and Punishment of
the Crime of Genocide, [1951] I.C.J. Rep. 15 (advisory opinion)....... 106, 578
Rex v. Dawson (1696), 13 St. Tr. 451 283
Reyat's Application for a Writ of Habeas Corpus, Re (22 March 1989),
CO/1157/88, MWC (Q.B.D.) 452
Rohrig, Brunner and Heinze (1950), 17 I.L.R. 393 (Neth. Ct. Cass.) 69
Romania (State) v. Cheng (1997), 158 N.S.R. (2d) 13, 114 C.C.C.
(3d) 289, [1997] N.S.J. No. 106 (S.C.), aff'd (1997), 162 N.S.R.
(2d) 395, 119 C.C.C. (3d) 561, [1997] N.S.J. No. 408 (C.A.) 452
Rutaganda (ICTR-96-3-T), Judgment and Sentence, 6 December 1999
(Int'l Crim. Trib. for Rwanda) 112, 113, 134

S v. De Blom (1977) 3 SA 513 (A) 158
S.S. Lotus (France v. Turkey) (1927) P.C.I.J. (Ser. A.) No. 10.............281, 285, 473
Saint John (City) v. Fraser-Brace Overseas, [1958] S.C.R. 263,
13 D.L.R. (2d) 177, [1958] S.C.J. No. 18.. 35
Schooner Exchange v. McFaddon, 11 U.S. (7 Cranch) 116 (1812) 570
Schreiber v. Canada (Attorney General), [1998] 1 S.C.R. 841,
158 D.L.R. (4th) 577, [1998] S.C.J. No. 42............................. 60, 495, 498, 511
Semanza (ICTR-97-20-A), Appeals Chamber Judgment, 20 May 2005
(Int'l Crim. Trib. for Rwanda) 116, 122
Semanza (ICTR-97-20-T), Judgment and Sentence, 15 May 2003
(Int'l Crim. Trib. for Rwanda) 112, 134, 244
Seromba (ICTR-2001-66-I), Trial Chamber Judgment, 13 December 2006
(Int'l Crim. Trib. for Rwanda) 112, 114, 122
Sesay, Kallon and Gbao, Case No. SCSL-04-15-T-619, Trial Chamber,
Decision of 25 February 2009 (Special Court for Sierra Leone) 204

Shepherd and Minister of Employment and Immigration, Re (1989),
    70 O.R. (2d) 765, 63 D.L.R. (4th) 687, [1989] O.J. No. 2056 (C.A.)............ 447
Sherk v. Canada (Attorney General) (2002), [2003] 2 W.W.R. 27,
    176 B.C.A.C. 49, 2002 BCCA 673... 488
Sherk v. Canada (Attorney General) (2003), 178 C.C.C. (3d) 297,
    109 C.R.R. (2d) 283, 2003 BCSC 1216.. 492–93
Simba (ICTR-01-76-A) Appeals Chamber Judgment, 27 November 2007
    (Int'l Crim. Trib. for Rwanda) 110
Simba (ICTR-01-76-T), Judgment and Sentence, 13 December 2005
    (Int'l Crim. Trib. for Rwanda) 114
Simić (IT-95-9-A), Appeals Chamber Judgment, 28 November 2006
    (Int'l Crim. Trib. for the former Yugoslavia)............................. 126, 141, 142
Simić (IT-95-9-T), Trial Chamber Judgment, 17 October 2003
    (Int'l Crim. Trib. for the former Yugoslavia)... 124–25
Situation in Uganda (ICC-02/04-53), Warrant of Arrest for Joseph Kony
    Issued on 8 July 2005 As Amended on 27 September 2005
    (Int'l Crim. Ct.)... 192, 198, 199
Sivakumar v. Canada (Minister of Citizenship and Immigration) (1993),
    [1994] 1 F.C. 433, 163 N.R. 197, [1993] F.C.J. No. 1145 (C.A.)................... 266
Smith v. Socialist People's Libyan Arab Jamahiriya, 113 I.L.R. 534
    (2d Circ. 1997) 61
Society of Composers, Authors & Music Publishers of Canada v.
    Canadian Assn. of Internet Providers, [2004] 2 S.C.R. 427,
    240 D.L.R. (4th) 193, 2004 SCC 45...405, 421, 424
Soering v. United Kingdom, Series A, No. 161 (1989)
    (Eur. Ct. Hum. Rts.)..xxi, 500, 503
Sommersett v. Stewart (1772), 98 E.R. 499 (K.B.)... 288
Stakić (IT-97-24-A), Appeals Chamber Judgment, 22 March 2006
    (Int'l Crim. Trib. for the former Yugoslavia)...................................... 126, 129
Stakić (IT-97-24-T), Trial Chamber Judgment, 31 July 2003
    (Int'l Crim. Trib. for the former Yugoslavia).........................109, 111, 114, 124
State of Arizona v. Willoughby (1995), 114 I.L.R. 586 (Ariz. S.C.) 63
State v. Beahan, [1992] 1 S.A.C.R. 307 (A) (Zimbabwe) 476
State v. Ebrahim, [1991] 2 S. Afr. L.R. 553, in translation at 95 I.L.R. 417 476
Stocké v. Federal Republic of Germany (1989), 95 I.L.R. 328
    (Eur. Comm. Hum. Rts.) 474
Strugar (IT-01-42-T), Trial Chamber Judgment, 31 January 2005
    (Int'l Crim. Trib. for the former Yugoslavia)...141
Stuckey (Re) (1999), 181 D.L.R. (4th) 144, 68 C.R.R. (2d) 51, [1999]
    B.C.J. No. 2271 (S.C.).. 493
Stuckey (Re) (2000), 184 D.L.R. (4th) 328, 144 C.C.C. (3d) 184,
    2000 BCSC 171 494
Suresh v. Canada (Minister of Citizenship and Immigration),
    [2002] 1 S.C.R. 3, 208 D.L.R. (4th) 1,
    2002 SCC 1 .... 37, 40, 271, 279, 294, 458, 503–4, 527

T. v. Immigration Officer, [1996] A.C. 742 (H.L.) 455, 456–57

Tadić (IT-94-1-A), Appeals Chamber Judgment, 15 July 1999
(Int'l Crim. Trib. for the former Yugoslavia)........ 122, 124, 134, 137, 140, 168

Tadić (IT-94-1-AR72), Decision on the Defence Motion for
Interlocutory Appeal on Jurisdiction, Appeals Chamber,
2 October 1995 (Int'l Crim. Trib. For the former
Yugoslavia) ....xxi, 99, 119, 132, 133, 146, 147–48, 167, 262

Tadić (IT-94-1-T), Decision on the Defence Motion on Jurisdiction,
Trial Chamber, 10 August 1995 (Int'l Crim. Trib. for the
former Yugoslavia) 167

Tadić (IT-94-1-T), Trial Chamber Opinion and Judgment, 7 May 1997
(Int'l Crim. Trib. for the former Yugoslavia)..................................... 128, 134

Taylor (SCSL-03-01-I-059), Appeals Chamber Decision on Immunity
Motion, 31 May 2004 (Special Court for Sierra Leone).................205, 555–57

Taylor (SCSL-03-01-T) (Special Court for Sierra Leone) 3, 204

Tele-Mobile Co. v. Ontario, [2008] 1 S.C.R. 305, 92 O.R. (3d) 478,
2008 SCC 12 495

Thailand v. Saxena (2006), 265 D.L.R. (4th) 55, 224 B.C.A.C. 43,
2006 BCCA 98, leave to appeal to S.C.C. refused, [2006]
S.C.C.A. No. 147, reconsideration denied (2009), 273 B.C.A.C. 41,
[2009] B.C.J. No. 1146, 2009 BCCA 223.. 505

Thomas c. R., (2006), 199 C.C.C. (3d) 188, 33 C.R. (6th) 336,
2005 QCCA 628 .... 509, 512

United Kingdom v. Ramsden (1996), 135 D.L.R. (4th) 693, 107 C.C.C.
(3d) 104, [1996] O.J. No. 1839 (Gen. Div.)... 492, 493

United Kingdom v. Ramsden (1996), 92 O.A.C. 270, 108 C.C.C.
(3d) 289, [1996] O.J. No. 2716 (C.A.), leave to appeal to S.C.C.
refused, [1996] S.C.C.A. No. 443 487

United Kingdom v. Wilson-Smith & Co., [2002] O.J. No. 5342 (S.C.J.).... 490, 508

United States of America v. Allard, [1987] 1 S.C.R. 564, 40 D.L.R.
(4th) 102, [1987] S.C.J. No. 20 501

United States of America v. Allard, [1991] 1 S.C.R. 861, 64 C.C.C.
(3d) 159, [1991] S.C.J. No. 30... 447–48

United States of America v. Amhaz, [2002] B.C.J. No. 3354,
2002 BCSC 118.. 490

United States of America v. Anekwu (2008), 79 B.C.L.R. (4th) 323,
232 C.C.C. (3d) 130, 2008 BCCA 138, leave to appeal to S.C.C.
granted, [2008] S.C.C.A. No. 246 464

United States of America v. Barbarash, [2002] B.C.J. No. 2803,
2002 BCSC 1721 .... 489, 490

United States of America v. Beach (1999), 134 Man. R. (2d) 56,
132 C.C.C. (3d) 156, [1999] M.J. No. 56 (C.A.) 492

United States of America v. Beach (2000), 185 D.L.R. (4th) 357,
[2000] 5 W.W.R. 190, [2000] M.J. No. 150 (C.A.) 493

United States of America v. Black, [2007] O.J. No. 1304 (S.C.J.) 491

United States of America v. Burns, [2001] 1 S.C.R. 283, 195 D.L.R.
(4th) 1, [2001] S.C.J. No. 8, 2001 SCC 7 .... xxii, 26, 39, 40, 60, 279, 468,
469, 503–504, 505, 506, 508, 527, 530

United States of America v. Cobb, [2001] 1 S.C.R. 587, 197 D.L.R.
(4th) 46, 2001 SCC 19 466

United States of America v. Cotroni, [1989] 1 S.C.R. 1469,
96 N.R. 321, [1989] S.C.J. No. 56 .... xxi, 445–46, 465, 470, 471, 501

United States of America v. El-Jabsheh (2002), 167 C.C.C. (3d) 82,
[2002] B.C.J. No. 1349, 2002 BCSC 246 490

United States of America v. Ferras; United States of America v. Latty,
[2006] 2 S.C.R. 77, 268 D.L.R. (4th) 1, 2006 SCC 33 .... 463, 464, 465, 466

United States of America v. Future Électronique Inc. (2000),
[2001] R.J.Q. 49, 151 C.C.C. (3d) 403, [2000] J.Q. no 5547
(C.A.), leave to appeal to S.C.C. refused, [2001] C.S.C.R. no. 82 489–90

United States of America v. Kavaratzis (2006), 209 O.A.C. 180,
208 C.C.C. (3d) 139, [2006] O.J. No. 1661 (C.A.) 441, 452

United States of America v. Kwok, [2001] 1 S.C.R. 532, 197 D.L.R.
(4th) 1, 2001 SCC 18 89

United States of America v. Licht (2002), 168 C.C.C. (3d) 287,
98 C.R.R. (2d) 291, 2002 BCSC 1151 516

United States of America v. Maydak, [2004] B.C.J. No. 2473,
2004 BCSC 1550.. 491

United States of America v. McDowell (2004), 237 D.L.R. (4th) 677,
183 C.C.C. (3d) 149, [2004] O.J. No. 1190 (C.A.), leave to appeal
to S.C.C. refused, [2004] S.C.C.A. No. 325... 464

United States of America v. McVey, [1992] 3 S.C.R. 475, 77 C.C.C.
(3d) 1, [1992] S.C.J. No. 95.. 447–48, 460

United States of America v. Nadarajah (2009), 95 O.R. (3d) 514,
243 C.C.C. (3d) 281, [2009] O.J. No. 946 (S.C.J.) 368

United States of America v. Orphanou, [2004] O.T.C. 167, 19 C.R.
(6th) 291, [2004] O.J. No. 622 (S.C.J.).. 490

United States of America v. Price (2007), 86 O.R. (3d) 762,
226 O.A.C. 45, 2007 ONCA 526 .... 489, 490, 491

United States of America v. Reumayr (2003), 184 B.C.A.C. 251,
176 C.C.C. (3d) 377, 2003 BCCA 375 471

United States of America v. Ross, [1995] R.J.Q. 1680, 100 C.C.C.
(3d) 320, [1995] Q.J. No. 506 (C.A.) 492, 493

United States of America v. Shepherd (1976), [1977] 2 S.C.R. 1067,
70 D.L.R. (3d) 136, [1976] S.C.J. No. 106... 463

United States of America v. Shulman, [2001] 1 S.C.R. 616, 197 D.L.R.
(4th) 69, 2001 SCC 21 466

United States of America v. Sigurdson (1998), 132 Man. R. (2d) 17,
[1998] M.J. No. 374 (Q.B.), aff'd (1999), 134 Man. R. (2d) 114 (C.A.) 489

United States of America v. Thomlinson (2007), 84 O.R. (3d) 161,
219 O.A.C. 322, [2007] O.J. No. 246 (C.A.) 465–66

United States of America v. Tsioubris, [2001] 1 S.C.R. 613,
197 D.L.R. (4th) 67, 2001 SCC 20 466
United States of America v. Wilson, [2002] B.C.J. No. 129,
2002 BCSC 124 .... 488, 489
United States v. Alvarez-Machain, 504 U.S. 655, 112 S. Ct. 2188 (1992) 475
United States v. Cargo of the Brig Malek Adhel, 43 U.S. 210 (1844) 282
United States v. Marino-Garcia, 679 F.2d 1373 (11th Cir. 1982) 77
United States v. Noriega, 746 F. Supp. 1506 (S.D. Fla. 1990) 441
United States v. Smith, 18 U.S. (5 Wheat.) 153 (1820) 283
United States v. Toscanino, 500 F.2d 267 (2d Circ. 1974) 477
United States v. Wright-Barker, 784 F.2d 161 (3d Circ. 1986) 441
United States v. Yunis (No. 2), 681 F. Supp. 909 (D.D.C. 1988) 68
Universal Jurisdiction Case (1958), 28 I.L.R. 341 (Austrian Sup. Ct.) 77
Universal Jurisdiction over Drug Offences (1987), 74 I.L.R. 166
(Germ. Fed. Sup. Ct.) 77

Vasiljević (IT-98-32-T), Trial Chamber Judgment, 29 November 2002
(Int'l Crim. Trib. for the former Yugoslavia).............................. 124, 128, 134

Wajid v. Canada (Minister of Citizenship and Immigration) (2000),
185 F.T.R. 308, [2000] F.C.J. No. 736 (T.D.) 266

Yamashita, In re, 327 U.S. 1 (1946) 571

Zazai v. Canada (Minister of Citizenship and Immigration) (2005),
259 D.L.R. (4th) 281, 50 Imm. L.R. (3d) 107, 2005 FCA 303 266
Zschiegner v. United States of America (2001), 194 N.S.R. (2d) 30,
154 C.C.C. (3d) 547, 2001 NSCA 74 495

INDEX

Abduction, 473–79. *See also* Extradition, abduction, and extraordinary rendition, alternatives to

Additional Protocols to the Geneva Conventions, 225, 251

Ad hoc tribunals, United Nations. *See* United Nations *ad hoc* tribunals, direct enforcement against core crimes

Admissibility of evidence gathered in foreign states, 509–37
admissibility of foreign-gathered evidence
catalogues of factors, 513, 514
no test for, 513
Afghanistan law, governing activities of Canadian forces personnel, 525
avoiding extraterritorial application of the *Canadian Charter of Rights and Freedoms*, 515
Canada-US Mutual Legal Assistance Treaty (MLAT), 515
evidence in accordance with law of requesting state, 515
Canadian Charter of Rights and Freedoms (Charter), 536
applies to trial held in Canada, 511

evidence gathered by foreign officials, excluded, 511
s. 32 stage, 521
territorially limited, 526
trial fairness stage, 521
Canadian forces personnel, 525
Canadian officials, 515
investigative activities in foreign states, 516
Canadian police, policy goal, participation in transnational investigations, 533
Canadian Security Intelligence Service (CSIS), 524
Canadian Security Intelligence Service Act, 524
Controlled Drugs and Substances Act (CDSA), 519
Criminal Code, 524, 525
domestic law, extraterritorial application, 531
evidence
Canadian Charter of Rights and Freedoms, 509, 510, 511
caselaw developed, 509
gathered by Canadian officials, 515–23

gathered by foreign officials, 509–15
foreign officials, 509
foreign states, 509
international criminal cooperation obligations, 516
international humanitarian law (IHL), 526
police, joint or cooperative investigations, 531
testimony, caregivers, 515
Afghanistan, 1, 265, 280, 362, 525, 527, 537
African Union, 183, 221, 482
Agreement for the Prosecution and Punishment of Major War Criminals of the European Axis, and Establishing the Charter of the International Military Tribunal (IMT Charter), 5
Aggression, 152–56
    defined, 155
    Draft Code of Crimes against the Peace and Security of Mankind, 154
    Kellogg-Briand Pact of 1928, 153
    Nuremberg Tribunal, 153
    prosecuting individuals, making aggressive war, 153
    Rome Statute, 155, 156
    Special Working Group on the Crime of Aggression, 155, 156
    UN Charter, 154, 155
Aircraft. *See* Jurisdiction, international and transnational crime
Al-Qaeda, 359, 362, 363
Antarctic. *See* Jurisdiction, international and transnational crime
AP I. *See First Protocol to the Geneva Conventions*
AP II. *See Second Protocol to the Geneva Conventions*
Apartheid, 293–95
    1968 *Convention on Non-Applicability of Statutory Limitations to War Crimes and Crimes against Humanity*, 293
    1973 *International Convention on the Suppression and Punishment of the Crime of Apartheid*, 293

Apartheid Convention, 12, 178, 294, 295
    Canada, 295
    crime against humanity, 293
    Genocide Convention, 294
    South Africa, 293
    UN, 294
Apartheid Convention, 12, 178, 294, 295
Arab Convention on the Suppression of Terrorism, 298
Arar, Maher, 480
Arctic region. *See* Jurisdiction, international and transnational crime
Aut dedere aut judicare, 19, 20, 96, 97, 98, 139, 216, 307, 309, 310, 348, 349, 351, 353, 358, 361, 365, 369, 372, 375, 376, 399, 448, 515

bin Laden, Osama, 362, 363
Bosnia and Herzegovina, 168, 211, 477, 551

CAH Act. *See Crimes Against Humanity and War Crimes Act*
Cambodia, 10, 207, 208, 389, 391
Canadian Charter of Rights and Freedoms (Charter), 16, 26, 28, 29, 38, 40, 41, 42, 67, 229, 232, 237, 238, 253, 254, 255, 256, 260, 279, 280, 292, 314, 329, 409, 458, 465, 466, 469, 470, 479, 489, 490, 491, 493, 495, 496, 594
Canadian Security Intelligence Service (CSIS), 26, 267, 328, 524, 525, 527
CAT. *See* United Nations *Convention against Torture and other Cruel, Inhuman and Degrading Treatment or Punishment (CAT)*
CDSA. *See Controlled Drugs and Substances Act*
Central African Republic, 181, 183, 192, 198
Charter. *See Canadian Charter of Rights and Freedoms*
Charter of the International Military Tribunal (IMT Charter), 7, 118, 120, 128, 132, 147, 161, 162, 163, 164, 217, 232, 266, 549
Chicago Convention on International Civil Aviation, 61

Child sex tourism, transnational,
        388–90. *See also* Children
    1989 United Nations *Convention on
        the Rights of the Child (UNCRC)*,
        389
    1999 *Convention concerning the Pro-
        hibition and Immediate Action for
        the Elimination of the Worst Forms
        of Child Labour (ILO Convention)*,
        390
    Canadian implementing legislation,
        391–92
    child labour, worst forms of, defin-
        ition, 390
    child pornography, sexual exploita-
        tion and sale and possession of,
        390
    child prostitution 389, 390
    child's organs, transfer for profit, 390
    children
        engaging in forced labour, 390
        sexual exploitation of, 388
    Commercial Exploitation of Chil-
        dren, Second Congress against,
        389
    Criminal Code
        prosecution of Canadian citizens,
        391
    Human Trafficking Protocol, 390
    international law, 388–90
    *Optional Protocol to the Convention on
        the Rights of the Child on the Sale
        of Children, Child Prostitution and
        Child Pornography*, 389
    Stockholm Conference, 1996, 391
    UNICEF, 389
Children, 67, 108, 113, 114, 125, 152,
        183, 290, 318, 325, 326, 327, 388,
        389, 390, 391, 393, 398, 403, 404,
        408
Chile, 76, 273, 580, 584
CICAD. *See* Inter-American Drug Abuse
        Control Commission
Citizenship Act, 71, 228, 229, 267, 432
Coastal states. *See* Jurisdiction, inter-
        national and transnational crime
*Code of Crimes against the Peace and
        Security of Mankind*, 9
Commission on Crime Prevention and
        Criminal Justice, 12

Commission on the Responsibility of
        the Authors of War and on the
        Enforcement Penalties, 5
*Comprehensive Convention on Internation-
        al Terrorism*, 297
Computer. *See* Cybercrime, trans-
        national
Conspiracy, 437–43
    Criminal Code, 437
    inchoate offences, 437
    murder, conspiring to commit, 438,
        439
    offences, 437
Constitution Act, 1867, 28
Contiguous zone. *See* Jurisdiction, inter-
        national and transnational crime
Continental shelf. *See* Jurisdiction, inter-
        national and transnational crime
*Convention concerning the Prohibition and
        Immediate Action for the Elimina-
        tion of the Worst Forms of Child
        Labour (ILO Convention)*, 390, 391
*Convention for the Prevention and Punish-
        ment of the Crime of Genocide. See
        Genocide Convention*
*Convention for the Suppression of Unlaw-
        ful Acts against the Safety of Mari-
        time Navigation (SUA Convention)*,
        284, 287, 346, 347, 348, 349, 429
*Convention for the Suppression of Unlaw-
        ful Seizure of Aircraft (Hague
        Convention)*, 344
*Convention on Combating Bribery of
        Foreign Officials in International
        Business Transactions*, 32
*Convention on Laundering, Search, Seiz-
        ure and Confiscation of the Proceeds
        of Crime*, 380
Convention on the High Seas, 282
*Convention on the Non-Applicability
        of Statutory Limitations to War
        Crimes and Crimes against Human-
        ity*, 119
*Convention on the Prevention and Punish-
        ment of Crimes against Internation-
        ally Protected Persons, Including
        Diplomatic Agents*, 352, 354

Convention on the Rights of the Child on the Sale of Children, Child Prostitution and Child Pornography, Optional Protocol to the, 67, 389

Convention on the Status of Refugees (Refugee Convention), 265

Core crimes, direct enforcement against, 159–213. *See also* Aggression; Crimes against humanity; Genocide; War crimes

Crimes against humanity, 117–30
  Charter of the International Military Tribunal (IMT Charter), 120
  formulation, 118
  Civilian Population Protocol to the Geneva Conventions (AP I), 121
  definition and jurisdiction, 119–20
  Genocide Convention, 120
  history, 117–19
  contextual elements, 121
  Convention on the Non-Applicability of Statutory Limitations to War Crimes and Crimes against Humanity, 119
  definition, 117
  deportation, 126
  enslavement, 125
  extermination, 125
  ICTR Statute, 119–20
  ICTY Statute, 120
  imprisonment, 126
  jurisdiction, 117
  mental element, 123–24
  murder, *assassinat*, 124
  Nazi depredations, 118
  nullem crimen sine lege, 118
  Nuremberg trials, 119
  other inhumane acts, 129
  persecution, 128–29
    anti-Semitic, 129
    definition, ethnic cleansing, 128
    International Military Tribunal (IMT) Charter, 128
    Nazi regime, 128
    Rome Statute, 128
  rape
    definition, 127
    ICC Elements, 127
    Iraqi High Tribunal, 128
    Rome Statute, 127

  Special Court for Sierra Leone (SCSL), 128
  United Nations Transitional Administration in East Timor (UNTAET) Serious Crimes Panels, 128
  Rome Statute, 120, 129–30
  torture, 126–27
  United Nations *Convention against Torture (CAT)*, 126
  widespread or systematic attack, 122–23

Crimes Against Humanity and War Crimes Act (CAH Act), 9, 23, 32, 36, 78, 101, 214, 215, 234, 241, 242, 245, 247, 250, 251, 252, 253, 260, 261, 267, 428, 590, 591, 592, 593, 595, 596

Criminal Code, 28, 33, 36, 37, 38, 61, 67, 69, 78, 85, 86, 87, 88, 225, 227, 228, 229, 234, 235, 242, 245, 247, 257, 259, 278, 286, 292, 322, 328, 330, 335, 341, 342, 345, 349, 351, 356, 358, 363, 366, 367, 378, 385, 391, 404, 410, 415, 422, 424, 427, 430, 431, 432, 433, 437, 463, 486, 487, 487, 489, 524, 525, 590, 593

Crimes, Core. *See* Aggression; Crimes against humanity; Genocide; War crimes

Crimes, Domestic. *See* Domestic crimes "purely" with transnational element

Crimes, International. *See* Apartheid; Piracy; Slavery; Terrorism

Crimes, Suppression of. *See* Suppression of crime, international cooperation in the

Croatia, 168, 551

CSIS. *See* Canadian Security Intelligence Service

Cybercrime, transnational 392–405
  2002 Guidelines for the Security of Information Systems and Networks: Towards a Culture of Security, 397
  Additional Protocol to the Convention on Cybercrime, 402
  aut dedere obligation, 399
  Canada Evidence Act, 403
  Canadian implementation, 403–5

categories
  computer as storage device, 393
  computer as tool, 393
classifications of substantive criminal
    offences, 397
computer as target, 393
computer data and systems, 397
  offences
    computer-related, 398
    content-related, 398
    infringements of copyright and
      related rights, 398
Convention on Cybercrime, 396, 397,
    400, 402, 404
Criminal Code, 404
Council of Europe (CoE), 400
European Convention on Extradition,
    401
*European Convention on Human
    Rights,* 401
international law, 392–403
Internet luring, 403
jurisdiction, 394–95, 398
offences against the confidentiality,
    integrity and availability of
police forces, 403
RCMP, 403
term, 393
transborder investigation, 401
Yokohama Global Commitment, 389
*Cybercrime Convention. See European
    Convention on Cybercrime*

Darfur. *See* Sudan, the
Democratic Republic of the Congo
    (DRC), 74, 75, 152, 181, 183, 192,
    198, 199, 221, 572, 573
Deportation. *See* Extradition, deporta-
    tion and mutual legal assistance
Distinguishing international and trans-
    national criminal law, 12–21
  international crimes, 17–19
    definition, 17
      subcategories, 18
        individual responsibility, 18
        no direct liability of indi-
          viduals, 18
  Pentagon, 11 September 2001, 1
  transnational crimes of domestic
    concern, 20–21

transnational crimes of international
    concern, 19–20
  aut dedere aut judicare mechan-
    ism, 19
  extraterritorial jurisdiction, 20
  qualified territorial jurisdiction, 21
  suppression conventions, 19
World Trade Center, 11 September
    2001, 1
Domestic crimes "purely" with trans-
    national element, 407–9
  extraterritorial jurisdiction, 409
  prescriptive jurisdiction, 409
  qualified territoriality, 408
Double jeopardy. *See Ne bis in idem*
DRC. *See* Democratic Republic of the
    Congo
Drug trafficking, transnational, 370–79
  1961 *Single Convention on Narcotic
    Drugs*, 372
  1971 *UN Convention on Psychotropic
    Substances*, 372
  1972 *Protocol Amending the Single
    Convention on Narcotic Drugs*, 372
    aut dedere aut judicare mechan-
      ism, 375
  Canada's drug strategy, 377
    Canadian implementing legisla-
      tion, 377–79
  *Controlled Drugs and Substances Act
    (CDSA)*, 377
  illicit drugs, 371
  Inter-American Drug Abuse Control
    Commission (CICAD), 377
  International law, 370–77
  jurisdiction, 375
  League of Nations, regulating narcot-
    ics, 371
  licit drugs, illicit trade in, 370
  organized crime, 371
  Psychotropic Substances Convention,
    377
  Psychotropic substances, 373
  trafficking illegal substances, 370
  United Nations Commission on Nar-
    cotic Drugs, 371
  *United Nations Convention against
    Illicit Traffic in Narcotic Drugs
    and Vienna Narcotics Convention*,
    373–74

United Nations Economic and Social Council (ECOSOC), 371
United Nations Office on Drug Crime (UNODC), 372

East Timor, 10, 209
ECHR. See European Convention for the protection of Human Rights and Fundamental Freedoms
EEZ. See Exclusive economic zone
EGO. See Evidence-gathering order
Elements of crimes. See International Criminal Court, Elements of Crimes
Enforcement, international and transnational criminal law 21–23
    direct, 21–23
    distinction between direct and indirect, 22
    indirect, 21–23
    Rome Statute, 22
Enforcement, jurisdiction
    Canada, ships
        high seas, 95
    criminal law, 93
    extradition, 94
    foreign state, 94
    police forces, 95
    state cooperation, 94
    treaty-based prescriptive and aut dedere aut judicare, 96, 97, 98
        "conditional" universal jurisdiction, 96
            differences between universal jurisdiction, 98
        Terrorist Bombing Convention, 97
        treaty-based prescriptive and enforcement jurisdiction, 96
Ethnic cleansing, 110, 128, 165, 210, 243. See also Genocide
European Convention for the Protection of Human Rights and Fundamental Freedoms (ECHR), 45, 401, 474
European Convention on Cybercrime (Cybercrime Convention), 396, 397, 400, 401, 402, 404, 405
European Convention on Extradition, 401, 457
European Convention on Mutual Assistance in Criminal Matters, 482

European Cybercrime Convention. See European Convention on Cybercrime (Cybercrime Convention)
European Union, 24, 221, 304, 383, 448, 481, 482
Evidence, admissibility of, gathered in foreign states. See Admissibility of evidence gathered in foreign states
Evidence-Gathering Orders (EGOs). See Mutual legal assistance, evidence-gathering orders
Exclusive economic zone (EEZ). See Jurisdiction, international and transnational crime
Extradition, 447–72
    aut dedere aut judicare provisions, 449
    Canada, bilateral and multilateral extradition treaties, 460
    Canada-US Extradition Treaty, 462
    Canadian law, 460–72
    Canadian Charter of Rights and Freedoms, 469, 470
    crime suppression, goal of extradition, 449
    Criminal Code, 463
    discrimination, 457
        1957 European Convention on Extradition, 457
    double criminality and extraditable offences, 450–52
    double jeopardy, 459–60
    "eliminative" or "no list" approach, 462
    evidentiary requirements, 453
    extraditable offences, double criminality and, 450
    Extradition Act, 460, 462–71
        authority to proceed, 462–63
        judicial phase, 463–66
        ministerial phase, 467–71
    "extradition agreement," defined, 462
    extradition judge, 463, 466, 467
    International Assistance Group, Justice Canada, 462
    International Criminal Court (ICC), 461
    International Criminal Tribunal for Rwanda (ICTR), 461

International Criminal Tribunal for the former Yugoslavia (ICTY), 461
international law, 447
  history, 447–49
  "irregular rendition," 447
Jay Treaty of 1794, 460
military/fiscal offences, 458–59
Model Treaty on Extradition, United Nations (UN Model Treaty), 448
ne bis in idem, 459–60
offences, military/fiscal 458–59
  UN Model Treaty, 459
principles of extradition law, 449–60
  discrimination, 457
  double criminality and extraditable offences, 450–52
  double jeopardy/*ne bis in idem*, 459–60
  evidentiary requirements, 453–54
  military/fiscal offences, 458
  political offence exception, 454–57
  reciprocity, 452
  "rule of non-inquiry," 457–58
  specialty and re-extradition, 453
reciprocity, 452
"record of the case," 465, 466
request to foreign state or entity for surrender of fugitive, 471
right of specialty, 471
"rule of non-inquiry," 457–58
"Shepherd test," 463
specialty and re-extradition, 453
suppression conventions
  Vienna Narcotics Convention, 448
surrender
  decision based on relevant factors, 470–71
  Minister
    may refuse to order, 468–69
    must refuse to order, 468
    requesting state, to, 467
treaties between states, 448
  Commonwealth, 448
  Organization of American States (OAS), 448
  Organization of African Unity (OAU), 448
United Nations Convention against Transnational Organized Crime (TOC Convention), 448

Webster-Ashburton Treaty of 1842, 460
Extradition, abduction and extraordinary rendition, alternatives to, 472–81
  1984 United Nations *Convention against Torture (CAT)*, 480
  "universally condemned offences," 478
  abduction, 473–79
  alternatives, reasons, 472,
  Arar, Maher
    illegal rendition, 480
  Canadian Charter of Rights and Freedoms, 479
  caselaw approach
    "abuse of process," 475, 476
    mala captus bene detentus, 475
  European Convention for the Protection of Human, Rights and Fundamental Freedoms (ECHR), 474
    art. 5(1), violation, 474
  extraordinary rendition, 479–81
  global war on terror, 481
  Harvard Research Draft, 473
  Rome Statute, 478
  Temporary Committee on the Alleged Use of European Countries by the CIA for the Transport and Illegal Detention of Prisoners, 481
  UN Human Rights Committee, violation, *International Covenant on Civil and Political Rights (ICCPR)*, 474
Extradition Act (1877), 460
Extradition Act, 32, 229, 324, 460, 462, 471
Extradition, deportation and mutual legal assistance
  Canada
    abolition of death penalty as principle of fundamental justice, 503
    extradition and deportation practices, 504
    extradition or deportation, individuals facing death penalty or torture, 505
  Canada-US extradition treaty, 502
  Canadian Charter of Rights and Freedoms

apply to extradition process, 501
  assessing Ministerial orders for
    surrender, 502
death penalty upon extradition, 502
deportation, 498–509
extradition, 498–509
*International Covenant on Civil and
  Political Rights (ICCPR)*, 504
International criminal cooperation,
  human rights, and the application
  of the *Charter*, extradition, deportation and mutual legal assistance,
  498–509
mutual legal assistance (MLA),
  498–509, 507
*Mutual Legal Assistance in Criminal
  Matters Act (MLA Act)*, 508
potential conflict between extradition
  and human rights protection, 501
"shocks the conscience" test, 502,
  505
Supreme Court of Canada
  balancing exercise, 501
  caselaw and authoritative opin-
    ions, 507
  constitutional methodology, 506
  international law methodology,
    507
Extraterritorial criminal jurisdiction,
  over prescriptively transnational
  crimes, 425–37
1963 *Tokyo Convention on Offences
  and Certain Other Acts Occurring
  on Board Aircraft*, 436
  "flight" definition, 436
*Agreement Concerning Cooperation on
  the Civil International Space Station*, 430
aircraft, 434, 436
Antarctica, 430
avoiding lawlessness
  high seas, 429
  territorial gaps, 429–30
Canada and extraterritorial jurisdiction, 425–28
Citizenship Act, 432
Code of Service Discipline, 431
controlling behaviour of representatives of Canada, 430–32

*Convention for the Suppression of
  Unlawful Acts against the Safety of
  Maritime Navigation*, 429
*Crimes Against Humanity and War
  Crimes Act (CAH Act)*, 428
Criminal Code, 427, 429, 431, 433
  fixed platforms, 429
  ships, 429
  treason, high, committed outside
    of Canada, 432
exclusive economic zones (EEZ)
  continental shelves, 436
extensions of jurisdiction, nationality
  principle, 431
extraterritorial provisions, 432
fixed platforms, 434, 436
Foreign Enlistment Act, 433
*Immigration and Refugee Protection Act
  (IRPA)*, 432
implementing international treaties,
  428–30
International Space Station (ISS), 430
international treaties, 428
Interpretation Act, 426
lawless spaces, 430
Libman test, 433, 434
National Defence Act, 431
"non-extraterritorial" offences,
  433–34
Oceans Act, 430
offences, "non-extraterritorial,"
  433–34
outer space, 429
  objects in, 430
  Outer Space Treaty, 429
Permanent Court of International
  Justice, 425
persons abroad, 430
persons representing Canada, governmental capacity, 430
platforms, fixed, 434, 436
policy goals, 427
"prohibitive rule," 425
protection of Canadian interests,
  432–33
*Protocol for the Suppression of Unlaw-
  ful Acts against the Safety of Fixed
  Platforms Located on the Continental Shelf*, 429
Public Service Employment Act, 431

Security Offences Act, 432
  range of offences, 433
ships, aircraft and fixed platforms,
  434–37
  flag state, 434
  "floating islands," 435
  nationality, state in which regis-
    tered, 435
space travel, 430
Statute of Westminster ,425
suppression conventions, Canada, 428
Torture Convention, 428
*United Nations Convention on the Law
  of the Sea (UNCLOS)* 435
  high seas collisions, navigational
    incidents, 436
Extraordinary rendition. *See* Extradition, abduction, and extraordinary rendition, alternatives to

Firearms, illicit manufacturing of and
  trading in. *See* Organized crime,
  transnational
First Geneva Convention (GC I), 4, 138,
  568
*First Protocol to the Geneva Conventions
  (AP I)*, 121
Flag states. *See* Jurisdiction, internation-
  al and transnational crime
Floating islands. *See* Jurisdiction, inter-
  national and transnational crime
Fourth Geneva Convention, 126

GC I. See First Geneva Convention
GC II. See Second Geneva Convention
GC III. See Third Geneva Convention
GC IV. See Fourth Geneva Convention
Geneva Convention of 1929, 224
Geneva Conventions (1949), 4, 7, 73, 77,
  96, 100, 131, 132, 135, 138, 139,
  140, 141, 143, 144, 147, 149, 151,
  170, 175, 178, 208, 215, 216, 225,
  251, 261, 262, 305, 306, 349, 528,
  568, 569, 572, 574, 579, 592
Geneva Conventions Act, 78, 225, 226,
  229, 252, 590, 592, 595, 596
Genocide, 105–17
  acts constituting, 112–14
    causing serious bodily harm or
      mental harm, 113

children, forcibly transferring, 114
  deliberately inflicting condi-
    tions of life calculated to
    destroy the group, 113–14
  imposing measures intended to
    prevent, 114
  killing, 113
complicity, 116
definition, 108
dolus specialis, 109
erga omnes obligation, 106
ethnic cleansing, 110
ethnic group, definition, 111
Genocide Convention, 106, 108, 110,
  111, 112, 115, 116
history, 105–7
*ICC Elements (International Criminal
  Court Elements of Crimes)*, 117
inchoate and incomplete offences,
  115
*International Convention on the
  Prevention and Punishment of
  the Crime of Genocide*, 106
jurisdiction, 108–9
jus cogens principle, 106
mental element, 109
national group, definition, 111
offences, inchoate and incomplete,
  115
protected group, defining the 111
racial group, definition, 111
religious group, definition, 112
Rome Statute, 107, 108, 116–17
special intent, 109
  travaux preparatoires, 115
Genocide Convention, 7, 25, 31, 42,
  73,106, 108, 109, 110, 111, 112,
  115, 116 120, 173, 177, 215, 217,
  225, 243, 244, 245, 262, 293, 294,
  551, 577, 578, 579

Hague Convention IV of 1907, 146, 147
Hague Conventions, 4, 5, 6, 138, 147, 148,
  344, 345, 346
Hijacking Convention, 307
Holocaust, 217, 578
Hostages, 143, 144, 145, 349, 350
*Hostages Convention. See International
  Convention against the Taking of
  Hostages*

Human rights
  application of *Charter*
    international criminal cooper-
      ation, 497–538
  impact of, 25–27
    Canadian Security Intelligence
      Service (CSIS,) 26
    Genocide Convention, 25
    offenders, 25
    universally condemned offences,
      26
Hussein, Saddam, 3, 212
Hutu, 112, 171, 176

ICC. *See* International Criminal Court
ICC Elements. See *International Criminal
  Court Elements of Crimes*
ICRC. *See* International Committee of
  the Red Cross
ICTR. *See International Criminal Tribunal
  for Rwanda*
ICTR Statute. *See Statute of the Inter-
  national Criminal Tribunal for
  Rwanda*
ICTY. *See International Crinimal Tribunal
  for the former Yugoslavia*
ICTY Statute. *See Statute of the Inter-
  national Criminal Tribunal for the
  former Yugoslavia*
ILO Convention. *See Convention concern-
  ing the Prohibition and Immediate
  Action for the Elimination of the
  Worst Forms of Child Labour*
*Immigration and Refugee Protection Act
  (IRPA)*, 86, 264, 329, 330, 332,
  432, 496
Immunities
  Canadian implementation, 589–98
    crimes against humanity, 592–93
      defined, 592, 593
    diplomatic immunity as a special
      case, 596–98
      *Foreign Missions and Inter-
        national Organizations Act*,
        597 "reasonable period,"
        598
      *Vienna Convention on Consular
        Relations*, 596, 597
      *Vienna Convention on Diplo-
        matic Relations*, 596, 597

  *Foreign Missions and International
    Organizations Act*, 597
    grave crime defined, 598
    s. 3, 598
    *Vienna Convention on Con-
      sular Relations, Schedule
      to Foreign Missions and
      International Organizations
      Act*, 598
    *Vienna Convention on Diplo-
      matic Relations, Schedule
      to Foreign Missions and
      International Organizations
      Act*, 598
  genocide, 593
  *Vienna Convention on Consular
    Relations*, 598
  *Vienna Convention on Diplomatic
    Relations*, 598
  war crimes, 590–92
    Convention against Torture, 589
    *Crimes Against Humanity and
      War Crimes Act (CAH Act)*,
      590
    Geneva Conventions, 592
    Geneva Conventions Act, 592
    Rome Statute, 591, 592
  criminal prosecution, from, 539–99
    diplomatic immunity, 540
    immunity from prosecution
      functional (immunity *ratione
        materiae*), 540
      personal (immunity *ratione
        personae*/absolute immun-
        ity), 540
  domestic courts, before, 567–89
    crimes against humanity, 579–80
      Geneva Conventions, 579
      Genocide Convention, 579
      Rome Statute, 579
    Criminal Justice Act 1988, 585
    Geneva Conventions, 568–69
    International Criminal Police Or-
      ganization (INTERPOL), 573
    Nuremberg Principles, 571
    obligation to criminal grave
      breaches, 568–69
    Rome Statute, 567
    torture, 580–89

Convention against Torture, 580,
    582, 583, 584, 586, 587,
    588, 589
UN Secretary-General, 550
*Vienna Convention on the Law of
    Treaties*, 574
war crimes, 568–77
    Democratic Republic of the
        Congo (DRC), 572
    Geneva Conventions, 568–69
international law, 541–46
    Ad hoc Committee on Jurisdic-
        tional Immunities of State and
        Their Property, 542
    immunity *ratione materiae*,
        544–46
        individual, state official acting
            in official capacity, 545
        limited number of acts, 545
    immunity *ratione personae*, 543–44
        attaches to certain high gov-
            ernment offices, 543
        heads of government, no dis-
            tinction between personal
            or official acts, 544
        heads of state and diplomats,
            544
        personal immunity, 543–44
    International Law Commission
        (ILC), 542
    *United Nations Convention on the
        Jurisdictional Immunities of
        States and Their Property*, 542
international tribunals, before,
    546–67
    ad hoc criminal tribunals, 549–55
        Bosnia and Herzegovina, 551
        Croatia, 551
        general, 549–55
        Kambanda (ICTR), 554
        Karadžić (ICTY), 552
        Kosovo, 551
        Milosević (ICTY), 551–52
    *Charter of the International Mil-
        itary Tribunal (IMT Charter)*,
        547
    Commission on the Responsibility
        of the Authors of the War and
        on Enforcement of Penalties,
        546

crimes committed in
    Balkan war, 549
    Rwanda, 549
    Yugoslavia, former, 549
immunities from criminal pros-
    ecution
    immunity before domestic
        courts, 567
    war crimes, 568
International Criminal Court as
    special case, 558–66
International Military Tribunal
    (MTFE), Far East,
    accused of crimes in, 547
Internationalized tribunals
    Special Court for Sierra Leone
        (SCSL), 555–58
Kambanda (ICTR) 554–55
Peace Conference of 1919, 546
Report of the Commission, estab-
    lishing international tribunal,
    prosecute officials, 547
Rome Statute, 565, 566
    cooperation with respect to
        waiver of immunity and
        consent to irrelevance of
        official capacity, 559–60
    surrender, 560–62
Rwanda, 554
    guilty plea, 554
Sierra Leone, internationalized
    tribunals, Special Court for
    (SCSL), 555–58
*Statute of the Special Court for
    Sierra Leone*, 555
    Appeals Chamber, 556
    Nuremberg Principles, 556
    UN Secretary-General, 556
Treaty of Versailles, 546
IMT Charter. See Charter of the Inter-
    national Military Tribunal
*Inter-American Convention against Cor-
    ruption (OAS Convention against
    Corruption)*, 337, 338, 342
*Inter-American Convention against the
    Illicit Trafficking and Production of
    Firearms, Ammunition, Explosives
    and Other Related Materials*, 333
Inter-American Drug Abuse Control
    Commission (CICAD), 372, 377

Inter-American Torture Convention, 274
International and transnational criminal
    law, sources of, 27–46
Canada, customary international law,
    33–37
    creation and ascertainment
        crystallization, 34
        customary obligations, 34
        declare or codify, 34
        jus cogens, 34
        opinio juris, 34
        persistent objectors, 34
        reception, 35
Canadian Charter of Rights and Free-
    doms, s. 11(g)
    "general principles," 41
    International Covenant on Civil and
        Political Rights (ICCPR), 41
    "international law," 41
    nullum crimen sine lege, 41
    principle of legality, 41
    doctrine of "incorporation" or
        "adoption," 35
    United Nations Convention on the
        Law of the Sea (UNCLOS), 35
domestic sources
    Canada, 28
        Canadian Charter of Rights and
            Freedoms, 28, 29
        Constitution Act 1867, s. 91, 28
        Criminal Code, 28
        judge-made common law, 28
        legislative statutes 28
        international law, 27–29
        transnational international law, 27
international law sources
    Canada, 29–42
        reception in, 29
        Statute of the International Court
            of Justice, art. 38(1), 29
        treaty law, 30–33
other sources
    Canadian Charter of Rights and
        Freedoms, s. 11(g), 38, 41
    comity, international, 40
    Draft Code of Crimes against the
        Peace and Security of Mankind,
        39–40
    lex ferenda, 39
    Model Treaty on Extradition, 40

nullum crimen sine lege, 38
soft law, 39–40
Statute of the International Court of
    Justice, 37
    judicial decisions, 38
    teachings of the most highly
        qualified publicists of the
        various nations, 39
subjects of
    European Convention on Human
        Rights, 44
    European Court of Human
        Rights, 44
    Genocide Convention, Canada
        ratified, 42
    individual liability, versus state
        responsibility, 42
    individuals
        "objects" of the law, 43
        "subjects" of the law, 43
    international criminal law
        state responsibility versus
            individual liability, 42
        subjects of, 42
liability, individual versus state re-
    sponsibility, 42
Nuremberg Tribunal, 44
responsibility, state, 42
state responsibility
    doctrine of, 43
    versus individual liability, 42
treaty law
    Canada, 30–32
        creation and legal effect, 30–32
            accession, 31
            jus cogens norm, 31
            pacta sunt servand, 30
            party, 31
            ratification, 31
            reception, 32
            reservations, 31
            signatory, 31
            suspension, 31
            termination, 31
            Vienna Convention on the
                Law of Treaties 1969, 30
            War Crimes Act, 32
    Convention on Combating Bribery of
        Foreign Officials in International
        Business Transactions, 32

Extradition Act, 32
Genocide Convention, Canada
    party to, 31
*Mutual Legal Assistance in Crim-
    inal Matters Act*, 32
International Committee of the Red
    Cross (ICRC), 131, 177, 215
*International Convention against the Tak-
    ing of Hostages (Hostages Conven-
    tion)*, 350
*International Convention for the Suppres-
    sion of Acts of Nuclear Terrorism*,
    296, 364, 366
*International Convention on the Preven-
    tion and Punishment of the Crime of
    Genocide. See Genocide Convention*
International courts, jurisdiction
    *Crimes Against Humanity and War
        Crimes Act (CAH Act)*, 100
    Geneva Conventions, 96
        jus cogens status, 96
        suppression conventions, 96
    International Criminal Tribunal for
        Rwanda (ICTR), 100
    jurisdiction of international courts,
        99
    Rome Statute, 100, 101
    Sierra Leone Court, 99
    *Statute of the International Criminal
        Tribunal for the former Yugoslavia
        (ICTY Statute)*, 99
    suppression conventions, 96
        goals, 97
    treaty-based prescriptive and en-
        forcement jurisdiction
    United Nations Interim Administra-
        tion Mission in Kosovo (UNMIK),
        99
International Criminal Court (ICC),
    176–202
    age of prosecution, 190
    *Agreement on Privileges and Immun-
        ities of the Court*, 180
    Apartheid Convention, 178
    Assembly of States Parties (ASP), 180
    Bush administration, 183, 184
    Central African Republic, 183
    China, 195
    Clinton administration, 183
    Cold War, 177

Darfur, the Sudan, 182, 194, 198
Democratic Republic of the Congo,
    183, 189
*Draft Code of Crimes against the Peace
    and Security of Mankind*, 177
drug trafficking and terrorism, 188
Elements of Crimes, 114, 117, 125,
    127–28, 151, 180, 182, 238, 262,
    290–91
"fallback" court, 197
Geneva Conventions, 178
Genocide Convention, 177
Hague Invasion Act, 184
"horizontal" model, 197
International Committee of the Red
    Cross (ICRC), 177
"lateral" relationship, ICC and states,
    197
legal persons, 189
like-minded caucus, 179
Lord's Resistance Army (LRA), 181,
    193
narcotics
    producers and traffickers, 177
    traffickers, Caribbean, 187
natural persons, 189
Non-Aligned Movement (NAM), 179
Nuremberg Principles, 177
Obama administration, 184
"on the territory," 188, 189
Preparatory Committee (PrepCom),
    178–79
proprio motu powers, 181
Report of the International Commis-
    sion of Inquiry, 194
Rome Conference, 183
Rome Statute, 176, 179, 180, 181, 183,
    184, 185, 186, 188, 190, 191, 192,
    193, 194, 195, 196, 197, 199, 200
Rules of Procedure and Evidence (RPE),
    180, 186
Security Council, United Nations, 193
special *rapporteur*, 178
Trinidad and Tobago, 177
Truth and Reconciliation Commis-
    sion, South Africa, 199
Uganda, 191, 193, 199
UN Charter, 176, 193
unwilling to investigate or prosecute,
    198

Uganda, DRC (Democratic Republic of the Congo) and Central African Republic, 192
US, 195
"vertical" model, 197
Vienna Narcotics Convention, 178
International Criminal Court Elements of Crimes (ICC Elements), 114, 117, 125, 127–28, 151, 180, 182, 238, 262, 290–91
International Criminal Police Organization (INTERPOL), 11, 24, 573
International Criminal Tribunal for Rwanda (ICTR), 3, 8, 18, 21, 39, 45, 100, 105, 107, 108, 109, 111, 146, 168, 171, 172, 173, 174, 175, 176, 197, 203, 205, 241, 242, 245, 251, 461, 462, 485, 550, 554, 555, 566
International Criminal Tribunal for the former Yugoslavia (ICTY), 3, 8, 18, 21, 26, 39, 45, 104, 105, 107, 108, 109, 110, 112, 119, 121, 122, 124 125, 127, 128, 129, 133, 135, 136, 145, 148, 150, 151, 165, 166, 169, 170, 171, 172, 174, 175, 176, 187, 197, 203, 205, 211, 241, 242, 274, 461, 462, 477, 478, 485, 550, 551, 552, 553, 555, 563, 566
International crimes. *See* Apartheid; Piracy; Slavery; Terrorism
International Military Tribunal Charter. See Charter of the International Military Tribunal
International Space Station (ISS). *See* Jurisdiction, international and transnational crime
International Transfer of Offenders Act, 324
Internationalized courts, direct enforcement against core crimes
age of prosecution, juvenile offenders, 206
All People's Congress (APC), 203
Ba'athist regime, 212
Bosnia and Herzegovina War Crimes Chamber and Serbian War Crimes Chamber, 211
Cambodia Extraordinary Chambers, 207–8

chambers, 205, 211
core international crimes, 212
East Timor 209–10
Extraordinary Chambers in the Courts of Cambodia (ECCC), 207
Geneva Conventions, 208
Indonesia, 209
International Criminal Court (ICC), 202–12
"special" courts, 202
International Independent Investigation Commission, 209
Iraqi High Tribunal, Internationalized Courts (IHT), 211–12
Iraqi Transnational Assembly, 211
jurisdiction, temporal, 208
Khmer Rouge, 207, 208
"killing fields," 208
Kosovo, 210
Kurds, 212
Lebanon, Special Tribunal for (STL), 208–9
Lomé Peace Agreement, 203
Revolutionary United Front (RUF), 203
Serbia War Crimes Chamber, 211
Serbian ethnic cleansing, 210
serious crime panel, 209
Shiite rebellion, 212
Sierra Leone, Special Court for, 203–6
creation, 203
history, 203
jurisdiction, 206–7
structure, 205
Statute of the Special Tribunal, 208
United Nations Interim Administration Mission in Kosovo (UNMIK), 210
United Nations Transnational Administration in East Timor (UNTAET), 209
UNMIK Regulations, 210
War Crimes Chamber, Republic of Serbia, 211
War Crimes Chamber of the State Court in Sarajevo, 211
Yugoslavia, Former: Bosnia and Herzegovina War Crimes Chamber and Serbia War Crimes Chamber, Internationalized Courts, 211

Internet. *See* Jurisdiction, international
  and transnational crime
Iraq, 3, 10, 200, 211, 212
  Iraqi High Tribunal (IHT), 211–12
*IRPA. See Immigration and Refugee Protec-
  tion Act*

Jurisdiction, international and transnational crime
  defined, 50
  domestic, 51
  enforcement, 54
  extraterritorial, 52
  historical perspective, 49
  international crime, 48
  judicial 54
  national level, 49
  prescriptive, 53, 54
    airspace, above state's territory, 61
    "allocating competences," 56
    Canada
      aircraft 61
      Arctic region, 61
      ice, 61
    *Chicago Convention on Internation-
      al Civil Aviation*, 61
    jurisdiction, concurrent, 59
    nationality principle, 66
      accused person, 66
      *Agreement Concerning Co-
        operation on the Civil Inter-
        national Space Station*, 91
      Antarctic Treaty, 77
      baselines, 84
      Canadian-flagged vessel, 89
      *Coastal Fisheries Protection
        Act*, 87
      coastal states, 83
      Code of Service Discipline, 68
      common law states, nationality
        principle, 67
      constructive presence, 90
      *Controlled Drugs and Substances
        Act (CDSA)*, 86
      Crew Code of Conduct, 92
      *Crimes Against Humanity and
        War Crimes Act (CAH Act)*,
        78
      Criminal Code, 68, 67, 74, 78,
        85, 86, 87, 88

Customs Act, 86
European Space Agency, 91
extend prescriptive jurisdiction, 71
flag states, 83, 89
foreign citizens,
  employed by armed forces, 67
  employed by government, 67
Geneva Conventions, 73, 77
Geneva Conventions Act, 78
Genocide Convention, 73
hot pursuit, 89
*Immigration and Refugee Protec-
  tion Act (IRPA)*, 86
Income Tax Act, 86
innocent passage, 84
internal waters, 84
International Space Station
  (ISS), 91
Internet, jurisdiction over, 92
jurisdiction
  at sea, 82
  contiguous zone, 86
  continental shelf, 88
  exclusive economic zone
    (EEZ), 87
  high seas, 88
  hot pursuit, 89
  internal waters and the ter-
    ritorial sea, 84
  Internet, 92
  space, 91
jus cogens status, 77
maritime zone, 89–90
mother ship, 90
National Defence Act, 68
Northwest Atlantic Fisheries
  Organization (NAFO)
  Regulatory Area, 87
nullum crimen sine lege principle, 67
Nuremberg Tribunal, 72
Oceans Act, Canada, 83, 84, 85,
  86, 87, 88
*Optional Protocol to the Con-
  vention on the Rights of the
  Child on the Sale of Children,
  Child Prostitution and Child
  Pornography*, 67
Outer Space Treaty of 1967, 91

passive personality,
    hijacking offences, US, 68
    safe havens for offenders, 69
    victim, 68
permanent residents, 67
Public Service Employment Act,
    68
realpolitik, 79
Registration Convention, 91
res communis, 77, 83
resident aliens, 67
Rome Statute, 78
*Royal Canadian Mounted Police
    Act*, 68
Security Offences Act, 70
space, jurisdiction, 91
substantial and *bona fide* con-
    nection, 78, 81
territorial sea, 84
territory
    defined states with coast-
        lines, 84
    defined without coastlines,
        84
UN *Fish Stocks Agreement*, 87
*United Nations Convention on
    the Law of the Sea (UN-
    CLOS)*, 72, 83
universal jurisdiction
    absolute universal jurisdic-
        tion, 74
    Canada, 78
    common crimes, 77
    custodial universal jurisdic-
        tion, 74
    prosecution under, 75
vessels
    jurisdiction over, 83
    non-commercial govern-
        ment, 88
    suspected of piracy, 89
    warships, 88
Permanent Court of International
    Justice (PCIJ), 56
principles of extraterritorial juris-
    diction, 66
prohibitive rules, proving exist-
    ence of, 57
qualified territoriality, 62

objective territoriality prin-
    ciple, 63
    effects doctrine, 64
subjective territoriality prin-
    ciple, 62
state sovereignty, 60
territorial jurisdiction, bedrock
    rule, 60
territorial principle, 59
*Tokyo Convention on Offences and
    Certain Other Act Committed on
    Board Aircraft*, 61
treaties, 58
transnational crime, 48

Kellogg-Briand Pact of 1928, 6, 153
Kosovo, 10, 99, 210, 551

League of Nations, 161, 282, 289, 296,
    299, 371
Lebanon, 10, 208
    Special Tribunal for Lebanon
        (STL), 208–209
Lord's Resistance Army (LRA), 181, 182,
    193
LRA. *See* Lord's Resistance Army

Maritime zone. *See* Jurisdiction, inter-
    national and transnational crime
MLA. *See* Mutual legal assistance
*MLA Act. See Mutual Legal Assistance in
    Criminal Matters Act*
MLAT. *See* Mutual legal assistance
Migrants, smuggling of, 330–33
    1988 *Vienna Narcotics Convention*, 331
    Canadian implementing legislation,
        332
    definition, 331
    false documents offences, 332
    Human Trafficking Protocol, 332
    International Maritime Organization
        (IMO) Interim Measures, 331
    international law, 330–32
    Migrant Smuggling Protocol, 330
    *United Nations Convention on the Law
        of the Sea (UNCLOS)*, 331
Money laundering. *See* Proceeds of
    crime and money laundering,
    transnational
Montreal Convention, 345, 346, 347, 352

Mutual legal assistance, 482–96
  1959 *European Convention on Mutual Assistance in Criminal Matters*, 482
  2000 *United Nations Convention against Transnational Organized Crime (TOC)*, 483
  "agreement" defined, 485
  appeals, 494
  Canadian Charter of Rights and Freedoms (Charter), 489, 495
  Canadian law, 483
  challenging the EGO, 492
  challenging the warrant, the sending hearing, 487
  costs, 494
  Criminal Code, 489
  Evidence-Gathering Orders (EGOs), 487
    challenging the, 492–94
    issuing, 491–92
  hearing, grounds to challenge, 490
  International Assistance Group (IAG), Justice Canada, 485
  MLAT, goal of, 483
  Model Treaty on Mutual Legal Assistance in Criminal Matters, United Nations, 483
  Mutual Legal Assistance in Criminal Matters Act (MLA Act), 485, 486, 489, 495–96
  mutual legal assistance treaty (MLAT) regimes, 482
  OAS Convention on Mutual Assistance in Criminal Matters, 485
  search warrants, issuing of, 486
    Criminal Code, 486, 487
  Vienna Narcotics Convention, 482, 485
Mutual Legal Assistance in Criminal Matters Act, 32, 324, 342, 485, 486, 487, 489, 508, 514

Narcotics, 9, 11, 20, 22, 23, 70, 85, 90, 96, 177, 187, 188, 316, 359, 371, 374, 377, 379, 384, 439, 440, 441, 442, 512
Narcotics Convention, 1988. See *Vienna Narcotics Convention*
Nationality principle. *See* Jurisdiction, international and transnational crime

Nazi war criminals, 162, 215, 267. *See also* Nuremberg and Tokyo Tribunals, direct enforcement against core crimes
Ne bis in idem, 201, 257, 401, 459
Nuclear Terrorism Convention. See *International Convention for the Suppression of Acts of Nuclear Terrorism*
Nullum crimen sine lege principle, 38, 41, 67
Nuremberg and Tokyo Tribunals, direct enforcement against core crimes, 159–213
  Charter of the International Military Tribunal (IMT Charter), 161
  Germany, acts of aggression, 162
  International Military Tribunal for the Far East (IMTFE), 163
  Japanese occupation, 161
  Kellogg-Briand Pact, 163
  London Agreement, 161, 162
  Nazi regime, 161
  Nazi war criminals, 162
  Nuremberg Tribunal, 160
  Potsdam Declaration 163
  Tokyo Charter, 163
  Tokyo Tribunal, 160
  Treaty of Lausanne, 161
  Treaty of Versailles, 161
  United Nations *ad hoc* tribunals, 160
Nuremberg Principles, 7, 177, 215, 551, 556, 571
Nuremberg Tribunal, 44, 72, 199, 47, 153. *See also* Nuremberg and Tokyo Tribunals, direct enforcement against core crimes

OAS Convention against Corruption. See *Inter-American Convention against Corruption*
OAS Convention. See *Organization of American States Convention*
OAU (Organization of African Unity) Convention. See *OAU Convention on the Prevention and Combating of Terrorism*
OAU Convention on the Prevention and Combatting of Terrorism, 298

Oceans Act, 83, 84, 85, 86, 87, 88, 430, 436, 437
OECD Convention. *See Organisation for Economic Cooperation and Development Convention*
OIC Convention, 298
Organisation for Economic Cooperation and Development Convention (OECD Convention), 320, 337, 338, 340, 341
Organization of American States Convention (OAS Convention), 335
Organized crime, transnational, 314–42
  1996 *Inter-American Convention against Corruption (OAS Convention against Corruption)*, 337
  1997 *Inter-American Convention against the Illicit Trafficking and Production of Firearms, Ammunition, Explosives and Other Related Materials*, 333
  2000 Inter-Ministerial National Agenda on Organized Crime, 322
  Act to amend the Criminal Code (organized crime and law enforcement), 322
  "corruption" of public officials, 320
  laundering of proceeds of crime, 319–20
  Measures to Combat Organized Crime Initiative, 322
  "organized criminal group," 318
  participation in an organized criminal group, 319
  "serious" crime, definition, 318
  TOC Convention, bifurcated approach, 317
  witnesses, intimidation of and tampering with 320
  Convention on Combating Bribery of Foreign Public Officials in International Business Transactions (OECD Convention against Corruption), 337
  corruption, 336–42
  Canadian implementing legislation, 340–42
  Corruption of Foreign Public Officials Act (CFPOA), 340

Criminal Code, 335, 341
Export and Import Permits Act, 335
Firearms Act, 335
firearms, illicit manufacturing of and trading in, 333–36
  Canadian implementing legislation, 335–36
  international law, 333–35
Firearms Protocol, TOC Convention, 333
G8 Summit Meeting, Halifax 1995, 315
Income Tax Act, 340
international law, 317–21, 336–40
Mutual Legal Assistance in Criminal Matters Act, 342
Organization of American Sates Convention (OAS Convention), 335
organized crime offences, 317–24
  Canadian implementing legislation, 321–24
smuggling of migrants, 330–33
  1988 *Vienna Narcotics Convention*, 331
  Canadian implementing legislation, 332
  definition, 331
  false documents offences, 332
  Human Trafficking Protocol, 332
  international law, 330–32
  International Maritime Organization (IMO) Interim Measures, 331
  Migrant Smuggling Protocol, 330
  United Nations Convention on the Law of the Sea (UNCLOS), 331
trafficking in persons, 324–30
  Canadian Border Security Service (CBSA,) 328
  Canadian implementing legislation, 327–30
  Canadian International Development Agency (CIDA), 328
  Canadian Security Intelligence Service (CSIS), 328
  Human Trafficking Protocol, 326, 328, 329
  Immigration and Refugee Protection Act (IRPA), 329
  Interdepartmental Working Group on Trafficking in Persons (IWGTIP), 327

international law, 324–27
RCMP, 328
Status of Women Canada, 328
UN Office on Drugs and Crime
    (UNODOC,) 314
*United Nations Convention against
    Corruption (UNCAC)*, 315, 316,
    337
*United Nations Convention against
    Transnational Organized Crime
    (TOC Convention)*, 315
United Nations General Assembly
    (UNGA), 315
Wassenaar Arrangement, 334
Outer space. *See* Jurisdiction, inter-
    national and transnational crime

Peace of Westphalia of 1648, 3, 4
Persons, trafficking in, 324–30
    Canadian Border Security Service
        (CBSA,) 328
    Canadian implementing legislation,
        327–30
    Canadian International Development
        Agency (CIDA), 328
    Canadian Security Intelligence Ser-
        vice (CSIS), 328
    Human Trafficking Protocol, 326, 328,
        329
    *Immigration and Refugee Protection Act
        (IRPA)*, 329
    Interdepartmental Working Group on
        Trafficking in Persons (IWGTIP),
        327
    international law, 324–27
    Royal Canadian Mounted Police
        (RCMP), 328
    Status of Women Canada, 328
Piracy, 281–87
    animus furundi, 283
    Canadian law, 286–87
        *Convention on the Suppression of
            Unlawful Acts against the Safety
            of Maritime Navigation*, 287
        Criminal Code 286
        piratical acts, 287
    *Convention for the Suppression of
        Unlawful Acts against the Safety of
        Maritime Navigation*, 284
    definition, 281, 282

Harvard Research team, 282
High Seas Convention, 282
history, 281
jurisdiction over, 285–86
League of Nations, 282
Rome Statute, 283
Somali territorial waters, 285
South America, coast of, 284
South China Sea, coast of, 285
Strait of Malacca, coast of, 285
*United Nations Convention on the Law
    of the Sea (UNCLOS)*, 282
West Africa, coast of, 284
Preparatory Committee for an Internation-
    al Criminal Court (PrepCom), 9
Principles of extradition law, 449–60
    discrimination, 457
    double criminality and extraditable
        offences, 450–52
    double jeopardy/*ne bis in idem*, 459–60
    evidentiary requirements, 453–54
    military/fiscal offences, 458
    political offence exception, 454–57
    reciprocity, 452
    "rule of non-inquiry," 457–58
    specialty and re-extradition, 453
Proceeds of crime and money laun-
    dering, transnational, 379–88
    1988 *Vienna Narcotics Convention*,
        380, 384
    1999 *Terrorist Financing Convention*,
        381
    2003 UN Model Terrorist Financing
        Bill, 381
    Anti-Terrorism Act, 386
    Basel Committee on Banking Super-
        vision (Basel Committee), 383
    Canadian implementing legislation,
        384–88
    Caribbean Financial Action Task
        Force (CFATF), 384
    *Controlled Drugs and Substances Act
        (CDSA)*, 386
    *Convention on Laundering, Search,
        Seizure and Confiscation of the
        Proceeds of Crime*, 380
    Corruption Convention, 381
    *Corruption of Foreign Public Officials
        Act (CFPOA)*, 386
    Criminal Code, 384

"proceeds of crime" defined, 385
Cross-Border Currency and Monetary
    Instruments Reporting Regulations,
    388
Egmont Group, 384
Financial Action Task Force (FATF),
    381–82
    40 Recommendations, 382, 388
"financial devastation," 379
Financial Transaction and Report
    Analysis Centre (FINTRAC), 388
illicit narcotics trade 384
    organized crime groups, 384
international law, 379–84
Proceeds of Crime (Money Laundering)
    and Terrorist Financing Act, 387,
    388
"professional" launderers, 380
Seized Property Management Act, 386
Suspicious Transaction Reporting
    Regulations, 388
Terrorist Financing, Special Recom-
    mendations on, 383
United Nations Convention against
    Transnational Organized Crime,
    381
UNODC, Anti Money Laundering
    Unit, (AMLU) 381
Prosecution, national, core crimes, 214–68
    ad hoc tribunals, 214
    African Union, 221
    Argentina, 217, 218
    aut dedere mechanism, 216
    Canadian legislation, Crimes Against
        Humanity and War Crimes Act
        (CAH Act), 214
    Charter of the International Military
        Tribunal Charter (IMT Charter),
        217
    Cold War, 216, 219
    Crimes Against Humanity and War
        Crimes Act, 2000 (CAH Act), 233–63
        Act respecting genocide, crimes
            against humanity and war
            crimes and to implement the
            Rome Statute of the Internation-
            al Criminal Court, and to make
            consequential amendments to
            other Acts, 234
        ad hoc tribunals, 255

Additional Protocols to the Geneva
    Conventions, 251
autrefois convict, 257
Canadian Border Services Agency
    (CBSA), 233
Canadian Charter of Rights and
    Freedoms, 238, 253, 254, 255
Canadian evidence law, presump-
    tion of innocence, 256
complicity and inchoate offences,
    253–55
core crimes, domestic versions, 237
Crimes against Humanity and
    War Crimes Program, 233
crimes, definitions, 238
    intent, 238
Criminal Code, 235, 245, 253, 255,
    256
defined, 246
Department of Justice, 233
Elements of the Crimes, 252
Geneva Conventions, 261
    Additional Protocols, 261
Geneva Conventions Act, 252
genocide
    advocating/incitement to geno-
        cide, 243–46
    definition, 243
Genocide Convention, 245
ICC Elements of Crimes (ICC Ele-
    ments), 238
in absentia, 257
international caselaw, 241
International Criminal Tribunal
    for Rwanda (ICTR), 241
International Criminal Tribu-
    nal for the former Yugoslavia
    (ICTY), 241
Interpretation Act, 253
jurisdiction, 234, 236
    "custodial" universal jurisdic-
        tion, 235
    extraterritorial jurisdiction, 236
    offences
        outside Canada, 235
        within Canada, 235
Modern War Crimes Program, 233
offences against the administra-
    tion of justice, 259
other provisions, 258–59

procedure and defences, 255–58
Public Prosecution Service of
    Canada, 255
RCMP (Royal Canadian Mounted
    Police), 233
Rome Statute, 234, 235, 238, 239,
    240, 243, 246, 247, 250, 251,
    252, 255, 256, 258, 260
Rwanda, 251
    genocide, 244
    national, 259
Second Protocol to the Geneva Con-
    ventions (AP II), 251
Tutsi, 244
Universal Declaration of Human
    Rights, 234
war crime, defined, 250
war crimes program, mandate,
    233
WW II Program, 233
Draft Code of Crimes against the
    Peace and Security of Mankind,
    215, 219
enforcement models
    direct, 214
    indirect, 214
    post-war world, 215–23
European Union, 221
Geneva Conventions, 215, 216
Genocide Convention, 215, 217
Germany, territorial state, 218
Holocaust, 217
immigration-based mechanisms
    Canadian Security Intelligence
        Service (CSIS), 267
    Citizenship Act, 267
    exclusion from
        immigration, 264–65
        refugee status, 265–66
    Immigration and Refugee Board,
        decisions, 266
    Immigration and Refugee Protection
        Act (IRPA), 264
    Immigration and Refugee Protection
        Regulations, 265
    Justice Canada, 267
    loss of citizenship, 267
    RCMP (Royal Canadian Mounted
        Police), 267
    Refugee Convention, 265

war crimes program, cases heard,
    263
indirect enforcement, Canada,
    1945–1999, 223–32
    Act to amend the Criminal Code, the
        Immigration Act, 1976 and the
        Citizenship Act, 228, 229
    Additional Protocols to the Geneva
        Conventions, ratification of, 225
    British Commonwealth Relations
        Office, 224
    Canadian Charter of Rights and
        Freedoms (Charter), 229
    Canadian War Crimes Investiga-
        tion Units, 224
    Crimes against Humanity and
        War Crimes Section, Depart-
        ment of Justice
        creation of, 228
    Criminal Code, 227
    Department of Justice, 228
    Deschênes Commission, 227, 228,
        232
    Extradition Act, 229
    Geneva Convention of 1929, 224
    Geneva Conventions Act, 225, 226,
        229
    Geneva Conventions of 1949, rati-
        fied, 225
    Justice War Crimes Section, 230
    Lithuania, 226
    Modern War Crimes Section,
        Department of Citizenship and
        Immigration Canada (CIC), 232
    Nuremberg laws, retroactive, 232
    post-WW II developments, 223
    War Crimes Act, 224, 226
    war crimes, defined, 224
    war crimes trials, Aurich, Ger-
        many, 224
International Committee of the Red
    Cross (ICRC), 215
International Criminal Court (ICC),
    214
Israeli District Court of Jerusalem, 217
Jewish people, crimes against the, 217
Nazi war criminals, 215
Nuremberg and Tokyo Tribunals,
    214, 215
Organic Law No. 6/2985, Spain, 222

Rome Statute, 219, 220, 223
Senegal, 221
Spain, 220
UN ad hoc tribunal, creation of, 219
UN Convention on the Non-Applicabil-
    ity of Statutes of Limitation to War
    Crimes and Crimes against Human-
    ity, 216
United Nations, 215
War crimes investigation units, spe-
    cial, Canada, Denmark, Ethiopia,
    Norway, Netherlands, UK, 222
WW II criminals, prosecuting, 219
Yugoslav conflict, convictions of
    individuals, 220
Prostitution, enforced, 127, 129, 145,
    290, 292, 325, 389, 390
Protected Persons Convention. See
    Convention on the Prevention and
    Punishment of Crimes against
    Internationally Protected Persons,
    Including Diplomatic Agents
Protocol for the Suppression of Unlaw-
    ful Acts against the Safety of Fixed
    Platforms Located on the Continent-
    al Shelf (SUA Protocol), 346, 347

Qualified territoriality in Canadian law.
    See Territoriality in Canadian law,
    qualified

Rape
    definition, 127
    ICC Elements, 127
    Iraqi High Tribunal (IHT), 128
    Rome Statute, 127
    Special Court for Sierra Leone
        (SCSL), 128
    United Nations Transitional Admin-
        istration in East Timor (UNTAET)
        Serious Crimes Panels, 128
Refugee Convention. See Convention on the
    Status of Refugees
Registration Convention, 91

Rome Statute, 3, 9, 12, 18, 22, 24, 32, 36,
    37, 54, 78, 100, 101, 107, 108, 109,
    116, 119, 120, 123, 125, 126, 127,
    128, 129, 136, 144, 146, 148, 149,
    150 155, 156, 174, 176, 179, 180,
    181, 183, 184, 185, 186, 187, 188,
    189, 190, 191, 192, 193, 194, 195,
    196, 197, 199, 200, 201, 212, 219,
    220, 223, 234, 235, 238, 239, 240,
    243, 247, 249, 250, 251, 252, 253,
    255, 256, 258, 259, 260, 261, 262,
    275, 283, 290, 291, 293, 478, 558,
    559, 560, 561, 562, 563, 564, 565,
    566, 567, 568, 579, 590, 591
Rwanda, 2, 38, 99, 100, 109, 112, 136,
    160, 171, 172, 173, 174, 175, 176,
    194, 220, 241, 243, 251, 260, 261,
    262, 265, 353, 549, 554, 555, 575

SCSL. See Special Court for Sierra Leone
Second Geneva Convention (GC II), 131,
    138
Second Protocol to the Geneva Conventions
    (AP II), 135, 251
Senegal, 221
Serbia, 168, 169, 210, 211, 477
Ships. See Jurisdiction, international and
    transnational crime
Sierra Leone, 10, 203, 204, 205, 206, 207,
    555, 556
Slavery, 288–92
    Canadian law, in
    chattel, 290
    Criminal Code, 292
    definition, 288, 289
    erga omnes, 288
    history, 288
    jurisdiction over, 291–92
        unqualified universal jurisdiction,
        291
    jus cogens norm, 288
    League of Nations Slavery Convention,
        289
    Supplementary Convention on the Abo-
        lition of Slavery, the Slave Trade,
        and Institutions and Practices Simi-
        lar to Slavery, 1956, 289, 291
    UN Working Group on Contempor-
        ary Forms of Slavery, 290
Slavery Convention, 289

Smuggling of migrants. *See* Migrants, smuggling of; Organized Crime, transnational

Somalia, 353

Space, outer, *See* Jurisdiction, international and transnational crime

Special Court for Sierra Leone (SCSL), 146, 203–207, 555–58, 566

Special Tribunal for Lebanon (STL), 208–209

Statute of the International Criminal Tribunal for Rwanda (ICTR Statute), 119, 120,135, 136, 176, 261, 262, 554, 555

Statute of the International Criminal Tribunal for the former Yugoslavia (ICTY Statute), 100, 120, 135, 146, 147, 170, 555

Statute of the International Court of Justice (ICJ Statute), 129

Statutory Limitations Convention, 293, 294

STL. *See* Special Tribunal for Lebanon

SUA Convention. See Convention for the Suppression of Unlawful Acts against the Safety of Maritime Navigation

SUA Protocol. See Protocol for the Suppression of Unlawful Acts against the Safety of Fixed Platforms Located on the Continental Shelf

Sudan, The, 2, 181, 182, 184, 185, 194, 198, 562, 563, 564, 565

Supplementary Slavery Convention, 290, 291

Suppression conventions, 305–14
  1963 *Tokyo Aircraft Convention*, 307
  1988 *Vienna Narcotics Convention*, 307
  aut dedere obligations, 307
  central features, 307–11
    criminalize conduct, 307
    exert jurisdiction over offence, 308
    Hijacking Convention, 307
    Narcotics Convention, 311
    obligation to extradite alleged or suspected perpetrators, 308
    aut dedere aut judicare, 309
    Terrorist Bombings Convention, 308
  Geneva Conventions, 306
  history, 305
  human rights concerns, 311–14
    Canada, *Canadian Charter of Rights and Freedoms*, 314
    Terrorist Bombing Convention, 313
    United Nations Convention against Transnational Organized Crime (TOC Convention), 313
  obligation imposed by Rome, 306
  treaty crimes, 305
    basic goals, 306

Suppression of crime, international cooperation in the, 23–24
  bilateral extradition treaties, 23
  extradition, 23
  multilateral extradition treaties, 24
  mutual legal assistance, 24
  Rome Statute, 24
  states, 23

Taliban, 265, 359, 362, 363

Tamil Tigers, 279

Territoriality in Canadian law, qualified, 409–24
  Canadian courts, interpreting requirements of comity, 418
  Coastal Fisheries Protection Act, 415
  Competition Act, 416, 422
  Copyright Act, 421
  Criminal Code, 410, 422, 424
  extradition context, 419–20
  international comity, 417–20
  Libman and extraterritoriality, 420–23
  Libman test, 409–12, 424
  "real and substantial connection," 412–17
  territorial jurisidiction
    subjective, 420
    test, 412
  test, two-part "real and substantial link," 411

Terrorism, 295–301
  1977 *Additional Protocol I to the Geneva Conventions*, 298
  anti-terrorism instruments
    Arab Convention, 298
    OAU Convention, 298
    OIC Convention, 298

1997 *Terrorist Bombing Convention*, 296

2000 *Terrorist Financing Convention*, 296, 297, 299

2005 *Nuclear Terrorism Convention*, 296

Comprehensive Convention on International Terrorism, 297

definition, 297

League of Nations, ratification, 296

reaching agreement, definition, 296

UN General Assembly, 295

Terrorism, transnational, 343–70

9/11 attacks, 344

Achille Lauro
   Palestinian terrorists, 346

airplanes, civilian, as tools of terrorism, 344

Al-Qaeda, 359, 362, 363

Anti-Terrorism Act, 363, 367

Canada Evidence Act, 367

aut dedere aut judicare obligation, 348, 353, 358, 361, 365, 369

civil aviation, 344–46

Cold War, end of, 359, 354

Convention for the Suppression of Unlawful Acts against the Safety of Civil Aviation (Montreal Convention), 345

Convention for the Suppression of Unlawful Acts against the Safety of Maritime Navigation (SUA Convention), 346, 347, 348

Convention for the Suppression of Unlawful Seizure of Aircraft (Hague Convention), 344

Convention on the Physical Protection of Nuclear Material, 366

Convention on the Prevention and Punishment of Crimes against Internationally Protected Persons, Including Diplomatic Agents, 352

Convention on the Safety of United Nations and Associated Personnel, 354

Counter-Terrorism Committee (CTC), 343

Criminal Code, 345, 349, 351, 363, 366, 367

definitions
   "associated personnel," 356

"device," 365

"fixed platform," 347

"internationally protected person," 353

"radioactive material," 365

"nuclear material," 365

"United Nations operation," 356

"United Nations personnel," 356

devices, 356

Eastern bloc states, fall of, 359

Entebbe raid, 351

Financial Action Task Force (FATF)
   "Special Recommendations on Terrorist Financing," 362

Geneva Conventions, 349

Hague Convention, 344

high seas attacks, 347

hostage-taking, 349–52

International Atomic Energy Agency guidelines, 365

International Civil Aviation Organization (ICAO), 344

International Convention against the Taking of Hostages (Hostages Convention), 350

International Convention for the Suppression of Acts of Nuclear Terrorism, 364

International Convention for the Suppression of Terrorist Bombings, 357, 358, 360, 364

International Convention for the Suppression of the Financing of Terrorism, 360

internationally protected persons, 352–53

maritime terrorism, 346–49

Munich Olympics, 1972, 350

"new terrorism" jurisdiction, 369

nuclear terrorism, 364–66

Nuclear Terrorism Convention, 366

nuclear weapons, 364

Official Secrets Act, 367

Optional Protocol to the Convention on the Safety of United Nations and Associated Personnel, 355

Proceeds of Crime (Money Laundering) and Terrorist Financing Act, 367

Protected Persons Convention, 354

*Protocol for the Suppression of Unlaw-
ful Acts against the Safety of Fixed
Platforms Located on the Continent-
al Shelf (SUA Protocol)*, 346, 347
*Protocol for the Suppression of Unlaw-
ful Act of Violence at Airports Serv-
ing International Civil Aviation*,
345
Resolution 1373, 362
Russian initiative
*International Convention for the
Suppression of Acts of Nuclear
Terrorism*, 364
Security Council resolutions, 362
Security of Information Act, 367
SUA Convention, 348
SUA Protocol, 348
Taliban, 359, 362, 363
"terrorism offence" defined in *Crim-
inal Code*, 368
terrorist bombings, 356–59
terrorist financing, 359–64
Terrorist Financing Convention, 361,
362, 364
UN and associated personnel, 353–56
UN Charter, 351
UN Personnel Convention, 355
United Nations Act, 367
United Nations
Afghanistan Regulations, 363
global counter-terrorism strategy,
343
peacekeepers, 353
suppression of Terrorism Regula-
tions, 364
*United Nations Convention against
Transnational Organized Crime
(TOC Convention)*, 257
Terrorist Bombing Convention, 308, 360,
351, 357, 358, 365
Terrorist Financing Convention, 296, 297,
299, 361, 362, 363, 364, 366, 381
Third Geneva Convention (GC III), 148
TOC Convention. *See United Nations
Convention against Transnational
Organized Crime*
Tokyo Aircraft Convention. *See Tokyo
Convention on Offences and Certain
Other Acts Committed on Board
Aircraft*

*Tokyo Convention on Offences and Certain
Other Acts Committed on Board
Aircraft*, 61, 95, 307, 344, 436
Tokyo Tribunal, 21, 43, 99, 153, 159,
160, 214, 215. *See also* Nuremberg
and Tokyo Tribunals, direct enforcement against core crimes
Torture, 269–302
acts constituting, 275–76
European Court of Human Rights,
276
pain or suffering, 275
Afghanistan, 280
Canadian law
definition, 278
classifying as an international crime,
271
Criminal Code, 278
definition, 270
deport (*refoule*), 280
history, 270
intention, 274
*International Covenant on Civil and
Political Rights (ICCPR)*, 272
International Criminal Tribunal for
the former Yugoslavia (ICTY)
humiliation of victim, 274
jurisdiction over, 272–73
mental elements 274–75
Inter-American Torture Convention,
274
non-*refoulement* obligation, 279
other state obligations, 277–78
prohibition of 270
public official requirement, 277
refoulement, 279
Rome Statute, 275
Tamil Tigers, 279
*United Nations Convention against
Torture and other Cruel, Inhuman
and Degrading Treatment or Punishment (CAT)*, 271
United Nations General Assembly
(UNGA), 270
*Universal Declaration of Human
Rights*, 270
Torture Convention. *See United Nations
Convention against Torture and
other Cruel, Inhuman and Degrading Treatment or Punishment (CAT)*

Trafficking in drugs. *See* Drug trafficking, transnational
Trafficking in persons. *See* Organized
Crime, Transnational; Persons,
trafficking in
Treason, 67, 70, 71, 432, 455
Treaty law
Canada, 30–32
creation and legal effect, 30–32
accession, 31
jus cogens norm, 31
pacta sunt servand, 30
party, 31
ratification, 31
reception, 32
reservations, 31
signatory, 31
suspension, 31
termination, 31
*Vienna Convention on the Law
of Treaties*, 1969, 30
War Crimes Act, 32
*Convention on Combating Bribery of
Foreign Officials in International
Business Transactions*, 32
Extradition Act, 32
Genocide Convention, Canada party
to, 31
*Mutual Legal Assistance in Criminal
Matters Act (MLA Act)*, 32
Treaty of Lausanne, 5, 161
Treaty of Versailles, 5, 161, 546
Trinidad and Tobago, 9, 177
Tutsi, 112, 171, 244, 260

Uganda, 181, 185, 188, 191, 192, 193,
198, 199
UN Personnel Convention, 354, 355, 356
UNCAC. *See United Nations Convention
against Corruption*
UNCLOS. *See United Nations Convention
on the Law of the Sea*
UNCRC. *See United Nations Convention
on the Rights of the Child*
UNICEF, 389
United Nations, 3, 7, 12, 32, 106, 160,
165, 185, 193, 207, 210, 215, 304,
333, 353, 371, 380, 448, 483, 549,
555

United Nations *ad hoc* tribunals, direct
enforcement against core crimes,
165–76
Additional Protocol II (AP II), 175
chambers, 175
Conference for Security and Cooperation in Europe (CSCE), 165
creation, 165
Dayton Agreement, 167
history, 165
jurisdiction, 170–71
North Atlantic Treaty Organization (NATO), 167
structure, 169
Geneva Conventions, 170, 175
Genocide Convention, 173
Hutu, 171, 176
International Criminal Tribunal for
the former Yugoslavia (ICTY),
165, 167
commission of experts, 165
International Criminal Tribunal for
Rwanda (ICTR), 168, 171–76
creation, 171
history, 171
jurisdiction, 175
prosecutors, 169
registry, 169, 175
Rome Statute, 174
structure, 175
chambers, 169
office of the prosecutor, 169
Tutsi, 171
UN Office of Internal Oversight
Services, 172
UN Security Council, 171
war crimes chambers, Bosnia and
Herzegovina, Croatia, Republic of
Serbia, 168
Yugoslavia, former, 170
*United Nations Convention against Cor-
ruption (UNCAC)*, 315, 320, 337,
338, 339, 340, 341, 342
United Nations *Convention against Torture and Other Cruel, Inhuman and
Degrading Treatment or Punishment
(CAT)*, 11, 12, 76, 126, 127, 271,
272, 273, 274, 275, 276, 277, 278,
279, 280, 297, 310, 428, 504

United Nations Convention against Trans-national Organized Crime (TOC Convention), 313, 315, 316, 317, 319, 320, 321, 322, 323, 324, 326, 328, 329, 330, 333, 337, 338, 340, 342, 357, 358, 381, 390, 403, 448

United Nations Convention on the Juris-dictional Immunities of States and Their Property, 542

United Nations Convention on the Law of the Sea (UNCLOS), 35, 72, 83, 87, 88, 89, 282, 285, 286, 287, 291, 331, 347, 375, 435, 436,

United Nations *Convention on the Rights of the Child (UNCRC)*, 389

United Nations Transitional Administra-tion in East Timor (UNTAET), 128, 209-10

UNTAET. *See* United Nations Transi-tional Administration in East Timor

VCLT. *See Vienna Convention on the Law of Treaties*

Vessels. *See* Jurisdiction, international and transnational crime

Vienna Convention on Consular Relations, 596, 597, 598

Vienna Convention on Diplomatic Rela-tions, 596, 597, 598

Vienna Convention on the Law of Treaties (VCLT), 30, 44, 574

Vienna Narcotics Convention, 178, 307, 311, 331, 373, 374, 375, 377, 378, 380, 381, 384, 386, 448, 482, 485

War crimes, 130–52
  armed conflict, 133
    international, 134
  aut dedere aut judicare mechanism, 139
  definition, 131
  existence of and nexus to armed conflict, 133–37
  first trial, 131
  Geneva Conventions, 131, 135, 138, 144
    Additional Protocols I and II, 131,138
      art. 4 prohibitions, 145
      grave breaches regime, 140

      compelling protected per-son to serve in forces of hostile power, 142
      extensive destruction and appropriation of prop-erty, 141
      taking civilians as hostages, 143
      torture or inhumane treat-ment, including bio-logical experiments, 141
      unlawful combatants, 143
      unlawful deportation or transfer or unlawful confinement, 142
      wilful killing, 140
      wilfully causing great suffering or serious injury to body or health, 141
      wilfully depriving a pris-oner of war or civilian the rights of a fair and, regular trial 142
    civilians in occupied territories (*GC IV*), 131
    prisoners of war (*GC III*), 131
    Second Protocol to the (AP II), 135
    sick and shipwrecked sailors (*GC II*), 131
    wounded soldiers (*GC I*), 131
  Hague Conventions, 138
  Hague law, 131
  ICTR Statute, 135
  ICTY Statute, 135
  International Committee of the Red Cross (ICRC), 131
  international versus international armed conflict, 134
  jurisdiction, war crimes, 130
    requirements, 133
  Law of Geneva, 132
  Law of the Hague, 132
  mental element, 137–38
  Rome Statute, 136, 149–52
    Geneva Conventions, in the, 151
    war crimes in the, 3, 149
      art. 8, 149
      elements of the crimes (ICC Elements), 151

Rwanda, 136
Statute of the ICTR, 135
Statute of the ICTY, 135
Vietnam conflict, 139
violations of the law or customs of
war, 146–49
*Charter of the International Mil-
itary Tribunal (IMT Charter)*,
146, 147
Geneva Conventions, 147
Hague Convention IV, 146
Hague law-based war crimes,
Hague Regulations, 148–49
Hague Regulations recognized by
the Nuremberg Tribunal, 147
ICTY Statute, 147
Yugoslavia, the former, 137
Warships. *See* Jurisdiction, international
and transnational crime
Witness Protection Program Act, 324

Yugoslavia, 2, 8, 99, 100, 109, 137, 165,
167, 170, 171, 194, 211, 241, 265,
353, 461, 477, 549, 550, 551, 555

ABOUT THE AUTHOR

Robert J. Currie is a faculty member of the Schulich School of Law at Dalhousie University, where he teaches International Criminal Law, International Advocacy, Evidence, and Civil Procedure. He studied at both St. Francis Xavier University and the Norman Paterson School of International Affairs at Carleton University, and has degrees in law from Dalhousie and the University of Edinburgh. Prior to his academic appointment, Professor Currie had a civil litigation practice at the Atlantic Canadian firm McInnes Cooper, where he appeared before all levels of court in Nova Scotia. He has been a member of the Nova Scotia Bar since 2000.

Professor Currie has authored or co-authored numerous articles and comments in the area of international and transnational criminal law, and his work has been cited by Canadian courts, including the Supreme Court of Canada. He has acted as a consultant in many capacities, and since 2009 has been a Commissioner of the Law Reform Commission of Nova Scotia. In 2008, Professor Currie was honoured with the Dalhousie Law Students' Society and Alumni Association Award for Excellence in Teaching.